TAKING SIDES

Clashing Views in

United States History, Volume 2, Reconstruction to the Present

FOURTEENTH EDITION

Selected, Edited, and with Introductions by

Larry Madaras
Howard Community College

and

James M. SoRelle
Baylor University

Connect
Learn
Succeed™

D0141252

TAKING SIDES: CLASHING VIEWS IN UNITED STATES HISTORY, VOLUME 2:
RECONSTRUCTION TO THE PRESENT, FOURTEENTH EDITION

Published by McGraw-Hill, a business unit of The McGraw-Hill Companies, Inc., 1221 Avenue
of the Americas, New York, NY 10020. Copyright © 2011 by The McGraw-Hill Companies, Inc. All
rights reserved. Previous edition(s) 2009, 2007, and 2005. No part of this publication may be
reproduced or distributed in any form or by any means, or stored in a database or retrieval
system, without the prior written consent of The McGraw-Hill Companies, Inc., including, but not
limited to, in any network or other electronic storage or transmission, or broadcast for distance
learning.

Some ancillaries, including electronic and print components, may not be available to customers
outside the United States.

Taking Sides® is a registered trademark of the McGraw-Hill Companies, Inc.
Taking Sides is published by the **Contemporary Learning Series** group within the McGraw-Hill
Higher Education division.

1 2 3 4 5 6 7 8 9 0 DOC/DOC 1 0 9 8 7 6 5 4 3 2 1 0

MHID: 0-07-805002-2
ISBN: 978-0-07-805002-2
ISSN: 2156-9452 (print)
ISSN: 2156-9460 (online)

Managing Editor: *Larry Loeppke*
Senior Developmental Editor: *Jill Meloy*
Senior Permissions Coordinator: *Shirley Lanners*
Senior Marketing Communications Specialist: *Mary Klein*
Marketing Coordinator: *Alice Link*
Senior Project Manager: *Jane Mohr*
Design Coordinator: *Brenda A. Rolwes*
Cover Graphics: *Rick D. Noel*

Compositor: MPS Limited, a Macmillan Company
Cover Image: © Library of Congress

Library of Congress Cataloging-in-Publication Data

Main entry under title:
    Taking sides: clashing views on controversial issues in American history, volume ii,
    reconstruction to the present/selected, edited, and with introductions by Larry Madaras and
    James W. SoRelle—14th ed.

Includes bibliographical references and index.
    1. United States—History—1865– I. Madaras, Larry, *comp*. II. SoRelle, James M., *comp*.
                                                                                            973

Editors/Academic Advisory Board

Members of the Academic Advisory Board are instrumental in the final selection of articles for each edition of TAKING SIDES. Their review of articles for content, level, and appropriateness provides critical direction to the editors and staff. We think that you will find their careful consideration well reflected in this volume.

TAKING SIDES: Clashing Views in

UNITED STATES HISTORY, VOLUME 2, RECONSTRUCTION TO THE PRESENT

Fourteenth Edition

EDITORS

Larry Madaras
Howard Community College
and
James M. SoRelle
Baylor University

ACADEMIC ADVISORY BOARD MEMBERS

Editors/Academic Advisory Board continued

Preface

The success of the past thirteen editions of *Taking Sides: Clashing Views in United States History* has encouraged us to remain faithful to its original objectives, methods, and format. Our aim has been to create an effective instrument to enhance classroom learning and to foster critical thinking. Historical facts presented in a vacuum are of little value to the educational process. For students, whose search for historical truth often concentrate on *when* something happened rather than on *why,* and on specific events rather than on the *significance* of those events, *Taking Sides* is designed to offer an interesting and valuable departure. The understanding that the reader arrives at based on the evidence that emerges from the clash of views encourages the reader to view history as an *interpretive* discipline, not one of rote memorization.

As in previous editions, the issues are arranged in chronological order and can be easily incorporated into any American history survey course. Each issue has an issue *introduction,* which sets the stage for the debate that follows in the pro and con selections and provides historical and methodological background to the problem that the issue examines. Each issue concludes with a *postscript,* which ties the readings together, briefly mentions alternative interpretations, and supplies detailed *suggestions for further reading* for the student who wishes to pursue the topics raised in the issue. Also, Internet site addresses (URLs), which should prove useful as starting points for further research, have been provided on the *Internet References* page that accompanies each unit opener. At the back of the book is a listing of all the *contributors to this volume* with a brief biographical sketch of each of the prominent figures whose views are debated here.

Changes to This Edition

In this edition, we have continued our efforts to maintain a balance between the traditional political, diplomatic, and cultural issues and the new social history, which depicts a society that benefited from the presence of African Americans, women, and workers of various racial and ethnic backgrounds. With this in mind, we present six new issues, some at the request of teachers who wanted some of the earlier issues revisited. These include: "Did Reconstruction Fail as a Result of Racism?" (Issue 1); "Were the Nineteenth-Century Big Businessmen 'Robber Barons'?" (Issue 3); "Were the Populists Irrational Reactionaries?" (Issue 6); "Did President Roosevelt Deliberately Withhold Information About the Attack on Pearl Harbor from the American Commanders?" (Issue 12). Other issues were reconceptualized. These include: "Was the American Labor Movement Radical?" (Issue 4) and "Did the New Deal Prolong the Great Depression?" (Issue 11). Two issues remained the same with new articles. See "Was Woodrow Wilson Responsible for the Failure of the United States to Join the League of Nations?" (Issue 9) and "Was Rock and Roll Responsible for Dismantling America's Traditional Family, Sexual, and Racial Customs in the 1950s and 1960s?" (Issue 14). The last issue is new and asks a basic question: "Is the United States a Declining Power?" (Issue 18).

A word to the instructor *An Instructor's Resource Guide With Test Questions* (multiple-choice and essay) is available through the publisher for the instructor using *Taking Sides* in the classroom. A general guidebook, *Using Taking Sides in the Classroom,* which discusses methods and techniques for integrating the pro-con approach into any classroom setting, is also available. An online version of *Using Taking Sides in the Classroom* and a correspondence service for *Taking Sides* adopters can be found at http://www.mhcls.com/usingts/.

Taking Sides: Clashing Views in United States History is only one title in the *Taking Sides* series. If you are interested in seeing the table of contents for any other titles, please visit the *Taking Sides* Web site at www.mhhe.com/cls.

Acknowledgments Many individuals have contributed to the successful completion of past editions. We appreciate the evaluations submitted to McGraw-Hill/CLS by those who have used *Taking Sides* in the classroom. Special thanks to those who responded with specific suggestions for the previous editions:

Gary Best
University of Hawaii–Hilo

James D. Bolton
Coastline Community College

Mary Borg
University of Northern Colorado

John Whitney Evans
College of St. Scholastica

Mark Hickerson
Chaffey College

Maryann Irwin
Diablo Valley College

Tim Koerner
Oakland Community College

Gordon Lam
Sierra College

Jon Nielson
Columbia College

Andrew O'Shaugnessy
University of Wisconsin–Oshkosh

Manian Padma
DeAnza College

Elliot Pasternack
Middlesex County College (N.J.)

Robert M. Paterson
Armstrong State College

Charles Piehl
Mankato State University

Ethan S. Rafuse
University of Missouri–Kansas City

John Reid
Ohio State University–Lima

Murray Rubinstein
CUNY Baruch College

Neil Sapper
Amarillo College

Preston She
Plymouth State College

Jack Traylor
William Jennings Bryan College

We are particularly indebted to Maggie Cullen, Cindy SoRelle, the late Barry A. Crouch, Virginia Kirk, Joseph and Helen Mitchell, and Jean Soto, who shared their ideas for changes, pointed us toward potentially useful historical works, and provided significant editorial assistance. Lynn Wilder performed indispensable typing duties connected with this project. Susan E. Myers, Ela Ciborowski, and Karen Higgins in the library at Howard Community College provided essential help in acquiring books and articles on interlibrary loan. Finally, we are sincerely grateful for the commitment, encouragement, and patience provided over the years by David Dean, former list manager for the *Taking Sides* series; David Brackley, former senior developmental editor; and the entire staff of McGraw-Hill/CLS. Indispensable to this project are Ted Knight, the former list manager, and Jill Meloy, the current editor-in-charge of the *Taking Sides* series.

Larry Madaras
Howard Community College

James M. SoRelle
Baylor University

Contents In Brief

Contents

George M. Fredrickson concludes that racism, in the form of the doctrine of white supremacy, colored the thinking not only of southern whites but of most white northerners as well and produced only halfhearted efforts by the Radical Republicans in the postwar period to sustain a commitment to black equality. Heather Cox Richardson argues that the failure of Radical Reconstruction was primarily a consequence of a national commitment to a free-labor ideology that opposed an expanding central government that legislated rights to African Americans that other citizens had acquired through hard work.

Professor of history David T. Courtright argues that the cattle, mining, and lumbering Western frontiers were extremely violent because these regions were populated by young, single, and transient males who frequented saloons and prostitutes, and engaged in fights. Professor Robert R. Dykstra argues that Dodge City had a low crime rate in the decade 1876–1885, and in the murder case of *Kansas v. Gill*, it conducted a jury trial "according to conventions nurtured through a thousand years of Anglo-American judicial traditions."

According to Howard Zinn, the new industrialists such as John D. Rockefeller, Andrew Carnegie, and J. P. Morgan adopted business practices that encouraged monopolies and used the powers of the government to control the masses from rebellion. John S. Gordon argues that the nineteenth-century men of big business such as John D. Rockefeller and Andrew Carnegie developed through the oil and steel industries consumer products that improved the lifestyle of average Americans.

Issue 4.   Was the American Labor Movement Radical?   78

Although stopping short of a frontal attack on capitalism, Professor Leon Fink argues that the Knights of Labor envisioned a kind of workingman's democracy that would ensure minimal standards of health and safety at the industrial workplace. Historian Carl N. Degler maintains that the American labor movement accepted capitalism and reacted conservatively to the radical organizational changes brought about in the economic system by big business.

Issue 5.   Were Late Nineteenth-Century Immigrants "Uprooted"?   103

Oscar Handlin asserts that immigrants to the United States in the late nineteenth century were alienated from the cultural traditions of the homeland they had left as well as from those of their adopted country. Mark Wyman argues that as many as four million immigrants to the United States between 1880 and 1930 viewed their trip as temporary and remained tied psychologically to their homeland to which they returned once they had accumulated enough wealth to enable them to improve their status back home.

Issue 6.   Were the Populists Irrational Reactionaries?   125

According to Richard Hofstadter the Populists created a conspiracy theory around the issues of industrialism that activated a virulent strain of nativism and anti-Semitism, and revealed their desire to return to a rural utopia that they associated with the early nineteenth century. Charles Postel characterizes the Populists as forward-thinking reformers who hoped to use the government to manage an increasingly modern, technologically sophisticated, and globally connected society for the benefit of ordinary citizens.

Donald Spivey contends that Booker T. Washington alienated both students and faculty at Tuskegee Institute by establishing an authoritarian system that failed to provide an adequate academic curriculum to prepare students for the industrial workplace. Robert J. Norrell insists that Booker T. Washington, while limited by the racial climate of the day in what he could accomplish, nevertheless spoke up for political and civil rights, decried mob violence, and defended black education as a means of promoting a more positive image for African Americans in an era dominated by the doctrine of white supremacy.

Professor of history Richard M. Abrams maintains that progressivism was a failure because it tried to impose a uniform set of values upon a culturally diverse people and never seriously confronted the inequalities that still exist in American society. Professors of history Arthur S. Link and Richard L. McCormick argue that the Progressives were a diverse group of reformers who confronted and ameliorated the worst abuses that emerged in urban industrial America during the early 1900s.

Professor John M. Cooper argues that the stroke that partially paralyzed Woodrow Wilson during his speaking tour in 1919 hampered the president's ability to compromise with the Republicans over the terms of America's membership in the League of Nations if the Senate ratified the Treaty of Versailles. William G. Carleton believed that Woodrow Wilson understood the role that the United States would play in world affairs.

David E. Kyvig admits that alcohol consumption declined sharply in the prohibition era but that federal actions failed to impose abstinence among an increasingly urban and heterogeneous populace that resented and resisted restraints on their individual behavior. J. C. Burnham states that the prohibition experiment was more a success than a failure and contributed to a substantial decrease in liquor consumption, reduced arrests for alcoholism, fewer alcohol-related diseases and hospitalizations, and destroyed the old-fashioned saloon that was a major target of the law's proponents.

Professor Burton W. Folsom, Jr., argues the New Deal prolonged the Great Depression because its antifree market program of high taxes and special-interest spending to certain banks, railroads, farmers, and veterans created an antibusiness environment of regime uncertainty. Professor of history Roger Biles contends that, in spite of its minimal reforms and nonrevolutionary programs, the New Deal created a limited welfare state that implemented economic stabilizers to avert another depression.

Retired rear admiral Robert A. Theobald argues that President Franklin D. Roosevelt deliberately withheld information from the commanders at Pearl Harbor in order to encourage the Japanese to make a surprise attack on the weak U.S. Pacific Fleet. Historian Roberta Wohlstetter contends that even though naval intelligence broke the Japanese code, conflicting signals and the lack of a central agency coordinating U.S. intelligence information made it impossible to predict the Pearl Harbor attack.

Correlation Guide

The *Taking Sides* series presents current issues in a debate-style format designed to stimulate student interest and develop critical thinking skills. Each issue is thoughtfully framed with an issue summary, an issue introduction, and a postscript. The pro and con essays—selected for their liveliness and substance—represent the arguments of leading scholars and commentators in their fields.

Taking Sides: Clashing Views in United States History, Volume 2: Reconstruction to the Present, 14/e is an easy-to-use reader that presents issues on important topics such as *immigration, racial equality, the Great Depression, the Vietnam War,* and *the Cold War.* For more information on *Taking Sides* and other *McGraw-Hill Contemporary Learning Series* titles, visit www.mhhe.com/cls.

This convenient guide matches the issues in **Taking Sides: United States History, Volume 2, 14/e** with the corresponding chapters in two of our best-selling McGraw-Hill History textbooks by Brinkley and Davidson et al.

Taking Sides: United States History, Volume 2, 14/e	The Unfinished Nation: A Concise History of the American People, Volume 2: From 1865, 6/e by Brinkley	Experience History, Volume 2: Since 1865, 7/e by Davidson, et al.
Issue 1: Did Reconstruction Fail as a Result of Racism?	**Chapter 15:** Reconstruction and the New South	**Chapter 17:** Reconstructing the Union, 1865–1877
Issue 2: Was the Wild West More Violent Than the Rest of the United States?	**Chapter 16:** The Conquest of the Far West **Chapter 18:** The Age of the City	**Chapter 18:** The New South & the Trans-Mississippi West, 1870–1914
Issue 3: Were the Nineteenth-Century Big Businessmen "Robber Barons"?	**Chapter 17:** Industrial Supremacy **Chapter 18:** The Age of the City	**Chapter 19:** The New Industrial Order, 1870–1914
Issue 4: Was the American Labor Movement Radical?	**Chapter 17:** Industrial Supremacy	**Chapter 19:** The New Industrial Order, 1870–1914
Issue 5: Were Late-Nineteenth-Century Immigrants "Uprooted"?	**Chapter 18:** The Age of the City	**Chapter 20:** The Rise of an Urban Order, 1870–1914
Issue 6: Were the Populists Irrational Reactionaries?	**Chapter 19:** From Crisis to Empire	**Chapter 21:** The Political System under Strain at Home and Abroad, 1877–1900
Issue 7: Did Booker T. Washington's Philosophy and Actions Betray the Interests of African Americans?	**Chapter 15:** Reconstruction and the New South **Chapter 20:** The Progressives	**Chapter 21:** The Political System under Strain at Home and Abroad, 1877–1900 **Chapter 22:** The Progressive Era, 1890–1920 **Chapter 24:** The New Era, 1920–1929

(Continued)

Taking Sides: United States History, Volume 2, 14/e	The Unfinished Nation: A Concise History of the American People, Volume 2: From 1865, 6/e by Brinkley	Experience History, Volume 2: Since 1865, 7/e by Davidson, et al.
Issue 8: Did the Progressives Fail?	**Chapter 20:** The Progressives	**Chapter 22:** The Progressive Era, 1890–1920
Issue 9: Was Woodrow Wilson Responsible for the Failure of the United States to Join the League of Nations?	**Chapter 21:** America and the Great War	**Chapter 23:** The United States and the Collapse of the Old World Order, 1901–1920 **Chapter 24:** The New Era, 1920–1929
Issue 10: Was Prohibition a Failure?	**Chapter 20:** The Progressives **Chapter 22:** The New Era **Chapter 24:** The New Deal	**Chapter 24:** The New Era, 1920–1929
Issue 11: Did the New Deal Prolong the Great Depression?	**Chapter 23:** The Great Depression **Chapter 24:** The New Deal **Chapter 26:** America in a World at War	**Chapter 25:** The Great Depression and the New Deal, 1929–1939 **Chapter 26:** America's Rise to Globalism, 1927–1945
Issue 12: Did President Roosevelt Deliberately Withhold Information About the Attack on Pearl Harbor from the American Commanders?	**Chapter 25:** The Global Crisis, 1921–1941 **Chapter 26:** America in a World at War	**Chapter 25:** The Great Depression and the New Deal, 1929–1939 **Chapter 26:** America's Rise to Globalism, 1927–1945
Issue 13: Was President Truman Responsible for the Cold War?	**Chapter 26:** America in a World at War **Chapter 27:** The Cold War	**Chapter 27:** Cold War America, 1945–1954
Issue 14: Was Rock and Roll Responsible for Dismantling America's Traditional Family, Sexual, and Racial Customs in the 1950s and 1960s?	**Chapter 28:** The Affluent Society **Chapter 30:** The Crisis of Authority	**Chapter 28:** The Suburban Era, 1945–1963 **Chapter 29:** Civil Rights & Uncivil Liberties, 1947–1969
Issue 15: Did President John F. Kennedy Demonstrate a Strong Commitment to Civil Rights?	**Chapter 29:** Civil Rights, Vietnam, and the Ordeal of Liberalism	**Chapter 29:** Civil Rights & Uncivil Liberties, 1947–1969
Issue 16: Did President Nixon Negotiate a "Peace with Honor" in Vietnam in 1973?	**Chapter 29:** Civil Rights, Vietnam, and the Ordeal of Liberalism **Chapter 30:** The Crisis of Authority	**Chapter 30:** The Vietnam Era, 1963–1975
Issue 17: Has the Women's Movement of the 1970s Failed to Liberate American Women?	**Chapter 30:** The Crisis of Authority	**Chapter 30:** The Vietnam Era, 1963–1975 **Chapter 31:** The Conservative Challenge, 1976–1992
Issue 18: Is the United States a Declining Power?	**Chapter 31:** From "The Age of Limits" to the Age of Reagan **Chapter 32:** The Age of Globalization	**Chapter 31:** The Conservative Challenge, 1976–1992 **Chapter 32:** Nation of Nations in a Global Community, 1989–Present

Introduction

The Study of History

Larry Madaras

James M. SoRelle

In a pluralistic society such as ours, the study of history is bound to be a complex process. How an event is interpreted depends not only on existing evidence but also on the perspective of the interpreter. Consequently, understanding history presupposes the evaluation of information, a task that often leads to conflicting conclusions. An understanding of history, then, requires the acceptance of the idea of historical relativism. Relativism means the redefinition of our past is always possible and desirable. History shifts, changes, and grows with new and different evidence and interpretations. As is the case with the law and even with medicine, beliefs that were unquestioned 100 or 200 years ago have been discredited or discarded since.

Relativism then encourages revisionism. There is a maxim that says, "The past must remain useful to the present." Historian Carl Becker argued that every generation should examine history for itself, thus ensuring constant scrutiny of our collective experience through new perspectives. History, consequently, does not remain static, in part because historians cannot avoid being influenced by the times in which they live. Almost all historians commit themselves to revising the views of other historians by either disagreeing with earlier interpretations or creating new frameworks that pose different questions.

Schools of Thought

Three predominant schools of thought have emerged in American history since the first graduate seminars in history were given at the Johns Hopkins University in Baltimore, Maryland, in the 1870s. The *progressive* school dominated the professional field in the first half of the twentieth century. Influenced by the reform currents of populism, progressivism, and the New Deal, these historians explored the social and economic forces that energized America. The progressive scholars tended to view the past in terms of conflicts between groups, and they sympathized with the underdog.

The post–World War II period witnessed the emergence of a new group of historians who viewed the conflict thesis as overly simplistic. Writing against the backdrop of the Cold War, these *neoconservative* and *consensus* historians argued that Americans possess a shared set of values and that the areas of agreement within the nation's basic democratic and capitalistic framework are more important than the areas of disagreement.

In the 1960s, however, the civil rights movement, women's liberation, and the student rebellion (with its condemnation of the war in Vietnam) fragmented the consensus of values upon which historians of the 1950s centered their interpretations. This turmoil set the stage for the emergence of another group of scholars. *New Left* historians began to reinterpret the past once again. They emphasized the significance of conflict in American history, and they resurrected interest in those groups ignored by the consensus school. In addition, New Left history is still being written.

The most recent generation of scholars, however, focuses upon social history. Their primary concern is to discover what the lives of "ordinary Americans" were really like. These new social historians employ previously overlooked court and church documents, house deeds and tax records, letters and diaries, photographs, and census data to reconstruct the everyday lives of average Americans. Some employ new methodologies, such as quantification (enhanced by advanced computer technology) and oral history, while others borrow from the disciplines of political science, economics, sociology, anthropology, and psychology for their historical investigations.

The proliferation of historical approaches, which are reflected in the issues debated in this book, has had mixed results. On the one hand, historians have become so specialized in their respective time periods and methodological styles that it is difficult to synthesize the recent scholarship into a comprehensive text for the general reader. On the other hand, historians now know more about new questions or ones that previously were considered to be germane only to scholars in other social sciences. Although there is little agreement about the answers to these questions, the methods employed and the issues explored make the "new history" a very exciting field to study.

The topics that follow represent a variety of perspectives and approaches. Each of these controversial issues can be studied for its individual importance to American history. Taken as a group, they interact with one another to illustrate larger historical themes. When grouped thematically, the issues reveal continuing motifs in the development of American history.

Entrepreneurs, Laborers, Immigrants, African Americans, and Farm Workers

Issue 3 explores the dynamics of the modern American economy through investigations of the nineteenth-century entrepreneurs. Were these industrial leaders robber barons, as portrayed by contemporary critics and many history texts? Or, were they industrial statesmen and organizational geniuses? The late radical historian Howard Zinn views the new industrialists as "robber barons" who adopted business practices that encouraged monopolies and used the power of government to control the masses from rebellion. But, John Steele Gordon, a business historian, argues that men such as Rockefeller and Carnegie developed, through the oil and steel industries, consumer products that improved the lifestyle of average Americans.

In the wake of industrialization during the late 1800s, the rapid pace of change created new working conditions for the labor class. How did laborers react to these new changes? Did they lose their autonomy in large corporations? Did they accept or reject the wage system? Were they pawns of the economic cycles of boom and bust, to be hired and fired at will? Did they look for an alternative to capitalism by engaging in strikes, establishing labor unions, or creating a socialist movement? In Issue 4, Carl N. Degler maintains that American workers accepted capitalism and the changes that it brought forth. Though stopping short of a frontal attack on capitalism, Professor Leon Fink argues that the Knights of Labor envisioned a kind of "workingman's democracy" that would ensure minimal standards of health and safety at the industrial workplace. By the beginning of the twentieth century, however, the organizational innovations of Rockefeller and the assembly-line techniques pioneered by Henry Ford had revolutionized American capitalism.

The vast majority of these factory workers came from the farms and cities of Europe. Massive immigration to the United States in the late nineteenth and early twentieth centuries introduced widespread changes in American society. Moreover, the presence of increasing numbers of immigrants from southern and eastern Europe, many of them Catholics and Jews, seemed to threaten native-born citizens, most of whom were Protestant and of northern and western European ancestry. Asian immigrants, mainly from China or Japan, added to nativist feats. In Issue 5, Oscar Handlin argues that the immigrants were alienated from their Old World cultures as they adjusted to an unfamiliar and often hostile environment. But Professor Mark Wyman argues that immigrants never gave up the fight for their personal autonomy. He points out that many immigrants to the United Sates believed their stay in America would be temporary, a fact that limited their efforts at assimilation and reinforced ties to their original homelands to which many of them returned once they had acquired some wealth.

Two issues cover the failure of the newly freed slaves to achieve political and legal equality. By 1900, most African Americans were not allowed to vote and were segregated into the poorest agricultural jobs as sharecroppers and tenant farmers. Did Reconstruction Fail as a Result of Racism? George M. Fredrickson, in Issue 1, concludes that racism in the form of the doctrine of white supremacy, colored the thinking not only of southern whites but of most white northerners as well and produced only halfhearted efforts by the Radical Republicans in the postwar period to sustain a commitment to black equality. Heather Cox Richardson argues that the failure of Radical Reconstruction was primarily a consequence of a national commitment to a free-labor ideology that opposed the expanding central government that legislated rights to African Americans that other citizens that acquired through hard work.

One of the most controversial figures in American history was the early-twentieth-century African American leader Booker T. Washington. Was Washington too accommodating toward white values and goals and too accepting of the political disfranchisement and social segregation that took away the basic freedoms that African Americans earned after their emancipation from slavery? In Issue 7, Donald Spivey argues that Washington not only subordinated political, social, and civil rights to economic goals, but also failed to provide the training necessary to allow students to become capable, skilled artisans. Robert J. Norrell, on the other hand, insists that Washington frequently challenged the political, economic, and social status quo of African Americans both publicly and behind the scenes.

No group seemed further away from urban-industrial America than the cowboys, farmers, miners, and lumberjacks who worked on America's last frontier. Issue 2 asks whether the Wild West was real or a mythical image created by novelists, movies, radio, television, and Wild West shows. Professor of history David T. Courtright argues that the cattle, mining, and lumbering western frontiers were extremely violent because these regions were populated by young, single, and transient males who frequented saloons and prostitutes, and engaged in fights with the local Indians and Chinese, as well as with each other. Professor Robert R. Dykstra argues that Dodge City had a low crime rate in the decade 1876–1885, and in the murder case of Kansas V. Gill, it conducted a jury trial "according to conventions nurtured through a thousand years of Anglo-American judicial traditions."

Political and Social Successes and Failures, 1890–1945

Issue 6 discusses the first major political reform movement of the late nineteenth century. According to Richard Hofstadter, the populists were not democratic reformers but reactionaries who created a conspiracy theory around the issues of industrialism and the "money question," which activated a virulent strain of nativism and anti-Semitism and revealed their desire to return to a rural utopia that they associated with the early nineteenth century. Charles Postel characterizes the Populists as forward-thinking reformers who hoped to use the government to manage an increasingly modern, technologically sophisticated, and globally connected society for the benefit of ordinary citizens.

The Progressive movement is examined in Issue 8. Richard M. Abrams attributes the failure of the movement to its limited scope. He maintains that it imposed a uniform set of values on a diverse people and did not address the inequalities that prevailed in American society. Arthur S. Link and Richard L. McCormick, however, emphasize the reforms introduced by the progressives that checked the abuses of industrialization and urbanization during the early 1900s.

Issue 10 discusses one of the major progressive "social control" reforms—Prohibition. The "noble experiment" to prohibit the manufacture, sale, and transportation of alcoholic beverages had a rather short life. Originally passed in 1919, the Prohibition amendment was repealed fourteen years later. To this day, it remains the only amendment ever to have been removed from the Constitution. John C. Burnham revises the traditional image of the decade of the 1920s as the "lawless years." He points out that when the "Prohibition experiment" was passed, two-thirds of the states, which encompassed over half of the population, were already dry. The purpose of the legislation, he argues, was to control the political and social practices of the immigrant working classes who lived in the cities. He denies that crime increased dramatically in the decade, attributing the so-called crime waves to the overblown accounts in the newspapers and newsreels. Gambling, rather than the sale of illegal liquor, remained the major source of revenue for organized crime. Burnham also marshals statistical evidence to document a decline in per capita drinking in the early 1920s as well as in the diseases and deaths related to alcohol. David Kyvig concedes that Prohibition "sharply reduced the consumption of alcohol in the United States." But images of lawbreaking through Hollywood films and newsreels and the inability of law enforcement officials in all levels of government to enforce a law, especially unpopular in American cities, "disenchanted many Americans and moved some to an active effort to bring an end to the dry law."

The Great Depression of the 1930s remains one of the most traumatic events in U.S. history. The characteristics of that decade are deeply etched in American folk memory, but the remedies that were applied to those social and economic ills—known collectively as the New Deal—are not easy to evaluate. In Issue 11, Roger Biles contends that the economic stabilizers created by the New Deal programs prevented the recurrence of the Great Depression. Burton J. Folsom, Jr., on the other hand, criticizes the New Deal from a twenty-first century conservative perspective. In his view, because New Deal agencies were anti-business, they overregulated the economy and did not allow the free enterprise system to work out the depression that FDR's programs prolonged.

Code, conflicting signals and the lack of a central agency coordinating U.S. intelligence information made it impossible to predict the Pearl Harbor attack.

World War II brought the end of Nazi Germany and imperial Japan. It was the war that was really supposed to end all wars. FDR, haunted by the ghost of Woodrow Wilson, hoped that the United Nations could resolve national conflicts. Unfortunately, an unintended consequence was the reemergence of the rivalry between the United States and the Soviet Union. Who started the Cold War? Was it inevitable, or should one side take more of the blame? In Issue 12, Professor Arnold A. Offner argues that President Harry S. Truman was a parochial nationalist whose limited vision of foreign affairs precluded negotiations with the Russians over cold war issues. But John Gaddis, the most important American scholar of the cold war, argues that after a half century of scholarship, Joseph Stalin was uncompromising and primarily responsible for the cold war.

No discussion of American foreign policy is complete without some consideration of the Vietnam War. Was America's escalation inevitable in 1965? Did the government accomplish a "peace with honor" when it withdrew American troops from Vietnam in 1973 in exchange for the return of our POWs? In Issue 16, President Nixon believes that the South Vietnamese government would not have lost the civil war in 1975 had not the United States Congress cut off aid. But, Professor Larry Berman argues that Nixon knew the agreement was flawed. But the President intended to bomb North Vietnam troops to prevent the collapse of South Vietnam until he left office.

Social, Cultural, and Economic Changes Since 1945

Carl N. Degler has labeled the years from 1945 to 1963 as the age of "anxiety and affluence." Issue 14 deals with this unique period in U.S. history. The population explosion that took place after World War II led to a youth culture who challenged the value system of their parents. Tensions between parents and children have always existed in America. Do different tastes in dress and music reflect revolutionary or surface changes? Professor Jody Pennington, a Danish professor of American Studies, argues that the emergence of rock and roll in the 1950s along with new forms of consumerism expressed "the inner conflict between conservative and rebellious forces for high school teenagers who wanted to rebel against their parents yet still grow up to be them. But writer J. Ronald Oakley sees less rebellion. He argues that although the life-styles of youth departed from their parents, their basic ideas and attitudes were still the conservative ones that mirrored the conservatism of the affluent age in which they grew up.

The situation for African Americans has vastly improved since the civil rights revolution of the 1950s and 1960s. But did it improve educational, polit-ical, and economic opportunities for minorities? Issue 15 discusses how Presi-dent John F. Kennedy was caught off guard when the civil rights movement escalated in the 1960s with non-violent demonstrations. How did Kennedy respond? Was he a reluctant reformer and did he finally demonstrate a strong commitment to civil rights? Carl M. Brauer asserts that President John F. Kennedy carried out an unambiguous commitment to civil rights that far exceeded anything his immediate predecessors had done which included efforts to end discrimination in voting, education, hiring practices, public facilities, and housing. Nick Bryant claims that President Kennedy took an overly cautious approach to civil rights matters to avoid a confrontation with white southern Democrats in Congress and relied too heavily on symbolic, largely cosmetic changes that left him with a meager legacy of civil rights accomplishments.

A direct lineage of the civil rights revolution was the Women's Libera-tion Movement of the 1970s. Did it help or harm women? In Issue 17, writer and lecturer F. Carolyn Garglia argues that women should stay at home and practice the values of "true motherhood" because contemporary feminists have discredited marriage, devalued traditional homemaking, and encour-aged sexual promiscuity. But feminist and activist scholar Sara M. Evans takes a much more positive view of the women's movements for suffrage and liberation in the past 100 years. Despite their class, racial, religious, ethnic, and regional differences, Evans argues that women in America experienced major transformations in their private and public lives in the twentieth century.

The reader concludes with a major current debate about our history. Is the United States a declining power? Are we going the way of Rome in the third century? Or England in the twentieth century? In the first selection in Issue 18, Professor Andrew J. Bacevich, a West Point graduate and Vietnam veteran, believes that the United States has enlarged the power of the presidency and abuses its military power to create an informal empire in the energy-rich Persian Gulf in its pursuit of a consumer-dominated good life. But Dr. Fareed Zakaria, a political commentator for CNN, believes the United States is still a great power in the post-industrial world because of its tremendous advantages in education, immigration and scientific innovation.

Conclusion

The process of historical study should rely more on thinking than on memorizing data. Once the basics of who, what, when, and where are determined, historical thinking shifts to a higher gear. Explanation, analysis, evaluation, comparison, and contrast take command. These skills not only increase our knowledge of the past, but they also provide general tools for the comprehension of all the topics about which human beings think.

The diversity of a pluralistic society, however, creates some obstacles to comprehending the past. The spectrum of differing opinions on any particular subject eliminates the possibility of quick and easy answers. In the final analysis, conclusions are often built through a synthesis of several different interpretations, but even then they may be partial and tentative.

The study of history in a pluralistic society allows each citizen the opportunity to teach independent conclusions about the past. Since most, if not all, historical issues affect the present and future, understanding the past becomes necessary if society is to progress. Many of today's problems have a direct connection with the past. Additionally, other contemporary issues may lack obvious direct antecedents, but historical investigation can provide illuminating analogies. At first, it may appear confusing to read and to think about opposing historical views, but the survival of our democratic society depends on such critical thinking by acute and discerning minds.

Internet References . . .

Journal Sites

Important journal articles and book reviews that reflect the most recent scholarship on all the issues can be found on the following site:

http://H-NE.msu.edu

Freedmen's Bureau Online

This Web site contains more than one hundred transcriptions of reports on murders, riots, and "outrages" (any criminal offense) that occurred in the former Confederate states from 1865 to 1868.

http://www.freedmensbureau.com/

John D. Rockefeller and the Standard Oil Company

This site, created by Swiss entrepreneur Francois Micheloud, provides a highly detailed history of the American oil industry, with John D. Rockefeller as a main focus.

http://www.micheloud.com./FXM/SO/rock.htm

World Wide Web Virtual Library

This site focuses on labor and business history.

http://www.iisg.nl/~w3vl/

International Channel

Immigrants helped to create modern America. Visit this interesting site to experience "the memories, sounds, even tastes of Ellis Island."

http://www.i-channel.com/

American Family Immigration History Center

Records on the more than 25 million passengers and crew members who passed through Ellis Island between 1892 and 1924 are available here.

http://www.ellisisland.org

(Gene) Autry National Center

4700 Western Heritage Way, Los Angeles, CA 90027; phone (323) 667-2000
This site contains information about one of the most important museums and collections of Western and Indian history.

http://www.autrynationalcenter.org

1896: The Presidential Campaign

The election of 1896 was one of the most contentious in U.S. history. When Republican William McKinley defeated William Jennings Bryan on November third, there were no fewer than six candidates on the ballot and the country was in the throes of an economic depression. This Web site provides close to 100 political cartoons surrounding the election campaigns.

http://projects.vassar.edu/1896/1896home.html

The Gilded Age

*E*conomic expansion and the seemingly unlimited resources available in postbellum America offered great opportunity and created new political, social, and economic challenges. Political freedom and economic opportunity provided incentives for immigration to America. But after an initial burst of freedom, African Americans were segregated from mainstream America and limited in their political and economic rights and opportunities. The need for cheap labor to run the machinery of the Industrial Revolution created an atmosphere for potential exploitation that was intensified by the concentration of wealth in the hands of a few capitalists. The labor movement took root, with some elements calling for an overthrow of the capitalist system, while others sought to establish political power within the existing system. Strains began to develop between immigrant and native-born workers as well as between workers and owners, husbands and wives, and parents and their children.

With the growth of industry, urban problems became more acute. Improvements in water and sewage, street cleaning, housing, mass transit, and fire and crime prevention developed slowly because incredible population growth strained municipal services. Urban governments had limited powers, which often fell under the control of political bosses. Historians disagree as to whether or not attempts to remedy these problems through a brokered political system were successful. Meanwhile, the last frontier had been reached with the end of the Indian wars. Were the Western communities more violent than the large industrial cities of the 1890s? Or have radio, television, and the movies portrayed a mythical West?

- Did Reconstruction Fail as a Result of Racism?
- Was the Wild West More Violent Than the Rest of the United States?
- Were the Nineteenth-Century Big Businessmen "Robber Barons"?
- Was the American Labor Movement Radical?
- Were Late-Nineteenth-Century Immigrants "Uprooted"?
- Were the Populists Irrational Reactionaries?

ISSUE 1

Did Reconstruction Fail as a Result of Racism?

YES: George M. Fredrickson, from *The Black Image in the White Mind: The Debate on Afro-American Character and Destiny, 1817–1914* (Harper & Row, 1971)

NO: Heather Cox Richardson, from *The Death of Reconstruction: Race, Labor, and Politics in the Post–Civil War North, 1865–1901* (Harvard University Press, 2001)

ISSUE SUMMARY

YES: George M. Fredrickson concludes that racism, in the form of the doctrine of white supremacy, colored the thinking not only of southern whites but of most white northerners as well and produced only halfhearted efforts by the Radical Republicans in the postwar period to sustain a commitment to black equality.

NO: Heather Cox Richardson argues that the failure of Radical Reconstruction was primarily a consequence of a national commitment to a free-labor ideology that opposed an expanding central government that legislated rights to African Americans that other citizens had acquired through hard work.

Given the complex issues of the post–Civil War years, it is not surprising that the era of Reconstruction (1865–1877) is shrouded in controversy. For the better part of a century following the war, historians typically characterized Reconstruction as a total failure that had proved detrimental to all Americans—northerners and southerners, whites and blacks. According to this traditional interpretation, a vengeful Congress, dominated by radical Republicans, imposed military rule upon the southern states. Carpetbaggers from the North, along with traitorous white scalawags and their black accomplices in the South, established coalition governments that rewrote state constitutions, raised taxes, looted state treasuries, and disenfranchised former Confederates while extending the ballot to the freedmen. This era finally ended in 1877 when courageous southern white Democrats successfully "redeemed" their region from "Negro rule" by toppling the Republican state governments.

This portrait of Reconstruction dominated the historical profession until the 1960s. One reason for this is that white historians (both northerners and southerners) who wrote about this period operated from two basic assumptions: (1) The South was capable of solving its own problems without federal government interference; and (2) the former slaves were intellectually inferior to whites and incapable of running a government (much less one in which some whites would be their subordinates). African American historians, such as W. E. B. DuBois, wrote several essays and books that challenged this negative portrayal of Reconstruction, but their works seldom were taken seriously in the academic world and rarely were read by the general public. Still, these black historians foreshadowed the acceptance of revisionist interpretations of Reconstruction, which coincided with the successes of the civil rights movement (or "Second Reconstruction") in the 1960s.

Without ignoring obvious problems and limitations connected with this period, revisionist historians identified a number of accomplishments of the Republican state governments in the South and their supporters in Washington, D.C. For example, revisionists argued that the state constitutions that were written during Reconstruction were the most democratic documents that the South had seen up to that time. Also, although taxes increased in the southern states, the revenues generated by these levies financed the rebuilding and expansion of the South's railroad network, the creation of a number of social service institutions, and the establishment of a public school system that benefited African Americans as well as whites. At the federal level, Reconstruction achieved the ratification of the Fourteenth and Fifteenth Amendments, which extended significant privileges of citizenship (including the right to vote) to African Americans, both North and South. Revisionists also placed the charges of corruption leveled by traditionalists against the Republican regimes in the South in a more appropriate context by insisting that political corruption was a *national* malady. Although the leaders of the Republican state governments in the South engaged in a number of corrupt activities, they were no more guilty than several federal officeholders in the Grant administration, or the members of New York City's notorious Tweed Ring (a Democratic urban political machine), or even the southern white Democrats (the Redeemers) who replaced the radical Republicans in positions of power in the former Confederate states. Finally, revisionist historians sharply attacked the notion that African Americans dominated the reconstructed governments of the South.

In the essays that follow, George M. Fredrickson and Heather Cox Richardson present thought-provoking analyses of the influence racism played in the failure of Reconstruction. In the first selection, Fredrickson contends that the doctrine of white supremacy that galvanized southern opposition to the political, economic, and social empowerment of African Americans after the war also dominated the thinking of white northerners, including many Radical Republicans. As a consequence, racism prevented the success of efforts to incorporate African Americans fully into American society on an equitable basis.

Heather Cox Richardson offers a postrevisionist interpretation of the failure of Reconstruction and contends that the key barrier to postwar assistance for African Americans was the nation's commitment to a free-labor ideology. Believing that social equality derived from economic success, most Americans opposed legislation, such as the Civil Rights Act of 1875, which appeared to provide special interest legislation solely for the benefit of the former slaves.

3

YES

George M. Fredrickson

The Black Image in the White Mind: The Debate on Afro-American Character and Destiny, 1817–1914

Race and Reconstruction

Once freed, the black population of the South constituted a new element that had to be incorporated somehow into the American social and political structure. Some Radical Republicans and veterans of the antislavery crusade regarded justice and equality for the freedmen as a fulfillment of national ideals and a desirable end in itself. For a larger number of loyal Northerners the question of Negro rights was, from first to last, clearly subordinate to the more fundamental aim of ensuring national hegemony for Northern political, social, and economic institutions. But even those who lacked an ideological commitment to black equality could not avoid the necessity of shaping a new status for the Southern blacks; for there they were in large numbers, capable of being either a help or a hindrance to the North's effort to restore the Union and secure the fruits of victory.

Before 1863 and 1864, Northern leaders had been able to discuss with full seriousness the possibility of abolishing slavery while at the same time avoiding the perplexing and politically dangerous task of incorporating the freed blacks into the life of the nation. President Lincoln and other moderate or conservative Republicans, feeling the pulse of a racist public opinion, had looked to the reduction or elimination of the black population through colonization or emigration as a way of approaching the racial homogeneity which they associated with guaranteed national unity and progress. By itself the Emancipation Proclamation had not destroyed such hopes, but events soon made the colonization schemes irrelevant and inappropriate. . . .

Whatever the motivation of Radical Reconstruction and however inadequate its programs, it was a serious effort, the first in American history, to incorporate Negroes into the body politic. As such, it inevitably called forth bitter opposition from hardcore racists, who attempted to discredit radical measures by using many of the same arguments developed as part of the proslavery argument in the prewar period.

The new cause was defined as "white supremacy"—which in practice allowed Southern whites to reduce the freedmen to an inferior caste, as they had attempted to do by enacting the "Black Codes" of 1865. To further this cause in 1868, [John] Van Evrie simply reissued his book *Negroes and Negro "Slavery"* with a topical introduction and under the new title *White Supremacy and Negro Subordination.* [Josiah] Nott also entered the Reconstruction controversy. In an 1866 pamphlet he reasserted the "scientific" case for inherent black inferiority as part of an attack on the Freedmen's Bureau and other Northern efforts to deal with the Southern race question. "If the whites and blacks be left alone face to face," he wrote, "they will soon learn to understand each other, and come to proper terms under the law of necessity."

Edward A. Pollard, a Richmond journalist and prewar fire-eater, also attacked Northern Reconstruction proposals on racial grounds. His book *The Lost Cause Regained,* published in 1868, contended that "the permanent, natural inferiority of the Negro was the true and *only* defense of slavery" and lamented the fact that the South had wasted its intellectual energy on other arguments. Before the war, Pollard had advocated a revival of the slave trade because it would deflate the pretensions of uppity house servants and town Negroes by submerging them in a flood of humble primitives; he now endorsed Van Evrie's thesis that white democracy depended on absolute black subordination, and concluded his discussion of Negro racial characteristics by asserting that the established "fact" of inferiority dictated "the true *status* of the Negro." Other propagandists of white supremacy, North and South, joined the fray. A writer named Lindley Spring attacked Radical Reconstruction in 1868 with a lengthy discourse on the benighted and savage record of blacks in Africa; and a Dr. J. R. Hayes excoriated the proposed Fifteenth Amendment in 1869 with a rehash of all the biological "evidence" for Negro incapacity.

Inevitably, the pre-Adamite theory of Dr. Samuel A. Cartwright and Jefferson Davis was trotted out. In 1866 Governor Benjamin F. Perry of South Carolina made it the basis of a defense of white supremacy; and in 1867 a Nashville publisher named Buckner Payne, writing under the pseudonym "Ariel," revived a controversy among racists by expounding the doctrine at some length in a pamphlet entitled *The Negro: What Is His Ethnological Status?* Payne not only asserted that the Negro was "created before Adam and Eve" as "a *separate* and *distinct* species of the *genus homo,*" but also argued that it was because some of the sons of Adam intermarried with this inferior species, related, as it was, to the "higher orders of the monkey," that God had sent the flood as a punishment for human wrongdoing. Like almost all the racist respondents to Reconstruction, he contended that Negro equality would lead inevitably to amalgamation, and that miscegenation, in addition to resulting in the debasement of the white race, would bring on catastrophic divine intervention: "The states and people that favor this equality and amalgamation of the white and black races, *God will exterminate. . . .* A man can not commit so great an offense against his race, against his country, against his God, . . . as to give his daughter in marriage to a negro—a *beast. . . .*"

Most of the propagandists who attacked Radical measures on extreme racist grounds had a prewar record as apologists for slavery, but Hinton Rowan Helper attracted the greatest attention because of his fame or notoriety as an antebellum critic of slavery. As we have seen, Helper had never concealed his anti-Negro sentiments. A letter of 1861 summed up his philosophy: "A trio of unmitigated and demoralizing nuisances, constituting in the aggregate, a most foul and formidable obstacle to our high and mighty civilization in America are Negroes, Slavery, and Slaveholders. . . .

> Death to Slavery!
> Down with the Slaveholders!
> Away with the Negroes!"

Having done justice to the first two imperatives in *The Impending Crisis,* Helper turned after the war to the third. His *Nojoque,* published in 1867, may have been the most virulent racist diatribe ever published in the United States. It contemplated with relish the time when "the negroes, and all the other swarthy races of mankind," have been "completely fossilized." To speed up the divinely ordained process of racial extermination, Helper proposed as immediate steps the denial of all rights to Negroes and their complete separation from the whites. All this of course went in the teeth of the emerging Reconstruction policies of what had been Helper's own party, and throughout the book he excoriated "the Black Republicans" for departing from the attitudes of the prewar period, a time when Republicans had billed themselves as "the white man's party." His heroes were "White Republicans" like Secretary of State Seward and those few Republicans in the House and Senate who had remained loyal to President Johnson and joined the Democrats in efforts to prevent Federal action on behalf of Negro equality.

The active politicians—mostly Democrats—who opposed Radical Reconstruction were quite willing to resort to racist demagoguery, although they generally avoided the excesses of polemicists like Payne and Helper. President Johnson, for example, played subtly but unmistakably on racial fears in his veto messages of 1866; and later, in his third annual message to Congress, he put his views squarely on the line: ". . . it must be acknowledged that in the progress of nations negroes have shown less capacity for self-government than any other race of people. No independent government of any form has ever been successful in their hands. On the contrary whenever they have been left to their own devices they have shown an instant tendency to relapse into barbarism. . . . The great difference between the two races in physical, mental, and moral characteristics will prevent an amalgamation or fusion of them together in one homogeneous mass. . . . Of all the dangers which our nation has yet encountered, none are equal to those which must result from the success of the effort now making to Africanize the [Southern] half of our country." Equally blatant were the Northern Democratic Congressmen who made speeches against Radical measures which appealed directly to the prejudices of white workingmen. As Representative John W. Chanler of New York put it, in attacking an 1866 proposal to give the vote to Negroes in the District of Columbia: "White democracy makes war on every class, caste, and race which assails its sovereignty or would undermine the mastery of the white working man, be he ignorant or learned, strong or weak. Black democracy does not exist. The black race have never asserted and maintained their inalienable right to be a people, anywhere, or at any time."

In addition to such crude appeals to "white democracy," Democratic spokesmen in Congress provided detailed and pretentious discourses on the "ethnological" status of the Negro, drawn from writers like Nott and Van Evrie. The most notable of such efforts was the speech Representative James Brooks of New York delivered on December 18, 1867, in opposition to the First Reconstruction Act. "You have deliberately framed a bill," he accused the Radicals, "to overthrow this white man's government of our fathers and to erect an African Government in its stead. . . . The negro is not the equal of the white man, much less his master; and this I can demonstrate anatomically, physiologically and psychologically too, if necessary. Volumes of scientific authority establish the fact. . . ." Brooks then proceeded "in the fewest words possible to set forth scientific facts." He discoursed at length on "the hair or wool of the negro," on "the skull, the brain, the neck, the foot, etc.," and on the perils of miscegenation. In considering the last topic, he conceded that "the mulatto with white blood in his veins often has the intelligence and capacity of a white man," but added that he could not consent to suffrage for mulattoes because to do so would violate the divine decree "that all are to be punished who indulge in a criminal admixture of races, so that beyond the third or fourth generation there could be no further mulatto progeny." Having covered black and brown physiology, Brooks went on in standard racist fashion to portray Negro history as a great emptiness.

In general such anti-Negro arguments were simply ignored by the proponents of Radical Reconstruction, who, by and large, tried to avoid the whole question of basic racial characteristics. But Brook's speech, perhaps the most thorough presentation of the racist creed ever offered in Congress, could not go unanswered. In a brief reply, Thaddeus Stevens dismissed Brook's views as contradicting the Biblical doctrine of the unity of mankind. Resorting to sarcasm and impugning Brook's loyalty, Stevens agreed that Negroes were indeed "barbarians," because they had "with their own right hands, in defense of liberty, stricken down thousands of the friends of the gentleman who has been enlightening us today." Disregarding Brooks's point about the "intelligence and capacity of mulattoes," Stevens proposed to match Frederick Douglass against Brooks in an oratorical contest. A more serious and extended reply to Brooks was made from the Republican side of the aisle by John D. Baldwin of Massachusetts. Baldwin's speech is significant because it clearly reveals both the strengths and weaknesses of the Radical position on race as a factor in Reconstruction.

In the first place, Baldwin contended, Brooks's argument was largely a *non sequitur;* for "the question presented in these discussions is not a question concerning the equality or the inequality of human races . . . it is a question concerning human rights. It calls on us to decide whether men shall be equal before the law and have equality in their relations to the Government of their country." Races, like individuals, might indeed differ in their capacities, but this should not affect their fundamental rights. In reply to Brooks's claim that miscegenation would result from equality, Baldwin suggested that it was much more likely to result from degradation such as had occurred under slavery, a system which provided a "fatal facility" for "the mixture of races." As for

Brooks's position on political rights, it meant in effect that all Negroes should be excluded from suffrage while "even the most ignorant and brutal white man" should be allowed to vote: "If he should propose to guard the ballot by some exclusion of ignorance or baseness, made without regard to race or class, candid men would listen to him and discuss that proposition." But Brooks was propounding, according to Baldwin, a concept of white privilege and "divine right" completely incompatible with the American egalitarian philosophy. Eventually Baldwin touched gingerly on the question of inherent racial differences and conceded the point that the races were not alike, but argued that "it is quite possible that we shall find it necessary to revise our conception of what constitutes the superiority of race." The prevailing conception, he noted, had resulted from an admiration for the ability to conquer and dominate; but were such aggressive qualities "really the highest, the most admirable development of human nature?" Pointing to the recent rise of a higher regard for the gentler, more peaceable virtues, Baldwin suggested "that each race and each distinct family of mankind has some peculiar gift of its own in which it is superior to others; and that an all-wise Creator may have designed that each race and family shall bring its own peculiar contribution to the final completeness of civilization. . . ." Although he did not discuss directly how the racial character of whites and Negroes differed, he was clearly invoking the romantic racialist conceptions that had long been popular among Radicals and abolitionists.

At first glance it would appear that Baldwin's speech constituted an adequate response to the racist critique of Radical Reconstruction, despite his avoidance of Brooks's specific physiological, anatomical, and historical arguments. It was indeed "rights" that the Radicals were attempting to legislate and not the identity of the races. But if, as Baldwin conceded, the races had differing "gifts"—with the whites holding a monopoly of the kind of qualities that led to dominance and conquest—then the competitive "test" of racial capabilities that the Radicals envisioned as resulting from their program would, to follow their own logic, lead inevitably to white domination, even without the support of discriminatory laws. Furthermore, their tendency to accept the concept of innate racial differences and their apparent repulsion to intermarriage were invitations to prejudice and discrimination on the part of those whites— presumably the overwhelming majority of Americans—who were less likely to respond to romantic appeals to racial benevolence than to draw traditional white-supremacist conclusions from any Radical admissions that blacks were "different" and, in some sense, unassimilable.

✦

A few Radicals and abolitionists had early and serious doubts about the efficacy and underlying assumptions of the Reconstruction Acts of 1867 and 1868. They suspected that quick readmission of Southern states into the Union under constitutions providing for Negro suffrage and the disfranchisement of prominent ex-Confederates would not by itself give blacks a reasonable opportunity to develop their full capacities and establish a position of genuine equality. Some understanding of this problem had been reflected in the land confiscation proposals of men like Thaddeus Stevens and Wendell Phillips. But it was the Radicals who worked for extended periods among the freedmen in the South who gained the fullest awareness of what needed to be done beyond what most Congressional proponents of Radical Reconstruction thought was necessary. Charles Stearns, an abolitionist who attempted to establish a co-operative plantation in Georgia as a step toward Negro land-ownership, attacked the notion that legal and political rights were all that was required to give the black man a fair, competitive position. In *The Black Man of the South, and the Rebels,* published in 1872, Stearns denounced Greeley's philosophy of "root hog or die," arguing that even a hog could not root without a snout. In his view, provisions for land and education, far beyond anything that was then available to the blacks, were absolutely essential. Arguing that "the black man possesses all the natural powers that we possess," he pointed out that the blacks had not yet recovered from the degrading effects of slavery and were unable, even under Radical Reconstruction, to compete successfully or maintain their rights in the face of a bitterly hostile Southern white population.

Albion W. Tourgée, an idealistic "carpetbagger" who settled in North Carolina and became a judge under its Radical regime, was an eloquent and persistent spokesman for the same point of view. Tourgée, who eventually made his experiences and perceptions the basis of a series of novels, sensed from the beginning that the Radical program, as it finally emerged from Congress, constituted a halfhearted commitment to Negro equality which was doomed to fail in the long run. In a letter to the *National Anti-Slavery Standard* in October, 1867, he announced his opposition to the "Plan of Congress" that was taking shape. "No law, no constitution, no matter how cunningly framed," he wrote, "can shield the poor man of the South from the domination of that very aristocracy from which rebellion sprang, when once states are established here. Anarchy or oligarchy is the inevitable result of reconstruction. Serfdom or bloodshed must necessarily follow. The 'Plan of Congress,' so called, if adopted, would deliver the free men of the South, bound hand and foot to their old-time, natural enemies." The Southern Republican Party, Tourgée was saying, was composed largely of impoverished blacks and lower-class whites. Even if assured of temporary political dominance by the disfranchisement of ex-Confederates, these men would soon find themselves at the mercy of the large landowners, who were in a position to apply economic pressure and undo the reforms of Reconstruction. With rare realism, Tourgée argued in effect that political power could not be maintained on the basis of suffrage alone but must be bolstered by adequate economic and social power— and this was precisely what Southern Republicans lacked.

Tourgée's predictions of course came true. As the North looked on, manifesting an increasing reluctance to interfere—a growing desire to wash its hands of the whole matter—Southern white "redeemers" toppled one Radical government after another between 1870 and 1877 and established white-supremacist regimes. Southern Radicalism, supported largely by black votes and ruling through shifting and unstable alliances of Northern "carpetbaggers," Southern white "scalawags," and emergent black spokesmen, had no chance of withstanding the economic, political, and paramilitary opposition of the white majority. In his 1879 Reconstruction novel, *A Fool's Errand,* Tourgée provided an acute assessment of what the Northern leadership had done and why it failed to achieve its original objectives:

> After having forced a proud people to yield what they had for more than two centuries considered a right,—the right to hold the African race in bondage,—they proceeded to outrage a feeling as deep and fervent as the zeal of Islam or the exclusiveness of the Hindoo caste, by giving the ignorant, the unskilled and dependent race—a race which could not have lived a week without the support or charity of the dominant one—equality of political right. Not content with this, they went farther, and by erecting the rebellious territory into self-regulating and sovereign states, they abandoned these parties to fight out the question of predominance without the possibility of national interference, they said to the colored man in the language of one of the pseudo-philosophers of that day, 'Root, hog, or die!'

The Negro never had a chance in this struggle, as the entire novel makes clear. His ignorance and poverty made him no match for the white conservative forces.

What Tourgée and a few others—notably Representative George W. Julian of Indiana—would have preferred as a plan of reconstruction was a comparatively long-term military occupation or territorial rule of the South, which would have guaranteed "Regeneration before Reconstruction." This "territorial tutelage" would have lasted for an indeterminate period, perhaps as long as twenty or thirty years—long enough to give the North a chance to prepare the freedmen for citizenship through extensive programs of education and guidance, presumably including some form of economic assistance, while at the same time working for a diminution of the racial prejudice and "disloyalty" of the whites. But such an approach was rendered impossible both by pressures which impelled Republican politicians to seek readmission of loyalist-dominated Southern states to the Union in time for the election of 1868 and by the underlying social and racial attitudes that have been described. According to the dominant "self-help" ideology, no one, regardless of his antecedents, had a claim on society for economic security or special protection, or was entitled to a social status that he had not earned through independent struggle and hard work; the just penalty for laziness, inefficiency, or vice was severe social and economic deprivation, and it was becoming an open question at this time whether society's most abysmal "failures" should even retain their full right to participate in the political process. Having been provided with Federal laws and Constitutional amendments which supposedly guaranteed his legal equality, the black man was expected to make his own way and find his "true level" with a minimum of interference and direct assistance. When the Reconstruction governments foundered, many in the North were quick to say that the blacks had had their fair chance, had demonstrated their present incapacity for self-government, and could justifiably be relegated, for the time being at least, to an inferior status.

Tourgée probably understood better than anyone how tenuous and conditional the Northern commitment to Negro equality had been. His book *An Appeal to Caesar,* published in 1884, contended that the Northern people "have always reflected the Southern idea of the negro in everything except as to his natural right to be free and to exercise the rights of the freedman. From the first [the North] seems to have been animated by the sneaking notion that after having used the negro to fight its battles, freed him as the natural result of a rebellion based on slavery, and enfranchised him to constitute a political foil to the ambition and disloyalty of his former master, it could at any time unload him upon the states where he chanced to dwell, wash its hands of all further responsibility in the matter, and leave him to live or die as chance might determine."

The Death of Reconstruction: Race, Labor, and Politics in the Post–Civil War North, 1865–1901

Civil Rights and the Growth of the National Government, 1870–1883

Northern Republican disillusionment with African-American attitudes toward social issues compounded the Northern association of Southern freedmen with labor radicals who advocated confiscation of wealth. Taking place during and immediately after the South Carolina tax crisis, the civil rights debates of the 1870s seemed to confirm that African-Americans were turning increasingly to legislation to afford them the privileges for which other Americans had worked individually. Civil rights agitation did more than simply flesh out an existing sketch of disaffected black workers, however; it suggested that advocates of African-American rights were actively working to expand the national government to cater to those who rejected the free labor ideal.

"Civil rights," in the immediate aftermath of the war, meant something different than it gradually came to mean over the next several years. *Harper's Weekly* distinguished between "natural rights" to life, liberty, and "the fruits of . . . honest labor," and "civil rights," which were critical to a freedperson's ability to function as a free worker. Civil rights, it explained, were "such rights as to sue, to give evidence, to inherit, buy, lease, sell, convey, and hold property, and others. Few intelligent persons in this country would now deny or forbid equality of natural and civil rights," it asserted in 1867. The 1866 Civil Rights Act, written by the man who had drafted the Thirteenth Amendment, Illinois senator Lyman Trumbull, was intended to secure to African-Americans "full and equal benefit of all laws and proceedings for the security of person and property as is enjoyed by white citizens." It guaranteed only that the legal playing field would be level for all citizens; state legislatures could not enact legislation endangering a black person's right to his life or his land. By 1867, hoping to woo conservative Republican voters into the Democratic camp and to undercut the justification for black suffrage, even moderate Democrats claimed to be willing to back civil rights for African-Americans "with every token of sincerity . . . from a free and spontaneous sense of justice."

"Social" equality was a different thing—it was a result of a person's economic success rather than a condition for it. It was something to be earned by whites and blacks alike. Directly related to economic standing, a man's social standing rose as he prospered. A good social position also required that a person possess other attributes that the community valued. A place in upwardly mobile American society required religious observance and apparently moral behavior, as well as the habits of thrift and economy dictated by a plan for economic success. This gradual social elevation became a mirror of gradual economic elevation through hard work as a traditional free laborer.

Immediately after the Civil War, as Democrats insisted that black freedom would usher in social mixing between races and intermarriage, almost all Northern Republicans emphatically denied that emancipation was intended to have any effect on social issues and reiterated that African-Americans must rise in society only through the same hard effort that had brought other Americans to prominence. In 1867, a correspondent to the radical *Cincinnati Daily Gazette* from Louisiana painted a complimentary portrait of Louisiana African-Americans, then concluded that they had neither the expectation nor the desire for "social equality, that favorite bugbear." They would ridicule any attempt to break down social distinctions by legislation, knowing that the government could give them only political equality, the writer claimed, quoting his informants as saying, "Our own brains, our own conduct, is what we must depend upon for our future elevation; each one of us striving for himself and laboring to improve his mental and moral condition." Adding credence to the correspondent's representations, the Georgia Freedmen's Convention of 1866 resolved, "We do not in any respect desire social equality beyond the transactions of the ordinary business of life, inasmuch as we deem our own race, equal to all our wants of purely social enjoyment."

As the Republicans enacted legislation promoting the interests of African-Americans, however, racist Democrats insisted they were forcing social interaction to promote African-Americans artificially, at the expense of whites. When the Civil Rights Act of 1866 took effect, Democrats charged that the Republican concept of black equality before the law meant Republicans believed that blacks and whites were entirely equal. The *New York World* predicted interracial marriages; the *Columbus (Ohio) Crisis* insisted that a black orator in Richmond had told his black audience to "vote for the man who will bring you into his parlor, who will eat dinner with you, and who, if you want her, will let you marry his daughter." In 1868, *De Bow's Review* argued that negro suffrage meant that African-Americans would "next meet us at the marriage altar and in the burial vault," where they would "order the white ancestors' bones to be disinterred and removed elsewhere, and their own transferred into these hitherto held sacred white family sepulchers."

In response to Democratic attacks, in 1868 the *New York Times* reiterated that Republicans planned only for African-Americans to share the rights and opportunities of typical free laborers. It maintained that "reconstruction did not fly in the face of nature by attempting to impose social . . . equality," it simply established political and legal equality. These rights would eventually "obliterate" social prejudices as white men sought black votes. The next year the *Times* approvingly reported that abolitionist agitator Wendell Phillips had said that "the social equality of the black race will have to be worked out by their own exertion." Frederick Douglass put out the best idea, it continued later, namely: "Let the negro alone."

ᴥᴥᴥ

Republican insistence that social equality would work itself out as freedpeople worked their way up to prosperity could not provide an answer for the overwhelming discrimination African-Americans faced. While many black and white Southerners accepted the established patterns of segregation, those practices meant that African-Americans' public life was inferior to that of their white counterparts. Black people could not sit on juries in most of the South, they could not be certain of transportation on railroads or accommodation at inns, their schools were poor copies of white schools. In addition to creating a climate of constant harassment for African-Americans, discrimination, especially discrimination in schooling, seemed to hamper their ability to rise economically. The Fourteenth and Fifteenth Amendments had made all Americans equal before the law, but they could not guarantee equal access to transportation, accommodations, or schools, and while many ex-slaves accepted conditions as an improvement on the past and dismissed civil rights bills as impractical, those African-Americans who had worked hard to become members of the "better classes" deeply resented their exclusion from public facilities. "Education amounts to nothing, good behavior counts for nothing, even money cannot buy for a colored man or woman decent treatment and the comforts that white people claim and can obtain," complained Mississippi Sheriff John M. Brown. Prominent African-Americans called for legislation to counter the constant discrimination they faced.

African-American proponents of a new civil rights law to enforce non-discrimination in public services had a champion in the former abolitionist Senator Charles Sumner of Massachusetts. An exceedingly prominent man, the tall, aloof Sumner was the nation's leading champion of African-American rights after the war and had advocated a civil rights measure supplementary to the Civil Rights Act of 1866 since May 1870, when he introduced to the Senate a bill (S. 916) making the federal government responsible for the enforcement of equal rights in public transportation, hotels, theaters, schools, churches, public cemeteries, and juries.

But Sumner's sponsorship of a civil rights bill immediately made more moderate congressmen wary of it; his enthusiasm for black rights frequently made him advocate measures that seemed to remove African-Americans from the free labor system and make them favored wards of a government that was expanding to serve them. Only two months after the ratification of the fifteenth Amendment had reassured moderate Republicans and Democrats alike that they had done everything possible to make all men equal in America, Sumner told the Senate that black men were not actually equal enough, but that his new bill would do the trick. When it passes, he said, "I [will] know nothing further to be done in the way of legislation for the security of equal rights in this Republic." . . .

⚬⟨◉⟩⚬

By 1874, most Republicans were ready to cut the freedpeople's ties to the government in order to force African-Americans to fall back on their own resources and to protect the government from the machinations of demagogues pushing special-interest legislation. When Mississippi Republicans asked President Grant in January 1874 to use the administration to shore up their state organization, the *Philadelphia Inquirer* enthusiastically reported his refusal. Grant "remove[d] his segar from his mouth and enunciate[d] a great truth with startling emphasis," according to a writer for the newspaper. The president said it was "time for the Republican party to unload." The party could not continue to carry the "dead weight" of intrastate quarrels. Grant was sick and tired of it, he told listeners. "This nursing of monstrosities has nearly exhausted the life of the party. I am done with them, and they will have to take care of themselves." The *Philadelphia Inquirer* agreed that the federal government had to cease to support the Southern Republican organizations of freedpeople and their demagogic leaders. The *New York Daily Tribune* approved Grant's similar hands-off policy in Texas, thrilled that "there [was] no longer any cause to apprehend that another State Government will be overturned by Federal bayonets."

Benjamin Butler's role as the House manager of the civil rights bill only hurt its chances, for he embodied the connection between freedpeople and a government in thrall to special interests. The symbol of the "corruption" of American government, Butler was popularly credited with strong-arming the House into recognizing the Louisiana representatives backed by the Kellogg government, which was generally believed to be an illegal creation of Louisiana's largely black Republican party, supported not by the people of the state but by federal officers. Honest men wanted to destroy "the principle which Mr. Butler and his followers represent," wrote the *New York Daily Tribune* and others. "The force in our politics of which he is the recognized exponent, and of which thousands of our politicians of less prominence are the creatures." "Butlerism" meant gaining power by promising an uneducated public patronage or legislation in their favor, and all but the stalwart Republicans and Democratic machine politicians hoped for the downfall of both Butler and what he represented.

Despite the fact that it was prosperous African-Americans who advocated the bill, it appeared to opponents that the civil rights bill was an extraordinary piece of unconstitutional legislation by which demagogues hoped to hold on to power in the South, and thus in the nation, by catering to the whims of disaffected African-Americans who were unwilling to work. The proposed law seemed to offer nothing to the nation but a trampled constitution, lazy freedpeople, and a growing government corrupted into a vehicle for catering to the undeserving.

The civil rights bill would probably never have passed the Senate had it not been for the sudden death of Charles Sumner on March 11, 1874. Before he died, Sumner charged fellow Massachusetts senator George F. Hoar to "take care of the civil-rights bill,—my bill, the civil-rights bill, don't let it fail." Even Republican enemies of the bill eulogized the "great man"; the *Chicago Tribune* reflected that "there is no man, friend or enemy, who does not pause to pay respect to the memory of Charles Sumner." African-Americans across the country mourned Sumner's death and called for the passage of his "last and grandest work," and on April 14, 1874, from the Committee on the Judiciary, Senator Frederick T. Frelinghuysen reported Sumner's civil rights bill protecting African-Americans from discrimination in public facilities, schools, and juries. The committee's amendments placed firmly in the national legal apparatus responsibility for overseeing violations of the proposed law. In caucus on May 8, some Republican senators objected to "certain features" of the bill but expressed a desire to act "harmoniously" on the measure. In the next caucus, the Republicans decided to support the bill without amendments.

After an all-night session of the Senate, a handful of African-American men in the galleries applauded as the Senate passed the bill on May 23, 1874, by a vote of twenty-nine to sixteen. Rumors circulated that the president had "some doubts about signing it" if it should pass the House, and many Republicans indicated they would not mind the loss of the bill. "Respect for the dead is incumbent on us all," snarled the *New York Times*, "—but legislation should be based on a careful and wise regard for the welfare of the living, not upon 'mandates,' real or fictitious, of the dead." Referring to the apparent African-American control of Southern governments, the *Times* asked whether the freedman "stands in need of protection from the white man, or the white man stands in need of protection from him." The House Judiciary Committee could not agree on its own civil rights measure and decided to replace its bill with the Senate's. The House then tabled the bill for the rest of the session, despite the continued urging of "leading colored men" that Benjamin Butler get it taken up and passed. . . .

The civil rights bill was rescued from oblivion only by Democratic wins in the 1874 elections. Republican congressmen's desire to consolidate Reconstruction before the Democrats arrived barely outweighed party members' fears that the measure was an attempt of corrupt politicians to harness the black vote by offering African-Americans extraordinary benefits that would undermine their willingness to work. When the lame-duck Congress reconvened in December 1874, House Republican leader Benjamin Butler tried to pass a bill protecting freedmen at the polls and an army appropriations bill to shore up stalwart Republicans in the South. Democrats filibustered. Butler was unable to get a suspension of the rules to maneuver around them as fifteen Republicans joined the opposition, worried that Butler's attempt to suspend the rules was simply a means "to get through a lot of jobbing measures under cover of Civil Rights and protection of the South." With his reputation as a special-interest broker, Butler had a terrible time getting the civil rights bill off the Speaker's table. Finally Republicans agreed to let Butler take it to the floor in late January.

The galleries were full as the House discussed the bill in early February. After omitting provisions for integrated schools, churches, and cemeteries, the House passed the bill on February 5 by a vote of 162 to 100. While African-Americans in favor of a civil rights bill were horrified at the sacrifice of the school clause, all but the most radical Republicans approved the omission. "The bill . . . is worthy [of] the support of every congressman who wishes to deal equitably with the citizens of the United States, white and black," wrote even the *Boston Evening Transcript*. "This measure simply provides for the education of the blacks, and does not force their children into association with white scholars," at the same time demanding that the schools be equal. "The Republicans can stand upon such a platform as that," the *Transcript* chided unwilling party members. "The great desire and solicitude of the people are to support 'civil rights' and so execute in good faith the constitutional pledges of the nation." After initial reluctance, the Senate passed the school amendment by a vote of 38 to 62, and despite Democratic plans to talk the bill to death, the Senate repassed the civil rights bill without further amendment on February 27, 1875, with Democrats in the opposition. Grant signed the civil rights bill into law on March 1, 1875.

While some radical papers like the *Boston Evening Transcript* defended the bill—wondering "[i]f the blacks and whites cannot shave and drink together . . . how can they remain tolerably peaceful in the same community?"—its passage drew fire from conservative and moderate Northern Republicans who still read into the measure a larger political story of the corruption of a growing government by those determined to advance through government support rather than through productive labor. The *New York Times* noted that Nothern African-Americans were "quiet, inoffensive people who live for and to themselves, and have no desire to intrude where they are not welcome." In the South, however, it continued, "there are many colored men and women who delight in 'scenes' and cheap notoriety." It was these people, the "negro politician, . . . the ignorant field hand, who, by his very brutality has forced his way into, and disgraces, public positions of honor and trust—men . . . who have no feeling and no sensibility," who would "take every opportunity of inflicting petty annoyances upon their former masters." The author concluded that the law would not be enforceable, and that "it is a great mistake to seek to impose new social customs on a people by act of Congress." Noticing the immediate efforts of Southerners to circumvent the law by giving up public licenses and legislating against public disturbances, the *San Francisco Daily Alta California* agreed that the act was likely to produce more trouble than equality, and reiterated that social equality must be earned rather than enforced by law.

The true way for African-Americans to achieve equality, Republicans argued, was to work. The *New York Times* approvingly quoted an African-American minister in the South who reiterated the idea that laborers must rise socially only as they acquired wealth and standing. The *Times* recorded his warning that "character, education, and wealth will determine their position, and all the laws in the world cannot give them a high position if they are not worthy of it." Even a correspondent for the staunchly Republican *Cincinnati Daily Gazette* reflected that "Sambo . . . can go to the hotels, ride in first-class cars, and enjoy a box in the theater. To what good is all this? . . . He needs now, to be let alone, and let work out his own destiny, aided only as his wants make him an object of charity. . . .

In 1883, the U.S. Supreme Court considered five civil rights cases, one each from Tennessee, New York, Kansas, Missouri, and California. On October 15, 1883, the court decided that the Civil Rights Act of 1875 was unconstitutional because federal authority could overrule only state institutional discrimination, not private actions; Justice John Marshall Harlan of Kentucky cast the only dissenting vote. With the decision, Northern Republicans stated that they had never liked the law, because it removed African-Americans from the tenets of a free labor society, using the government to give them benefits for which others had to work. The *New York Times* declared that African-Americans "should be treated on their merits as individuals precisely as other citizens are treated in like circumstances" and admitted that there was, indeed, "a good deal of unjust prejudice against" them. But the *Times* remained skeptical that legislation could resolve the problem. Even newspapers like the *Hartford Courant*, which supported the law, said it did so only because it proved that Americans were sincere in their quest for equal rights. Three days later that newspaper mused that the law had been necessary only for "the reorganization of a disordered society," and that freedpeople no longer needed its protection. The *Philadelphia Daily Evening Bulletin* agreed that public sentiment had changed so dramatically that the law was now unnecessary. Even the radical African-American *Cleveland Gazette*, which mourned the court's decision, agreed that the law was a dead letter anyway. The *New York Times* welcomed the decision, going so far as to charge the law with keeping "alive a prejudice against the negroes . . . which without it would have gradually died out."

Instead of supporting the Civil Rights Act, Republicans reiterated the idea that right-thinking African-Americans wanted to succeed on their own. The *New York Times* applauded the public address of the Louisville, Kentucky National Convention of Colored Men that concentrated largely on the needs of Southern agricultural labor and referred not at all to civil rights. That the convention had pointedly rejected chairman Frederick Douglass's draft address, which had included support for civil rights legislation, made the *Times* conclude that most attendees were "opposed to the extreme views uttered by Mr. Douglass," and that the great African-American leader should retire, since his "role as a leader of his race is about played out."

Despite the *Times*'s conclusion, African-Americans across the country protested the decision both as individuals and in mass meetings, reflecting, "It is a mercy that Charles Sumner is not alive to mourn for his cherished Civil Rights bill." At a mass meeting in Washington, D.C., Frederick Douglass admonished that the decision "had inflicted a heavy calamity on the 7,000,000 of colored people of this country, and had left them naked and defenceless against the action of a malignant, vulgar and pitiless prejudice." When the African Methodist Episcopal (AME) Church Conference of Western States, in session in Denver, discussed the decision, delegates made "incendiary" speeches and "[a] Bishop declared that if the negroes' rights were thus trampled upon a revolution would be the result." . . .

Republicans and Democrats agreed that the only way for African-Americans to garner more rights was to work to deserve them, as all others did in America's free labor system. The *Philadelphia Daily Evening Bulletin* repeated this view:

> [F]urther advancement depends chiefly upon themselves, on their earnest pursuit of education, on their progress in morality and religion, on their thoughtful exercise of their duties as citizens, on their persistent practice of industry, on their self-reliance, and on their determination to exalt themselves, not as proscribed or despised Africans, but as American men clothed with the privileges of citizenship in the one great republic of the earth. They have it in their power to secure for themselves, by their own conduct, more really important "rights" than can be given to them by any formal legislation of Congress.

The Democratic *Hartford Weekly Times* agreed, and asserted that true black leaders, "not men like Fred. Douglass, who are 'professional' colored men, and who have been agitating something and been paid for it all of their lives," approved of the decision. "They say there is no such thing as social equality among white men, and that the colored man cannot get it by law, but by the way he conducts himself."

Republican and Democratic newspapers highlighted those African-Americans who cheerfully told their neighbors "to acquire knowledge and wealth as the surest way of obtaining our rights." From Baltimore came the news that "Mr. John F. Cook, a colored man of character, who deservedly enjoys the respect of this entire community, who has held and administered with marked ability for years the responsible office of Collector of Taxes for the District of Columbia," told a reporter that he had no fears of white reprisals after the decision, expecting whites to accord to African-Americans "what legislation could never accomplish." "These are golden words, and if all men of his race were like Mr. Cook there would never be any trouble on this subject," concluded the Republican *Philadelphia Daily Evening Bulletin*.

Even many Northern Democrats painted their own picture of an egalitarian free labor society that had no need of a civil rights law. First they restated the idea that Republican efforts for African-Americans had simply been a ploy to control the government by marshalling the black vote. Trying to make new ties to African-American voters, the Democratic *San Francisco Examiner* emphasized that Republicans had only wanted to use the black vote to create a Republican empire and that the reversal showed that Republicanism no longer offered advantages to black citizens. A reporter noted that members of the black community had said that "it was about time to shake off the Republican yoke and act in politics as American citizens, not as chattels of a party who cared but for their votes."

While the rhetoric of the *San Francisco Examiner* repeated long-standing Democratic arguments, it also reinforced the idea that some hardworking African-Americans had indeed prospered in America, and that these upwardly mobile blacks were fully accepted even in Democratic circles. In San Francisco, the paper noted, "there are . . . many intelligent and educated men and women of African descent." Using the Republican pattern of according prosperous African-Americans names, descriptions, and their own words, it interviewed the Reverend Alexander Walters, whom it described respectfully as an educated and well-traveled young man, and happily printed both his assertion that in cities across the nation and "in the West . . . race prejudice has died out," and his prediction that the court's decision would drive black voters from the Republican party. Similarly, it quoted P. A. Bell, "the veteran editor of the *Elevator*, the organ of the colored people," as saying that in California—a Democratic state—"we people are treated just as well as if there were fifty Civil Rights bills."

With the overturning of the 1875 Civil Rights Act, mainstream Republicans and Democrats, black and white, agreed that there must be no extraordinary legislation on behalf of African-Americans, who had to work their way up in society like everyone else. Stalwart Republicans who advocated additional protection for black citizens were seen as either political demagogues who wanted the black vote to maintain their power or misguided reformers duped by stories of white atrocities against freedpeople. Northern black citizens who advocated civil rights legislation, like Frederick Douglass, were either scheming politicians who, like their white counterparts, needed the votes of uneducated African-Americans, or they were disaffected workers who believed in class struggle and wanted to control the government in order to destroy capital.

Southern blacks seemed to be the worst of all these types. They appeared to want to increase the government's power solely in order to be given what others had earned, and to do so, they were corrupting government by keeping scheming Republican politicos in office.

POSTSCRIPT

Did Reconstruction Fail as a Result of Racism?

There can be little doubt that racism played some role in the failure of the Radical Republicans to realize their most ambitious goals for integrating African Americans into the mainstream of American society in the years following the Civil War. After all, white supremacy was a powerful doctrine. At the same time, we should not so cavalierly dismiss some of the more positive conclusions reached by that first generation of revisionist historians who built upon W. E. B. DuBois's characterization of Reconstruction as a "splendid failure." For example, Kenneth Stampp's *The Era of Reconstruction, 1865–1877* (Alfred A. Knopf, 1965) ends with the following statement: "The Fourteenth and Fifteenth Amendments, which could have been adopted only under the conditions of radical reconstruction, make the blunders of that era, tragic though they were, dwindle into insignificance. For if it was worth a few years of civil war to save the Union, it was worth a few years of radical reconstruction to give the American Negro the ultimate promise of equal civil and political rights." Eric Foner, too, recognizes something of a silver lining in the nation's post–Civil War reconstruction process. In *Reconstruction: America's Unfinished Revolution, 1863–1877* (Harper & Row, 1988), Foner claims that Reconstruction, though perhaps not all that radical, offered African Americans at least a temporary vision of a free society. Similarly, in *Nothing But Freedom: Emancipation and Its Legacy* (Louisiana State University Press, 1984), Foner advances his interpretation by comparing the treatment of ex-slaves in the United States with that of newly emancipated slaves in Haiti and the British West Indies. Only in the United States, he contends, were the freedmen given voting and economic rights. Although these rights had been stripped away from the majority of black southerners by 1900, Reconstruction had, nevertheless, created a legacy of freedom that inspired succeeding generations of African Americans.

On the other hand, C. Vann Woodward, in "Reconstruction: A Counterfactual Playback," an essay in his thought-provoking *The Future of the Past* (Oxford University Press, 1988), shares Fredrickson's pessimism about the outcome of Reconstruction. For all the successes listed by the revisionists, he argues that the experiment failed. He challenges Foner's conclusions by insisting that former slaves were as poorly treated in the United States as they were in other countries. He also maintains that the confiscation of former plantations and the redistribution of land to the former slaves would have failed in the same way that the Homestead Act of 1862 failed to generate equal distribution of government lands to poor white settlers.

Thomas Holt's *Black Over White: Negro Political Leadership in South Carolina During Reconstruction* (University of Illinois Press, 1977) is representative of state and local studies that employ modern social science methodology to yield new perspectives. Although critical of white Republican leaders, Holt (who is African American) also blames the failure of Reconstruction in South Carolina on free-born mulatto politicians, whose background distanced them economically, socially, and culturally from the masses of freedmen. Consequently, these political leaders failed to develop a clear and unifying ideology to challenge white South Carolinians who wanted to restore white supremacy.

The study of the Reconstruction period benefits from an extensive bibliography. Traditional accounts of Reconstruction include William Archibald Dunning's *Reconstruction, Political and Economic, 1865–1877* (Harper & Brothers, 1907); Claude Bowers's *The Tragic Era: The Revolution After Lincoln* (Riverside Press, 1929); and E. Merton Coulter's, *The South During Reconstruction, 1865–1877* (Louisiana State University Press, 1947), the last major work written from the Dunning (or traditional) point of view. Some of the earliest revisionist views appeared in the scholarly works of African American historians such as W. E. B. DuBois, *Black Reconstruction in America: An Essay Toward a History of the Part Which Black Folk Played in the Attempt to Reconstruct Democracy in America, 1860–1880* (Harcourt, Brace, 1935), a Marxist analysis; John Hope Franklin, *Reconstruction: After the Civil War* (University of Chicago Press, 1961); and Kenneth M. Stampp, *The Era of Reconstruction, 1865–1877* (Alfred A. Knopf, 1965). Briefer overviews are available in Forrest G. Wood, *The Era of Reconstruction, 1863–1877* (Harlan Davidson, 1975); and Michael Perman, *Emancipation and Reconstruction, 1862–1879* (Harlan Davidson, 1987). One of the best-written studies of a specific episode during the Reconstruction years is Willie Lee Rose's *Rehearsal for Reconstruction: The Port Royal Experiment* (Bobbs-Merrill, 1964), which describes the failed effort at land reform in the sea islands of South Carolina. Richard Nelson Current's *Those Terrible Carpetbaggers: A Reinterpretation* (Oxford University Press, 1988) is a superb challenge to the traditional view of these much-maligned Reconstruction participants. Finally, for collections of interpretive essays on various aspects of the Reconstruction experience, see Staughton Lynd, ed., *Reconstruction* (Harper & Row, 1967); Seth M. Scheiner, ed., *Reconstruction: A Tragic Era?* (Holt, Rinehart and Winston, 1968); and Edwin C. Rozwenc, ed., *Reconstruction in the South,* 2d ed. (Heath, 1972).

ISSUE 2

Was the Wild West More Violent Than the Rest of the United States?

YES: David T. Courtright, from "Frontiers," in Ronald Gottesman and Richard Maxwell Brown, eds., *Violence in America: An Encyclopedia, vol. 1* (Charles Scribner's Sons, 1999)

NO: Robert R. Dykstra, from "To Live and Die in Dodge City: Body Counts, Law and Order and the Case of Kansas v. Gill," in Michael A. Bellesiles, ed., *Lethal Imagination, Violence and Brutality in American History* (New York University Press, 1999)

ISSUE SUMMARY

YES: Professor of history David T. Courtright argues that the cattle, mining, and lumbering Western frontiers were extremely violent because these regions were populated by young, single, and transient males who frequented saloons and prostitutes, and engaged in fights.

NO: Professor Robert R. Dykstra argues that Dodge City had a low crime rate in the decade 1876–1885, and in the murder case of *Kansas v. Gill*, it conducted a jury trial "according to conventions nurtured through a thousand years of Anglo-American judicial traditions."

$\mathbf{I}$n 1893, the young historian Frederick Jackson Turner (1861–1932) delivered an address before the American Historical Association entitled *The Significance of the Frontier in American History*. Turner's essay not only sent him from Wisconsin to Harvard University, but also became one of the most important essays ever written in American history. According to Turner's thesis, American civilization was different from European civilization because the continent contained an abundance of land that was settled in four waves of migration from 1607 through 1890. During this process, the European heritage was shed, and the American characteristics of individualism, mobility, nationalism, and democracy developed.

This frontier theory of American history did not go unchallenged. Some historians argued that Turner's definition of the frontier was too vague and imprecise; he underestimated the cultural forces that came to the West from Europe and the eastern states; he neglected the forces of urbanization and industrialization in opening the West; he placed an undue emphasis on sectional development and neglected class struggles for power; finally, his provincial view of American history prolonged the isolationist views of a nation that became involved in world affairs in the twentieth century.

Younger historians have begun to question the traditional interpretation of Western expansion. For example, older historians believed that growth was good and automatically brought forth progress. New historians such as William Cronin, Patricia Limerick, and others, however, have questioned this assumption in examining the disastrous ecological effects of American expansionism, such as the elimination of the American buffalo and the depletion of forests.

Turner's romantic view of the frontier became popularized in the literature of the West from the 1860s through modern times. As America went through its Industrial Revolution with factories manned by immigrants pouring in from Europe and Asia and second- and third-generation farmers diminishing in numbers, a mythic view of the frontier developed. The publishing house of Beadle and Adams had five million of its dime novels in circulation. Its most prolific hero was William F. Cody, a real person glamorized as "Buffalo Bill, the King of the Border Men." Buffalo Bill or his ghostwriters produced 121 novels—all with the same formula. Cody's Wild West shows toured the United States and Europe and featured reenactments of such famous episodes as Custer's Last Stand "at the battle of Little Bighorn in 1876." Buffalo Bill even hired the aged Sitting Bull one season to ride around the arena once per show. The rest of the time, Sitting Bull sat in his tent signing autographs in the fashion of today's retired athletes.

The prototype Western for the twentieth century and beyond is found in Owen Wister's novel *The Virginian*. Written in 1902, it went through six printings its first year and remains in print today. The hero, a southerner gone to Wyoming, is forced at the end to kill his former best friend and his rustling partner. *The Virginian* legitimized the use of violence on the frontier. The good guys would use force only when necessary against the bad. Since Wister, novelists such as Louis L'Amour (whose 80-plus novels have sold over 100 million copies), motion pictures, radio, and television have perpetuated the mythical West.

"The United States," says Richard Hofstadter, "has a history but not a tradition of domestic violence" for two reasons. First, it lacks an ideological and geographical center; second, "we have a remarkable lack of memory where violence is concerned and left most of our excesses a part of our buried history. . . . What is most exceptional about the Americans is not the voluminous record of their violence, but their extraordinary ability, in the face of that record, to persuade themselves that they are among the best-behaved and best-regulated of peoples."

Since Professor Hofstadter wrote those words in 1971, a number of studies have attempted to systematically study the American history of violence. One major question is whether or not the late-nineteenth-century West was more violent than other parts of the country.

YES

David T. Courtright

Frontiers

The Two Types of Frontiers

Type I	Type II
farming, farm building	mining, ranching, other extraction
families, usually nuclear	individuals
balanced gender distribution	80 to 90 percent (or more) male
a few over forty-five years old	almost none over forty-five years old
many children	few children
high birthrate	low birthrate
women less highly valued	women more highly valued
relatively permanent	transient
limited vice	widespread commercialized vice
peaceful	violent
colonizing	imperialist, exploitative

Source: An elaboration of Walter Nugent, "Frontiers and Empires in the Late Nineteenth Century." *Western Historical Quarterly* 20 (1989): 401.

A Stabbing in Idaho

Don Maguire was a Rocky Mountain trader who made his money selling guns, knives, dice, cards, and various other items at a 1,000 percent profit. He kept a journal, which has been edited by the historian Gary Topping. This entry, composed in a hurried, stream-of-consciousness style, was written in the course of an 1877 trip to the mining town of Atlanta, Idaho:

> The two noted characters of the town Coyote Smith and Poker Smith. My attention was first drawn to Coyote Smith. While he was engaged in a quarrel with two carpenters who were working lumber in front of a saloon, he being drunk made much disturbance and at the same time vowing to whip the two carpenters whereupon one of them gave him a kick in the hip. This set him wild. He snarled for a revolver swearing to kill the two. A revolver he could not procure. Midway up the street entered into a second altercation with Poker Smith and seizing a carving knife from the counter of a restaurant he made a stroke [passage obliterated] to sever the jugular vein for Poker Smith but missing

his aim the knife struck the collar bone broke and his hand running down the blade he received a horrible wound cutting his hand from the hollow between the thumb and forefinger nearly to the wrist blood flowed freely from both parties but neither was fatally injured. There were no arrests made.

"No arrests made" was the outcome of many a similar confrontation. This sort of affray kept the local surgeon busy, not necessarily the sheriff or vigilance committee. One of the busiest surgeons was George Kenny of Salmon City, Idaho. Before he was through, he managed to fill half a coffee mug with bullets dug from miners.

> *Source:* "A Trader in the Rocky Mountains: Don Maguire's 1877 Diary."
> *Idaho Yesterdays* 27 (summer 1983): 2–4, 7 (quotation). Where indicated
> by Maguire's capitalization, periods have been inserted; the spelling
> of one word, "seizing" for "siezing," has been corrected.

In the last decades of the twentieth century the concept of the frontier had become for many U.S. historians the equivalent of an insult in a crowded saloon: an invitation to fight. Many a blow had been leveled at Frederick Jackson Turner's famous account of European-descended whites "advancing" into "free lands" along an "empty" frontier, a notion of national progress that was condemned as oblivious to the existence of the native peoples. Some indignant historians refrained from using the word *frontier* altogether, an extreme reaction that jettisoned a useful analytical concept. Properly understood in a neutral, ecological sense as a shifting, generally westward-moving zone of interaction between indigenous and nonindigenous populations, the idea of the frontier is useful in making sense of the historical pattern of violence in the United States. In fact, it is indispensable.

Peaceful and Not-So-Peaceful Frontiers

The frontier violence of fact and legend was mostly a product of developing regions with an excess of young single males. The historian Walter Nugent calls these type II frontiers and contrasts them with type I farming frontiers, which were generally peaceful, not to say dull. The people of the farming frontiers were the "colorless many, . . . too busy trying to raise families and eke out a living to become legendary." The denizens of the cattle towns and mining camps were the "colorful few," whose lives were more often cut short by accidents, drunken violence, or hygienic neglect.

Type II frontiers were most common in ranching country and in the mining and lumbering regions of the cordillera, the vast elevated region from the eastern Rocky Mountains to the western foothills of the Sierra Nevada and Cascade ranges. With the exception of Mormon-settled Utah, type I frontiers were found in rainier areas with good soil and readier access to the East. In their very earliest stages, they were pioneered by men who came ahead of their families to scout the land, build primitive shelters, and pave the way for agriculture. As soon as they judged conditions to be satisfactory, these men brought their fiancées or wives and children to join them. Though raids by Native Americans or outlaws might bring moments of terror (and retreat to safer lands), populations consisting mostly of young farming families enjoyed relatively stable social lives.

Type II frontiers were far more volatile. In any society young men in their late teens and twenties are responsible for a disproportionate amount of violence and disorder. Statistically, populations that consist mostly of young men have shown a tendency toward violent crime. This is not only because the young men are so numerous or brimful of testosterone, but also because so many of them are unattached. In type II frontiers there simply were not enough eligible women.

In normal circumstances, marriage acts as a brake on rambunctious male behavior: the boys get hitched and settle down. The cliché is grounded in both sociology and evolutionary psychology. When men acquire wives and families, they have more to lose and so behave more cautiously. Other things being equal, a married frontiersman thought twice before wading into the thick of a barroom fray. A married frontiersman was less likely to be in a barroom in the first place.

Vice, another prominent characteristic of type II frontier towns, was linked to violence in several ways. Unattached laborers—cowboys, miners, lumberjacks, fur trappers, navvies, teamsters—were the natural prey of gamblers, pimps, prostitutes, and whiskey peddlers, all of whom followed the frontier. Many vice figures were armed and hardened criminals who used violence or its threat to settle disputes over poker stakes and dance-hall girls. Vice institutions were flash points for trouble.

Nowhere was this clearer than in the Chinatowns of western cities and towns. Chinatowns were, among other things, recreational vice districts for the overwhelmingly male Cantonese laborers who poured into California and other western states and territories after the discovery of gold. They featured gambling parlors, brothels, and opium dens that were controlled by organized gangs called tongs. Tong enforcers (called highbinders or hatchet men) used muscle to collect gambling debts and prevent indentured prostitutes ("slave girls") from running away with customers. They waged pitched battles with other tongs to maintain control of the vice operations, much as rival gangs of bootleggers would later do during Prohibition. The homicide arrest rate for the Chinese in Portland, Oregon, in the 1870s was roughly four times that of the general population, a reflection of the abnormally high ratio of Chinese men to women and the consequent flourishing of vice and organized crime. The Chinese were also preyed upon by white robbers, extortionists, and bullies who found them easy and politically popular targets. The *English-Chinese Phrase Book* (1875, revised 1877) distributed by Wells, Fargo and Company included grimly useful sentences such as "He came to his death by homicide," "He was choked to death with a lasso, by a robber," "He was killed by an assassin," and "He was smothered in his room."

Outside Chinatown the saloon was the central establishment of vice. Spree drinking was common, particularly among workers who had just been paid. When they drank too much, they became careless and clumsy, likelier to give or take offense in dangerous circumstances. Clare McKanna, who studied nearly one thousand homicide cases in three western counties from 1880 to 1920, found that seven in ten of the perpetrators had been drinking, as had about six in ten of the victims. More than one-third of the male victims died in saloons or in the streets in front of them. Thirty-two of them had been shot by bartenders (mostly with pistols, not, according to legend, with a shotgun from behind the counter), while sixteen of the dead were themselves bartenders. Most of the killings took place in the evening or on the weekend, that is, the times when tipsy men were apt to be congregating in saloons and other places of bibulous recreation.

Drunken brawls were not necessarily homicidal. What made them so lethal was the frontier habit of carrying knives or especially guns. Handguns were responsible for 63 percent of the homicides in McKanna's sample; handguns, rifles, and shotguns were responsible for 75 percent. Ready access to deadly (and often concealed) weapons greatly increased the odds that a simple assault would escalate to homicide. Most frontier killings and maimings were sordid, unpremeditated affairs that arose from jostling or insults among touchy men who had had too much to drink.

Gun toting also carried the risk of accidental death. The *Caldwell Post,* a cattle-town newspaper, estimated that five cowboys were killed by accidental gun discharges for every one who was shot intentionally. An unjacketed .44- or .45-caliber bullet did tremendous damage. Many of those who survived gun mishaps had to live with terrible injuries: blasted groins, shot-away knees, missing faces, and the like.

Measuring the Violence

The most frequently studied measure of frontier violence is the homicide rate. Killings usually made it into newspapers and official documents and thus into the historical record, while lesser crimes such as assaults were often unremarked or unprosecuted. As Robert Dykstra has argued, even in legendary places like Dodge City the number of murders was actually small, owing to the smallness of their populations. Men did not duel in the streets every noon, nor was killing, criminal or otherwise, a common event.

In proportional terms, however, frontier killings were much more frequent than in the East. When homicide is expressed as a ratio (conventionally the number of cases per 100,000 people per year), type II frontier communities had rates that were at least an order of magnitude greater than those prevailing in eastern cities or midwestern agricultural regions. The homicide rate of Fort Griffin, a central Texas frontier town frequented by cowboys, buffalo hunters, and soldiers, was 229 per 100,000 in the 1870s. That of Boston, a long-settled eastern city whose population included proportionately more women, children, and old people, was only about 6.

Some of the most clear-cut evidence comes from California. Roger McGrath has calculated that the homicide rate for the mining town of Bodie (90 percent male) was 116 per 100,000 from 1878 to 1882, years when eastern homicide rates rarely exceeded single digits. (By contrast, the robbery rates in Bodie and nearby Aurora, Nevada, were comparable to, and burglary rates lower than, those of eastern cities—a reflection, perhaps, of the fear of armed retaliation by potential victims.) Kevin Mullen has estimated that the San Francisco homicide rate ranged from 28 to 80 per 100,000, with an average of about 49, during the city's tumultuous early years (1849–1856). The rate thereafter subsided to a range of 4 to 13 per 100,000 during the 1860s. The main reason for the shift was that the disproportionately youthful and male population characteristic of the early gold rush gradually gave way to a more balanced population that included more women, children, and old people.

This was in fact a universal pattern. Type II settlements did not retain their unbalanced populations forever. Within a decade or two the surplus men moved on to new frontiers, died prematurely, or married and settled down. Women, who were initially scarce, married and began bearing children at an early age, often in their teens. These children were roughly divided between boys and girls. Eventually the children married and further normalized the population. With the increasing numbers of women and children came institutions—schools, churches, and the Woman's Christian Temperance Union—that militated against vice and violence and improved the moral climate of the once-raucous frontier towns.

Frontier violence is thus best understood as a passing migratory anomaly. The nature of the labor demand drew youthful male workers to ranching, mining, and other type II frontier regions. These young men found themselves thrown together in competitive masculine company, isolated from familial influences, tempted by predaceous vice and payday sprees, and at least temporarily unable to find women to marry. When these circumstances changed—when the type II frontiers came to resemble more nearly the type I frontiers—the propensity toward public violence abated or at least stabilized at a lower level.

Cultural Influences

There is more to the story of frontier violence than population structure. Cultural factors also help to explain why men were so quick to fight other men and why there was so much conflict with Native Americans.

Men who come from cultures that stress personal honor are more likely to become involved in fights than those who do not. Such cultures emphasize the importance of responding to any perceived insult or slight, however trivial, lest a man lose face in the eyes of others who determine his social worth. The approved response is to display physical courage, to fight the offender, or, in certain upper-class contexts, to challenge him to a duel. The addition of deadly weapons to the honor imperative, epitomized by a Colorado grave marker, "He called Bill Smith a liar," explains why hotheaded killings were common on the frontier.

Those portions of the frontier settled or traversed by southerners were especially prone to hotheaded killings. The religiously motivated European immigrants who first journeyed to New England and the littoral regions of the middle colonies—Puritans, Quakers, German Pietists, and the like—were not particularly concerned about honor. However, the Cavaliers who settled in the

Chesapeake colonies were. (Maryland's homicide rate from 1657 to 1680 was more than twice that of Massachusetts, though this probably reflects excess males as well as cultural differences.) The Scots, Scots-Irish, border English, and Finns who settled along the backwoods frontier were also highly honor-conscious. They were accustomed to weapons and warfare, because they or their ancestors had come from remote and often violent rural areas on the hardscrabble periphery of northern and western Europe.

As the frontier moved westward, most new settlers situated themselves in places climatically similar to those whence they came. New Englanders moved to Ohio, southerners to the Gulf Plain, and so on. Until the twentieth century, migration tended to follow lines of latitude, as did cultural attitudes toward honor. Frontier regions settled by northerners were less violent than those settled by migrants from the South or Midlands. "All old-timers who know the West will tell you that they did not have so many killings and shooting scrapes after they got up North as they did in Texas," recalled E. C. "Teddy Blue" Abbott in his cowboy memoir, *We Pointed Them North: Recollections of a Cowpuncher* (1939; p. 231). The figures back him up. The statewide homicide rate in Texas was 32 per 100,000 in 1878, far higher than in northern climes.

Conflict with Native Americans

Many frontiersmen, northern as well as southern, had definite ideas about Anglo-Saxon racial superiority and the self-evident correctness of manifest destiny. At best, Native Americans were objects of suspicion; at worst, they were savages, disgusting, incorrigible, and even diabolical obstacles to the advance of civilization. Such extreme ethnocentrism naturally made it easier to justify killing them and appropriating their lands. The classic case was California, where miners enslaved, raped, or simply shot down Native Americans for no better reason, wrote one French missionary, than "to try their pistols." Miners, ranchers, and militiamen—the latter much more lethal to Native Americans than the better-disciplined regular soldiers—together accounted for more than forty-five hundred killings of Native Americans in California between 1848 and 1880.

Of course, the Native Americans in California and elsewhere fought back, often matching and surpassing whites in the ferocity of their attacks. Apaches were known to kindle slow fires under the heads of suspended captives. Tales of such atrocities confirmed the whites' conviction that the elimination of hostile Native Americans was in principle no different from hunting predatory animals. Even when Native Americans were accorded the formalities of a trial, bias against them practically guaranteed convictions. For example, every Apache accused of killing a white in Gila County, Arizona, in the late 1880s was convicted. The only Apaches who were acquitted or had their cases dismissed were those accused of killing other Apaches. For those found guilty, a long sentence was often tantamount to the death penalty. Well over one-third of all Native Americans sent off to prison in Arizona and California were dead within five years.

Native Americans were at a marked demographic disadvantage in their conflict with whites. Their numbers progressively dwindled because of their vulnerability to imported Old World diseases such as smallpox. Too many women and dependents were another military handicap. Braves were in short supply, a legacy of intertribal warfare and, more speculatively, of the greater susceptibility of males to infectious disease. Native American women and dependents were less mobile than the braves and therefore easier to attack. The tactic of destroying villages rather than going after elusive bands of warriors, which emerged in Massachusetts and Virginia as early as the 1620s and 1630s, was used repeatedly in the eighteenth and nineteenth centuries and led to such notorious and lopsided Native American defeats as Sand Creek (1864), Washita (1868), and Wounded Knee (1890).

Ecological violence by Europeans brought further hardship to Native Americans. Hunting was a popular pastime among frontiersmen, particularly during the nineteenth century. Competitive in masculine company and keen on proving their prowess, Europeans often killed more than was necessary to feed their families or sell to others. The rotting carcasses of thousands of Plains buffalo were a stark reminder of the excess slaughter and a signal source of Native American distress. Give the hunters bronze medals with a dead buffalo on one side and a discouraged Native American on the other, General Philip Sheridan admonished the Texas legislature. "Let them kill, skin, and sell until the buffalo are exterminated," he declared. "Then your prairies can be covered with speckled cattle, and the festive cowboy, who follows the hunter as a second forerunner of an advanced civilization."

Native Americans themselves were drawn into overhunting so they could barter meat and skins for European trade goods, thus heightening conflict with other tribes. One of those trade goods, alcohol, had horrific consequences. European memoirs are full of accounts of drunken Native Americans selling their squaws into prostitution, going on wild binges, stumbling into fires, cutting one another to pieces. One theory to account for this extreme behavior is that Native Americans had no knowledge of distilled alcohol before contact with Europeans and thus no store of social knowledge about drinking. Native Americans learned to drink hard liquor from the worst possible tutors: fur trappers, traders, mule skinners, and other denizens of the type II frontier. When they saw white men swill whiskey and become dangerously, obstreperously drunk, they did likewise and suffered the same consequences.

Government's Failure to Control Frontier Violence

Selling liquor to Native Americans was illegal in most places from colonial times on. Neither the British nor the American government was able to suppress the trade, however. The U.S. government, nominally responsible for policing the western territories, was seldom able adequately to enforce any policy to protect Native Americans. The frontier was vast, the settlers numerous and greedy, and the resources of the federal government limited. The army was spread too thin to control the movements of frontiersmen or to prevent them from trespassing on treaty lands. Local courts and juries were invariably sympathetic toward white defendants and hostile toward Native Americans.

In the early stages of frontier expansion, legal institutions were either lacking or inadequate. One response to this situation, patterned after the Regulator movement in South Carolina in 1767–1769 (in which backcountry settlers organized to restore law and order and establish institutions of local government), was vigilantism, or organized extralegal movements against robbers, rustlers, counterfeiters, and other outlaws. The historian Richard Maxwell Brown counted 326 such movements in the country between 1767 and 1904, the majority of which were in southern and southwestern territories and states, the single most important of which was Texas.

When vigilante actions were limited in scope and controlled by local elites, they often served socially constructive purposes. Selected malefactors were whipped, branded, banished, or sometimes hanged in public dramas that affirmed the values of property and order. But vigilantism could also miscarry. In California, racial minorities, particularly Hispanics, made up a disproportionate percentage of those subjected to lynch courts, which were especially swift and merciless if the victims were white. Vigilantism also ran the risk of triggering private warfare, when friends and relatives of the lynch victims sought revenge against the vigilante faction, or of miscarriages of justice, when personal enemies were killed under the guise of the popular will. Vigilantism, in short, was a poor substitute for professional police and regular courts and had been widely superseded by the close of the nineteenth century.

Frontier Violence After 1900

Frontier violence is not entirely a thing of the past. The night, for example, is a present-day frontier where colonization has been made possible by cars and electric lights. Charles Lindbergh wrote in his autobiography that the most spectacular change he had seen in the earth's surface in all his decades of flying was the sprinkling of myriad lights across the United States on a clear night. These lights were signs of "conquest," of human movement into the frontier of darkness. But that movement is highly selective. Midnight finds mostly young men on the streets—and higher rates of drunkenness, accidents, assault, rape, and murder than in the daylight hours. Nighttime, in brief, resembles a type II frontier.

In some respects, inner cities also resemble a type II frontier. Urban women are hardly outnumbered by men, as they were on the nineteenth-century frontier. Nevertheless, many young innercity males, for economic, subcultural, and demographic reasons, delay marriage or avoid the institution altogether. An increasing number of them have grown up in single-parent households and so have experienced little parental guidance and supervision. Those who have joined gangs, acquired weapons, and become involved with drug traffic and other forms of organized vice are statistically among the most violence-prone members of society, just like their type II frontier counterparts. Indeed, urban ghettos can be thought of as artificial and unusually violent frontier societies: vice-ridden combat zones in which groups of armed, unsupervised touchy bachelors, high on alcohol and other drugs, menace one another and the local citizenry.

Some historians have also seen analogies between twentieth-century U.S. involvement in Pacific wars—particularly against Filipino rebels, Japanese soldiers, and Vietnamese communists—and the earlier frontier campaigns against Native Americans. In all these cases, young American men, remote from what they called civilization, were pitted against enemies they deemed treacherous and racially inferior. The conflicts quickly assumed a ferocious quality reminiscent of the worst episodes of the wars against Native Americans. Indeed, the parallel was made explicit in the language of the Vietnam War, when young GIs spoke of forays into "Indian country" and code-named their operations Texas Star and Cochise Green (a reference to the chief of the Chiricahua Apache who waged relentless war against the U.S. Army).

These GIs have grown up in the golden age of the Western, a hugely successful genre in the publishing, film, radio, and television industries (also advertising: a square-jawed cowboy beat out a crusty taxi driver as the emblem of Philip Morris's legendary Marlboro cigarette campaign). That whole generation had been saturated with images of stylized violence and morally simplistic frontier stories of cowboys, Indians, desperadoes, and six-shooters. Did the public's fascination with these stories of frontier violence contribute to the high rates of violence in the United States relative to other industrial democracies? Did it matter that America's mythic hero was a man with a gun, an attitude, and a Stetson hat?

The answer is a qualified yes. We become who we are by emulating other figures in our environment, including the electronic environment with its celebrities and "action figures." Communications researchers have discovered that, for many people, these figures become role models: people act like them, dress like them, talk like them, even talk *to* them. Insofar as larger-than-life frontier figures, played by the likes of John Wayne and James Arness, entered and shaped mass consciousness, they reinforced the belief that gun violence was an appropriate means for resolving conflicts. It is doubtful, however, that their influence was greater than more fundamental social and economic factors—racism, ghetto isolation, subcultures of poverty, deindustrialization, secularization, family decline, homicidal sensitivity about honor, lax gun control laws, drug abuse, and drug trafficking—that have contributed to the ongoing reputation of the United States as a violent land.

Colonel House Nearly Gets Himself Killed

Edward Mandell House (1858–1938) is best known as Woodrow Wilson's adviser and confidant, a man so close to the president that Wilson once called him "my second personality . . . my independent self." But House, who came of age in Texas's most violent era and who counted it nothing to carry a gun, almost did not make it to Washington. In 1879 he was visiting a mining camp near Como, Colorado:

> It was like all other camps of that sort—rough men and rougher women, gambling, drinking, and killing. I was in a saloon, talking to a man whom I had known in Texas, when . . . a big, brawny individual

came into the room and began to abuse me in violent terms. I had never seen the man before and could not imagine why he was doing this. I retreated, and he followed. I had my overcoat on at the time and had my hand on my six-shooter in my pocket and cocked it. The owner of the saloon jumped over the bar between us. In five seconds more, I would have killed him. An explanation followed which cleared up the mystery. He had taken me for some one else against whom he had a grudge, and whom he had seen but once. I learned later that he was a popular ex-sheriff of Summit county and that if I had killed him I should have been lynched within the hour.

It always amuses me when I see the bad men in plays depicted as big, rough fellows with their trousers in their boots and six-shooters buckled around their waists. As a matter of fact, the bad men I have been used to in southern Texas were as unlike this as daylight from dark. They were usually gentle, mild-mannered, mild-spoken, and often delicate-looking men. They were invariably polite, and one not knowing the species would be apt to misjudge them to such an extent that a rough word or an insult would sometimes be offered. This mistake of judgment was one that could never be remedied, for a second opportunity was never given.

Source: Charles Seymour, ed., *The Intimate Papers of Colonel House.*
New York: Houghton Mifflin, 1926, pp. 24–25.

Robert R. Dykstra

 **NO**

To Live and Die in Dodge City: Body Counts, Law and Order, and the Case of Kansas v. Gill

Never mind that during its celebrated decade as a tough cattle town only fifteen persons died violently in Dodge City, 1876–1885, for an average of just 1.5 killings per cowboy season. Today, three decades after the first release of the homicide data, frontier Dodge City remains a universal metaphor for slaughter and civic anarchy.

Professional historians of the American West are, of course, presumed to know better. And yet there have been recent hints of scholarly skepticism about Dodge City's modest body count. In 1994, for instance, a very prominent essay on frontier violence discussed Dodge and the other Kansas cattle towns without so much as noting in passing their low absolute numbers of killings.

This odd disregard is puzzling. One explanation might be that the homicide data are deemed irrelevant to the question of frontier violence. This is simply hard to credit. A second might be that the data do not conform to the New Western History paradigm, which tends to insist that things were always worse than we thought. That notion can be argued either way. A third possibility is that the data are somehow suspect, and thus better left unmentioned until the question can somehow be settled once and for all. This last possibility, more than the persistence of the Dodge City metaphor among those who learned their Western history in darkened theaters, suggests the value of a revisit to the real, if legendary, town in question.

All the Homicide News Fit to Print

Dodge City was indeed a legend in its own time. It was where livestock herded up from Texas to the railroad tracks in Kansas would be sold, shipped east to market, or walked onward to the ranges of the northern Great Plains. The summertime influx of transients—well-heeled drovers and cattle brokers, festive cowboys, predatory gamblers, and sporting women—more than equaled the town's resident population. But a police force of multiple officers, their salaries totaling nearly half of Dodge City's entire municipal budget, closely supervised the behavior of these itinerants by enforcing strict gun-control laws.

The richest man in town, merchant Robert M. Wright, had been present in the bad old days when, in its unorganized first year of existence, Dodge had been the scene of several violent deaths. Wright and his entrepreneurial colleagues had not feared for their lives; they feared for their pocketbooks—that is, their local property values—as the newspapers of eastern Kansas delighted in such energetic headlines as "HOMICIDE AT DODGE CITY. A Notorious Desperado Killed" or "SHOT DEAD. Another Tragedy at Dodge City," or in such sly one-liners as "Only two men killed at Dodge City last week."

But with an expectation of the Texas cattle trade's coming to Dodge, local businessmen foresaw that the influx of new transients would only magnify all problems related to law and order. They therefore established a municipal government late in 1875, levied taxes to pay for it, and criminalized gun toting by private citizens. A photograph taken a few years later shows the town's busiest corner, downtown Front Street at its intersection with Bridge Street, the main thoroughfare in and out of Dodge. In the left background stand R. M. Wright's brick store and the facade of the celebrated Long Branch Saloon. In the middle foreground the superstructure of a town well displays a prominent sign: "The Carrying of Fire Arms Strictly PROHIBITED." As this proximity suggests handgun violence was considered bad for business, an emphatic collective belief of Dodge City's business and professional elite that ultimately explains the low body count.

Scholars' attempts to dilute the significance of such body counts first appeared in the 1980s. "These statistics seem to indicate that the cattle towns were not particularly violent," wrote Roger McGrath. "However, a note of caution is appropriate. Dykstra compiled his statistics exclusively from the local newspapers." The subtext here: How can we be sure that more murders and justifiable homicides than reported did not occur?

There is no known official list of violent deaths at Dodge. Pending discovery of any such compendium, we must depend on a few reasonable assumptions about those reported by the press. The first is the absolute and primal newsworthiness of violent death. However enthusiastically they might conspire in cover-ups and damage control regarding local social conflict, Dodge City's journalists seemed no more able to resist a good homicide story than any circulation-chasing New York or Chicago city editor.

A second assumption involves the substantial array of local weekly newspapers that offer a fairly intimate summary of life in Dodge during the trail-driving era. The *Dodge City Times* began publishing in May 1876, just in time for the town's first cattle-trading season. The *Ford County Globe* joined it in January 1878. The *Dodge City Democrat* appeared in December 1883. And the *Kansas Cowboy* moved to Dodge from Ness County in June 1884. True enough, the first ten months of the *Times,* save for a single issue, are not extant. For 1876, one must extrapolate from the absence of murderous dispatches about Dodge in the press of eastern Kansas; so far, none has been discovered. But certainly from March 1877 to the close of the Texas cattle trade at Dodge City late in 1885, all newspaper runs are virtually complete. Every nineteenth-century village should be so well documented.

A third guiding assumption seems equally reasonable. Cattle-town homicides, when they occasionally occur, are almost always reported in some detail, as the story of Henry Heck's demise will show. This attention lends weight to the notion that news concerning violent death tended to be revealed rather than suppressed.

Deadly Competition: Miami (1980) versus Dodge (1880)

A rather more comprehensive criticism of the cattle-town death statistics also appeared in the 1980s. This critique questioned the significance of the absolute numbers themselves, and argued for replacing them with homicide rates of the type annually devised by the FBI to measure urban violence. For today's metropolitan areas, each case of "murder and non-negligent manslaughter" (excluding justifiable homicides by the police) is calculated as a proportion of every 100,000 of population. The simple formula is

$$hr = (100,000/N_p)N_h,$$

where hr equals homicide rate, N_p equals population, and N_h equals number of homicides. Since the 1940s the FBI has used this formula in running a kind of annual negative sweepstakes in which the losing city becomes America's most violent community, the murder capital of the world. In 1980, for example, greater Mami's homicide rate soared to 32.7—the nation's highest that year.

But, as a few scholars began to note, a murder rate of 32.7 is not very high when contrasted with similarly calculated homicide rates back in time. That for late-thirteenth-century London, noted James Given, was about the same as the yearly average for Miami, 1948–1952. Barbara Hanawalt similarly discovered that the rate for London in the early fourteenth century soared even higher, to something between 36.0 and 51.3. Then, uncritically borrowing the two medievalists' methodology, Roger McGrath discovered that the average annual homicide rate at nineteenth-century Bodie, California, a mining camp, was a stratospheric 116.0.

These historians have been compromised by the statistical fallacy of small numbers. In 1980, Miami's absolute number of homicides exceeded 500, while Hanawalt's yearly average for London was only 18 and McGrath's body count for Bodie over several years was a measly 29. It was London's modest population (an estimated 35,000 to 50,000) and Bodie's small population (no more than 5,000 in any year) that caused their homicide rates to surpass modern Miami's.

As to tiny Dodge City—population 1,275 in 1880—its FBI homicide rate calculates out at an enormous 78.4 for that year, compared with Miami's 32.7 exactly a century later. Yet, the absolute numbers of murders on which these ratios are based are these: Dodge, 1; Miami, 515. In other words, if a bullet fired by John ("Concho") Gill had missed Henry C. Heck instead of striking him in the chest, Dodge City's 1880 murder rate would have been zero instead of soaring to more than twice that of the 1980 murder capital of the world.

But one may argue that a single killing in a village like frontier Dodge may have had more traumatic psychological impact on its residents than Miami's 515 homicides must have had on its citizens in 1980. This proposition is supported by such personal testaments as Elizabeth Salamon's account of a double murder in her quiet New Jersey town in 1997 ("a killing has occurred in our midst and we will never be the same"), the emotional agony in awaiting identification of the shooter ("at night, my husband and I try to sleep, but sleep does not come easily"), and her guilty elation when she learns that the killer himself has died violently ("when murder hits this close to home, a dark heart is a regrettable residual"). And the general idea accords with what scholars have occasionally noted about the sociological equivalence of small and large places concerning such things as population fertility and rural-urban value conflicts.

But how does the argument fare in any specific contrast between 1980s Miami and 1880s Dodge? The *Miami Herald* for late December of 1980 is studded with allusions to the "record 555 homicides in Dade County this year," as reported by the local medical examiner's office—a figure that evidently includes 40 justifiable homicides by the police that would not be included in the FBI calculation. The newspaper reported that things are much worse in California, where Los Angeles County's homicides had reached a record 2,130 for the year. (Unfortunately for the *Herald,* however, greater Miami's smaller population imposed a 32.7 murder rate as against only 23.3 for Los Angeles.)

In any event, such defensive finger-pointing did not help much. The mood of urgency within Miami's political and economic leadership was palpable. Announcing itself "very concerned about the high incidence of homicides and other acts of violence occurring in certain liquor establishments," Miami's city council urged that they be put out of business, and a special police task force convened to identify these evil influences. "It will help when we get sufficient manpower aboard," complained the chief of Miami's patrol division. As if in anticipation, a federation of local homeowner associations formed a blue-ribbon Citizens Action Council "to pressure state and local legislators to bolster programs to counter Dade's rising crime rate." At the behest of the Citizens Crime Commission of Greater Miami, the Dade County Metro Council endorsed the new group, which planned to meet with judges, state legislators, and Governor Bob Graham. One of the commissioners set the agenda by demanding that Graham convene a special legislative session to appropriate a hundred million dollars for Dade's "war on crime." "For too long," he conceded, "the word 'war' has been overworked. . . . Nevertheless, our city can quite accurately be described at this moment as a battleground of war." Such was the local response to Miami's 32.7 murder rate for 1980.

In contrast, the public mood of Dodge City in late 1880 in the wake of its 78.4 homicide rate is much less alarmist. True enough, Concho Gill's killing of Henry Heck of November 17 caused a sensation, especially in view of the fact that nobody had died violently at Dodge in more than a year. Both weekly newspapers expressed considerable indignation. N. B. Klaine, the dour and moralistic editor of the Times who moonlighted as Ford County's probate judge, broke the story on Saturday, November 20, complete with sinister overtones:

> **MURDER IN DODGE CITY.**
> On Tuesday night a murder was committed in this city, in that part of town south of the railroad track. . . . It has been some time since a murder has been committed in Dodge City, but the shooting Tuesday night offers no parallel to any of the crimes committed here. There was no provocation, and it is hinted that the unfortunate Heck was the victim of a conspiracy, the facts of which may be developed upon the trial of the murderer.

On November 23, in its turn, the *Globe* ran a much more forthcoming account that contained most of what we know of the killing's background. The paper was managed by D.M. Frost, a practicing attorney, and his journalistic associate Lloyd Shinn, who doubled as Dodge Township justice of the peace. From the breezy vernacular tone of the article, we may be almost certain that its author was Shinn rather than the more earnest Frost. The piece opens as follows:

> **HENRY C. HECK KILLED.**
> John Gill, Alias Concho, Establishes
> Himself as a Killer
>
> On last Wednesday morning the report that a killing had taken place in the city the night previous, was rife on the streets at an early hour. The report was soon confirmed and everybod[y] felt that Dodge had still some of the bloody instinct for which she was so famous in the lawless days of her infancy, when money was as dross and whisky four bits a drink.

But to the locals, as to any reasonably sensitive historian, the death of Henry Heck was much more than just a blemish on Dodge City's 1880 crime-control statistics. A human life had been taken, an industrious citizen was gone, the community diminished.

The Unredeemed Lover

Where does the story begin?

In southwestern Kansas. In the year 1876 or 1877.

Henry C. Heck arrived in Dodge. We know that he was single, the Ohio-born son of German immigrants, twenty-four or twenty-five years old. In fairly short order he became the trusted employee of H. B. ("Ham") Bell, the owner of a popular livery stable, a man not much older than himself. The two evidently became close friends. Heck, according to Lloyd Shinn's account, was often "left in charge of the extensive livery and other business, whenever Mr. Bell was absent from the city." Bell's "other business" increased considerably in June 1978, when he had a local contractor build him a dance hall, the Varieties Theatre, on Locust Street in the "notorious" south side of town. The establishment was a success from the start, and a month after its opening the *Globe* reported that "the Texas boys and visitors generally still continue to throng the Varieties nightly."

Ham Bell placed Heck in charge of this enterprise. In a legal deposition of early 1879, in which he adroitly distanced himself from entrepreneurial proximity, Bell described the place as "kept by Henry Heck." It is, he wrote, "a long frame building with a hall and bar in front and sleeping rooms in the rear." A contemporary photograph shows a low room with dark, wood-paneled ceiling and large side windows. In the foreground a bar extends along the right wall, three gaming tables stand beyond the bar, and a dance floor lies beyond the tables. Presumably the bedrooms are behind the wall in the back.

Management of the Varieties naturally brought Henry into close—not to say intimate—association with several young women (one as young as fourteen) identified by Ham Bell as "prostitutes, who belonged to the house and for the benefit of it solicited the male visitors to dance." And, Bell added, "The rooms in the rear [are] occupied, both during the dancing hours and after, both day and night[,] by the women for the purpose of prostitution."

In short, Heck's was not a particularly savory occupation, although it entailed much responsibility. Overseeing the bar and kitchen; tallying receipts; dispensing payments to liquor and grocery wholesalers, to the cook and bartenders and musicians, and (of course) to the young women. And keeping order, a task that brought him several close acquaintanceships among the police—successive marshals Ed Masterson and Charlie Bassett, the various assistant marshals (Wyatt Earp, for one), and the rank-and-file officers—who kept a watchful eye on the Varieties and its two competitors, the Lady Gay and the Comique, especially during the wee hours when spirits were high and inhibitions low.

There soon arose a complication. One of the young women, a violet-eyed blonde named Caroline ("Callie") Moore, had captured Henry's affections. "Nearly ever since Mr. Heck has resided in this county," wrote Shinn, ". . . this woman has been his faithful companion, according to the approved method of this class of Dodge City lotus eaters." Read: Henry and Callie lived together. And in time they planned a joint future beyond the confines of Dodge south of the tracks. Ham Bell had acquired a ranch twelve miles below town where the Camp Supply trail toward Texas intersected Mulberry Creek. Later, when trying to sell it, Bell laconically described Mulberry Ranch as "good range, good water running by the place, a well of good water at the door, good corral 100 feet square, good house 22 × 35." But better still was its situation: "a No. 1 location for keeping passersby, and cattle or sheep." Heck agreed to lease Mulberry Ranch. In the latter part of 1879 Heck and Callie Moore quit Ham Bell's employ and settled at the ranch. Here, as Lloyd Shinn puts it in words that suggest strong community approval, Heck "was raising a little stock which was being steadily accumulated by his industry and prudence." And "for nearly a year," wrote Shinn, Moore "performed the duties which usually fall to the lot of a rural housewife." Her life seemed a model of common-law domesticity.

But, we may guess, bright prairie flowers and frisky colts and wonderful sunsets and a convivial parade of teamsters stopping for dinner cannot forever compensate for the relative isolation of agricultural pioneering, which had defeated many a woman of stronger psychological construction than Callie Moore. Ranch life may have begun to pall. In any event, in September 1880, while on a shopping trip to town that no doubt included a visit to old friends and old haunts, she met Concho Gill, an unemployed cowboy whom the newspapers refer to as a gambler—a common cattle-town usage for any man who frequents saloons to play cards for money.

Gill, aged twenty-three, was the Texas-born son of an Irish immigrant father and a mother from Mississippi. The father must have died, for the mother was married to James D. Young, a Mississippi-born preacher. Gill's nickname probably refered to an adolescence in frontier Concho County of west-central Texas. Gill stood a half inch short of six feet, had a fair complexion, hazel eyes, and black hair. He could read and write, and "was a quiet man," said Shinn, "and not considered quarrelsome or dangerous." When visited in June 1880 by the Dodge City census taker, Gill was sharing a Front Street building with four other unattached males, each in his own apartment: two sheep raisers, another unemployed cowboy, and the manager of the local stockyard.

On that same day Gill also said he was sick, suffering from scurvy. This is not as unlikely an illness for a cowboy as it might seem today, when the disease is occasionally encountered among infants and the very elderly. But scurvy had been diagnosed as recently as the 1850s among frontier settlers lacking sustained access to foods rich in vitamin C—citrus fruits, tomatoes, vegetables. Adult symptoms include swollen, bleeding gums and loose teeth, bleeding under the skin and into the joints, mental depression, fatigue, and increased susceptibility to infection. Unless treated, the disease is fatal. Yet, as physicians of the time well knew, scurvy is easily cured; since the early sixteenth century lime juice was the infallible remedy, and fresh vegetables—especially potatoes and wild salad greens—were by the 1860s prescribed as effective preventives.

So why was Concho Gill sick in June and again in November? In a community blessed with doctors and druggists and grocery stores? Perhaps he suffered from some more serious malady than just a vitamin C deficiency. It is possible that he had a misdiagnosed case of gonorrhea or secondary-stage syphilis (not uncommon among cowboys), some of whose symptoms—joint pain, skin blotches, depression, lassitude—resemble those of scurvy.

Concho's illness, whatever it was, did not diminish his attractiveness to Callie Moore; in fact, a touch of chronic illness possibly added a certain Byronic allure, prompting some maternal impulse, perhaps. In any event, according to Shinn, Moore was immediately smitten. "His dark brown eyes, classic features, and complexion bronzed by a southern sun, together with [a prospect of] the indolent life of a gambler's paramour, were too dazzling to be resisted, when compared with kitchen drudgery, and the society of her more homely lover." Soon the young woman bid a permanent farewell to Mulberry Ranch, moving back to Dodge and in with Gill.

Moore's betrayal devastated Heck. He turned to drink, but it did no good. He at last resorted to an ultimatum. On Saturday, November 13, Heck told

Moore that she had three days to return to him or leave Dodge City forever. Or else.

Late in the evening of November 16 Henry Heck came to Dodge City to separate Callie Moore from Concho Gill. But some things, as John Demos reminds us, we have to imagine. We know nothing of how Heck managed his wait. But wait he did, as an unseasonably early winter gripped the village. Perhaps he had proposed their old workplace, the Varieties Theatre, as a rendezvous, where he now lingered, occasionally greeting friends, but moody, on edge, drinking too much. At last she arrived, accompanied by a companion, Sallie Frazier, a middle-aged woman of color who, we can imagine, hovered protectively as a tearful Moore faced her former lover. The young woman reaffirmed that she would neither get out of Dodge nor leave Gill. She and Frazier turned to go. Heck says that if she does not return to him by midnight he will, as both women later remember his words, kill Concho Gill "before morning."

At midnight, Heck gathered himself into his coat and stepped out into the night, somewhat unsteadily perhaps, his mood as bitter as the weather. He trudged through fallen snow, crossing the railroad track toward Front Street and the intermittent glow of its all-night saloons. He made his way to Gill's apartment and, without announcing himself, began kicking in the front door.

Inside, Gill had been sick for the past ten days. Moore was building a fire in the stove. A friend, one Charlie Milde, was also present in the room. Aroused from bed, Gill grabbed a pistol and went to the door. It flew open and he fired twice.

One bullet struck Henry Heck in the right breast just below the nipple, perforating the lung.

Heck retreated back into the darkness. We do not know how he spent the next half hour—perhaps dazed, bewildered by shock. Probably there was no pain: his neural synapses have shut down. Perhaps he rested, leaning upright in an alleyway, out of the wind, uncontrollably trembling. Perhaps he collapsed unconscious until the snow against his cheek finally brought him around. He roused himself and stumbled toward a lamp-lit saloon. He entered, and after calling for a drink told the night bartender that Gill had shot him. He left the saloon for a moment, returned, dropped to the floor, and expired "without a groan." It had taken him forty-five minutes to die.

This love story from early Dodge City is over. But the consequences were not, and they provide us with an important cultural reading of frontier justice in Dodge City.

The Judgment of Concho Gill

As the dying Henry Heck silently stumbled along Front Street, Assistant Marshal Neil Brown, alerted by the gunshots, arrived at Gill's apartment. He confiscated the fatal pistol, ordered Gill to dress, and escorted him to jail.

Later that morning of November 17, a coroner's inquest convened, as required for any death happening by violence or under suspicious circumstances. The coroner's jury was heavy with law-enforcement types characteristically impatient with troublemakers. The county coroner himself, Col.

John W. Straughn, doubled as a deputy sheriff. The six jurors included Ham Bell, now the deputy U.S. marshal in Dodge; blacksmith Pat Sugh-rue, a former Dodge Township constable and future Ford County sheriff; and merchant A. B. Webster, soon to run for mayor on a law-and-order platform. W. J. Miller, a local cattle raiser; James Mufty, an unemployed carpenter; and Fred Berg, a baker, rounded out the jury. They presumably viewed the body and then took testimony from bartender A. J. Tuttle, Officer Brown, Charlie Milde, and Callie Moore.

Although the victim literally broke into Gill's domicile, he may not have been armed. Tuttle testified that Heck was not carrying a weapon when he took his last drink. The jurors returned a verdict of felonious homicide, thereby asserting that the killing had been done without justification or excuse and signaling that Gill was in very serious trouble indeed. The following day editor N. B. Klaine, in his role as probate judge, appointed Under-Sheriff Fred Singer as administrator of the deceased's estate. As for Callie Moore, she "is still true to her imprisoned lover," noted Lloyd Shinn, "and supplies him daily with tempting viands."

The excitement subsided, life resumed its normal rhythms. Cattle continued loading down at the freight yard, and wagons bearing livestock feed, hay, and millet, arrived daily from outlying farms. U.S. Senator P. B. Plumb was in town several hours on his way home from Colorado. Saloon-owner Chaulk Beeson's sojourning parents departed for Iowa "well pleased with their visit." The respectable "dancing people" of the town announced plans to organize a social club. "Professor" W. H. LyBrand, hotel proprietor and former bandmaster, was recruiting an orchestra "to supply music for the holidays." On Thanksgiving Day churchgoers held interdenominational services and the Methodists hosted an oyster supper. The following afternoon children presented "literary exercises" at the grammar school. A baby was born to businessman A. J. Anthony and his wife. "Mother and son are doing well," it was reported. All of which suggests that frontier Dodge had more in common with fictional Grover's Corners, New Hampshire ("nice town, y'know what I mean?"), than with modern Miami.

And in contrast to Miami's plea for more cash for cops late in 1980, Dodge City's municipal council late in 1880 continued pressing the mayor to cut police expenditures. The reason was liquor prohibition, adopted as a constitutional amendment in November's general election, ending the legal sale of intoxicants in Kansas. With saloon license fees far and away the most important source of municipal income, citizens did not view the loss of revenue with equanimity. By mid-December 1880 the village found itself more than $2,200 in debt, with unpaid bills shortly hiking the total to $3,239. More than a hundred taxpayers panicked, petitioning the council for a referendum on dissolving the municipal corporation entirely. The council scheduled a vote for New Year's Eve. The *Ford County Globe* approved this drastic proposition, warning that saloon closings would leave Dodge City "without resources except such as might be derived from direct taxation. . . . This would swell the total tax upon the property owners of the city to about eight cents on the dollar." But cooler heads prevailed, and on December 31 a low voter turnout doomed this solution to the crisis.

Meanwhile, Concho Gill's fate was being decided. On December 1, Gill appeared at a preliminary examination before Lloyd Shinn, in his role as justice of the peace, to determine if sufficient evidence existed to warrant his trial by a higher court. Col. Thomas S. Jones appeared for the accused, County Attorney Mike Sutton, Dodge City's most prominent attorney, for the people. Owing to the absence of one witness, the defense requested a continuance, which Shinn granted. The hearing resumed on the fourth. We lack details; both newspapers evidently considered the testimony old news. On December 7, Shinn ruled that the evidence merited binding Gill over for trial at the January 1881 term of district court. Shinn set bail at $3,000. The charge was first-degree manslaughter, meaning that Gill allegedly killed Heck, in the words of the law, "without a design to effect death," at a moment when Heck was "engaged in the perpetration or [the] attempt to perpetrate [a] crime or misdemeanor, not amounting to a felony."

Justice Shinn's reasoning is discernible. Heck's death clearly had not been murder: provocating circumstances closely preceding the shooting—the unlawful attack by Heck on the defendant's door—had caused Gill to react on impulse, in the heat of the moment. Yet it also seemed to Shinn not to be a case of justifiable homicide, although Kansas law gave as one definition a killing "committed by any person . . . in resisting any attempt to murder such person, or to commit any felony upon him or her, or in any dwelling house in which such person shall be."

Gill probably assumed that Heck had a gun. But—and this was a major qualifier—whether Heck was or was not armed, Gill had had an obligation to "retreat to the wall," to avail himself of any reasonable avenue of escape, even if that was only a few feet of floor space, before employing deadly force. That Concho may have failed to understand this virtually universal responsibility was simply his bad luck. As it happened, Texas was unlike most other states. Where Gill came from, the law said a man did not have to retreat from an attacker any farther than "the air at his back." Unfortunately for Gill, Kansas was not Texas.

State of Kansas v. John Gill alias Concho opened at the courthouse in Dodge on January 17, 1881—two months to the day after the shooting. Again we lack details, although Judge Samuel R. Peters's summary for the record preserves the essential procedural facts. Again Mike Sutton prosecuted, Colonel Jones defended. As late as December 21 the charge was still first-degree manslaughter, punishable by "confinement and hard labor for a term not less than five years nor more than twenty-one years." But since then Mike Sutton, for some reason, had upped the charge to first-degree murder, punishable by death. The accusation Sutton filed with the court asserted that Gill "feloniously, willfully and of his deliberate and premeditated malice did kill and murder one Henry Heck contrary to law." Gill pleaded not guilty, he and Jones still probably confident that his act could be seen as self-defense.

A jury was empaneled, consisting of twelve men from outside the corporate boundaries of Dodge, the most prominent of them being the prosperous sheep rancher R. W. Tarbox. After hearing the evidence and arguments of counsel and being instructed in writing by the court, the jury retired to deliberate.

The next day it rendered its verdict: Gill was guilty not of first-degree murder but of murder in the second degree—a killing "committed purposely and maliciously, but without deliberation and premeditation," and punishable by "confinement and hard labor for not less than ten years."

The jurors evidently concluded that Gill had killed Heck with no set design to take life but that, nevertheless, there was a purpose to kill (or at least a purpose to inflict injury without caring whether it caused death or not) formed instantaneously in Gill's mind. And they must have been unimpressed by testimony suggesting that Gill had been so provoked by Heck's behavior as to reduce the crime to manslaughter.

Colonel Jones immediately moved for a new trial on the ground that the verdict was "contrary to evidence"—that is, the jurors had mistakenly interpreted the weight of the testimony in the case. Judge Peters pondered that for three days, then brought attorneys and defendant together again on January 21. He denied the motion to retry, and sentenced Gill to fifteen years' hard labor in the Kansas State Penitentiary. Concho was taken into custody, and the next day Sheriff George Hinkle and Under-Sheriff Singer took him off to Lansing.

The Rest of the Story

In March 1884, somebody—presumably Mike Sutton, the man who had successfully prosecuted Concho Gill three years earlier—addressed a petition to Governor George W. Glick. "We the undersigned Citizens of Ford County Kansas respectfully ask your excellency to commute the sentence of John Gill now confined in the penitentiary of the State of Kansas, under a sentence for fifteen years," Sutton wrote. "Since his incarceration his health has failed, and there is strong probability that . . . he will not live until the expiration of his term." But, the petition added, "The crime for which said John Gill was convicted was committed by him under a misapprehension . . . that the man he killed was hunting him [in order] to kill him."

This document resulted from a visit to Dodge City by Gill's stepfather, the Reverend Young. Probably after conferring with Callie Moore (now Mrs. C. F. Lane) and Sallie Frazier, he brought them to Sutton. The former county attorney took depositions from the two women, and then had these sworn to before E. D. Swan, a notary public. Incredibly enough, it seems, the knowledge that Heck had specifically threatened Gill's life, and that Gill knew it, had not been presented at the trial; apparently this was the first Sutton learned of it. Thus he drafted the petition, which the Rev. Mr. Young then circulated.

Soon thirty-six names graced the document. The signatories included Dodge City's mayor and its city clerk; *Times* editor and now postmaster N. B. Klaine; W. F. Petillon, Ford County's registrar of deeds; Sheriff Pat Sughrue, who had been a member of the coroner's jury that had initiated the case against Gill; Assistant City Marshal David ("Mysterious Dave") Mather; merchants R. M. Wright, H. M. Beverley, and a scattering of other commercial men; lawyers Sutton, Swan, and T. S. Jones, who had defended Gill; baker Fred Berg, who also had sat on the coroner's jury; plus a butcher, a druggist, two hoteliers, a bookkeeper, and two of the town's more respectable saloon own-ers. Although admitting that "I was not here at the time," Police Judge R. E. Burns added a note that "from Statements of Responsible citizens I believe this petition should be granted." In addition, Jones and Petillon each wrote sup-porting letters to Governor Glick.

"Everyone here seems to sympathize with him," said Petillon of the Rev-erend Young, and journalist Klaine agreed. "Time seems to efface unpleasant memories," he philosophized, "as well as to soften prejudices and produce sympathy." The tendency of cattle-town people to find excuses for leniency in cases of shooting homicides was belatedly asserting itself.

In his letter, Colonel Jones added an interesting interpretation of the trial. Gill "would have been promptly acquitted," he told the governor, "had a it not been for the evidence of a personal enemy." The identity of this enemy is unknown. One may guess that it was Heck's friend Ham Bell, who may have been responsible for the severe stance taken by the coroner's jury, who then had less influence over the more lenient Shinn decision but who later yet may have convinced Mike Sutton to escalate the charge against Gill to first-degree murder. What testimony Bell may have offered is also unknown; perhaps it maintained that Heck's killing was the result of a conspiracy, as suggested in the first news report of the death. In any event, Mike Sutton's implicit repudiation of his role in Gill's conviction included the suggestion that he, as county attorney, had been duped by somebody into wholly discounting Gill's claim of self-defense. For him, the two women's affidavits now proved definitive.

Gill's stepfather evidently hand carried the petition, the two affidavits, and the two supporting letters to Topeka, delivering them to Governor Glick. The governor said that prior to any formal application to commute, Young must give public notice in plenty of time for those with objections to make them known. On April 3 and 10, therefore, the *Dodge City Times* printed the required notice, editor Klaine certified its publication, and lawyer Swan sent copies of both to the governor. Formal application to commute his stepson's sentence would be made by Young on April 16, 1884.

But in the end the governor refused the request for unknown reasons. Concho did not die in prison, but he did stay for another seven years. On August 19, 1891, his sentence at last commuted, he emerged from the Kansas penitentiary after having served ten and one-half years for the murder of Henry Heck.

Body Counts or Murder Rates?

The point of the story of *Kansas v. Gill* is that the people of Dodge City took Heck's death seriously, and instituted deliberate legal action against his slayer according to conventions nurtured through a thousand years of Anglo-American judicial tradition. The judgment of Concho Gill was, as it was meant to be, a series of civic rituals assuring villagers that although situated on the geographic extremity of civilization, theirs was a fully domesticated society, culturally located well within the larger American community.

As for public fear, neither in Miami in December 1980 nor in Dodge in December 1880 did any important number of citizens cower behind locked doors. But Miami's business community clearly had been terrified by how its spiraling homicides would affect property values and tourism; Dodge City's businessmen, although attuned to the need to attract new residents and capital investment, were not. The important cause of these different responses was hardly the contrast between homicide rates of 32.7 and 78.4 but between body counts of 515 (or 555) and 1.

Let anthropologist Lawrence Keeley have the penultimate word on murder rates versus body counts. Keeley's recent book criticizing the "peaceful-savage" myth displays a wealth of evidence on the lethal nature of tribal life. Its relevance to the present discussion is that its author employs death rates somewhat similar to those calculated for the FBI crime reports, leading him to relish a number of absurd comparisons. For example, he judges a chance Blackfoot massacre of a 52-man Assiniboine raiding party more lethal (100.0 percent killed) than the loss of 21,392 British soldiers on the horrifying first day of the Battle of the Somme (only 13.5 percent killed). Obviously, the statistical fallacy of small numbers is in full flower here.

But Keeley has a ready reply. The unsophisticated, he says, are always "more impressed by absolute numbers than ratios." And he asks if, consistent with such views, any reader would rather undergo a critical medical operation at a "small, rural, Third-World clinic"—where the number of inadvertent deaths from surgery is numerically small but the death rate high—than at a large American "university or urban hospital" where such deaths are more frequent but the rate low. According to the same reasoning, would anyone prefer to fly regularly on small planes rather than airliners? And would one prefer to live on an Indian reservation than in a large city, "since the annual absolute number of deaths from homicide, drug abuse, alcoholism, cancer, heart disease, and automobile accidents will always be far fewer on the reservations than in major cities and their suburbs"?

There are, for the sake of argument, answers. Most health insurance would not pay for elective surgery in a jungle hospital, so that point is moot. But yes, those wealthy enough to own airplanes regularly and routinely defy the odds. And yes again, many persons would rather live in Navaho country than in parts of Manhattan.

But more to the point of this essay, a great majority of fully informed time-travelers surely would feel safer cruising the all-night saloons of Dodge City in 1880 than barhopping in Little Havana, Coconut Grove, or downtown Miami a hundred years later. And that is a ratio beyond dispute.

POSTSCRIPT

Was the Wild West More Violent Than the Rest of the United States?

David T. Courtwright believes that the frontier was a very violent place. He qualifies his answer by accepting the distinction of Professor Walter Nugent, who distinguishes between the two types of frontiers: type one, which centered on farming, and type two, which focused on mining, ranching, and other extractive industries. The author argues that type one had minimal violence because of its concentration of large nuclear families engaged in farming. On the other hand, the more volatile type-two frontiers of mining and cattle raising were manned by young, single males who often brawled in bar fights that were caused by excessive drinking, gambling, and womanizing.

Courtwright also takes a quick look at the violence that occurred on the multicultural West stressed in the writings of the new Western historians. He argues that Native Americans and whites engaged in some serious atrocities committed by both sides. He also discusses high crime rates among the Chinese in San Francisco because of tong (gang) battles.

Justice was limited in type-two frontier communities. The army was spread too thin, and local governments concentrated on property claims. Consequently, vigilante movements or quasi-legal groups emerged to enforce the law. Professor Richard Maxwell Brown, who has spent a lifetime writing books and articles about these movements, has calculated that 326 such movements emerged in the country between 1767 and 1904. Most of these movements occurred in the southern and southwestern territories and states, with Texas being the most violent.

Richard Maxwell Brown divides Western violence into roughly three periods. Period one, which is what this issue is concerned with, extends from 1850 to 1910. It parallels the tumult brought about by the Industrial Revolution. Brown employs the concept Western Civil War of Incorporation (WCWI) to interpret the feuds between Yankees and ex-Confederates, cattlemen and land barons, and Republicans and Democrats who use violence to gain power in the last American frontier. See Brown's summative article on "Violence" in Clyde A. Milner, II, et al., eds., *The Oxford History of the American West* (Oxford University Press, 1994).

Ironically, in recent years, historians have tried to lay to rest the myths about gunfighters. Writers such as Joseph Rosa have argued the term "gunfight" did not come into popular usage until the 1890s. The number of killings by Wild Bill Hickok was really seven or eight, not between 30 and 85. Even psychopathic killers like John Wesley Hardin and Billy the Kid had the

numbers of killings inflated over the years by pop writers and the movie industry. The bar-room brawl, not "the stereotypical walkdown of motion picture
fame," was responsible for most of the violence. And when gunfights took
place, the most famous killers were often outnumbered and ambushed. See
Joseph G. Rosa, *The Gunfighter: Man or Myth* (University of Oklahoma Press,
1969), and Gary L. Roberts, "The West's Gunmen," *American West* (January
1972, 10–15, 64; March 1972, 18–23, 61–62), and "Gunfighters and Outlaws,
Western," in Ronald Gottesman and Richard Maxwell Brown, eds., *Violence in
America: An Encyclopedia, vol. 1* (Charles Scribner's Sons, 1999).

Robert R. Dykstra was one of the first historians to challenge the image
of the West as a section more violent than the rest of the country. His study
of *The Cattletowns* (Knopf, 1968, 1983) rejected the view that the five towns of
Abilene, Caldwell, Dodge City, Ellsworth, and Wichita were hellholes. In fact,
from 1870 to 1885 only a total of 45 killings took place. The homicides varied
widely from accidental deaths to those that involved law officers, cowboys,
and gamblers, among others. Of the shootings that took place, "less than a
third of them returned the fire."

Dykstra has been criticized on numerous grounds. First of all, he did
not count the 17-plus murders committed in three of the five towns in the
years prior to his study, a point the author concedes. Secondly, he has been
challenged by studies of other communities whose authors compare the high
crime rates of some of these Western counties and communities with the lower
crime rates of nineteenth- and twentieth-century cities. Finally, Dykstra has
been taken to task for relying on contemporary newspaper accounts for his
main sources.

The author has responded vigorously to these charges. He challenges
writers who use the FBI statistical rate of crimes per 100,000 by claiming the
samples of a town or county are too small and, therefore, one less murder can
radically skew the homicide ratio downward. In addition, the comparisons may
be between apples and oranges. As Harold J. Weiss, Jr., points out in his valuable article, "Overdosing and Underestimating: A Look at a Violent and Not-
So-Violent American West," *Quarterly of the National Association for Outlaw and
Lawman History* (April–June 2003), "Have western historical writers used the same
database? Information about criminal homicides can be collected in several ways;
those committed; those reported to the police; those cleared by police arrests;
those that resulted in an indictment by a Grand Jury; those that came to trial;
those that ended in a court conviction; and those that involve prison time."

Dykstra also believes that contemporary newspapers reported every
homicide in as much detail as possible. Would a nineteenth-century newspaper miss a major crime any more than the nightly local news broadcasts,
which comb the police blotter for every gruesome homicide?

Dykstra's most recent assessments of the newest literature on Western
violence are (1) "Overdosing on Dodge City," *Western Historical Quarterly* (Winter 1996); (2) "Violence, Gender and Methodology in the 'New' Western History," *Reviews in American History* (March 1999); and (3) "Body Counts and
Murder Rates: The Contested Statistics of Western Violence," *Reviews in American History* (December 2003).

The most recent assessment, "Guns, Murder, and Probability: How Can We Decide Which Figures to Trust," *Reviews in American History* (June 2007) by Randolph Roth, challenges Dykstra's theory of the statistical fallacy of small numbers. A recent study by Clare V. McKanna, Jr., *Race and Homicide in Nineteenth Century California* (University of Nevada Press, 2002), examines seven counties in California and the one by David Peterson Del Mar, *Beaten Down: A History of Interpersonal Violence in the West* (University of Washington Press, 2002), studies all of Oregon. These figures, says Roth, constitute representative samples similar to contemporary pollsters who use small numbers to predict elections. Both books argue that very high crime rates existed in the nineteenth-century West.

Students interested in pursuing the subject further should consult the following bibliographical articles and books: Indispensable and balanced are Harold J. Weiss, Jr., "Overdosing and Underestimating: A Look at a Violent and Not-So-Violent American West," *Quarterly of the National Association for Outlaw and Lawman History, Inc.* (April–June 2003) and Michael A. Bellesiles, "Western Violence," in William Deverell, ed., *A Companion to the American West* (Blackwell Publishing, 2004), which plays down Western violence, while Robert McGrath is ambivalent in *Gunfighters, Highwaymen and Vigilantes: Violence in the Frontier* (University of California Press, 1984). Giles Vandal's *Rethinking Southern Violence: Homicides in Post–Civil War Louisiana, 1866–1884* (Ohio State University Press, 2000) offers a comprehensive look at the 4,986 recorded homicides in a southern state mostly against African Americans committed collectively by whites who refused to accept the new political order of the Reconstruction era.

More general are Michael A. Bellesiles, ed., *Lethal Imagination: Violence and Brutality in American History* (New York University Press, 1999), and the three-volume reference work in alphabetical order by Ronald Gottesman and Richard M. Brown, eds., *Violence in America: An Encyclopedia* (Charles Scribner's Sons, 1999). Easier to locate are two anthologies written in the shadow of the violent 1960s: Hugh Davis Graham and Ted Robert Gurrs, eds., *Violence in America: Historical and Comparative Perspectives* (New American Library, 1969) and Richard Hofstadter and Michael Wallace, eds., *American Violence: A Documentary History* (Random House, 1971), which argues that America has a history, but not a tradition, of violence.

ISSUE 3

Were the Nineteenth-Century Big Businessmen "Robber Barons"?

YES: Howard Zinn, from "Robber Barons and Rebels," in *A People's History of the United States* (HarperCollins, 1999)

NO: John S. Gordon, from "Was There Ever Such a Business!" in *An Empire of Wealth: The Epic History of American Economic Power* (Harper Perennial, 2004)

ISSUE SUMMARY

YES: According to Howard Zinn, the new industrialists such as John D. Rockefeller, Andrew Carnegie, and J. P. Morgan adopted business practices that encouraged monopolies and used the powers of the government to control the masses from rebellion.

NO: John S. Gordon argues that the nineteenth-century men of big business such as John D. Rockefeller and Andrew Carnegie developed through the oil and steel industries consumer products that improved the lifestyle of average Americans.

Between 1860 and 1914, the United States was transformed from a country of farms, small towns, and modest manufacturing concerns to a modern nation dominated by large cities and factories. During those years, the population tripled, and the nation experienced astounding urban growth. A new proletariat emerged to provide the necessary labor for the country's developing factory system. Between the Civil War and World War I, the value of manufactured goods in the United States increased 12-fold, and the capital invested in industrial pursuits multiplied 22 times. In addition, the application of new machinery and scientific methods to agriculture produced abundant yields of wheat, corn, and other foodstuffs, despite the decline in the number of farmers.

Why did this industrial revolution occur in the United States during the last quarter of the nineteenth century? What factors contributed to the rapid pace of American industrialization? In answering these questions, historians often point to the first half of the 1800s and the significance of the "transportation revolution," which produced better roads, canals, and railroads to move people and goods more efficiently and cheaply from one point to another.

Technological improvements such as the Bessemer process, refrigeration, electricity, and the telephone also made their mark in the nation's "machine age." Government cooperation with business, large-scale immigration from Europe and Asia, and the availability of foreign capital for industrial investments provided still other underpinnings for this industrial growth. Finally, American industrialization depended upon a number of individuals in the United States who were willing to organize and finance the nation's industrial base for the sake of anticipated profits. These, of course, were the entrepreneurs.

Regardless of how American entrepreneurs are perceived, there is no doubt that they constituted a powerful elite and were responsible for defining the character of society in the Gilded Age. For many Americans, these businessmen represented the logical culmination of the country's attachment to laissez-faire economics and rugged individualism. In fact, it was not unusual at all for the nation's leading industrialists to be depicted as the real-life models for the "rags-to-riches" theme epitomized in the self-help novels of Horatio Alger.

Closer examination of the lives of most of these entrepreneurs, however, reveals the mythical dimensions of this American idea. Simply put, the typical business executive of the late nineteenth century did not rise up from humble circumstances, a product of the American rural tradition or the immigrant experience, as frequently claimed. Rather, most of these big businessmen were of Anglo-Saxon origin and reared in a city by middle-class parents. According to one survey, over half of the leaders had attended college at a time when even the pursuit of a high school education was considered unusual. In other words, instead of having to pull themselves up by their own bootstraps from the bottom of the social heap, these individuals usually started their climb to success at the middle of the ladder or higher.

American public attitudes have reflected a schizophrenic quality with regard to the activities of the industrial leaders of the late nineteenth century. Were these entrepreneurs "robber barons," who employed any means necessary to enrich themselves at the expense of their competitors? Or were they "captains of industry" whose shrewd and innovative leadership brought order out of industrial chaos and generated great fortunes that enriched the public welfare through the workings of various philanthropic agencies that these leaders established? Although the "robber barons" stereotype emerged as early as the 1870s, it probably gained its widest acceptance in the 1930s when, in the midst of the Great Depression, many critics were proclaiming the apparent failure of American capitalism. Since the depression, however, some historians, including Allan Nevins, Alfred D. Chandler, and Maury Klein, have sought to revise the negative assessments offered by earlier generations of scholars. In the hands of these business historians, the late nineteenth-century businessmen have become "industrial salesmen" who skillfully oversaw the process of raising the United States to a preeminent position among the nations of the world.

The following selections reveal the divergence of scholarly opinion as it applies to the nineteenth century entrepreneurs who came to epitomize both the success and excess of corporate capitalism in the United States.

Robber Barons And Rebels

In the year 1877, the signals were given for the rest of the century: the blacks would be put back; the strikes of white workers would not be tolerated; the industrial and political elites of North and South would take hold of the country and organize the greatest march of economic growth in human history. They would do it with the aid of, and at the expense of, black labor, white labor, Chinese labor, European immigrant labor, female labor, rewarding them differently by race, sex, national origin, and social class, in such a way as to create separate levels of oppression—a skillful terracing to stabilize the pyramid of wealth.

Between the Civil War and 1900, steam and electricity replaced human muscle, iron replaced wood, and steel replaced iron (before the Bessemer process, iron was hardened into steel at the rate of 3 to 5 tons a day; now the same amount could be processed in 15 minutes). Machines could now drive steel tools. Oil could lubricate machines and light homes, streets, factories. People and goods could move by railroad, propelled by steam along steel rails; by 1900 there were 193,000 miles of railroad. The telephone, the typewriter, and the adding machine speeded up the work of business.

Machines changed farming. Before the Civil War it took 61 hours of labor to produce an acre of wheat. By 1900, it took 3 hours, 19 minutes. Manufactured ice enabled the transport of food over long distances, and the industry of meatpacking was born.

Steam drove textile mill spindles; it drove sewing machines. It came from coal. Pneumatic drills now drilled deeper into the earth for coal. In 1860, 14 million tons of coal were mined; by 1884 it was 100 million tons. More coal meant more steel, because coal furnaces converted iron into steel; by 1880 a million tons of steel were being produced; by 1910, 25 million tons. By now electricity was beginning to replace steam. Electrical wire needed copper, of which 30,000 tons were produced in 1880; 500,000 tons by 1910.

To accomplish all this required ingenious inventors of new processes and new machines, clever organizers and administrators of the new corporations, a country rich with land and minerals, and a huge supply of human beings to do the back-breaking, unhealthful, and dangerous work. Immigrants would come from Europe and China, to make the new labor force. Farmers unable to buy the new machinery or pay the new railroad rates would move to the cities.

Between 1860 and 1914, New York grew from 850,000 to 4 million, Chicago from 110,000 to 2 million, Philadelphia from 650,000 to 1½ million.

In some cases the inventor himself became the organizer of businesses—like Thomas Edison, inventor of electrical devices. In other cases, the businessman compiled other people's inventions, like Gustavus Swift, a Chicago butcher who put together the ice-cooled railway car with the ice- cooled warehouse to make the first national meatpacking company in 1885. James Duke used a new cigarette-rolling machine that could roll, paste, and cut tubes of tobacco into 100,000 cigarettes a day; in 1890 he combined the four biggest cigarette producers to form the American Tobacco Company.

While some multimillionaires started in poverty, most did not. A study of the origins of 303 textile, railroad, and steel executives of the 1870s showed that 90 percent came from middle- or upper-class families. The Horatio Alger stories of "rags to riches" were true for a few men, but mostly a myth, and a useful myth for control.

Most of the fortune building was done legally, with the collaboration of the government and the courts. Sometimes the collaboration had to be paid for. Thomas Edison promised New Jersey politicians $1,000 each in return for favorable legislation. Daniel Drew and Jay Gould spent $1 million to bribe the New York legislature to legalize their issue of $8 million in "watered stock" (stock not representing real value) on the Erie Railroad.

The first transcontinental railroad was built with blood, sweat, politics and thievery, out of the meeting of the Union Pacific and Central Pacific railroads. The Central Pacific started on the West Coast going east; it spent $200,000 in Washington on bribes to get 9 million acres of free land and $24 million in bonds, and paid $79 million, an overpayment of $36 million, to a construction company which really was its own. The construction was done by three thousand Irish and ten thousand Chinese, over a period of four years, working for one or two dollars a day.

The Union Pacific started in Nebraska going west. It had been given 12 million acres of free land and $27 million in government bonds. It created the Credit Mobilier company and gave them $94 million for construction when the actual cost was $44 million. Shares were sold cheaply to Congressmen to prevent investigation. This was at the suggestion of Massachusetts Congressman Oakes Ames, a shovel manufacturer and director of Credit Mobilier, who said: "There is no difficulty in getting men to look after their own property." The Union Pacific used twenty thousand workers—war veterans and Irish immigrants, who laid 5 miles of track a day and died by the hundreds in the heat, the cold, and the battles with Indians opposing the invasion of their territory.

Both railroads used longer, twisting routes to get subsidies from towns they went through. In 1869, amid music and speeches, the two crooked lines met in Utah.

The wild fraud on the railroads led to more control of railroad finances by bankers, who wanted more stability—profit by law rather than by theft. By the 1890s, most of the country's railway mileage was concentrated in six huge systems. Four of these were completely or partially controlled by the House of Morgan, and two others by the bankers Kuhn, Loeb, and Company.

J. P. Morgan had started before the war, as the son of a banker who began selling stocks for the railroads for good commissions. During the Civil War he bought five thousand rifles for $3.50 each from an army arsenal, and sold them to a general in the field for $22 each. The rifles were defective and would shoot off the thumbs of the soldiers using them. A congressional committee noted this in the small print of an obscure report, but a federal judge upheld the deal as the fulfillment of a valid legal contract.

Morgan had escaped military service in the Civil War by paying $300 to a substitute. So did John D. Rockefeller, Andrew Carnegie, Philip Armour, Jay Gould, and James Mellon. Mellon's father had written to him that "a man may be a patriot without risking his own life or sacrificing his health. There are plenty of lives less valuable."

It was the firm of Drexel, Morgan and Company that was given a U.S. government contract to float a bond issue of $260 million. The government could have sold the bonds directly; it chose to pay the bankers $5 million in commission.

On January 2, 1889, as Gustavus Myers reports:

> . . . a circular marked "Private and Confidential" was issued by the three banking houses of Drexel, Morgan & Company, Brown Brothers & Company, and Kidder, Peabody & Company. The most painstaking care was exercised that this document should not find its way into the press or otherwise become public. . . . Why this fear? Because the circular was an invitation . . . to the great railroad magnates to assemble at Morgan's house, No. 219 Madison Avenue, there to form, in the phrase of the day, an iron-clad combination . . . a compact which would efface competition among certain railroads, and unite those interests in an agreement by which the people of the United States would be bled even more effectively than before.

There was a human cost to this exciting story of financial ingenuity. That year, 1889, records of the Interstate Commerce Commission showed that 22,000 railroad workers were killed or injured.

In 1895 the gold reserve of the United States was depleted, while twenty-six New York City banks had $129 million in gold in their vaults. A syndicate of bankers headed by J. P. Morgan & Company, August Belmont & Company, the National City Bank, and others offered to give the government gold in exchange for bonds. President Grover Cleveland agreed. The bankers immediately resold the bonds at higher prices, making $18 million profit.

A journalist wrote: "If a man wants to buy beef, he must go to the butcher. . . . If Mr. Cleveland wants much gold, he must go to the big banker."

While making his fortune, Morgan brought rationality and organization to the national economy. He kept the system stable. He said: "We do not want financial convulsions and have one thing one day and another thing another day." He linked railroads to one another, all of them to banks, banks to insurance companies. By 1900, he controlled 100,000 miles of railroad, half the country's mileage.

Three insurance companies dominated by the Morgan group had a billion dollars in assets. They had $50 million a year to invest—money given by ordinary people for their insurance policies. Louis Brandeis, describing this in his book *Other People's Money* (before he became a Supreme Court justice), wrote: "They control the people through the people's own money."

John D. Rockefeller started as a bookkeeper in Cleveland, became a merchant, accumulated money, and decided that, in the new industry of oil, who controlled the oil refineries controlled the industry. He bought his first oil refinery in 1862, and by 1870 set up Standard Oil Company of Ohio, made secret agreements with railroads to ship his oil with them if they gave him rebates—discounts—on their prices, and thus drove competitors out of business.

One independent refiner said: "If we did not sell out. . . . we would be crushed out. . . . There was only one buyer on the market and we had to sell at their terms." Memos like this one passed among Standard Oil officials: "Wilkerson & Co. received car of oil Monday 13th. . . . Please turn another screw." A rival refinery in Buffalo was rocked by a small explosion arranged by Standard Oil officials with the refinery's chief mechanic.

The Standard Oil Company, by 1899, was a holding company which controlled the stock of many other companies. The capital was $110 million, the profit was $45 million a year, and John D. Rockefeller's fortune was estimated at $200 million. Before long he would move into iron, copper, coal, shipping, and banking (Chase Manhattan Bank). Profits would be $81 million a year, and the Rockefeller fortune would total two billion dollars.

Andrew Carnegie was a telegraph clerk at seventeen, then secretary to the head of the Pennsylvania Railroad, then a broker in Wall Street selling railroad bonds for huge commissions, and was soon a millionaire. He went to London in 1872, saw the new Bessemer method of producing steel, and returned to the United States to build a million-dollar steel plant. Foreign competition was kept out by a high tariff conveniently set by Congress, and by 1880 Carnegie was producing 10,000 tons of steel a month, making $1½ million a year in profit. By 1900 he was making $40 million a year, and that year, at a dinner party, he agreed to sell his steel company to J. P. Morgan. He scribbled the price on a note: $492,000,000.

Morgan then formed the U.S. Steel Corporation, combining Carnegie's corporation with others. He sold stocks and bonds for $1,300,000,000 (about 400 million more than the combined worth of the companies) and took a fee of 150 million for arranging the consolidation. How could dividends be paid to all those stockholders and bondholders? By making sure Congress passed tariffs keeping out foreign steel; by closing off competition and maintaining the price at $28 a ton; and by working 200,000 men twelve hours a day for wages that barely kept their families alive.

And so it went, in industry after industry—shrewd, efficient businessmen building empires, choking out competition, maintaining high prices, keeping wages low, using government subsidies. These industries were the first beneficiaries of the "welfare state." By the turn of the century, American Telephone and telegraph had a monopoly of the nation's telephone system, International Harvester made 85 percent of all farm machinery, and in every other industry resources became concentrated, controlled. The banks had interests in so many of these monopolies as to create an interlocking network of powerful corporation directors, each of whom sat on the boards of many other corporations. According to a Senate report of the early twentieth century, Morgan at his peak sat on the board of forty-eight corporations; Rockefeller, thirty-seven corporations.

Meanwhile, the government of the United States was behaving almost exactly as Karl Marx described a capitalist state: pretending neutrality to maintain order, but serving the interests of the rich. Not that the rich agreed among themselves; they had disputes over policies. But the purpose of the state was to settle upper-class disputes peacefully, control lower-class rebellion, and adopt policies that would further the long-range stability of the system. The arrangement between Democrats and Republicans to elect Rutherford Hayes in 1877 set the tone. Whether Democrats or Republicans won, national policy would not change in any important way.

When Grover Cleveland, a Democrat, ran for President in 1884, the general impression in the country was that he opposed the power of monopolies and corporations, and that the Republican party, whose candidate was James Blaine, stood for the wealthy. But when Cleveland defeated Blaine, Jay Gould wired him: "I feel . . . that the vast business interests of the country will be entirely safe in your hands." And he was right.

One of Cleveland's chief advisers was William Whitney, a millionaire and corporation lawyer, who married into the Standard Oil fortune and was appointed Secretary of the Navy by Cleveland. He immediately set about to create a "steel navy," buying the steel at artificially high prices from Carnegie's plants. Cleveland himself assured industrialists that his election should not frighten them: "No harm shall come to any business interest as the result of administrative policy so long as I am President . . . a transfer of executive control from one party to another does not mean any serious disturbance of existing conditions."

The presidential election itself had avoided real issues; there was no clear understanding of which interests would gain and which would lose if certain policies were adopted. It took the usual form of election campaigns, concealing the basic similarity of the parties by dwelling on personalities, gossip, trivialities. Henry Adams, an astute literary commentator on that era, wrote to a friend about the election:

> We are here plunged in politics funnier than words can express. Very great issues are involved. . . . But the amusing thing is that no one talks about real interests. By common consent they agree to let these alone. We are afraid to discuss them. Instead of this the press is engaged in a most amusing dispute whether Mr. Cleveland had an illegitimate child and did or did not live with more than one mistress.

In 1887, with a huge surplus in the treasury, Cleveland vetoed a bill appropriating $100,000 to give relief to Texas farmers to help them buy seed grain during a drought. He said: "Federal aid in such cases . . . encourages the expectation of paternal care on the part of the government and weakens the sturdiness of our national character." But that same year, Cleveland used his gold surplus to pay off wealthy bondholders at $28 above the $100 value of each bond—a gift of $45 million.

The chief reform of the Cleveland administration gives away the secret of reform legislation in America. The Interstate Commerce Act of 1887 was supposed to regulate the railroads on behalf of the consumers. But Richard Olney, a lawyer for the Boston & Maine and other railroads, and soon to be Cleveland's Attorney General, told railroad officials who complained about the Interstate Commerce Commission that it would not be wise to abolish the Commission "from a railroad point of view." He explained:

> The Commission . . . is or can be made, of great use to the railroads. It satisfies the popular clamor for a government supervision of railroads, at the same time that that supervision is almost entirely nominal. . . . The part of wisdom is not to destroy the Commission, but to utilize it.

Cleveland himself, in his 1887 State of the Union message, had made a similar point, adding a warning: "Opportunity for safe, careful, and deliberate reform is now offered; and none of us should be unmindful of a time when an abused and irritated people . . . may insist upon a radical and sweeping rectification of their wrongs."

Republican Benjamin Harrison, who succeeded Cleveland as President from 1889 to 1893, was described by Matthew Josephson, in his colorful study of the post-Civil War years, *The Politicos*: "Benjamin Harrison had the exclusive distinction of having served the railway corporations in the dual capacity of lawyer and soldier. He prosecuted the strikers [of 1877] in the federal courts . . . and he also organized and commanded a company of soldiers during the strike. . . ."

Harrison's term also saw a gesture toward reform. The Sherman Anti-Trust Act, passed in 1890, called itself "An Act to protect trade and commerce against unlawful restraints" and made it illegal to form a "combination or conspiracy" to restrain trade in interstate or foreign commerce. Senator John Sherman, author of the Act, explained the need to conciliate the critics of monopoly: "They had monopolies . . . of old, but never before such giants as in our day. You must heed their appeal or be ready for the socialist, the communist, the nihilist. Society is now disturbed by forces never felt before. . . ."

When Cleveland was elected President again in 1892, Andrew Carnegie, in Europe, received a letter from the manager of his steel plants, Henry Clay Frick: "I am very sorry for President Harrison, but I cannot see that our interests are going to be affected one way or the other by the change in administration." Cleveland, facing the agitation in the country caused by the panic and depression of 1893, used troops to break up "Coxey's Army," a demonstration of unemployed men who had come to Washington, and again to break up the national strike on the railroads the following year.

Meanwhile, the Supreme Court, despite its look of somber, black-robed fairness, was doing its bit for the ruling elite. How could it be independent, with its members chosen by the President and ratified by the Senate? How could it be neutral between rich and poor when its members were often former wealthy lawyers, and almost always came from the upper class? Early in the nineteenth century the Court laid the legal basis for a nationally regulated economy by establishing federal control over interstate commerce, and the legal basis for corporate capitalism by making the contract sacred.

In 1895 the Court interpreted the Sherman Act so as to make it harmless. It said a monopoly of sugar refining was a monopoly in manufacturing, not commerce, and so could not be regulated by Congress through the Sherman Act (*U.S. v. E. C. Knight Co.*). The Court also said the Sherman Act could be used against interstate strikes (the railway strike of 1894) because they were in restraint of trade. It also declared unconstitutional a small attempt by Congress to tax high incomes at a higher rate (*Pollock v. Farmers' Loan & Trust Company*). In later years it would refuse to break up the Standard Oil and American Tobacco monopolies, saying the Sherman Act barred only "unreasonable" combinations in restraint of trade.

A New York banker toasted the Supreme Court in 1895: "I give you, gentlemen, the Supreme Court of the United States—guardian of the dollar, defender of private property, enemy of spoliation, sheet anchor of the Republic."

Very soon after the Fourteenth Amendment became law, the Supreme Court began to demolish it as a protection for blacks, and to develop it as a protection for corporations. However, in 1877, a Supreme Court decision (*Munn v. Illinois*) approved state laws regulating the prices charged to farmers for the use of grain elevators. The grain elevator company argued it was a person being deprived of property, thus violating the Fourteenth Amendment's declaration "nor shall any State deprive any person of life, liberty, or property without due process of law." The Supreme Court disagreed, saying that grain elevators were not simply private property but were invested with "a public interest" and so could be regulated.

One year after that decision, the American Bar Association, organized by lawyers accustomed to serving the wealthy, began a national campaign of education to reverse the Court decision. Its presidents said, at different times: "If trusts are a defensive weapon of property interests against the communistic trend, they are desirable." And: "Monopoly is often a necessity and an advantage."

By 1886, they succeeded. State legislatures, under the pressure of aroused farmers, had passed laws to regulate the rates charged farmers by the railroads. The Supreme Court that year (*Wabash v. Illinois*) said states could not do this, that this was an intrusion on federal power. That year alone, the Court did away with 230 state laws that had been passed to regulate corporations.

By this time the Supreme Court had accepted the argument that corporations were "persons" and their money was property protected by the due process clause of the Fourteenth Amendment. Supposedly, the Amendment had been passed to protect Negro rights, but of the Fourteenth Amendment cases brought before the Supreme Court between 1890 and 1910, nineteen dealt with the Negro, 288 dealt with corporations.

The justices of the Supreme Court were not simply interpreters of the Constitution. They were men of certain backgrounds, of certain interests. One of them (Justice Samuel Miller) had said in 1875: "It is vain to contend with Judges who have been at the bar the advocates for forty years of railroad companies, and all forms of associated capital. . . ." In 1893, Supreme Court Justice David J. Brewer, addressing the New York State Bar Association, said:

> It is the unvarying law that the wealth of the community will be in the hands of the few. . . . The great majority of men are unwilling to endure that long self-denial and saving which makes accumulations possible . . . and hence it always has been, and until human nature is remodeled always will be true, that the wealth of a nation is in the hands of a few, while the many subsist upon the proceeds of their daily toil.

This was not just a whim of the 1880s and 1890s—it went back to the Founding Fathers, who had learned their law in the era of *Blackstone's Commentaries*, which said: "So great is the regard of the law for private property, that it will not authorize the least violation of it; no, not even for the common good of the whole community."

Control in modern times requires more than force, more than law. It requires that a population dangerously concentrated in cities and factories, whose lives are filled with cause for rebellion, be taught that all is right as it is. And so, the schools, the churches, the popular literature taught that to be rich was a sign of superiority, to be poor a sign of personal failure, and that the only way upward for a poor person was to climb into the ranks of the rich by extraordinary effort and extraordinary luck.

In those years after the Civil War, a man named Russell Conwell, a graduate of Yale Law School, a minister, and author of best-selling books, gave the same lecture, "Acres of Diamonds," more than five thousand times to audiences across the country, reaching several million people in all. His message was that anyone could get rich if he tried hard enough, that everywhere, if people looked closely enough, were "acres of diamonds." A sampling:

> I say that you ought to get rich, and it is your duty to get rich. . . . The men who get rich may be the most honest men you find in the community. Let me say here clearly . . . ninety-eight out of one hundred of the rich men of America are honest. That is why they are rich. That is why they are trusted with money. That is why they carry on great enterprises and find plenty of people to work with them. It is because they are honest men. . . .
> I sympathize with the poor, but the number of poor who are to be sympathized with is very small. To sympathize with a man whom God has punished for his sins . . . is to do wrong . . . let us remember there is not a poor person in the United States who was not made poor by his own shortcomings. . . .

Conwell was a founder of Temple University. Rockefeller was a donor to colleges all over the country and helped found the University of Chicago. Huntington, of the Central Pacific, gave money to two Negro colleges, Hampton Institute and Tuskegee Institute. Carnegie gave money to colleges and to libraries.

Johns Hopkins was founded by a millionaire merchant, and millionaires Cornelius Vanderbilt, Ezra Cornell, James Duke, and Leland Stanford created universities in their own names.

The rich, giving part of their enormous earnings in this way, became known as philanthropists. These educational institutions did not encourage dissent; they trained the middlemen in the American system—the teachers, doctors, lawyers, administrators, engineers, technicians, politicians—those who would be paid to keep the system going, to be loyal buffers against trouble.

In the meantime, the spread of public school education enabled the learning of writing, reading, and arithmetic for a whole generation of workers, skilled and semiskilled, who would be the literate or force of the new industrial age. It was important that these people learn obedience to authority. A journalist observer of the schools in the 1890s wrote: "The unkindly spirit of the teacher is strikingly apparent; the pupils, being completely subjugated to her will, are silent and motionless, the spiritual atmosphere of the classroom is damp and chilly."

Back in 1859, the desire of mill owners in the town of Lowell that their workers be educated was explained by the secretary of the Massachusetts Board of Education:

> The owners of factories are more concerned than other classes and interests in the intelligence of their laborers. When the latter are well-educated and the former are disposed to deal justly, controversies and strikes can never occur, nor can the minds of the masses be prejudiced by demagogues and controlled by temporary and factious considerations.

Joel Spring, in his book *Education and the Rise of the Corporate State*, says: "The development of a factory-like system in the nineteenth-century schoolroom was not accidental."

This continued into the twentieth century, when William Bagley's *Classroom Management* became a standard teacher training text, reprinted thirty times. Bagley said: "One who studies educational theory aright can see in the mechanical routine of the classroom the educative forces that are slowly transforming the child from a little savage into a creature of law and order, fit for the life of civilized society."

It was in the middle and late nineteenth century that high schools developed as aids to the industrial system, that history was widely required in the curriculum to foster patriotism. Loyalty oaths, teacher certification, and the requirement of citizenship were introduced to control both the educational and the political quality of teachers. Also, in the latter part of the century, school officials—not teachers—were given control over textbooks. Laws passed by the states barred certain kinds of textbooks. Idaho and Montana, for instance, forbade textbooks propagating "political" doctrines, and the Dakota territory ruled that school libraries could not have "partisan political pamphlets or books."

Against this gigantic organization of knowledge and education for orthodoxy and obedience, there arose a literature of dissent and protest, which had to make its way from reader to reader against great obstacles. Henry George, a self-educated workingman from a poor Philadelphia family, who became a newspaperman and an economist, wrote a book that was published in 1879 and sold millions of copies, not only in the United States, but all over the world. His book *Progress and Poverty* argued that the basis of wealth was land, that this was becoming monopolized, and that a single tax on land, abolishing all others, would bring enough revenue to solve the problem of poverty and equalize wealth in the nation. Readers may not have been persuaded of his solutions, but they could see in their own lives the accuracy of his observations:

> It is true that wealth has been greatly increased, and that the average of comfort, leisure and refinement has been raised; but these gains are not general. In them the lowest class do not share. . . . This association of poverty with progress is the great enigma of our times. . . . There is a vague but general feeling of disappointment; an increased bitterness among the working classes; a widespread feeling of unrest and brooding revolution. . . . The civilized world is trembling on the verge of a great movement. Either it must be a leap upward, which will open the way to advances yet undreamed of, or it must he a plunge downward which will carry us back toward barbarism. . . .

A different kind of challenge to the economic and social system was given by Edward Bellamy, a lawyer and writer from western Massachusetts, who wrote, in simple, intriguing language, a novel called *Looking Backward*, in which the author fells asleep and wakes up in the year 2000, to find a socialistic society in which people work and live cooperatively. *Looking Backward,* which described socialism vividly, lovingly, sold a million copies in a few years, and over a hundred groups were organized around the country to try to make the dream come true.

It seemed that despite the strenuous efforts of government, business, the church, the schools, to control their thinking, millions of Americans were ready to consider harsh criticism of the existing system, to contemplate other possible ways of living. They were helped in this by the great movements of workers and farmers that swept the country in the 1880s and 1890s. These movements went beyond the scattered strikes and tenants' struggles of the period 1830–1877. . . . They were nationwide movements, more threatening than before to the ruling elite, more dangerously suggestive. It was a time when revolutionary organizations existed in major American cities, and revolutionary talk was in the air.

John S. Gordon  **NO**

Was There Ever Such a Business!

The industrial empires that were created by the robber barons appeared more and more threatening in their economic power as they merged into ever-larger companies. In the latter half of the 1890s, this trend toward consolidation accelerated. In 1897 there were 69 corporate mergers; in 1898 there were 303; the next year 1,208. Of the seventy-three "trusts" with capitalization of more than $10 million in 1900, two-thirds had been created in the previous three years.

In 1901 J. P. Morgan created the largest company of all, U.S. Steel, merging Andrew Carnegie's empire with several other steel companies to form a new company capitalized at $1.4 billion. The revenues of the federal government that year were a mere $586 million. The sheer size of the enterprise stunned the world. Even the *Wall Street Journal* confessed to "uneasiness over the magnitude of the affair," and wondered if the new corporation would mark "the high tide of industrial capitalism." A joke made the rounds where a teacher asks a little boy about who made the world. "God made the world in 4004 B.C.," he replied, "and it was reorganized in 1901 by J. P. Morgan."

But when Theodore Roosevelt entered the White House in September 1901, the laiseez-faire attitude of the federal government began to change. In 1904 the government announced that it would sue under the Sherman Antitrust Act—long thought a dead letter—to break up a new Morgan consolidation, the Northern Securities Corporation. Morgan hurried to Washington to get the matter straightened out.

"If we have done anything wrong," Morgan told the president, fully encapsulating his idea of how the commercial world should work, "send your man to my man and they can fix it up."

"That can't be done," Roosevelt replied.

"We don't want to fix it up," his attorney general, Philander Knox, explained. "We want to stop it."

From that point on, the federal government would be an active referee in the marketplace, trying—not always successfully, to be sure—to balance the needs of efficiency and economies of scale against the threat of overweening power in organizations that owed allegiance only to their stockholders, not to society as a whole.

In 1907 the federal government took on the biggest "trust" of all, Standard Oil. The case reached the Supreme Court in 1910 and was decided the following

From *An Empire of Wealth: The Epic History of American Economic Power* by John Steele Gordon (Harper Perennial, 2004). Copyright © 2004 by John Steele Gordon. Reprinted by permission of HarperCollins Publishers.

year, when the Court ruled unanimously that Standard Oil was a combination in restraint of trade. It ordered Standard Oil broken up into more than thirty separate companies.

The liberal wing of American politics hailed the decision, needless to say, but in one of the great ironies of American economic history, the effect of the ruling on the greatest fortune in the world was only to increase it. In the two years after the breakup of Standard Oil, the stock in the successor companies doubled in value, making John D. Rockefeller twice as rich as he had been before.

Nothing so epitomized the economy of the late nineteenth-century Western world as steel. Its production became the measure of a country's industrial power, and its uses were almost without limit. Its influence in other sectors of the economy, such as railroads and real estate, was immense. But steel was hardly an invention of the time. Indeed, it has been around for at least three thousand years. What was new was the cost of producing it.

Pig iron, the first step in iron and steel production, is converted into bar iron by remelting it and mixing it with ground limestone to remove still more impurities. Cast iron is then created by pouring this into molds, producing such items as frying pans, cookstoves, and construction members. Cast iron was widely used in urban construction in the antebellum period, but it had serious drawbacks. Extremely strong in compression, cast iron makes excellent columns. But, because it is very brittle, it is weak in tension, making it unsuitable for beams. For them, wrought iron was needed.

Wrought iron is made by melting pig iron and stirring it repeatedly until it achieves a pasty consistency and most of the impurities have been volatilized. The laborers who worked these furnaces were known as puddlers and were both highly skilled and highly paid. After the metal is removed from the puddling furnace, it is subjected to pressure and rolled and folded over and over—in effect, it is kneaded like bread dough—until it develops the fibrous quality that makes wrought iron much less brittle than cast iron and thus moderately strong in tension. Wrought iron is quite soft compared to cast iron but it is also ductile, able to be drawn out and hammered into various shapes, just as copper can be.

Wrought iron, of course, was much more expensive to produce than cast iron but could be used for making beams, bridges, ships, and, most important to the nineteenth-century economy after 1830, railroad rails. The Industrial Revolution simply could not have moved into high gear without large quantities of wrought iron.

Steel, which is iron alloyed with just the right amount of carbon under suitable conditions, has the good qualities of both cast and wrought iron. It is extremely strong and hard, like cast iron, while it is also malleable and withstands shock like wrought iron. And it is far stronger in tension than either, and thus makes a superb building material.

But until the mid-nineteenth century, the only way to make steel was in small batches from wrought iron, mixing the iron with carbon and heating it for a period of days. Thus its use was limited to very high-value items such as sword blades, razors, and tools, where its ability to withstand shock and take and hold a sharp edge justified its high cost. At mid-century, roughly 250,000 tons of steel were being made by the old methods in Europe, and only about 10,000 tons in the United States.

Then, in 1856, an Englishman named Henry Bessemer (later Sir Henry) invented the Bessemer converter, which allowed steel to be made directly and quickly from pig iron. As so often happens in the history of technological development, the initial insight was the result of an accidental observation. Bessemer had developed a new type of artillery shell, but the cast-iron cannons of the day were not strong enough to handle it. He began experimenting in hopes of developing a stronger metal, and one day a gust of wind happened to hit some molten iron. The oxygen in the air, combining with the iron and carbon in the molten metal, raised the temperature of the metal and volatilized the impurities. Most of the carbon was driven off. What was left was steel.

Bessemer, realizing what had happened, immediately set about designing an industrial process that would duplicate what he had observed accidentally. His converter was a large vessel, about ten feet wide by twenty feet high, with trunnions so that its contents could be poured. It was made of steel and lined with firebrick. At the bottom, air could be blasted through holes in the firebrick into the "charge," as the mass of molten metal in the crucible was called, converting it to steel in a stupendous blast of flame and heat. With the Bessemer converter, ten to thirty tons of pig iron could be turned into steel every twelve to fifteen minutes in what is one of the most spectacular of all industrial processes.

The labor activist John A. Fitch wrote in 1910 that "there is a glamor about the making of steel. The very size of things—the immensity of the tools, the scale of production—grips the mind with an overwhelming sense of power. Blast furnaces, eighty, ninety, one hundred feet tall, gaunt and insatiable, are continually gaping to admit ton after ton of ore, fuel, and stone. Bessemer converters dazzle the eye with their leaping flames. Steel ingots at white heat, weighing thousands of pounds, are carried from place to place and tossed about like toys. . . . [C]ranes pick up steel rails or fifty-foot girders as jauntily as if their tons were ounces. These are the things that cast a spell over the visitor in these workshops of Vulcan."

One of the visitors to Henry Bessemer's steelworks in Sheffield, England, in 1872, was a young Scottish immigrant to America, Andrew Carnegie. He was mightily impressed—so impressed, in fact, that in the next thirty years he would ride the growing demand for steel to one of the greatest American fortunes.

Carnegie had been born in Dunfermline, a few miles northwest and across the Firth of Forth from Edinburgh, in 1835. His father was a hand weaver who owned his own loom, on which he made intricately patterned damask cloth. Dunfermline was a center of the damask trade, and skilled weavers such as William Carnegie could make a good living at it.

But the Industrial Revolution destroyed William Carnegie's livelihood. By the 1840s power looms could produce cloth such as damask much more cheaply than handlooms. While there had been 84,560 handloom weavers in Scotland in 1840, there would be only 25,000 ten years later. William Carnegie would not be one of them.

The elder Carnegie sank into despair, and his far tougher-minded wife took charge of the crisis. She had gotten a letter from her sister, who had immigrated to America, settling in Pittsburgh. "This country's far better for the working man," her sister wrote, "than the old one, & there is room enough & to spare, notwithstanding the thousands that flock to her borders." In 1847, when Andrew was twelve, the Carnegie family moved to Pittsburgh.

The Carnegies were in the first wave of one of the great movements of people in human history, known as the Atlantic migration. At first most of the immigrants came from the British Isles, especially Ireland after the onset of the Great Famine of the 1840s. Later Germany, Italy, and Eastern Europe provided immigrants in huge numbers, more than two million in 1900 alone.

In its size and significance the Atlantic migration was the equal of the barbarian movements in late classic times that helped bring the Roman Empire to an end. But while many of the barbarian tribes had been pushed by those behind them, the more than thirty million people who crossed the Atlantic to settle in America between 1820 and 1914 were largely pulled by the lure of economic opportunity.

Many, such as the land-starved Scandinavians who settled in the Upper Middle West, moved to rural areas and established farms. But most, at least at first, settled in the country's burgeoning cities, in the fast-spreading districts that came to be called slums (a word that came into use, in both Britain and America, about 1825). For the first time in American history, a substantial portion of the population was poor. But most of the new urban poor were not poor for long.

These slums, by modern standards, were terrible almost beyond imagination, with crime- and vermin-ridden, sunless apartments that often housed several people, sometimes several families, to a room and had only communal privies behind the buildings. In the 1900 census, when conditions in the slums had much improved from mid-century, one district in New York's Lower East Side had a population of more than fifty thousand but only about five hundred bathtubs.

Such housing, however, was no worse—and often better—than what the impoverished immigrants left behind in Europe, and as Mrs. Carnegie's sister— and millions like her—reported back home, the economic opportunities were far greater. The labor shortage so characteristic of the American economy since its earliest days had not abated. So the average stay for an immigrant family in the worst of the slums was less than fifteen years, before they were able to move to better housing in better neighborhoods and begin the climb into the American middle class.

The migration of people to the United States in search of economic opportunity has never ceased, although legal limits were placed on it beginning in the early 1920s. And this vast migration did far more than help provide the labor needed to power the American economy. It has given the United States the most ethnically diverse population of any country in the world. And because of that, it has provided the country with close personal connections with nearly every other country on the globe, an immense economic and political advantage.

The Carnegies moved into two rooms above a workshop that faced a muddy alleyway behind Mrs. Carnegie's sister's house in Allegheny City, a neighborhood of Pittsburgh. Mrs. Carnegie found work making shoes, and Mr. Carnegie worked in a cotton mill. Andrew got a job there as well, as a bobbin boy earning $1.20 a week for twelve-hour days, six days a week.

Needless to say, it didn't take the bright and ambitious Andrew Carnegie fifteen years to start up the ladder. By 1849 he had a job as a telegraph messenger boy, earning $2.50 a week. This gave him many opportunities to become familiar with Pittsburgh and its business establishment, and Carnegie made the most of them. Soon he was an operator, working the telegraph himself and able to interpret it by ear, writing down the messages directly. His salary was up to $25 a month.

In 1853, in a classic example of Louis Pasteur's dictum that chance favors the prepared mind, Thomas A. Scott, general superintendent of the Pennsylvania Railroad, a frequent visitor to the telegraph office where Carnegie worked, needed a telegraph operator of his own to help with the system being installed by the railroad. He chose Carnegie, not yet eighteen years old. By the time Carnegie was thirty-three, in 1868, he had an annual income of $50,000, thanks to the tutelage of Thomas Scott and numerous shrewd investments in railway sleeping cars, oil, telegraph lines, and iron manufacturing. But after his visit to Bessemer's works in Sheffield, he decided to concentrate on steel.

⚜

It had been pure chance that had brought the Carnegie family to Pittsburgh, but its comparative advantages would make it the center of the American steel industry.

Set where the Allegheny and Monongahela rivers join to form the Ohio and provide easy transportation over a wide area, Pittsburgh had been founded, as so many cities west of the mountains were, as a trading post. Shortly after the Revolution, Pittsburgh began to exploit the abundant nearby sources of both iron ore and coal and specialize in manufacturing. While the rest of the country still relied on wood, coal became the dominant fuel in Pittsburgh, powering factories that were turning out glass, iron, and other energy-intensive products. As early as 1817, when the population was still only six thousand, there were 250 factories in operation, and the nascent city, with already typical American boosterism, was calling itself the "Birmingham of America." Because of the cheap coal, Pittsburgh exploited the steam engine long before it began to displace water power elsewhere, and most of its factories were steam-powered by 1830.

There was, however, a price to be paid for the cheap coal, which produces far more smoke than does wood. About 1820, when Pittsburgh was still a relatively small town, a visitor wrote that the smoke formed "a cloud which almost amounts to night and overspreads Pittsburgh with the appearance of gloom and melancholy." By the 1860s even Anthony Trollope, London-born and no stranger to coal smoke, was impressed with the pall. Looked down on from the surrounding hills. Trollope reported, some of the tops of the churches could be seen, "But the city itself is buried in a dense cloud. I was never more in love with smoke and dirt than when I stood here and watched the darkness of night close in upon the floating soot which hovered over the house-tops of the city." As the Industrial Revolution gathered strength, other American cities became polluted with coal smoke and soot, but none so badly as Pittsburgh.

The most important coal beds in the Pittsburgh area were those surrounding the town of Connellsville, about thirty miles southeast of the city. What made Connellsville coal special was that it was nearly perfect for converting into coke. Indeed it is the best coking coal in the world.

Coke is to coal exactly what charcoal is to wood: heated in the absence of air to drive off the impurities, it becomes pure carbon and burns at an even and easily adjusted temperature. And either charcoal or coke is indispensable to iron and steel production. As the iron industry in Pittsburgh grew, it turned more and more to coke, the production of which was far more easily industrialized than was charcoal.

By the time Andrew Carnegie was moving into steel, Henry Clay Frick, who had been born in West Overton, Pennsylvania, not far from Connellsville, in 1849, was moving into coke. Like Carnegie, Frick was a very hardheaded businessman and willing to take big risks for big rewards. And like Carnegie, he was a millionaire by the time he was thirty. Unlike Carnegie, however, he had little concern with public opinion or the great social issues of the day. Carnegie always wanted to be loved and admired by society at large. Frick was perfectly willing to settle for its respect. Unlike Carnegie, he rarely granted newspaper interviews and never wrote articles for publication.

By the 1880s the Carnegie Steel Company and the H. C. Frick Company dominated their respective industries, and Carnegie was by far Frick's biggest customer. In late 1881, while Frick was on his honeymoon in New York, Carnegie, who loved surprises, suddenly proposed a merger of their companies at a family lunch one day. Frick, who had no inkling the proposal was coming, was stunned. So was Carnegie's ever-vigilant mother, now in her seventies. The silence that ensued was finally broken by what is perhaps the most famous instance of maternal concern in American business history.

"Ah, Andra," said Mrs. Carnegie in her broad Scots accent, "that's a very fine thing for Mr. Freek. But what do we get out of it?"

Needless to say, Carnegie had calculated closely what he would get out of it. First, the Carnegie Steel Company would get guaranteed supplies of coke at the best possible price; second, he would get the surpassing executive skills of Henry Clay Frick; and third, he would further the vertical integration of the steel industry in general and his company in particular.

Vertical integration simply means bringing under one corporation's control part or all of the stream of production from raw materials to distribution. It had been going on since the dawn of the Industrial Revolution (Francis Cabot Lowell had been the first to integrate spinning and weaving in a single building) but greatly accelerated in the last quarter of the nineteenth century as industrialists sought economies of scale as well as of speed to cut costs.

Carnegie and Frick shared a simple management philosophy: (1) Innovate constantly and invest heavily in the latest equipment and techniques to drive down operating costs. (2) Always be the low-cost producer so as to remain profitable in bad economic times. (3) Retain most of the profits in good times to take advantage of opportunities in bad times as less efficient competitors fail.

One such opportunity arose in 1889, by which time Frick was chairman of the Carnegie steel companies (Carnegie himself never held an executive position in the companies he controlled, but as the holder of a comfortable majority of the stock, he was always the man in charge). That year Frick snapped up the troubled Duquesne Steel Works, paying for it with $1 million in Carnegie company bonds due to mature in five years. By the time the bonds were paid off, the plant had paid for itself five times over.

Much of the technological advances that Carnegie was so quick to use came from Europe's older and more established steel industries, just as, nearly a century earlier, the American cloth industry had piggybacked on Britain's technological lead. As one of Carnegie's principal lieutenants, Captain W. M. Jones, explained to the British Iron and Steel Institute as early as 1881, "While your metallurgists as well as those of France and Germany, have been devoting their time and talents to the discovery of new processes, we have swallowed the information so generously tendered through the printed reports of the Institute, and we have selfishly devoted ourselves to beating you in output."

And beat them they did. In 1867 only 1,643 tons of Bessemer steel was produced in the United States. Thirty years later, in 1897, the tonnage produced was 7,156,957, more than Britain and Germany combined. By the turn of the century the Carnegie Steel Company alone would outproduce Britain. It would also be immensely profitable. In 1899 the Carnegie Steel Company, the low-cost producer in the prosperous and heavily protected American market, made $21 million in profit. The following year profits doubled. No wonder Andrew Carnegie exclaimed at one point, "Was there ever such a business!"

And steel was also transforming the American urban landscape. When stone was the principal construction material of large buildings, they could not rise much above six stories, even after the elevator was perfected in the 1850s, because of the necessary thickness of the walls. It was church steeples that rose above their neighbors and punctuated the urban skyline. But as the price of steel declined steadily as the industry's efficiency rose—by the 1880s the far longer-lasting steel railroad rails cost less than the old wrought-iron rails—more and more buildings were built with steel skeletons and could soar to the sky. Between the 1880s and 1913 the record height for buildings was broken as often as every year as "skyscrapers" came to dominate American urban skylines in an awesome display of the power of steel. . . .

While the late-nineteenth-century American economy was increasingly built by and with steel, it was increasingly fueled by oil. In 1859, the year Edwin Drake drilled the first well, American production amounted to only 2,000 barrels. Ten years later it was 4.25 million and by 1900, American production would be nearly 60 million barrels. But while production rose steadily, the price of oil was chaotic, sinking as low as 10 cents a barrel—far below the cost of the barrel itself—and soaring as high as $13.75 during the 1860s. One reason for this was the vast number of refineries then in existence. Cleveland alone had more than thirty, many of them nickel-and-dime, ramshackle operations.

Many people, while happy to exploit the new oil business, were unwilling to make large financial commitments to it for fear that the oil would suddenly dry up. The field in northwestern Pennsylvania was very nearly the only one in the world until the 1870s, when the Baku field in what was then southern Russia opened up. There would be no major new field in the United States until the fabulous Spindletop field in Texas was first tapped in 1902.

But a firm named Rockefeller, Flagler, and Andrews, formed to exploit the burgeoning market for petroleum products, especially kerosene, took the gamble of building top-quality refineries. Like Carnegie, it intended to exploit being the low-cost producer, with all the advantages of that position. The firm also began buying up other refineries as the opportunity presented itself.

The firm realized that there was no controlling the price of crude oil but that it could control, at least partly, another important input into the price of petroleum products: transportation. It began negotiating aggressively with the railroads to give the firm rebates in return for guaranteeing high levels of traffic. It was this arrangement that often allowed the firm to undersell its competitors and still make handsome profits, further strengthening the firm's already formidable competitive position.

In 1870 one of the partners, Henry Flagler, convinced the others to change the firm from a partnership to a corporation, which would make it easier for the partners to continue to raise capital to finance their relentless expansion while retaining control. The new corporation, named Standard Oil, was capitalized at $1 million and owned at that time about 10 percent of the country's oil refining capacity. By 1880 it would control 80 percent of a much larger industry.

The expansion of Standard Oil became one of the iconic stories of late-nineteenth-century America, as its stockholders became rich beyond imagination and its influence in the American economy spread ever wider. Indeed, the media reaction to Standard Oil and John D. Rockefeller in the Gilded Age is strikingly similar to the reaction to the triumph of Microsoft and Bill Gates a hundred years later. It is perhaps a coincidence that Rockefeller and Gates were just about the same age, their early forties, when they became household names and the living symbols of a new and, to some, threatening economic structure.

The image of Standard Oil that remains even today in the American folk memory was the product of a number of writers and editorial cartoonists who often had a political agenda to advance first and foremost. The most brilliant of these was Ida Tarbell, whose *History of the Standard Oil Company,* first published in *McClure's* magazine in 1902, vividly depicted a company ruthlessly expanding over the corporate bodies of its competitors, whose assets it gobbled up as it went.

That is by no means a wholly false picture, but it is a somewhat misleading one. For one thing, as the grip of Standard Oil relentlessly tightened on the oil industry, prices for petroleum products *declined* steadily, dropping by two-thirds over the course of the last three decades of the nineteenth century. It is simply a myth that monopolies will raise prices once they have the power to do so. Monopolies, like everyone else, want to maximize their profits, not their prices. Lower prices, which increase demand, and increased efficiency, which cuts costs, is usually the best way to achieve the highest possible profits. What makes monopolies (and most of them today are government agencies, from motor vehicle bureaus to public schools) so economically evil is the fact that, without competitive pressure, they become highly risk-aversive—and therefore shy away from innovation—and notably indifferent to their customers' convenience.

Further, Standard Oil used its position as the country's largest refiner not only to extract the largest rebates from the railroads but also to induce them to deny rebates to refiners that Standard Oil wanted to acquire. It even sometimes forced railroads to give it secret rebates not only on its own oil, but on that shipped by its competitors as well, essentially a tax on competing with Standard Oil. (This is about as close as the "robber barons" ever came to behaving like, well, robber barons.) It thus effectively presented these refiners with Hobson's choice: they could agree to be acquired, at a price set by Standard Oil, or they could be driven into bankruptcy by high transportation costs.

The acquisition price set, however, was a fair one, arrived at by a formula developed by Henry Flagler, and consistently applied. Sometimes, especially if the owners of the refinery being acquired had executive talents that Standard wished to make use of, the price was a generous one. Further, the seller had the choice of receiving cash or Standard Oil stock. Those who chose the latter— and there were hundreds—became millionaires as they rode the stock of the Standard Oil Company to capitalist glory. Those who took the cash often ended up whining to Ida Tarbell.

None of this, of course, was illegal, and that was the real problem. In the late nineteenth century people such as Rockefeller, Flagler, Carnegie, and J. P. Morgan were creating at a breathtaking pace the modern corporate economy, and thus a wholly new economic universe. They were moving far faster than society could fashion, through the usually slow-moving political process, the rules needed to govern that new universe wisely and fairly. But that must always be the case in democratic capitalism, as individuals can always act far faster than can society as a whole. Until the rules were written—largely in the first decades of the twentieth century—it was a matter of (in the words of Sir Walter Scott)

> The good old rule, the simple plan
> That they should take who have the power
> And they should keep who can.

Part of the problem is that there is a large, inherent inertia in any political system, and democracy is no exception. Politicians, after all, are in the reelection business, and it is often easier to do nothing than to offend one group or another. So while the American economy had changed profoundly since the mid-nineteenth century, the state incorporation laws, for instance, had not. As an Ohio corporation, Standard Oil was not allowed to own property in other states or to hold the stock of other corporations. As it quickly expanded throughout the Northeast, the country, and then across the globe, however, Standard Oil necessarily acquired property in other states and purchased other corporations.

The incorporation laws, largely written in an era before the railroads and telegraph had made a national economy possible, were no longer adequate to meet the needs of the new economy. To get around the outdated law, Henry Flager, as secretary of Standard Oil, had himself appointed as trustee to hold the property or stock that Standard Oil itself could not legally own. By the end of the 1870s, however, Standard owned dozens of properties and companies in other states, each, in theory, held by a trustee who was in some cases Flagler and in other cases other people. It was a hopelessly unwieldy corporate structure.

In all probability, it was Flagler—a superb executive—who found the solution. Instead of each subsidiary company having a single trustee, with these trustees scattered throughout the Standard Oil empire, the same three men, all at the Cleveland headquarters, were appointed trustees for all the subsidiary companies. In theory, they controlled all of Standard Oil's assets outside Ohio. In fact, of course, they did exactly what they were told.

Thus was born the business trust, a form that was quickly imitated by other companies that were becoming national in scope. The "trusts" would be one of the great bogeymen of American politics for the next hundred years, but, ironically, the actual trust form of organization devised by Henry Flagler lasted only until 1889. That year New Jersey—seeking a source of new tax revenue—became the first state to modernize its incorporation laws and bring them into conformity with the new economic realities. New Jersey now permitted holding companies and interstate activities, and companies flocked to incorporate there, as, later, they would flock to Delaware, to enjoy the benefits of a corporation-friendly legal climate. Standard Oil of New Jersey quickly became the center of the Rockefeller interests, and the Standard Oil Trust, in the legal sense, disappeared.

‿◈‿

With the growth of American industry, the nature of American foreign trade changed drastically. The United States remained, as it remains today, a formidable exporter of agricultural and mineral products. Two new ones were even added in the post-Civil War era: petroleum and copper. But it also became a major exporter of manufactured goods that it had previously imported. In 1865 they had constituted only 22.78 percent of American exports. By the turn of the twentieth century they were 31.65 percent of a vastly larger trade. The percentage of world trade, meanwhile, that was American in origin doubled in these years to about 12 percent of total trade.

Nowhere was this more noticeable than in iron and steel products, the cutting edge of late-nineteenth-century technology. Before the Civil War the United States exported only $6 million worth of iron and steel manufactures a year. In 1900 it exported $121,914,000 worth of locomotives, engines, rails, electrical machinery, wire, pipes, metalworking machinery, boilers, and other goods. Even sewing machines and typewriters were being exported in quantity. . . .

This country has never developed an aristocracy,because the concept of primogeniture, with the eldest son inheriting the bulk of the fortune, never took hold. Thus great fortunes have always been quickly dispersed among heirs in only a few generations. The American super rich are therefore always nouveau riche and often act accordingly, giving new meaning in each generation to the phrase *conspicuous consumption*. In the Gilded Age, they married European titles, built vast summer cottages and winter retreats that cost millions but were occupied only a few weeks a year. . . .

POSTSCRIPT

Were the Nineteenth-Century Big Businessmen "Robber Barons"?

The field of business history can be divided into three major interpretations: (1) the robber baron or anti-big business viewpoint; (2) the entrepreneurial statesman or pro-big business account; (3) the organizational or bureaucratic functional framework that deems irrelevant the robber baron and entrepreneurial arguments.

The robber baron interpretation emerged from the muckrakers of the Progressive Era (1897–1917) who were critical of the immoral methods used by businessmen such as J. J. Hill, John D. Rockefeller, and Andrew Carnegie to gain control over the railroads, the oil, and steel processing industries. The book that did the most to fix the stereotype of the late nineteenth-century businessman as a predator was Matthew Josephson's *The Robber Barons: The Great American Capitalists, 1861–1901* (Harcourt Brace and World, 1934, 1962). He admitted that "large-scale production replaced the scattered, decentralized mode of production; industrial enterprises became more concentrated, more 'efficient' technically and essentially 'cooperative' where they had been purely individualistic and lamentably wasteful." While this may have been a good thing, Josephson argues that the negatives far outweighed the positives. Ultimately, he concluded, the "extremes of management and stupidity would make themselves felt. . . . The alternations of prosperity and poverty would be more violent and mercurial, speculation and breakdown each more excessive; while the inherent contradictions within society pressed with increasing intolerable force against the bonds of the old order."

Josephson's view was challenged by the new group of business historians who emerged in the 1940s and 1950s, but they were isolated from mainstream historians so that some form of the "robber baron" interpretation continued into the high school and college texts through the 1960s. New left historians such as Gabriel Kolko's *The Triumph of Conservatism: A Reinterpretation of American History* (Macmillan, 1963) kept it alive as he blamed big business for the militarism, poverty, and racism that still existed in the 1960s.

In 1981, Howard Zinn, a socialist, Marxist, and an activist historian wrote *A People's History of the United States* (HarperCollins, 1980, 1999). The book became an instant success and sold over a million copies. In one of the ironies of history, it made Zinn, the anti-business Marxist, a millionaire. Upon his death in February 2010, at the age of 87, *A People's History of the United States* climbed to number four on *The New York Times'* paperback nonfiction bestseller list.

Zinn's chapter, reprinted as the first reading, is self-explanatory. He details all the arguments used earlier by Josephson and Kolko. He believes that big businessmen led by Rockefeller and Carnegie worked hand in hand with the financier J. P. Morgan who functioned as a quasi-Federal Reserve System before it was created in 1913. Morgan's banking house financed numerous mergers and controlled most of the boards of these corporations through the "interlocking directorates" of Morgan's officials who staffed the pools and trusts that held the stock.

Professor Zinn also believes that both political parties, the Congress and Presidents Cleveland and Harrison, fought over such non-important issues, such as the tariff and Cleveland's mistresses and illegitimate child, and ignored important issues such as the low wages, poor housing, and horrible safety issues for the working class. In Zinn's view, the state militia, the courts, the churches, and even the education system, both colleges and high schools, were designed to produce executives for the corporations and workers for the factories. In short, Zinn's view of American history, especially this period, is very depressing. Critics have faulted Zinn's interpretation as too one-sided and lacks the diversity of viewpoints, especially divisions between small and large businessmen and small and large farmers, the pressures put upon Congress, the Justice Department who staffed the Antitrust Division in charge of enforcing the Sherman Act, and the members of the Interstate Commerce Commission who were supposed to regulate the railroads.

The Josephson–Zinn interpretation did not go unchallenged. The Harvard Business School in the 1930s and writers such as the famous journalist and popular historian Allan Nevins, whose two-volume biography of John D. Rockefeller in 1940 and rewritten in 1953, stressed his positive attributes. Rockefeller was not a robber baron, maintained Nevins, but an entrepreneurial statesman who imposed upon American industry "a more rational and efficient pattern." He and others like him were motivated not by wealth but by competition, achievement, and the "imposition of their will over a given environment." Had it not been for men like Rockefeller, the industries that developed in steel, oil, textiles, chemicals and electricity gave us such a competitive advantage that we were able to win both world wars in the twentieth century.

The two interpretations came to a head in 1954 when the *Saturday Review* published the enlightened article "Should American History Be Rewritten? A Debate Between Allan Nevins and Matthew Josephson," vol. 37 (February 6, 1954), pp. 7–10, 44–49. See also Hal Bridges, "The Robber Baron Concept in American History," *Business History Review*, vol. 32 (Spring 1958), pp. 1–13, and Maury Klein's critique of Josephson, "A Robber Historian," *Forbes* (October 26, 1987). John S. Gordon's chapter in Carnegie and Rockefeller's *An Empire of Wealth* is the antithesis of Zinn. An independent scholar who has written numerous books and articles, especially for *American Heritage*, Gordon extols a highly positive view of the men of big business. He stresses the innovations in production and organization as well as the new technologies that Carnegie used, for example, when he brought to America from Scotland the Bessemer steel process used to refine steel into iron ore. Gordon definitely takes the pro-business stance. He argues that monopolies in the private sector, want to maximize profits, not their prices, "It is simply a myth that they will raise prices once they have the power to do so." For example, as Standard Oil became the sole monopoly in the oil industry, "prices for petroleum products declined steadily, dropping by two-thirds over the course of the last three decades of the nineteenth century."

Critics of Gordon and the entrepreneurial statesmen point of view challenged Gordon's rosy picture of development and question whether workers could have been paid a living wage, and provided a clean and safe working environment and at the same time have produced a creative and dynamic economy.

The third school of business history was the organizational school. Led by Alfred D. Chandler, Jr., this view avoided the morality tale between robber barons and entrepreneurs and stressed how large-scale corporations vertically organized themselves with departments that stretched from production, accounting, marketing, sales and distribution. Key to Chandler's view was the importance of the new national urban markets that had developed by 1900. The best place to start with Chandler is "The Beginning of 'Big Business' in American Industry," *Business History Review*, vol. 33 (Spring 1959), pp. 1–31.

Chandler almost single-handedly reshaped the way in which historians write about corporations when he employed organizational theories of decision making borrowed from the sociologists and applied them to case studies of corporate America. For example, see *Strategy and Structure: Chapters in the History of American Industrial Enterprise* (MIT Press, 1962); *The Visible Hand: The Managerial Revolution in American Business* (Harvard University Press, 1977); and *Scale and Scope: The Dynamics of Industrial Capitalism* (Harvard University Press, 1990). Chandler's most important essays are collected in Thomas K. McCraw, ed., *The Essential Alfred Chandler: Essays Toward a Historical Theory of Big Business* (Harvard Business School Press, 1988). For an assessment of Chandler's approach and contributions, see Louis Galambos, "The Emerging Organizational Synthesis in Modern American History," *Business History Review* (Autumn 1970) and Thomas K. McCraw, "The Challenge of Alfred D. Chandler, Jr.: Retrospect and Prospect," *Reviews in American History* (March 1987).

Chandler's critics have complained that he ignored the role of the individual entrepreneur in developing particular industries. In "Entrepreneurial Persistence through the Bureaucratic Age," *Business History Review*, vol. 51 (Winter 1977), pp. 415–43, Professor Harold C. Livesay tries to reconcile an organizational and entrepreneurial approach via case studies of Andrew Carnegie, Michigan National Bank President Howard Stoddard, and Henry Ford II and his post-World War II revival of the Ford Motor Company. Two important articles examine the main currents in business history today. Mary Klein, "Coming Full Circle: The Study of Big Business since 1950," *Enterprise and Society*, vol. 2 (September 2001), pp. 425–460, contrasts the broader external approach pushed by Professors Thomas C. Cochran and William Miller, *The Age of Enterprise: A Social History of Industrial America*, revised ed. (Harper & Row, 1961) with the internal bureaucratic approach of Alfred Chandler. In a very detailed and sophisticated article useful for history majors with a business emphasis, see Naomi R. Lamoreaux, Daniel M. G. Raff, and Peter Temin, "Beyond Markets and Hierarchies: Toward a New Synthesis of Business History," *American Historical Review* (April 2003), pp. 404–433. The authors argue that some of Chandler's vertically integrated corporations lost control of their markets in the 1980s and, therefore, more flexible frameworks needed to be developed to explain current and past behaviors of corporations.

Biographies of the titans of industry remain popular with the general public. The authors are sympathetic to their subject. See Joseph Frazier Wall, *Andrew Carnegie* (Oxford University Press, 1970); Harold C. Livesay, *Andrew Carnegie and the Rise of Big Business* (Little, Brown, 1975, 1990); James T. Baker, *Andrew Carnegie: Robber Baron as American Hero* (Wadsworth, Thompson Learning, 2003); Ron Chernow, *Titan: The Life of John D. Rockefeller, Sr.* (Random House, 1998); Jean Strouse, *Morgan: American Financier* (Random House, 1999); Robert Sobel and David B. Sicilia, *The Entrepreneurs: An American Adventure* (Houghton–Mifflin, 1986); and Harold C. Livesay, *American Made: Men Who Shaped the American Economy* (Little, Brown, 1986).

Finally, labor historian Steve Fraser offers a critical review of T. J. Stiles, *The First Tycoon* (Knopf, 2009) in "The Misunderstood Robber Baron," *The Nation* (November 30, 2009). If Cornelius Vanderbilt, builder of the Erie Railroad, was lionized as a great entrepreneur, how much concern did he show for the thousands of workers who were killed building the railroad because they worked excessively long hours for paltry wages? See also the exchange between Stiles and Fraser in letters to the editor, *The Nation* (December 14, 2009).

ISSUE 4

Was the American Labor Movement Radical?

YES: Leon Fink, from *Workingmen's Democracy: The Knights of Labor and American Politics* (University of Illinois Press, 1983)

NO: Carl N. Degler, from *Out of Our Past: The Forces That Shaped Modern America*, 3rd ed. (Harper & Row, 1984)

ISSUE SUMMARY

YES: Although stopping short of a frontal attack on capitalism, Professor Leon Fink argues that the Knights of Labor envisioned a kind of workingman's democracy that would ensure minimal standards of health and safety at the industrial workplace.

NO: Historian Carl N. Degler maintains that the American labor movement accepted capitalism and reacted conservatively to the radical organizational changes brought about in the economic system by big business.

The two major labor unions that developed in the late nineteenth century were the Knights of Labor and the American Federation of Labor (AFL). Because of hostility toward labor unions, the Knights of Labor functioned for 12 years as a secret organization. Between 1879 and 1886 the Knights of Labor grew from 10,000 to 700,000 members. Idealistic in many of its aims, the union supported social reforms such as equal pay for men and women, the prohibition of alcohol and the abolition of conflict and child labor. Economic reforms included the development of workers' cooperatives, public ownership of utilities, and a more moderate, eight-hour workday. The Knights declined after 1886 for several reasons. Although it was opposed to strikes, the union received a black eye as did the whole labor movement when it was blamed for the bombs that were thrown at the police during the 1886 Haymarket Square riot in Chicago. According to most historians, other reasons that are usually associated with the decline of the Knights include the failure of some cooperative businesses, conflict between skilled and unskilled workers, and, most important, competition from the AFL. By 1890 the Knight's membership had dropped to 100,000. It died in 1917.

A number of skilled unions got together in 1896 and formed the AFL. Samuel Gompers was elected its first president, and his philosophy permeated the AFL during his 37 years in office. He pushed for practical reforms—better hours, wages, and working conditions. Unlike the Knights, the AFL avoided associations with political parties, workers' cooperatives, unskilled workers, immigrants, and women. Decision-making power was in the hands of locals rather than the central board. Gompers was heavily criticized by his contemporaries, and later by historians, for his narrow craft unionism. But despite the depression of the 1890s, membership increased from 190,000 to 500,000 by 1900, to 1,500,000 by 1904, and to 2,000,000 by the eve of World War I.

Gompers's cautiousness is best understood in the context of his times. The national and local governments were in the hands of men who were sympathetic to the rise of big business and hostile to the attempts of labor to organize. Whether it was the railroad strike of 1877, the Homestead steel strike of 1892, or the Pullman car strike of 1894, the pattern of repression was always the same. Companies would cut wages, workers would go out on strike, scab workers would be brought in, fights would break out, companies would receive court injunctions, and the police and state and federal militia would beat up the unionized workers. After a strike was broken, workers would lose their jobs or would accept pay cuts and longer workdays.

On the national level, Theodore Roosevelt became the first President to show any sympathy for the workers. As a police commissioner in New York City and later as governor of New York, Roosevelt observed firsthand the deplorable occupational and living conditions of the workers. Although he avoided recognition of the collective bargaining rights of labor unions, Roosevelt forced the anthracite coal owners in Pennsylvania to mediate before an arbitration board for an equitable settlement of a strike with the mine workers.

In 1905, a coalition of socialists and industrial unionists formed America's most radical labor union: the Industrial Workers of the World (IWW). There were frequent splits within this union and much talk of violence. But in practice, the IWW was more interested in organizing unskilled workers into industrial unions than in fighting, as were the earlier Knights of Labor and the later Congress of Industrial Organizations. Strikes were encouraged to improve the daily conditions of the workers through long-range goals, which included reducing the power of the capitalists by increasing the power of the workers.

In the first selection, Professor Leon Fink argues that the Knights of Labor envisioned a kind of workingmen's democracy which would bring about minimal standards of health and safety in the industrial workplace. Although the Knights didn't espouse socialism, the union did search for alternatives to the hourly wage system, which had become a standard feature in the new assembly line factories. In the second reading, Stanford University Emeritus Professor Carl N. Degler believes that American workers accepted capitalism and, like business unionist Samuel Gompers, were interested in obtaining better hours, wages, and working conditions. Socialism was rejected, he argues, because workers believed they were achieving economic and social mobility under capitalism.

Workingmen's Democracy: The Knights of Labor and American Politics

Two well-traveled routes into the Gilded Age are likely to leave the present-day visitor with the same puzzled and unsatisfied feeling. One itinerary pursuing the political history of the era begins in 1876 with the official end of Reconstruction and winds through the election of William McKinley in 1896. The other route, this one taking a social prospectus, departs with the great railroad strikes of 1877 and picks its way through the drama and debris of an industrializing society. The problem is that the two paths never seem to meet. Compartmentalization of subject matter in most textbooks into "politics," "economic change," "social movements," and so on only papers over the obvious unanswered question—what impact did an industrial revolution of unprecedented magnitude have on the world's most democratic nation?

The question, of course, permits no simple answer. By most accounts the political era inaugurated in 1876 appears, except for the Populist outburst of the mid-1890s, as a conservative, comparatively uneventful time sandwiched between the end of Radical Reconstruction and the new complexities of the twentieth century. With the Civil War's financial and social settlement out of the way, a society desperately wanting to believe that it had removed its last barriers to social harmony by and large lapsed into a period of ideological torpor and narrow-minded partisanship. Political contests, while still the national pastime (national elections regularly drew 80 percent, state and local elections 60–80 percent of eligible voters, 1876–96), seem to have dwelt less on major social issues than on simple party fealty. Fierce rivalries engendered by the sectional, ethnocultural, and economic interest group divisions among the American people increasingly were presided over and manipulated by party professionals. To be sure, genuine policy differences—e.g., over how best to encourage both industry and trade, the degree of danger posed by the saloon, honesty in government—fueled a venomous political rhetoric. As echoed by both national parties from the late 1870s through the early 1890s, however, a complacent political consensus had emerged, stressing individual opportunity,

From *Workingmen's Democracy: The Knights of Labor and American Politics* by Leon Fink (University of Illinois Press, 1983), pp. xi–xiv, 3–4, 5–9, 11, 12–13, 14, 228–230 (excerpts). Copyright © 1983 by the Board of Trustees of the University of Illinois. Reprinted by permission of University of Illinois Press.

rights in property, and economic freedom from constraints. The welfare of the American Dream, in the minds of both Democrats and Republicans, required no significant governmental tinkering or popular mobilization. Acknowledging the parties' avoidance of changing social and economic realities, a most compelling recent commentary on the late nineteenth-century polity suggests that the "distinct, social need" of the time was in part filled by heightened partisanship and the act of political participation itself.

In contrast to the ritualistic quality of politics, the contemporary social world seems positively explosive. Consolidation of America's industrial revolution touched off an era of unexampled change and turmoil. As work shifted decisively away from agriculture between 1870 and 1890, the manufacturing sector, with a spectacular increase in the amount of capital invested, the monetary value of product, and the number employed, sparked a great economic leap forward. By 1880 Carroll D. Wright, U.S. Commissioner of Labor Statistics, found that the application of steam and water power to production had so expanded that "at least four-fifths" of the "nearly 3 millions of people employed in the mechanical industries of this country" were working under the factory system. It was not just the places of production but the people working within them that represented a dramatic departure from preindustrial America. While only 13 percent of the total population was classified as foreign-born in 1880, 42 percent of those engaged in manufacturing and extractive industries were immigrants. If one adds to this figure workers of foreign parentage and of Afro-American descent, the resulting nonnative/nonwhite population clearly encompassed the great majority of America's industrial work force. Not only, therefore, had the industrial revolution turned a small minority in America's towns and cities into the direct employers of their fellow citizens, but the owners of industry also differed from their employees in national and cultural background. This sudden transformation of American communities, accompanied as it was by a period of intense price competition and unregulated swings in the business cycle, provided plentiful ingredients for social unrest, first manifest on a national scale in the railroad strike of 1877.

The quintessential expression of the labor movement in the Gilded Age was the Noble and Holy Order of the Knights of Labor, the first mass organization of the American working class. Launched as one of several secret societies among Philadelphia artisans in the late 1860s, the Knights grew in spurts by the accretion of miners (1874–79) and skilled urban tradesmen (1879–85). While the movement formally concentrated on moral and political education, cooperative enterprise, and land settlement, members found it a convenient vehicle for trade union action, particularly in the auspicious economic climate following the depression of the 1870s. Beginning in 1883, local skirmishes escalated into highly publicized confrontations with railroad financier Jay Gould, a national symbol of new corporate power. Strikes by Knights of Labor telegraphers and railroad shopmen touched off an unprecedented wave of strikes and boycotts that carried on into the renewed depression in 1884–85 and spread to thousands of previously unorganized semiskilled and unskilled laborers, both urban and rural. The Southwest Strike on Gould's Missouri and Texas-Pacific railroad lines together with massive urban eight-hour campaigns in 1886 swelled a tide of unrest that has become known as the "Great Upheaval." The turbulence aided the efforts of organized labor, and the Knights exploded in size, reaching more than three-quarters of a million members. Although membership dropped off drastically in the late 1880s, the Knights remained a powerful force in many areas through the mid-1890s. Not until the Congress of Industrial Organizations revival of the 1930s would the organized labor movement again lay claim to such influence within the working population.

At its zenith the movement around the Knights helped to sustain a national debate over the social implications of industrial capitalism. Newspaper editors, lecturers, and clergymen everywhere addressed the Social Question. John Swinton, the leading labor journalist of the day, counted Karl Marx, Hawaii's King Kalakaua, and the Republican party's chief orator, Robert G. Ingersoll, among the enlightened commentators on the subject. Even the U.S. Senate in 1883 formally investigated "Relations between Labor and Capital." Nor was the debate conducted only from on high. In laboring communities across the nation the local press as well as private correspondence bore witness to no shortage of eloquence from the so-called inarticulate. One of the busiest terminals of communications was the Philadelphia office of Terence Vincent Powderly, General Master Workman of the Knights of Labor. Unsolicited personal letters expressing the private hopes and desperations of ordinary American citizens daily poured in upon the labor leader: an indigent southern mother prayed that her four young girls would grow up to find an honorable living, an unemployed New York cakemaker applied for a charter as an organizer, a Cheyenne chief sought protection for his people's land, an inventor offered to share a new idea for the cotton gin on condition that it be used cooperatively.

Amidst spreading agitation, massed strength, and growing public awareness, the labor issues ultimately took tangible political form. Wherever the Knights of Labor had organized by the mid-1880s, it seemed, contests over power and rights at the workplace evolved into a community-wide fissure over control of public policy as well. Indeed, in some 200 towns and cities from 1885 to 1888 the labor movement actively fielded its own political slates. Adopting "Workingmen's," "United Labor," "Union Labor," "People's Party," and "Independent" labels for their tickets, or alternatively taking over one of the standing two-party organizations in town, those local political efforts revealed deep divisions within the contemporary political culture and evoked sharp reactions from traditional centers of power. Even as manufacturers' associations met labor's challenge at the industrial level, business response at the political level was felt in the dissolution of party structures, creation of antilabor citizens' coalitions, new restrictive legislation, and extralegal law and order leagues. In their ensemble, therefore, the political confrontations of the 1880s offer a most dramatic point of convergence between the world leading out of 1876 and that stretching from 1877. As a phenomenon simultaneously entwined in the political and industrial history of the Gilded Age the subject offers an opportunity to redefine the main issues of the period. . . .

Working-Class Radicalism in the Gilded Age:
Defining a Political Culture

The labor movement of the Gilded Age, not unlike its nineteenth-century British counterpart, spoke a "language of class" that was "as much political as economic." In important ways an eighteenth-century republican political inheritance still provided the basic vocabulary. The emphasis within the movement on equal rights, on the identity of work and self-worth, and on secure, family-centered households had informed American political radicalism for decades. A republican outlook lay at the heart of the protests of journeymen-mechanics and women millworkers during the Jacksonian period; it likewise inspired abolitionist and the women's suffrage and temperance movements and even contributed to the common school crusade. Within the nineteenth-century political mainstream this tradition reached its height of influence in the free labor assault of the Radical Republicans against slavery. The fracture of the Radical Republican bloc, as David Montgomery has demonstrated, signaled a break in the tradition itself. The more conspicuous and politically dominant side of the schism reflected the growing ideological conservatism of America's industrialists and their steady merger into older socioeconomic elites. A less complacent message, however, also percolated through the age of Hayes, Harrison, and Hanna. Taking place largely outside the party system, this renewed radicalism found a home within an invigorated labor movement.

Working-class radicalism in the Gilded Age derived its principles—as grouped around economic, national-political, and cultural themes—from the period of the early revolutionary-democratic bourgeoisie. Implicitly, labor radicals embraced a unifying conception of work and culture that Norman Birnbaum has labeled the *Homo faber* ideal: "an artisanal conception of activity, a visible, limited, and directed relationship to nature." The *Homo faber* ethic found its political embodiment in Enlightenment liberalism. "From that source," notes Trygve R. Tholfson in a recent commentary on mid-Victorian English labor radicalism, "came a trenchant rationalism, a vision of human emancipation, the expectation of progress based on reason, and an inclination to take the action necessary to bring society into conformity with rationally demonstrable principles." In the late nineteenth century Enlightenment liberalism was harnessed to a historical understanding of American nationalism, confirmed by both the American Revolution and the Civil War. Together these political, economic, and moral conceptions coalesced around a twin commitment to the citizen-as-producer and the producer-as-citizen. For nearly a century Americans had been proud that their country, more than anywhere else in the world, made republican principles real. In this respect the bloody war over slavery served only to confirm the ultimate power of the ideal.

Certain tendencies of the Gilded Age, however, heralded for some an alarming social regression. The permanency of wage labor, the physical and mental exhaustion inflicted by the factory system, and the arrogant exercise of power by the owners of capital threatened the rational and progressive march of history. "Republican institutions," the preamble to the constitution of the Knights of Labor declared simply, "are not safe under such conditions." "We have openly arrayed against us," a Chicago radical despaired in 1883, "the powers of the world, most of the intelligence, all the wealth, and even law itself." . . .

In response the labor movement in the Gilded Age turned the plowshares of a consensual political past into a sword of class conflict. "We declare," went the Knights' manifesto, "an inevitable and irresistible conflict between the wage-system of labor and republican system of government." To some extent older demons seemed simply to have reappeared in new garb, and, as such, older struggles beckoned with renewed urgency. A Greenback editor in Rochester, New Hampshire, thus proclaimed that "patriots" who overturn the "lords of labor" would be remembered next to "the immortal heroes of the revolution and emancipation." . . .

To many other outside observers in the 1880s, the American working class—in terms of organization, militancy, and collective self-consciousness— appeared more advanced than its European counterparts. A leader of the French Union des Chambres syndicales Ouvrières compared the self-regarding, individualist instincts of the French workers to those of the Americans enrolled in the Knights of Labor (Ordre des Chevaliers du Travail):

> Unfortunately, the French worker, erratic as he is enthusiastic, of an almost discouraging indolence when it is a question of his own interests, does not much lend himself to organization into a great order like yours. He understands nevertheless their usefulness, even cites them as an example each time that he has the occasion to prove the possibility of the solidarity of workers; but when it comes to passing from the domain of theory to that of practice, he retreats or disappears. Thirsty for freedom he is always afraid of alienating any one party while contracting commitments toward a collectivity; mistrustful, he is afraid of affiliating with a group whose positions might not correspond exactly to those inscribed on his own flag; undisciplined, he conforms with difficulty to rules which he has given to himself. . . . He wants to play it safe and especially will not consent to any sacrifice without having first calculated the advantages it will bring to him.

Eleanor Marx and Edward Aveling returned from an 1886 American tour with a glowing assessment of the workers' mood. Friedrich Engels, too, in the aftermath of the eight-hour strikes and the Henry George campaign, attached a special preface to the 1887 American edition of *The Condition of the Working Class in England in 1844*:

> In European countries, it took the working class years and years before they fully realized the fact that they formed a distinct and, under the existing social conditions, a permanent class of modern society; and it took years again until this class-consciousness led them to form themselves into a distinct political party, independent of, and opposed to, all the old political parties, formed by the various sections of the ruling classes. On the more favored soil of America, where no medieval ruins bar the way, where history begins with the elements of the modern bourgeois society as evolved in the seventeenth century, the working class passed through these two stages of its development within ten months.

Nor was it only in the eyes of eager well-wishers that the developments of the 1880s seemed to take on a larger significance. Surveying the map of labor upheaval, the conservative Richmond *Whig* wrote in 1886 of "socialistic and agrarian elements" threatening "the genius of our free institutions." The Chicago *Times* went so far in its fear of impending revolution as to counsel the use of hand grenades against strikers.

Revolutionary anticipations, pro or con, proved premature. That was true at least partly because both the movement's distant boosters as well as its domestic detractors sometimes misrepresented its intentions. Gilded Age labor radicals did not self-consciously place themselves in opposition to a prevailing economic system but displayed a sincere ideological ambivalence toward the capitalist marketplace. On the one hand, they frequently invoked a call for the "abolition of the wage system." On the other hand, like the classical economists, they sometimes spoke of the operation of "natural law" in the marketplace, acknowledged the need for a "fair return" on invested capital, and did not oppose profit per se. Employing a distinctly pre-Marxist economic critique that lacked a theory of capital accumulation or of surplus value, labor leaders from Ira Steward to Terence Powderly tried nevertheless to update and sharpen the force of received wisdom. The Knights thus modified an earlier radical interpretation of the labor-cost theory of value, wherein labor, being the source of all wealth, should individually be vested with the value of its product, and demanded for workers only an intentionally vague "proper share of the wealth they create." In so doing they were able to shift the weight of the analysis (not unlike Marx) to the general, collective plight of the laboring classes. In their eyes aggregation of capital together with cutthroat price competition had destroyed any semblance of marketplace balance between employer and employee. Under the prevailing economic calculus labor had been demoted into just another factor of production whose remuneration was determined not by custom or human character but by market price. In such a situation they concluded, as Samuel Walker has noted, that "the contract was not and could not be entered into freely. . . . The process of wage determination was a moral affront because it degraded the personal dignity of the workingman." This subservient position to the iron law of the market constituted "wage slavery," and like other forms of involuntary servitude it had to be "abolished."

Labor's emancipation did not, ipso facto, imply the overthrow of capitalism, a system of productive relations that the Knights in any case never defined. To escape wage slavery workers needed the strength to redefine the social balance of power with employers and their allies—and the will and intelligence to use that strength. One after another the Knights harnessed the various means at their disposal—education, organization, cooperation, economic sanction, and political influence—to this broad end: "To secure to the workers the full enjoyment [note, not the full return] of the wealth they create, sufficient leisure in which to develop their intellectual, moral and social faculties, all of the benefits of recreation, and pleasures of association; in a word to enable them to share in the gains and honors of advancing civilization."

A wide range of strategic options was represented within the counsels of the labor movement. One tendency sought to check the rampant concentration of wealth and power with specific correctives on the operation of the free market. Radical Greenbackism (with roots in Kelloggism and related monetary theories), Henry George's single tax, and land nationalization, each of which commanded considerable influence among the Knights of Labor, fit this category. Another important tendency, cooperation, offered a more self-reliant strategy of alternative institution-building, or, as one advocate put it, "the organization of production without the intervention of the capitalist." Socialism, generally understood at the time as a system of state as opposed to private ownership of production, offered a third alternative to wage slavery. Except for a few influential worker-intellectuals and strong pockets of support among German-Americans, however, Socialism (for reasons which will become clearer in the next chapter) carried comparatively little influence in the 1880s. The argument of veteran abolitionist and labor reformer Joseph Labadie—"To say that state socialism is the rival of co-operation is to say that Jesus Christ was opposed to Christianity"—met a generally skeptical reception. Particularly in the far West, self-identified anarchists also agitated from within the ranks of the Order.

If Gilded Age labor representatives tended to stop short of a frontal rejection of the political-economic order, there was nevertheless no mistaking their philosophic radicalism. Notwithstanding differences in emphasis, the labor movement's political sentiments encompassed both a sharp critique of social inequality and a broad-based prescription for a more humane future. Indeed, the labor representative who shrugged off larger philosophical and political commitments in favor of a narrow incrementalism was likely to meet with incredulity. One of the first, and most classic, enunciations of business unionism, for example, received just this response from the Senate Committee on Labor and Capital in 1883. After taking testimony from workers and labor reformers across the country for six months, the committee, chaired by New Hampshire Senator Henry Blair, interviewed Adolph Strasser, president of the cigar-makers' union. Following a disquisition on the stimulating impact of shorter working hours on workers' consumption patterns, Strasser was asked if he did not contemplate a future beyond the contemporary exigencies of panic and overproduction, "some time [when] every man is to be an intelligent man and an enlightened man?" When Strasser did not reply, Senator Blair interceded to elaborate the question. Still, Strasser rebuffed the queries, "Well, our organization does not consist of idealists . . . we do [not] control the production of the world. That is controlled by employers, and that is a matter for them." Senator Blair was taken aback.

> Blair. I was only asking you in regard to your ultimate ends.
>   Witness. We have no ultimate ends. We are going on from day to day. We are fighting only for immediate objects—objects that can be realized in a few years. . . .
>   Blair. I see that you are a little sensitive lest it should be thought that you are a mere theorizer. I do not look upon you in that light at all.
>   Witness. Well, we say in our constitution that we are opposed to theorists, and I have to represent the organization here. We are all practical men.
>   Blair. Have you not a theory upon which you have organized?

Witness. Yes, sir: our theory is the experience of the past in the United States and in Great Britain. That is our theory, based upon actual facts. . . .

Blair. In other words you have arrived at the theory which you are trying to apply?

Witness. We have arrived at a practical result.

Blair. But a practical result is the application of a theory is it not?

On a cultural level, labor's critique of American society bore the same relation to Victorian respectability that its political radicalism bore to contemporary liberalism. In both cases the middle-class and working-class radical variants derived from a set of common assumptions but drew from them quite different, even opposing, implications. No contemporary, for example, took more seriously than the Knights of Labor the cultural imperatives toward productive work, civic responsibility, education, a wholesome family life, temperance, and self-improvement. The intellectual and moral development of the individual, they would have agreed with almost every early nineteenth-century lyceum lecturer, was a precondition for the advancement of democratic civilization. In the day of Benjamim Franklin such values may well have knit together master craftsmen, journeymen, and apprentices. In the age of the factory system, however, the gulf between employer and employee had so widened that the lived meanings of the words were no longer the same. . . .

For the Knights the concept of the producing classes indicated an ultimate social division that they perceived in the world around them. Only those associated with idleness (bankers, speculators), corruption (lawyers, liquor dealers, gamblers), or social parasitism (all of the above) were categorically excluded from membership in the Order. Other social strata such as local merchants and manufacturers were judged by their individual acts, not by any inherent structural antagonism to the workers' movement. Those who showed respect for the dignity of labor (i.e., who sold union-made goods or employed union workers at union conditions) were welcomed into the Order. Those who denigrated the laborer or his product laid themselves open to the righteous wrath of the boycott or strike. Powderly characteristically chastised one ruthless West Virginia coal owner, "Don't die, even if you do smell bad. We'll need you in a few years as a sample to show how *mean* men used to be."

This rather elastic notion of class boundaries on the part of the labor movement was reciprocated in the not inconsequential number of shopkeepers and small manufacturers who expressed sympathy and support for the labor movement. . . .

Idealization of hearth and home, a mainstay of familial sentimentality in the Gilded Age, also enjoyed special status within the labor movement. For here, as clearly as anywhere in the radicals' world view, conventional assumptions had a critical, albeit ambivalent, edge in the context of changing social circumstances. Defense of an idealized family life as both moral and material mainstay of society served as one basis of criticism of capitalist industry. Machinist John Morrison argued before the Senate investigating committee that the insecurities of the unskilled labor market were so threatening family life as to make the house "more like a dull prison instead of a home." A self-educated Scottish-born leader of the type-founders, Edward King, associated trade union morality with the domestic "sentiments of sympathy and humanity" against the "business principles" of the age. Almost unanimously, the vision of the good life for labor radicals included the home. . . .

The importance of the domestic moral order to the late nineteenth-century radical vision also translated into an unparalleled opening of the labor movement to women. As Susan Levine has recently documented, the Knights of Labor beckoned both to wage-earning women and workingmen's wives to join in construction of a "cooperative commonwealth," which, without disavowing the Victorian ideal of a separate female sphere of morality and domestic virtue, sought to make that sphere the center of an active community life.

Both their self-improving and domestic commitments converged in the working-class radicals' antipathy to excessive drinking. The Knights' oath of temperance, which became known as "the Powderly pledge," appealed in turn to intellectual development and protection of the family as well as to the collective interests of the labor movement. Like monopoly, the bottle lay waiting to fasten a new form of slavery upon the free worker. In another sense, as David Brundage has suggested, the growing capitalization of saloons together with expansion of saloon-linked variety theatre directly threatened a family-based producers' community. While most radicals stopped short of prohibition, exhortations in behalf of temperance were commonplace. In part it was a matter of practical necessity. Tension between the mores of traditional plebeian culture and the need for self-discipline by a movement striving for organization and power were apparent. . . .

In general, then, the labor movement of the late nineteenth century provided a distinct arena of articulation and practice for values that crossed class lines. Two aspects of this use of inherited values for radical ends merit reemphasis. First, to the extent that labor radicalism shared in the nineteenth century's cult of individualism, it established a social and moral framework for individual achievement. The culture of the labor movement stressed the development of individual capacity, but not competition with other individuals; while striving to elevate humanity, it ignored what S. G. Boritt has identified as the essence of the Lincoln-sanctified American Dream—the individual's "right to rise." The necessary reliance by the labor movement upon collective strength and community sanction militated against the possessive individualism that anchored the world of the workers' better-off neighbors. By its very nature, the labor movement set limits to the individual accumulation of wealth extracted from others' efforts and represented, in Edward King's words, "the graduated elimination of the personal selfishness of man."

Second, in an age of evolutionary, sometimes even revolutionary, faith in progress and the future (a faith generally shared by labor radicals), the movement made striking use of the past. Without renouncing the potential of industrialism for both human liberty and material progress, radicals dipped selectively into a popular storehouse of memory and myth to capture alternative images of human possibility. The choice of the name "Knights of Labor" itself presented images of chivalry and nobility fighting the unfeeling capitalist marketplace. Appeals to the "nobility of toil" and to the worker's "independence" conjured up the proud village smithy—not the degradation of labor in the factory system. Finally, celebrations of historic moments of human liberation and political advancement challenged a political-economic orthodoxy beholden to notions of unchanging, universal laws of development. Indeed, so conspicuously sentimental were the celebrations of Independence Day and Memorial Day that Powderly had to defend the Order from taunts of "spread-eagleism" and "Yankee doodleism."

This sketch of working-class radicalism in the Gilded Age raises one final question. Whose movement—and culture—was it? In a country as diverse as the United States, with a labor force and labor movement drawn from a heterogeneous mass of trades, races, and nationalities, any group portrait runs the risk of oversimplification. The varying contours of the late nineteenth-century working class do require specific inquiry, to which the next several chapters of this work contribute. Nevertheless, the Knights of Labor did provide a vast umbrella under which practically every variety of American worker sought protection. As such, the dynamic of the Order itself offers important clues to the general social context in which working-class radicalism as defined here flourished. . . .

This dominant stream within the labor movement included people who had enjoyed considerable control over their jobs, if not also economic autonomy, men who often retained claim to the tools as well as the knowledge of their trade. They had taken seriously the ideal of a republic of producers in which hard work would contribute not only to the individual's improved economic standing but also to the welfare of the community. So long as they could rely on their own strength as well as their neighbors' support, this skilled stratum organized in an array of craft unions showed economic and political resilience. But the spreading confrontations with national corporate power, beginning in the 1870s, indicated just how much erosion had occurred in the position of those who relied on custom, skill, and moral censure as ultimate weapons. Industrial dilution of craft skills and a direct economic and political attack on union practices provided decisive proof to these culturally conservative workingmen of both the illegitimacy and ruthlessness of the growing power of capital. It was they, according to every recent study of late nineteenth-century laboring communities, who formed the backbone of local labor movements. The Knights were, therefore, first of all a coalition of reactivating, or already organized, trade unions. . . .

For reasons of their own masses of workers who had not lost full and equal citizenship—for they had never possessed it—joined the skilled workers within the Knights. Wherever the Order achieved political successes, it did so by linking semiskilled and unskilled industrial workers to its base of skilled workers and leaders. The special strength of the Knights, noted the Boston *Labor Leader* astutely, lay "in the fact that the whole life of the community is drawn into it, that people of all kinds are together. . ., and that they all get directly the sense of each others' needs." . . .

. . .The Knights of Labor envisioned a kind of workingmen's democracy. The organized power of labor was capable of revitalizing democratic citizenship and safeguarding the public good within a regulated marketplace economy. Through vigilant shop committees and demands such as the eight-hour day, organized workers—both men and women—would ensure minimal standards of safety and health at the industrial workplace, even as they surrounded the dominant corporate organizational model of business with cooperative models of their own. A pride in honest and useful work, rational education, and personal virtue would be nurtured through a rich associational life spread out from the workplace to meeting hall to the hearth and home. Finally, the integrity of public institutions would be vouchsafed by the workingmen in politics. Purifying government of party parasitism and corruption, cutting off the access to power that allowed antilabor employers to bring the state apparatus to their side in industrial disputes, improving and widening the scope of vital public services, and even contemplating the takeover of economic enterprises that had passed irreversibly into monopoly hands—by these means worker-citizens would lay active claim to a republican heritage.

The dream was not to be. At the workplace management seized the initiative toward the future design and control of work. A managerial revolution overcoming the tenacious defenses of the craft unions transferred autonomy over such matters as productivity and skill from custom and negotiation to the realm of corporate planning. Except for the garment trades and the mines, the national trade unions had generally retreated from the country's industrial heartland by 1920. In the local community as well, the differences, even antagonisms, among workers often stood out more than did the similarities. Segmentation of labor markets, urban ethnic and socioeconomic residential segregation, cultural as well as a protectionist economic disdain for the new immigrants, and the depoliticization of leisure time (i.e., the decline of associational life sponsored by labor organizations) all contributed toward a process of social fragmentation. In such circumstances working-class political cooperation proved impossible. The Socialist party and the Progressive slates could make little more than a dent in the hold of the two increasingly conservative national parties over the electorate. Only with the repolarization of political life beginning in 1928 and culminating in the New Deal was the relation of labor and the party system again transformed. By the late 1930s and 1940s a revived labor movement was beginning, with mixed success, to play the role of a leading interest group and reform conscience within the Democratic party.

This impressionistic overview permits one further observation of a quite general nature. One of the favorite tasks of American historians has been to explain why the United States, alone among the nations of the Western world, passed through the industrial revolution without the establishment of a class consciousness and an independent working-class political movement. Cheap land, the cult of individualism, a heterogeneous labor force, social mobility, and the federal separation of powers comprise several of the numerous explanations that have been offered. While not directly denying the importance of any of the factors listed above, this study implicitly suggests a different approach to the problem of American exceptionalism.

The answer appears to lie less in a permanent structural determinism—whether the analytic brace be political, economic, or ideological—than in a dynamic and indeed somewhat fortuitous convergence of events. To understand the vicissitudes of urban politics, we have had to keep in mind the action on at least three levels: the level of working-class social organization (i.e., the nature and strength of the labor movement), the level of business response, and the level of governmental response. During the Gilded Age each of these areas took an incendiary turn, but only briefly and irregularly and most rarely at the same moment. The 1880s, as R. Laurence Moore has recently reiterated, were the international seedtime for the strong European working-class parties of the twentieth century. In America, too, the momentum in the 1880s was great. Indeed, examined both at the level of working-class organization and industrial militancy, a European visitor might understandably have expected the most to happen here first. At the political level, as well, American workers were in certain respects relatively advanced. In the 1870s and in the 1880s they established independently organized local labor regimes well before the famous French Roubaix or English West Ham labor-Socialist town councils of the 1890s. Then, a combination of forces in the United States shifted radically away from the possibilities outlined in the 1880s. The labor movement fragmented, business reorganized, and the political parties helped to pick up the pieces. The initiatives from without directed at the American working class from the mid-1890s through the mid-1920s—part repression, part reform, part assimilation, and part recruitment of a new labor force—at an internationally critical period in the gestation of working-class movements may mark the most telling exceptionalism about American developments.

It would in any case be years before the necessary conditions again converged and labor rose from the discredited icons of pre-Depression America with a new and powerful political message. Workplace, community, and ballot box would all once again be harnessed to a great social movement. But no two actors are ever in quite the same space at the same time. The choices open to the CIO, it is fair to say, were undoubtedly influenced both by the achievement and failure of their counterparts a half-century earlier. . . .

Carl N. Degler

 **NO**

Out of Our Past

The Workers' Response

To say that the labor movement was affected by the industrialization of the postwar years is an understatement; the fact is, industrial capitalism created the labor movement. Not deliberately, to be sure, but in the same way that a blister is the consequence of a rubbing shoe. Unions were labor's protection against the forces of industrialization as the blister is the body's against the irritation of the shoe. The factory and all it implied confronted the working-man with a challenge to his existence as a man, and the worker's response was the labor union.

There were labor unions in America before 1865, but, as industry was only emerging in those years, so the organizations of workers were correspondingly weak. In the course of years after Appomattox, however, when industry began to hit a new and giant stride, the tempo of unionization also stepped up. It was in these decades, after many years of false starts and utopian ambitions, that the American labor movement assumed its modern shape.

Perhaps the outstanding and enduring characteristic of organized labor in the United States has been its elemental conservatism, the fantasies of some employers to the contrary notwithstanding. Indeed, it might be said that all labor unions, at bottom, are conservative by virtue of their being essentially reactions against a developing capitalism. Though an established capitalist society views itself as anything but subversive, in the days of its becoming and seen against the perspective of the previous age, capitalism as an ideology is radically subversive, undermining and destroying many of the cherished institutions of the functioning society. This dissolving process of capitalism is seen more clearly in Europe than in America because there the time span is greater. But, as will appear later, organized labor in the United States was as much a conservative response to the challenge of capitalism as was the European trade union movement.

Viewed very broadly, the history of modern capitalism might be summarized as the freeing of the three factors of production—land, labor, and capital—from the web of tradition in which medieval society held them. If capitalism was to function, it was necessary that this liberating process take place. Only when these basic factors are free to be bought and sold according to the dictates of the profit motive can the immense production which capitalism promises be realized. An employer, for example, had to be free to dismiss labor when the balance sheet required it, without being compelled to retain workers because society or custom demanded it. Serfdom, with its requirement that the peasant could not be taken from the land, was an anachronistic institution if capitalism was to become the economic ideology of society. Conversely, an employer needed to be unrestricted in his freedom to hire labor or else production could not expand in accordance with the market. Guild restrictions which limited apprenticeships were therefore obstacles to the achievement of a free capitalism.

The alienability of the three factors of production was achieved slowly and unevenly after the close of the Middle Ages. By the nineteenth century in most nations of the West, land had become absolutely alienable—it could be bought and sold at will. With the growth of banking, the development of trustworthy monetary standards, and finally the gold standard in the nineteenth century, money or capital also became freely exchangeable. Gradually, over the span of some two centuries, the innovating demands of capitalism stripped from labor the social controls in which medieval and mercantilistic government had clothed it. Serfdom as an obstacle to the free movement of labor was gradually done away with; statutes of laborers and apprenticeships which fixed wages, hours, and terms of employment also fell into disuse or suffered outright repeal. To avoid government interference in the setting of wage rates, the English Poor Law of 1834 made it clear that the dole to the unemployed was always to be lower than the going rate for unskilled labor. Thus supply and demand would be the determinant of wage levels. Both the common law and the Combination Acts in the early nineteenth century in England sought to ensure the operation of a free market in labor by declaring trade unions to be restraints on trade.

Like land and capital, then, labor was being reduced to a commodity, freely accessible, freely alienable, free to flow where demand was high. The classical economists of the nineteenth century analyzed this long historical process, neatly put it together, and called it the natural laws of economics.

To a large extent, this historical development constituted an improvement in the worker's status, since medieval and mercantilist controls over labor had been more onerous than protective. Nevertheless, something was lost by the dissolution of the ancient social ties which fitted the worker into a larger social matrix. Under the old relationship, the worker belonged in society; he enjoyed a definite if not a high status; he had a place. Now he was an individual, alone; his status was up to him to establish; his urge for community with society at large had no definite avenue of expression. Society and labor alike had been atomized in pursuit of an individualist economy. Herein lay the radical character of the capitalist ideology.

That the workingman sensed the radical change and objected to it is evident from what some American labor leaders said about their unions. Without rejecting the new freedom which labor enjoyed, John Mitchell, of the Mine Workers, pointed out that the union "stands for fraternity, complete and absolute." Samuel Gompers' eulogy of the social microcosm which was the trade union has the same ring. "A hundred times we have said it," he wrote, "and we say it again, that trade unionism contains within itself the potentialities of working class regeneration." The union is a training ground for democracy and provides "daily object lessons in ideal justice; it breathes into the working classes the spirit of unity"; but above all, it affords that needed sense of community. The labor union "provides a field for noble comradeship, for deeds of loyalty, for self-sacrifice beneficial to one's fellow-workers." In the trade union, in short, the workers could obtain another variety of that sense of community, of comradeship, as Gompers put it, which the acid of individualistic capitalism had dissolved.

And there was another objection to the transformation of labor into an exchangeable commodity. The theoretical justification for the conversion of the factors of production into commodities is that the maximum amount of goods can be produced under such a regime. The increased production is deemed desirable because it would insure greater amounts of goods for human consumption and therefore a better life for all. Unfortunately for the theory, however, labor cannot be separated from the men who provide it. To make labor a commodity is to make the men who provide labor commodities also. Thus one is left with the absurdity of turning men into commodities in order to give men a better life! . . .

Seen in this light, the trade union movement stands out as a truly conservative force. Almost instinctively, the workers joined labor unions in order to preserve their humanity and social character against the excessively individualistic doctrines of industrial capitalism. Eventually, the workers' organizations succeeded in halting the drive to the atomized society which capitalism demanded, and in doing so, far from destroying the system, compelled it to be humane as well as productive.

The essential conservatism of the labor movement is to be seen in particular as well as in general. The organizations of American labor that triumphed or at least survived in the course of industrialization were conspicuous for their acceptance of the private property, profit-oriented society. They evinced little of the radical, anticapitalist ideology and rhetoric so common among European trade unions. Part of the reason for this was the simple fact that all Americans—including workers—were incipient capitalists waiting for "the break." But at bottom it would seem that the conservatism of American labor in this sense is the result of the same forces which inhibited the growth of socialism and other radical anticapitalist ideologies. . . .

"The overshadowing problem of the American labor movement," an eminent labor historian has written, "has always been the problem of staying organized. No other labor movement has ever had to contend with the fragility so characteristic of American labor organizations." So true has this been that even today the United States ranks below Italy and Austria in percentage of workers organized (about 25 percent as compared, for instance, with Sweden's 90 percent). In such an atmosphere, the history of organized labor in America has been both painful and conservative. Of the two major national organizations of workers which developed in the latter half of the nineteenth century, only the cautious, restrictive, pragmatic American Federation of Labor [A.F. of L.] lived into the twentieth century. The other, the Knights of Labor, once the more powerful and promising, as well as the less accommodating in goals and aspirations, succumbed to Selig Perlman's disease of fragility.

Founded in 1869, the Noble Order of the Knights of Labor recorded its greatest successes in the 1880s, when its membership rolls carried 700,000 names. As the A.F. of L. was later to define the term for Americans, the Knights did not seem to constitute a legitimate trade union at all. Anyone who worked, except liquor dealers, bankers, lawyers, and physicians, could join, and some thousands of women workers and Negroes were members in good standing of this brotherhood of toilers. But the crucial deviation of the Knights from the more orthodox approach to labor organization was its belief in worker-owned producers' co-operatives, which were intended to make each worker his own employer. In this way, the order felt, the degrading dependence of the worker upon the employer would be eliminated. "There is no good reason," Terence V. Powderly, Grand Master Workman of the order, told his followers, "why labor cannot, through co-operation, own and operate mines, factories and railroads."

In this respect the order repudiated the direction in which the America of its time was moving. It expressed the small-shopkeeper mentality which dominated the thinking of many American workers, despite the obvious trend in the economy toward the big and the impersonal. As the General Assembly of 1884 put it, "our Order contemplates a radical change, while Trades' Unions . . . accept the industrial system as it is, and endeavor to adapt themselves to it. The attitude of our Order to the existing industrial system is necessarily one of war." Though the order called this attitude "radical," a more accurate term, in view of the times, would have been "conservative" or "reactionary."

In practice, however, the Knights presented no more of a threat to capitalism than any other trade union. Indeed, their avowed opposition to the strike meant that labor's most potent weapon was only reluctantly drawn from the scabbard. The Constitution of 1884 said, "Strikes at best afford only temporary relief"; members should learn to depend on education, co-operation, and political action to attain "the abolition of the wage system."

Though the order officially joined in political activity and Grand Master Workman Powderly was at one time mayor of Scranton, its forays into politics accomplished little. The experience was not lost on shrewd Samuel Gompers, whose American Federation of Labor studiously eschewed any alignments with political parties, practicing instead the more neutral course of "rewarding friends and punishing enemies."

In a farewell letter in 1893, Powderly realistically diagnosed the ills of his moribund order, but offered no cure: "Teacher of important and much-needed reforms, she has been obliged to practice differently from her teachings. Advocating arbitration and conciliation as first steps in labor disputes she has been forced to take upon her shoulders the responsibilities of the aggressor first and, when hope of arbitrating and conciliation failed, to beg of the opposing side to do what we should have applied for in the first instance. Advising against strikes we have been in the midst of them. While not a political party we have been forced into the attitude of taking political action."

For all its fumblings, ineptitude, and excessive idealism, the Knights did organize more workers on a national scale than had ever been done before. At once premature and reactionary, it nonetheless planted the seeds of industrial unionism which, while temporarily overshadowed by the successful craft organization of the A.F. of L., ultimately bore fruit in the C.I.O. [Committee for Industrial Organization]. Moreover, its idealism, symbolized in its admission of Negroes and women, and more in tune with the mid-twentieth century than the late nineteenth, signified its commitment to the ideals of the democratic tradition. For these reasons the Knights were a transitional type of unionism somewhere between the utopianism of the 1830s and the pragmatism of the A.F. of L. It seemed to take time for labor institutions to fit the American temper.

In the course of his long leadership of the American Federation of Labor, Samuel Gompers welcomed many opportunities to define the purposes of his beloved organization. . . .

"The trade unions are the business organizations of the wage-earners," Gompers explained in 1906, "to attend to the business of the wage-earners." Later he expressed it more tersely: "The trade union is not a Sunday school. It is an organization of wage-earners, dealing with economic, social, political and moral questions." As Gompers' crossing of swords with Hillquit demonstrated, there was no need or place for theories. "I saw," the labor leader wrote years later, in looking back on his early life in the labor movement, "the danger of entangling alliances with intellectuals who did not understand that to experiment with the labor movement was to experiment with human life. . . . I saw that the betterment of workingmen must come primarily through workingmen."

In an age of big business, Samuel Gompers made trade unionism a business, and his reward was the survival of his Federation. In a country with a heterogeneous population of unskilled immigrants, reviled and feared Negroes, and native workers, he cautiously confined his fragile organization to the more skilled workers and the more acceptable elements in the population. The result was a narrow but lasting structure.

Though never ceasing to ask for "more," the A.F. of L. presented no threat to capitalism. "Labor Unions are *for* the workingman, but against no one," John Mitchell of the United Mine Workers pointed out. "They are not hostile to employers, not inimical to the interests of the general public. . . . There is no necessary hostility between labor and capital," he concluded. Remorselessly pressed by Morris Hillquit as Gompers was, he still refused to admit that the labor movement was, as Hillquit put it, "conducted against the interests of the employing people." Rather, Gompers insisted, "It is conducted for the interests of the employing people." And the rapid expansion of the American economy bore witness to the fact that the Federation was a friend and not an enemy of industrial capitalism. Its very adaptability to the American scene—its conservative ideology, if it was an ideology at all—as Selig Perlman has observed, contained the key to its success. "The unionism of the American Federation of Labor 'fitted' . . . because it recognized the virtually inalterable conservatism of the American community as regards private property and private initiative in economic life."

This narrow conception of the proper character of trade unionism—job consciousness, craft unionism, lack of interest in organizing the unskilled, the eschewing of political activity—which Gompers and his Federation worked out for the American worker continued to dominate organized labor until the earthquake of the depression cracked the mold and the Committee for Industrial Organization issued forth.

Nobody Here But Us Capitalists

"By any simple interpretation of the Marxist formula," commented Socialist Norman Thomas in 1950, "the United States, by all odds the greatest industrial nation and that in which capitalism is most advanced, should have had long ere this is a very strong socialist movement if not a socialist revolution. Actually," he correctly observed, "in no advanced western nation is organized socialism so weak." Nor was this the first time Socialists had wondered about this. Over eighty years ago, in the high noon of European socialism, Marxist theoretician Werner Sombart impatiently put a similar question: *"Warum gibt es in den Vereinigten Staaten keinen Sozialismus?"*

The failure of the American working class to become seriously interested in socialism in this period or later is one of the prominent signs of the political and economic conservatism of American labor and, by extension, of the American people as a whole. This failure is especially noteworthy when one recalls that in industrialized countries the world over—Japan, Italy, Germany, Belgium, to mention only a few—a Socialist movement has been a "normal" concomitant of industrialization. Even newly opened countries like Australia and New Zealand have Labour parties. Rather than ask, as Americans are wont to do, why these countries have nurtured such frank repudiators of traditional capitalism, it is the American deviation from the general pattern which demands explanation.

In large part, the explanation lies in the relative weakness of class consciousness among Americans. Historically, socialism is the gospel of the *class-conscious* working class, of the workingmen who feel themselves bound to their status for life and their children after them. It is not accidental, therefore, that the major successes of modern socialism are in Europe, where class lines have been clearly and tightly drawn since time immemorial, and where the possibility of upward social movement has been severely restricted in practice if not in law. Americans may from time to time have exhibited class consciousness and even class hatred, but such attitudes have not persisted, nor have they been typical. As Matthew Arnold observed in 1888, "it is indubitable that rich men are regarded" in America "with less envy and hatred than rich men in Europe." A labor leader like Terence Powderly was convinced that America was without classes. "No matter how much we may say about classes and class distinction, there are no classes in the United States. . . . I have always refused to admit that we have classes in our country just as I have refused to admit that the labor of a man's hand or brain is a commodity." And there was a long line of commentators on American society, running back at least to Crèvecoeur, to illustrate the prevalence of Powderly's belief.

The weakness of American class consciousness is doubtless to be attributed, at least in part, to the fluidity of the social structure. Matthew Arnold, for example, accounted for the relative absence of class hatred on such grounds, as did such very different foreign observers as Werner Sombart and Lord Bryce. The British union officials of the Mosely Commission, it will be recalled, were convinced of the superior opportunities for success enjoyed by American Workers. Stephan Thernstrom in his study of Newburyport gave some meas-ure of the opportunities for economic improvement among the working class when he reported that all but 5 percent of those unskilled workers who per-sisted from 1850 to 1900 ended the period with either property or an improve-ment in occupational status.

Men who are hoping to move upward on the social scale, and for whom there is some chance that they can do so, do not identify themselves with their present class. "In worn-out, king-ridden Europe, men stay where they are born," immigrant Charles O'Conor, who became an ornament of the New York bar, contended in 1869. "But in America a man is accounted a failure, and certainly ought to be, who has not risen about his father's station in life." So long as Horatio Alger means anything to Americans, Karl Marx will be just another German philosopher.

The political history of the United States also contributed to the fail-ure of socialism. In Europe, because the franchise came slowly and late to the worker, he often found himself first an industrial worker and only later a voter. It was perfectly natural, in such a context, for him to vote according to his economic interests and to join a political party avowedly dedicated to those class interests. The situation was quite different in America, however, for political democracy came to America prior to the Industrial Revolution. By the time the industrial transformation was getting under way after 1865, all adult males could vote and, for the most part, they had already chosen their political affiliations without reference to their economic class; they were Republicans or Democrats first and workers only second—a separation between politics and economics which has become traditional in America. "In the main," wrote Lord Bryce about the United States of the 1880s, "political questions proper have held the first place in a voter's mind and questions affecting his class second." Thus, when it came to voting, workers registered their convictions as citizens, not as workingmen. (In our own day, there have been several nota-ble failures of labor leaders to swing their labor vote, such as John L. Lewis' attempt in 1940 and the C.I.O.'s in 1950 against Senator Taft and the inability of union leaders to be sure they could hold their members to support Hubert Humphrey in the Presidential election of 1968.) To most workers, the Social-ist party appeared as merely a third party in a country where such parties are political last resorts.

Nor did socialism in America gain much support from the great influx of immigration. It is true that many Germans came to this country as convinced Socialists and thus swelled the party's numbers, but they also served to pin the stigma of "alien" upon the movement. Even more important was the fact that the very heterogeneity of the labor force, as a result of immigration, often made animosities between ethnic groups more important to the worker than class antagonism. It must have seemed to many workers that socialism, with its central concern for class and its denial of ethnic antagonism, was not deal-ing with the realities of economic life.

In the final reckoning, however, the failure of socialism in America is to be attributed to the success of capitalism. The expanding economy provided opportunities for all, no matter how meager they might appear or actually be at times. Though the rich certainly seemed to get richer at a prodigious rate, the poor, at least, did not get poorer—and often got richer. Studies of real wages between 1865 and 1900 bear this out. Though prices rose, wages generally rose faster, so that there was a net gain in average income for workers during the last decades of the century. The increase in real wages in the first fifteen years of the twentieth century was negligible—but, significantly, there was no decline. The high wages and relatively good standard of living of the American worker were patent as far as the twenty-three British labor leaders of the Mosely Commission were concerned. The American is a "better educated, better housed, better clothed and more energetic man than his British brother," concluded the sponsor, Alfred Mosely, a businessman himself.

But America challenged socialism on other grounds than mere material things. Some years ago an obscure Socialist, Leon Samson, undertook to account for the failure of socialism to win the allegiance of the American working class; his psychological explanation merits attention because it illuminates the influence exercised by the American Dream. Americanism, Samson observes, is not so much a tradition as it is a doctrine; it is "what socialism is to a socialist." Americanism to the American is a body of ideas like "democracy, liberty, opportunity, to all of which the American adheres rationalistically much as a socialist adheres to his socialism—because it does him good, because it gives him work, because, so he thinks, it guarantees him happiness. America has thus served as a substitute for socialism."

Socialism has been unable to make headway with Americans, Samson goes on, because "every concept in socialism has its substitutive countercept in Americanism." As Marxism holds out the prospect of a classless society, so does Americanism. The opportunities for talent and the better material life which socialism promised for the future were already available in America and constituted the image in which America was beheld throughout the world. The freedom and equality which the oppressed proletariat of Europe craved were a reality in America—or at least sufficiently so to blunt the cutting edge of the Socialist appeal. Even the sense of mission, of being in step with the processes of history, which unquestionably was one of the appeals of socialism, was also a part of the American Dream. Have not all Americans cherished their country as a model for the world? Was not this the "last, best hope of earth"? Was not God on the side of America, as history, according to Marx, was on the side of socialism and the proletariat?

Over a century ago, Alexis de Tocqueville predicted a mighty struggle for the minds of men between two giants of Russia and the United States. In the ideologies of socialism and the American Dream, his forecast has been unexpectedly fulfilled.

POSTSCRIPT

Was the American Labor Movement Radical?

$\mathbf{F}$ink presents a very sophisticated analysis of how the Knights of Labor traced its values back to the republican ideology of the late eighteenth-century enlightenment thinkers. The Knights embraced a unified conception of work and culture which extolled the virtues of individual hard work, love of family, and love of country. All members of the producing classes were invited to join, including businessmen. According to Fink, excluded were "only those associated with idleness (bankers, speculators) and corruption (lawyers, liquor dealers, gamblers)."

During the 1880s the Knights employed a "pre-Marxist economic critique" of the industrial system. There were discussions about the "abolition of the wage system" and the analysis shifted away from the problems of the individual workers to the "general, collective, plight of labor." Yet Fink admits that the Knights never made a frontal attack on capitalism.

The question of why the United States never developed a major socialist movement or labor party has been the subject of much speculation. A good starting point is John H. Laslett and Seymour Martin Lipset, eds., *Failure of a Dream: Essays in the History of American Socialism* (Anchor Press/Doubleday, 1974), a collection of articles that generally reinforces Degler's arguments. Political scientist Theodore J. Lowi argues that our political system of federalism is the primary reason in "Why Is There No Socialism in the United States?" *Society* (January/February 1985). Historian Eric Foner tears down all explanations and asks, "Why Has There Been No Socialist Transformation in Any Advanced Capitalist Society?" *History Workshop* (Spring 1984). Finally, see Rick Halpern and Jonathan Morris, eds., *American Exceptionalism? U.S. Working Class Formation in an International Context* (St. Martin's Press, 1997).

To learn more about the rise and fall of the Knights of Labor, see the case studies in Leon Fink's *Workingmen's Democracy: The Knights of Labor and American Politics* (University of Illinois Press, 1983). See also Fink's collection of articles *In Search of the Working Class* (University of Illinois Press, 1994). Three other noteworthy books on the Knights of Labor are Robert E. Weir, *Beyond Labor's Veil: The Culture of the Knights of Labor* (Pennsylvania State University Press, 1996); Kim Voss, *The Making of American Exceptionalism: The Knights of Labor and Class Formation in the Nineteenth Century* (Cornell University Press, 1993); and Bruce Laurie, *Artisans Into Workers: Labor in Nineteenth-Century America* (Hill and Wang, 1989).

Professor Carl Degler takes a different approach to this issue. He agrees with the traditional labor historians that the American worker accepted capitalism and wanted a bigger piece of the pie. But he reverses the radial-conservative dichotomy as applied to the conflict between the worker and the businessman. In his view, the real radicals were the industrialists who created a more mature system of capitalism. Labor merely fashioned a conservative response to the radical changes brought about by big business. The system led to its demise. Its place was taken by the American Federation of Labor, whose long-time leader Samuel Gompers was famous for his acceptance of the wage system and American capitalism. Labor merely fashioned a conservative response to the radial changes brought about by big business. The system led to its demise. Its place was taken by the American Federation of Labor, whose long-time leader Samuel Gompers was famous for his acceptance of the wage system and American capitalism. The American Federation of Labor adopted practical goals; it strove to improve the lot of the worker by negotiating for better hours, wages, and working conditions. "In an age of big business," says Degler, "Samuel Gompers made trade unionism a business, and his reward was the survival of his Federation."

In explaining the failure of socialism in America, Degler argues that Americans lacked a working-class consciousness because they believed in real mobility. Also, a labor party failed to emerge because Americans developed their commitment to the two-party system before the issues of the industrial revolution came to the forefront. The influx of immigrants from a variety of countries created the heterogeneous labor force, and animosities between rival ethnic groups appeared more real than class antagonisms. "In the final reckoning," says Degler, "the failure of socialism in America is to be attributed to the success of capitalism."

For the past three decades, historians have begun to study the social and cultural environment of the American working class. The approach is modeled after E. P. Thompson's highly influential and sophisticated Marxist analysis, *The Making of the English Working Class* (1963), a work that is the capstone of an earlier generation of British and French social historians. The father of the "new labor history" in the United States is the late Herbert G. Gutman, whose articles collected in *Work, Culture, and Society* (Knopf, 1976) and *Power and Culture: Essays On the American Working Class* (Pantheon, 1987) are the starting point for every student of the period. It was Gutman who first discussed American workers as a group separate from the organized union movement. Gutman's distinction between pre-industrial and industrial values laid the groundwork for a whole generation of scholars who have engaged in case studies of both union and nonunion workers in both urban and rural areas of America.

Gutman's framework differs from mainstream American historians' more traditional approach in several ways. Gutman abandons the division of American history at the Civil War/Reconstruction fault line. He proposes a threefold division for free, white workers: (1) the premodern early industrial period from 1815 to 1843; (2) the transition to capitalism, which encompasses the years 1843–1893; and (3) the development of a full-blown industrial system, which took place from the late 1890s through World War I. Gutman's unique periodization enables us to view the evolution of the free, white, nonunion worker, whose traditional values withstood the onslaughts of an increasingly large-scale dehumanized factory system that emphasized productivity and efficiency until the depression of 1893.

Gutman also challenges the view that workers were helpless pawns of the owners and that they were forced to cave in every time a strike took place. He shows that on a local level in the 1880s, immigrant workers not only joined unions but also usually won their strikes. This is because small shopkeepers and workers in other industries often supported those who were out on strike. Gutman also argues from census data of the 1880s that immigrant families were more stable and less prone to divorce and desertion than native-born families. Gutman applied many of these insights to slaves in his prizewinning book *The Black Family in Slavery and Freedom* (Pantheon, 1976).

Labor histories influenced by Thompson and Gutman should be sampled first in the following collections of articles: Daniel J. Lieb, ed., *The Labor History Reader* (University of Illinois, 1985); Michael H. Frisch and Daniel J. Walkowitz, eds., *Working Class America: Essays on Labor, Community, and American Society* (University of Illinois, 1983); Charles Stephenson and Robert Asher, eds., *Life and Labor: Dimensions of American Working Class History* (State University of New York Press, 1986); and Milton Cantor, ed., *American Working Class Culture: Explorations in American Labor and Social History* (Greenwood Press, 1979).

Two journals have devoted entire issues to the American labor movement: the fall 1989 issue of *The Public Historian* and the February 1982 issue of *Social Education*. Students who wish to sample the diverse scholarships on the American workers should consult "A Round Table: Labor, Historical, Pessimism, and Hegemony," *Journal of American History* (June 1988).

ISSUE 5

Were Late Nineteenth-Century Immigrants "Uprooted"?

YES: Oscar Handlin, from *The Uprooted: The Epic Story of the Great Migrations That Made the American People,* 2nd ed. (Little, Brown and Company, 1973)

NO: Mark Wyman, from *Round-Trip to America: The Immigrants Return to Europe, 1880–1930* (Cornell University Press, 1993)

ISSUE SUMMARY

YES: Oscar Handlin asserts that immigrants to the United States in the late nineteenth century were alienated from the cultural traditions of the homeland they had left as well as from those of their adopted country.

NO: Mark Wyman argues that as many as four million immigrants to the United States between 1880 and 1930 viewed their trip as temporary and remained tied psychologically to their homeland to which they returned once they had accumulated enough wealth to enable them to improve their status back home.

Immigration has been one of the most powerful forces shaping the development of the United States since at least the early seventeenth century. In fact, it should not be overlooked that even the ancestors of the country's Native American population were migrants to this "New World" some 37,000 years ago. There can be little doubt that the United States is a nation of immigrants, a reality reinforced by the motto "E Pluribus Unum" (one from many), which is used on the Great Seal of the United States and on several U.S. coins.

The history of immigration to the United States can be organized into four major periods of activity: 1607–1830, 1830–1890, 1890–1924, and 1968 to the present. During the first period, the seventeenth and eighteenth centuries, there were a growing number of European migrants who arrived in North America, mostly from the British Isles, as well as several million Africans who were forced to migrate to colonial America as a consequence of the Atlantic slave trade. While increased numbers of non-English immigrants arrived in America in the eighteenth century, it was not until the nineteenth century that large numbers of immigrants from other northern and western European countries, as well as from China, arrived and created significant population diversity. Two European groups predominated during this second major period: As a result of the potato famine, large numbers of Irish Catholics emigrated in the 1850s, and for a variety of religious, political, and economic reasons, so did many Germans. Chinese immigration increased, and these immigrants found work in low-paying service industries, such as laundries and restaurants, and as railroad construction workers.

The Industrial Revolution of the late nineteenth century sparked a third wave of immigration. Immigrants by the millions began pouring into the United States attracted by the unskilled factory jobs that were becoming more abundant. Migration was encouraged by various companies whose agents distributed handbills throughout Europe, advertising the ready availability of good-paying jobs in America. This phase of immigration, however, represented something of a departure from previous ones as most of these "new immigrants" came from southern and eastern Europe. This flood continued until World War I, after which mounting xenophobia culminated in the passage by Congress in 1924 of the National Origins Act, which restricted the number of immigrants into the country to 150,000 annually, and which placed quotas on the numbers of immigrants permitted from each foreign country.

In the aftermath of World War II, restrictions were eased for several groups, especially those who survived the Nazi death camps or who sought asylum in the United States in the wake of the aggressive movement into Eastern Europe by the Soviet Union after the war. But restrictions against Asians and Africans were not lifted until the Immigration Reform Act of 1965, which set in motion a fourth phase of immigration history. In contrast to earlier migrations, the newest groups have come from Latin America and Asia.

Efforts to curb immigration to the United States reflect an anxiety and ambivalence that many Americans have long held with regard to "foreigners." Anxious to benefit from the labor of these newcomers but still hesitant to accept the immigrants as full-fledged citizens entitled to the same rights and privileges as native-born residents, Americans have on a number of occasions discovered that they had an "immigrant problem." Harsh anti-immigrant sentiment based on prejudicial attitudes toward race, ethnicity, or religion has periodically boiled over into violence and calls for legislation to restrict immigration.

What effect did these kinds of attitudes have on those who migrated to the United States in search of a life better than the one they experienced in their native lands? What happened to their Old World customs and traditions? How fully did immigrants assimilate into the new culture they encountered in the United States? Was the United States, in fact, a melting pot for immigrants, as some have suggested?

In the following readings, Oscar Handlin argues that the immigrants were uprooted from their Old World cultures as they attempted to adjust to an unfamiliar and often hostile environment in the United States. Mark Wyman points out that many immigrants to the United States believed that their stay in America would be temporary, a fact that limited their efforts at assimilation and reinforced ties to their original homelands.

The Shock of Alienation

. . . As the passing years widened the distance, the land the immigrants had left acquired charm and beauty. Present problems blurred those they had left unsolved behind; and in the haze of memory it seemed to these people they had formerly been free of present dissatisfactions. It was as if the Old World became a great mirror into which they looked to see right all that was wrong with the New. The landscape was prettier, the neighbors more friendly, and religion more efficacious; in the frequent crises when they reached the limits of their capacities, the wistful reflection came: *This would not have happened there.*

The real contacts were, however, disappointing. The requests—that back there a mass be said, or a wise one consulted, or a religious medal be sent over—those were gestures full of hope. But the responses were inadequate; like all else they shrank in the crossing. The immigrants wrote, but the replies, when they came, were dull, even trite in their mechanical phrases, or so it seemed to those who somehow expected these messages to evoke the emotions that had gone into their own painfully composed letters. Too often the eagerly attended envelopes proved to be only empty husks, the inner contents valueless. After the long wait before the postman came, the sheets of garbled writing were inevitably below expectations. There was a trying sameness to the complaints of hard times, to the repetitious petty quarrels; and before long there was impatience with the directness with which the formal greeting led into the everlasting requests for aid.

This last was a sore point with the immigrants. The friends and relatives who had stayed behind could not get it out of their heads that in America the streets were paved with gold. *Send me for a coat. . . . There is a piece of land here and if only you would send, we could buy it. . . . Our daughter could be married, but we have not enough for a dowry. . . . We are ashamed, everyone else gets . . . much more frequently than we.* Implicit in these solicitations was the judgment that the going-away had been a desertion, that unfulfilled obligations still remained, and that the village could claim assistance as a right from its departed members.

From the United States it seemed there was no comprehension, back there, of the difficulties of settlement. It was exasperating by sacrifices to scrape together the remittances and to receive in return a catalogue of new needs, as if there were not needs enough in the New World too. The immigrants never

From *The Uprooted: The Epic Story of the Great Migrations That Made the American People*, 2nd ed. by Oscar Handlin (Little, Brown and Company, 1951, 1973), excerpts from pp. 260–266, 270–274, 279–285. Copyright © 1951, 1973 by Oscar Handlin. Reprinted by permission of Little, Brown and Company/Hachette Book Group USA and the author.

shook off the sense of obligation to help; but they did come to regard their Old Countrymen as the kind of people who depended on help. The trouble with the Europeans was, they could not stand on their own feet.

The cousin green off the boat earned the same negative appraisal. Though he be a product of the homeland, yet here he cut a pitiable figure; awkward manners, rude clothes, and a thoroughgoing ineptitude in the new situation were his most prominent characteristics. The older settler found the welcome almost frozen on his lips in the face of such backwardness.

In every real contact the grandeur of the village faded; it did not match the immigrants' vision of it and it did not stand up in a comparison with America. When the picture came, the assembled family looked at it beneath the light. This was indeed the church, but it had not been remembered so; and the depressing contrast took some of the joy out of remembering.

The photograph did not lie. There it was, a low building set against the dusty road, weather-beaten and making a candid display of its ill-repair. But the recollections did not lie either. As if it had been yesterday that they passed through those doors, they could recall the sense of spaciousness and elevation that sight of the structure had always aroused.

Both impressions were true, but irreconcilable. The mental image and the paper representation did not jibe because the one had been formed out of the standards and values of the Old Country, while the other was viewed in the light of the standards and values of the New. And it was the same with every other retrospective contact. Eagerly the immigrants continued to look back across the Atlantic in search of the satisfactions of fellowship. But the search was not rewarded. Having become Americans, they were no longer villagers. Though they might willingly assume the former obligations and recognize the former responsibilities, they could not recapture the former points of view or hold to the former judgments. They had seen too much, experienced too much to be again members of the community. It was a vain mission on which they continued to dispatch the letters; these people, once separated, would never belong again.

⚫⚫⚫

Their home now was a country in which they had not been born. Their place in society they had established for themselves through the hardships of crossing and settlement. The process had changed them, had altered the most intimate aspects of their lives. Every effort to cling to inherited ways of acting and thinking had led into a subtle adjustment by which those ways were given a new American form. No longer Europeans, could the immigrants then say that they belonged in America? The answer depended upon the conceptions held by other citizens of the United States of the character of the nation and of the role of the newcomers within it.

In the early nineteenth century, those already established on this side of the ocean regarded immigration as a positive good. When travel by sea became safe after the general peace of 1815 and the first fresh arrivals trickled in, there was a general disposition to welcome the movement. The favorable attitude persisted even when the tide mounted to the flood levels of the 1840s and 1850s. The man off the boat was then accepted without question or condition.

The approval of unlimited additions to the original population came easily to Americans who were conscious of the youth of their country. Standing at the edge of an immense continent, they were moved by the challenge of empty land almost endless in its extension. Here was room enough, and more, for all who would bend their energies to its exploitation. The shortage was of labor and not of acres; every pair of extra hands increased the value of the abundant resources and widened opportunities for everyone.

The youth of the nation also justified the indiscriminate admission of whatever foreigners came to these shores. There was high faith in the destiny of the Republic, assurance that its future history would justify the Revolution and the separation from Great Britain. The society and the culture that would emerge in this territory would surpass those of the Old World because they would not slavishly imitate the outmoded forms and the anachronistic traditions that constricted men in Europe. The United States would move in new directions of its own because its people were a new people.

There was consequently a vigorous insistence that this country was not simply an English colony become independent. It was a nation unique in its origins, produced by the mixture of many different types out of which had come an altogether fresh amalgam, the American. The ebullient citizens who believed and argued that their language, their literature, their art, and their polity were distinctive and original also believed and argued that their population had not been derived from a single source but had rather acquired its peculiar characteristics from the blending of a variety of strains.

There was confidence that the process would continue. The national type had not been fixed by its given antecedents; it was emerging from the experience of life on a new continent. Since the quality of men was determined not by the conditions surrounding their birth, but by the environment within which they passed their lives, it was pointless to select among them. All would come with minds and spirits fresh for new impressions; and being in America would make Americans of them. Therefore it was best to admit freely everyone who wished to make a home here. The United States would then be a great smelting pot, great enough so that there was room for all who voluntarily entered; and the nation that would ultimately be cast from that crucible would be all the richer for the diversity of the elements that went into the molten mixture.

The legislation of most of the nineteenth century reflected this receptive attitude. The United States made no effort actively to induce anyone to immigrate, but neither did it put any bars in the way of their coming. Occasional laws in the four decades after 1819 set up shipping regulations in the hope of improving the conditions of the passage. In practice, the provisions that specified the minimum quantities of food and the maximum number of passengers each vessel could carry were easily evaded. Yet the intent of those statutes was to protect the travelers and to remove harsh conditions that might discourage the newcomers.

Nor were state laws any more restrictive in design. The seaports, troubled by the burdens of poor relief, secured the enactment of measures to safeguard their treasuries against such charges. Sometimes the form was a bond to guarantee that the immigrant would not become at once dependent upon public support; sometimes it was a small tax applied to defray the costs of charity. In either case there was no desire to limit entry into the country; and none of these steps had any discernible effect upon the volume of admissions.

Once landed, the newcomer found himself equal in condition to the natives. Within a short period he could be naturalized and acquire all the privileges of a citizen. In some places, indeed, he could vote before the oath in court so transformed his status. In the eyes of society, even earlier than in the eyes of the law, he was an American. . . .

❦

As the nineteenth century moved into its last quarter, a note of petulance crept into the comments of some Americans who thought about this aspect of the development of their culture. It was a long time now that the melting pot had been simmering, but the end product seemed no closer than before. The experience of life in the United States had not broken down the separateness of the elements mixed into it; each seemed to retain its own identity. Almost a half-century after the great immigration of Irish and Germans, these people had not become indistinguishable from other Americans; they were still recognizably Irish and German. Yet even then, newer waves of newcomers were beating against the Atlantic shore. Was there any prospect that all these multitudes would ever be assimilated, would ever be Americanized?

A generation earlier such questions would not have been asked. Americans of the first half of the century had assumed that any man who subjected himself to the American environment was being Americanized. Since the New World was ultimately to be occupied by a New Man, no mere derivative of any extant stock, but different from and superior to all, there had been no fixed standards of national character against which to measure the behavior of newcomers. The nationality of the new Republic had been supposed fluid, only just evolving; there had been room for infinite variation because diversity rather than uniformity had been normal.

The expression of doubts that some parts of the population might not become fully American implied the existence of a settled criterion of what was American. There had been a time when the society had recognized no distinction among citizens but that between the native and the foreign-born, and that distinction had carried no imputation of superiority or inferiority. Now there were attempts to distinguish among the natives between those who really belonged and those who did not, to separate out those who were born in the United States but whose immigrant parentage cut them off from the truly indigenous folk.

It was difficult to draw the line, however. The census differentiated after 1880 between natives and native-born of foreign parents. But that was an inadequate line of division; it provided no means of social recognition and offered no basis on which the *true Americans* could draw together, identify themselves as such.

Through these years there was a half-conscious quest among some Americans for a term that would describe those whose ancestors were in the

United States before the great migrations. Where the New Englanders were, they called themselves Yankees, a word that often came to mean non-Irish or non-Canadian. But Yankee was simply a local designation and did not take in the whole of the old stock. In any case, there was no satisfaction to such a title. Its holders were one group among many, without any distinctive claim to Americanism, cut off from other desirable peoples prominent in the country's past. Only the discovery of common antecedents could eliminate the separations among the really American.

But to find a common denominator, it was necessary to go back a long way. Actually no single discovery was completely satisfactory. Some writers, in time, referred to the civilization of the United States as Anglo-Saxon. By projecting its origins back to early Britain, they implied that their own culture was always English in derivation, and made foreigners of the descendants of Irishmen and Germans, to say nothing of the later arrivals. Other men preferred a variant and achieved the same exclusion by referring to themselves as "the English-speaking people," a title which assumed there was a unity and uniqueness to the clan which settled the home island, the Dominions, and the United States. Still others relied upon a somewhat broader appellation. They talked of themselves as Teutonic and argued that what was distinctively American originated in the forests of Germany; in this view, only the folk whose ancestors had experienced the freedom of tribal self-government and the liberation of the Protestant Reformation were fully American.

These terms had absolutely no historical justification. They nevertheless achieved a wide currency in the thinking of the last decades of the nineteenth century. Whatever particular phrase might serve the purpose of a particular author or speaker, all expressed the conviction that some hereditary element had given form to American culture. The conclusion was inescapable: to be Americanized, the immigrants must conform to the American way of life completely defined in advance of their landing.

꒰ꗯ꒱

There were two counts to the indictment that the immigrants were not so conforming. They were, first, accused of their poverty. Many benevolent citizens, distressed by the miserable conditions in the districts inhabited by the laboring people, were reluctant to believe that such social flaws were indigenous to the New World. It was tempting, rather, to ascribe them to the defects of the newcomers, to improvidence, slovenliness, and ignorance rather than to inability to earn a living wage.

Indeed to those whose homes were uptown the ghettos were altogether alien territory associated with filth and vice and crime. It did not seem possible that men could lead a decent existence in such quarters. The good vicar on a philanthropic tour was shocked by the moral dangers of the dark un-lighted hallway. His mind rushed to the defense of the respectable young girl: *Whatever her wishes may be, she can do nothing—shame prevents her from crying out.* The intention of the reformer was to improve housing, but the summation nevertheless was, *You cannot make an American citizen out of a slum.*

The newcomers were also accused of congregating together in their own groups and of an unwillingness to mix with outsiders. The foreign-born flocked to the great cities and stubbornly refused to spread out as farmers over the countryside; that alone was offensive to a society which still retained an ideal of rusticity. But even the Germans in Wisconsin and the Scandinavians in Minnesota held aloofly to themselves. Everywhere, the strangers persisted in their strangeness and willfully stood apart from American life. A prominent educator sounded the warning: *Our task is to break up their settlements, to assimilate and amalgamate these people and to implant in them the Anglo-Saxon conception of righteousness, law, and order.*

It was no simple matter to meet this challenge. The older residents were quick to criticize the separateness of the immigrant but hesitant when he made a move to narrow the distance. The householders of Fifth Avenue or Beacon Street or Nob Hill could readily perceive the evils of the slums but they were not inclined to welcome as a neighbor the former denizen of the East Side or the North End or the Latin Quarter who had acquired the means to get away. Among Protestants there was much concern over the growth of Catholic, Jewish, and Orthodox religious organizations, but there was no eagerness at all to provoke a mass conversion that might crowd the earlier churches with a host of poor foreigners. When the population of its neighborhood changed, the parish was less likely to try to attract the newcomers than to close or sell its building and move to some other section.

Indeed there was a fundamental ambiguity to the thinking of those who talked about "assimilation" in these years. They had arrived at their own view that American culture was fixed, formed from its origins, by shutting out the great mass of immigrants who were not English or at least not Teutonic. Now it was expected that those excluded people would alter themselves to earn their portion in Americanism. That process could only come about by increasing the contacts between the older and the newer inhabitants, by sharing jobs, churches, residences. Yet in practice, the man who thought himself an Anglo-Saxon found proximity to the other folk just come to the United States uncomfortable and distasteful and, in his own life, sought to increase rather than to lessen the gap between his position and theirs.

There was an escape from the horns of this unpleasant dilemma. It was tempting to resolve the difficulty by arguing that the differences between Americans on the one hand and Italians or Jews or Poles on the other were so deep as to admit of no conciliation. If these other stocks were cut off by their own innate nature, by the qualities of their heredity, then the original breed was justified both in asserting the fixity of its own character and in holding off from contact with the aliens. . . .

The fear of everything alien instilled by the First World War brought to fullest flower the seeds of racist thinking. Three enormously popular books by an anthropologist, a eugenist, and a historian revealed to hundreds of thousands of horrified Nordics how their great race had been contaminated by contact with lesser breeds, dwarfed in stature, twisted in mentality, and ruthless in the pursuit of their own self-interest.

These ideas passed commonly in the language of the time. No doubt many Americans who spoke in the bitter terms of race used the words in a figurative sense or in some other way qualified their acceptance of the harsh doctrine. After all, they still recognized the validity of the American tradition of equal and open opportunities, of the Christian tradition of the brotherhood of man. Yet, if they were sometimes troubled by the contradiction, nevertheless enough of them believed fully the racist conceptions so that five million could become members of the Ku Klux Klan in the early 1920s. . . .

꧁꧂

The activities of the Klan were an immediate threat to the immigrants and were resisted as such. But there was also a wider import to the movement. This was evidence, at last become visible, that the newcomers were among the excluded. The judgment at which the proponents of assimilation had only hinted, about which the racist thinkers had written obliquely, the Klan brought to the open. The hurt came from the fact that the mouthings of the Kleagle were not eccentricities, but only extreme statements of beliefs long on the margin of acceptance by many Americans. To the foreign-born this was demonstration of what they already suspected, that they would remain as alienated from the New World as they had become from the Old.

Much earlier the pressure of their separateness had begun to disturb the immigrants. As soon as the conception of Americanization had acquired the connotation of conformity with existing patterns, the whole way of group life of the newcomers was questioned. Their adjustment had depended upon their ability as individuals in a free society to adapt themselves to their environment through what forms they chose. The demand by their critics that the adjustment take a predetermined course seemed to question their right, as they were, to a place in American society.

Not that these people concerned themselves with theories of nationalism, but in practice the hostility of the "natives" provoked unsettling doubts about the propriety of the most innocent actions. The peasant who had become a Polish Falcon or a Son of Italy, in his own view, was acting as an American; this was not a step he could have taken at home. To subscribe to a newspaper was the act of a citizen of the New World, not of the Old, even if the journal was one of the thousand published by 1920 in languages other than English. When the immigrants heard their societies and their press described as un-American they could only conclude that they had somehow become involved in an existence that belonged neither in the old land nor in the new.

Yet the road of conformity was also barred to them. There were matters in which they wished to be like others, undistinguished from anyone else, but they never hit upon the means of becoming so. There was no pride in the surname, which in Europe had been little used, and many a new arrival was willing enough to make a change, suitable to the new country. But August Björkegren was not much better off when he called himself Burke, nor the Blumberg who became Kelly. The Lithuanians and Slovenes who moved into the Pennsylvania mining fields often endowed themselves with nomenclature of the older settlers, of the Irish and Italians there before them. In truth, these people found it difficult to know what were the "American" forms they were expected to take on.

What they did know was that they had not succeeded, that they had not established themselves to the extent that they could expect to be treated as if they belonged where they were.

If he was an alien, and poor, and in many ways helpless, still he was human, and it rankled when his dignity as a person was disregarded. He felt an undertone of acrimony in every contact with an official. Men in uniform always found him unworthy of respect; the bullying police made capital of his fear of the law; the postmen made sport of the foreign writing on his letters; the streetcar conductors laughed at his groping requests for directions. Always he was patronized as an object of charity, or almost so.

His particular enemies were the officials charged with his special oversight. When misfortune drove him to seek assistance or when government regulations brought them to inspect his home, he encountered the social workers, made ruthless in the disregard of his sentiments by the certainty of their own benevolent intentions. Confident of their personal and social superiority and armed with the ideology of the sociologists who had trained them, the emissaries of the public and private agencies were bent on improving the immigrant to a point at which he would no longer recognize himself.

The man who had dealings with the social workers was often sullen and unco-operative; he disliked the necessity of becoming a case, of revealing his dependence to strangers. He was also suspicious, feared there would be no understanding of his own way of life or of his problems; and he was resentful, because the powerful outsiders were judging him by superficial standards of their own. The starched young gentleman from the settlement house took stock from the middle of the kitchen. Were there framed pictures on the walls? Was there a piano, books? He made a note for the report: *This family is not yet Americanized; they are still eating Italian food.*

The services are valuable, but taking them is degrading. It is a fine thing to learn the language of the country; but one must be treated as a child to do so. *We keep saying all the time, This is a desk, this is a door. I know it is a desk and a door. What for keep saying it all the time? My teacher is a very nice young lady, very young. She does not understand what I want to talk about or know about.*

The most anguished conflicts come from the refusal of the immigrants to see the logic of their poverty. In the office it seems reasonable enough: people incapable of supporting themselves would be better off with someone to take care of them. It is more efficient to institutionalize the destitute than to allow them, with the aid of charity, to mismanage their homes. But the ignorant poor insist on clinging to their families, threaten suicide at the mention of the Society's refuge, or even of the hospital. What help the woman gets, she is still not satisfied. Back comes the ungrateful letter. *I don't ask you to put me in a poorhouse where I have to cry for my children. I don't ask you to put them in a home and eat somebody else's bread. I can't live here without them. I am so sick for them. I could live at home and spare good eats for them. What good did you give me to send me to the poorhouse? You only want people to live like you but I will not listen to you no more.*

A few dedicated social workers, mostly women, learned to understand the values in the immigrants' own lives. In some states, as the second generation became prominent in politics, government agencies came to co-operate with and protect the newcomers. But these were rare exceptions. They scarcely softened the rule experience everywhere taught the foreign-born, that they were expected to do what they could not do—to live like others.

For the children it was not so difficult. They at least were natives and could learn how to conform; to them the settlement house was not always a threat, but sometimes an opportunity. Indeed they could adopt entire the assumption that national character was long since fixed, only seek for their own group a special place within it. Some justified their Americanism by discovery of a colonial past; within the educated second generation there began a tortuous quest for eighteenth-century antecedents that might give them a portion in American civilization in its narrower connotation. Others sought to gain a sense of participation by separating themselves from later or lower elements in the population; they became involved in agitation against the Orientals, the Negroes, and the newest immigrants, as if thus to draw closer to the truly native. Either course implied a rejection of their parents who had themselves once been green off the boat and could boast of no New World antecedents.

The old folk knew then they would not come to belong, not through their own experience nor through their offspring. The only adjustment they had been able to make to life in the United States had been one that involved the separateness of their group, one that increased their awareness of the differences between themselves and the rest of the society. In that adjustment they had always suffered from the consciousness they were strangers. The demand that they assimilate, that they surrender their separateness, condemned them always to be outsiders. In practice, the free structure of American life permitted them with few restraints to go their own way, but under the shadow of a consciousness that they would never belong. They had thus completed their alienation from the culture to which they had come, as from that which they had left.

Mark Wyman

The America Trunk Comes Home

The emigrant who once boarded a ship for America was returning, and with him came the "America trunk" that had been loaded so carefully for the outgoing voyage. In Finland, this *American arkku* was filled when it came home with everything from glass dishes to locks from a baby's first haircut to such prized American objects as a phonograph player or double-bitted axe. Its contents were the talk of the neighborhood, valued for decades as mementos.

The America trunk is an apt symbol of both emigration and remigration, of immigrants coming to America and returning to their homelands. The symbol persists, for the trunk occupies hallowed positions today in homes of third-generation Americans who cling to an image of their ancestral saga; in many European homes, similarly, the chest that came back is still revered as a remnant, a piece of that dream which once drew an emigrant across the seas.

But there was more, much more, symbolized in the America trunk. Within its recesses were tools or clothes that carried memories of hard struggles abroad. It provided a continuing connection with America, and because the United States increasingly played a leading role in international affairs, remigrants would be called on to interpret that role. They became *americani* and "Yanks"; America's importance raised their importance. And the items they valued enough to carry back in trunks would provide clues to what America's impact would be: was it tools the returners brought? or books on political theory, nationalist aspirations, labor organization, new churches? Or were the contents of the America trunk to be used to impress neighbors, perhaps to be sold to help purchase a shop or an extra piece of land? Modern students of immigration who seek answers to such questions are no different than Charles Dickens, who gazed at the emigrants returning home to Europe on his ship in 1842 and admitted that he was "curious to know their histories, and with what expectations they had gone out to America, and on what errands they were going home, and what their circumstances were.". . .

The Ubiquitous Remigrant

The trunks were but one small part, like the tip of an iceberg, of the enormity of the movement of people, objects, and ideas back to Europe.

Percentage rates of return ranged from 30 to 40 percent for such groups as the Italians, down to 10 percent among the Irish. Using these as a rough

From *Round Trip to America: The Immigrants Return to Europe, 1880–1930* by Mark Wyman (Cornell University Press, 1993), pp. 189, 191–197, 204–209. Copyright © 1993 by Cornell University. Reprinted by permission of Cornell University Press.

guide, it is possible to estimate that the total return to Europe may have been as high as four million repatriated emigrants during the 1880–1930 era of mass immigration into North America.

Examined within individual countries, these massive totals mean that one in twenty residents of Italy was a returned emigrant at the time of World War I, and shortly thereafter in a Norwegian county of heavy emigration it was found that one-fourth of all males over age fifteen had lived at least two years in America. Such high numbers signify that for the next sixty years visitors to European villages would encounter former residents of Scranton or Cleveland or Detroit, happy to describe their American experiences, wanting to know how the baseball pennant race was shaping up. . . .

A More-Reachable America

The years 1880–1930 stand out in the immigrant experience. Europeans crossed to North America in ever-increasing numbers as major improvements appeared in transportation. For generations before, however, an extensive pattern of short-term, work-seeking migration had existed in most areas of Europe, from Macedonians heading out to jobs around the Mediterranean to Irishmen and women crossing to England and Scotland for farm work. These nearby treks continued into the era of mass transatlantic emigration, as was evident in Polish totals: at the peak of Polish emigration to the United States in 1912–13, 130,000 left for America—compared to 800,000 heading for seasonal work elsewhere in Europe. It is true that development of the oceangoing steamship, coupled with an increasing flow of news and publicity about American jobs, helped shift the destinations of many short-term migrants to the West, across the Atlantic. North and South America were becoming more closely fitted into the Atlantic economy and, if this meant that midwestern pork could now be packed for consumers in Germany, it also signified that Germans from those same consuming areas, and Poles, Italians, and Finns, could easily travel to find employment in those same U.S. packing plants.

These developments welded mass migration closely to the variations, booms, and busts of American industry. To these immigrants, America became basically the site of factory employment, gang labor on a railroad section, a job underground following a coal seam. One Italian could talk of his American experiences only in terms of trains, rails, and crossties, "as if all of America was nothing but a braid of tracks," a countryman reported.

As the trio of concerns of *journey, job hunt, and employment* became more predictable, less dangerous, the trip to America could then be viewed as something other than a lifetime change. Like short-term labor migration within Europe, it became a means to improve life at home, through earning enough to achieve a higher status or more solid position in the village. It was not so much the start of a new life as another step in the process of social mobility. These factors in turn dictated that life in the American "workshop" would be temporary for many.

. . . In all, it is impossible to know what percentage of immigrants planned to return home, but it is not reaching far beyond the evidence to estimate that a majority in the 1880–1930 period initially expected to turn their backs on life and labor overseas once they had accumulated some wealth. Various things caused most to change their minds: in the United States these included realizing that opportunities in America outstripped those at home, gaining a better job, becoming accustomed to a higher standard of living, the arrival of news from abroad that removed the necessity for return, or gradual Americanization through learning the language, acquiring American friends, falling in love with a local girl.

Sometimes the shifts in expectations could be traced through a progression of names, as in the case of a Lithuanian immigrant couple who lived in coal towns in Pennsylvania and Illinois, always planning to return to Lithuania until they moved on to Oklahoma and decided to settle down. Their first two children were born in 1896 and 1900, when they still expected to go back to Europe, and were accordingly named Gediminas and Juozas. The third arrived in 1912, when they had become Americans. They named him Edwin.

But until that decision was made, until the carefully plotted return plans were finally abandoned, then every act, every expenditure had to be undertaken with an eye toward repatriation. This fact dawned gradually on an American in 1903 as he traveled about Italy and found that returned emigrants were much different, better persons at home; they had lived in brutal conditions in the United States because of "a feeling among them that they were merely temporizing . . .; that they had come to America to make a few hundred dollars to send or take back to Italy; and that it did not make much difference what they ate, wore or did, just so long as they got the money and got back." Their day-to-day existence in the United States would not improve until they were "drawn into the real American life" and changed their minds about going back to Europe.

Dreams of the village were especially strong among such persons; their thoughts were directed eastward toward home, even while they lived and worked in the West. This longing made assimilation difficult, and ethnic identities were further maintained by life in immigrant enclaves, blocking or discouraging connections with American institutions. Such isolation drew the fire of many Americans and settled members of the Old Immigration. Angered at the spectacle of U.S. dollars being carried overseas, they were also appalled by living conditions among those expecting to return. Labor unions suffered from the influx of these low-wage immigrants who often rejected invitations to join their fight for better wages and conditions. For years the unions approached the newcomers from two directions, often at the same time: seeking to organize the aliens while attacking them as strikebreakers and cheap competition. And the continued exodus of remigrants added to the pressure on union leaders to side with the restrictionist movement. . . .

As these immigrants held back from identifying with their new country of residence, many became part of a subculture within their own immigrant culture; that is, the temporary immigrant did even less than other immigrants to learn English, adapt to American ways, join American organizations. This reluctance further stimulated nativist attacks, which reached a climax with the restriction legislation of the postwar 1920s. Remigrants were not the only cause of the nativist surge, but their lifestyles in America helped fuel the restrictionist drive and they became one of the nativists' easiest targets.

Praise and Scorn at Home

As they returned to Europe the remigrants found a mixed welcome. Constructing new-style houses of brick rather than wood, many wore fancy clothes and endeavored to climb the social ladder. But villagers often looked askance at these people who seemed all too often to be putting on airs. One critic was the father of later emigrant Stoyan Christowe, who observed the well-dressed remigrants parading around their Bulgarian village and spat out, "An ox is an ox even if you put golden horns on him."

Their stories were often too fantastic, too farfetched. Norwegians began referring to them as *Amerikaskroner*—"tall tales from America." One man recalled his uncle's return to Norway in 1929 and his strange revelations about the things he had seen: "He told us about the Christmas trees that went round and round, he talked about streetcars, he talked of electric lights, he told of huge buildings, skyscrapers, he told us how they built them, he talked about the communications, railroads that went to every corner in the land, he told us about an industrial society which was so different from what we knew that it was like a completely different world." Was it all believable? Perhaps not. More recently, a returned emigrant showed his Norwegian grade school pupils a U.S. postcard with a photo graph of a giant Pacific Northwest log on a logging truck, the driver standing proudly on top. When he translated the postcard's legend, "Oregon Toothpick," one child retorted, "I've always heard that Americans have big mouths."

Their money was a reality that could not be denied, however. The cash carried home, together with the vast sums mailed back by those still toiling across the ocean, helped stabilize the economies of Europe and served as a stimulus for local booms. Business experience and connections became the most obvious gains from remigration in many districts, especially in Germany. Land, apartment houses, taverns, shops, and other firms were purchased by those coming home with "golden horns." For a time in Bydgoszcz, a Polish city in Pomerania, seventy agencies worked primarily to help remigrants obtain or sell properties. Two generations later the flow of retirees back from America would stimulate similar activities through their Social Security checks and factory pensions.

Most who returned in the 1880–1930 era went into agriculture, and this activity was at the center of much of the debate over their impact. Certainly agriculture was extremely backward in many areas; one estimate by returning Norwegians was that farming in Norway was fifty years behind that in the United States. But would returned emigrants be the ones to launch the required changes? Remigrants rushed to buy farmland, and large-scale commercialization of land became one of the most noted results of the vast emigration and return. But early evidence indicated that remigrants then continued or even expanded traditional and backward farming practices.

In contrast, areas such as Prussia and the English Midlands, where farm progress was extensive in the late nineteenth century, featured either the growth of larger land units with major investments of capital or the contrary development of smaller but more specialized farms that used the latest in farm technology and benefited from growing consumer demand. A student of the transformation of British agriculture notes increased farming complexity through use of artificial manures and new seeds and livestock breeds and adds that this "no doubt . . . also required flexibility of mind." But flexibility of mind regarding agricultural improvements may have been missing among many remigrants coming back to traditional farming in such areas as southern Italy or Poland. Few had worked on American farms, and this fact alone predicted that their impact on the Continent's agriculture would be minimal. Sporadic improvements and changes were widely publicized, but these were unusual, like the tomatoes planted by some Finns or the new flowers appearing in Polish gardens. Only in certain areas, such as parts of Scandinavia, could it be said that the remigrants were a definite mainstay of drives to modernize agriculture.

But in other occupations and situations, where emigrants had been able to learn American methods, improvements were obvious. To begin with, more vigorous work habits were widely noted. Also, many carried home sewing machines, which led to improvements in clothing, and holiday garb began to be worn more regularly. Homemaking benefited: when Irish women returned, they refused to continue traditional hearth cooking because it only permitted meat to be boiled; soon they installed grates or bought ranges. Personal hygiene improved, and a Hungarian report indicated that remigrants even kept their windows open at night, rejecting the traditional belief that night air held evils.

Many threw themselves into various campaigns for government change: Irish Home Rulers sought to throw off British control, Slovaks and Croatians pushed for separate nations, some Finns who had attended the Duluth Work People's College wanted to destroy capitalism. Others agitated for the development of public schools, and the remigrants' presence helped spread English through Gaelic-speaking areas of Ireland and in many other districts across Europe. Returned emigrants began to appear as members of village councils, school boards, even national legislatures; three of them became prime ministers, of Norway, Latvia, and Finland. . . .

Conclusions

In an examination of the remigrant from 1880 to 1930, before leaving Europe, at work in America, and after the return home, nine broad conclusions emerge:

1. The temporary immigrant was in truth far different from the immigrant who planned to stay. The expectations of any immigrant were all-important in directing his or her job-seeking, assimilation, and adjustment to American life, and the immigrant who stepped onto American sail planning permanent residence saw these goals differently than did the short-term industrial migrant. The latter was basically a *sojourner,* defined by sociologists as a deviant form

of the stranger, who remains psychologically in his homeland while living somewhere else, culturally isolated, tied physically but not mentally to a job. He may have changed his mind eventually, but until that point he lived the life of one who saw his future back in Europe.

Employment became the critical part of the remigrant's American existence. Like a New England girl arriving to work briefly in the Lowell mills in the 1830s, or a Turkish *Gastarbeiter* in Germany today, the temporary industrial migrant in the 1880–1930 period saw the world through different eyes than did (or does) the worker planning to remain. To ignore this fact and its implications is to miss a major facet of immigration's impact and an important explanation of immigrants' failure to assimilate despite lengthy residence abroad. Failing to take it into account would also make it difficult to understand why so many who returned home took up farming rather than the industrial occupations they had known overseas. If one task of the historian is to see the past from different angles, then following the contrary path of the temporary immigrant can provide an important new perspective.

2. The American immigration story becomes less unified, more diverse, when remigrants are considered within the broad picture of the peopling of a continent. There was little in common between the Bohemian family settling the Nebraska prairies in the 1890s and Bohemian men arriving for a year's work in a Chicago stockyard. Assimilation was soon forced on those farming in Nebraska; it was not even a remote goal of most of those lining up for their wages each fortnight in Chicago. One immigrant is not always equal to another—an obvious fact, but one made both more apparent and more significant when the remigrant experience is considered. . . .

3. There were many Americas contained within the broad vision of the United States by the 1880s, but America as the symbol of economic opportunity increasingly became uppermost for immigrants, especially those planning a temporary stay. Democracy was of little importance to a sojourner dreaming of adding to his piece of earth in the Mezzogiorno. When economic opportunity and democracy were seen as two branches of the same trunk, however, one could buttress the other in forming an image of the nation. But a remigrant who had witnessed few examples of democracy in his twelve-hour days in a steel mill would consider America in a different light than would another new resident escaping from religious unrest and finding herself in the competitive free-for-all of U.S. church denominations. Economic opportunity became the representative American symbol to millions.

4. The basis of American nativism was not opposition to return migration, but it gained several major arguments in the course of reacting to temporary immigrants. Nativists began to erupt in anger as thousands and thousands of short-term residents avoided assimilation and escaped abroad with their American earnings. The exodus goaded many Americans into ever stronger condemnations of immigration in general, and the identification of European remigrants with Chinese sojourners became complete. This provided an opening for earlier, permanent immigrants to condemn later arrivals and to become in effect immigrant nativists. Anti-foreign sentiment among U.S. labor groups leaned especially hard on the temporary immigrant.

5. The striving for status—to hold onto a vanishing position, or even to climb higher—emerges as one of the main forces behind remigration as well as emigration. Remigrants often left Europe to seek a higher status at home; they did not seek a permanent existence and better status in America. The New World may have represented a horn of plenty, but its wealth would be more useful back in Europe. Basic subsistence could be met, and after that the possibility of becoming landowners of importance in the village. Immigrants knew enough about life in the United States to understand the saying, "America for the oxen, Europe for the peasant." It was in Europe, not America, that the opportunity to reach a new level of existence waited.

6. The remigrant's importance in stimulating further immigration may have eclipsed even that of the much-maligned steamship agent. A large-scale exodus developed mainly from European areas where there had been an earlier emigration, which had produced a return flow of successes with money to purchase land and to construct "American houses." These acts promoted America with more impact than did handbills posted on village walls. There is also evidence of what might be called "emigration families," providing members from each generation who spent time in the United States and then returned, their tales handed down to stimulate others to try America later. The process was then repeated, generation after generation, and the remigrant ancestors became long-term role models. Their example competed with the emigrant letter as the chief propagandist of emigration. And the picture of America as a horn of plenty became indelibly fastened on a people who grew up hearing American stories around the winter hearth.

7. The return flow must be counted as a major reason that Europe's enormous exodus to America did not result in a net loss for the home society. Some form of general decline might have been expected for a continent that lost 36 million of its most active and future-oriented citizens to the United States from 1820 to 1975. The same could have been predicted for other regions that sent their people to America; one might even apply it to Mexico and the Caribbean nations today. But instead of causing a deterioration, the era of mass emigration proved overall to be one of general advance and progress for the people of many nations. This pattern continues. Certainly many things, tangible and intangible, have contributed to this result, but one is the extensive return flow of people, money, and ideas. As a Polish priest concluded from his study of the emigration from Miejsce parish in 1883, the returns from America meant that the exodus was "not a loss but a gain for this province." It could be said for most of Europe.

The Continent benefited as well from the return of organizational and political skills, as men and women of all ideologies and aspirations came back to launch labor unions and community organizations and to become involved in political affairs. Churches were challenged and new philosophies began to circulate. When Finland and Latvia achieved independence amid scenes of enormous chaos, leadership in each new country fell to those already experienced in labor and political struggles in America. Norway also chose a remigrant as its prime minister to lead the country through the dark days of depression and World War II. Many others coming back occupied government posts in municipalities as well as in national regimes.

The remigrants brought change in many forms. New words were carried home: modern Finnish has been enriched by many remigrant words and phrases, according to recent studies. Beyond this, many of those returning to Europe displayed an openness, an attitude that shook off the old and helped transform the peasant world. And remigration contributed further to a mingling of cultures which encouraged change as well as helping bring a gradual integration of the cultures of Europe and America.

The United States is more than just people transferred from Europe; Europe is guided by more than influences from America. But the two-way exchange was one crucial factor in the historical development of both, and the remigrant helped in both directions, a continuing link between two cultures.

8. American "exceptionalism," the view that the American experience has been unique and that developments in the United States were basically different from those elsewhere, is dealt a further blow by the remigration story. The United States was not a land where every immigrant came to stay; it was a country seen by many foreigners as a means rather than an end. As such, the American immigration pageant contained many scenes known elsewhere, for temporary stays as well as permanent moves have long been part of human migrations.

Parallels are numerous. Just as was often the case in the United States, temporary migrants were unpopular in the Ruhr, where German unions fought Poles, employers put aliens in the dirtiest jobs, and officials sought their removal. Swiss workers assaulted Italians in 1896, the government meanwhile blocked their naturalization, and welfare groups refused to give aid. This was nativism run wild. Riots erupted against Italian workers in France from the 1880s on; in 1893, fifty Italians were killed and 150 wounded during an attack by French miners at the Aigues-Mortes salt-works. There was physical violence in the United States, but as in Europe the opposition to those planning to return usually took other forms: unions sought their dismissal, politicians argued for bans on their employment, and editorial writers aimed darts at those who carried off national wealth. . . .

9. Finally, the story of the returned immigrant brings the historian face to face with the importance of human feelings, human emotions, in world events. Scholars often stress impersonal forces when discussing developments involving masses of people. But the fact that several million immigrants could turn around and leave a land with a higher standard of living and all the glitter of modernization, to cross the ocean again and return to a backward peasant village, with its distinctive culture and traditions, stands as supreme testimony to the pull of kin and home.

The Psalmist cried, "How shall we sing the Lord's song in a strange land?" And the longing to be within the family circle, in the familiar pathways and fields of home, has always been part of the human condition. The human heart must be given equal rank here with cold economic statistics and the pleadings of steamship agents. For the sense of being lost, away from moorings, left thousands of immigrants with the feeling that nothing seemed right in the New World—not holidays, not religious rites, not even the summer sunrise. They like the Psalmist felt lost in a strange land. The Swedish novelist of emigration, Vilhelm Moberg, reflected on these feelings in his autobiographical novel *A Time on Earth:*

> Man must have a root in the world; he must belong somewhere. He cannot abandon the land where he was born and adopt another country as his birthplace. Prattle about old and new mother countries is prattle only, and a lie. Either I have a country of my own, or I have not. Mother country is singular, never plural.
>
> The country you knew as child and young man was the country you left. That was your fate; you could never find another homeland.

In the final analysis, the story of the returned immigrants is a record of the endurance of home and family ties. It provides further evidence that, for many, immigration demonstrated the strength and unity of the family—both in going to America and in returning—rather than the family's weakening or destruction. For it was to rejoin their people, to walk again on their own land, to sit in the parish church once more, that the temporary immigrants repacked their America trunks and booked passage again, this time for home. The journey to America had been round-trip. And as they had helped shape life in the United States, its world of work, its image of itself and of foreigners, now they would affect the lives of their own families, their villages, their homelands. It would be a different future on both continents because of the returned immigrants.

POSTSCRIPT

Were Late Nineteenth-Century Immigrants "Uprooted"?

Oscar Handlin has been recognized as the most influential scholar on immigration history since his doctoral dissertation won the Dunning Prize when he was only twenty-six years old. Published as *Boston's Immigrants: A Study in Acculturation* (Harvard University Press, 1941), this was the first study of immigration to integrate sociological concepts within a historical framework. A decade later, Handlin published *The Uprooted,* in which he combined the interdisciplinary framework with a personal narrative of the immigrants' history. Although many historians criticized this approach, the book earned Handlin a Pulitzer Prize.

John Bodnar's *The Transplanted,* while offering a contrasting metaphor for the immigration experience to the United States, shares with Handlin's work an attempt to present a general account of that experience, to portray the immigrants in a sympathetic light and to employ an interdisciplinary approach by borrowing concepts from the social sciences. Handlin and Bodnar, however, differ in their perspectives about America's ethnic past. Handlin views the immigrants as people who were removed from their particular Old World cultures and who assimilated into the New World value system within two generations. In contrast, Bodnar argues that some first-generation immigrants may have shed their traditional culture quickly upon arrival in the United States, but more continued to maintain a viable lifestyle in their adopted homeland that focused upon the family household and the neighboring ethnic community. "Not solely traditional, modern or working class," says Bodnar, "it was a dynamic culture, constantly responding to changing needs and opportunities and grounded in a deep sense of pragmatism and mutual assistance."

The Harvard Encyclopedia of American Ethnic Groups (Harvard University Press, 1980), edited by Stephan Thernstrom and Oscar Handlin, is a valuable collection of articles on every ethnic group in the United States. It also contains twenty-nine thematic essays on such subjects as prejudice, assimilation, and folklore. Also useful and more manageable is Stephanie Bernardo, *The Ethnic Almanac* (Doubleday, 1981), whose purpose is to "amuse, inform and entertain you with facts about your heritage and that of your friends, neighbors and relatives." Leonard Dinnerstein and David Reimers's *Ethnic Americans: A History of Immigration and Assimilation,* 2nd ed. (Harper & Row, 1982), is a short but accurate text, while Joe R. Feagan's *Racial and Ethnic Relations,* 2nd ed. (Prentice Hall, 1985), is a useful sociological text that examines the major ethnic groups through assimilationist and power-conflict models.

In the last generation, dozens of studies have focused on the experiences of particular immigrant groups in the United States. See, for example, Moses Rischin, *The Promised City: New York's Jews, 1870–1914* (Harvard University Press, 1962); Jack Chen, *The Chinese in America* (Harper & Row, 1980); Matt S. Meier and Feliciano Rivera, *The Chicanos: A History of Mexican Americans* (Hill and Wang, 1972); Humbert Nelli, *Italians in Chicago, 1880–1930: A Study of Ethnic Mobility* (Oxford University Press, 1970); and Thomas Kessner, *The Golden Door: Italian and Jewish Immigrant Mobility in New York City, 1880–1915* (Oxford University Press, 1977). The reaction to the immigration of the late nineteenth century can be observed in Jacob Riis's contemporary account of New York City, *How the Other Half Lives* (1890; reprint, Hill and Wang, 1970), and in John Higham's *Strangers in the Land: Patterns of American Nativism, 1860–1925* (Rutgers University Press, 1955), which is considered the best work on anti-immigrant prejudice in this time period.

ISSUE 6

Were the Populists Irrational Reactionaries?

YES: Richard Hofstadter, from *The Age of Reform: From Bryan to F.D.R.* (Alfred A. Knopf, 1955 and 1972)

NO: Charles Postel, from *The Populist Vision* (Oxford University Press, 2007)

ISSUE SUMMARY

YES: According to Richard Hofstadter the Populists created a conspiracy theory around the issues of industrialism that activated a virulent strain of nativism and anti-Semitism, and revealed their desire to return to a rural utopia that they associated with the early nineteenth century.

NO: Charles Postel characterizes the Populists as forward-thinking reformers who hoped to use the government to manage an increasingly modern, technologically sophisticated, and globally connected society for the benefit of ordinary citizens.

Industrialism produced significant changes and affected every major group in American society. Manufacturers and laborers obviously experienced the impact of these new forces, but industrial influences were felt beyond the confines of the nation's growing cities. Industrialism also altered the lives of rural Americans who depended upon the soil for their livelihoods. Although they hoped to benefit from new markets and increased prosperity, the reality for most American farmers was greater poverty. After 1815, the independent, self-sufficient farmer began his retreat into American mythology in the wake of the relentless advance of commercial agriculture.

Between 1860 and 1900, American farmers confronted a steady downward spiral of agricultural prices, especially among major cash crops like wheat, corn, and cotton. Greater efficiency created higher production levels which in turn drove prices to lower levels. Meanwhile, farmers and their families had to purchase manufactured goods, many of which were inflated artificially in price by existing tariff schedules. Purchasing new land and better machinery to offset declining prices only compounded the problem and created a new one—the difficulty of repaying credit. By 1890, many farmers were losing their lands to foreclosure and were forced into tenancy or sharecropping; others abandoned the countryside for the city.

The discontent bred by these factors led American farmers to conclude that the best solution lay in organization. This was a momentous decision on the part of a group of citizens who for generations had expressed a commitment to individualism of the most rugged sort. But with industrialists forming managers' associations and urban workers pushing for the recognition of their unions, many farmers decided to follow suit. Initial attempts to organize resulted in the National Grange of the Patrons of Husbandry in the 1860s, a social group, and the Alliance movement of the 1870s and 1880s. Finally, farmers attempted to organize an effective political movement in the 1890s, which culminated in the People's, or Populist's, Party. The Populists mounted opposition to the forces that threatened to make beggars of agricultural and urban workers alike, but with the defeat of William Jennings Bryan in the presidential election of 1896, Populism passed quickly from the scene. Nevertheless, many of the ideas and programs advanced by the People's Party subsequently were secured by reformers in the twentieth century.

Who were the Populists? How were their goals and ideology molded by the times in which they lived? How did the Populist Party react to the urban, industrial values that seemed to be dominating American society in the late nineteenth century? Was the revolt of the Populists in large part an effort to return American society to the simpler utopia that they believed had characterized the United States in the early 1800s? These are some of the questions addressed in the essays that follow.

Richard Hofstadter credits the Populist Party with releasing reform sentiments that fueled the protests of the Progressive era and for being the first political movement to insist upon federal responsibility for the common good of American society. At the same time, Hofstadter claims, Populism was provincial, nationalistic, nativistic, and anti-Semitic, characteristics that Hofstadter ascribes to a group of reactionary agrarians living uncomfortably in a modern, industrialized nation. According to Charles Postel, the Populists were neither irrational nor reactionary. Their vision for the United States involved the use of an active federal government as an agency of the majority, rather than the corporate and wealthy elite, in order to insure fair access to the benefits of modernity.

In addition to Hicks' work cited above, the origins of the farmers' revolt of the late nineteenth century are explored in D. Sven Nordin, *Rich Harvest: A History of the Grange, 1867–1900* (University Press of Mississippi, 1974); Robert C. McMath, Jr., *Populist Vanguard: A History of the Southern Farmers' Alliance* (University of North Carolina Press, 1975); Michael Schwartz, *Radical Protest and Social Structure: The Southern Farmers' Alliance and Cotton Tenancy, 1880–1890* (Academic, 1976); Stephen Hahn, *The Roots of Southern Populism: Yeoman Farmers and the Transformation of the Georgia Upcountry, 1850–1890* (Oxford University Press, 1983); and Donna Barnes, *Farmers in Rebellion: The Rise and Fall of the Southern Farmers' Alliance and People's Party in Texas* (University of Texas Press, 1984).

The Folklore of Populism

The Two Nations

For a generation after the Civil War, a time of great economic exploitation and waste, grave social corruption and ugliness, the dominant note in American political life was complacency. Although dissenting minorities were always present, they were submerged by the overwhelming realities of industrial growth and continental settlement. The agitation of the Populists, which brought back to American public life a capacity for effective political indignation, marks the beginning of the end of this epoch. In the short run the Populists did not get what they wanted, but they released the flow of protest and criticism that swept through American political affairs from the 1890s to the beginning of the first World War.

Where contemporary intellectuals gave the Populists a perfunctory and disdainful hearing, later historians have freely recognized their achievements and frequently overlooked their limitations. Modern liberals, finding the Populists' grievances valid, their programs suggestive, their motives creditable, have usually spoken of the Populist episode in the spirit of Vachel Lindsay's bombastic rhetoric:

> Prairie avenger, mountain lion,
> Bryan, Bryan, Bryan, Bryan,
> Gigantic troubadour, speaking like a siege gun,
> Smashing Plymouth Rock with his boulders from the West.

There is indeed much that is good and usable in our Populist past. While the Populist tradition had defects that have been too much neglected, it does not follow that the virtues claimed for it are all fictitious. Populism was the first modern political movement of practical importance in the United States to insist that the federal government has some responsibility for the common weal; indeed, it was the first such movement to attack seriously the problems created by industrialism. The complaints and demands and prophetic denunciations of the Populists stirred the latent liberalism in many Americans and startled many conservatives into a new flexibility. Most of the "radical" reforms in the Populist program proved in later years to be either harmless or useful. In at least one important area of American life a few Populist leaders

From *The Age of Reform: From Byron to F.D.R.* by Richard Hofstadter (Alfred A. Knopf 1955, 1972), pp. 60–65, 70, 75–83, 91–93 (notes omitted). Copyright © 1955, 1972 by Richard Hofstadter. Reprinted by permission of Alfred A. Knopf, a division of Random House, Inc.

in the South attempted something profoundly radical and humane—to build a popular movement that would cut across the old barriers of race—until persistent use of the Negro bogy distracted their following. To discuss the broad ideology of the Populists does them some injustice, for it was in their concrete programs that they added most constructively to our political life, and in their more general picture of the world that they were most credulous and vulnerable. Moreover, any account of the fallibility of Populist thinking that does not acknowledge the stress and suffering out of which that thinking emerged will be seriously remiss. But anyone who enlarges our portrait of the Populist tradition is likely to bring out some unseen blemishes. In the books that have been written about the Populist movement, only passing mention has been made of its significant provincialism; little has been said of its relations with nativism and nationalism; nothing has been said of its tincture of anti-Semitism.

The Populist impulse expressed itself in a set of notions that represent what I have called the "soft" side of agrarianism. These notions, which appeared with regularity in the political literature, must be examined if we are to re-create for ourselves the Populist spirit. To extract them from the full context of the polemical writings in which they appeared is undoubtedly to oversimplify them; even to name them in any language that comes readily to the historian of ideas is perhaps to suggest that they had a formality and coherence that in reality they clearly lacked. But since it is less feasible to have no labels than to have somewhat too facile ones, we may enumerate the dominant themes in Populist ideology as these: the idea of a golden age; the concept of natural harmonies; the dualistic version of social struggles; the conspiracy theory of history; and the doctrine of the primacy of money. . . .

The utopia of the Populists was in the past, not the future. According to the agrarian myth, the health of the state was proportionate to the degree to which it was dominated by the agricultural class, and this assumption pointed to the superiority of an earlier age. The Populists looked backward with longing to the lost agrarian Eden, to the republican America of the early years of the nineteenth century in which there were few millionaires and, as they saw it, no beggars, when the laborer had excellent prospects and the farmer had abundance, when statesmen still responded to the mood of the people and there was no such thing as the money power. What they meant—though they did not express themselves in such terms—was that they would like to restore the conditions prevailing before the development of industrialism and the commercialization of agriculture. It should not be surprising that they inherited the traditions of Jacksonian democracy, that they revived the old Jacksonian cry: "Equal Rights for All, Special Privileges for None," or that most of the slogans of 1896 echoed the battle cries of 1836. General James B. Weaver, the Populist candidate for the presidency in 1892, was an old Democrat and Free-Soiler, born during the days of Jackson's battle with the United States Bank, who drifted into the Greenback movement after a short spell as a Republican, and from there to Populism. His book, *A Call to Action,* published in 1892, drew up an indictment of the business corporation which reads like a Jacksonian polemic. Even in those hopeful early days of the People's Party, Weaver projected no grandiose plans for the future, but lamented the course of recent history, the growth of economic oppression, and the emergence of great contrasts of wealth and poverty, and called upon his readers to do "All in [their] power to arrest the alarming tendencies of our times."

Nature, as the agrarian tradition had it, was beneficent. The United States was abundantly endowed with rich land and rich resources, and the "natural" consequence of such an endowment should be the prosperity of the people. If the people failed to enjoy prosperity, it must be because of a harsh and arbitrary intrusion of human greed and error. "Hard times, then," said one popular writer, "as well as the bankruptcies, enforced idleness, starvation, and the crime, misery, and moral degradation growing out of conditions like the present, being unnatural, not in accordance with, or the result of any natural law, must be attributed to that kind of unwise and pernicious legislation which history proves to have produced similar results in all ages of the world. It is the mission of the age to correct these errors in human legislation, to adopt and establish policies and systems, in accord with, rather than in opposition to divine law." In assuming a lush natural order whose workings were being deranged by human laws, Populist writers were again drawing on the Jacksonian tradition, whose spokesmen also had pleaded for a proper obedience to "natural" laws as a prerequisite of social justice.

Somewhat akin to the notion of the beneficence of nature was the idea of a natural harmony of interests among the productive classes. To the Populist mind there was no fundamental conflict between the farmer and the worker, between the toiling people and the small businessman. While there might be corrupt individuals in any group, the underlying interests of the productive majority were the same; predatory behavior existed only because it was initiated and underwritten by a small parasitic minority in the highest places of power. As opposed to the idea that society consists of a number of different and frequently clashing interests—the social pluralism expressed, for instance, by Madison in the *Federalist*—the Populists adhered, less formally to be sure, but quite persistently, to a kind of social dualism: although they knew perfectly well that society was composed of a number of classes, for all practical purposes only one simple division need be considered. There were two nations. "It is a struggle," said Sockless Jerry Simpson, "between the robbers and the robbed." "There are but two sides in the conflict that is being waged in this country today," declared a Populist manifesto. "On the one side are the allied hosts of monopolies, the money power, great trusts and railroad corporations, who seek the enactment of laws to benefit them and impoverish the people. On the other are the farmers, laborers, merchants, and all other people who produce wealth and bear the burdens of taxation. . . . Between these two there is no middle ground." "On the one side," said Bryan in his famous speech against the repeal of the Sherman Silver Purchase Act, "stand the corporate interests of the United States, the moneyed interests, aggregated wealth and capital, imperious, arrogant, compassionless. . . . On the other side stand an unnumbered throng, those who gave to the Democratic party a name and for whom it has assumed to speak." The people versus the interests, the public versus the plutocrats, the toiling multitude versus the money power—in various phrases this central antagonism was expressed. From this simple social classification it seemed to follow that once the techniques of misleading the people were exposed, victory over the money power ought to be easily accomplished, for in sheer numbers the people were overwhelming. "There is no power on earth that can defeat us," said General Weaver during the optimistic days of the campaign of 1892. "It is a fight between labor and capital, and labor is in the vast majority." . . .

History as Conspiracy

. . . There was something about the Populist imagination that loved the secret plot and the conspiratorial meeting. There was in fact a widespread Populist idea that all American history since the Civil War could be understood as a sustained conspiracy of the international money power. . . .

Wherever one turns in the Populist literature of the nineties one can find this conspiracy theory expressed. It is in the Populist newspapers, the proceedings of the silver conventions, the immense pamphlet literature broadcast by the American Bimetallic League, the Congressional debates over money; it is elaborated in such popular books as Mrs. S. E. V. Emery's *Seven Financial Conspiracies which have Enslaved the American People* or Gordon Clark's *Shylock: as Banker, Bondholder, Corruptionist, Conspirator.*

Mrs. Emery's book, first published in 1887, and dedicated to "the enslaved people of a dying republic," achieved great circulation, especially among the Kansas Populists. According to Mrs. Emery, the United States had been an economic Garden of Eden in the period before the Civil War. The fall of man had dated from the war itself, when "the money kings of Wall Street" determined that they could take advantage of the wartime necessities of their fellow men by manipulating the currency. "Controlling it, they could inflate or depress the business of the country at pleasure, they could send the warm life current through the channels of trade, dispensing peace, happiness, and prosperity, or they could check its flow, and completely paralyze the industries of the country." With this great power for good in their hands, the Wall Street men preferred to do evil. Lincoln's war policy of issuing greenbacks presented them with the dire threat of an adequate supply of currency. So the Shylocks gathered in convention and "perfected" a conspiracy to create a demand for their gold. The remainder of the book was a recital of a series of seven measures passed between 1862 and 1875 which were alleged to be a part of this continuing conspiracy, the total effect of which was to contract the currency of the country further and further until finally it squeezed the industry of the country like a hoop of steel.

Mrs. Emery's rhetoric left no doubt of the sustained purposefulness of this scheme—described as "villainous robbery," and as having been "secured through the most soulless strategy." She was most explicit about the so-called "crime of 1873," the demonetization of silver, giving a fairly full statement of the standard greenback-silverite myth concerning that event. As they had it, an agent of the Bank of England, Ernest Seyd by name, had come to the United States in 1872 with $500,000 with which he had bought enough support in Congress to secure the passage of the demonetization measure. This measure was supposed to have greatly increased the value of American four per cent bonds held by British capitalists by making it necessary to pay them in gold only. To it Mrs. Emery attributed the panic of 1873, its bankruptcies, and its train of human disasters: "Murder, insanity, suicide, divorce, drunkenness and all forms of immorality and crime have increased from that day to this in the most appalling ratio."

"Coin" Harvey, the author of the most popular single document of the whole currency controversy, *Coin's Financial School*, also published a novel, *A Tale of Two Nations*, in which the conspiracy theory of history was incorporated into a melodramatic tale. In this story the powerful English banker Baron Rothe plans to bring about the demonetization of silver in the United States, in part for his own aggrandizement but also to prevent the power of the United States from outstripping that of England. He persuades an American Senator (probably John Sherman, the *bête noire* of the silverites) to co-operate in using British gold in a campaign against silver. To be sure that the work is successful, he also sends to the United States a relative and ally, one Rogasner, who stalks through the story like the villains in the plays of Dion Boucicault, muttering to himself such remarks as "I am here to destroy the United States—Cornwallis could not have done more. For the wrongs and insults, for the glory of my own country, I will bury the knife deep into the heart of this nation." Against the plausibly drawn background of the corruption of the Grant administration, Rogasner proceeds to buy up the American Congress and suborn American professors of economics to testify for gold. He also falls in love with a proud American beauty, but his designs on her are foiled because she loves a handsome young silver Congressman from Nebraska who bears a striking resemblance to William Jennings Bryan!

One feature of the Populist conspiracy theory that has been generally overlooked is its frequent link with a kind of rhetorical anti-Semitism. The slight current of anti-Semitism that existed in the United States before the 1890s had been associated with problems of money and credit. During the closing years of the century it grew noticeably. While the jocose and rather heavy-handed anti-Semitism that can be found in Henry Adams's letters of the 1890s shows that this prejudice existed outside Populist literature, it was chiefly Populist writers who expressed that identification of the Jew with the usurer and the "international gold ring" which was the central theme of the American anti-Semitism of the age. The omnipresent symbol of Shylock can hardly be taken in itself as evidence of anti-Semitism, but the frequent references to the House of Rothschild make it clear that for many silverites the Jew was an organic part of the conspiracy theory of history. Coin Harvey's Baron Rothe was clearly meant to be Rothschild; his Rogasner (Ernest Seyd?) was a dark figure out of the coarsest anti-Semitic tradition. "You are very wise in your way," Rogasner is told at the climax of the tale, "the commercial way, inbred through generations. The politic, scheming, devious way, inbred through generations also." One of the cartoons in the effectively illustrated *Coin's Financial School* showed a map of the world dominated by the tentacles of an octopus at the site of the British Isles, labeled: "Rothschilds." In Populist demonology, anti-Semitism and Anglophobia went hand in hand.

The note of anti-Semitism was often sounded openly in the campaign for silver. A representative of the New Jersey Grange, for instance, did not hesitate to warn the members of the Second National Silver Convention of 1892 to watch out for political candidates who represented "Wall Street, and the Jews of Europe." Mary E. Lease described Grover Cleveland as "the agent of Jewish bankers and British gold." Donnelly represented the leader of the governing Council of plutocrats in *Cæsar's Column,* one Prince Cabano, as a powerful Jew, born Jacob Isaacs; one of the triumvirate who lead the Brotherhood of Destruction is also an exiled Russian Jew, who flees from the apocalyptic carnage with a hundred million dollars which he intends to use to "revive the ancient splendors of the Jewish race, in the midst of the ruins of the world." One of the more elaborate documents of the conspiracy school traced the power of the Rothschilds over America to a transaction between Hugh McCulloch, Secretary of the Treasury under Lincoln and Johnson, and Baron James Rothschild. "The most direful part of this business between Rothschild and the United States Treasury was not the loss of money, even by hundreds of millions. It was the resignation of the country itself INTO THE HANDS OF ENGLAND, as England had long been resigned into the hands of HER JEWS."

Such rhetoric, which became common currency in the movement, later passed beyond Populism into the larger stream of political protest. By the time the campaign of 1896 arrived, an Associated Press reporter noticed as "one of the striking things" about the Populist convention at St. Louis "the extraordinary hatred of the Jewish race. It is not possible to go into any hotel in the city without hearing the most bitter denunciation of the Jews as a class and of the particular Jews who happen to have prospered in the world." This report may have been somewhat overdone, but the identification of the silver cause with anti-Semitism did become close enough for Bryan to have to pause in the midst of his campaign to explain to the Jewish Democrats of Chicago that in denouncing the policies of the Rothschilds he and his silver friends were "not attacking a race; we are attacking greed and avarice which know no race or religion."

It would be easy to misstate the character of Populist anti-Semitism or to exaggerate its intensity. For Populist anti-Semitism was entirely verbal. It was a mode of expression, a rhetorical style, not a tactic or a program. It did not lead to exclusion laws, much less to riots or pogroms. There were, after all, relatively few Jews in the United States in the late 1880s and early 1890s, most of them remote from the areas of Populist strength. It is one thing, however, to say that this prejudice did not go beyond a certain symbolic usage, quite another to say that a people's choice of symbols is of no significance. Populist anti-Semitism does have its importance—chiefly as a symptom of a certain ominous credulity in the Populist mind. It is not too much to say that the Greenback-Populist tradition activated most of what we have of modern popular anti-Semitism in the United States. From Thaddeus Stevens and Coin Harvey to Father Coughlin, and from Brooks and Henry Adams to Ezra Pound, there has been a curiously persistent linkage between anti-Semitism and money and credit obsessions. A full history of modern anti-Semitism in the United States would reveal, I believe, its substantial Populist lineage, but it may be sufficient to point out here that neither the informal connection between Bryan and the Klan in the twenties nor Thomas E. Watson's conduct in the Leo Frank case were altogether fortuitous. And Henry Ford's notorious anti-Semitism of the 1920s, along with his hatred of "Wall Street," were the foibles of a Michigan farm boy who had been liberally exposed to Populist notions.

The Spirit Militant

The conspiratorial theory and the associated Anglophobic and Judophobic feelings were part of a larger complex of fear and suspicion of the stranger that haunted, and still tragically haunts, the nativist American mind. This feeling, though hardly confined to Populists and Bryanites, was none the less exhibited by them in a particularly virulent form. Everyone remote and alien was distrusted and hated—even Americans, if they happened to be city people. The old agrarian conception of the city as the home of moral corruption reached a new pitch. Chicago was bad; New York, which housed the Wall Street bankers, was farther away and worse; London was still farther away and still worse. This traditional distrust grew stronger as the cities grew larger, and as they were filled with immigrant aliens. As early as 1885 the Kansas preacher Josiah Strong had published *Our Country,* a book widely read in the West, in which the cities were discussed as a great problem of the future, much as though they were some kind of monstrous malignant growths on the body politic. Hamlin Garland recalled that when he first visited Chicago, in the late 1880s, having never seen a town larger than Rockford, Illinois, he naturally assumed that it swarmed with thieves. "If the city is miles across," he wondered, "how am I to get from the railway station to my hotel without being assaulted?" While such extreme fears could be quieted by some contact with the city, others were actually confirmed—especially when the farmers were confronted with city prices. Nativist prejudices were equally aroused by immigration, for which urban manufacturers, with their insatiable demand for labor, were blamed. "We have become the world's melting pot," wrote Thomas E. Watson. "The scum of creation has been dumped on us. Some of our principal cities are more foreign than American. The most dangerous and corrupting hordes of the Old World have invaded us. The vice and crime which they have planted in our midst are sickening and terrifying. What brought these Goths and Vandals to our shores? The manufacturers are mainly to blame. They wanted cheap labor: and they didn't care a curse how much harm to our future might be the consequence of their heartless policy." . . .

As we review these aspects of Populist emotion, an odd parallel obtrudes itself. Where else in American thought during this period do we find this militancy and nationalism, these apocalyptic forebodings and drafts of world-political strategies, this hatred of big businessmen, bankers, and trusts, these fears of immigrants and urban workmen, even this occasional toying with anti-Semitic rhetoric? We find them, curiously enough, most conspicuous among a group of men who are in all obvious respects the antithesis of the Populists. During the late 1880s and the '90s there emerged in the eastern United States a small imperialist elite representing, in general, the same type that had once been Mugwumps, whose spokesmen were such solid and respectable gentlemen as Henry and Brooks Adams, Theodore Roosevelt, Henry Cabot Lodge, John Hay, and Albert J. Beveridge. While the silverites were raging openly and earnestly against the bankers and the Jews, Brooks and Henry Adams were expressing in their sardonic and morosely cynical private correspondence the same feelings, and acknowledging with bemused irony their kinship at this point with the mob. While Populist Congressmen and newspapers called for war with England or Spain, Roosevelt and Lodge did the same, and while Mrs. Lease projected her grandiose schemes of world partition and tropical colonization, men like Roosevelt, Lodge, Beveridge, and Mahan projected more realistic plans for the conquest of markets and the annexation of territory. While Populist readers were pondering over Donnelly's apocalyptic fantasies, Brooks and Henry Adams were also bemoaning the approaching end of their type of civilization, and even the characteristically optimistic T. R. could share at moments in "Brooks Adams' gloomiest anticipations of our gold-ridden, capitalist-bestridden, usurer-mastered future." Not long after Mrs. Lease wrote that "we need a Napoleon in the industrial world who, by agitation and education, will lead the people to a realizing sense of their condition and the remedies," Roosevelt and Brooks Adams talked about the threat of the eight-hour movement and the danger that the country would be "enslaved" by the organizers of the trusts, and played with the idea that Roosevelt might eventually lead "some great outburst of the emotional classes which should at least temporarily crush the Economic Man."

Not only were the gentlemen of this imperialist elite better read and better fed than the Populists, but they despised them. This strange convergence of unlike social elements on similar ideas has its explanation, I believe, in this: both the imperialist elite and the Populists had been bypassed and humiliated by the advance of industrialism, and both were rebelling against the domination of the country by industrial and financial capitalists. The gentlemen wanted the power and status they felt due them, which had been taken away from their class and type by the *arriviste* manufacturers and railroaders and the all-too-potent banking houses. The Populists wanted a restoration of agrarian profits and popular government. Both elements found themselves impotent and deprived in an industrial culture and balked by a common enemy. On innumerable matters they disagreed, but both were strongly nationalistic, and amid the despairs and anxieties of the nineties both became ready for war if that would unseat or even embarrass the moneyed powers, or better still if it would topple the established political structure and open new opportunities for the leaders of disinherited farmers or for ambitious gentlemen. But if there seems to be in this situation any suggestion of a forerunner or analogue of modern authoritarian movements, it should by no means be exaggerated. The age was more innocent and more fortunate than ours, and by comparison with the grimmer realities of the twentieth century many of the events of the nineties take on a comic-opera quality. What came in the end was only a small war and a quick victory; when the farmers and the gentlemen finally did coalesce in politics, they produced only the genial reforms of Progressivism; and the man on the white horse turned out to be just a graduate of the Harvard boxing squad, equipped with an immense bag of platitudes, and quite willing to play the democratic game.

Charles Postel

 **NO**

The Populist Vision

"**Y**ou shall not crucify mankind upon a cross of gold." With this indictment of the financial establishment, William Jennings Bryan, a young congressman from Nebraska, electrified the delegates to the Democratic Convention
gathered under the hot roof of the Chicago Coliseum in July of 1896. On the
fifth ballot, Bryan won a surprise nomination as the presidential candidate. The
nomination marked a historic shift in party alignment, with the Democratic
party embracing a platform of minting silver, a federal income tax, and other
reforms demanded by rural and labor constituencies. Two weeks later, at its
convention in St. Louis, the People's party also endorsed Bryan for president.

For Republicans, and a considerable number of "sound money" Democrats, the Populist endorsement confirmed their worst fears about the Bryan
campaign. They viewed the Populists and their reckless currency doctrines as
instruments of "anarchy" and "lawlessness." Theodore Roosevelt, the police
commissioner of New York City at the time, believed that the Populists were
"plotting a social revolution," and to check their efforts at "subversion" he
proposed lining up twelve Populist leaders against a wall and "shooting them
dead." Similarly apocalyptic and fearful language characterized the hard-
fought election campaign that pitted the Democratic-Populist Bryan against
the "goldbug" Republican William McKinley.

Bryan's loss that November inflicted wounds on the People's party from
which it never recovered. Populism failed in presidential politics. It failed to
sustain a viable presence at the polls. And it failed to maintain any semblance
of cohesion, as the movement slid into rancorous discord over who was to
blame. "Middle-of-the-road" Populists accused the architects of "fusion" with
the Democrats of betraying principles. The "fusionists" accused their critics of
failing to recognize political realities. The faithful of both camps continued
to keep the People's party name alive into the twentieth century. But their
small numbers only confirmed that what had once been a powerful social and
political movement was no longer so. Populism failed, leaving in its wake the
question of why.

Lawrence Goodwyn has provided the most stirring explanation: the
"democratic promise" of Populism fell victim to an insidious and Judas-like
"shadow movement" ("fusionists") that betrayed honest and straight "middle-
of-the-road" Populism to the tender mercies of corporate power. Such a

From *The Populist Vision* by Charles Postel (Oxford University Press, 2007), pp. 269–271,
280–284, 286–289. Copyright © 2007 by Oxford University Press. Reprinted by permission of
Oxford University Press, Ltd. www.oup.co.uk.

rendering makes for gripping tragedy. However, it has little to do with the interior fault lines of Populist politics and ideology. It also fails to take into account the external obstacles that the movement faced. Among other things, the Populists had to break the formidable grip in which the two established parties held the political system. This presented a challenge that the People's party came as close to meeting as any third party had since prior to the Civil War. That the Populists realized the electoral strength that they did is at least partly attributable to their innovative melding of "middle-of-the-road" and "fusionist" tactics. Such flexibility was facilitated by the Populists' distrust of partyism, a distrust that also contributed to the Populists' undoing.

Goodwyn's tragedy fits within the larger narrative of the defeat of traditional society by modernity: Populism failed because the wheels of history rolled over it. When social and cultural historians portray late nineteenth-century social movements as expressions of resistance to the market and modernity, it is difficult to avoid the conclusion that such movements, despite the heroism and humanity they may have revealed, were doomed from the outset by an inexorable historical process. In a provocative dissent, James Livingston recognizes comedy where others see tragedy. For Livingston, . . . Populism represented the premodern and republican past. But, unlike the others, he rejects the notion that the destruction of that past frames the tragic narrative of the twentieth century. Modernity offered democratic and progressive possibilities, Livingston contends, and farm and labor movements—with their soft-money doctrines and fear of "concentrated market power"—opposed the advent of the modern market society. The demands of modernity, Livingston implies, required the "eradication of Populism."

The setbacks suffered by the People's party at the polls, however, must not be read as extended referenda on the historical rights or wrongs of the Populist program. Populist electoral setbacks said little about the historic necessity, much less inevitability, of gold or silver, greenbacks or subtreasury loans. Summing up the defeat of the Populists and other late nineteenth-century reform movements, Gretchen Ritter writes that their loss was not determined by either destiny or nature. Their defeat "was not dictated by the anonymous forces of historical progress and economic modernity." Rather, she concludes, "political choice, structural constraints, and historical contingency shaped the fate of the antimonopolists."

Nor did the Populists lose because their views were unrealistic. True, their rhetoric could be far-fetched. Their discussion of the currency, for example, although grounded in plausible assumptions about the benefits of inflation, could also be utopian, paranoid, or apocalyptic. This, however, cannot explain the movement's failures, because the movement had no monopoly on delusional thinking. If anything, the Populists were outdone in this respect by academic and corporate elites who convinced themselves of numerous absurdities. Gold standard advocates, for example, could match any contenders when it came to absurd and paranoid arguments, as they dogmatically insisted that any deviation from a gold-based currency would immediately dispatch civilization to the hell fires of anarchy. Such flights of fancy—"superstition" as the Populists rightly called it—circulated as profound wisdom among American scholars and business leaders. As C. Vann Woodward noted, "The political crisis of the nineties evoked hysterical responses and apocalyptic delusions in more than one quarter." The Populist electoral failure therefore provides for a poor measure of the fanciful or overwrought. But it does say a great deal about which quarter had what political resources in terms of political machinery, mass media, bribery, and fraud—and the will to energetically use such resources.

Populism's failure must also be viewed in light of what came after. In the wake of the defeat of the People's party, a wave of reform soon swept the country. Progressive Era legislation in the first years of the new century expanded the role of government in American life and laid the foundations of modern political development. Populism provided an impetus for this modernizing process, with many of their demands co-opted and refashioned by progressive Democrats and Republicans. By a turn of fate, Populism proved far more successful dead than alive. At the same time, the process of co-optation and refashioning produced a reconfiguration of the social dynamics of reform. The Populist vision for a modern America was increasingly eclipsed by a corporate vision. . . .

The passage of the Federal Reserve Act of 1913 pointed to the direction of the shifting nexus of reform. Aroused to action by the financial panic of 1907, a wide range of banking, industrial, farming, and other business leaders sought to modernize America's archaic and patchwork monetary and financial systems. The banking establishment sought to protect the prerogatives of corporate managers and their control over the new system. The farm lobby and reform Democrats from the West and the South sought to ensure that rural constituencies would be given equitable access. The final product reflected concessions to all parties. Provisions long sought by rural reform included a more elastic currency to facilitate circulation and economic expansion. Later in the twentieth century, the need for such elasticity was well established in financial orthodoxy, although in 1913 some members of the financial establishment continued to denounce the notion as Populist financial heresy. The Federal Reserve Act also provided for a regulated and standardized system of rural lending, making a reality of farmers' demands for access to reliable lines of credit.

In significant ways, however, the Federal Reserve Act represented the eclipse of Populist ideals. The money question, as the Farmers' Alliance Committee on the Monetary System had explained, was ultimately about the "levers of power" and who controlled them. People's party leader Herman Taubeneck had expressed the same idea: "Who shall issue the necessary paper money and control its volume? This is the pivot upon which the money question revolves. It is the pith, the marrow, the alpha and omega of this great subject." To put the levers of control in the hands of the public, the Populists believed, required centralization. It meant replacing the federally chartered and corporately owned banks of the National Banking System with a federal subtreasury system and other institutions centered in the Treasury and Post Office departments in Washington. Alternative proposals circulated within the Farmers' Alliance, including a scheme for regional centralization with a "Cotton States Bank" and a "Grain States Bank" under the direction of regional "Mother Banks." The

People's party, however, insisted on centralizing the power to issue money and credit in the national bureaucracy in Washington.

In this regard, the Populists were no less "centralizers" than their corporate opponents. James Livingston argues that only the corporate elite and their intellectual allies favored monetary centralization because they alone represented modernity, whereas the Populist coalition of farmers and laborers stood for premodern "dispersed assets." But simply because the corporate elite claimed that their views were the only ones that conformed to the requirements of modernity did not necessarily make it so. The Populists were equally committed, if not more committed, to centralization as a means to rationalize and modernize the nation's monetary and credit systems. They looked to the Bank of France as a model, a system that was centralized, rationalized, bureaucratic, and modern, and that formed quite independently of corporate industry. If monetary centralization provides a test of modernity, then the Populists were at least a step ahead of most of their adversaries.

In terms of the levers of power, however, the Federal Reserve System bore little resemblance to the Populist ideal. The problem lay not with centralization, but in the structural distribution of control. If anything, the devolution of responsibilities to regional reserve banks only weakened the possibility of public accountability. The requirement that gave bankers and their business allies a majority on the regional boards of directors did the same. Most strikingly, the enormous power conferred on an unelected Federal Board of Directors epitomized how far monetary "science" had evolved toward an exclusive enterprise. Populists believed that the regulation of the money supply could and must be understood by the people whose business interests and livelihoods were affected by it. Expert statisticians and economists provided an essential service. But when properly compiled and presented, "any mechanic" could understand the essential rules governing currency volume, production, and demand. Gathered in their meeting lodges, farmers and laborers could master the "science of money" and thereby wrest the levers of monetary power from the corporate elite. Such was the Populist vision that faded into memory as a handful of financial wizards took the reins at the Federal Reserve.

The Country Life Movement reflected a change in the social dynamics of rural reform. In the 1880s and 1890s, rural modernization was largely driven by rural people. In the first years of the new century, urban people—government officials, academics, ministers, business leaders—grew alarmed at what they perceived as rural backwardness. The Roosevelt administration set up a Commission on Country Life to explore paths to "better farming, better business, and better living on the farm." The Commission's 1909 report warned that the "incubus of ignorance and inertia is so heavy and widespread" in rural America "as to constitute a national danger." The report pointed to stagnant farm productivity, crude business methods, appalling sanitation and hygiene, overworked women, poor schools, and primitive churches. Country Life reformers looked for remedies. They exuded a sublime self-confidence that through education and regulation, social ills could be healed and those deemed dangerously on the margins could be safely integrated into the progressive society. Much as upper- and middle-class

Progressives had set their sights on "cleaning up" the urban slums, now they would also bring modernity to the rural districts.

The recommendations of the Country Life Commission translated into policy that, for the most part, enjoyed support among rural constituencies. The Smith-Lever Act of 1914 formalized a national system of agricultural extension services to help farmers apply scientific and business methods. Federal and state agencies committed resources to fact-finding surveys and to a broad campaign to improve rural homes, schools, and churches. Progressive Era urban reformers focused on many of the goals of rural modernization that rural Populism had articulated a generation before—a fact that was both the greatest strength and the most glaring weakness of the Country Life Movement.

A number of farm reformers resented what they perceived as an act of usurpation. They pointed out that for years farm organizations had pointed to the same rural deficiencies and the same needs for reform the Country Life Commission presented as new discoveries. Nahum J. Bachelder of the national Grange caustically noted that the Grange itself was a "country life commission," and one with greater knowledge of rural conditions. Bachelder suggested that perhaps the Grange should set up a "commission on city life" to study deficiencies in urban life. Farm reformers who had spent their lives toiling in the traces of rural modernization often resented the paternalistic assumptions that inspired the Country Life Movement.

Country Life reformers paid special attention to improving the lot of rural women. Their proposals closely resembled those heard in the Farmer's Alliance in the 1880s and 1890s to modernize women's lives. They sought to place women's work in the home and garden on systematic and business lines, to boost efficiency by equipping kitchens and laundries with the latest appliances, and to improve women's cultural, social, and economic opportunities. However, when rural women and men discussed these issues among themselves in their suballiance meetings, it carried a different meaning from the concerted campaign of university professors, trained ministers, and other perceived outsiders. Despite their best efforts to reassure their rural subjects of their good intentions, the urban-based reformers often appeared as zealous missionaries seeking, as the Country Life Commission put it, "to teach persons how to live." Farmwomen at times responded coolly to expert lectures on hygiene and health. After wearing themselves out scrubbing and cleaning, they had reason to resent the exhortations from learned professors about clean homes and the civilizing effects of "combating dirt."

Urban reformers expressed similarly paternalistic and condescending attitudes toward the rural church. Again, the agrarian reformers of the previous generation had addressed the same deficiencies of the country churches that the Country Life reformers did. They, too, had criticized the "intense sectarian consciousness" that tended to put doctrine and creed above the social needs of the farmers. As the Country Life Commission put it, the country church failed as "effective agents in the social evolution of their communities." The Populists had felt similarly, and many of them had abandoned the church in search of other avenues of spiritual expression. The Country Life Movement, however, looked to reorganize the country church on the urban model, as urban professors and ministers tried to replace the small rural church with a new, modern, and consolidated church.

Predictably, the urban-based campaign for rural modernization opened fissures of distrust. Although rural people tended to support Progressive Era reforms, they also questioned the intentions of academics, urban ministers, and state and federal government agents seeking to refashion their homes, schools, and churches. Skepticism occasionally led to resistance. Historians have noted that the 1925 Tennessee law against teaching evolution in the public schools, for example, was driven less by ideological objections to Darwin than by an effort to reassert majority will over matters of education and religion in the face of intervention by perceived outsiders.

Meanwhile, academics, church officials, and government experts undertook extensive surveys of "rural problems." Among the problems they sought to resolve was why farmers responded with such ambivalence to urban efforts at rural uplift. Part of the explanation lay with farmers' skepticism about the intentions of their self-appointed urban benefactors. At the same time, a working assumption of the burgeoning field of rural sociology was the need to look deeper into the peculiar features of the rural environment and rural mind that led farmers to resist innovation, science, and progress. For modernity to come to the American countryside, it would take the concerted efforts of scientific experts and state agencies to convince the farmers to go along.

As the influence of urban-based elites in rural reform grew, the reform impulse was channeled along a narrower and more exclusive path. The Farmers' Alliance had originally promised to organize cotton, wheat, and other producers as a class. Rich and poor farmers alike would find strength in business organization. Alliance enterprises quickly demonstrated, however, that such organization was far more accessible to prosperous and land-owning farmers than cash-poor and debt-strapped small farmers and tenants. The Progressive Era system of business organization tilted even more sharply in favor of the former, and largely excluded the latter. The broad Populist "confederation of industrial orders" gave way to a narrower coalition of the propertied and the exclusively white. . . .

The Progressive reformers of the early twentieth century saw themselves uplifting the human condition, shaping popular modes of thought, and engineering the society of the future. The efforts of the Country Life Movement to remake rural life reflected a vision that agrarian scholar James C. Scott describes in a broader context as "high modernism." The concept of "high modernism," Scott writes, is "best conceived as a strong (one might even say muscle-bound) version of the beliefs in scientific and technical progress that were associated with industrialization in Western Europe and in North America from roughly 1830 until World War I." It displayed "a supreme self-confidence about continued lineal progress" and "increasing control over nature." "High modernism," Scott concludes, was a "sweeping vision of how the benefits of technical and scientific progress might be applied—usually through the state—in every field of human activity."

Bringing Scott's concept to bear on American rural history, Deborah Fitzgerald writes that "high modernist" urban leaders of the 1920s and 1930s persuaded reluctant farmers to "become modern." By her account agricultural college professors, government agents, bankers, and other business leaders sought "to bring agriculture kicking and screaming into the modern world." In other words, modernity was imposed from the outside on a largely static rural environment.

Fitzgerald's narrative poses a number of outstanding questions, especially about earlier developments. What does it say about late nineteenth-century social conflict and the historic role of Populism and similar movements? Would the term "high modernism" apply to the Populist vision, at least as Scott defines it? No less than their industrial counterparts, Leonidas Polk, Charles Macune, Mary Elizabeth Lease, Marion Cannon, Reuben Kolb, Herman Taubeneck, Marion Butler, Thomas Nugent, Marion Todd, William Peffer, and a host of other Populist leaders displayed a "muscle-bound" belief in progress, science, and technology. Their "evolutionary imagination" gave them enormous self-confidence that the course of progress was both lineal and knowable. They believed in the human capacity, through government action and otherwise, to harness nature and cure a broad range of society's ills. And they acted accordingly as agricultural commissioners, politicians, state appointees, and executives of powerful farm organizations.

Yet, if the Populist leaders counted among the "high modernists" of their day, they were of a special type. Unlike the Country Life Movement of the early twentieth century, rural Populism grew from rural roots. These roots were evident in the network of men and women—Populism's "organic intellectuals"—that sustained the movement's systems of lectures and rural newspapers and brought a modernizing vision to farmers' homes and meeting lodges. Where the Country Life Movement looked to improve the lot of others, the Populists were modernizers from within. They spoke in the language of self-help and sought improvements on the principle of self-activation.

The Populists incorporated into their modernizing vision mass organizations enrolling millions of common working people. In late nineteenth- and twentieth-century Europe, Asia, Latin America, and Africa "high modernists" of various types—socialists, radicals, nationalists, populists—built their modern systems on labor, peasant, and other mass organizations. In the United States, the Populists took extraordinary strides toward making mass organizations of farmers and laborers the mainspring of their vision of social reconstruction. The Farmers' Alliance and associated "industrial orders" gave flesh to the majoritarian, if not entirely democratic, principles that Populism pursued.

Where the Country Life leaders may have felt most comfortable in the university laboratory or business board meeting, the Macunes and Polks of Populism were at home in gatherings of people with callused hands and sunburned necks. Manual labor was part of the ethos that shaped the possibilities for a broad and inclusive coalition. Many rural Populists disapproved of strikes and labor boycotts and erected walls of hostility against immigrant and Chinese workers in particular. Yet the emergence of labor Populism within the ranks of railway employees, miners, and other sections of the working class revealed that Populism had the potential of an expansive organizational alliance.

As social engineers, the Populists were second to none in terms of earnest commitment and scope of vision. The Populist movement contained too many diverse and contradictory elements to speak of a single Populist social blueprint.

Some of these elements, such as Bellamy's Nationalism, represented influential mental constructs more than a practical system of reform. Other elements were not unique to the Populists at all but were broadly pursued by modernizers among business, academic, and political leaders. This was especially true in regard to race, with all of the ominous implications that entailed.

Nonetheless, the sum of Populist strivings leaves a distinct outline of what their "cooperative commonwealth" might have looked like. In regard to the nation's business, the Populists hoped to take the materials at hand—the latest technologies and organizational systems—and use them to rationalize markets and regulate and centralize the channels of commerce and finance. Their vision involved a complex and dynamic combination of public and private, cooperative and corporate, municipal and nationalized property relations. Progressive Era models contained elements of this complexity. However, the Populist version was more flexible in terms of encroachments on private and corporate prerogatives. This included a major role for the self-organization of labor within the management and structure of the economy, a role that American corporate managers would fiercely—and successfully—resist.

The Populists wanted an active government to ensure fair access to the benefits of modernity. By way of the referendum and the initiative and other political reforms, Populists sought to reshape government as an agency of the majority rather than of the corporate and wealthy minority. A federal income tax on high incomes was part of the Populist goal of checking the concentration of wealth and spreading the abundance of farm and factory to those who produced it. But there was a reason why so much of the Populist imagination focused on publicly owned and subsidized systems of postal delivery, telecommunications, railways, and the perfection of the public system of education. The Populist republic would squarely and equitably place even the rural "clodhopper" on the national and international grid of modern culture and knowledge.

For the 1892 electoral canvass, Thomas Watson published a campaign book under the title *Not a Revolt; It Is a Revolution*. Populism would usher in "a new order of things," "re-mark the lines of life," and bring a complete "revolution in the old systems." In the fever of electoral warfare, both friends and foes of the third-party movement tended to accept similar terms: for better or for worse, a Populist victory at the polls meant a momentous transformation of American society. Through the prism of time, it is apparent that a Populist triumph would have been less of a revolution than advertised. A Populist United States would have taken evolutionary steps to reform and rationalize the capitalist system. Perhaps it would have placed American institutions on paths akin to those of Canada or even Denmark—significant changes but hardly the overthrow of existing conditions. Yet, Populism did indeed represent something momentous. It mobilized millions of ordinary men and women in an effort to steer the political and economic institutions of an increasingly modern, technologically sophisticated, and globally connected society. The significance of this movement lay in the act of trying.

POSTSCRIPT

Were the Populists Irrational Reactionaries?

Richard Hofstadter's thesis represented the first major challenge to the favorable interpretation of the Populists presented in John D. Hicks, *The Populist Revolt: A History of the Farmers' Alliance and the People's Party* (University of Minnesota Press, 1931). This critique was extended, however, by Victor C. Ferkiss, a political scientist, whose "Populist Influences in American Fascism," *Western Political Quarterly* (June 1957) argued that the Populist movement was not based upon egalitarian goals of human freedom. In fact, Ferkiss concluded, by encouraging majority rule over governmental institutions, the Populists committed them selves to a "plebiscitary democracy" very similar to that proposed for Germany by Adolf Hitler. A rejoinder to Ferkiss' argument appears in Walter T. K. Nugent, *The Tolerant Populists: Kansas Populism and Nativism* (University of Chicago Press, 1963). In this effort to rehabilitate the Populist image, Nugent concluded that in Kansas, agrarian reformers were not xenophobic, anti-Semitic, or consumed by the bugaboo of a conspiracy of the "money interests." For an insightful analysis of Hofstadter's rendering of Populism within the context of the historian's craft, see Robert M. Collins, "The Originality Trap: Richard Hofstadter on Populism," *Journal of American History 76* (June 1989):150–167.

Internet References . . .

Booker T. Washington Papers

The complete 14-volume set of Washington's papers is available on this Web site, including the well-known "Atlanta Compromise Address" and his autobiography *Up from Slavery.* Texts include books, articles, speeches, and correspondence covering the years 1860 to 1915.

http://www.historycooperative.org/btw/index.html

Gilded Age and Progressive Era Resources

General Resources on the Gilded Age and Progressive Era.

http://www.tntech.edu:8080/www/acad/hist/gilprog.html

Alcohol, Temperance & Prohibition

This useful Web site offers a wide range of primary source material for researching the history of the prohibition movement, temperance, and alcoholism.

http://dl.lib.brown.edu/temperance/

Anti-Saloon League, 1893–1933

These printed materials are representative of the public campaigns of the Anti-Saloon League from 1893 to 1933. A six-page history of the League and the temperance movement and six biographical essays of movement leaders provide context.

http://wpl.lib.oh.us.:80/AntiSaloon/

The 1920s

This Web site aims to raise awareness about an amazing time in history.

http://www.louisville.edu/~kprayb01/1920s.html

New Deal Network

Offering more than 20,000 items, this Web site focuses on objects, documents, and images relevant to the New Deal. "Document Library" contains more than 900 newspaper and journal articles, speeches, letters, reports, advertisements, and other textual materials that treat a broad array of subjects.

http://www.newdeal.feri.org

After the Day of Infamy: "Man on the Street" Interviews Following the Attack on Pearl Harbor

More than 12 hours of audio interviews conducted in the days following the December 7, 1941, attack on Pearl Harbor in January and February 1942 are included on this Web site. Interviews include the voices of 200 "ordinary Americans" recorded in 10 places across the United States. December recordings were made by fieldworkers contacted by the Library of Congress Radio Research Project to gather opinions of a diverse group of citizens regarding American entrance in the war.

http://memory.loc.gov/ammem/afcphhtml/afcphhome.html

The Response to Industrialism and Reform, War, and Depression

*T*he maturing of the industrial system, a major economic depression, agrarian unrest, and labor violence all came to a head in 1898 with the Spanish–American War. The Progressives brought about major domestic reforms to ameliorate the worst abuses of rapid industrial growth and urbanization. American presidents advanced a proactive foreign policy, but the nation's role as a mediator of global conflicts was pushed to the limit when Woodrow Wilson tried to get the United States to join the League of Nations at the end of World War I.

The most serious problems of inequality were never addressed by the Progressives. African Americans began fighting for civil and political rights. Spokespersons for blacks emerged, but their programs for advancement frequently touched off controversy among both black and white people. There was controversy over whether the prohibition movement curbed drinking or whether it created a climate of lawlessness in the 1920s.

The onset of a more activist federal government accelerated with the Great Depression. In the midst of widespread unemployment, Franklin D. Roosevelt was elected on a promise to give Americans a "New Deal." Every sector of the economy was affected by the proliferation of the alphabet soup New Deal agencies, and historians continue to debate whether the New Deal measures ameliorated or prolonged the Great Depression.

The impending World War killed the New Deal by 1939. With the fall of France to the Germans in 1940, FDR tried to abandon the traditional foreign policy of isolationism by aiding allies in Europe and Asia without becoming involved in the war. The effort failed, and the Japanese attacked Pearl Harbor and destroyed most of the Pacific fleet.

- Did Booker T. Washington's Philosophy and Actions Betray the Interests of African Americans?
- Did the Progressives Fail?
- Was Woodrow Wilson Responsible for the Failure of the United States to Join the League of Nations?
- Was Prohibition a Failure?
- Did the New Deal Prolong the Great Depression?
- Did President Roosevelt Deliberately Withhold Information About the Attack on Pearl Harbor from the American Commanders?

ISSUE 7

Did Booker T. Washington's Philosophy and Actions Betray the Interests of African Americans?

YES: Donald Spivey, from *Schooling for the New Slavery: Black Industrial Education, 1868–1915* (Greenwood Press, 1978)

NO: Robert J. Norrell, from "Understanding the Wizard: Another Look at the Age of Booker T. Washington," in W. Fitzhugh Brundage, ed., *Booker T. Washington and Black Progress: Up From Slavery 100 Years Later* (University of Florida Press, 2003)

ISSUE SUMMARY

YES: Donald Spivey contends that Booker T. Washington alienated both students and faculty at Tuskegee Institute by establishing an authoritarian system that failed to provide an adequate academic curriculum to prepare students for the industrial workplace.

NO: Robert J. Norrell insists that Booker T. Washington, while limited by the racial climate of the day in what he could accomplish, nevertheless spoke up for political and civil rights, decried mob violence, and defended black education as a means of promoting a more positive image for African Americans in an era dominated by the doctrine of white supremacy.

In the late nineteenth and early twentieth centuries, most black Americans' lives were characterized by increased inequality and powerlessness. Although the Thirteenth Amendment had fueled a partial social revolution by emancipating approximately four million southern slaves, the efforts of the Fourteenth and Fifteenth Amendments to provide all African Americans with the protections and privileges of full citizenship had been undermined by the U. S. Supreme Court.

Seventy-five percent of all African Americans resided in rural areas by 1910. Ninety percent lived in the South, where they suffered from abuses associated with the sharecropping and crop-lien systems, political disfranchisement, and antagonistic race relations, which often boiled over into acts of violence, including race riots and lynchings. Black southerners who moved north in the decades preceding World War I to escape the ravages of racism instead discovered a society in which the color line was drawn more rigidly to limit black opportunities. Residential segregation led to the emergence of racial ghettos. Jim Crow also affected northern education, and competition for jobs produced frequent clashes between black and white workers. By the early twentieth century, then, most African Americans endured a second-class citizenship reinforced by segregation laws (both customary and legal) in the "age of Jim Crow."

Prior to 1895, the foremost spokesman for the nation's African American population was former slave and abolitionist Frederick Douglass, whose crusade for blacks emphasized the importance of civil rights, political power, and immediate integration. August Meier has called Douglass "the greatest living symbol of the protest tradition during the 1880s and 1890s." At the time of Douglass's death in 1895, however, this tradition was largely replaced by the emergence of Booker T. Washington. Born into slavery in Virginia in 1856, Washington became the most prominent black spokesman in the United States as a result of a speech delivered in the year of Douglass's death at the Cotton States Exposition in Atlanta, Georgia. Known as the "Atlanta Compromise," this address, with its conciliatory tone, found favor among whites and gave Washington, who was the president of Tuskegee Institute in Alabama, a reputation as a "responsible" spokesman for black America.

What did Booker T. Washington really want for African Americans? Did his programs realistically address the difficulties confronted by blacks in a society where the doctrine of white supremacy was prominent? Is it fair to describe Washington simply as a conservative whose accommodationist philosophy betrayed his own people? Did the "Sage of Tuskegee" consistently adhere to his publicly stated philosophy of patience, self-help, and economic advancement?

One of the earliest and most outspoken critics of Washington's program was his contemporary, W. E. B. Du Bois. In a famous essay in *The Souls of Black Folk* (1903), Du Bois leveled an assault upon Washington's narrow educational philosophy for blacks and his apparent acceptance of segregation. By submitting to disfranchisement and segregation, Du Bois charged, Washington had become an apologist for racial injustice in the United States. He also claimed that Washington's national prominence had been bought at the expense of black interests throughout the nation.

In the first of the following selections, Donald Spivey offers a more recent interpretation that follows the critical assessment of Du Bois. He portrays Booker T. Washington as an authoritarian "overseer" who imposed a militaristic system at Tuskegee and who alienated students and faculty by insisting upon a program that not only subordinated political, social, and civil rights to economic goals but also failed to provide the training necessary to allow students to become capable, skilled artisans.

In the second selection, Robert J. Norrell concludes that Washington never stopped trying to act on behalf of African American interests. He denies that Washington was simply an accommodationist and claims that there was a fundamental similarity between Washington's direct and indirect challenges to white supremacy on the one hand and the substance of the protests sponsored by the National Association for the Advancement of Colored People (NAACP) on the other.

Shine, Booker, Shine: The Black Overseer of Tuskegee

Perhaps Paulo Freire had Booker T. Washington in mind when he wrote in his classic study on education, "The oppressed have been destroyed precisely because their situation has reduced them to things. In order to regain their humanity they must cease to be things and fight as men. . . . They cannot enter the struggle as objects in order later to become men." To Booker T. Washington the sensible thing for blacks to do was to fashion a coalition with whites in power to make themselves indispensable "objects" to the prosperity of the nation. His conception of the proper course for blacks rested upon the blacks' own exploitability. He believed that the profit motive dictated American thought and action. Those who proved themselves antagonistic would remain powerless or be annihilated; those who proved themselves of value would be rewarded. Thus, he contended that social, political, and civil rights were secondary issues for blacks—subordinate to and dependent upon the race's economic importance. This philosophy of uplift through submission drew heated criticism from many black leaders. What is not a familiar story is that in his championing of these ideas, Washington alienated many of his Tuskegee students and faculty members and never gained the full support of the white South. . . .

Like the good overseer, and like his mentor, Samuel Chapman Armstrong, Booker T. sought to make his students superb laborers, that is, totally reliable. He criticized Tuskegee students who showed any signs of being unreliable. "Young men come here [Tuskegee Institute] and want to work at this industry or that, for a while, and then get tired and want to change to something else." To be a good worker, Washington professed, one must understand "the Importance of Being Reliable."

Booker Washington worked diligently to please the dominant white society, to make his blacks "the best labor in the world." He watched his students' every move. He was a stickler for precision and detail. The Founder emphasized such things to the Tuskegee student body and teachers as the proper positioning of brooms. Washington sent a notice to three department heads: "Will you kindly see that all brooms in your department are kept on their proper end. I notice that this is not done now." One faculty member responded on top of the Founder's memo: "This must be a mistake." It was not. Booker Washington demanded that everyone, including Mrs. Washington, place and store brooms with the brush end up.

The Founder placed every aspect of the student's life at Tuskegee under a strict regime of rules and regulations. Committees were formed that conducted daily examinations of the students' rooms and personal belongings. Careful attention was given to whether or not all had toothbrushes. One committee reported that it had noted some "absence of tooth brushes and tooth mugs." The Founder received other reports on the toothbrush situation. "There is a very large number of students that use the tooth brush only to adorn the washstand," one of Washington's student informers reported.

The slightest trace of dirt or grime was call for alarm and disciplinary action at Tuskegee. A committee appointed to inspect one of the dorms noted, "The wood work needs scrubbing and dusting thoroughly." The committee also reported that beds were not properly made in military fashion and some of the linen needed ironing and was improperly folded. Students who left their beds unmade were often punished by not receiving dinner.

When Tuskegee students did dine, they did so under stringent rules and regulations. Talking during meals was permitted only at precise intervals designated by the ringing of bells.

The list of regulations ended with Rule Number 15: "For the violation of the above rules you will be severely punished."

Naturally, students sometimes fell short of the mark. Captain Austin, a stickler for detail, noted that student discipline during meals needed improvement. And no detail escaped his military eye: "Students continue to eat after bell rings and this together with the noise made by the knives and forks tinkling against the plates make it very difficult to hear the adjutant read the notices." In Austin's report to Booker Washington, which contained dining violations, he stated that the men students had become "careless in dress." He complained also about the behavior of women students in the dining hall. "The girls," Austin reported, "are exceedingly boisterous and rough when rising from their tables."

Search and seizure comprised part of the everyday life at Tuskegee. Men and women alike were searched for liquor, obscene materials, or anything else that in some way might contribute to the breakdown of rules or affect the school's "reputation." Searching of students' rooms and personal belongings became official policy at Tuskegee in 1906, when it was written into the School Code.

Booker Washington gave the students' social life the closest scrutiny. The institute forbade male and female students from associating after classes. The woman students received constant reminders from the Dean of Women to remain "moral and pure." This same advice was given to the men students by the Commandant of Cadets. Separate walkways across campus were designated for male and female to guarantee the two kept separated. Male students were forbidden to walk around or near the girls' dormitory after dusk. This was done, as one school official put it, to "prevent the promiscuous mingling of boys and girls."

Washington was working to make Tuskegee students into the type of blacks that the white South relished. Their training was primarily in "how to behave" rather than in how to become skilled tradesmen. To be a skilled crafts-man requires proficiency in mathematical and verbal skills. The school's cur-riculum, however, was industrial almost to the total exclusion of the academic. What academic studies that did exist were secondary and often optional. That the school would commit itself to this type of program was clear from the staff that Washington employed at the school. Most of the faculty members were Hampton graduates, and they knew more about discipline than trades.

The *Southern Workman* reported that Hampton graduates held most of the key posts at Tuskegee Institute, noting the fact that the school's principal was "Hampton's most distinguished graduate." Washington issued a directive in 1908 to his departmental heads in which he stated that he wanted the school to "employ each year a reasonable number of Hampton graduates." He added that he "did not want the number of Hampton graduates decreased on the teaching force at Tuskegee."

The Founder was not completely closeminded in hiring personnel for teaching positions at Tuskegee, but instructors he hired from academic insti-tutions often failed to fit well into his educational scheme because he sub-ordinated every aspect of Tuskegee's educational program to the industrial schooling idea of producing tractable blacks. Blacks from academic universities like Howard, Fisk, and Atlanta were employed at the school. Roscoe Conkling Bruce, a product of Harvard University who headed the so-called academic curriculum at Tuskegee, found that the institute's commitment to preparing students as common laborers was total. Bruce thought that perhaps some of the students might be material for professional careers. He complained about educating students "chiefly in accordance with the demands for labor."

Another thorn in Washington's side was a young instructor in the aca-demic department named Leslie P. Hill, who had been hired by Bruce. Hill obviously failed to adjust to the second-class status of academic studies at Tuskegee. He initiated innovative approaches to his teaching of educational theory, history, and philosophy. However, the Founder regarded Hill as hostile to the educational philosophy of the school. Washington, in his explanation for firing Hill, remarked that the young Harvard graduate seemed to feel that the methods employed at Tuskegee were "either wrong or dangerous."

If he had many of the school's instructors in mind, Hill was absolutely right. Higher education at Tuskegee was a sad joke. Hill recognized that the general atmosphere discouraged serious effort among the industrial faculty. He noted that courses lacked outlines, instructors failed to use facilities properly, and that many of them lacked the competence to teach the skills for which they were hired.

Roscoe Bruce found the entire Tuskegee situation quite perplexing. He understood that Tuskegee was an industrial school—a fact, Bruce remarked, that he was "often reminded of." But he said that he failed to see how students who received little to no academic training would be able to carry on up-to-date craft positions. He wrote to the principal, "You see, the truth is that the carpenter is not taught enough mathematics, the machinist enough physics, or the farmer enough chemistry for the purpose of his particular work." Bruce also found it discouraging that there was no distinction made in the school's curriculum between those students who were going to be teachers and the ones "who plan to make horseshoes or to paint houses."

Washington conceded that some difficulties existed with the industrial idea of education, but that he had said so in his book, *Up From Slavery.*

> I told those who doubted the wisdom of the plan [industrial education] that I knew our first buildings would not be so comfortable or so complete in their finish as buildings erected by the experienced hands of outside workmen, but that in the teaching of civilization, self-help, and self-reliance, the erection of the buildings by the students themselves would more than compensate for any lack of comfort or fine finish.

His point, no doubt, was that problems are to be expected but they will be solved in time.

Regardless of what Booker T. said, Tuskegee was not preparing its students to take their place as skilled artisans in the industrial world. The school maintained a general policy of allowing students to graduate without even having finished a trade course. One report indicated that some positions calling for manual skills had become open to blacks in the South and that the opportunities for the Tuskegee graduates were "greater than ever," but that the students were not properly prepared for these jobs.

Roscoe C. Bruce reported to Washington on another separate occasion in which he complained that upon visiting the Girls' Laundry Department he was struck by the lack of any real skills training. Bruce said that the students did not seem to be receiving instruction in the art of the task but in fact simply performed menial chores.

W.T.B. Williams of the General Education Board conducted a survey of Tuskegee in 1906 and concluded that the student who completed the course of studies had what might be equivalent to a ninth grade education in the public school system. He considered there to be a general lack of training and preparation at the school. In addition, said Williams, "the majority of the students are barely able to read the Bible." He said in conclusion, "Considering the elementary nature of much of this work and the maturity of the students, the daily requirements seem pretty light."

The lack of quality in instruction and academic training at Tuskegee drove Roscoe Bruce to resign in 1906. Washington replaced him with J.R.E. Lee, who fit well into the Tuskegee idea. But Lee's own correspondence reveals the lack of serious academic or skills education at the school. Lee noted that the students who had attended one or two years of education at the general education schools, such as Fisk or Atlanta, were able to go immediately to the senior ranks at Tuskegee. Lee admitted that the work required of students at those schools was "far above the work required here [at Tuskegee]."

The lack of a positive, achievement-oriented atmosphere at Tuskegee had a negative effect on students and teachers. In 1912, one Tuskegee instructor openly admitted that the students they produced were ill-equipped to pursue a skilled occupation in industry. He thought that perhaps the problem lay with the teachers. He begged that they "give more time and attention" to their duties.

Instructors, on the other hand, blamed the problem on the students. Teachers in the industrial classes claimed that the students lacked the necessary attitude to become tradesmen, that they took their assignments lightly and performed them poorly. The instructor in basic construction and design accused the students of not following floor plans and of being sloppy and lazy in the performance of their tasks.

However, the teachers seemed more preoccupied with social matters than with correcting their students' deficiencies. "The young women teachers engage in frivolities hardly in keeping with their calling," W.T.B. Williams reported. "They are good women but not seriously concerned about the work in hand. They seem to give far more attention to dress rather than to almost anything else. . . ."

The female instructors were not alone. The men could stand on their own in terms of being frivolous. They repeatedly hosted gala social outings. One example was the going away party for Booker T. Washington, Jr., given in his honor by the faculty men. It was an elaborate and extravagant affair with orchestra, "seating arrangements patterned after that in the Cabinet Room of the White House," and dinner crowned with "Fried Chicken, Booker T. Washington, Jr. Style."

After a visit to Tuskegee in 1904, Robert Curtis Ogden commented on the "peculiar" social attitude of the school's faculty. He and his other white companions had been guests of honor at a faculty-hosted concert of classical music. Ogden, commenting later to Booker Washington about the concert, said that he believed his guests appreciated the entertainment, but that they would have enjoyed seeing more of the teachers and students at work rather than watching their hosts do their "level best to be like white folks and not natural."

Tuskegee's faculty was imitative of whites, but they were black and not the omnipotent authority symbol that, for example, Hampton's all-white staff was to its students. Tuskegee students, justifiably, found faults with the faculty, the education they received, and the conditions of campus life. They voiced their displeasure. The class in agricultural science at Tuskegee was taught by the renowned George Washington Carver, and he could not escape the growing discontent among students. One student complained that he had come to Tuskegee to learn the most advanced techniques in farming from George Washington Carver but found that the professor seemed to be more interested in producing "hired hands." The student remarked that overall he felt that he was "not receiving progressive instruction."

In addition, students challenged the strict discipline of the school in subtle ways. Julio Despaigne, Washington's key informant in the dorms, reported, "The students have the habit of making their beds at the morning good for when the inspector comes that he can find it well, and in the afternoon they disorder them and put clean and dirty clothes on them."

The rebellion of the students against the oppressive social restrictions of the institute manifested itself in different subtle ways. Some students began skipping chapel to meet with members of the opposite sex. Others volunteered for duties that held a high likelihood of putting them in contact with the opposite sex; a favorite assignment among male and female students was night duty at the school's hospital. Those fortunate enough to draw that duty were on their honor not to fraternize. The administration, however, soon found out the hospital was being used as a place for social carousing. Walter McFadden and Katie Paterson received an official reprimand from the administration "for questionable socializing while on night duty together at the hospital."

Some male students placed latches on their doors to keep night inspectors from entering while they, allegedly, broke school rules. This was met with quick action on the part of the administration. The Executive Council decided that because of

> the misconduct, gambling and so forth, which is indulged in on the part of certain young men who place night latches on their doors and lock themselves into their rooms from teachers' and officers' attempts to get into the room and who jump out of the windows before they can be detected in their mischief: because of this it has been found necessary to remove all the night latches from the doors.

The women students of the laundry class asserted themselves against unfair practices. They could not understand why they should be paid less than their labor was worth. They objected to the hard work with low pay. The young women said that they had the work of both students and teachers to do including that of the summer teachers and that on one occasion they had remained until five o'clock on Saturday evening in order to supply the boys with their week's laundry. "We hope you will not think of us as complainers," they closed in their letter to Booker Washington, "but, simply as children striving to perform their duty; and, at the same time receive some recompense in return. We are asking for higher wages. May we have it?" The Founder's answer was to appoint a committee to investigate their complaint, with the quiet result that nothing ever came of it.

The students' discontent gradually gave way to outright hostility against the school. Students stole from the institution, broke windows, wrecked dormitories, defaced walls, and on several occasions debased the school chapel. Some tried to avoid school and work by pretending to be ill. The institute's physician reported to Booker Washington, "I wish you also to bear in mind that a large number of the students who come to the hospital are not calling because they are ill, but are simply giving way to some imaginary ills, or else taking advantage of the easy method of losing an hour or two from work." One student spoke bluntly to Washington about the feeling among many of the students that to be successful at the school it was required to become "slaves of you [Mr. Washington] and Tuskegee." A group of native-born African students, accused of challenging the authority of one of their instructors and later brought before Washington for discipline, criticized the education they were receiving at Tuskegee and the attitude of teachers, including the Founder himself, who they said "acted as a master ordering his slaves." They concluded: "We do not intend no longer to remain in your institution. . . ."

Students openly rebelled against the school's disciplinary practices. Charles H. Washington, a member of the senior class, considered the prying eyes of the faculty into every aspect of the individual student's private life to be too much for him. He told a faculty member point-blank to pass on the word that they "are to cease meddling with his affairs."

During the last ten years of Washington's reign at Tuskegee, from 1905 to his death in 1915, faculty members alluded to a growing student hostility against them. They became fearful for their personal safety, believing that students were carrying weapons and ready to use them. The situation at Tuskegee became more tense with the passing of each day. Students acted discourteously to instructors in and out of class. A group of faculty members reported to Washington that pupils had become so rebellious that they "never felt safe in appearing before the students."

In the tradition of the overseer whose position is dependent upon his ability to keep those under his charge in line, Washington met student discontent each step of the way with a tightening of rules and regulations. But student unrest continued. The result was that discipline at Tuskegee during the latter part of his administration approached absurdity. Students were suspended for talking without permission, failing to dress according to standards, or even for "failing to take a napkin to the dining hall." Young men students were chastised for "putting their hands in their pockets," and failing to obey that rule, the administration sought to offer "such inducements as will make them do so."

That the punishment students received outweighed the offense is clearly indicated in the case of Lewis Smith, whom a fellow student accused of "over indiscrete conduct with Emma Penny of the same class." Smith, a senior and slated to graduate as class salutatorian, was brought before the administration for allegedly attempting to hug and kiss Miss Penny. Although he denied the charges and his testimony was substantiated by a fellow classmate, the administration saw fit to punish Smith. He was denied the distinction of graduating as class salutatorian.

Smith was lucky. He could have been suspended or expelled—favorite disciplinary measures during the latter years of Booker T.'s rule over Tuskegee Institute. A case in point is the 1912 flag incident. A few members of the senior class of that year decided to celebrate by flying their class flag over Tompkins Hall. They made the unpardonable mistake, however, of not obtaining the administration's permission. School officials considered the students' act a conspiracy against the institute's authority, an "organized movement on the part of some of the members of the senior class . . . and that this was not carried out on the spur of the moment." The accused students begged for mercy and swore that they acted out of no intent to challenge school authority or embarrass the administration. One of the accused vowed they would rather have had their "heads severed from their bodies" than to do anything against Tuskegee. The young men were suspended.

The slightest infraction on the part of the student, or even suspicion of having broken a rule, was reason enough for the Washington administration to notify parents. This had near disastrous results in the case of Charles Bell, a senior who was brought before the administration on the suspicion of having engaged in "sexual misconduct" with a young woman named Varner of the same class. Both denied the charges. There was no eyewitness testimony or other "proof" that Bell and Varner had done anything wrong, except the fact that they were often seen together. The administration, nevertheless, passed its suspicions on to Miss Varner's father. He showed up later on campus with his gun, saying that he would shoot Bell on sight. Bell was forced to leave the institute until the situation quieted.

When Tuskegee students did pose a real threat to the sovereignty of Booker Washington, he showed no mercy. In 1903, a group of Tuskegee students launched a strike against the school. The material on the strike, and it is extremely sketchy, does indicate that the participants objected to the entire Tuskegee order of things. They wanted more academic training, better instruction, more opportunity to learn trades, and an easing of rules and regulations. Washington's response was undiluted: "No concessions."

In an official but insubstantial report on the strike to the school's white financial backers, Booker T. contended that a few malcontents had occupied one of the school's buildings, thinking that this was the way to be heard. The students were not upset with the institute, he said, "nor were they in opposition to any industrial work," but "objected to being required to devote too much time to both industrial work and studies with too little time for preparation." The strike apparently ended as quickly as it had begun once the administration served notice that all those who failed to return to work immediately would be expelled.

Those who obtained an "education" at Tuskegee did so in accordance with the industrial schooling idea and under the watchful eyes of Booker Taliaferro Washington. Student dissatisfaction did nothing to change the Founder's mind about the rightness of the type of educational philosophy he professed and protected. His administration practiced a stiff brand of discipline that it never backed down from. But students, on occasion, continued to try and voice their complaints. Perhaps it is understandable, then, why the Washington administration felt it might be necessary to establish a "guard house" for the purpose of confining its student incorrigibles. It did just that in 1912.

Booker T.'s educational practices were based on his desire to please whites and gain their support. The Founder worked to make whites more a part of the school's operations. He invited them to visit the institute on every occasion. He believed that the school's annual commencement exercises afforded an excellent opportunity to win goodwill from the local whites. "I think it would be well for you to spend a week in Montgomery among the white and colored people," Washington advised a fellow faculty member. "I am very anxious that in addition to the colored people we have a large representative class of whites to attend Commencement." In fact, the Founder considered paying the fares of white visitors to the commencement exercises. The school advertised the commencement of 1904 in the *Tuskegee News*.

Washington did everything possible to bring in more local white support. When Washington received advice from a "reliable source" that if he kept the number of Jews down in attendance at commencement, more local whites would probably come, he responded: "Of course I do not want to keep the Jews away, but I think it would be a good plan to increase the number of Gentiles if possible."

The Founder received unsolicited advice on how to gain more local and national support. One Northerner wrote him suggesting that the school would gain more support if it devoted itself exclusively to the production of domestic servants. The writer suggested that the program should stress "cooking, waiting on table, cleaning silver and washing windows, sewing, dusting, washing and ironing."

In his response, Washington made it clear that Tuskegee did this and more:

> At this institution we give training in every line of domestic work, hence any girl who finishes our course should be able to perform any of the usual duties connected with a servant's life, but one of the most important things to be accomplished for the colored people now is the getting of them to have correct ideas concerning labor, that is to get them to feel that all classes of labor, whether of the head or hand, are dignified. This lesson I think Tuskegee, in connection with Hampton, has been successful in teaching the race.

And, like Hampton, Tuskegee aimed to do more than serve as an agency to place individual domestics. Washington in conclusion said that the most economical thing to be done was to send out a set of people not only trained in hand but thoroughly equipped in mind and heart so that they themselves could go out and start smaller centers or training schools. He believed that it would be of greater service to the whole country "if we can train at Tuskegee one girl who could go out and start a domestic training school in Atlanta, Baltimore, or elsewhere, than we would be doing by trying to put servants directly into individual houses which would be a never ending task.". . .

Booker T. Washington never intentionally did anything to upset or anger Southern whites. He repledged his love for the South and his obedience to its traditions in *My Larger Education,* published four years before his death. The Founder said in that work, "I understand thoroughly the prejudices, the customs, the traditions of the South—and, strange as it may seem to those who do not wholly understand the situation, I love the South." The philosophy of "uplift" for blacks that he preached across the nation and taught at Tuskegee Institute was in accordance with that love and the prevailing racial, economic order. His role was like that of the black overseer during slavery who, given the position of authority over his fellow slaves, worked diligently to keep intact the very system under which they both were enslaved.

Understanding the Wizard: Another Look at the Age of Booker T. Washington

From his day to ours, Booker T. Washington has been viewed as a symbol of the age in which he lived, but he has proved to be an elastic emblem, one pulled and stretched to mean different things to different people. Washington clearly recognized his symbolic role and acted always to shape its meaning, but often he failed to persuade his audience of the object lessons he meant to teach. When Washington's autobiography *Up From Slavery* appeared in 1901, William Edward Burghardt Du Bois began to critique the Tuskegee principal as a black leader chosen by whites. Du Bois wrote that Washington had taken the idea of industrial training for blacks and "broadened it from a by-path into a veritable Way of Life." Washington thought the older black schools that offered a liberal education were "wholly failures, or worthy of ridicule," which was partly why, Du Bois claimed, other blacks had "deep suspicion and dislike" for the Tuskegeean. "Among the Negroes, Mr. Washington is still far from a popular leader." In *The Souls of Black Folk* in 1903, Du Bois perfected his critique, asserting that Washington's program "practically accepts the alleged inferiority of the Negro races." In the 1895 Atlanta Exposition speech—Du Bois dubbed it the "Atlanta Compromise," a pejorative that would prove enduring—Washington had, he insisted, accepted the denial of black citizenship rights. Washington was "striving nobly to make Negro artisans, business men, and property-owners; but it is utterly impossible, under modern competitive methods, for the workingmen and property-owners to defend their rights and exist without the right of suffrage."

In the years after Washington's death in 1915, many readers of *Up From Slavery* would come to a more positive evaluation of the book and its author, and little was added to Du Bois's critique of Washington until 1951, when C. Vann Woodward's sharp irony in *Origins of the New South* seconded Du Bois's criticism of Washington's materialist values: "The businessman's gospel of free enterprise, competition, and *laissez faire* never had a more loyal exponent than the master of Tuskegee." Louis R. Harlan, a Woodward student, stepped forward as the most influential interpreter of Washington with the publication in 1972 of the first installments of both his two-volume biography of Washington and the fourteen-volume *Booker T. Washington Papers.* Professor Harlan criticized Washington's failure to protest the wrongs he witnessed against African Americans, writing that he "acquiesced in segregation," accepted "complacently" the denial of equal rights after Reconstruction, rose to power only because whites chose him to lead blacks, and offered leadership that amounted to a "setback of his race." Professor Harlan emphasized the hypocrisy of Washington's public disavowal of politics at the same time he was working constantly to influence federal appointments in the South. Precisely because Harlan drove his thesis so well and paraded a variety of vivid symbols before the readers about the "faustian" Wizard, he shaped almost all the writing on post-Reconstruction race relations published after 1972. Still, Harlan mainly put Washington in two contexts: the conflict with Do Bois, and Washington's influence in Republican politics. Placing Washington in other historical contexts, however, can yield different understandings. What follows is an attempt to broaden the contextual framework in which Washington's life and work are judged.

◦◦◦

One crucial context for understanding Booker T. Washington was the thinking of whites in the 1880s and 1890s about the future of race relations. Intellectuals and politicians writing to shape public opinion, from both North and South, had turned increasingly hostile toward African Americans. . . .

These intensely hostile views toward African Americans found their way to the average person in the South through the white-owned newspapers in that region, which gave the suggestion of the all-encompassing nature of race trouble in the United States. In his study of shall-town newspapers in the South, Thomas D. Clark found that most papers in the 1880s and 1890s clearly reflected the "Negro-as-beast" thinking of the time. The editors revealed "a general fear of the Negro," whom they often depicted as uncivilized, a "wild, ignorant animal . . . [a] black sensual fiend, whose intense hatred of the white race would cause him to strike with wild demoniacal fury at an unguarded moment.". . .

In his 1895 Atlanta Exposition speech, Washington challenged the images then current in white intellectual and cultural presentations of African Americans, insisting that blacks were a people of "love and fidelity" to whites, a "faithful, law-abiding, and unresentful" people. In its larger thrust, the Atlanta speech represented Washington's attempt to counter the presumption on the part of the white South, and much of the rest of the nation, that African Americans had declined in character and morality in freedom. The overarching message that Washington intended was not acceptance of disfranchisement and segregation but rather a message of progress, of movement forward and upward. In Atlanta, Washington began to offer Americans a new point of view in order to challenge the ideology of white supremacy.

In the years after the Atlanta speech, Washington often spoke up for civil and political rights. This is contrary to Professor Harlan's contention that "his public utterances were limited to what whites approved" and that

Washington's actions on behalf of civil and political rights were exclusively part of his "secret life" of arranging court challenges and organizing protests but taking no public part. In fact, in 1896 Washington told the *Washington Post* that forcing blacks "to ride in a 'Jim Crow' car that is far inferior to that used by the white people is a matter that cannot stand much longer against the increasing intelligence and prosperity of the colored people." In a speech at a Spanish–American War Peace jubilee in Chicago before 16,000 people, Washington asserted that the United States had won all its battles but one, "the effort to conquer ourselves in the blotting out of racial prejudice.... Until we thus conquer, ourselves. I make no empty statement when I say that we shall have, especially in the Southern part of our country, a cancer gnawing at the heart of the Republic, that shall one day prove as dangerous as an attack from an army without or within." In 1899, in response to the horrific Sam Hose lynching in Newnan, Georgia, Washington wrote to the *Birmingham Age-Herald* that he opposed "mob violence under all circumstances. Those guilty of crime should be surely, swiftly and terribly punished, but by legal methods." In June of that year, he published a long article on lynching that appeared in many southern and northern newspapers in which he offered statistics to show that only a small portion of those lynched were even charged with rape. Lynching did not deter crime, Washington insisted; it degraded whites who participated, and it gave the South a bad name throughout the world.

As he became recognized after 1895 as the most prominent African American—and as he consciously accepted the role as leader of his race— Washington constantly gave speeches and interviews and wrote to try to improve the image of African Americans. In practice, creating an ideology to challenge white supremacy usually amounted to influencing what the public media reported about blacks. By the late 1890s Washington frequently sent press releases to both black and white newspapers that either pointed to black achievements that contradicted the "Negro-as-beast" image by showing black success or suggesting actions that contradicted blacks' negative image. Washington seemed always to know what modern-day publicists teach public figures in a critical spotlight: Answering criticism often only fuels the public-relations crisis. He quoted Oliver Wendell Holmes: "Controversy equalizes wise men and fools, and the fools know it." Thus, whether the criticism came from whites or blacks, Washington's first instinct was to keep his response to himself.

Running through all Washington's public efforts to counter the intensely anti-black feeling in the South in the late 1890s was a defense of black education. In virtually every speech, magazine article, or newspaper interview, and in many of the press releases sent out from Tuskegee, Washington dwelt on the great and growing value of African American education, and only some of his emphases promoted industrial education. Having observed the removal of blacks from politics in Mississippi and South Carolina and having fought disfranchisement in Louisiana and lost, Washington by 1900 privately doubted that anything could halt the powerful momentum of the movement to take away black suffrage. The attack on black education that intensified over the course of the 1890s, however, represented an even more fundamental assault, one that Washington had to turn back, or the purpose of his life was defeated.

Senator Benjamin R. Tillman of South Carolina constantly declared that "it is foolish to my mind to disfranchise the Negro on account of illiteracy and turn right around and compel him to become literate.

Up From Slavery represented Washington's ultimate statement of black progress. "No one can come into contact with the race for twenty years as I have done in the heart of the South," he wrote, "without being convinced that the race is constantly making slow but sure progress materially, educationally, and morally." Washington had made himself, and he clearly understood that his life personified the progress that he wanted whites to believe about African Americans in general. Tuskegee Institute was to be seen as an objective demonstration of black progress. From the time that he emerged as a national figure and the leader of his race at Atlanta in 1895, through the publication of *Up From Slavery* in 1901, Washington held fast to the idea that African Americans were going up, not down.

⚜

The local context in which Booker T. Washington worked always circumscribed his options. Like many Black Belt towns during Reconstruction, Tuskegee had been the scene of violent racial conflict over political power. The founding of Tuskegee Institute in 1881 represented an effort for peaceful accommodation between the dominant local whites and a defeated and unhappy black community. The white leaders mainly responsible for helping blacks obtain the initial state support for the new school had earlier helped to direct the vigilantes terrorizing Republican voters and officeholders. The message of the local history was clear: Washington's school, the object lesson of black progress, could only survive if it had the support, or at least the toleration, of the white community. . . .

White hostility to black education was growing more intense in the South at the turn of the century. By 1903, when James K. Vardaman was elected governor of Mississippi, Booker T. Washington was alarmed about what might happen to black education, because the election had demonstrated that "the majority of white people in Mississippi oppose Negro education of any character." Industrial education was growing increasingly controversial. In 1901 the governor of Georgia expressed his view that while Washington was a "good negro . . . I am opposed to putting negroes in factories and offices. When you do that you will cause dissatisfaction between the two races and such things might lead to a race war. The field of agriculture is the proper one for the negro." In *The Leopard's Spots,* Dixon's all-knowing white minister claims that industrial education increases the Negro's danger to white society. "Industrial training gives power. If the Negro ever becomes a serious competitor of the white labourer in the industries of the South, the white man will kill him."

⚜

Booker T. Washington's presence at a White House dinner in October 1901 drastically and permanently undermined his acceptance in the white South. There, he would never return to the level of popularity that he had achieved prior to the dinner. The dinner caused leading figures to erupt in outrage. . . .

Although threatening letters poured into Tuskegee and rumors of Washington's impending assassination circulated for years, Tuskegee's principal forged ahead with the purpose that had taken him to the White House in the first place, the naming of federal appointments in the South. Washington had already prevailed on Roosevelt to name Thomas Goode Jones, his ally and the former Democratic governor of Alabama, to the federal judiciary because Jones had, Washington wrote Roosevelt, "stood up in the constitutional convention and elsewhere for a fair election law, opposed lynching, and has been outspoken for the education of both races." In 1903 Washington began a protracted defense of Roosevelt's appointment of William Crum, a black Republican, to be collector of the port of Charleston, South Carolina, against the determined opposition of Senator Tillman. That same year, after Vardaman had ridiculed whites in Indianola, Mississippi, for "tolerating a nigger wench" as postmistress, which caused the woman in question to resign, Washington encouraged Roosevelt not to accept her resignation. All the while he was leading a vigorous, South-wide campaign against the spreading "lily-white" movement in the Republican party, an effort of southern white Republicans to become as "white" as the Democrats. From Roosevelt's entry into the White House at least through the 1908 presidential election, Washington worked constantly to get and maintain black political influence in the Republican party.

Washington's determination to retain African American political influence has earned him the scorn of historians who have seen hypocrisy in his defense of black officeholding while seeming to disavow the importance of suffrage for African Americans. But it may also be understood as the resolve of a man who believed that it was only just that African Americans get some political positions. Washington believed that those few appointments encouraged blacks to feel that they were not entirely removed from American democracy. It also possibly represented the actions of a man who viewed himself as a race leader in competition with other race leaders—Tillman and Vardaman, for example—and he wanted his race to win occasionally. . . .

Throughout 1903 and 1904, Washington continued to push for black appointments, especially a permanent position for Dr. Crum. From 1901 to 1908, southern newspapers focused on no public issue more consistently than Roosevelt's patronage appointments, and there was virtually no support for his position from white-owned newspapers. In Alabama in 1903, judge Jones presided over criminal trials of men charged with peonage, which occasioned condemnation of Jones, Roosevelt, and Booker T. Washington in the southern press. Time and again, editorials and articles referred back to the White House dinner, a perfect symbol of the way that black political influence led to demands for social equality. Further agitating white concerns about political participation during these years was the proposal of the Indiana congressman Edgar Crumpacker, starting in 1901, to reduce the congressional representation of the southern states that had disfranchised black voters. Booker T. Washington opposed the reduction because he thought it would validate and further encourage disfranchisement, and it was not passed in the Congress, but "Crumpackerism" provided southern politicians and editorialists with evidence of continuing northern "meddling" in whites' control of politics in the South. As such it fueled southern whites' hypersensitivity about protecting white supremacy. . . .

◦◦◦

After 1905 Washington continued on all the same lines, but his intensity waned as events relentlessly buried his optimism. Although the constitutional limits on funding black education had been defeated, Washington worried about the decimation of black primary schools as local school districts across the South discriminated against black children in the allocation of money for teachers, buildings, and books. "In the country districts I am quite sure that matters are going backward," he wrote privately in 1906. "In many cases in Alabama teachers are being paid as little as Ten dollars per month. This of course means no school." Catastrophic events in 1906 further damaged the person viewed as the leader of the race. The Atlanta riot in September and Roosevelt's wholesale dismissal of black soldiers charged with rioting at Brownsville, Texas, in November represented such injustice that African Americans and sympathetic whites in the North questioned the leadership of the man presumably in charge of protecting black rights. Roosevelt added insult to injury in a presidential address in December that grossly exaggerated black criminality and pandered to the common stereotype. Kelly Miller of Howard University wrote to Washington that Roosevelt's speech did "more to damn the Negro to everlasting infamy than all the maledictions of Tillman, Vardaman, [and] Dixon" and predicted that Washington would be held responsible for Roosevelt's behavior. "When Mr. Roosevelt requested you to act as his adviser and when you accepted that delicate responsibility, the world may be expected to believe that he is guided by the advice of his own seeking." With the symbolism of equality that the White House dinner had represented to African Americans now exploded by Roosevelt's bigotry, Washington lost authority as the leader of his race at the same time that the Niagara Movement solidified northern black opposition to him. He never recovered from these reverses, though typically he never acknowledged his defeat.

◦◦◦

The contextual evidence presented herein suggests that Booker T. Washington had great obstacles before him as he tried to lead his race in the 1890s and early twentieth century, and by no honest measure can he be seen as an overall success. His most basic goal was to demonstrate a trajectory of progress among African Americans at a time when the thoroughly white-supremacist society believed that blacks were declining into criminality and even oblivion. He faced a public discourse and a popular culture that were relentlessly set against him. He confronted personal and political enemies in the South who fought to keep him from projecting an ideology of black progress and who, starting in

1901, stirred race hate by attacking Washington for his defense of black office-holders and education. Those attacks undermined his ability to pursue his symbolic action on behalf of black progress, though he never stopped trying.

These reconsiderations of Washington's reputation should make historians think again about how this period of American history is presented. Washington often has been portrayed as the symbol of the age of segregation, he of course standing for acquiescence in Jim Crow. In light of evidence presented herein of Washington's active challenges, direct and indirect, to white supremacy, that understanding seems wrong. So do those views, including ones expressed by Professors Woodward and Harlan, which characterize Washington as "conservative." At the least they represent an unacceptably imprecise meaning for the term. Washington clearly was set against "conserving" the white-supremacist society and culture in which he lived. His purpose was to change things for African Americans. He could only be considered a conservative in his support of the capitalist system.

The designation of Washington as an "accommodationist" also has to be questioned in the light of the evidence herein. He worked too hard to resist and to overcome white supremacy to call him an accommodationist, even if some of his white-supremacist southern neighbors so construed some of his statements. Having conditions forced on him, with threat of destruction clearly the cost of resistance, does not constitute a fair definition of accommodation. The protest-versus-accommodation dichotomy has functioned as virtually a Manichaean divide in writing about African American leadership. The tendency to make protest leaders the good guys and accommodators the bad guys reflects the sentiments at large in society since the Civil Rights Movement. If Booker T. Washington has been the main historical antecedent for accommodationism as the misguided opposite of protest, and if in fact "accommodationism" misrepresents much of his real work, then writing about American race relations must be reevaluated. Indeed, there have been few if any black "leaders" in American history who were not protest leaders in some measure. It is only by comparing degrees of protest commitment, or preferring certain styles of protest to others, that distinctions are drawn (and often overdrawn). This divide has also been understood as between "idealism" and "realism," and historians have favored idealists in writing about black leaders, perhaps because of their self-identity with Washington's critics. In the early 1920s, Kelly Miller noted that "there always existed a small group of assertive Negroes . . . composed mainly of college bred men of liberal culture who were unwilling to compromise their intellectual integrity by surrendering the abstract claim of political rights. They could not tolerate the suggestion of inferiority which Washington's program implied. . . . The man with the theory always has the advantage of the man with the thing, in abstract disquisition. Since Mr. Washington's death, this group has gained the ascendancy in dominating the thought and opinion of the race, but has not been able to realize to the least degree the rights and recognition so vehemently demanded."

The protest-accommodation dichotomy has obscured the fundamental similarity of the substance of Washington's action to the protests agenda put forward starting in 1909 by the National Association for the Advancement of

Colored People (NAACP). Washington made public protests against discrimination on railroads, lynching, unfair voting qualifications, discriminatory funding in education, segregated housing legislation, and discrimination by labor unions—the latter two protests coming after 1910. He arranged and personally provided partial funding for lawsuits challenging disfranchisement, jury discrimination, and peonage. And he campaigned constantly against the pernicious images projected in the media and popular culture about blacks, including the 1915 protest against *Birth of a Nation*. He attempted to organize a national black newspaper. The NAACP would have the same protest concerns about segregated public accommodations, lynching, the criminal justice system, and economic discrimination, and it would bring legal challenges to protect blacks' right to vote, get an education, and have fair access to housing. It would also condemn regularly the ugly stereotypes prevalent in American life, starting with *Birth of a Nation* and continuing through *Amos 'n' Andy* on radio in the early 1930s, Hollywood films in the 1940s, and *Amos 'n' Andy* on television in the 1950s. The NAACP did, of course, establish a national publication, *Crisis*, that accomplished much of what Washington had in mind. Washington's anticipation of virtually all the NAACP protest agenda suggests that a consensus of what needed to be done to protect black rights had been identified as early as 1900, and he and the NAACP had in turn pursued it.

It seems that much common ground lay beneath the two men slugging it out for leadership of the race. Beyond the civil rights strategies that they both embraced in one way or another, they shared a similar despair at the inability of whites to see the achievement of so much decency and intelligence among African Americans. Although Du Bois held the African past in higher regard than Washington did, they both were convinced that people of African descent had been readily civilized. Both were deeply dismayed by the disjuncture between their own achievements and the awful reputation of African Americans as a group among whites. Although Washington did not voice it openly, he and Du Bois understood in similar ways the downward trajectory of black prospects between 1900 and 1908. They agreed that intelligence among African Americans had to be manifest in order to overcome the race's reputation for weakness and poor character, and they also believed that the development of a cadre of black leaders and achievers was necessary to accomplish that. To be sure, they had somewhat different ideas of how to develop African American exemplars, but the nurturing of "human capital" clearly was the first goal of each as a race leader. It is partly because each man distrusted the other so much personally and was so determined to see the other as a major obstruction to his own purposes that their similarities of thought and strategy have been overlooked.

Led by Du Bois, however, historians confused the style with the substance of Booker T. Washington. Many historians have shown a narrow-mindedness about black leaders' styles: African American leaders must always be "lions" like Frederick Douglass, Du Bois, Martin Luther King Jr., or Jesse Jackson. They cannot be "foxes" or "rabbits," else they will be accused of lacking manhood. On the level of sound logic, historians must be honest in recognizing that protest has yielded the desired results more episodically than consistently.

Other strategies for change have worked better at other times, and external influences have also been the prime determinant of change at some points. It is misleading to teach that change is the result exclusively, or even predominantly, of protest.

But then Washington also misled when he taught that economic uplift would ultimately bring the return of political rights. In a hundred different ways he expressed his faith that a black person who acquired economic independence would command the respect of white neighbors and ultimately with it would come the full rights of citizenship. But he never seems to have acknowledged, not even privately, what was clear from the anti-industrial-education arguments made by Dixon and others at the turn of the century—that most whites objected fundamentally to the rise in status represented by a black skilled worker, business proprietor, or landowner. To concede that would have undermined his economic strategy. And there was no other realistic avenue for progress; certainly, neither politics nor protest would work in the South of 1901. Instead, he did what any good public-relations man does—he ignored the facts that did not fit his presentation of reality. He insisted that blacks would rise in status through education and economic success. To a certain extent, events after his death vindicated his faith: World wars, great migrations, and a vastly expanded national government did bring enough economic opportunity to free many African Americans from the South's hostility to all black economic progress. But those events also brought a greater chance for political solutions, and it would be political action in the 1960s that ended segregation and disfranchisement.

Notwithstanding the sympathetic attitude toward Booker T. Washington herein, let it be understood that he failed in his larger purpose of persuading whites that African Americans were progressing rather than degenerating. His public relations campaign simply could not overcome the intense political and cultural authority of white supremacy that mounted in the 1890s and held sway in the early twentieth century. But neither did the efforts of the NAACP in that regard succeed until World War II, when the national resolve to defeat racist enemies resulted in a commitment, some of it based in government propaganda, to the rejection of racial stereotypes in American culture. The removal of anti-black stereotypes from mass culture that began during World War II enabled the acceptance of African American equality in the 1950s and 1960s. Washington did not succeed in remaking the black image in the American mind, but he identified it as a necessary challenge that others did meet. He should be credited with anticipating the "modern" world in which image was more readily manipulated, and sometimes more important, than reality. His efforts to shape his own symbolism, and that of African Americans as a group, should be marked as a shrewd and valiant effort to lift his people.

POSTSCRIPT

Did Booker T. Washington's Philosophy and Actions Betray the Interests of African Americans?

Discussions of race relations in the late nineteenth- and early twentieth-century United States invariably focus on the ascendancy of Booker T. Washington, his apparent accommodation to existing patterns of racial segregation, and the conflicting traditions within black thought, epitomized by the clash between Washington and Du Bois. Seldom, however, is attention given to black nationalist thought in the "Age of Booker T. Washington."

Black nationalism, centered on the concept of racial solidarity, has been a persistent theme in African American history, and it reached one of its most important stages of development between 1880 and 1920. In the late 1800s Henry McNeal Turner and Edward Wilmot Blyden encouraged greater interest in the repatriation of black Americans to Africa, especially Liberia. This goal continued into the twentieth century and culminated in the "Back-to-Africa" program of Marcus Garvey and his Universal Negro Improvement Association. Interestingly, Booker T. Washington also exhibited nationalist sentiment by encouraging blacks to withdraw from white society, develop their own institutions and businesses, and engage in economic and moral uplift. Washington's nationalism concentrated on economic self-help and manifested itself in 1900 with the establishment of the National Negro Business League.

A thorough assessment of the protest and accommodation views of black Americans is presented in August Meier, *Negro Thought in America, 1880–1915* (University of Michigan Press, 1963). Rayford Logan, in *The Betrayal of the Negro: From Rutherford B. Hayes to Woodrow Wilson* (Macmillan, 1965), describes the last quarter of the nineteenth century as "the nadir" for black life. By far the best studies on Booker T. Washington are two volumes by Louis R. Harlan: *Booker T. Washington: The Making of a Black Leader, 1856–1901* (Oxford University Press, 1972) and *Booker T. Washington: The Wizard of Tuskegee, 1901–1915* (Oxford University Press, 1983). In addition, Harlan has edited the 13-volume *Booker T. Washington Papers* (University of Illinois Press, 1972–1984). For assessments of two of Booker T. Washington's harshest critics, see Stephen R. Fox's *The Guardian of Boston: William Monroe Trotter* (Atheneum, 1970) and David Levering Lewis's two Pulitzer Prize winning volumes, *W. E. B. Du Bois: Biography of a Race, 1868–1919* (Henry Holt, 1993) and *W. E. B. Du Bois: The Fight for Equality and the American Century, 1919–1963* (Henry Holt, 2000).

John H. Bracey, Jr., August Meier, and Elliott Rudwick, in *Black Nationalism in America* (Bobbs-Merrill, 1970), provide an invaluable collection of documents pertaining to black nationalism. See also Edwin S. Redkey, *Black*

Exodus: Black Nationalist and Back-to-Africa Movements, 1890–1910 (Yale University Press, 1969), and Hollis R. Lynch, *Edward Wilmot Blyden: Pan-Negro Patriot, 1832–1912* (Oxford University Press, 1967). Diverse views of Marcus Garvey, who credited Booker T. Washington with inspiring him to seek a leadership role on behalf of African Americans, are found in Edmund David Cronon, *Black Moses: The Story of Marcus Garvey and the Universal Negro Improvement Association* (University of Wisconsin Press, 1955); Tony Martin, *Race First: The Ideological and Organizational Struggles of Marcus Garvey and the UNIA* (Greenwood Press, 1976); and Judith Stein, *The World of Marcus Garvey: Race and Class in Modern Society* (Louisiana State University Press, 1986). Some of Garvey's own writings are collected in Amy Jacques-Garvey, ed., *Philosophy and Opinions of Marcus Garvey* (1925; reprint; Atheneum, 1969).

Race relations in the late nineteenth century are explored in C. Vann Woodward, *The Strange Career of Jim Crow,* 2nd rev. ed. (Oxford University Press, 1966), a volume that sparked a lively historiographical debate concerning the origins of segregation. Of the numerous challenges to the Woodward thesis that a full-blown pattern of racial segregation did not emerge until 1890, Howard N. Rabinowitz's *Race Relations in the Urban South, 1865–1890* (Oxford University Press, 1978) is one of the most insightful. Robert J. Norrell provides the most recent overview of American race relations in *The House I Live In: Race in the American Century* (Oxford University Press, 2005). In addition, a number of monographs have appeared over the past four decades, which explore the development of the African American presence in the nation's major cities. Among the best of these urban studies are Gilbert Osofsky, *Harlem: The Making of a Ghetto: Negro New York, 1890–1930* (Harper & Row, 1966); Allan H. Spear, *Black Chicago: The Making of a Negro Ghetto, 1890–1920* (University of Chicago Press, 1967); Kenneth L. Kusmer, *A Ghetto Takes Shape: Black Cleveland, 1870–1930* (University of Illinois Press, 1976); and George C. Wright, *Life Behind a Veil: Blacks in Louisville, Kentucky, 1865–1930* (Louisiana State University Press, 1985).

ISSUE 8

Did the Progressives Fail?

YES: Richard M. Abrams, from "The Failure of Progressivism," in Richard Abrams and Lawrence Levine, eds., *The Shaping of the Twentieth Century,* 2nd ed. (Little, Brown, 1971)

NO: Arthur S. Link and Richard L. McCormick, from *Progressivism* (Harlan Davidson, 1983)

ISSUE SUMMARY

YES: Professor of history Richard M. Abrams maintains that progressivism was a failure because it tried to impose a uniform set of values upon a culturally diverse people and never seriously confronted the inequalities that still exist in American society.

NO: Professors of history Arthur S. Link and Richard L. McCormick argue that the Progressives were a diverse group of reformers who confronted and ameliorated the worst abuses that emerged in urban industrial America during the early 1900s.

*P*rogressivism is a word used by historians to define the reform currents in the years between the end of the Spanish-American War and America's entrance into the Great War in Europe in 1917. The so-called Progressive movement had been in operation for over a decade before the label was first used in the 1919 electoral campaigns. Former president Theodore Roosevelt ran as a third-party candidate in the 1912 election on the Progressive party ticket, but in truth the party had no real organization outside of the imposing figure of Theodore Roosevelt. Therefore, as a label, "progressivism" was rarely used as a term of self-identification for its supporters. Even after 1912, it was more frequently used by journalists and historians to distinguish the reformers of the period from socialists and old-fashioned conservatives.

The 1890s was a crucial decade for many Americans. From 1893 until almost the turn of the century, the nation went through a terrible economic depression. With the forces of industrialization, urbanization, and immigration wreaking havoc upon the traditional political, social, and economic structures of American life, changes were demanded. The reformers responded in a variety of ways. The proponents of good government believed that democracy was threatened because the cities were ruled by corrupt political machines while the state legislatures were dominated by corporate interests. The cure was to purify democracy and place government directly in the hands of the people through such devices as the initiative, referendum, recall, and the direct election of local school board officials, judges, and U.S. senators.

Social justice proponents saw the problem from a different perspective. Settlement workers moved into cities and tried to change the urban environment. They pushed for sanitation improvements, tenement house reforms, factory inspection laws, regulation of the hours and wages of women, and the abolition of child labor.

A third group of reformers considered the major problem to be the trusts. They argued for controls over the power of big business and for the preservation of the free enterprise system. Progressives disagreed on whether the issue was size or conduct and on whether the remedy was trust-busting or the regulation of big business. But none could deny the basic question: How was the relationship between big business and the U.S. government to be defined?

How successful was the Progressive movement? What triggered the reform impulse? Who were its leaders? How much support did it attract? More important, did the laws that resulted from the various movements fulfill the intentions of its leaders and supporters?

In the following selections, Richard M. Abrams distinguishes the Progressives from other reformers of the era, such as the Populists, the Socialists, the mainstream labor unions, and the corporate reorganization movement. He then argues that the Progressive movement failed because it tried to impose a uniform set of middle-class Protestant moral values upon a nation that was growing more culturally diverse, and because the reformers supported movements that brought about no actual changes or only superficial ones at best. The real inequalities in American society, says Abrams, were never addressed.

In contrast, Arthur S. Link and Richard L. McCormick view progressivism from the point of view of the reformers and rank it as a qualified success. They survey the criticisms of the movement made by historians since the 1950s and generally find them unconvincing. They maintain that the Progressives made the first real attempts to change the destructive direction in which modern urban-industrial society was moving.

YES

Richard M. Abrams

The Failure of Progressivism

Our first task is definitional, because clearly it would be possible to beg the whole question of "failure" by means of semantical niceties. I have no intention of being caught in that kind of critics' trap. I hope to establish that there was a distinctive major reform movement that took place during most of the first two decades of this century, that it had a mostly coherent set of characteristics and long-term objectives, and that, measured by its own criteria—not criteria I should wish, through hindsight and preference, to impose on it—it fell drastically short of its chief goals.

One can, of course, define a reform movement so broadly that merely to acknowledge that we are where we are and that we enjoy some advantages over where we were would be to prove the "success" of the movement. In many respects, Arthur Link does this sort of thing, both in his and William B. Catton's popular textbook, *American Epoch,* and in his article, "What Happened to the Progressive Movement in the 1920s?" In the latter, Link defines "progressivism" as a movement that "began convulsively in the 1890s and waxed and waned afterward to our own time, to insure the survival of democracy in the United States by the enlargement of governmental power to control and offset the power of private economic groups over the nation's institutions and life." Such a definition may be useful to classify data gathered to show the liberal sources of the enlargement of governmental power since the 1890s; but such data would not be finely classified enough to tell us much about the *non*-liberal sources of governmental power (which were numerous and important), about the distinctive styles of different generations of reformers concerned with a liberal society, or even about vital distinctions among divergent reform groups in the era that contemporaries and the conventional historical wisdom have designed as progressive. . . .

Now, without going any further into the problem of historians' definitions which are too broad or too narrow—there is no space here for such an effort—I shall attempt a definition of my own, beginning with the problem that contemporaries set themselves to solve and that gave the era its cognomen, "progressive." That problem was *progress*—or more specifically, how American society was to continue to enjoy the fruits of material progress without the accompanying assault upon human dignity and the erosion of the conventional values and moral assumptions on which the social order appeared to rest. . . .

To put it briefly and yet more specifically, a very large body of men and women entered into reform activities at the end of the nineteenth century to translate "the national credo" (as Henry May calls it) into a general program for social action. Their actions, according to Richard Hofstadter, were "founded upon the indigenous Yankee-Protestant political tradition [that] assumed and demanded the constant disinterested activity of the citizen in public affairs, argued that political life ought to be run, to a greater degree than it was, in accordance with general principles and abstract laws apart from and superior to personal needs, and expressed a common feeling that government should be in good part an effort to moralize the lives of individuals while economic life should be intimately related to the stimulation and development of individual character."

The most consistently important reform impulse, among many reform impulses, during the progressive era grew directly from these considerations. It is this reform thrust that we should properly call "the progressive movement." We should distinguish it carefully from reform movements in the era committed primarily to other considerations.

The progressive movement drew its strength from the old mugwump reform impulse, civil service reform, female emancipationists, prohibitionists, the social gospel, the settlement-house movement, some national expansionists, some world peace advocates, conservation advocates, technical efficiency experts, and a wide variety of intellectuals who helped cut through the stifling, obstructionist smokescreen of systematized ignorance. It gained powerful allies from many disadvantaged business interests that appealed to politics to redress unfavorable trade positions; from some ascendant business interests seeking institutional protection; from publishers who discovered the promotional value of exposes; and from politicians-on-the-make who sought issues with which to dislodge long-lived incumbents from their place. Objectively it focused on or expressed (1) a concern for responsive, honest, and efficient government, on the local and state levels especially; (2) recognition of the obligations of society—particularly of an affluent society—to its underprivileged; (3) a desire for more rational use of the nation's resources and economic energies; (4) a rejection, on at least intellectual grounds, of certain social principles that had long obstructed social remedies for what had traditionally been regarded as irremediable evils, such as poverty; and, above all, (5) a concern for the maintenance or restoration of a consensus on what conventionally had been regarded as *fixed moral* principles. "The first and central faith in the national credo," writes Professor May, "was, as it always had been, the reality, certainty, and eternity of moral values. . . . A few thought and said that ultimate values and goals were unnecessary, but in most cases this meant that they believed so deeply in a consensus on these matters that they could not imagine a serious challenge." Progressives shared this faith with most of the rest of the country, but they also conceived of themselves, with a grand sense of stewardship, as its heralds, and its agents.

The progressive movement was (and is) distinguishable from other Contemporary reform movements not only by its devotion to social conditions regarded, by those within it as well as by much of the generality, as *normative,* but also by its definition of what forces threatened that order. More specifically, progressivism directed its shafts at five principal enemies, each in its own way representing reform:

1. The socialist *reform movement*—because, despite socialism's usually praiseworthy concern for human dignity, it represented the subordination of the rights of private property and of individualistic options to objectives that often explicitly threatened common religious beliefs and conventional standards of justice and excellence.
2. The corporate reorganization of American business, which I should call the *corporate reform movement* (its consequence has, after all, been called "the corporate revolution")—because it challenged the traditional relationship of ownership and control of private property, because it represented a shift from production to profits in the entrepreneurial definition of efficiency, because it threatened the proprietary small-business character of the American social structure, because it had already demonstrated a capacity for highly concentrated and socially irresponsible power, and because it sanctioned practices that strained the limits of conventionality and even legality.
3. *The labor union movement*—because despite the virtues of unionized labor as a source of countervailing force against the corporations and as a basis for a more orderly labor force, unionism (like corporate capitalism and socialism) suggested a reduction of individualistic options (at least for wage-earners and especially for small employers), and a demand for a partnership with business management in the decision-making process by a class that convention excluded from such a role.
4. *Agrarian radicalism*, and populism in particular—because it, too, represented (at least in appearance) the insurgency of a class conventionally believed to be properly excluded from a policy-making role in the society, a class graphically represented by the "Pitchfork" Bens and "Sockless" Jerrys, the "Cyclone" Davises and "Alfalfa" Bills, the wool hat brigade and the rednecks.
5. *The ethnic movement*—the demand for specific political and social recognition of ethnic or ex-national affiliations—because accession to the demand meant acknowledgment of the fragmentation of American society as well as a retreat from official standards of integrity, honesty, and efficiency in government in favor of standards based on personal loyalty, partisanship, and sectarian provincialism.

Probably no two progressives opposed all of these forces with equal animus, and most had a noteworthy sympathy for one or more of them. . . .

So much for what progressivism was not. Let me sum it up by noting that what it rejected and sought to oppose necessarily says much about what it was—perhaps even more than can be ascertained by the more direct approach.

My thesis is that progressivism failed. It failed in what it—or what those who shaped it—conceived to be its principal objective. And that was, over and above everything else, to restore or maintain the conventional consensus on a particular view of the universe, a particular set of values, and a particular constellation of behavioral modes in the country's commerce, its industry, its social relations, and its politics. Such a view, such values, such modes were challenged by the influx of diverse religious and ethnic elements into the nation's social and intellectual stream, by the overwhelming economic success and power of the corporate form of business organization, by the subordination of the work-ethic bound up within the old proprietary and craft enterprise system, and by the increasing centrality of a growing proportion of low-income, unskilled, wage-earning classes in the nation's economy and social structure. Ironically, the *coup de grâce* would be struck by the emergence of a philosophical and scientific rationale for the existence of cultural diversity within a single social system, a rationale that largely grew out of the very intellectual ferment to which progressivism so substantially contributed.

Progressivism sought to save the old view, and the old values and modes, by educating the immigrants and the poor so as to facilitate their acceptance of and absorption into the Anglo-American mode of life, or by excluding the "unassimilable" altogether; by instituting antitrust legislation or, at the least, by imposing regulations upon corporate practices in order to preserve a minimal base for small proprietary business enterprise; by making legislative accommodations to the newly important wage-earning classes—accommodations that might provide some measure of wealth and income redistribution, on-the-job safety, occupational security, and the like—so as to forestall a forcible transfer of policy-making power away from the groups that had conventionally exercised that power; and by broadening the political selection process, through direct elections, direct nominations, and direct legislation, in order to reduce tensions caused unnecessarily by excessively narrow and provincial cliques of policymakers. When the economic and political reforms failed to restore the consensus by giving the previously unprivileged an ostensible stake in it, progressive energies turned increasingly toward using the force of the state to proscribe or restrict specifically opprobrious modes of social behavior, such as gaming habits, drinking habits, sexual habits, and Sabbatarian habits. In the ultimate resort, with the proliferation of sedition and criminal syndicalist laws, it sought to constrict political discourse itself. And (except perhaps for the disintegration of the socialist movement) *that* failed, too.

One measure of progressivism's failure lies in the xenophobic racism that reappeared on a large scale even by 1910. In many parts of the country, for example, in the far west and the south, racism and nativism had been fully blended with reform movements even at the height of progressive activities there. The alleged threats of "coolie labor" to American living standards, and of "venal" immigrant and Negro voting to republican institutions generally, underlay the alliance of racism and reform in this period. By and large, however, for the early progressive era the alliance was conspicuous only in the south and on the west coast. By 1910, signs of heightening ethnic animosities, most notably anti-Catholicism, began appearing in other areas of the country as well. As John Higham has written, "It is hard to explain the rebirth of anti-Catholic ferment [at this time] except as an outlet for expectations which progressivism raised and then failed to fulfill." The failure here was in part the inability of reform to deliver a meaningful share of the social surplus to the groups left out of the general national progress, and in part the inability of reform to achieve its objective of assimilation and consensus.

The growing ethnic animus, moreover, operated to compound the difficulty of achieving assimilation. By the second decade of the century, the objects of the antagonism were beginning to adopt a frankly assertive posture. The World War, and the ethnic cleavages it accentuated and aggravated, represented only the final blow to the assimilationist idea; "hyphenate" tendencies had already been growing during the years before 1914. It had only been in 1905 that the Louisville-born and secular-minded Louis Brandeis had branded as "disloyal" all who "keep alive" their differences of origin or religion. By 1912, by now a victim of anti-Semitism and aware of a rising hostility toward Jews in the country, Brandeis had become an active Zionist; before a Jewish audience in 1913, he remarked how "practical experience" had convinced him that "to be good Americans, we must be better Jews, and to be better Jews, we must become Zionists."

Similarly, American Negroes also began to adopt a more aggressive public stance after having been subdued for more than a decade by antiblack violence and the accommodationist tactics suggested in 1895 by Booker T. Washington. As early as 1905, many black leaders had broken with Washington in founding the Niagara Movement for a more vigorous assertion of Negro demands for equality. But most historians seem to agree that it was probably the Springfield race riot of 1908 that ended illusions that black people could gain an equitable share in the rewards of American culture by accommodationist or assimilationist methods. The organization of the NAACP in 1909 gave substantive force for the first time to the three-year-old Niagara Movement. The year 1915 symbolically concluded the demise of accommodationism. That year, the Negro-baiting movie, "The Birth of a Nation," played to massive, enthusiastic audiences that included notably the president of the United States and the chief justice of the Supreme Court; the KKK was revived; and Booker T. Washington died. The next year, black nationalist Marcus Garvey arrived in New York from Jamaica.

Meanwhile, scientific knowledge about race and culture was undergoing a crucial revision. At least in small part stimulated by a keen self-consciousness of his own "outsider" status in American culture, the German-Jewish immigrant Franz Boas was pioneering in the new anthropological concept of "cultures," based on the idea that human behavioral traits are conditioned by historical traditions. The new view of culture was in time to undermine completely the prevailing evolutionary view that ethnic differences must mean racial inequality. The significance of Boas's work after 1910, and that of his students A. L. Kroeber and Clyde Kluckhohn in particular, rests on the fact that the racist thought of the progressive era had founded its intellectual rationale on the monistic, evolutionary view of culture; and indeed much of the progressives' anxiety over the threatened demise of "the American culture" had been founded on that view.

Other intellectual developments as well had for a long time been whittling away at the notion that American society had to stand or fall on the unimpaired coherence of its cultural consensus. Yet the new work in anthropology, law, philosophy, physics, psychology, and literature only unwittingly under-mined that assumption. Rather, it was only as the ethnic hostilities grew, and especially as the power of the state came increasingly to be invoked against dis-senting groups whose ethnic "peculiarities" provided an excuse for repression, that the new intelligence came to be developed. "The world has thought that it must have its culture and its political unity coincide," wrote Randolph Bourne in 1916 while chauvinism, nativism, and antiradicalism were mounting; now it was seeing that cultural diversity might yet be the salvation of the liberal society—that it might even serve to provide the necessary countervailing force to the power of the state that private property had once served (in the schema of Locke, Harrington, and Smith) before the interests of private property became so highly concentrated and so well blended with the state itself.

The telltale sign of progressivism's failure was the violent crusade against dissent that took place in the closing years of the Wilson administration. It is too easy to ascribe the literal hysteria of the postwar years to the dislocations of the War alone. Incidents of violent repression of labor and radical activities had been growing remarkably, often in step with xenophobic outbreaks, for several years before America's intervention in the War. To quote Professor Higham once more. "The seemingly unpropitious circumstances under which antiradi-calism and anti-Catholicism came to life [after 1910] make their renewal a subject of moment." It seems clear that they both arose out of the sources of the reform ferment itself. When reform failed to enlarge the consensus, or to make it more relevant to the needs of the still disadvantaged and disaffected, and when in fact reform seemed to be encouraging more radical challenges to the social order, the old anxieties of the 1890s returned.

The postwar hysteria represented a reaction to a confluence of anxiety-laden developments, including the high cost of living, the physical and social dislocations of war mobilization and the recruitment of women and Negroes into war production jobs in the big northern cities, the Bolshevik Revolution, a series of labor strikes, and a flood of radical literature that exaggerated the capabilities of radical action. "One Hundred Per Cent Americanism" seemed the only effective way of meeting all these challenges at once. As Stanley Coben has written, making use of recent psychological studies and anthro-pological work on cultural "revitalization movements"; "Citizens who joined the crusade for one hundred per cent Americanism sought, primarily, a unify-ing forte which would halt the apparent disintegration of their culture. . . . The slight evidence of danger from radical organizations aroused such wild fear only because Americans had already encountered other threats to cultural stability."

Now, certainly during the progressive era a lot of reform legislation was passed, much that contributed genuinely to a more liberal society, though more that contributed to the more absolutistic moral objectives of progres-sivism. Progressivism indeed had real, lasting effects for the blunting of the sharper edges of self-interest in American life, and for the reduction of the harsher cruelties suffered by the society's underprivileged. These achievements deserve emphasis, not least because they derived directly from the progressive habit of looking to standards of conventional morality and human decency for the solution of diverse social conflicts. But the deeper nature of the problem Confronting American society required more than the invocation of conventional standards; the conventions themselves were at stake, especially as they bore upon the allocation of privileges and rewards. Because most of the progressives never confronted that problem, in a way their efforts were doomed to failure.

In sum, the overall effect of the period's legislation is not so impressive. For example, all the popular government measures put together have not conspicuously raised the quality of American political life. Direct nominations and elections have tended to make political campaigns so expensive as to reduce the number of eligible candidates for public office to (1) the independently wealthy; (2) the ideologues, especially on the right, who can raise the needed campaign money from independently wealthy ideologues like themselves, or from the organizations set up to promote a particular ideology; and (3) party hacks who payoff their debt to the party treasury by whistle-stopping and chicken dinner speeches. Direct legislation through the Initiative and Referendum device has made cities and states prey to the best-financed and organized special-interest group pressures, as have so-called nonpartisan elections. Which is not to say that things are worse than before, but only that they are not conspicuously better. The popular government measures did have the effect of shaking up the established political organizations of the day, and that may well have been their only real purpose.

But as Arthur Link has said, in his text, *The American Epoch,* the popular government measures "were merely instruments to facilitate the capture of political machinery. . . . They must be judged for what they accomplished or failed to accomplish on the higher level of substantive reform." Without disparaging the long list of reform measures that passed during the progressive era, the question remains whether all the "substantive reforms" together accomplished what the progressives wanted them to accomplish.

Certain social and economic advantages were indeed shuffled about, but this must be regarded as a short-term achievement for special groups at best. Certain commercial interests, for example, achieved greater political leverage in railroad policy-making than they had had in 1900 through measures such as the Hepburn and Mann-Elkins Acts—though it was not until the 1940s that any real change occurred in the general rate structure, as some broad regional interests had been demanding at the beginning of the century. Warehouse, farm credits, and land-bank acts gave the diminishing numbers of farm owners enhanced opportunities to mortgage their property, and some business groups had persuaded the federal government to use national revenues to educate farmers on how to increase their productivity (Smith–Lever Act, 1914); but most farmers remained as dependent as ever upon forces beyond their control—the bankers, the middlemen, the international market. The FTC, and the Tariff Commission established in 1916, extended the principle of using government agencies to adjudicate intra-industrial conflicts ostensibly in the national interest, but these agencies would develop a lamentable tendency of deferring to and even confirming rather than moderating the power of each industry's dominant interests. The Federal Reserve Act made the currency more flexible, and that certainly made more sense than the old system, as even the bankers agreed. But depositers would be as prey to defaulting banks as they had been in the days of the Pharaoh—bank deposit insurance somehow was "socialism" to even the best of men in this generation. And despite Woodrow Wilson's brave promise to end the banker's stifling hold on innovative small business, one searches in vain for some provision in the FRA designed specifically to encourage small or new businesses. In fact, the only constraints on the bankers' power that emerged from the era came primarily from the ability of the larger corporations to finance their own expansion out of capital surpluses they had accumulated from extortionate profits during the War.

A major change almost occurred during the war years when organized labor and the principle of collective bargaining received official recognition and a handful of labor leaders was taken, temporarily, into policy-making councils (e.g., in the War Labor Board). But actually, as already indicated, such a development, if it had been made permanent, would have represented a defeat, not a triumph, for progressivism. The progressives may have fought for improved labor conditions, but they jealously fought against the enlargement of union power. It was no aberration that once the need for wartime productive efficiency evaporated, leading progressives such as A. Mitchell Palmer, Miles Poindexter, and Woodrow Wilson himself helped civic and employer organizations to bludgeon the labor movement into disunity and docility. (It is possible, I suppose, to argue that such progressives were simply inconsistent, but if we understand progressivism in the terms I have outlined above I think the consistency is more evident.) Nevertheless, a double irony is worth noting with respect to progressivism's objectives and the wartime labor developments. On the one hand, the progressives' hostility to labor unions defeated their own objectives of (1) counterbalancing the power of collectivized capital (i.e., corporations), and (2) enhancing workers' share of the nation's wealth. On the other hand, under wartime duress, the progressives did grant concessions to organized labor (e.g., the Adamson Eight-Hour Railway Labor Act, as well as the WLB) that would later serve as precedents for the very "collectivization" of the economic situation that they were dedicated to oppose.

Meanwhile, the distribution of advantages in the society did not change much at all. In some cases, from the progressive reformers' viewpoint at least, it may even have changed for the worse. According to the figures of the National Industrial Conference Board, even income was as badly distributed at the end of the era as before. In 1921, the highest 10 percent of income recipients received 38 percent of total personal income, and that figure was only 34 percent in 1910. (Since the share of the top 5 percent of income recipients probably declined in the 1910–20 period, the figures for the top 10 percent group suggest a certain improvement in income distribution at the top. But the fact that the share of the lowest 60 percent also declined in that period, from 35 percent to 30 percent, confirms the view that no meaningful improvement can be shown.) Maldistribution was to grow worse until after 1929.

American farmers on the whole and in particular seemed to suffer increasing disadvantages. Farm life was one of the institutional bulwarks of the mode of life the progressives ostensibly cherished. "The farmer who owns his land" averred Gifford Pinchot, "is still the backbone of the Nation; and one of the things we want most is more of him, . . . [for] he is the first of home-makers." If only in the sense that there were relatively fewer farmers in the total population at the end of the progressive era, one would have to say farm life in the United States had suffered. But, moreover, fewer owned their own farms. The number of farm tenants increased by 21 percent from 1900 to 1920; 38.1 percent of all farm operators in 1921 were tenants; and the figures look even worse when one notices that tenancy *declined* in the most *impoverished* areas during this period, suggesting that the family farm was surviving mostly in the more marginal agricultural areas. Finally, although agriculture had enjoyed some of its most prosperous years in history in the 1910–20 period, the 21 percent of the nation's gainfully employed who were in agriculture in 1919 (a peak year) earned only 16 percent of the national income.

While progressivism failed to restore vitality to American farming, it failed also to stop the vigorous ascendancy of corporate capitalism, the most conspicuous challenge to conventional values and modes that the society faced at the beginning of the era. The corporation had drastically undermined the very basis of the traditional rationale that had supported the nation's freewheeling system of resource allocation and had underwritten the permissiveness of the laws governing economic activities in the nineteenth century. The new capitalism bypassed the privately owned proprietary firm, it featured a separation of ownership and control, it subordinated the profit motive to varied and variable other objectives such as empire-building, and, in many of the techniques developed by financial brokers and investment bankers, it appeared to create a great gulf between the making of money and the producing of useful goods and services. Through a remarkable series of judicial sophistries, this nonconventional form of business enterprise had become, in law, a person, and had won privileges and liberties once entrusted only to men, who were presumed to be conditioned and restrained by the moral qualities that inhere in human nature. Although gaining legal dispensations from an obliging Supreme Court, the corporation could claim no theoretical legitimacy beyond the fact of its power and its apparent inextricable entanglement in the business order that had produced America's seemingly unbounded material success.

Although much has been written about the supposed continuing vitality of small proprietary business enterprise in the United States, there is no gainsaying the continued ascendancy of the big corporation nor the fact that it still lacks legitimation. The fact that in the last sixty years the number of small proprietary businesses has grown at a rate that slightly exceeds the rate of population growth says little about the character of small business enterprise today as compared with that of the era of the American industrial revolution; it does nothing to disparage the apprehensions expressed in the antitrust campaigns of the progressives. To focus on the vast numbers of automobile dealers and gasoline service station owners, for example, is to miss completely their truly humble dependence upon the very few giant automobile and oil companies, a foretold dependence that was the very point of progressives' anticorporation, antitrust sentiments. The progressive movement must indeed be credited with placing real restraints upon monopolistic tendencies in the United States, for most statistics indicate that at least until the 1950s business concentration showed no substantial increase from the turn of the century (though it may be pertinent to note that concentration ratios did increase significantly in the decade immediately following the progressive era). But the statistics of concentration remain impressive—just as they were when John Moody wrote *The Truth About the Trusts* in 1904 and Louis Brandeis followed it with *Other People's Money* in 1914. That two hundred corporations (many of them interrelated) held almost one-quarter of all business assets, and more than 40 percent of all corporate assets in the country in 1948; that the fifty largest manufacturing corporations held 35 percent of all industrial assets in 1948, and 38 percent by 1962; and that a mere twenty-eight corporations or one one-thousandth of a percentage of all nonfinancial firms in 1956 employed 10 percent of all those employed in the nonfinancial industries, should be sufficient statistical support for the apprehensions of the progressive era—*just as it is testimony to the failure of the progressive movement to achieve anything substantial to alter the situation.*

Perhaps the crowning failure of progressivism was the American role in World War I. It is true that many progressives opposed America's intervention, but it is also true that a great many more supported it. The failure in progressivism lies not in the decision to intervene but in the futility of intervention measured by progressive expectations.

Arthur S. Link and
Richard L. McCormick

 **NO**

Progressivism in History

Convulsive reform movements swept across the American landscape from the 1890s to 1917. Angry farmers demanded better prices for their products, regulation of the railroads, and the destruction of what they thought was the evil power of bankers, middlemen, and corrupt politicians. Urban residents crusaded for better city services and more efficient municipal government. Members of various professions, such as social workers and doctors, tried to improve the dangerous and unhealthy conditions in which many people lived and worked. Businessmen, too, lobbied incessantly for goals which they defined as reform. Never before had the people of the United States engaged in so many diverse movements for the improvement of their political system, economy, were calling themselves *progressives*. Ever since, historians have used the term *progessivism* to describe the many reform movements of the early twentieth century.

Yet in the goals they sought and the remedies they tried, the reformers were a varied and contradictory lot. Some progressives wanted to increase the political influence and control of ordinary people, while other progressives wanted to concentrate authority in experts. Many reformers tried to curtail the growth of large corporations; others accepted bigness in industry on account of its supposed economic benefits. Some progressives were genuinely concerned about the welfare of the "new" immigrants from southern and eastern Europe; other progressives sought, sometimes frantically, to "Americanize" the newcomers or to keep them out altogether. In general, progressives sought to improve the conditions of life and labor and to create as much social stability as possible. But each group of progressives had its own definitions of improvement and stability. In the face of such diversity, one historian, Peter G. Filene, has even argued that what has been called the progressive movement never existed as a historical phenomenon ("An Obituary for 'The Progressive Movement,'" *American Quarterly,* 1970).

Certainly there was no *unified* movement, but, like most students of the period, we consider progessivism to have been a real, vital, and significant phenomenon, one which contemporaries recognized and talked and fought about. Properly conceptualized, progressivism provides a useful framework for the history of the United States in the late nineteenth and early twentieth centuries.

One source of confusion and controversy about progressives and progressivism is the words themselves. They are often used judgmentally to describe people and changes which historians have deemed to be "good," "enlightened," and "farsighted." The progressives themselves naturally intended the words to convey such positive qualities, but we should not accept their usage uncritically. It might be better to avoid the terms progressive and progressivism altogether, but they are too deeply embedded in the language of contemporaries and historians to be ignored. Besides, we think that the terms have real meaning. In this [selection] the words will be used neutrally, without any implicit judgment about the value of reform.

In the broadest sense, progressivism was the way in which a whole generation of Americans defined themselves politically and responded to the nation's problems at the turn of the century. The progressives made the first comprehensive efforts to grapple with the ills of a modern urban-industrial society. Hence the record of their achievements and failures has considerable relevance for our own time.

Who Were the Progressives?

Ever since the early twentieth century, people have argued about who the progressives were and what they stood for. This may seem to be a strange topic of debate, but it really is not. Progressivism engaged many different groups of Americans, and each group of progressives naturally considered themselves to be the key reformers and thought that their own programs were the most important ones. Not surprisingly, historians ever since have had trouble agreeing on who really shaped progressivism and its goals. Scholars who have written about the period have variously identified farmers, the old middle classes, professionals, businessmen, and urban immigrants and ethnic groups as the core group of progressives. But these historians have succeeded in identifying *their* reformers only by defining progressivism narrowly, by excluding other reformers and reforms when they do not fall within some specific definition, and by resorting to such vague, catch-all adjectives as "middle class." . . .

The advocates of the middle-class view might reply that they intended to study the leaders of reform, not its supporters, to identify and describe the men and women who imparted the dominant character to progressivism, not its mass base. The study of leadership is surely a valid subject in its own right and is particularly useful for an understanding of progressivism. But too much focus on leadership conceals more than it discloses about early twentieth-century reform. The dynamics of progressivism were crucially generated by ordinary people—by the sometimes frenzied mass supporters of progressive leaders, by rank-and-file voters willing to trust a reform candidate. The chronology of progressivism can be traced by events which aroused large numbers of people—a sensational muckraking article, an outrageous political scandal, an eye-opening legislative investigation, or a tragic social calamity. Events such as these gave reform its rhythm and its power.

Progressivism cannot be understood without seeing how the masses of Americans perceived and responded to such events. Widely circulated magazines gave people everywhere the sordid facts of corruption and carried the clamor for reform into every city, village, and county. State and national election campaigns enabled progressive candidates to trumpet their programs. Almost no literate person in the United States in, say, 1906 could have been unaware that ten-year-old children worked through the night in dangerous factories, or that many United States senators served big business. Progressivism was the only reform movement ever experienced by the whole American nation. Its national appeal and mass base vastly exceeded that of Jacksonian reform. And progressivism's dependence on the people for its objectives and timing has no comparison in the executive-dominated New Deal of Franklin D. Roosevelt or the Great Society of Lyndon B. Johnson. Wars and depressions had previously engaged the whole nation, but never reform. And so we are back to the problem of how to explain and define the outpouring of progressive reform which excited and involved so many different kinds of people.

A little more than a decade ago, Buenker and Thelen recognized the immense diversity of progressivism and suggested ways in which to reorient the study of early twentieth-century reform. Buenker observed that divergent groups often came together on one issue and then changed alliances on the next ("The Progressive Era: A Search for a Synthesis," *Mid-America,* 1969). Indeed, different reformers sometimes favored the same measure for distinctive, even opposite, reasons. Progressivism could be understood only in the light of these shifting coalitions. Thelen, in his study of Wisconsin's legislature, also emphasized the importance of cooperation between different reform groups. "The basic riddle in Progressivism," he concluded, "is not what drove groups apart but what made them seek common cause."

There is a great deal of wisdom in these articles, particularly in their recognition of the diversity of progressivism and in the concept of shifting coalitions of reformers. A two-pronged approach is necessary to carry forward this way of looking at early twentieth-century reform. First, we should study, not an imaginary unified progressive movement, but individual reforms and give particular attention to the goals of their diverse supporters, the public rationales given for them, and the results which they achieved. Second, we should try to identify the features which were more or less common to different progressive reforms.

The first task—distinguishing the goals of a reform from its rhetoric and its results—is more difficult than it might appear to be. Older interpretations of progressivism implicitly assumed that the rhetoric explained the goals and that, if a proposed reform became law, the results fulfilled the intentions behind it. Neither assumption is a sound one: purposes, rationale, and results are three different things. Samuel P. Hays' influential article, "The Politics of Reform in Municipal Government in the Progressive Era" (*Pacific Northwest Quarterly,* 1964), exposed the fallacy of automatically equating the democratic rhetoric of the reformers with their true purposes. The two may have coincided, but the historian has to demonstrate that fact, not take it for granted. The unexamined identification of either intentions or rhetoric with results is also invalid, although it is still a common feature of the scholarship on progressivism. Only within the last decade have historians begun to examine the actual achievements of the reformers. To carry out this first task, in the following . . . we will distinguish between the goals and rhetoric of individual reforms and will discuss the results of reform whenever the current literature permits. To do so is to observe the ironies, complexities, and disappointments of progressivism.

The second task—that of identifying the common characteristics of progressivism—is even more difficult than the first but is an essential base on which to build an understanding of progressivism. The rest of this [selection] focuses on identifying such characteristics. The place to begin that effort is the origins of progressivism. . . .

The Character and Spirit of Progressivism

Progressivism was characterized, in the first place, by a distinctive set of attitudes toward industrialism. By the turn of the century, the overwhelming majority of Americans had accepted the permanence of large-scale industrial, commercial, and financial enterprises and of the wage and factory systems. The progressives shared this attitude. Most were not socialists, and they undertook reform, not to dismantle modern economic institutions, but rather to ameliorate and improve the conditions of industrial life. Yet progressivism was infused with a deep outrage against the worst consequences of industrialism. Outpourings of anger at corporate wrongdoing and of hatred for industry's callous pursuit of profit frequently punctuated the course of reform in the early twentieth century. Indeed, antibusiness emotion was a prime mover of progressivism. That the acceptance of industrialism *and* the outrage against it were intrinsic to early twentieth-century reform does not mean that progressivism was mindless or that it has to be considered indefinable. But it does suggest that there was a powerful irony in progressivism: reforms which gained support from a people angry with the oppressive aspects of industrialism also assisted the same persons to accommodate to it, albeit to an industrialism which was to some degree socially responsible.

The progressives' ameliorative reforms also reflected their faith in progress—in mankind's ability, through purposeful action, to improve the environment and the conditions of life. The late nineteenth-century dissidents had not lacked this faith, but their espousal of panaceas bespoke a deep pessimism: "Unless this one great change is made, things will get worse." Progressive reforms were grounded on a broader assumption. In particular, reforms could protect the people hurt by industrialization, and make the environment more humane. For intellectuals of the era, the achievement of such goals meant that they had to meet Herbert Spencer head on and confute his absolute "truths." Progressive thinkers, led by Lester Frank Ward, Richard T. Ely, and, most important, John Dewey, demolished social Darwinism with what Goldman has called "reform Darwinism." They asserted that human adaptation to the environment did not interfere with the evolutionary process, but was, rather, part and parcel of the law of natural change. Progressive intellectuals and their popularizers produced a vast literature to condemn laissez faire and to promote the concept of the active state.

To improve the environment meant, above all, to intervene in economic and social affairs in order to control natural forces and impose a measure of order upon them. This belief in interventionism was a third component of progressivism. It was visible in almost every reform of the era, from the supervision of business to the prohibition of alcohol (John W. Chambers II, *The Tyranny of Change: America in the Progressive Era, 1900–1917,* 1980). Interventionism could be both private and public. Given their choice, most progressives preferred to work noncoercively through voluntary organizations for economic and social changes. However, as time passed, it became evident that most progressive reforms could be achieved only by legislation and public control. Such an extension of public authority made many progressives uneasy, and few of them went so far as Herbert Croly in glorifying the state in his *The Promise of American Life* (1909) and *Progressive Democracy* (1914). Even so, the intervention necessary for their reforms inevitably propelled progressives toward an advocacy of the use of governmental power. A familiar scenario during the period was one in which progressives called upon public authorities to assume responsibility for interventions which voluntary organizations had begun.

The foregoing describes the basic characteristics of progressivism but says little about its ideals. Progressivism was inspired by two bodies of belief and knowledge—evangelical Protestantism and the natural and social sciences. These sources of reform may appear at first glance antagonistic to one another. Actually, they were complementary, and each imparted distinctive qualities to progressivism.

Ever since the religious revivals from about 1820 to 1840, evangelical Protestantism had spurred reform in the United States. Basic to the reform mentality was an all-consuming urge to purge the world of sin, such as the sins of slavery and intemperance, against which nineteenth-century reformers had crusaded. Now the progressives carried the struggle into the modern citadels of sin—the teeming cities of the nation. No one can read their writings and speeches without being struck by the fact that many of them believed that it was their Christian duty to right the wrongs created by the processes of industrialization. Such belief was the motive force behind the Social Gospel, a movement which swept through the Protestant churches in the 1890s and 1900s. Its goal was to align churches, frankly and aggressively, on the side of the downtrodden, the poor, and working people—in other words, to make Christianity relevant to this world, not the next. It is difficult to measure the influence of the Social Gospel, but it seared the consciences of millions of Americans, particularly in urban areas. And it triumphed in the organization in 1908 of the Federal Council of Churches of Christ in America, with its platform which condemned exploitative capitalism and proclaimed the right of workers to organize and to enjoy a decent standard of living. Observers at the Progressive party's national convention of 1912 should not have been surprised to hear the delegates sing, spontaneously and emotionally, the Christian call to arms, "Onward, Christian Solders!"

The faith which inspired the singing of "Onward, Christian Soldiers!" had significant implications for progressive reforms. Progressives used moralistic appeals to make people feel the awful weight of wrong in the world and to exhort them to accept personal responsibility for its eradication. The resultant reforms could be generous in spirit, but they could also seem intolerant to the people who were "reformed." Progressivism sometimes seemed to envision life in a small town Protestant community or an urban drawing room—a vision sharply different from that of Catholic or Jewish immigrants. Not every progressive shared the evangelical ethos, much less its intolerance, but few of the era's reforms were untouched by the spirit and techniques of Protestant revivalism.

Science also had a pervasive impact on the methods and objectives of progressivism. Many leading reformers were specialists in the new disciplines of statistics, economics, sociology, and psychology. These new social scientists set out to gather data on human behavior as it actually was and to discover the laws which governed it. Since social scientists accepted environmentalist and interventionist assumptions implicitly, they believed that knowledge of natural laws would make it possible to devise and apply solutions to improve the human condition. This faith underpinned the optimism of most progressives and predetermined the methods used by almost all reformers of the time: investigation of the facts and application of social-science knowledge to their analysis; entrusting trained experts to decide what should be done; and, finally, mandating government to execute reform.

These methods may have been rational, but they were also compatible with progressive moralism. In its formative period, American social science was heavily infused with ethical concerns. An essential purpose of statistics, economics, sociology, and psychology was to improve and uplift. Leading practitioners of these disciplines, for example, Richard T. Ely, an economist at the University of Wisconsin, were often in the vanguard of the Social Gospel. Progressives blended science and religion into a view of human behavior which was unique to their generation, which had grown up in an age of revivals and come to maturity at the birth of social science.

All of progressivism's distinctive features found expression in muckraking—the literary spearhead of early twentieth-century reform. Through the medium of such new ten-cent magazines as *McClure's, Everybody's, and Cosmopolitan,* the muckrakers exposed every dark aspect and corner of American life. Nothing escaped the probe of writers such as Ida M. Tarbell, Lincoln Steffens, Ray Stannard Baker, and Burton J. Hendrick—not big business, politics, prostitution, race relations, or even the churches. Behind the exposes of the muckrakers lay the progressive attitude toward industrialism: it was here to stay, but many of its aspects seemed to be deplorable. These could be improved, however, if only people became aware of conditions and determined to ameliorate them. To bring about such awareness, the muckrakers appealed to their readers' consciences. Steffens' famous series, published in book form as *The Shame of the Cities* in 1904, was frankly intended to make people feel guilty for the corruption which riddled their cities. The muckrakers also used the social scientists' method of careful and painstaking gathering of data—and with devastating effects. The investigative function—which was later largely taken over by governmental agencies—proved absolutely vital to educating and arousing Americans.

All progressive crusades shared the spirit and used the techniques discussed here, but they did so to different degrees and in different ways. Some voiced a greater willingness to accept industrialism and even to extol its potential benefits; others expressed more strongly the outrage against its darker aspects. Some intervened through voluntary organizations; others relied on government to achieve changes. Each reform reflected a distinctive balance between the claims of Protestant moralism and of scientific rationalism. Progressives fought among themselves over these questions even while they set to the common task of applying their new methods and ideas to the problems of a modern society. . . .

In this analysis we have frequently pointed to the differences between the rhetoric, intentions, and results of progressive reform. The failure of reform always to fulfill the expectations of its advocates was not, of course, unique to the progressive era. Jacksonian reform, Reconstruction, and the New Deal all exhibited similar ironies and disappointments. In each case, the clash between reformers with divergent purposes, the inability to predict how given methods of reform would work in practice, and the ultimate waning of popular zeal for change all contributed to the disjuncture of rationale, purpose, and achievement. Yet the gap between these things seems more obvious in the progressive era because so many diverse movements for reform took place in a brief span of time and were accompanied by resounding rhetoric and by high expectations for the improvement of the American social and political environment. The effort to change so many things all at once, and the grandiose claims made for the moral and material betterment which would result, meant that disappointments were bound to occur.

Yet even the great number of reforms and the uncommonly high expectations for them cannot fully account for the consistent gaps which we have observed between the stated purposes, real intentions, and actual results of progressivism. Several additional factors, intrinsic to the nature of early twentieth-century reform, help to explain the ironies and contradictions.

One of these was the progressives' confident reliance on modern methods of reform. Heirs of recent advances in natural science and social science, they enthusiastically devised and applied new techniques to improve American government and society. Their methods often worked; on the other hand, progressive programs often simply did not prove capable of accomplishing what had been expected of them. This was not necessarily the reformers' fault. They hopefully used untried methods even while they lacked a science of society which was capable of solving all the great problems which they attacked. At the same time, the progressives' scientific methods made it possible to know just how far short of success their programs had sometimes fallen. The evidence of their failures thus was more visible than in any previous era of reform. To the progressives' credit, they usually published that evidence—for contemporaries and historians alike to see.

A second aspect of early twentieth-century reform which helps to account for the gaps between aims and achievements was the deep ambivalence of the progressives about industrialism and its consequences. Individual reformers were divided, and so was their movement as a whole.

Compared to many Americans of the late 1800s, the progressives fundamentally accepted an industrial society and sought mainly to control and ameliorate it. Even reformers who were intellectually committed to socialist ideas often acted the part of reformers, not radicals.

Yet progressivism was infused and vitalized, as we have seen, by people truly angry with their industrial society. Few of them wanted to tear down the modern institutions of business and commerce, but their anger was real, their moralism was genuine, and their passions were essential to the reforms of their time.

The reform movement never resolved this ambivalence about industrialism. Much of its rhetoric and popular passion pointed in one direction—toward some form of social democracy—while its leaders and their programs went in another. Often the result was confusion and bitterness. Reforms frequently did not measure up to popular, antibusiness expectations, indeed, never were expected to do so by those who designed and implemented them. Even conservative, ameliorative reformers like Theodore Roosevelt often used radical rhetoric. In doing so, they misled their followers and contributed to the ironies of progressivism.

Perhaps most significant, progressives failed to achieve all their goals because, despite their efforts, they never fully came to terms with the divisions and conflicts in American society. Again and again, they acknowledged the existence of social disharmony more fully and frankly than had nineteenth-century Americans. Nearly every social and economic reform of the era was predicated on the progressive recognition that diverse cultural and occupational groups had conflicting interests, and that the responsibility for mitigating and adjusting those differences lay with the whole society, usually the government. Such recognition was one of the progressives' most significant achievements. Indeed, it stands among the most important accomplishments of liberal reform in all of American history. For, by frankly acknowledging the existence of social disharmony, the progressives committed the twentieth-century United States to recognizing—and to lessening—the inevitable conflicts of a heterogeneous industrial society.

Yet the significance of the progressives' recognition of diversity was compromised by the methods and institutions which they adopted to diminish or eliminate social and economic conflict. Expert administrative government turned out to be less neutral than the progressives believed that it would be. No scientific reform could be any more impartial than the experts who gathered the data or than the bureaucrats who implemented the programs. In practice, as we have seen, administrative government often succumbed to the domination of special interests.

It would be pointless to blame the progressives for the failure of their new methods and programs to eradicate all the conflicts of an industrial society, but it is perhaps fair to ask why the progressives adopted measures which tended to disguise and obscure economic and social conflict almost as soon as they had uncovered it. For one thing, they honestly believed in the almost unlimited potentialities of science and administration. Our late twentieth-century skepticism of these wonders should not blind us to the faith with which the progressives embraced them and imbued them with what now seem magical properties. For another, the progressives were reformers, not radicals. It was one thing to recognize the existence of economic and social conflict, but quite another thing to admit that it was permanent. By and large, these men and women were personally and ideologically inclined to believe that the American society was, in the final analysis, harmonious, and that such conflicts as did exist could be resolved. Finally, the class and cultural backgrounds of the leading progressives often made them insensitive to lower-class immigrant Americans and their cultures. Attempts to reduce divisions sometimes came down to imposing middle-class Protestant ways on the urban masses. In consequence, the progressives never fulfilled their hope of eliminating social conflict. Reformers of the early twentieth century saw the problem more fully than had their predecessors, but they nonetheless tended to consider conflicts resolved when, in fact, they only had been papered over. Later twentieth-century Americans have also frequently deceived themselves in this way.

Thus progressivism inevitably fell short of its rhetoric and intentions. Lest this seem an unfairly critical evaluation, it is important to recall how terribly ambitious were the stated aims and true goals of the reformers. They missed some of their marks because they sought to do so much. And, despite all their shortcomings, they accomplished an enormous part of what they set out to achieve.

Progressivism brought major innovations to almost every facet of public and private life in the United States. The political and governmental systems particularly felt the effects of reform. Indeed, the nature of political participation and the uses to which it was put went through transitions as momentous as those of any era in American history. These developments were complex, as we have seen, and it is no easy matter to sort out who was helped and who was hurt by each of them or by the entire body of reforms. At the very least, the political changes of the progressive era significantly accommodated American public life to an urban-industrial society. On balance, the polity probably emerged neither more nor less democratic than before, but it did become better suited to address, or at least recognize, the questions and problems which arose from the cities and factories of the nation. After the progressive era, just as before, wealthier elements in American society had a disproportionate share of political power, but we can hardly conclude that this was the fault of the progressives.

The personal and social life of the American people was also deeply affected by progressivism. Like the era's political changes, the economic and social reforms of the early twentieth century were enormously complicated and are difficult to summarize without doing violence to their diversity. In the broadest sense, the progressives sought to mitigate the injustice and the disorder of a society now dominated by its industries and cities. Usually, as we have observed, the quests for social justice and social control were extricably bound together in the reformers' programs, with each group of progressives having different interpretations of these dual ends. Justice sometimes took second place to control. However, before one judges the reformers too harshly for that, it is well to remember how bad urban social conditions were in the late nineteenth century and the odds against which the reformers fought. It is also well to remember that they often succeeded in mitigating the harshness of urban-industrial life.

The problems with which the progressives struggled have, by and large, continued to challenge Americans ever since. And, although the assumptions and techniques of progressivism no longer command the confidence which early twentieth-century Americans had in them, no equally comprehensive body of reforms has ever been adopted in their place. Throughout this study, we have criticized the progressives for having too much faith in their untried methods. Yet, if this was a failing, it was also a source of strength, one now missing from reform in America. For the essence of progressivism lay in the hopefulness and optimism which the reformers brought to the tasks of applying science and administration to the high moral purposes in which they believed. The historical record of their aims and achievements leaves no doubt that there were many men and women in the United States in the early 1900s who were not afraid to confront the problems of a modern industrial society with vigor, imagination, and hope. They of course failed to solve all those problems, but no other generation of Americans has done conspicuously better in addressing the political, economic, and social conditions which it faced.

POSTSCRIPT

Did the Progressives Fail?

In spite of their differences, both Abrams's and Link and McCormick's interpretations make concessions to their respective critics. Link and McCormick, for example, admit that the intended reforms did not necessarily produce the desired results. Furthermore, the authors concede that many reformers were insensitive to the cultural values of the lower classes and attempted to impose middle-class Protestant ways on the urban masses. Nevertheless, Link and McCormick argue that in spite of the failure to curb the growth of big business, the progressive reforms did ameliorate the worst abuses of the new urban industrial society. Although the Progressives failed to solve all the major problems of their times, they did set the agenda that still challenges the reformers of today.

Abrams also makes a concession to his critics when he admits that "progressivism had real lasting effects for the blunting of the sharper edges of selfinterest in American life, and for the reduction of the harsher cruelties suffered by the society's underprivileged." Yet the thrust of his argument is that the progressive reformers accomplished little of value. While Abrams probably agrees with Link and McCormick that the Progressives were the first group to confront the problems of modern America, he considers their intended reforms inadequate by their very nature. Because the reformers never really challenged the inequalities brought about by the rise of the industrial state, maintains Abrams, the same problems have persisted to the present day.

Historians have generally been sympathetic to the aims and achievements of the progressive historians. Many, like Charles Beard and Frederick Jackson Turner, came from the Midwest and lived in model progressive states like Wisconsin. Their view of history was based on a conflict between groups competing for power, so it was easy for them to portray progressivism as a struggle between the people and entrenched interests.

It was not until after World War II that a more complex view of progressivism emerged. Richard Hofstadter's *Age of Reform* (Alfred A. Knopf, 1955) was exceptionally critical of the reformist view of history as well as of the reformers in general. Born of Jewish immigrant parents and raised in cities in New York, the Columbia University professor argued that progressivism was a moral crusade undertaken by WASP families in an effort to restore older Protestant and individualistic values and to regain political power and status. Both Hofstadter's "status revolution" theory of progressivism and his profile of the typical Progressive have been heavily criticized by historians. Nevertheless, he changed the dimensions of the debate and made progressivism appear to be a much more complex issue than had previously been thought.

Most of the writing on progressivism for the past 20 years has centered around the "organizational" model. Writers of this school have stressed the role of the "expert" and the ideals of scientific management as basic to an understanding of the Progressive Era. This fascination with how the city manager plan worked in Dayton or railroad regulation in Wisconsin or the public schools laws in New York City makes sense to a generation surrounded by bureaucracies on all sides. Two books that deserve careful reading are Robert Wiebe's *The Search for Order, 1877–1920* (Hill & Wang, 1967) and the wonderful collection of essays by Samuel P. Hayes, *American Political History as Social Analysis* (Knoxville, 1980), which brings together two decades' worth of articles from diverse journals that were seminal in exploring ethnocultural approaches to politics within the organizational model.

In a highly influential article written for the *American Quarterly* in spring 1970, Professor Peter G. Filene proclaimed, "An Obituary for the 'Progressive Movement.'" After an extensive review of the literature, Filene concluded that since historians cannot agree on its programs, values, geographical location, members, and supporters, there was no such thing as a Progressive movement. Few historians were bold enough to write progressivism out of the pantheon of American reform movements. But Filene put the proponents of the early twentieth-century reform movement on the defensive. Students who want to see how professional historians directly confronted Filene in their refusal to attend the funeral of the Progressive movement should read the essays by John D. Buenker, John C. Burnham, and Robert M. Crunden in *Progressivism* (Schenkman, 1977).

Three works provide an indispensable review of the literature of Progressivism in the 1980s. Link and McCormick's *Progressivism* (Harlan Davidson, 1983) deserves to be read in its entirety for its comprehensive yet concise coverage. More scholarly but still readable are the essays on the new political history in McCormick's *The Party Period and Public Policy: American Politics From the Age of Jackson to the Progressive Era* (Oxford University Press, 1986). The more advanced student should consult Daniel T. Rodgers, "In Search of Progressivism," *Reviews in American History* (December 1982). While admitting that Progressives shared no common creed or values, Rodgers nevertheless feels that they were able "to articulate their discontents and their social visions" around three distinct clusters of ideas: "The first was the rhetoric of antimonopolism, the second was an emphasis on social bonds and the social nature of human beings, and the third was the language of social efficiency."

ISSUE 9

Was Woodrow Wilson Responsible for the Failure of the United States to Join the League of Nations?

YES: John M. Cooper, Jr., from *Breaking the Heart of the World: Woodrow Wilson and the Fight for the League of Nations* (Cambridge University Press, 2001)

NO: William G. Carleton, from "A New Look at Woodrow Wilson," *The Virginia Quarterly Review* (Autumn 1962)

ISSUE SUMMARY

YES: Professor John M. Cooper argues that the stroke that partially paralyzed Woodrow Wilson during his speaking tour in 1919 hampered the president's ability to compromise with the Republicans over the terms of America's membership in the League of Nations if the Senate ratified the Treaty of Versailles.

NO: William G. Carleton believed that Woodrow Wilson understood the role that the United States would play in world affairs.

T he presidential polls of Arthur Schlesinger in 1948 and 1962 as well as the 1983 Murray-Blessing poll have ranked Wilson among the top 10 presidents. William Carleton considers him the greatest twentieth-century president, only two notches below Jefferson and Lincoln. Yet, among his biographers, Wilson has been treated ungenerously. They carp at him for being naïve, overly idealistic, and too inflexible. It appears that Wilson's biographers respect the man but do not like the person.

Wilson's own introspective personality may be partly to blame. He was, along with Jefferson and to some extent Theodore Roosevelt, America's most intellectual president. He spent nearly 20 years as a history and political science teacher and scholar at Bryn Mawr, Wesleyan, and at his alma mater, Princeton University. While his multi-volume *History of the United States* appears dated as it gathers dust on musty library shelves, his Ph.D. dissertation on *Congressional Government,* written as a graduate student at Johns Hopkins, remains a classic statement of the weakness of leadership in the American constitutional system.

There is one other reason why Wilson has been so critically analyzed by his biographers. Certainly, no president before or since has had less formal political experience than Wilson. Apparently, academic work does not constitute the proper training for the presidency. Yet, in addition to working many years as a college professor and a short stint as a lawyer, Wilson served eight distinguished years as the president of Princeton University. He turned it into one of the outstanding universities in the country. He introduced the preceptorial system, widely copied today, which supplemented course lectures with discussion conferences led by young instructors. He took the lead in reorganizing the university's curriculum. He lost two key battles. The alumni became upset when he tried to replace the class-ridden eating clubs with his "Quadrangle Plan," which would have established smaller colleges within the university system. What historians most remember about his Princeton career, however, was his losing fight with the Board of Trustees and Dean Andrew West concerning the location and eventual control over the new graduate school. Wilson resigned when it was decided to build a separate campus for the graduate school.

Shortly after Wilson left Princeton in 1910, he ran for governor of New Jersey and won his only political office before he became the president. As a governor, he gained control over the state Democratic Party and pushed through the legislature a litany of progressive measures—a primary and elections law, a corrupt practices act, workmen's compensation, utilities regulation, school reforms, and an enabling act that allowed certain cities to adopt the commission form of government. When he was nominated on the 46th ballot at the Democratic convention in 1912, Wilson had enlarged the power of the governor's office in New Jersey and foreshadowed the way in which he would manage the presidency.

During his first four years, he also fashioned a legislative program rivaled only by FDR's later "New Deal." The "New Freedom" pulled together conservative and progressive, rural and urban, as well as southern and northern Democrats in passing such measures as the Underwood-Simmons Tariff, the first bill to significantly lower tariff rates since the Civil War, and the Owens–Keating Child Labor Act. It was through Wilson's adroit maneuvering that the Federal Reserve System was established. This banking measure, the most significant in American history, established the major agency that regulates money supply in the country today. Finally, President Wilson revealed his flexibility when he abandoned his initial policy of rigid and indiscriminate trust busting for one of regulating big business through the creation of the Federal Trade Commission.

More controversial were Wilson's presidential roles as commander-in-chief of the armed forces and chief diplomat. Some have argued that Wilson did not pay enough attention to strategic issues in the war while other writers said he merged the proper dose of force and diplomacy. The issue here is whether or not Wilson bears the responsibility for the failure of the United States to join the League of Nations. John M. Cooper gives a qualified yes. Had Wilson negotiated with the Republicans as he did on other occasions, he might have gotten his peace treaty. But the stroke accelerated a stubborn streak that limited his negotiation skills. Professor William G. Carleton gives a spirited defense of Wilson's domestic and foreign policies in the second essay.

YES

John M. Cooper, Jr.

Breaking the Heart of the World

• • • **W**hat did it all mean? Did the outcome of the League fight do what Wilson said it would do? Did the failure of the United States to join the League "break the heart of the world"? Or were the obstacles to peacemaking so great, were the odds stacked so heavily against the restoration of world order, that it was an exercise in futility? Did those obstacles and odds make it, in the words of Shakespeare's Macbeth, "full of sound and fury, signifying nothing"? These questions define the two poles in the argument that lasted for the first four or five decades after the League fight.

Unlike most great historical arguments with lasting relevance, this one has led to broad agreement. Since the middle of the twentieth century, few historians or other analysts have doubted that the second set of answers to the question about what the League fight meant is the right one. The near consensus that has emerged around those answers usually employs a more polite phrasing than "sound and fury." It also includes a bow or two toward marginal differences that American membership in the League might have made. But, at bottom, few writers have challenged the notion that the course of American foreign policy and international relations would have been much the same regardless of the outcome of League fight.[1]

Ironically, Wilson's posthumous apotheosis in the 1940s and the sense of having belatedly heeded his warnings have contributed more than anything else to the prevalence of this view of the meaning of the League fight. As usually stated, the prevailing argument boils down to three interlocking propositions. First, Wilson was ahead of his time. Second, Americans were not ready after World War I to make the full-scale commitment to collective security and international enforcement that Wilson demanded. Third, it took World War II to drive home the lessons that Wilson had tried to teach. These propositions need to be examined both separately and together. Separately, each one reveals different assumptions about why the League fight turned out the way it did and what its lasting repercussions were. Together, they provide answers to the question of whether the outcome of the League fight did indeed break the heart of the world.

Each of these propositions is like the face of a three-sided pyramid. Each one takes its shape from the central question of what the League fight meant, yet at the same time each one presents its own distinctive aspect. The first proposition—that Wilson was ahead of his time—speaks directly to his personal role. That role has long since come to be judged as pivotal. Without Wilson, the League fight almost certainly would not have arisen in the first place. A less bold and visionary leader—one who was not ahead of his or her time—would not have attempted to do so much. Likewise, without Wilson, the League fight would almost certainly have ended in some kind of compromise. His unbending insistence upon joining an essentially political international organization with firm obligations under Article X ruled out any halfway house between that position and rejection of membership. In short, the correctness of Winston Churchill's early pronouncement about "this man's mind and spirit" seems incontrovertible.

But there is more to the proposition that Wilson was ahead of his time, and this is where controversy persists. At issue are the value and meaning placed upon his being ahead of his time. In one way, any strong leader must have the capacity for anticipating events and forecasting opportunities and dangers. This capacity is what Shakespeare meant by recognizing the "tide in the affairs of men which, taken at the flood, leads on to fortune" and what Bismarck meant by hearing the distant hoofbeat of the horse of history. Conversely, leaders must retain an appreciation of how willing and able their followers are to accompany them in great leaps forward. Most interpreters of Wilson in the League fight have stressed the negative aspect of his being ahead of his time. "Too far ahead" is the prevailing judgment, and the controversy revolves around why this appears to have been the case.

Two broad schools of interpretation have arisen to account for this perceived fault. One school is cultural and psychological; the other is circumstantial and physiological. The key word for the first school is "messianic." That word, in its view, captures Wilson's religiously based affliction with delusions of divine revelation and chosenness. He believed, so this argument goes, that he and he alone had both the capacity and the message to save the world. This is a cultural view of Wilson for two reasons. First, it sees him as a product of his own culture—the Anglo-American Protestant middle-class world that flourished in the second half of the nineteenth century. Second, this view grows out of the culture of those who have held it, the twentieth century "modernist" dispensation that arose in Europe before World War I and took firm hold there and in America starting in the 1920s. As applied to Wilson, this view found earliest expression in Keynes's depiction of him in *The Economic Consequences of the Peace* and was soon followed by similar treatment at the hands of Mencken and other "debunkers" of that decade.

The psychological side of this school also flowered early. Starting with the American literary critic Edmund Wilson in the mid-1920s, various writers have attributed Woodrow Wilson's alleged messianism to psychological deformations. As viewed through their Freudian lenses, Wilson emerged from his childhood with a severely damaged ego and unresolved oedipal conflict. Further, those maladjustments bred in him messianic delusions and compulsions toward figuratively mortal conflicts with father figures. This happened first in his academic career and later in politics, where Lodge in the League fight played the part of the last of these adversaries. In fact, Sigmund Freud himself painted just such a portrait of Wilson, in collaboration with the defector from the American delegation to the peace conference, William Bullitt. Their contribution did not come to light, however, until the 1960s. In the meantime, this essentially Freudian interpretation had already entered the mainstream of American political interpretation, in general through the writings of Harold Lasswell and in particular application to Wilson through the work of Alexander and Juliette George.[2]

This school of interpretation has several shortcomings. The main defect of the cultural interpretation is—to reverse Mark Twain's celebrated crack about Wagner's music ("It's not as bad as it sounds")—it is not as good as it sounds. This interpretation was present though not greatly developed in Keynes's depiction of Wilson in the *Economic Consequences of the Peace* and found fuller expression in the late 1930s in E. H. Carr's *The Twenty Years' Crisis*. More recently, others have stressed racial, gendered, and ethnocentric biases that supposedly crippled him in dealing with the more diverse and disorderly world of the twentieth century. Wilson, in these views, was the exponent of culture-bound, antiquated, hegemonic notions of order ill suited to the realities of the twentieth century.[3]

The main response to this interpretation is—at the risk of impoliteness—so what? Where else except from his own cultural background was Wilson going to get his ideas about world order? It is blatantly presentist and ahistorical to expect anything else. More important, do the origins and limitations of his ideas necessarily invalidate them? Perhaps so, but perhaps not. The alternatives to his vision of order, "pluralism" and "disorder," entailed ethnic and national conflicts, genocides, and world wars. Viewed in that light, Wilson's time-bound views do not look so bad, especially because his insistence upon flexible application of them and adjustment over time left room for growth and change.

Likewise, the stress on Wilson's psychological flaws has three major flaws of its own. First and most clearly, any reading of what Wilson said at almost any time during the League fight makes it difficult to sustain the allegation of messianism. For example, he never uttered the phrase "war to end all wars." That came from Lloyd George, as did "self-determination" as both a phrase and a general principle. Wilson, by contrast, made a limited and circumspect case for his program, as he had done earlier with the Fourteen Points and as he continued to do throughout the League fight. He stressed that the League marked only the indication of the direction and the beginning of the journey toward a more just and peaceful world. He called the League "a living thing," and he expected and wanted it to evolve over time. He repeatedly claimed that he would welcome a better alternative if his opponents could come up with one. To be sure, that was a rhetorical offer, but at a deeper level Wilson meant it sincerely. In laying stress on the obligation under Article X, he revealed that he cared far less about the particular provisions of the treaty and the Covenant and far more about ensuring his nation's commitment to an active role in preserving peace. The only way to reconcile such sophisticated, self-critical arguments with messianism is to impute fantastic deviousness and insincerity to Wilson. This requires a psychological stretch that only a few of his worst enemies in the League fight were willing to make.

The second flaw in this psychological interpretation is that it resembles the biblical parable of the mote and the beam. It detects and pounces on Wilson's supposed shortcomings while remaining oblivious to its own greater limitations. Its own "modernist" assumptions limit and disable this psychological interpretation. Those assumptions stress the supremacy of unconscious and emotional forces, combined with racial, class, and gendered biases. Thereby, Wilson and figures like him—who drew their assumptions from orthodox religious creeds and believed in disinterestedness and the power of reason—have become literally incomprehensible to this modernist sensibility. In fact, it was Wilson's grounding in that very culture of his time, especially his youthful immersion in some of the most sophisticated religious thinking of that day, that inoculated him against the messianic tendencies that did afflict others in the atmosphere of supercharged idealism and evangelism that suffused much of American political life from 1900 to 1920.[4]

The final flaw in this psychological interpretation is its downgrading of physiological factors. The need to see the "real" Wilson in his refusal to compromise during the League fight requires adherents to this school to scoff at suggestions that other circumstances in 1919 and 1920 may also have played an important role. Leaving aside the question of whether anyone's behavior at a particular time can reveal the "real" person, this refusal to give consideration to the major stroke that Wilson suffered appears willful or even perverse. How could such a devastating illness *not* have affected his behavior? How could the worst crisis of presidential disability in American history *not* have affected the outcome of the League fight? These objections become particularly acute when they are set against the events of January and February 1920. Then, virtually every League advocate and every member of the president's inner circle, including Tumulty, Dr. Grayson, and Mrs. Wilson, tried to persuade him to compromise. To imagine that a healthier Wilson would not have tried to bring the League fight to a better, more pleasant, more constructive conclusion requires another psychological stretch. It demands an insistence upon personality-warped messianism that borders on the ludicrous.[5]

The other broad school of interpretation of Wilson's being ahead of his time—the one that stresses circumstantial factors—answers that last, health-based objection to the cultural-psychological interpretation. But this second school of interpretation did not originate as a response to the first one. Rather, it initially stressed not his health, but other circumstances, as part of the Wilsonian position during and right after the League fight. Wilson was ahead of his time, this view holds, chiefly because so many of his contemporaries in the nation's political leadership refused to keep up with him. This view shifts the onus for an unsatisfactory outcome to the League fight over to the Republicans, particularly Lodge and, to a lesser degree, Root. These men stand accused of putting personal dislike of Wilson and pursuit of partisan advantage ahead of the greater good of the nation and the world. By contrast, Taft and others in the LEP stand as paragons of enlightenment and bipartisan harmony.[6]

The flaws in such a circumstantial case are not hard to see. Like the opposing school, this one also imputes hidden and ignoble motives to the actors whom it dislikes. It gives little credence to the sincerity and rationality of Lodge or Root when they raised what they regarded as practical and principled objections to Wilson's program. It also fails to recognize that, given their inconstancy in supporting that program, Taft, Lowell, and the Thirty-One Republicans of October 1920, were not so different from their fellow partisans. Furthermore, to deplore partisanship and exalt bipartisanship, as this school does, is to misunderstand the essentially adversarial nature of the American two-party system. Like this country's legal system, the two-party system demands vigorous conflict between the two sides, whereas bipartisanship usually requires abdication by one of the adversaries. This system has built-in limitations. These limitations become particularly acute in harnessing diverse coalitions within one or the other of only two parties and in processes that require supermajorities in one or both houses of Congress, such as the two-thirds needed for approval of constitutional amendments or consent to treaties. But to blame the outcome of the League fight on partisanship is like blaming the weather. To blame Lodge, Root, and others for acting like partisans is to blame them for doing what they were supposed to do.

The most serious flaw in this circumstantial interpretation is that it does not square with the facts of the League fight. In one way, the more culpable partisans were the Democrats. Many of them bowed to Wilson's dictation against their better judgment. Republican senators were scoring partisan points when they leveled such charges at their colleagues across the aisle before the votes on the treaty, but they were largely correct. On the Republican side, what seems noteworthy is not how staunchly the non-Irreconcilable senators opposed Wilson but how far, by their lights, they went to meet him. After the Round Robin and the Foreign Relations Committee's effort to amend the treaty, the Lodge reservations represented a considerable retreat for many of them. As for Lodge, despite his manifest negativism toward the League and hostile stance toward Wilson, he showed much greater flexibility than most interpreters have given him credit for or than he himself cared to remember. Both his dealings with Stephen Bonsal in November 1919 and even more his conduct in the bipartisan talks in January 1920 revealed a wavering in his total rejection of Article X and some openness toward compromise. Lodge did not come away from the League fight a beloved figure, but he was not at all the wily, underhanded villain of contemporary and later caricature.[7]

What this circumstantial view does stress correctly is that others besides Wilson contributed to his being ahead of his time. This view also correctly calls attention to the excessive heat of partisan conflict in 1919 and 1920. Much of that heat stemmed from the emotions that had been whipped up during the war and had not abated after the abrupt end of the fighting in November 1918. Simultaneously with the League fight, those emotions and other discontents were exploding into race riots and lynchings, massive labor strikes, and the Red Scare of 1919 and 1920. Much of the partisan heat of those years also stemmed from the uneasy position of both parties. Thanks largely to their own earlier internecine conflicts, the once-dominant Republicans had endured banishment from the White House and congressional majorities for the longest period in their party's history. Their victory in the 1918 elections raised their hopes, but they gained control of Congress only by narrow margins, and their best presidential prospect, Roosevelt, died in January 1919. By the same token, the Democrats approached the postwar situation with mingled hope and apprehension, and few of them had any stomach for questioning the leadership of their only president to win reelection since Andrew Jackson. In short, these political circumstances would have taxed the resources of even the ablest, healthiest leader who tried to pull off a foreign policy coup like Wilson's.

Clearly, the weightiest circumstance of all was that Wilson was not the healthiest of leaders during the League fight. Whether he was the ablest leader available is a different question and one that cannot be answered apart from considerations of his health. With the exception of Thomas A. Bailey, those who developed the circumstantial interpretation of Wilson's performance did not pay much attention to his health. Only with the work of Edwin Weinstein, a trained neurologist, in the 1970s did anyone confront head-on the question of what impact illness in general and the 1919 stroke in particular had on Wilson's behavior. The leading Wilson scholar and editor of *The Papers of Woodrow Wilson,* Arthur Link, soon joined Weinstein in promoting a more physiological interpretation of his life and career. Several of the published volumes of this series came to include extensive notes and appendixes both by Link and his fellow editors and by medical experts about the likely influences of his physical condition at different times but most significantly during the peace conference and the League fight.[8]

Such attention was long overdue in interpreting why Wilson behaved as he did in 1919 and 1920. Moreover, the emphasis on his health throughout his life broadened the inquiry beyond the narrow question of whether the stroke was responsible for his failure to compromise. Unfortunately, in their zeal to pursue their medical interpretation, Weinstein and Link gratuitously attacked the psychological school and provoked a series of furious rejoinders by the Georges, who enlisted a medical expert of their own. The ensuing melee showed neither side at its best, but when the dust had settled some agreement did emerge about the likely influences of Wilson's cardiovascular and neurological condition in 1919 and 1920. The most important area of agreement lay in examining his condition prior to as well as following the stroke. "Cerebrovascular accidents," especially ones such as Wilson suffered, have an antecedent pathology, which often includes "small strokes" and which, even without those, often affects the victim's personality and behavior. That pathology, together with the impact of age and fatigue, underscores the conclusion that Wilson was operating at a level far below his best standard of performance in the White House.[9]

Unfortunately, this stress on his health and the controversy with the psychological school created the impression that Link and Weinstein were putting all their interpretative eggs in one basket and that they were seeking to exculpate Wilson. That was not the case. Weinstein, in particular, mixed his medical interpretations with a psychological portrait of Wilson that differed in tone but not much in content from earlier views. This was a surpassingly important point that went unnoticed in the scholarly fracas. Whatever the impact of Wilson's stroke, its antecedent pathology, and its subsequent effects, that impact could only have occurred in conjunction with his psychological makeup. Put another way, a different person would have reacted differently to an illness like this.

It might seem tempting to try to reconcile the psychological and physiological interpretations by claiming that the stroke and its surrounding neurological condition simply accentuated his personality deformations and exacerbated his messianic tendencies. But such an attempt at reconciliation would only make a bad interpretation worse. The one sound element in that blending of views is the neurologists' finding that such strokes often exaggerate their victims' personality traits. Clearly, this was true with Wilson. Combined with the ill effects of his isolation from outside contacts, his stroke appears to have destroyed previously exercised compensations for tendencies toward self-righteousness and stubbornness. But the psychological injuries inflicted by the stroke did not turn him into a would-be messiah. Rather, the stroke, its treatment, and perhaps its preceding neurological effects operated on a different aspect of Wilson's personality. His condition rendered him incapable of compromise only partly because of stubbornness and self-righteousness and not at all from messianic delusions.

The best adjective to describe the aspect of Wilson's personality that was most significantly affected by his health is "promethean." He resembled the character in ancient Greek mythology, Prometheus, who defied the gods in order to steal fire from Olympus and bring it back as a gift to his fellow mortals. The promethean traits of boldness and willingness to gamble for great stakes formed central aspects of Wilson's character at least from middle age onward. Without such boldness, Wilson would have been an ordinary college president, not the most exciting academic innovator of his time. Without such boldness, he would not have gone into politics at all, rather than running for office for the first time at the age of fifty-three. Without such boldness, he might have become a humdrum governor, rather than a leading reformer ranked alongside such contemporary state-level "progressive" titans as La Follette and Hiram Johnson, as well as his party's presidential nominee within two years. Without such boldness, he might have been a cautious domestic president who felt his way slowly, instead of one of the three greatest legislative leaders in the White House in the twentieth century. Without such boldness, he might have pursued a cautious neutrality throughout the world war, instead of finally, for better or worse, intervening with full force in order to try to shape the postwar international order.[10]

Even without his role in the League fight, Wilson ranks as one of the most daring presidents in American history. Public images to the contrary notwithstanding, he moved much more boldly in the White House than his great rival Theodore Roosevelt had done. He may even have surpassed Franklin Roosevelt in his willingness to gamble for great stakes at home and abroad. Unquestionably, Wilson's biggest gamble was his basically political conception of the League of Nations combined with a strong American commitment to international enforcement. The promethean quality of his personality shone through more brightly there than anywhere else. His decision to go to Europe and stay for the whole peace conference, his refusal to take along senators or big-name Republicans who might get in his way, his seizing the moment to whip together the Draft Covenant with Article X at its heart, his defiance of the Round Robin, his speaking tour in September—all these actions bespoke the promethean character of Wilson's role in the League fight. Finally, tragically, even his fate was promethean. The gods punished Prometheus by chaining him for eternity to a rock, while vultures pulled out his innards. Both the physical disability and the psychological imbalance that the stroke inflicted were mortal equivalents to such divine punishment.

Whether such a promethean approach was wise in the abstract is a pertinent question. It is another way of asking whether Wilson got too far ahead of his time and, if so, whose fault that was. More concretely, it needs to be asked whether this was a wise approach given the state of Wilson's health. One who seeks to play the part of Prometheus had better be in possession of every possible strength and ability. Wilson was nowhere near such fighting trim. Even before his stroke, the flare-up at the Round Robin, the failure of the speech presenting the treaty to the Senate, the inability to reach out to sympathetic Republican senators, the slowness in hitting his oratorical stride, and the faltering on the speaking tour—all these sprang in some measure from failing health. Such physical shortcomings and their likely psychological effects would have hampered any leader at any time, but they proved devastating for a would-be promethean figure at such a critical juncture.

The stroke appears to have exacerbated this promethean trait by rendering Wilson literally incapable of compromise. With his stroke-warped judgment, he could not view his gamble on the League and Article X as anything but an all-or-nothing proposition. Half a loaf looked like poison to him. His delusions about some sort of "referendum" and running for a third term, together with the threat to withdraw from the peace treaty in the diplomatic note about Fiume, attested to his willingness to lose everything rather than settle for an inconclusive outcome to the League fight. Pride and convictions about the righteousness of his cause also gripped the stroke-plagued Wilson when he scorned compromise after compromise, but it was the gambler rather than the would-be messiah who found total, clearcut defeat better than an unsatisfying, muddled draw. Wilson could not do what he had once exhorted others to do. He could not accept "peace without victory."

The second proposition in the prevailing answer to questions about the meaning of the League fight—that the American people were not ready to assume Wilson's commitments—is a corollary to the first proposition about his being ahead of his time. This second proposition shifts attention from leaders to followers. Of these three propositions, this one has stirred the least controversy. Few interpreters have doubted that, indeed, the American people in 1919 and 1920 were unwilling to take up the burden that Wilson wanted to thrust upon them. . . .

Consideration of where the public stood during the League fight leads logically to the third proposition about its meaning—that it took World War II to get Americans to heed the Wilsonian message. This third proposition requires acceptance of the preceding one, and it strikes closest to the central question of what the League fight really meant. Agreeing with these two propositions requires believing that the League fight meant comparatively little. This belief assumes further that American membership in the League and greater participation in world politics would not have done much to forestall the breakdown of international order in the 1930s. A different outcome to the League fight, so this answer holds, would not have prevented World War II. Failure to follow Wilson did not "break the heart of the world." Here is the heart of the matter. The basic question remains: Is this so?

The strongest argument in support of this third proposition is the observation that things did happen that way. World War II evidently did induce near universal and lasting support for Wilsonian commitments to maintain international order and peace. Two questions immediately arise about this proposition. First, could anything else have induced such support? Second, what were the nature and consequences of the support that World War II did induce? . . .

One last consideration needs to be noted in answering the overriding Question of what the League meant. This is the matter of what was at stake.

The stakes that Wilson strove to win in the League fight were nothing less than to prevent a recurrence of the carnage that had raged from 1914 through 1918. Even without seeing with his own eyes, he grasped how truly death-dealing and calamitous modern industrial-technological warfare had become. He also recognized that death and wounding and destruction did not comprise the sum of this kind of war's evil effects. He saw that order had broken down not only among nations but also within them, releasing terrible passions that might feed into lurid ideologies.

Wilson does not need to be exalted to the status of a secular prophet in order to appreciate his vision. He understood Communism only dimly, although he recoiled from the Bolsheviks' revolutionary violence. He did not foresee Fascism and Nazism, although he feared the nationalist passions that he saw unleashed in Europe and elsewhere. He did not foresee nuclear weapons, although he did envision how conventional warfare could become even more terribly destructive, as it did in World War II, Korea, and Vietnam. Wilson did not need to be a prophet. It was enough for him to be a sensitive man who had glanced into the abyss that yawned ahead if people and nations did not mend their ways. He never claimed to be a messiah or to have surefire solutions. As he said repeatedly on his speaking tour for the League, he was offering only some insurance against a repetition of what had just ravaged the world. But, he insisted, any insurance, even limited, partial insurance, was better than none. This was the same man who had cried out to Frank Cobb of the New York *World* in March 1917, as he agonized over whether to intervene in the war, "If there is any alternative, for God's sake let's take it."

Did the outcome of the League fight "break the heart of the world"? Of course it did. It is not necessary to claim that a different outcome would have prevented the rise of Hitler, the Holocaust, World War II, or the dropping of the atomic bomb. Just to list those events and to remember other things that have occurred between the end of World War I and the last decade of the twentieth century is to gain an appreciation of what the stakes in the League fight really were. Just to recall those events is to see that Wilson was absolutely right to grasp at any insurance against such things happening. Decent and reasonable people disagreed with him. They did not see the stakes the way Wilson did, and they believed that what he was asking was excessive and dangerous. Wilson failed to be as flexible and persuasive as he should have been, and his illness turned him into the biggest obstacle to a more-constructive outcome. But two facts remain incontrovertible. For all their decency and intelligence, Wilson's opponents were wrong. For all his flaws and missteps, Wilson was right. He should have won the League fight. His defeat did break the heart of the world. . . .

Notes

1. For a recent expression of this view, see Ninkovich, *Wilsonian Century: U.S. Foreign Policy since 1900* (Chicago, 1999), p. 76.

2. See Sigmund Freud and William Bullitt, *Thomas Woodrow Wilson: A Psychological Study* (Boston, 1967); and Alexander George and Juliette George, *Woodrow Wilson and Colonel House: A Personality Study* (New York, 1956). Appropriately, the Georges were students of Lasswell's at the University of Chicago.

3. See E. H. Carr, *The Twenty Years' Crisis* (London, 1939), esp. 102–112. Two able recent presentations of this view of Wilson are in Lloyd E. Ambrosius, *Woodrow Wilson and the American Diplomatic Tradition: The Treaty Fight in Perspective* (New York, 1987); and David Steigerwald, *Wilsonian Idealism in America* (Ithaca, N.Y., 1994).

4. Examples of Wilson's contemporaries who can fairly be accused of messianic tendencies include not only that paragon of evangelical and conservative Protestantism, Bryan, but also such apparent religious skeptics as La Follette and Roosevelt. On Wilson's religious upbringing and pre-presidential political thought, see John M. Mulder, *Woodrow Wilson: The Years of Preparation* (Princeton, N.J., 1978); and Niels Aage Thorsen, *The Political Thought of Woodrow Wilson, 1875–1910* (Princeton, N.J., 1988).

5. To be fair to those who downgrade the influence of the stroke in particular, it should be noted that none other than Arthur Link once stated, "It is, therefore, possible, even probable, that Wilson would have acted as he did even had he not suffered his breakdown, for it was not in his nature to compromise away the principles in which he believed." Arthur S. Link, *Wilson the Diplomatist: A Look at His Major Foreign Policies* (Baltimore, 1957), 155. When he wrote those words, Link had evidently not completely discarded the critical, sometimes even harsh, view of Wilson that he expressed in the first volume of his biography, *Wilson: The Road to the White House* (Princeton, N.J., 1947), and in *Woodrow Wilson and the Progressive Era, 1910–1917* (New York, 1954). He later modified most of those criticisms of Wilson and reversed his evaluation of the effect of the stroke on Wilson's refusal to compromise in the League fight.

6. The stress on the nefarious influence of partisanship is one of the few points on which I disagree with the otherwise estimable and incisive treatment of the League fight in Thomas A. Bailey, *Woodrow Wilson and the Great Betrayal* (New York, 1945).

7. Although I am less sympathetic toward Lodge, I do agree in the main with the assessments of him in William Widenor's excellent *Henry Cabot*

Lodge and the Search for an American Foreign Policy (Berkeley, Calif., 1980), especially when he says, "We may reasonably assume that Lodge would have swallowed the League had he seen therein the means of securing a Republican victory" (309) and Lodge "had to be less forthright in expressing his views, had to be all things to all men" (322).

8. See Edwin Weinstein, "Woodrow Wilson's Neurological Illness," *Journal of American History*, LVII (Sept. 1970), 324–351, and *Woodrow Wilson: A Medical and Psychological Biography* (Princeton, N.J., 1981). Relevant notes and appendixes to the *Papers of Wilson* are cited above in the notes relating to Wilson's behavior in the summer of 1919 and the impact of the stroke.

9. On the controversy, see Edwin Weinstein, James William Anderson, and Arthur S. Link, "Woodrow Wilson's Political Personality: A Reappraisal," *Political Science Quarterly*, XCIII (Winter 1978–79), 585–598; George and George, "Woodrow Wilson and Colonel House: A Reply to Weinstein, Anderson, and Link," ibid., XCVI (Winter 1981–82), 641–643; George and George, "Issues in Wilson Scholarship: References to Early Strokes in the Papers of Woodrow Wilson," *Journal of American History*, LXX (March 1984), 845–853; Arthur S. Link, David W. Hirst, John Wells Davidson, and John E. Little, "Communication," ibid., 945–955. Alexander George, Michael T. Marmor, and Juliette George, "Communication," ibid., 955–956. For an appraisal of Weinstein's book and the first two items in this battle of the articles, see Dorothy Ross, "Woodrow Wilson and the Case for Psychohistory," ibid., LXIX (Dec. 1982), 639–668; and Lloyd E. Ambrosius, "Woodrow Wilson's Health and the Treaty Fight," *International History Review*, IX (February 1987), 73–84.

10. A remark that revealed this side of Wilson's personality came in 1910 when he told his brother-in-law Stockton Axson, after his defeat in the graduate school controversy at Princeton, "I am not interested in simply administering a club. Unless I can develop something I cannot get thoroughly interested." Axson memoir, "Princeton Controversy," Ray Stannard Baker Papers, Box 99.

William G. Carleton  **NO**

A New Look at Woodrow Wilson

All high-placed statesmen crave historical immortality. Woodrow Wilson craved it more than most. Thus far the fates have not been kind to Wilson; there is a reluctance to admit him to as great a place in history as he will have.

Congress has just gotten around to planning a national memorial for Wilson, several years after it had done this for Theodore Roosevelt and Franklin D. Roosevelt. Wilson is gradually being accepted as one of the nation's five or six greatest Presidents. However, the heroic mold of the man on the large stage of world history is still generally unrecognized.

There is a uniquely carping, hypercritical approach to Wilson. Much more than other historical figures he is being judged by personality traits, many of them distorted or even fancied. Wilson is not being measured by the yardstick used for other famous characters of history. There is a double standard at work here.

What are the common errors and misrepresentations with respect to Wilson? In what ways is he being judged more rigorously? What are the reasons for this? Why will Wilson eventually achieve giant stature in world history?

⋅⟨⊙⟩⋅

There are two criticisms of Wilson that go to the heart of his fame and place in history. One is an alleged inflexibility and intransigence, an inability to compromise. The other is that he had no real understanding of world politics, that he was a naïve idealist. Neither is true.

If Wilson were indeed as stubborn and adamant as he is often portrayed he would have been a bungler at his work, for the practice and art of politics consist in a feeling for the possible, a sense of timing, a capacity for give-and-take compromise. In reality, Wilson's leadership of his party and the legislative accomplishments of his first term were magnificent. His performance was brilliantly characterized by the very qualities he is said to have lacked: flexibility, accommodation, a sense of timing, and a willingness to compromise. In the struggles to win the Federal Reserve Act, the Clayton Anti-Trust Law, the Federal Trade Commission, and other major measures of his domestic program, Wilson repeatedly mediated between the agrarian liberals and the conservatives of his party, moving now a little to the left, now to the right, now back to the left. He learned by experience, cast aside pride of opinion,

From *Virginia Quarterly Review,* vol. 38, no. 4 (Autumn 1962), pp. 545–566. Copyright © 1962 by University of Virginia. Reprinted by permission.

accepted and maneuvered for regulatory commissions after having warned of their danger during the campaign of 1912, and constantly acted as a catalyst of the opposing factions of his party and of shifting opinion.

The cautious way Wilson led the country to military preparedness and to war demonstrated resiliency and a sense of timing of a high order. At the Paris Conference Wilson impressed thoughtful observers with his skill as a negotiator; many European diplomats were surprised that an "amateur" could do so well. Here the criticism is not that Wilson was without compromise but that he compromised too much.

Actually, the charge that Wilson was incapable of compromise must stand or fall on his conduct during the fight in the Senate over the ratification of the League of Nations, particularly his refusal to give the word to the Democratic Senators from the South to vote for the Treaty with the Lodge Reservations, which, it is claimed, would have assured ratification. Wilson, say the critics, murdered his own brain child. It is Wilson, and not Lodge, who has now become the villain of this high tragedy.

Now, would a Wilsonian call to the Southerners to change their position have resulted in ratification? Can we really by sure? In order to give Southerners time to readjust to a new position, the call from the White House would have had to have been made several weeks before that final vote. During that time what would have prevented Lodge from hobbling the League with still more reservations? Would the mild reservationists, all Republicans, have prevented this? The record shows, I think, that in the final analysis the mild reservationists could always be bamboozled by Lodge in the name of party loyalty. As the fight on the League had progressed, the reservations had become more numerous and more crippling. Wilson, it seems, had come to feel that there simply was no appeasing Lodge.

During the Peace Conference, in response to the Senatorial Round Robin engineered by Lodge, Wilson had reopened the whole League question and obtained the inclusion of American "safeguards" he felt would satisfy Lodge. This had been done at great cost, for it had forced Wilson to abandon his position as a negotiator above the battles for national advantages and to become a suppliant for national concessions. This had resulted in his having to yield points in other parts of the Treaty to national-minded delegations from other countries. When Wilson returned from Paris with the completed Treaty, Lodge had "raised the ante," the Lodge Reservations requiring the consent of other signatory nations were attached to the Treaty, and these had multiplied and become more restrictive in nature as the months went by. Would not then a "final" yielding by Wilson have resulted in even stiffer reservations being added? Was not Lodge using the Reservations to effect not ratification but rejection, knowing that there was a point beyond which Wilson could not yield?

Wilson seems honestly to have believed that the Lodge Reservations emasculated the League. Those who read them for the first time will be surprised, I think, to discover how nationally self-centered they were. If taken seriously, they surely must have impaired the functioning of the League. However, Wilson was never opposed to clarifying or interpretative reservations which would not require the consent of the other signatories. Indeed, he himself wrote the Hitchcock Reservations.

Even had the League with the Lodge Reservations been ratified, how certain can we really be that this would have meant American entrance into the League? Under the Lodge Reservations, every signatory nation had to accept them before the United States could become a member. Would all the signatories have accepted every one of the fifteen Lodge Reservations? The United States had no monopoly on chauvinism, and would not other nations have interposed reservations of their own as a condition to their acceptance of the Lodge Reservations?

At Paris, Wilson had personally experienced great difficulty getting his own mild "reservations" incorporated into the Covenant. Now, at this late date, would Britain have accepted the Lodge Reservation on Irish self-determination? In all probability. Would Japan have accepted the Reservation on Shantung? This is more doubtful. Would the Latin American states have accepted the stronger Reservation on the Monroe Doctrine? This is also doubtful. Chile had already shown concern, and little Costa Rica had the temerity to ask for a definition of the Doctrine. Would the British Dominions have accepted the Reservation calling for one vote for the British Empire or six votes for the United States? Even Lord Grey, who earlier had predicted that the signatories would accept the Lodge Reservations, found that he could not guarantee acceptance by the Dominions, and Canada's President of the Privy Council and Acting Secretary for External Affairs, Newton W. Rowell, declared that if this Reservation were accepted by the other powers Canada would withdraw from the League.

By the spring of 1920, Wilson seems to have believed that making the League of Nations the issue in the campaign of 1920 would afford a better opportunity for American participation in an effective League than would further concessions to Lodge. To Wilson, converting the Presidential election into a solemn referendum on the League was a reality. For months, because of his illness, he had lived secluded in the White House, and the memories of his highly emotional reception in New York on his return from Paris and of the enthusiasm of the Western audiences during his last speaking trip burned vividly bright. He still believed that the American people, if given the chance, would vote for the League without emasculating reservations. Does this, then, make Wilson naïve? It is well to remember that in the spring of 1920 not even the most sanguine Republican envisaged the Republican sweep that would develop in the fall of that year.

If the strategy of Wilson in the spring of 1920 was of debatable wisdom, the motives of Lodge can no longer be open to doubt. After the landslide of 1920, which gave the Republicans the Presidency and an overwhelming majority in a Senate dominated by Lodge in foreign policy, the Treaty was never resurrected. The Lodge Reservations, representing months of gruelling legislative labor, were cavalierly jettisoned, and a separate peace was made with Germany.

What, then, becomes of the stock charge that Wilson was intolerant of opposition and incapable of bending? If the truth of this accusation must rest on Wilson's attitude during the Treaty fight, and I think it must, for he showed remarkable adaptability in other phases of his Presidency, then it must fall. The situation surrounding the Treaty fight was intricately tangled, and there is certainly as much evidence on the side of Wilson's forbearance as on the side of his obstinacy.

A far more serious charge against Wilson is that he had no realistic understanding of world politics, that he was an impractical idealist whose policies intensified rather than alleviated international problems. Now what American statesman of the period understood world politics better than Wilson—or indeed in any way as well as he? Elihu Root, with his arid legalism? Philander Knox, with his dollar diplomacy? Theodore Roosevelt or Henry Cabot Lodge? Roosevelt and Lodge had some feel for power politics, and they understood the traditional balance of power, at least until their emotions for a dictated Allied victory got the better of their judgment: but was either of them aware of the implications for world politics of the technological revolution in war and the disintegration of the old balance of power? And were not both of them blind to a new force in world politics just then rising to a place of importance—the anti-imperialist revolutions, which even before World War I were getting under way with the Mexican Revolution and the Chinese Revolution of Sun Yat-sen?

Wilson is charged with having no understanding of the balance of power, but who among world statesmen of the twentieth century better sated the classic doctrine of the traditional balance of power than Wilson in his famous Peace Without Victory speech? And was it not Theodore Roosevelt who derided him for stating it? With perfectly straight faces Wilson critics, and a good many historians, tell us that TR, who wanted to march to Berlin and saddle Germany with a harsh peace, and FDR, who sponsored unconditional surrender, "understood" the balance of power, but that Wilson, who fought to salvage a power balance by preserving Germany from partition, was a simple-simon in world politics—an illustration of the double standard at work in evaluating Wilson's place in history.

Wilson not only understood the old, but with amazing clarity he saw the new, elements in world politics. He recognized the emergence of the anti-imperialist revolutions and the importance of social politics in the international relations of the future. He recognized, too, the implications for future world politics of the technological revolution in war, of total war, and of the disintegration of the old balance of power—for World War I had decisively weakened the effective brakes on Japan in Asia, disrupted the Turkish Empire in the Middle East and the Austro-Hungarian Empire in Europe, and removed Russia as a make-weight for the foreseeable future. Wilson believed that a truncated Germany and an attempted French hegemony would only add to the chaos, but he saw too that merely preserving Germany as a power unit would not restore the old balance of power. To Wilson, even in its prime the traditional balance of power had worked only indifferently and collective security would have been preferable, but in his mind the revolutionary changes in the world of 1919 made a collective-security system indispensable.

Just what is realism in world politics? Is it not the ability to use purposefully many factors, even theoretically contradictory ones, and to use them not singly and consecutively but interdependently and simultaneously, shifting the emphasis as conditions change? If so, was not Wilson a very great realist in world politics? He used the old balance-of-power factors, as evidenced by his fight to save Germany as a power unit and his sponsoring of a tripartite alliance of the United States, Britain, and France to guarantee France from any German aggression until such time as collective security would become effective. But he labored to introduce into international relations the new collective-security factors to supplement and gradually supersede in importance the older factors, now increasingly outmoded by historical developments. To label as doctrinaire idealist one who envisaged world politics in so broad and flexible a way is to pervert the meaning of words. . . .

Ranking the Presidents has become a popular game, and even Presidents like to play it, notably Truman and Kennedy. In my own evaluation, I place Wilson along with Jefferson and Lincoln as the nation's three greatest Presidents, which makes Wilson our greatest twentieth-century President. If rated solely on the basis of long-range impact on international relations, Wilson is the most influential of all our Presidents.

What are the achievements which entitle Wilson to so high a place? Let us consider the major ones, although of course some of these are more important than others.

. . . [B]etter than any responsible statesman of his day, Wilson understood and sympathized with the anti-imperialist revolutions and their aspirations for basic internal reforms. He withdrew American support for the Bankers' Consortium in China, and the United States under Wilson was the first of the great powers to recognize the Revolution of Sun Yat-sen. Early in his term he had to wrestle with the Mexican Revolution. He saw the need for social reform; avoided the general war with Mexico that many American investors, Catholics, and professional patriots wanted; and by refusing to recognize the counter-revolution of Huerta and cutting Huerta off from trade and arms while allowing the flow of arms to Carranza, Villa, and Zapata, he made possible the overthrow of the counter-revolution and the triumph of the Revolution. What merciless criticism was heaped on Wilson for insisting that Latin Americans should be positively encouraged to institute reforms and develop democratic practices. Yet today Americans applaud their government's denial of Alliance-for-Progress funds to Latin American countries which refuse to undertake fundamental economic and social reforms and flout democracy.

. . . [C]onfronted with the stupendous and completely novel challenge of having to mobilize not only America's military strength but also its civilian resources and energies in America's first total war, the Wilson Administration set up a huge network of administrative agencies, exemplifying the highest imagination and creativity in the art of practical administration. FDR, in his New Deal and in his World War II agencies, was to borrow heavily from the Wilson innovations.

. . . Wilson's Fourteen Points and his other peace aims constituted war propaganda of perhaps unparalleled brilliance. They thrilled the world. They gave high purpose to the peoples of the Allied countries and stirred their war efforts. Directed over the heads of the governments to the enemy peoples themselves, they produced unrest, helped bring about the revolutions that overthrew the Sultan, the Hapsburgs, and the Hohenzollerns, and hastened the end of the war.

. . . [T]he Treaty of Versailles, of which Wilson was the chief architect, was a better peace than it would have been (considering, among other things, the imperialist secret treaties of the Allies) because of Wilson's labors for a just peace. The League of Nations was founded, and this was to be the forerunner of the United Nations. To the League was assigned the work of general disarmament. The mandate system of the League, designed to prepare colonial peoples for self-government and national independence, was a revolutionary step away from the old imperialism. The aspirations of many peoples in Europe for national independence were fulfilled. (If the disruption of the Austro-Hungarian Empire helped destroy the old balance of power, it must be said that in this particular situation Wilson's doctrine of national autonomy only exploited an existing fact in the interest of Allied victory, and even had there been no Wilsonian self-determination the nationalities of this area were already so well developed that they could not have been denied independence after the defeat of the Hapsburgs. Wilson's self-determination was to be a far more *creative* force among the colonial peoples than among the Europeans.) The Treaty restrained the chauvinism of the Italians, though not as much as Wilson would have liked. It prevented the truncating of Germany by preserving to her the Left Bank of the Rhine. The war-guilt clause and the enormous reparations saddled on Germany were mistakes, but Wilson succeeded in confining German responsibility to civilian damage and the expenses of Allied military pensions rather than the whole cost of the war; and had the United States ratified the Treaty and participated in post-war world affairs, as Wilson expected, the United States would have been in a position to join Britain in scaling down the actual reparations bill and in preventing any such adventure as the French seizure of the Ruhr in 1923, from which flowed Germany's disastrous inflation and the ugly forces of German nihilism. (There is poignancy in the broken Wilson's coming out of retirement momentarily in 1923 to denounce France for making "waste paper" of the Treaty of Versailles.) Finally, if Shantung was Wilson's Yalta, he paid the kind of price FDR paid and for precisely the same reason—the collapse of the balance of power in the immediate area involved.

. . . [T]he chief claim of Wilson to a superlative place in history—and it will not be denied him merely because he was turned down by the United States Senate—is that he, more than any other, formulated and articulated the ideology which was the polestar of the Western democracies in World War I, in World War II, and in the decades of Cold War against the Communists. Today, well past the middle of the twentieth century, the long-time program of America is still a Wilsonian program: international collective security, disarmament, the lowering of economic barriers between nations (as in America's support for the developing West European community today), anti-colonialism, self-determination of nations, and democratic social politics as an alternative to Communism. And this was the program critics of Wilson called "anachronistic," a mere "throw-back" to nineteenth-century liberalism!

America today is still grappling with the same world problems Wilson grappled with in 1917, 1918, and 1919, and the programs and policies designed to meet them are still largely Wilsonian. But events since Wilson's time have made his solutions more and more prophetic and urgent. The sweep of the anti-imperialist revolutions propels us to wider self-determination and social politics. The elimination of space, the increasing interdependence of the world, the further disintegration of the balance of power in World War II, and the nuclear revolution in war compel us to more effective collective security and to arms control supervised by an agency of the United Nations.

There will be more unwillingness to identify Wilson with social politics abroad than with the other policies with which he is more clearly identified. Historians like to quote George L. Record's letter to Wilson in which he told Wilson that there was no longer any glory in merely standing for political democracy, that political democracy had arrived, that the great issues of the future would revolve around economic and social democracy. But Wilson stood in no need of advice on this score. Earlier than any other responsible statesman, Wilson had seen the significance of the Chinese Revolution of Sun Yat-sen and of the Mexican Revolution, and he had officially encouraged both. Wilson believed that economic and social reform was implicit in the doctrine of self-determination, especially when applied to the colonial peoples. He recognized, too, that the Bolshevist Revolution had given economic and social reform a new urgency in all parts of the world. He was also well aware that those who most opposed his program for a world settlement were the conservative and imperialist elements in Western Europe and Japan, that socialist and labor groups were his most effective supporters. He pondered deeply how closely and openly he could work with labor and socialist parties in Europe without cutting off necessary support at home. (This—how to use social democracy and the democratic left to counter Communism abroad and still carry American opinion—was to be a central problem for every discerning American statesman after 1945.) Months before he had received Record's letter, Wilson himself had expressed almost the same views as Record. In a long conversation with Professor Stockton Axson at the White House, Wilson acknowledged that his best support was coming from labor people, that they were in touch with world movements and were international-minded, that government ownership of some basic resources and industries was coming, even in the United States, and that it was by a program of social democracy that Communism could be defeated.

In 1918 two gigantic figures—Wilson and Lenin—faced each other and articulated the contesting ideologies which would shake the world during the century. Since then, the lesser leaders who have succeeded them have added little to the ideology of either side. We are now far enough into the century to see in what direction the world is headed, provided there is no third world war. It is not headed for Communist domination. It is not headed for an American hegemony. And it is not headed for a duality with half the world Communist and the other half capitalist. Instead, it is headed for a new pluralism. The emerging new national societies are adjusting their new industrialism to their own conditions and cultures; and their developing economies will be varying mixtures of privatism, collectivism, and welfarism. Even the Communist states differ from one another in conditions, cultures, stages of revolutionary development, and degrees of Marxist "orthodoxy" or "revisionism." And today, all national states, old and new, Communist and non-Communist, join the United Nations as a matter of course.

There will be "victory" for neither "side," but instead a world which has been historically affected by both. Lenin's international proletarian state failed to materialize, but the evolving economies of the underdeveloped peoples are being influenced by his collectivism. However, the facts that most of the emerging economies are mixed ones, that they are working themselves out within autonomous national frameworks, and that the multiplying national states are operating internationally through the United Nations all point to a world which will be closer to the vision of Wilson than to that of Lenin. For this reason Wilson is likely to become a world figure of heroic proportions, with an acknowledged impact on world history more direct and far-reaching than that of any other American.

POSTSCRIPT

Was Woodrow Wilson Responsible for the Failure of the United States to Join the League of Nations?

Professor William G. Carleton presents an impassioned defense of both Wilson's policies at Versailles as well as their implications for the future of American foreign policy. Carleton responds to the two main charges historians continue to level against Wilson: his inability to compromise and his naïve idealism. Unlike Professor Thomas A. Bailey, who in *Woodrow Wilson and the Great Betrayal* (Macmillan, 1945) blames Wilson for failing to compromise with senator Henry Cabot Lodge, Carleton excoriates the chairman of the Senate Foreign Relations Committee for adding "nationally self-centered" reservations that he knew would emasculate the League of Nations and most likely cause other nations to add reservations to the Treaty of Versailles. Wilson, says Carleton, was a true realist when he rejected the Lodge reservations.

Professor Carleton's article was in many ways a response to the realist critique of traditional American foreign policy put forth during the height of the cold war. Most influential were the series of lectures on *American Diplomacy, 1900–1950* (Mentor Books, 1951) by former diplomat George F. Kennan who protested vehemently about the "legalistic-moralistic" streak that permeated American foreign policy. Other realistic critics included influential journalist Walter Lippman and political scientist Robert Endicott Osgood and Hans Morgenthau. Osgood's study of *Ideals and Self-Interest in American Foreign Relations* (University of Chicago Press, 1953) established the realist/idealist dichotomy later utilized by former Secretary of State Henry Kissinger in his scholarly history of *Diplomacy* (Simon & Schuster, 1994). According to Kissinger, Wilson was reflective of an excessive moralism and naïveté, which Americans hold about the world even today. Rejecting the fact that the United States had a basic national interest in preserving the balance of power of Europe, Wilson told the American people that they were entering the war to "bring peace and safety to all nations and make the world itself at last free." Kissinger believes that Theodore Roosevelt, the realist, had a firmer handle on foreign policy than did Wilson, the idealist. But in the long run, Wilsonianism triumphed and has influenced every modern-day president's foreign policy.

Scholars have criticized the realist approach to Wilson for a number of reasons. Some say that it is "unrealistic" to expect an American president to ask for a declaration of war to defend abstract principles such as the balance of power or the American national interest. Presidents and other elected officials must have a moral reason if they expect the American public to support a foreign war in which American servicemen might be killed.

Many recent historians agree with David F. Trask that Wilson developed realistic and clearly articulated goals and coordinated his larger diplomatic aims with the use of force better than any other wartime U.S. president. See "Woodrow Wilson and the Reconciliation of Force and Diplomacy, 1917–1918," *Naval War College Review* (January/February 1975). Arthur S. Link, coeditor of the *Papers of Woodrow Wilson,* 69 vols. (Princeton, 1966–1993), gave a blow-by-blow response to Kennan in revised lectures given at Johns Hopkins University in *Woodrow Wilson: Revolution, War and Peace* (Harlan Davidson, 1979) nicely summarized in "The Higher Realism of Woodrow Wilson," in a book of essays with the same title (Vanderbilt University Press, 1971). . . . Finally, George Kennan acknowledges that his earlier criticism of Wilson had to be viewed within the context of the cold war. "I now view Wilson," he wrote in 1991, "as a man who, like so many other people of broad vision and acute sensitivities, was ahead of his time, and did not live long enough to know what great and commanding relevance his ideas would acquire before this century was out." See "Comments on the Paper, Entitled 'Kennan Versus Wilson'" by Thomas J. Knock in John M. Cooper et al., eds., *The Wilson Era: Essays in Honor of Arthur S. Link* (Harlan Davidson, 1991).

In his article, Professor Carleton advanced many of the arguments that historians Trask, Link, and Kennan later used defending Wilson's "higher realism." Rejecting the view of Wilson as a naïve idealist, Carleton maintains: "He recognized the emergence of the anti-imperialist revolutions . . . the importance of social politics in the international relations of the future . . . the implications for future world politics of the technological revolutions in war, of total war, and of the disintegration of the old balance of power."

Wilson's health has received serious scrutiny from scholars. In the early 1930s, Sigmund Freud and William C. Bullitt, a former diplomat, wrote a scathing and highly inaccurate biography of *Thomas Woodrow Wilson* (Houghton Mifflin, 1967) published posthumously in 1967. The book was poorly received and scathingly reviewed by Arthur S. Link, "The Case for Woodrow Wilson," in *The Higher Realism.* . . . The major controversy seems to be those who stress psychological difficulties—see Alexander and Juliette George, *Woodrow Wilson and Colonel House: A Personality Study* (Dover Press, 1956, 1964)—versus medical illnesses—see Edwin A. Weinstein, *Woodrow Wilson: A Medical and Psychological Biography* (Princeton University, 1981). For the best summaries of the controversy, see Thomas T. Lewis, "Alternative Psychological Interpretations of Woodrow Wilson," *Mid-America* (vol. 45, 1983); and Lloyd E. Ambrosius, "Woodrow Wilson's Health and the Treaty Fight, 1919–1920," *The International History Review* (February 1987). Phyllis Lee Levin, *Edith and Woodrow: The White House Years* (Scribners, 2001); and Robert J. Maddox, "Mrs. Wilson and the Presidency," *American History* (February 1973), make the case that we have already had America's first woman president. . . .

ISSUE 10

Was Prohibition a Failure?

YES: David E. Kyvig, from *Repealing National Prohibition,* 2nd ed. (The University of Chicago Press, 1979, 2000)

NO: J. C. Burnham, from "New Perspectives on the Prohibition 'Experiment' of the 1920s," *Journal of Social History, vol. 2* (Fall 1968)

ISSUE SUMMARY

YES: David E. Kyvig admits that alcohol consumption declined sharply in the prohibition era but that federal actions failed to impose abstinence among an increasingly urban and heterogeneous populace that resented and resisted restraints on their individual behavior.

NO: J. C. Burnham states that the prohibition experiment was more a success than a failure and contributed to a substantial decrease in liquor consumption, reduced arrests for alcoholism, fewer alcohol-related diseases and hospitalizations, and destroyed the old-fashioned saloon that was a major target of the law's proponents.

$\mathbf{A}$mericans, including many journalists and scholars, have never been shy about attaching labels to their history, and frequently they do so to characterize particular years or decades in their distant or recent past. It is doubtful, however, that any period in our nation's history has received as many catchy appellations as has the decade of the 1920s. Described at various times as the "Jazz Age," the "Roaring Twenties," the "prosperity decade," the "age of normalcy," or simply the "New Era," these are years that obviously have captured the imagination of the American public, including the chroniclers of the nation's past.

In 1920, the Great War was over, and President Woodrow Wilson received the Nobel Peace Prize despite his failure to persuade the Senate to adopt the Covenant of the League of Nations. The "Red Scare," culminating in the Palmer raids conducted by the Justice Department, came to an embarrassingly fruitless halt, and Republican Warren Harding won a landslide victory in the campaign for the presidency, an election in which women, buoyed by the ratification of the Nineteenth Amendment, exercised their suffrage rights for the first time in national politics. In Pittsburgh, the advent of the radio age was symbolized by the broadcast of election results by KDKA, the nation's first commercial radio station. F. Scott Fitzgerald and Sinclair Lewis each published their first important novels and thereby helped to usher in the most significant American literary renaissance since the early nineteenth century.

During the next nine years, Americans witnessed a number of amazing events: the rise and fall of the Ku Klux Klan; the trial, conviction, and execution of anarchists Nicola Sacco and Bartolomeo Vanzetti on murder charges and the subsequent legislative restrictions on immigration into the United States; battles over the teaching of evolution in the schools epitomized by the rhetorical clashes between William Jennings Bryan and Clarence Darrow during the Scopes trial in Dayton, Tennessee; the Harding scandals; "talking" motion pictures; and, in 1929, the collapse of the New York Stock Exchange, symbolizing the beginning of the Great Depression and bringing a startling end to the euphoric claims of business prosperity that had dominated the decade.

The 1920s are also remembered as the "dry decade," as a consequence of the ratification of the Eighteenth Amendment and the passage by Congress of the Volstead Act that prohibited the manufacture, sale, or transportation of alcoholic beverages. The implementation of national prohibition represented a continuation of the types of reforms designed by Progressives to improve the quality of life for the American citizenry; however, the illicit manufacture and trade of alcohol and the proliferation of speakeasies, where patrons seemed to flaunt the law with impunity, raise questions about the effectiveness of such legislation. Did prohibition work, or was it a noble, but failed, experiment? The selections that follow address this matter from different perspectives.

David Kyvig points out that the Volstead Act did not specifically prohibit the use or purchase of alcoholic beverages and that liquor continued to be provided by various sources, including gangland bootleggers, to meet consumer demand. Despite efforts to enforce the law, the federal government failed to create an adequate institutional network to insure compliance. Hence, although the consumption of alcohol did drop during the decade of the 1920s, legislation failed to eliminate drinking or to produce a feeling that such a goal was even within reach.

J. C. Burnham, on the other hand, argues that enforcement of the prohibition laws was quite effective in many places. Moreover, in addition to reducing the per capita consumption of alcohol, the enactment of prohibition legislation led to several positive social consequences. For example, during the 1920s, fewer people were arrested for public drunkenness, and there were substantially fewer Americans treated for alcohol-related diseases. All in all, he concludes, prohibition was more of a success than a failure.

YES

David E. Kyvig

America Sobers Up

When the Eighteenth Amendment took effect on January 17, 1920, most observers assumed that liquor would quickly disappear from the American scene. The possibility that a constitutional mandate would be ignored simply did not occur to them. "Confidence in the law to achieve a moral revolution was unbounded," one scholar of rural America has pointed out, explaining that "this was, after all, no mere statute, it was the Constitution." The assistant commissioner of the Internal Revenue Service, the agency charged with overseeing the new federal law, predicted that it would take six years to make the nation absolutely dry but that prohibition would be generally effective from the outset. Existing state and federal law enforcement agencies were expected to be able to police the new law. Initial plans called for only a modest special enforcement program, its attention directed to large cities where the principal resistance was anticipated. Wayne Wheeler of the Anti-Saloon League confidently anticipated that national prohibition would be respected, and estimated that an annual federal appropriation of five million dollars would be ample to implement it. The popular evangelist Billy Sunday replaced his prohibition sermon with one entitled "Crooks, Corkscrews, Bootleggers, and Whiskey Politicians—They Shall Not Pass." Wartime prohibition, which only banned further manufacture of distilled spirits and strong beer (with an alcohol content exceeding 2.75 percent) had already significantly reduced consumption. Few questioned the Volstead Act's capacity to eliminate intoxicants altogether. Americans accustomed to a society in which observation and pressure from other members of a community encouraged a high degree of conformity did not foresee that there would be difficulties in obtaining compliance with the law. They did not realize that the law would be resented and resisted by sizable elements in an increasingly urban and heterogeneous society where restraints on the individual were becoming far less compelling.

Within a few months it became apparent that not every American felt obliged to stop drinking the moment constitutional prohibition began. In response to consumer demand, a variety of sources provided at first a trickle and later a growing torrent of forbidden beverages. Physicians could legally prescribe "medicinal" spirits or beer for their patients, and before prohibition was six months old, more than fifteen thousand, along with over fifty-seven thousand pharmacists, obtained licenses to dispense liquor. Grape juice or

From *Repealing National Prohibition,* 2nd ed., by David E. Kyvig (University of Chicago Press, 1979, 2000) pp. 20–32, 35. Copyright © 1979 by David E. Kyvig. Reprinted by permission of the author.

concentrates could be legitimately shipped and sold and, if the individual pur-chaser chose, allowed to ferment. Distributors learned to attach "warning" labels, reporting that United States Department of Agriculture tests had deter-mined that, for instance, if permitted to sit for sixty days the juice would turn into wine of twelve percent alcohol content. The quadrupled output and rising prices of the California grape industry during the decade showed that many people took such warnings to heart.

Other methods of obtaining alcoholic beverages were more devious. Some "near-beer," which was legally produced by manufacturing genuine beer, then removing the three to five percent alcohol in excess of the approved one-half percent, was diverted to consumers before the alcohol was removed. In other instances, following government inspection, alcohol was reinjected into near-beer, making what was often called "needle beer." Vast amounts of alcohol produced for industrial purposes were diverted, watered down, and flavored for beverage purposes. To discourage this practice, the government directed that industrial alcohol be rendered unfit to drink by the addition of denaturants. Bootleggers did not always bother to remove such poisons, which cost some unsuspecting customers their eyesight or their lives.

Theft of perhaps twenty million gallons of good preprohibition liquor from bonded warehouses in the course of the decade, as well as an undeter-minable amount of home brewing and distilling, provided more palatable and dependable beverages. By 1930 illegal stills provided the main supply of liquor, generally a high quality product. The best liquor available was that smug-gled in from Canada and from ships anchored on "Rum Row" in the Atlantic beyond the twelve-mile limit of United States jurisdiction. By the late 1920s, one million gallons of Canadian liquor per year, eighty percent of that nation's greatly expanded output, made its way into the United States. British shipment of liquor to islands which provisioned Rum Row increased dramatically. Exports to the Bahamas, for example, went from 944 gallons in 1918 to 386,000 gallons in 1922. The tiny French islands of St. Pierre and Miguelon off the coast of Newfoundland imported 118,600 gallons of British liquor in 1922, "quite a respectable quantity," a British official observed, "for an island population of 6,000." Bootlegging, the illicit commercial system for distributing liquor, solved most problems of bringing together supply and demand. Government appeared unable—some claimed even unwilling—to halt a rising flood of intoxicants. Therefore, many observers at that time, and increasing numbers since the law's repeal, assumed that prohibition simply did not work. . . .

The Volstead Act specified how the constitutional ban on "intoxicating liquors . . . for beverage purposes" was to be enforced. What the statute did not say had perhaps the greatest importance. While the law barred manufacture, transport, sale, import, or export of intoxicants, it did not specifically make their purchase or use a crime. This allowed continued possession of intoxi-cants obtained prior to prohibition, provided that such beverages were only for personal use in one's own home. Not only did the failure outlaw use render prohibition harder to enforce by eliminating possession as *de facto* evidence of crime, but also it allowed the purchaser and consumer of alcoholic beverages to defend his own behavior. Although the distinction was obviously artificial, the consumer could and did insist that there was nothing illegal about his drinking, while at the same time complaining that failure of government efforts to suppress bootlegging represented a break down of law and order.

Adopting the extreme, prohibitionist view that any alcohol whatsoever was intoxicating, the Volstead Act outlawed all beverages with an alcoholic content of .5 percent or more. The .5 percent limitation followed a traditional standard used to distinguish between alcoholic and nonalcoholic beverages for purposes of taxation, but that standard was considered by many to be unrealistic in terms of the amount of alcohol needed to produce intoxication. Wartime prohibition, after all, only banned beer with an alcohol content of 2.75 percent or more. Many did not associate intoxication with beer or wine at all but rather with distilled spirits. Nevertheless, the only exception to the .5 percent standard granted by the Volstead Act, which had been drafted by the Anti-Saloon League, involved cider and fruit juices; these subjects of natural fermentation were to be illegal only if declared by a jury to be intoxicating in fact. The Volstead Act, furthermore, did permit the use of intoxicants for medicinal purposes and religious sacraments; denatured industrial alcohol was exempted as well.

The Eighteenth Amendment specified that federal and state governments would have concurrent power to enforce the ban on intoxicating beverages. Therefore the system which evolved to implement prohibition had a dual nature. Congress, anticipating general compliance with the liquor ban as well as cooperation from state and local policing agencies in dealing with those violations which did occur, created a modest enforcement program at first. Two million dollars was appropriated to administer the law for its first five months of operation, followed by $4,750,000 for the fiscal year beginning July 1, 1920. The Prohibition Bureau of the Treasury Department recruited a force of only about fifteen hundred enforcement agents. Every state except Maryland adopted its own antiliquor statute. Most state laws were modeled after the Volstead Act, though some dated from the days of state prohibition and several imposed stricter regulations or harsher penalties than did the federal statute. State and local police forces were expected to enforce these laws as part of their normal duties. Critics at the time and later who claimed that no real effort was made to enforce national prohibition because no large enforcement appropriations were forthcoming needed to consider the assumptions and police practices of the day. No general national police force, only specialized customs and treasury units, existed. Furthermore, neither federal nor state officials initially felt a need for a large special force to carry out this one task. The creators of national prohibition anticipated only a modest increase in the task facing law-enforcement officials.

Most Americans obeyed the national prohibition law. Many, at least a third to two-fifths of the adult population if Gallup poll surveys in the 1930s are any indication, had not used alcohol previously and simply continued to abstain. Others ceased to drink beer, wine, or spirits when to do so became illegal. The precise degree of compliance with the law is difficult to determine because violation levels cannot be accurately measured. The best index of the extent to which the law was accepted comes from a somewhat indirect indicator.

Consumption of beer, wine, and spirits prior to and following national prohibition was accurately reflected in the payment of federal excise taxes on alcoholic beverages. The tax figures appear reliable because bootlegging lacked sufficient profitability to be widespread when liquor was legally and conveniently obtainable. The amount of drinking during prohibition can be inferred from consumption rates once alcoholic beverages were again legalized. Drinking may have increased after repeal; it almost certainly did not decline. During the period 1911 through 1915, the last years before widespread state prohibition and the Webb—Kenyon Act began to significantly inhibit the flow of legal liquor, the per capita consumption by Americans of drinking age (15 years and older) amounted to 2.56 gallons of absolute alcohol. This was actually imbibed as 2.09 gallons of distilled spirits (45 percent alcohol), 0.79 gallons of wine (18 percent alcohol), and 29.53 gallons of beer (5 percent alcohol). In 1934, the year immediately following repeal of prohibition, the per capita consumption measured 0.97 gallons of alcohol distributed as 0.64 gallons of spirits, 0.36 gallons of wine, and 13.58 gallons of beer (4.5 percent alcohol after repeal). Total alcohol consumption, by this measure, fell by more than 60 percent because of national prohibition. Granting a generous margin of error, it seems certain that the flow of liquor in the United States was at least cut in half. It is difficult to know whether the same number of drinkers each consumed less or, as seems more likely, fewer persons drank. The crucial factor for this discussion is that national prohibition caused a substantial drop in aggregate alcohol consumption. Though the figures began to rise almost immediately after repeal, not until 1970 did the annual per capita consumption of absolute alcohol reach the level of 1911–15. In other words, not only did Americans drink significantly less as a result of national prohibition, but also the effect of the law in depressing liquor usage apparently lingered for several decades after repeal.

Other evidence confirms this statistical picture of sharply reduced liquor consumption under prohibition. After the Volstead Act had been in force for a half dozen years, social worker Martha Bensley Bruere conducted a nationwide survey of drinking for the National Federation of Settlements. Her admittedly impressionistic study, based upon 193 reports from social workers across the country, focused on lower-class, urban America. Social workers, who generally favored prohibition, perhaps overrated the law's effectiveness. Nevertheless, Bruere's book provided probably the most objective picture of prohibition in practice in the mid-1920s.

The Bruere survey reported that adherence to the dry law varied from place to place. The Scandinavians of Minneapolis and St. Paul continued to drink. On the other hand, prohibition seemed effective in Sioux Falls, South Dakota. In Butte, Montana, the use of intoxicants had declined, though bootleggers actively plied their trade. Idaho, Oregon, and Washington had generally accepted prohibition, and even in the West Coast wet bastion, San Francisco, working-class drinking appeared much reduced. The Southwest from Texas to Los Angeles was reported to be quite dry. The survey cited New Orleans as America's wettest city, with bootlegging and a general disregard of the law evident everywhere. In the old South, prohibition was said to be effectively enforced for Negroes but not whites. Throughout the Midwest, with some exceptions, residents of rural areas generally observed prohibition, but city dwellers appeared to ignore it. In the great metropolises of the North and East, with their large ethnic communities—Chicago, Detroit, Cleveland, Pittsburgh, Boston, New York, and Philadelphia—the evidence was overwhelming that the law was neither respected nor observed.

Throughout the country, Bruere suggested, less drinking was taking place than before prohibition. Significantly, she reported the more prosperous upper and middle classes violated the alcoholic beverage ban far more frequently than did the working class. Illicitly obtained liquor was expensive. Yale economist Irving Fisher, himself an advocate of prohibition, claimed that in 1928 on the average a quart of beer cost 80¢ (up 600 percent from 1916), gin $5.90 (up 520 percent), and corn whiskey $3.95 (up 150 percent) while average annual income per family was about $2,600. If nothing else, the economics of prohibition substantially reduced drinking by lower-class groups. Thus prohibition succeeded to a considerable degree in restraining drinking by the very social groups with whom many advocates of the law had been concerned. The Bruere study, therefore, offered cheer to drys. Yet her report also demonstrated that acceptance of prohibition varied with ethnic background and local custom as well as economics. Community opinion appeared more influential than federal or state laws or police activity. People in many parts of the United States voluntarily obeyed the Eighteenth Amendment, but elsewhere citizens chose to ignore it. In the latter part of the decade, violations apparently increased, both in small towns and large cities. In Detroit it reportedly became impossible to get a drink "unless you walked at least ten feet and told the busy bartender what you wanted in a voice loud enough for him to hear you above the uproar."

Any evidence to the contrary notwithstanding, national prohibition rapidly acquired an image, not as a law which significantly reduced the use of alcoholic beverages, but rather as a law that was widely flouted. One Wisconsin congressmen, writing to a constituent after a year of national prohibition, asserted, "I believe that there is more bad whiskey consumed in the country today than there was good whiskey before we had prohibition and of course we have made a vast number of liars and law violators through the Volstead Act." In part this commonly held impression stemmed from the substantial amount of drinking which actually did continue. Even given a 60 percent drop in total national alcohol consumption, a considerable amount of imbibing still took place. Yet the image also derived in part from the unusually visible character of those prohibition violations which did occur.

Drinking by its very nature attracted more notice than many other forms of law-breaking. It was, in the first place, generally a social, or group, activity. Moreover, most drinking took place, Bruere and others acknowledged, in urban areas where practically any activity was more likely to be witnessed. Bootleggers had to advertise their availability, albeit carefully, in order to attract customers. The fact that the upper classes were doing much of the imbibing further heightened its visibility. Several additional factors insured that many Americans would have a full, perhaps even exaggerated, awareness of the extent to which the prohibition law was being broken.

The behavior of those who sought to profit by meeting the demand for alcoholic beverages created an indelible image of rampant lawlessness. National prohibition provided a potentially very profitable opportunity for persons willing to take certain risks. "Prohibition is a business," maintained the best known and most successful bootlegger of all, Al Capone of Chicago. "All I do is supply a public demand." Obtaining a supply of a commodity, transporting it to a marketplace, and selling it for an appropriate price were commonplace commercial activities; carrying out these functions in the face of government opposition and without the protections of facilities, goods, and transactions normally provided by government made bootlegging an unusual business. Indeed bootleggers faced the problem—or the opportunity—that hijacking a competitor's shipment of liquor often presented the easiest and certainly the cheapest way of obtaining a supply of goods, and the victim of such a theft had no recourse to regular law enforcement agencies. Nor, for better or worse, could bootleggers expect government to restrain monopolistic practices, regulate prices, or otherwise monitor business practices. Consequently, participants in the prohibition-era liquor business had to develop their own techniques for dealing with competition and the pressures of the marketplace. The bootlegging wars and gangland killings, so vividly reported in the nation's press, represented, on one level, a response to a business problem. . . .

Violence was commonplace in establishing exclusive sales territories, in obtaining liquor, or in defending a supply. In Chicago, for instance, rival gangs competed intensely. Between September 1923 and October 1926, the peak period of struggle for control of the large Chicago market, an estimated 215 criminals died at the hands of rivals. In comparison, police killed 160 gangsters during the same period. Although by conventional business standards the violence level in bootlegging remained high, it declined over the course of the 1920s. Consolidation, agreement on markets, regularizing of supply and delivery all served to reduce turbulence. John Torrio and Al Capone in Chicago, Charles Solomon in Boston, Max Hoff in Philadelphia, Purple Gang in Detroit, the Mayfield Road Mob in Cleveland, and Joseph Roma in Denver imposed some order on the bootlegging business in their cities. The more than a thousand gangland murders in New York during prohibition reflect the inability of Arnold Rothstein, Lucky Luciano, Dutch Schultz, Frank Costello, or any other criminal leader to gain control and put an end to (literally) cut-throat competition in the largest market of all. . . .

Ironically, the federal government in its efforts to enforce national prohibition often contributed to the image of a heavily violated law. Six months after the Eighteenth Amendment took effect, for example, Jouett Shouse, an Assistant Secretary of the Treasury whose duties included supervising prohibition enforcement, announced that liquor smuggling had reached such (portions that it could no longer be handled by the 6,000 agents of the Customs Bureau. Shouse estimated that 35,000 men would be required to guard the coasts and borders against the flood of liquor pouring into the country. The Assistant Secretary attributed the problem to an unlimited market for smuggled whiskey and the 1,000 percent profits which could be realized from its sale.

During the 1920 presidential campaign, Republican nominee Warren G. Harding pledged to enforce the Volstead Act "as a fundamental principle of the American conscience," implying that the Wilson administration had neglected its duty. Despite his known fondness for drink, Harding attracted dry support with such statements while his opponent, the avowedly wet James A. Cox, floundered. Once inaugurated, President Harding tried to fulfill his campaign promise but met with little success. He explained to his wet Senate friend, Walter Edge of New Jersey, "Prohibition is a constitutional mandate and I hold it to be absolutely necessary to give it a fair and thorough trial." The president appointed the Anti-Saloon league's candidate, Roy A. Haynes, as commissioner of prohibition and gave the corpulent, eternally optimistic Haynes a generally free hand in selecting personnel to wage battle against bootlegging. Harding began to receive considerable mail from across the country complaining about the failure of the dry law. As reports of prohibition violations increased, Harding became more and more disturbed. Never much of a believer in prohibition himself, Harding had, nevertheless, been willing as a senator to let the country decide whether it wanted the Eighteenth Amendment, and now as president he deplored the wholesale breaking of the law. In early 1923, having gradually realized the importance of personal example, Harding gave up his own clandestine drinking. In a speech in Denver just prior to his death, Harding appealed rigorously for observance of prohibition in the interest of preventing lawlessness, corruption, and collapse of national moral fiber. "Whatever satisfaction there may be in indulgence, whatever objection there is to the so-called invasion of personal liberty," the president asserted, "neither counts when the supremacy of law and the stability of our institutions are menaced." Harding's rhetoric, although intended to encourage compliance with prohibition, furthered the image of a law breaking down.

A report by Attorney General Harry Daugherty to President Calvin Coolidge shortly after Harding's death suggested the extent to which the Volstead Act was being violated in its early years of operation. Daugherty indicated that in the first forty-one months of national prohibition, the federal government had initiated 90,330 prosecutions under the law. The number of cases had been rising: 5,636 were settled in April 1923, 541 more than in the initial six months of prohibition. The number of new cases doubled between fiscal 1922 and fiscal 1923. The government obtained convictions in 80 percent of the terminated cases. These figures showed, the attorney general argued, that prohibition enforcement was becoming increasingly effective. They could just as well be seen, however, as an indication of an enormous and increasing number of violations.

The prohibition cases brought into federal court most certainly represented only a small fraction of actual offenses. They nevertheless seemed to be more than the court and prison system could handle. In 1920, 5,095 of the 34,230 cases terminated in the federal courts involved prohibition violation; during 1929, 75,298 prohibition cases alone were concluded. In 1920, federal prisons contained just over 5,000 inmates; ten years later they contained over 12,000, more than 4,000 of whom were serving time for liquor violations. The courts were so overworked that they frequently resorted to the expedient of "bargain days." Under this system, on set days large numbers of prohibition violators would plead guilty after being given prior assurance that they would not receive jail sentences or heavy fines. By 1925, pleas of guilty, without jury trials, accounted for over 90 percent of the convictions obtained in federal courts. The legal system appeared overwhelmed by national prohibition.

As president, Calvin Coolidge found prohibition enforcement to be the same headache it had been for his predecessor. Like Harding, Coolidge was constantly under pressure from Wayne Wheeler and other dry leaders to improve enforcement. He received hundreds of letters deploring the rate of Volstead Act violations and urging forceful action. Coolidge merely acknowledged receipt of letters on the subject, avoiding any substantial response. As it did with many other issues, the Coolidge administration sought to avoid the prohibition question as much as possible. Other than seeking Canadian and British cooperation in halting smuggling, and holding White House breakfasts for prestigious drys, few federal initiatives were taken while Coolidge remained in office. The picture of rampant prohibition violation stood unchallenged.

Congress, once having adopted the Volstead Act and appropriated funds for its enforcement, assumed its job was done and avoided all mention of prohibition during the law's first year of operation. Evidence of violations, however, quickly provoked dry demands that Congress strengthen the prohibition law. Whenever Congress acted, it drew attention to the difficulties of abolishing liquor. When it failed to respond, as was more frequently the case, drys charged it with indifference to law breaking. Whatever it did, Congress proved unable to significantly alter prohibition's image.

After Harding's inauguration, Congress learned that retiring Attorney General A. Mitchell Palmer had ruled that the Volstead Act placed no limit on the authority of physicians to prescribe beer and wine for medicinal purposes." Senator Frank B. Willis of Ohio and Representative Robert S. Campbell of Kansas moved quickly to correct this oversight by introducing a bill that would forbid the prescription of beer and rigidly limit physicians' authority to prescribe wine and spirits. Only one pint of liquor would be permitted to be dispensed for a patient during any ten-day period, under their plan. Well-prepared dry spokesmen completely dominated the hearings on the Willis-Campbell bill, insisting that this substantial source of intoxicants be eliminated. Physicians and pharmacists protested that beer possessed therapeutic value and that Congress had no right to restrict doctors in their practice of medicine. Nevertheless, in the summer of 1921 the bill passed the House by a vote of 250 to 93, and the Senate by 39 to 20. The Willis-Campbell Act reflected congressional determination to shut off the liquor supply, but like the Volstead Act, it did not resolve the problem of imposing abstinence on those willing to ignore the law in order to have a drink.

For years, Congress continued to wrestle with the problem of creating and staffing an effective federal enforcement organization. The Volstead Act delegated responsibility for implementing national prohibition to an agency of the Bureau of Internal Revenue in the Department of the Treasury. The act exempted enforcement agents from civil service regulations, making them political appointees. The Anti-Saloon League, through its general counsel,

Wayne B. Wheeler, relentlessly pressed Harding and Coolidge to name its candidates to positions in the enforcement agency. The prohibition unit, beset by patronage demands and inadequate salaries, attracted a low caliber of appointees and a high rate of corruption. By 1926 one out of twelve agents had been dismissed for such offenses as bribery, extortion, solicitation of money, conspiracy to violate the law, embezzlement, and submission of false reports. A senator who supported prohibition argued lamely that this record was no worse than that of the twelve apostles, but he could not disguise the enforcement unit's very tarnished reputation.

Even if the agency had been staffed with personnel of better quality, its task would have been overwhelming. It received little cooperation from the Department of Justice, with which it shared responsibility for prosecuting violators. Furthermore, the prohibition unit lacked both the manpower and the money to deal with the thousands of miles of unpatrolled coastline, the millions of lawbreaking citizens, and the uncountable hordes of liquor suppliers. The agency focused its efforts on raiding speakeasies and apprehending bootleggers, but this task alone proved beyond its capacity and discouraged a series of prohibition commissioners.

Congress steadily increased enforcement appropriations but never enough to accomplish the goal. In 1927 prohibition agents were finally placed under civil service, and in 1930 the Prohibition Bureau was at last transferred to the Justice Department. As useful as these congressional steps may have been, they came long after the enforcement effort had acquired a dismal reputation and doubts as to whether prohibition could possibly be effective had become deeply ingrained.

Early in 1929 Congress made a determined effort to compel greater adherence to national prohibition. A bill introduced by Washington senator Wesley L. Jones drastically increased penalties for violation of the liquor ban. Maximum prison terms for first offenders were raised from six months to five years, and fines were raised from $1,000 to $10,000. The Jones "Five-and-Ten" Bill, as it was called, passed by lopsided majorities in Congress and signed into law by Coolidge days before he left office, did not improve prohibition's effectiveness but strengthened its reputation as a harsh and unreasonable statute.

During the 1920s the Supreme Court did more than either the Congress or the president to define the manner in which national prohibition would be enforced and thereby to sharpen the law's image. As a Yale law professor and earlier as president, William Howard Taft had opposed a prohibition amendment because he preferred local option, disliked any changes in the Constitution, and felt national prohibition would be unenforceable. But when the Eighteenth Amendment was ratified, Taft, a constant defender of the sanctity of democratically adopted law, accepted it completely and even became an advocate of temperance by law. He condemned critics of national prohibition, saying, "There isn't the slightest chance that the constitutional amendment will be repealed. You know that and I know it." As chief justice from 1921 until 1930, he sought to have the prohibition laws strictly enforced and took upon himself the writing of prohibition decisions. The opinions handed down by the Taft Court during the 1920s greatly influenced conceptions of the larger implications of the new law as well as the actual course of prohibition enforcement. . . .

While in reality national prohibition sharply reduced the consumption of alcohol in the United States, the law fell considerably short of expectations. It neither eliminated drinking nor produced a sense that such a goal was within reach. So long as the purchaser of liquor, the supposed victim of a prohibition violation, participated in the illegal act rather than complained about it, the normal law enforcement process simply did not function. As a result, policing agencies bore a much heavier burden. The various images of lawbreaking, from contacts with the local bootlegger to Hollywood films to overloaded court dockets, generated a widespread belief that violations were taking place with unacceptable frequency. Furthermore, attempts at enforcing the law created an impression that government, unable to cope with lawbreakers by using traditional policing methods, was assuming new powers in order to accomplish its task. The picture of national prohibition which emerged over the course of the 1920s disenchanted many Americans and moved some to an active effort to bring an end to the dry law.

J. C. Burnham  **NO**

New Perspectives on the Prohibition "Experiment" of the 1920s

Recently a number of historians have shown that the temperance movement that culminated in national prohibition was central to the American reform tradition. Such writers as James H. Timberlake have demonstrated in detail how the Eighteenth Amendment was an integral part of the reforms of the Progressive movement. Yet we commonly refer to the "prohibition experiment" rather than the "prohibition reform." This characterization deserves some exploration. The question can be raised, for example, why we do not refer to the "workmen's compensation law experiment."

One explanation may be that of all of the major reforms enacted into law in the Progressive period, only prohibition was decisively and deliberately repealed. The Sixteenth and Seventeenth Amendments are still on the books; the Eighteenth is not. For historians who emphasize the theme of reform, referring to prohibition as an experiment gives them the option of suggesting that its repeal involved no loss to society. To characterize the repeal of prohibition as a major reversal of social reform would seriously impair the view that most of us have of the cumulative nature of social legislation in the twentieth century.

We have been comfortable for many decades now with the idea that prohibition was a great social experiment. The image of prohibition as an experiment has even been used to draw lessons from history: to argue, for example, that certain types of laws—especially those restricting or forbidding the use of liquor and narcotics—are futile and probably pernicious. Recently, however, some new literature has appeared on prohibition, whose total effect is to demand a reexamination of our customary view.

The idea that prohibition was an experiment may not survive this renaissance of scholarship in which the reform and especially Progressive elements in the temperance movement are emphasized. But it is profitable, at least for the purposes of this article, to maintain the image of an experiment, for the perspectives available now permit a fresh evaluation of the experiment's outcome.

Specifically, the prohibition experiment, as the evidence stands today, can more easily be considered a success than a failure. While far from clear-cut, the balance of scholarly evidence has shifted the burden of proof to those who would characterize the experiment a failure. . . .

From *Journal of Social History,* vol. 2, no. 1, Autumn 1968/1969, pp. 51, 52, 55–68. Copyright © 1969 by Journal of Social History, George Mason University. Reprinted by permission.

The American prohibition experiment grew out of the transformation that the combination of Progressive reformers and businessmen wrought in the temperance movement. Beginning in 1907 a large number of state and local governments enacted laws or adopted constitutional provisions that dried up—as far as alcoholic beverages were concerned—a substantial part of the United States. The success of the anti-liquor forces, led by the Anti-Saloon League, was so impressive that they were prepared to strike for a national prohibition constitutional amendment. This issue was decided in the 1916 Congressional elections, although the Amendment itself was not passed by Congress until December 22, 1917. A sufficient number of states ratified it by January 16, 1919, and it took effect on January 16, 1920.

In actuality, however, prohibition began well before January, 1920. In addition to the widespread local prohibition laws, federal laws greatly restricted the production and sale of alcoholic beverages, mostly, beginning in 1917, in the guise of war legislation. The manufacture of distilled spirits beverages, for example, had been forbidden for more than three months when Congress passed the Eighteenth Amendment late in 1917. The Volstead Act of 1919, passed to implement the Amendment, provided by law that wartime prohibition would remain in effect until the Amendment came into force.

The Eighteenth Amendment prohibited the manufacturing, selling, importing, or transporting of "intoxicating liquors." It was designed to kill off the liquor business in general and the saloon in particular; but at the same time the Amendment was not designed to prohibit either the possession or drinking of alcoholic beverages. At a later time the courts held that even the act of buying liquor to be legal and not part of a conspiracy. Most of the local and state prohibition laws were similar in their provisions and intent. The very limited nature of the prohibition experiment must, therefore, be understood from the beginning.

At the time, a number of union leaders and social critics pointed out that the Eighteenth Amendment constituted class legislation; that is, the political strength of the drys lay among middle class Progressives who wanted, essentially, to remove the saloon from American life. The Amendment permitted those who had enough money to lay in all the liquor they pleased, but the impecunious workingman was to be deprived of his day-to-day or week-to-week liquor supply. The class aspect of prohibition later turned out to have great importance. Most of the recent revisionist writers have concentrated upon the interplay between prohibition and social role and status.

The primary difficulty that has stood in the way of properly assessing the prohibition experiment has been methods of generalization. Evidence gathered from different sections of the country varies so radically as to make weighing of evidence difficult. In addition, there has been a great deal of confusion about time: When did prohibition begin? What period of its operation should be the basis for judgment? The difficulties of time and place are particularly relevant to the fundamental question of enforcement.

As the country looked forward to prohibition after the elections of 1916, widespread public support, outside of a few urban areas, was expected to make prohibition a success both initially and later on. It was reasonable to expect that enforcement would be strict and that society both institutionally and informally would deal severely with any actions tending to revive the liquor trade. These expectations were realistic through the years of the war, when prohibition and patriotism were closely connected in the public mind. Only some years after the passage of the Volstead Act did hopes for unquestionably effective enforcement fade away. In these early years, when public opinion generally supported enforcement, the various public officials responsible for enforcement were the ones who most contributed to its breakdown. This breakdown in many areas in turn led to the evaporation of much public support in the country as a whole.

Successive Congresses refused to appropriate enough money to enforce the laws. Through its influence in Congress the Anti-Saloon League helped to perpetuate the starvation of the Prohibition Bureau and its predecessors in the name of political expediency. Huge sums spent on prohibition, the drys feared, would alienate many voters—and fearful Congressmen—more or less indifferent to prohibition. The prohibitionists therefore made the claim that prohibition was effective so that they would not have to admit the necessity of large appropriations for enforcement. A second act of irresponsibility of the Congresses was acquiescing in exempting the enforcement officers from Civil Service and so making the Prohibition Bureau part of the political spoils system. League officials who had written this provision into the Volstead Act hoped by using their political power to dictate friendly appointments, but the record shows that politics, not the League, dominated federal enforcement efforts. Not until 1927 did the Prohibition Bureau finally come under Civil Service.

The men charged with enforcement, the Presidents of the 1920s, were, until Hoover, indifferent to prohibition except as it affected politics. Wilson, although not a wet, vetoed the Volstead Act, and it was passed over his veto. Harding and Coolidge were notoriously uninterested in enforcing prohibition. When Hoover took office in 1929 he reorganized the administration of enforcement, and his effectiveness in cutting down well established channels of supply helped give final impetus to the movement for a re-evaluation of prohibition.

In some areas prosecutors and even judges were so unsympathetic that enforcement was impossible. Elsewhere local juries refused to convict in bootlegging cases. These local factors contributed greatly to the notable disparities in the effectiveness of prohibition from place to place.

By a unique concurrent enforcement provision of the Eighteenth Amendment, state and local officials were as responsible for enforcement as federal authorities. The Anti-Saloon League, because of its power in the states, expected to use existing law enforcement agencies and avoid huge federal appropriations for enforcement. Contrary to the expectations of the League, local officials were the weakest point in enforcement. Most of the states—but not all—enacted "little Volstead" acts; yet in 1927 only eighteen of the forty-eight states were appropriating money for the enforcement of such acts. Local enforcement in many Southern and Western areas was both severe and effective; in other areas local enforcement was even more unlikely than federal enforcement. For years the entire government of New Jersey openly defied the Eighteenth Amendment, and it was clear that the governor was not troubled a bit about his oath of office. Some states that had enforced their own prohibition laws before 1919 afterward made no attempt to continue enforcement.

With such extreme variations in the enforcement of prohibition over the United States, judging the overall success of the experiment on the basis of enforcement records is hazardous. Bootlegging in New York, Chicago, and San Francisco clearly was not necessarily representative of the intervening territory, and vice versa.

An easier basis for generalizing about the effectiveness of enforcement is the impact that prohibition had on consumption of alcohol. Here the second major complication mentioned crops up: the availability of liquor varied greatly from time to time and specifically from an initial period of effectiveness in 1919–1922 to a later period of widespread violation of the law, typically 1925–1927.

In the early years of national prohibition, liquor was very difficult to obtain. In the later years when the laws were being defied by well-organized bootleggers operating through established channels, the supply increased. By the late 1920s, for example, the domestic supply of hard liquor in northern California was so great that the price fell below the point at which it was profitable to run beverages in from Canada by ship. In the last years of prohibition it became very easy—at least in some areas with large populations—to obtain relatively good liquor. Many people, relying on their memories, have generalized from this later period, after about 1925, to all of the prohibition years and have come, falsely, to the conclusion that enforcement was neither real nor practical. Overall one can say that considering the relatively slight amount of effort put into it, enforcement was surprisingly effective in many places, and particularly in the early years.

Both so-called wet and dry sources agree that the amount of liquor consumed per capita decreased substantially because of prohibition. The best figures available show that the gallons of pure alcohol ingested per person varied widely over four different periods. In the period 1911–1914, the amount was 1.69 gallons. Under the wartime restrictions, 1918–1919, the amount decreased to .97. In the early years of national prohibition, 1921–1922, there was still further decrease to .73 gallons. In the later years of prohibition, 1927–1930, the amount rose to 1.14 gallons.

These figures suggest that great care must be used in making comparisons between "before" prohibition and "after." Statistics and memories that use 1920 as the beginning of prohibition are misleading, since not only were federal laws in force before then but there was also extensive state prohibition. The peak of absolute consumption of beer, for example, was reached in the years 1911–1914, not 1916–1918, much less 1919. The real "before" was sometime around 1910.

The best independent evidence of the impact of prohibition can be found in the available figures for certain direct and measurable social effects of alcohol consumption. The decrease from about 1915 to 1920–1922 in arrests for drunkenness, in hospitalization for alcoholism, and in the incidence of other diseases, such as cirrhosis of the liver, specifically related to drinking was remarkable. The low point of these indexes came in 1918–1921, and then they climbed again until the late 1920s. Because of confusion about when prohibition began, the significance of these well known statistics has seldom been appreciated: there is clear evidence that in the early years of prohibition not only did the use of alcohol decrease but American society enjoyed some of the direct benefits promised by proponents of prohibition.

Undoubtedly the most convincing evidence of the success of prohibition is to be found in the mental hospital admission rates. There is no question of a sudden change in physicians' diagnoses, and the people who had to deal with alcohol-related mental diseases were obviously impressed by what they saw. After reviewing recent hospital admission rates for alcoholic psychoses, James V. May, one of the most eminent American psychiatrists, wrote in 1922: "With the advent of prohibition the alcoholic psychoses as far as this country is concerned have become a matter of little more than historical interest. The admission rate in the New York state hospitals for 1920 was only 1.9 percent [as compared with ten percent in 1909–1912]." For many years articles on alcoholism literally disappeared from American medical literature.

In other words, after World War I and until sometime in the early 1920s, say, 1922 or 1923, when enforcement was clearly breaking down, prohibition was generally a success. Certainly there is no basis for the conclusion that prohibition was inherently doomed to failure. The emasculation of enforcement grew out of specific factors that were not organically related to the Eighteenth Amendment.

Nor is most of this analysis either new or controversial. Indeed, most of the criticism of prohibition has centered around assertions not so much that the experiment failed but that it had two more or less unexpected consequences that clearly show it to have been undesirable. The critics claim, first, that the Eighteenth Amendment caused dangerous criminal behavior; and, second, that in spite of prohibition more people drank alcohol than before. If a candid examination fails to confirm these commonly accepted allegations, the interpretation of prohibition as a failure loses most of its validity. Such is precisely the case.

During the 1920s there was almost universal public belief that a "crime wave" existed in the United States. In spite of the literary output on the subject, dealing largely with a local situation in Chicago, there is no firm evidence of this supposed upsurge in lawlessness. Two criminologists, Edwin H. Sutherland and C. H. Gehlke, at the end of the decade reviewed the available crime statistics, and the most that they could conclude was that "there is no evidence here of a 'crime wave,' but only of a slowly rising level." These admittedly inadequate statistics emphasized large urban areas and were, it should be emphasized, *not* corrected to reflect the increase in population. Actually no statistics from this period dealing with crime are of any value whatsoever in generalizing about crime rates. Apparently what happened was that in the 1920s the long existent "underworld" first became publicized and romanticized. The crime wave, in other words, was the invention of enterprising journalists feeding on some sensational crimes and situations and catering to a public to whom the newly discovered "racketeer" was a covert folk hero.

Even though there was no crime wave, there was a connection between crime and prohibition, as Frederick Lewis Allen suggested in his alliterative coupling of "Alcohol and Al Capone." Because of the large profits involved in bootlegging and the inability of the producers and customers to obtain police protection, criminal elements organized and exploited the liquor business just as they did all other illegal activities. It would be a serious distortion even of racketeering, however, to emphasize bootlegging at the expense of the central criminal-directed activity, gambling. Since liquor-related activities were not recognized as essentially criminal in nature by substantial parts of the population, it is difficult to argue that widespread violation of the Volstead Act constituted a true increase of crime. Nevertheless, concern over growing federal "crime" statistics, that is, bootlegging cases, along with fears based on hysterical journalism, helped to bring about repeal.

We are left, then, with the question of whether national prohibition led to more drinking than before. It should first be pointed out not only that the use of 1920 as the beginning of prohibition is misleading but that much of the drinking during the 1920s was not relevant to the prohibition of the Eighteenth Amendment and Volstead Act. Private drinking was perfectly legal all of the time, and possession of liquor that had been accumulated by the foresighted before prohibition was entirely lawful. The continued production of cider and wine at home was specifically provided for also. Indeed, the demand for wine grapes was so great that many grape growers who in 1919 faced ruin made a fortune selling their grapes in the first years of the Amendment. Ironically, many an old lady who made her own wine believed that she was defying prohibition when in fact the law protected her.

We still face the problem of reconciling the statistics quoted above that show that alcohol consumption was substantially reduced, at one point to about half of the pre-prohibition consumption, with the common observation of the 1920s that as many or more people were drinking than before.

What happened, one can say with hindsight, was predictable. When liquor became unavailable except at some risk and considerable cost, it became a luxury item, that is, a symbol of affluence and, eventually, status. Where before men of good families tended not to drink and women certainly did not, during the 1920s it was precisely the sons and daughters of the "nice" people who were patronizing the bootleggers and speakeasies, neither of which for some years was very effectively available to the lower classes. This utilization of drinking as conspicuous consumption was accompanied by the so-called revolution in manners and morals that began among the rebellious intellectuals around 1912 and reached a high point of popularization in the 1920s when the adults of the business class began adopting the "lower" social standards of their children.

We can now understand why the fact was universally reported by journalists of the era that "everyone drank, including many who never did before." Drinking, and often new drinking, was common among the upper classes, especially among the types of people likely to consort with the writers of the day. The journalists and other observers did indeed report honestly that they saw "everyone" drinking. They seldom saw the lower classes and almost never knew about the previous drinking habits of the masses. The situation was summed up by an unusually well-qualified witness, Whiting Williams, testifying before the Wickersham Commission. A vice-president of a Cleveland steel company, he had for many years gone in disguise among the working people of several areas in connection with handling labor problems. He concluded:

> . . . very much of the misconception with respect to the liquor problem comes from the fact that most of the people who are writing and talk-ing most actively about the prohibition problem are people who, in the nature of things, have never had any contact with the liquor prob-lem in its earlier pre-prohibition form and who are, therefore, unduly impressed with the changes with respect to drinking that they see on their own level; their own level, however, representing an extremely small proportion of the population.
>
> The great mass who, I think, are enormously more involved in the whole problem, of course, in the nature of things are not articulate and are not writing in the newspapers.

The important point is that the "everyone" who was reported to be drink-ing did not include working-class families, i.e., the pre-ponderant part of the population. Clark Warburton, in a study initiated with the help of the Asso-ciation Against the Prohibition Amendment, is explicit on this point: "The working class is consuming not more than half as much alcohol per capita as formerly." The classic study is Martha Bensley Bruère's. She surveyed social workers across the country, and the overwhelming impression (even taking account of urban immigrant areas where prohibition laws were flouted) was that working people drank very much less than before and further, as pre-dicted, that prohibition had, on the balance, substantially improved condi-tions among low-income Americans.

Even in its last years the law, with all of its leaks, was still effective in cut-ting down drinking among the workers, which was one of the primary aims of prohibition. Here, then, is more evidence of the success of the prohibition experiment. Certainly the Anti-Saloon League did succeed in destroying the old-fashioned saloon, the explicit target of its campaign.

Taking together all of this evidence of the success of prohibition, especially in its class differential aspects, we are still left with the question of why the law was repealed.

The story of repeal is contained largely in the growth of the idea that prohibition was a failure. From the beginning, a number of contemporary observers (particularly in the largest cities) saw many violations of the law and concluded that prohibition was not working. These observers were in the minority, and for a long time most people believed that by and large pro-hibition was effective. Even for those who did not, the question of repeal—once appeals to the Supreme Court had been settled—simply never arose. Bartlett C. Jones has observed, "A peculiarity of the Prohibition debate was the fact that repeal, called an absolute impossibility for much of the period, became irresistibly popular in 1932 and 1933. Not even enemies of prohibition considered absolute repeal as an alternative until quite late, although they upheld through all of these years their side of the vigorous public debate about the effectiveness and desirability of the prohibition laws.

In the early days of prohibition, the predominant attitudes toward the experiment manifested in the chief magazines and newspapers of the country were either ambivalent acceptance or, more rarely, impotent hostility. In 1923–1924 a major shift in the attitudes of the mass circulation information media occurred so that acceptance was replaced by nearly universal outright criticism accompanied by a demand for modification of the Volstead Act. The criticism was based on the assumption that Volsteadism, at least, was a failure. The suggested solution was legalizing light wines and beers.

The effectiveness of the shift of "public opinion" is reflected in the vigorous counterattack launched by the dry forces who too often denied real evils and asserted that prohibition was effective and was benefitting the nation. By claiming too much, especially in the late 1920s, the drys discredited that which was really true, and the literate public apparently discounted all statements that might show that prohibition was at least a partial success, partly on the rigidly idealistic basis that if it was a partial failure, it was a total failure.

Great impetus was given to sentiment hostile to prohibition by the concern of respectable people about the "crime wave." They argued, plausibly enough given the assumptions that there was a crime wave and that prohibition was a failure, that universal disregard for the Eighteenth Amendment was damaging to general respect for law. If the most respectable elements of society, so the argument went, openly showed contempt for the Constitution, how could anyone be expected to honor a mere statute? Much of the leadership of the "anti's" soon came from the bar associations rather than the bar patrons.

Coincident with this shift in opinion came the beginning of one of the most effective publicity campaigns of modern times, led by the Association Against the Prohibition Amendment. At first largely independent of liquor money, in the last years of prohibition the AAPA used all it could command. By providing journalists with reliable information, the AAPA developed a virtual monopoly on liquor and prohibition press coverage." In the late 1920s and early 1930s it was unusual to find a story about prohibition in small local papers that did not have its origin-free of charge, of course—with the AAPA.

The AAPA had as its announced goal the modification of the Volstead Act to legalize light wines and beers. The organization also headed up campaigns to repeal the "little Volstead" acts most states had enacted. By the late 1920s the AAPA beat the Anti-Saloon League at its own game, chipping away at the state level. State after state, often by popular vote, did away with the concurrent enforcement acts. Both the wets and the drys viewed state repeals and any modification of the Volstead Act as only steps toward full repeal. Perhaps they were correct; but another possibility does need examination.

Andrew Sinclair, in the most recent and thorough examination of the question, contends that modification of the Volstead Act to legalize light wines and beers would have saved the rest of the prohibition experiment. It is difficult to differ with Sinclair's contention that complete repeal of the Eighteenth Amendment was unprovoked and undesirable.

When President Hoover appointed the Wickersham Commission, public opinion was almost unanimous in expecting that the solution to the prohibition problem would be modification. The Commission's report strengthened the expectation. Not even the Association Against the Prohibition Amendment hoped for more than that, much less repeal. But suddenly an overwhelming surge of public sentiment brought about the Twenty-First Amendment denouement.

The cause of this second sudden shift in opinion was the Great Depression that began about 1929. Jones has shown convincingly that every argument used to bring about repeal in 1932–1933 had been well known since the beginning of prohibition. The class aspect of the legislation, which had been so callously accepted in 1920, was suddenly undesirable. The main depression-related argument, that legalization of liquor manufacture would produce a badly needed additional tax revenue, was well known in the 1910s and even earlier. These rationalizations of repeal were masks for the fact that the general public, baffled by the economic catastrophe, found a convenient scapegoat: prohibition. (The drys had, after all, tried to credit prohibition for the prosperity of the 1920s.) The grouns well of public feeling was irresistible and the entire "experiment, noble in motive and far-reaching in purpose," was not modified but thrown out with Volsteadism, bathwater, baby, and all.

Because the AAPA won, its explanations of what happened were accepted at face value. One of the lasting results of prohibition, therefore, was perpetuation of the stereotypes of the wet propaganda of the 1920s and the myth that the American experiment in prohibition (usually misunderstood to have outlawed personal drinking as well as the liquor business) was a failure. Blanketed together here indiscriminately were all of the years from 1918 to 1933.

More than thirty years have passed since the repeal of the Eighteenth Amendment. Surely the AAPA has now had its full measure of victory and it is no longer necessary for historians to perpetuate a myth that grew up in another era. For decades there has been no realistic possibility of a resurgence of prohibition in its Progressive form—or probably any other form.

The concern now is not so much the destruction of myth, however; the concern is that our acceptance of the myth of the failure of prohibition has prevented us from exploring in depth social and especially sociological aspects of the prohibition experiment. Recent scholarship, by treating prohibition more as a reform than an experiment, has shown that we have been missing one of the most interesting incidents of twentieth-century history.

POSTSCRIPT

Was Prohibition a Failure?

For many historians, the 1920s marked an era of change in the United States, from international involvement and war to isolationism and peace, from the feverish reform of the Progressive era to the conservative political retrenchment of "Republican ascendancy," from the entrenched values of Victorian America to the cultural rebellion identified with the proliferation of "flivvers," "flappers," and hip flasks. In 1931, Frederick Lewis Allen focused on these changes in his popular account of the decade, *Only Yesterday.* In a chapter entitled "The Revolution of Morals and Manners," Allen established a widely accepted image of the 1920s as a period of significant social and cultural rebellion. An excellent collection of essays that explores this issue is John Braeman, Robert H. Bremner, and David Brody, eds., *Change and Continuity in Twentieth Century America: The 1920s* (Ohio State University Press, 1968).

The history of the temperance and prohibition movements in the United States is effectively presented in Andrew Sinclair, *Prohibition: The Era of Excess* (Harper & Row, 1962); Joseph R. Gusfield, *Symbolic Crusade: Status Politics and the American Temperance Movement* (University of Illinois Press, 1963); James H. Timberlake, *Prohibition and the Progressive Movement* (1963); Norman H. Clark, *Deliver Us from Evil: An Interpretation of American Prohibition* (W. W. Norton; 1976); and Thomas R. Pegram, *Battling Demon Rum: The Struggle for a Dry America, 1800–1933* (Ivan R. Dee, 1998). Mark E. Lender and James Kirby Martin provide an excellent survey that includes a chapter on the rise and fall of the prohibition amendment in *Drinking in America* (The Free Press, 1982).

There are a number of important overviews of the 1920s. Among the more useful are John D. Hicks, *Republican Ascendancy, 1921–1933* (Harper & Row, 1960), a volume in The New American Nation Series; Roderick Nash, *The Nervous Generation: American Thought, 1917–1930* (Rand McNally, 1970); and two volumes by Paul Carter, *The Twenties in America,* 2nd ed. (Harlan Davidson, 1975) and *Another Part of the Twenties* (Columbia University Press, 1977). The classic sociological study by Robert and Helen Lynd, *Middletown: A Study in Contemporary American Culture* (Harcourt, Brace, 1929) explores the values of a group of "typical" Americans of the 1920s.

The economic history of the decade is discussed in George Soule, *Prosperity Decade: From War to Depression, 1917–1929* (Holt, Rinehart & Winston, 1947); Peter Fearon, *War, Prosperity, and Depression* (University of Kansas Press, 1987); and John Kenneth Galbraith, *The Great Crash, 1929,* rev. ed. (Houghton Mifflin, 1989). For a critical biography of the decade's most notable business leader, see Keith Sward, *The Legend of Henry Ford* (Rinehart, 1948).

The status of women in the decade after suffrage receives general treatment in William H. Chafe, *The Paradox of Change: American Women in the 20th Century* (Oxford University Press, 1991) and, more thoroughly, in Dorothy M. Brown, *Setting a Course: American Women in the 1920s* (Twayne, 1987). Discussions of feminism in the 1920s are competently presented in William L. O'Neill, *Everyone Was Brave: The Rise and Fall of Feminism in America* (University of Illinois Press, 1973); Susan D. Baker, *The Origins of the Equal Rights Amendment: Feminism Between the Wars* (Greenwood Press, 1981); and Nancy F. Cott, *The Grounding of Feminism* (Yale University Press, 1987). David M. Kennedy, *Birth Control in America: The Career of Margaret Sanger* (Yale University Press, 1970) examines an important issue that attracted the interest of many women's groups in the 1920s, while Jacqueline Dowd Hall, *Revolt Against Chivalry: Jessie Daniel Ames and the Women's Campaign Against Lynching* (Columbia University Press, 1979) explores the role of women in the area of race relations.

Race is also the focal point of several studies of the Harlem Renaissance. The best of these works include Nathan Irvin Huggins, *Harlem Renaissance* (Oxford University Press, 1971); David Levering Lewis, *When Harlem Was in Vogue* (Alfred A. Knopf, 1981); and Cary D. Wintz, *Black Culture and the Harlem Renaissance* (Rice University Press, 1988).

Recent scholarship on the Ku Klux Klan in the 1920s has focused on its grassroots participation in local and state politics. Klan members are viewed less as extremists and more as political pressure groups whose aims were to gain control of various state and local governmental offices. The best overview of this perspective is Shawn Lay, ed., *The Invisible Empire in the West: Toward a New Historical Appraisal of the Ku Klux Klan of the 1920s* (University of Illinois Press, 1992). For additional approaches to the KKK's activities in the "Roaring Twenties," see Charles C. Alexander, *The Ku Klux Klan in the Southwest* (University of Kentucky Press, 1965); Kenneth T. Jackson, *The Ku Klux Klan in the City, 1915–1930* (Oxford University Press, 1967); Kathleen M. Blee, *Women of the Klan: Racism and Gender in the 1920s* (University of California Press, 1991); and Nancy MacLean, *Behind the Mask of Chivalry: The Making of the Second Ku Klux Klan* (Oxford University Press, 1994).

ISSUE 11

Did the New Deal Prolong the Great Depression?

YES: Burton W. Folsom, Jr., from *New Deal or Raw Deal? How FDR's Economic Legacy Has Damaged America* (Simon & Schuster, 2008)

NO: Roger Biles, from *A New Deal for the American People* (Northern Illinois University Press, 1991)

ISSUE SUMMARY

YES: Professor Burton W. Folsom, Jr., argues the New Deal prolonged the Great Depression because its antifree market program of high taxes and special-interest spending to certain banks, railroads, farmers, and veterans created an antibusiness environment of regime uncertainty.

NO: Professor of history Roger Biles contends that, in spite of its minimal reforms and nonrevolutionary programs, the New Deal created a limited welfare state that implemented economic stabilizers to avert another depression.

The catastrophe triggered by the 1929 Wall Street debacle crippled the American economy, deflated the optimistic future most Americans assumed to be their birthright, and ripped apart the values by which the country's businesses, farms, and governments were run. During the next decade, the inertia of the Great Depression stifled their attempts to make ends meet.

The world depression of the 1930s began in the United States. The omnipotence of American productivity, the ebullient American spirit, and the self-deluding thought "it can't happen here" blocked out any consideration of an economic collapse that might devastate the capitalist economy and threaten U.S. democratic government.

All aspects of American society trembled from successive jolts; there were 4 million unemployed people in 1930 and 9 million more by 1932. Those who had not lost their jobs took pay cuts or worked for scrip. There was no security for those whose savings were lost forever when banks failed or stocks declined.

Manufacturing halted, industry shut down, and farmers destroyed wheat, corn, and milk rather than sell them at a loss. Worse, there were millions of homeless Americans—refugees from the cities roaming the nation on freight trains, victims of the drought or the Dust Bowl seeking a new life farther west, and hobo children estranged from their parents.

Business and government leaders alike seemed immobilized by the economic giant that had fallen to its knees. Herbert Hoover, the incumbent president at the start of the Great Depression, attempted some relief programs. However, they were ineffective considering the magnitude of the distress. The President's attempts at voluntary cooperation between business and labor to avoid layoffs or pay increases broke down by the severity of the depression in mid-1931. Hoover went further than previous presidents in using the power of the federal government, but efforts were too small and too late.

As governor of New York, Franklin D. Roosevelt (who was elected president in 1932) had introduced some relief measures, such as industrial welfare and a comprehensive system of unemployment remedies, to alleviate the social and economic problems facing the citizens of the state. Yet his campaign did little to reassure his critics that he was more than a rich boy who wanted to be the president. In light of later developments Roosevelt may have been the only presidential candidate to deliver more programs than he actually promised.

The New Deal attempted to jump-start the economy with dozens of recovery and relief measures. On inauguration day, FDR told the nation "the only thing we have to fear is fear itself." A bank holiday was immediately declared. Congress passed the Emergency Banking Act, which pumped Federal Reserve notes into the major banks and stopped the wave of bank failures. Later banking acts separated commercial and investment institutions, and the Federal Deposit Insurance Corporation (FDIC) guaranteed people's savings from a loss of up to $2,500 in member banks. A number of relief agencies were set up that provided work for youth and able-bodied men on various state and local building projects. Finally the Tennessee Valley Administration (TVA) was created to provide electricity in rural areas not serviced by private power companies.

In 1935 the Supreme Court ended the First New Deal by declaring both the Agriculture Adjustment Administration and National Recovery Act unconstitutional. In response to critics on the left who felt that the New Deal was favoring the large banks, big agriculture, and big business, FDR shifted his approach in 1935. The Second New Deal created the Works Project Administration (WPA), which became the nation's largest employer in its eight years of operation. Social Security was passed, and the government guaranteed monthly stipends for the aged, the unemployed, and dependent children. Labor pressured the administration for a collective bargaining bill. The Wagner Act established a National Labor Relations Board to supervise industry-wide elections. The steel, coal, automobile, and some garment industries were unionized as membership tripled from 3 million in 1933 to 9 million in 1939.

Did the New Deal prolong the Great Depression? Burton F. Folsom, Jr., argues in the affirmative because its alphabet soup agencies (all with three letters) created an antibusiness environment that rejected free market capitalism with special-interest spending financed by high taxes. Roger Biles contends its programs were nonrevolutionary and its reforms minimal. Nevertheless, he argues, the New Deal created a limited welfare state that implemented economic stabilizers to avert another depression.

YES

Burton W. Folsom, Jr.

New Deal or Raw Deal? How FDR's Economic Legacy Has Damaged America

The Making of the Myth: FDR and the New Deal

On May 9, 1939, Henry Morgenthau, Jr., the secretary of the treasury and one of the most powerful men in America, had a startling confession to make. He made this remarkable admission before the influential Democrats who ran the House Ways and Means Committee. As he bared his soul before his fellow Democrats, Morgenthau may have pondered the irony of his situation.

Here he was—a major cabinet head, a man of great authority. The source of his power, of course, was his intimate friendship with President Franklin Delano Roosevelt. Morgenthau was the president's longtime neighbor, close confidant, and—would be for over a decade—his loyal secretary of the treasury. Few men knew the president better, talked with him more, or defended him more faithfully. Eleanor Roosevelt once said Morgenthau was one of only two men who could tell her husband "categorically" that he was wrong and get away with it. Roosevelt and Morgenthau liked to banter back and forth at cabinet meetings, pass each other secret notes, meet regularly for lunch, and talk frequently on the phone. Morgenthau cherished a photo of himself and the president in a car, side by side, friends forever, with Roosevelt's inscription: "To Henry," it read, "from one of two of a kind."

But in May 1939, Morgenthau had a problem. The Great Depression—the most devastating economic catastrophe in American history—was not only persisting, in some ways it was getting worse. Unemployment, for example, the previous month had again passed the 20 percent mark. Here was Morgenthau, the secretary of the treasury, an expert on finance, a fount of statistics on the American economy during the 1930s; his best friend was the president of the United States and the author of the New Deal; key public policy decisions had to go through Morgenthau to get a hearing. And yet, with all this power, Morgenthau felt helpless. After almost two full terms of Roosevelt and the New Deal, here are Morgenthau's startling words—his confession—spoken candidly before his fellow Democrats on the House Ways and Means Committee:

We have tried spending money. We are spending more than we have ever spent before and it does not work. And I have just one interest, and if I am wrong . . . somebody else can have my job. I want to see this country prosperous. I want to see people get a job. I want to see people get enough to eat. We have never made good on our promises. . . . I say after eight years of this Administration we have just as much unemployment as when we started. . . . And an enormous debt to boot!

In these words, Morgenthau summarized a decade of disaster, especially during the years Roosevelt was in power. Indeed average unemployment for the whole year in 1939 would be higher than that in 1931, the year before Roosevelt captured the presidency from Herbert Hoover. Fully 17.2 percent of Americans, or 9,480,000, remained unemployed in 1939, up from 16.3 percent, or 8,020,000 in 1931. On the positive side, 1939 was better than 1932 and 1933, when the Great Depression was at its nadir, but 1939 was still worse than 1931, which at that time was almost the worst unemployment year in U.S. history. No depression, or recession, had ever lasted even half this long.

Put another way, if the unemployed in 1931 under Hoover would have been lined up one after the other in three separate lines side by side, they would have extended from Los Angeles across the country to the border of Maine. In 1939, eight years later, the three lines of unemployed Americans would have lengthened, heading from the border of Maine south to Boston, then to New York City, to Philadelphia, to Washington, D.C., and finally into Virginia. That line of unemployed people from the border of Maine into Virginia was mostly added when Roosevelt was president.

We can visualize this hypothetical line of unemployed Americans, but what about the human story of their suffering. Who were some of them, and what were they thinking? In the line at Chicago, we would encounter salesman Ben Isaacs. "Wherever I went to get a job, I couldn't get no job," Isaacs said of the prolonged depression. "I went around selling razor blades and shoe laces. There was a day I would go over all the streets and come home with fifty cents, making a sale. That kept going until 1940, practically." Letters to President Roosevelt tell other stories. For example, in Chicago, a twelve-year-old Chicago boy wrote the president, "We haven't paid the gas bill, and the electric bill, haven't paid grocery bill for 3 months. . . . My father he staying home. All the time he's crying because he can't find work. I told him why are you crying daddy, and daddy said why shouldn't I cry when there is nothing in the house." In our hypothetical unemployment line at Latrobe, Pennsylvania, we might see the man who wrote in 1934, "No home, no work, no money. We cannot go along this way. They have shut the water supply from us. No means of sanitation. We cannot keep the children clean and tidy as they should be." From Augusta, Georgia, in 1935 came this letter to the president: "I am eating flour bread and drinking water, and no grease and nothing in the bread. . . . I aint even got bed[d]ing to sleep on. . . ." But even he was better off than the man from Beaver Dam, Virginia, who wrote the president, "We right now, have no work, no winter bed clothes. . . . Wife don't even have a winter coat. What are we going to do through these cold times coming on? Just looks we will have to freeze and starve together."

High unemployment was just one of many tragic areas that made the 1930s a decade of disaster. The *Historical Statistics of the United States,* compiled by the Census Bureau, fills out the rest of the grim picture. The stock market, which picked up in the mid-1930s, had a collapse later in the decade. The value of all stocks dropped almost in half from 1937 to 1939. Car sales plummeted one-third in those same years, and were lower in 1939 than in any of the last seven years of the 1920s. Business failures jumped 50 percent from 1937 to 1939; patent applications for inventions were lower in 1939 than for any year of the 1920s. Real estate foreclosures, which did decrease steadily during the 1930s, were still higher in 1939 than in any year during the next two decades.

Another disaster sign in the 1930s was the spiraling national debt. The United States had budget surpluses in 1930 and 1931, but soon government spending ballooned and far outstripped revenue from taxes. The national debt stood at $16 billion in 1931; by the end of the decade the debt had more than doubled to more than $40 billion. Put another way, the national debt during the last eight years of the 1930s, less than one decade, grew more than it had in the previous 150 years of our country's existence. From 1776 to 1931, the spending to support seven wars and at least five recessions was more than offset by the debt acquired during the 1930s. Put yet another way, if Christopher Columbus, on that October day when he discovered the New World, could have arranged to put $100 a minute in a special account to defray the American debt, by 1939 his account would not yet have accumulated enough cash to pay for just the national debt acquired in the 1930s alone. In other words, if we were to pay $100 a minute (in 1930s dollars) into a special '30s debt account, we would need more than 450 years to raise enough money to pay off the debt of that decade.

The economic travail of the New Deal years can also be seen in the seven consecutive years of unbalanced trade from 1934 to 1940. Much of our government spending during the decade went to prop up prices of wheat, shirts, steel, and other exports, which in turn, because of the higher prices, made them less desirable as exports to other countries. From 1870 to 1970, only during the depression years plus the year 1888 did the United States have an unfavorable balance of trade.

Hard times are often followed by social problems. The United States in the 1930s was no exception. For example, the American birthrate dropped sharply, and the country's population increased only 7 percent in that decade. During the more prosperous 1920s, by contrast, the birthrate was higher and the country's population increased 16 percent.

For many Americans, the prolonged Great Depression of the 1930s became a time of death. As one eighty-year-old wrote, "Now [December 1934] there are a lot of us [who] will choose suicide in preference to being herded into the poor house." Apparently, thousands of Americans agreed with her, because suicides increased from 1929 to 1930 and remained high throughout the 1930s. Equally sad were the people who gave up on life after prolonged despair and took their lives more subtly, through an accidental fall, reckless driving, or being hit by a train. All three of these categories hit record numbers of deaths per capita during the New Deal years.

The loss of the will to live was also reflected in life expectancy during the 1930s. When Franklin Roosevelt became president in 1933, life expectancy in the United States was 63.3 years. Since 1900, it had steadily increased sixteen years—almost half a year each year of the first third of the twentieth century. In 1940, however, after more than seven years of the New Deal, life expectancy had dropped to 62.9 years. Granted, the slight decline during these years was not consistent—two of the seven years showed an increase over 1933. But the steady increase in life expectancy from 1900 to 1933 and from 1940 to the end of the century was clearly interrupted only during the New Deal years.

The halt in improved life expectancy hit blacks even harder than whites. In 1933, black Americans could expect to live only 54.7 years, but in 1940 that had dropped to 53.1 years. Both before and after the Great Depression, the gap in life expectancy between blacks and whites had narrowed, but from 1933 to 1940 it actually widened. Strong indications are that blacks suffered more than whites during Roosevelt's first term as president.

Someone might survey the wreckage from the 1930s and say, "Okay, maybe the whole decade of the thirties was a disaster. But since the Great Depression was a worldwide catastrophe, doesn't that diminish America's blame for its bad numbers?" The Great Depression did, of course, rock most of the world, but some nations performed better than others in limiting damage and restoring economic growth. Fortunately, the League of Nations collected data from many nations throughout the 1930s on industrial production, unemployment, national debt, and taxes. How did the United States compare with other countries? The answer: in all four of these key indexes the U.S. did very poorly, almost worse than any other nation studied. Most nations of Europe weathered the Great Depression better than the United States did.

In a decade of economic disaster, such as the 1930s, a decline in morality is a significant danger. If record numbers of people are hungry, out of jobs, and taxed higher than ever before, will the charity, honesty, and integrity necessary to hold a society together begin to crumble as well? The *Historical Statistics of the United States* offers some help in answering this question. Homicides increased slightly during the 1930s. There were more than 10,000 murders a year only seven times from 1900 to 1960, and all seven years were in the 1930s. Arrests during this decade roughly doubled: almost 300,000 were made in 1932, and this steadily increased, reaching a peak of almost 600,000 in 1939. Divorce rates increased as well, especially during the late 1930s, and the number of cases of syphilis treated almost doubled, although cases of gonorrhea were roughly constant.

Statistics can't tell the whole story of the changing mores of the 1930s. Many persons openly threatened to steal—or thought about stealing—to make ends meet during the Great Depression. Joblessness also led to "jumping trains" either to find work elsewhere or just to roam the country. R. S. Mitchell of the Missouri Pacific Railroad testified before the U.S. Senate that young men who jumped trains often encountered "hardened criminals" on these rides, who were a "bad influence" on the character of these youths. The *Historical*

Statistics further shows that deaths to trespassers on railroads were at their highest ever during the depression years of 1933 to 1936.

Roosevelt and the Historians

Did the New Deal, rather than helping to cure the Great Depression, actually help prolong it? That is an important question to ask and ponder. Almost all historians of the New Deal rank Roosevelt as a very good to great president and the New Deal programs as a step in the right direction. With only a few exceptions, historians lavish praise on Roosevelt as an effective innovator, and on the New Deal as a set of programs desperately needed and very helpful to the depressed nation.

An example of this adulation is the appraisal by Henry Steele Commager and Richard B. Morris, two of the most distinguished American historians of the twentieth century. Commager, during a remarkable career at Columbia University and Amherst College, wrote over forty books and became perhaps the bestselling historian of the century. From the first year of Roosevelt's presidency, Commager lectured and wrote articles in defense of the New Deal. Richard Morris, his junior partner at Columbia, was a prolific author and president of the American Historical Association. Here is Commager and Morris's assessment of Roosevelt and the New Deal:

> The character of the Republican ascendancy of the twenties had been pervasively negative; the character of the New Deal was overwhelmingly positive. "This nation asks for action, and action, now," Roosevelt said in his first inaugural address, and asked for "power to wage war against the emergency." . . .
>
> It is the stuff of good history, this—a leadership that was buoyant and dynamic; a large program designed to enable the government to catch up with a generation of lag and solve the problems that crowded upon it; a people quickened into resolution and self-confidence; a nation brought to realize its responsibilities and its potentialities. How it lends itself to drama! The sun rises on a stricken field; the new leader raises the banner and waves it defiantly at the foe; his followers crowd about him, armies of recruits emerge from the shadows and throng into the ranks; the bands play, the flags wave, the army moves forward, and soon the sound of battle and the shouts of victory are heard in the distance. In perspective we can see that it was not quite like that, but that was the way it seemed at the time.

Commager and Morris's assessment highlights four main points of defense for Roosevelt and the New Deal that have been adopted by most historians for the last seventy years: first, the 1920s were an economic disaster; second, the New Deal programs were a corrective to the 1920s, and a step in the right direction; third, Roosevelt (and the New Deal) were very popular; and fourth, Roosevelt was a good administrator and moral leader.

These four points constitute what many historians call "the Roosevelt legend." Since the works of Arthur M. Schlesinger, Jr., and William Leuchtenburg have been essential in shaping and fleshing out this view of Roosevelt, I will quote from them liberally. . . .

In fact, the most recent Schlesinger poll (1996) ranks Roosevelt and Lincoln as *the* greatest presidents in U.S. history. He and his New Deal have become American idols. As Conlin writes, "From the moment F. D. R. delivered his ringing inaugural address—the clouds over Washington parting on cue to let the March sun through, it was obvious that he was a natural leader." Even before Roosevelt died, Conlin notes, "he was ranked by historians as among the greatest of the chief executives. . . . No succeeding generation of judges has demoted him." Leuchtenburg concludes, "Few would deny that Franklin Delano Roosevelt continues to provide the standard by which every successor has been, and may well continue to be, measured."

Of course, historians are often nigglers and all students of Roosevelt and his presidency have some complaints. What's interesting is that most of these complaints are that Roosevelt should have done more than he did, not less. "The havoc that had been done before Roosevelt took office," Leuchtenburg argues, "was so great that even the unprecedented measures of the New Deal did not suffice to repair the damage." Therefore, to Leuchtenburg and others, the New Deal was only "a halfway revolution" that should have gone further. Some historians say FDR should have done more deficit spending during the recession of 1937; some chide him for not supporting civil rights more strongly; some point to abuse or corruption in some of the programs; and some say he should have done much more to redistribute wealth. The New Deal was, many historians conclude, a conservative revolution that saved capitalism and preserved the existing order. Some New Deal historians of the 1980s, 1990s, and 2000s—loosely called the "constraints school"—argue that the New Deal did promote many needed changes, but that Roosevelt was constrained in what he could accomplish and therefore he did as much reform as circumstances would permit.

These recent criticisms of Roosevelt and the New Deal slightly alter but do not diminish the Roosevelt legend. The four points of defense are currently intact, and are usually found in most histories of the New Deal and in virtually all of the American history textbooks today. . . .

After his 1996 presidential poll, Schlesinger was more confident in Roosevelt than ever. Of the thirty-two experts consulted, thirty-one gave FDR the highest rating of "Great" and one ranked him "Near Great," the second highest rating. "For a long time FDR's top standing enraged many who had opposed his New Deal," Schlesinger wrote. "But now that even Newt Gingrich pronounces FDR the greatest president of the century, conservatives accept FDR at the top with stoic calm." Along these lines, historian David Hamilton, who edited a book of essays on the New Deal, observed, "Conservative critiques [of the New Deal] have drawn less attention in recent years. . . ." In other words, according to Schlesinger and many historians, the debate is over as the Roosevelt legend is established even among conservative historians.

The historical literature tends to support Schlesinger. The books and articles on Roosevelt and the New Deal are now so extensive, however, that it is almost impossible to read it all. Historian Anthony Badger has come as close as any modern historian to mastering the New Deal literature, and his book *The*

New Deal: The Depression Years, 1933–1940 is an essential tool to the modern historian trying to sort out all the writing on the subject. Badger looks fondly at Schlesinger and Leuchtenburg, the two key historians to shape the historical writing on the New Deal:

> At a time when there were few specialist monographs, both authors [Schlesinger and Leuchtenburg] displayed a remarkably sure touch in identifying the critical issues at stake in the most diverse New Deal activities. Both demonstrated an enviable mastery of a vast range of archival material. No one is ever likely to match the richness of Schlesinger's dramatic narrative. No one is ever likely to produce a better one volume treatment of the New Deal than Leuchtenburg's.

Thus, the Roosevelt legend seems to be intact. And as long as it is intact, the principles of public policy derived from the New Deal will continue to dominate American politics. As historian Ray Allen Billington noted, the New Deal "established for all time the principle of positive government action to rehabilitate and preserve the human resources of the nation." Yet, as we have seen, there is that nagging observation in 1939 by Henry Morgenthau, the secretary of the treasury, the friend of Roosevelt's and the man in the center of the storm. With great sadness, he confessed, "We are spending more than we have ever spent before and it does not work. . . . We have never made good on our promises."

Since national unemployment during the previous month of April 1939 was 20.7 percent, Morgenthau's admission has the ring of truth to it.

Is it possible that the Roosevelt legend is really the Roosevelt myth?. . .

What Finally Did End the Great Depression

If Roosevelt's New Deal programs did not break the Great Depression, then what did? Most historians have argued that America's entry into World War II was the key event that ended it. Federal spending drastically increased as twelve million U.S. soldiers went to war, and millions more mobilized in the factories to make war material. As a result, unemployment plummeted and, so the argument goes, the Great Depression receded.

William Leuchtenburg, who has written the standard book on the New Deal, claims, "The real impetus to recovery was to come from rapid, large-scale spending." Roosevelt, according to Leuchtenburg, was reluctant to take this step. When, at last, Pearl Harbor was bombed, "The war proved that massive spending under the right conditions produced full employment."

Recently, David M. Kennedy, in his Pulitzer Prize-winning book on Roosevelt, echoed Leuchtenburg's argument. "Roosevelt," Kennedy insisted, "remained reluctant to the end of the 1930s to engage in the scale of compensatory spending adequate to restore the economy to pre-Depression levels, let alone expand it." At the end of his book, Kennedy concluded, "It was a war that had brought [Americans] as far as imagination could reach, and beyond, from the ordeal of the Great Depression. . . ." More specifically, "The huge expenditures for weaponry clinched the Keynesian doctrine that government spending could underwrite prosperity. . . ."

Economists, Keynes notwithstanding, have always been less willing to believe this theory than historians. F.A. Hayek, who won the Nobel Prize in economics, argued against this view in 1944 in *The Road to Serfdom*. Economist Henry Hazlitt, who wrote for the *New York Times* during the Roosevelt years, observed, "No man burns down his own house on the theory that the need to rebuild it will stimulate his energies." And yet, as historians and others viewed World War II, "they see almost endless benefits in enormous acts of destruction. They tell us how much better off economically we all are in war than in peace. They see 'miracles of production' which it requires a war to achieve." Thus, in Hazlitt's argument, the United States merely shifted capital from private markets, where it could have made consumer goods, to armament factories, where it made tanks, bombs, and planes for temporary use during war.

Along these lines, economist Robert Higgs has observed, "Unemployment virtually disappeared as conscription, directly and indirectly, pulled more than 12 million potential workers into the armed forces and millions of others into draft-exempt employment, but under the prevailing conditions, the disappearance of unemployment can hardly be interpreted as a valid index of economic prosperity." A supporting point for this idea is that real private investment and real personal consumption sharply declined during the war. Stock market prices, for example, in 1944 were still below those of 1939 in real dollars.

If not World War II, what did end the Great Depression? This question is still open to research and original thinking. Higgs argues," It is time for economists and historians to take seriously the hypothesis that the New Deal prolonged the Great Depression by creating an extraordinarily high degree of regime uncertainty in the minds of investors." Roosevelt, as we have seen, regularly attacked business and steadily raised income tax rates, corporate tax rates, and excise taxes during the 1930s. He added the undistributed profits tax and conducted highly publicized tax cases that sent many investors to prison. During World War II, Roosevelt softened his rhetoric against businessmen, whom he needed to wage the war, but he did issue an executive order for a 100 percent tax on all personal income over $25,000. When Roosevelt died, and Truman became president, the hostile rhetoric toward businessmen further declined and no new tax hikes were added. During the war, in fact, Roosevelt had switched from attacking rich people to letting big corporations monopolize war contracts. Under Truman, businessmen were even more optimistic. They expanded production, and the U.S. economy was thus able to absorb the returning soldiers and those who had previously worked to make war equipment.

That, in a nutshell, is Higgs's thesis, and he has two persuasive pieces of evidence on his side. First, many leading industrialists of the 1930s openly explained how the president's efforts to tax and regulate were stifling the nation's economic expansion. For example, Lammot Du Pont, who revolutionized the textile industry in the 1940s with the invention of nylon, was one of many businessmen who complained about Roosevelt's policies. "Uncertainty rules the tax situation, the labor situation, the monetary situation, and practically every legal condition under which industry must operate," Du Pont protested in 1937. "Are new restrictions to be placed on capital, new limits on profits? . . . It is impossible to even guess at the answers."

Second, Higgs cites poll data that show a sharp increase in optimism about business after Roosevelt died and Truman became president. For example, the American Institute of Public Opinion (AIPO) did solid polling of attitudes on business and its findings are impressive. In March 1939, for example, AIPO asked a national sample, "Do you think the attitude of the Roosevelt administration toward business is delaying business recovery?" More than twice as many respondents said "yes" as said "no." In May 1945, however, one month after Roosevelt's death, the AIPO pollsters asked, "Do you think Truman will be more favorable or less favorable toward business than Roosevelt was?" On this poll, Truman had eight times more yeses than nos. *Forbes* and *Fortune* also did polls of businessmen and found similar results. What that meant was that after the war, American businessmen expanded production and thereby absorbed into the workforce the returning soldiers. The Great Depression was over at last.

Other nations recovered from the Great Depression more quickly than did the United States. During the late 1930s, the League of Nations collected statistics from the United States and from many other nations on industrial recovery. Much of that data support the idea that Roosevelt's New Deal created economic uncertainty and was in fact uniquely unsuccessful as a recovery program. In the table below, we can see some of the aftermath of the depression within a depression in 1937, when the stock market lost one-third of its value. During late 1938, the United States had some recovery, but in early 1939 recovery again lagged. By May 1939, unemployment again reached 20 percent, industrial production had fallen about 10 percent from the first of the year, and Henry Morgenthau confessed, "We are spending more than we have ever spent before and it does not work."

. . . The U.S. economy was in a tailspin six years after FDR became president and the country suffered more unemployment than most of the other ones studied by the League of Nations.

Some historians, trying to defend Roosevelt, point out that unemployment in the United States slightly dropped each year from 1933 to 1937, which suggests some progress in fighting the Depression. Unemployment was 25.2 percent in 1933, 22 percent in 1934, 20.3 percent in 1935, 17 percent in 1936, and 14.3 percent in 1937. That 14.3 percent, however, is alarmingly high and—outside of the 1930s—was only exceeded for a brief period in all of American history during the Panic of 1893. What's worse, the business uncertainty during Roosevelt's second term stifled that modest recovery of his first term.

To be fair, if we describe the downward move of unemployment during Roosevelt's first term, we must present the steady upward move of unemployment during most of his second term. Unemployment was 15.0 percent in September 1936, 15.1 percent in January 1937, 17.4 percent in January 1938, 18.7 percent in January 1939, and 20.7 percent in April 1939. Thus, more than six years after Roosevelt took office, and almost ten years after the stock market crash of 1929, unemployment topped the 20 percent mark. The League of

Industrial Production in the United States Date (1929 = 100)	
June 1938	65
December 1938	87
January 1939	85
February 1939	82
March 1939	82
April 1939	77
May 1939	77
June 1939	81

Sources: League of Nations, *World Economic Survey, 1938/39* (Geneva, 1939), 110–11.

Nations study, which tried to explain the poor performance of the U.S. economy, cited the "uneasy relations between business and the [Roosevelt] Administration." As Yale economist Irving Fisher bluntly wrote Roosevelt, "You have also delayed recovery."

Why was the performance of the U.S. economy—especially relative to other nations—so miserable? What were some of the ingredients in America's unique "regime uncertainty"? The first place to start is tax policy. One reason that the United States lagged behind other countries in recovery from the Great Depression is that Roosevelt strongly emphasized raising revenue by excise taxes. According to another League of Nations study, the U.S. increased its revenue from excise taxes more rapidly than did any of the other nine nations surveyed. Britain and France, for example, decreased their dependency on excise taxes from 1929 to 1938. Japan, Germany, Italy, and Hungary did increase their excise revenues, but only slightly. The United States, however, had a whopping 328 percent increase in excise revenue from 1929 to 1938. "The very large increases of yield [in tax revenue] which are shown in the case of Belgium [310 percent] and the United States [328 percent] are due to substantial increases in the rate of duty," the study concluded. Since these taxes fell heavier on lower incomes, that may have contributed to the poorer rate of recovery from the Great Depression by the United States.

Other tax problems contributed to "regime uncertainty." Corporate taxes went up, the estate tax was increased to a top rate of 70 percent, and the United States alone among nations passed an undistributed profits tax. Businessmen watched the top rate of the federal income tax increase from 24 to 63 percent in 1932 under Hoover and then to 79 percent in 1935 under Roosevelt. The president regularly castigated businessmen and threatened to raise rates further. On April 27, 1942, Roosevelt issued an executive order that would tax all personal income over $25,000 at 100 percent. All "excess income," the president argued/should go to win the war." Furthermore, Roosevelt's use of the IRS to prosecute wealthy Americans, especially Republicans, created incentives for businessmen to shift their investments into areas of lesser taxation. All of this created "regime uncertainty," and the Great Depression persisted throughout the 1930s. As we have seen in the League of Nations study, in 1929 the United States had the lowest level of unemployment of any of the sixteen nations surveyed. The U.S. dropped to eighth place by 1932, eleventh place in 1937, and then to thirteenth place in 1938.

In retrospect, we can see that Roosevelt's special-interest spending created insatiable demands by almost all groups of voters for special subsidies. That, in itself, created regime uncertainty. Under the RFC, for example, the federal government made special loans to banks and railroads; then the AAA had price supports for farmers; soon the operators of silver mines were demanding special high prices for their product. At one level, as we have seen, Roosevelt used these subsidies as political tools to reward friends and punish enemies. But beyond that, where would the line be drawn? Who would get special taxpayer subsidies and who would not? As Walter Waters, who led the veterans' march on Washington in 1932, observed, "I noticed, too, that the highly organized lobbies in Washington for special industries were producing results: loans were being granted to their special interests and these lobbies seemed to justify their existence. Personal lobbying paid, regardless of the justice or injustice of their demand."

Roosevelt became trapped in a debt spiral of special-interest spending. He often did not try to escape because of the political benefits received when he supported subsidy bills to targeted interest groups. In 1935, when the veterans came clamoring again for a special subsidy, Roosevelt cast only a tepid veto—how could he justify the cash to all the other groups, but deny the veterans? Therefore, an obliging Congress voted the veterans a special bonus of $2 billion—a sum exceeding 6 percent of the entire national debt. As the *St. Louis Post-Dispatch* observed," Here is a superb example of how a powerful minority, in this case the veterans' organizations, has been able . . . to win Congress over to a proposition in defiance of logic, good sense and justice." Such an unwarranted subsidy was, the editor feared, a "grave defect in our system." We can better understand Henry Morgenthau's frustration in May 1939. He could just as easily have said, "We have tried spending and it creates frantic lobbying and a never-ending cycle of more spending."

A New Deal for the American People

At the close of the Hundred Days, Franklin D. Roosevelt said, "All of the proposals and all of the legislation since the fourth day of March have not been just a collection of haphazard schemes, but rather the orderly component parts of a connected and logical whole." Yet the president later described his approach quite differently. "Take a method and try it. If it fails admit it frankly and try another. But above all, try something." The impetus for New Deal legislation came from a variety of sources, and Roosevelt relied heavily at various times on an ideologically diverse group of aides and allies. His initiatives reflected the contributions of, among others, Robert Wagner, Rexford Tugwell, Raymond Moley, George Norris, Robert LaFollette, Henry Morgenthau, Marriner Eccles, Felix Frankfurter, Henry Wallace, Harry Hopkins, and Eleanor Roosevelt. An initial emphasis on recovery for agriculture and industry gave way within two years to a broader-based program for social reform; entente with the business community yielded to populist rhetoric and a more ambiguous economic program. Roosevelt suffered the opprobrium of both the conservatives, who vilified "that man" in the White House who was leading the country down the sordid road to socialism, and the radicals, who saw the Hyde Park aristocrat as a confidence man peddling piecemeal reform to forestall capitalism's demise. Out of so many contradictory and confusing circumstances, how does one make sense of the five years of legislative reform known as the New Deal? And what has been its impact on a half century of American life?[1]

A better understanding begins with the recognition that little of the New Deal was new, including the use of federal power to effect change. Nor, for all of Roosevelt's famed willingness to experiment, did New Deal programs usually originate from vernal ideas. Governmental aid to increase farmers' income, propounded in the late nineteenth century by the Populists, surfaced in Woodrow Wilson's farm credit acts. The prolonged debates over McNary-Haugenism in the 1920s kept the issue alive, and Herbert Hoover's Agricultural Marketing Act set the stage for further federal involvement. Centralized economic planning, as embodied in the National Industrial Recovery Act, flowed directly from the experiences of Wilson's War Industries Board; not surprisingly, Roosevelt chose Hugh Johnson, a veteran of the board, to head the National Recovery Administration. Well established in England and Germany before the First World War, social insurance appeared in a handful of states—notably Wisconsin—before

From *A New Deal for the American People* by Roger Biles (Northern Illinois University Press, 1991). Copyright © 1991 by Northern Illinois University Press. Reprinted by permission.

the federal government became involved. Similarly, New Deal labor reform took its cues from the path-breaking work of state legislatures. Virtually alone in its originality, compensatory fiscal policy seemed revolutionary in the 1930s. Significantly, however, Roosevelt embraced deficit spending quite late after other disappointing economic policies and never to the extent Keynesian economists advised. Congress and the public supported the New Deal, in part, because of its origins in successful initiatives attempted earlier under different conditions.

Innovative or not, the New Deal clearly failed to restore economic prosperity. As late as 1938 unemployment stood at 19.1 percent and two years later at 14.6 percent. Only the Second World War, which generated massive industrial production, put the majority of the American people back to work. To be sure, partial economic recovery occurred. From a high of 13 million unemployed in 1933, the number under Roosevelt's administration fell to 11.4 million in 1934, 10.6 million in 1935, and 9 million in 1936. Farm income and manufacturing wages also rose, and as limited as these achievements may seem in retrospect, they provided sustenance for millions of people and hope for many more. Yet Roosevelt's resistance to Keynesian formulas for pump priming placed immutable barriers in the way of recovery that only war could demolish. At a time calling for drastic inflationary methods, Roosevelt introduced programs effecting the opposite result. The NRA restricted production, elevated prices, and reduced purchasing power, all of which were deflationary in effect. The Social Security Act's payroll taxes took money from consumers and out of circulation. The federal government's $4.43 billion deficit in fiscal year 1936, impressive as it seemed, was not so much greater than Hoover's $2.6 billion shortfall during his last year in office. As economist Robert Lekachman noted, "The 'great spender' was in his heart a true descendant of thrifty Dutch Calvinist forebears." It is not certain that the application of Keynesian formulas would have sufficed by the mid-1930s to restore prosperity, but the president's cautious deflationary policies clearly retarded recovery.[2]

Although New Deal economic policies came up short in the 1930s, they implanted several "stabilizers" that have been more successful in averting another such depression. The Securities and Exchange Act of 1934 established government supervision of the stock market, and the Wheeler-Rayburn Act allowed the Securities and Exchange Commission to do the same with public utilities. Severely embroiled in controversy when adopted, these measures have become mainstays of the American financial system. The Glass–Steagall Banking Act forced the separation of commercial and investment banking and broadened the powers of the Federal Reserve Board to change interest rates and limit loans for speculation. The creation of the Federal Deposit Insurance Corporation (FDIC) increased government supervision of state banks and significantly lowered the number of bank failures. Such safeguards restored confidence in the discredited banking system and established a firm economic foundation that performed well for decades thereafter.

The New Deal was also responsible for numerous other notable changes in American life. Section 7(a) of the NIRA, the Wagner Act, and the Fair Labor Standards Act transformed the relationship between workers and business and breathed life into a troubled labor movement on the verge of total extinction.

In the space of a decade government laws eliminated sweatshops, severely curtailed child labor, and established enforceable standards for hours, wages, and working conditions. Further, federal action eliminated the vast majority of company towns in such industries as coal mining. Although Robert Wagner and Frances Perkins dragged Roosevelt into labor's corner, the New Deal made the unions a dynamic force in American society. Moreover, as Nelson Lichtenstein has noted, "by giving so much of the working class an institutional voice, the union movement provided one of the main political bulwarks of the Roosevelt Democratic party and became part of the social bedrock in which the New Deal welfare state was anchored."[3]

Roosevelt's avowed goal of "cradle-to-grave" security for the American people proved elusive, but his administration achieved unprecedented advances in the field of social welfare. In 1938 the president told Congress: "Government has a final responsibility for the well-being of its citizenship. If private co-operative endeavor fails to provide work for willing hands and relief for the unfortunate, those suffering hardship from no fault of their own have a right to call upon the Government for aid; and a government worthy of its name must make fitting response." The New Deal's safety net included low-cost housing; old-age pensions; unemployment insurance; and aid for dependent mothers and children, the disabled, the blind, and public health services. Sometimes disappointing because of limiting eligibility requirements and low benefit levels, these social welfare programs nevertheless firmly established the principle that the government had an obligation to assist the needy. As one scholar wrote of the New Deal, "More progress was made in public welfare and relief than in the three hundred years after this country was first settled."[4]

More and more government programs, inevitably resulting in an enlarged administrative apparatus and requiring additional revenue, added up to a much greater role for the national government in American life. Coming at a time when the only Washington bureaucracy most of the people encountered with any frequency was the U.S. Postal Service, the change seemed all the more remarkable. Although many New Deal programs were temporary emergency measures, others lingered long after the return of prosperity. Suddenly, the national government was supporting farmers, monitoring the economy, operating a welfare system, subsidizing housing, adjudicating labor disputes, managing natural resources, and providing electricity to a growing number of consumers. "What Roosevelt did in a period of a little over 12 years was to change the form of government," argued journalist Richard L. Strout. "Washington had been largely run by big business, by Wall Street. He brought the government to Washington." Not surprisingly, popular attitudes toward government also changed. No longer willing to accept economic deprivation and social dislocation as the vagaries of an uncertain existence, Americans tolerated—indeed, came to expect—the national government's involvement in the problems of everyday life. No longer did "government" mean just "city hall."[5]

The operation of the national government changed as well. For one thing, Roosevelt's strong leadership expanded presidential power, contributing to what historian Arthur Schlesinger, Jr., called the "imperial presidency." Whereas Americans had in previous years instinctively looked first to Capitol Hill, after Roosevelt the White House took center stage in Washington. At the same time, Congress and the president looked at the nation differently. Traditionally attentive only to one group (big business), policymakers in Washington began responding to other constituencies such as labor, farmers, the unemployed, the aged, and to a lesser extent, women, blacks, and other disadvantaged groups. This new "broker state" became more accessible and acted on a growing number of problems, but equity did not always result. The ablest, richest, and most experienced groups fared best during the New Deal. NRA codes favored big business, and AAA benefits aided large landholders; blacks received relief and government jobs but not to the extent their circumstances merited. The long-term result, according to historian John Braeman, has been "a balkanized political system in which private interests scramble, largely successfully, to harness governmental authority and/or draw upon the public treasury to advance their private agendas."[6]

Another legacy of the New Deal has been the Roosevelt revolution in politics. Urbanization and immigration changed the American electorate, and a new generation of voters who resided in the cities during the Great Depression opted for Franklin D. Roosevelt and his party. Before the 1930s the Democrats of the northern big-city machines and the solid South uneasily coexisted and surrendered primacy to the unified Republican party. The New Deal coalition that elected Roosevelt united behind common economic interests. Both urban northerners and rural southerners, as well as blacks, women, and ethnic immigrants, found common cause in government action to shield them from an economic system gone haywire. By the end of the decade the increasing importance of the urban North in the Democratic party had already become apparent. After the economy recovered from the disastrous depression, members of the Roosevelt coalition shared fewer compelling interests. Beginning in the 1960s, tensions mounted within the party as such issues as race, patriotism, and abortion loomed larger. Even so, the Roosevelt coalition retained enough commitment to New Deal principles to keep the Democrats the nation's majority party into the 1980s.[7]

Yet for all the alterations in politics, government, and the economy, the New Deal fell far short of a revolution. The two-party system survived intact, and neither fascism, which attracted so many followers in European states suffering from the same international depression, nor communism attracted much of a following in the United States. Vital government institutions functioned without interruption and if the balance of powers shifted, the nation remained capitalistic; free enterprise and private ownership, not socialism, emerged from the 1930s. A limited welfare state changed the meld of the public and private but left them separate. Roosevelt could be likened to the British conservative Edmund Burke, who advocated measured change to offset drastic alterations—"reform to preserve." The New Deal's great achievement was the application of just enough change to preserve the American political economy.

Indications of Roosevelt's restraint emerged from the very beginning of the New Deal. Rather than assume extraordinary executive powers as Abraham Lincoln had done in the 1861 crisis, the president called Congress into special session. Whatever changes ensued would come through normal governmental activity. Roosevelt declined to assume direct control of the economy, leaving the nation's resources in the hands of private enterprise. Resisting the blandishments of radicals calling for the nationalization of the banks, he provided the means for their rehabilitation and ignored the call for national health insurance and federal contributions to Social Security retirement benefits. The creation of such regulatory agencies as the SEC confirmed his intention to revitalize rather than remake economic institutions. Repeatedly during his presidency Roosevelt responded to congressional pressure to enact bolder reforms, as in the case of the National Labor Relations Act, the Wagner-Steagall Housing Act, and the FDIC. The administration forwarded the NIRA only after Senator Hugo Black's recovery bill mandating 30-hour workweeks seemed on the verge of passage.

As impressive as New Deal relief and social welfare programs were, they never went as far as conditions demanded or many liberals recommended. Fluctuating congressional appropriations, oscillating economic conditions, and Roosevelt's own hesitancy to do too much violence to the federal budget left Harry Hopkins, Harold Ickes, and others only partially equipped to meet the staggering need. The president justified the creation of the costly WPA in 1935 by "ending this business of relief." Unskilled workers, who constituted the greatest number of WPA employees, obtained but 60 to 80 percent of the minimal family income as determined by the government. Roosevelt and Hopkins continued to emphasize work at less than existing wage scales so that the WPA or PWA never competed with free labor, and they allowed local authorities to modify pay rates. They also continued to make the critical distinction between the "deserving" and "undeserving" poor, making sure that government aided only the former. The New Deal never challenged the values underlying this distinction, instead seeking to provide for the growing number of "deserving" poor created by the Great Depression. Government assumed an expanded role in caring for the disadvantaged, but not at variance with existing societal norms regarding social welfare.

The New Deal effected no substantial redistribution of income. The Wealth Tax Act of 1935 (the famous soak-the-rich tax) produced scant revenue and affected very few taxpayers. Tax alterations in 1936 and 1937 imposed no additional burdens on the rich; the 1938 and 1939 tax laws actually removed a few. By the end of the 1930s less than 5 percent of Americans paid income taxes, and the share of taxes taken from personal and corporate income levies fell below the amount raised in the 1920s. The great change in American taxation policy came during World War II, when the number of income tax payers grew to 74 percent of the population. In 1942 Treasury Secretary Henry Morgenthau noted that "for the first time in our history, the income tax is becoming a people's tax." This the New Deal declined to do.[8]

Finally, the increased importance of the national government exerted remarkably little influence on local institutions. The New Deal seldom dictated and almost always deferred to state and local governments—encouraging, cajoling, bargaining, and wheedling to bring parochial interests in line with national objectives. As Harry Hopkins discovered, governors and mayors angled to obtain as many federal dollars as possible for their constituents but with no strings attached. Community control and local autonomy, conditions thought to be central to American democracy, remained strong, and Roosevelt understood the need for firm ties with politicians at all levels. In his study of the New Deal's impact on federalism, James T. Patterson concludes: "For all the supposed power of the New Deal, it was unable to impose all its guidelines on the autonomous forty-eight states. . . . What could the Roosevelt administration have done to ensure a more profound and lasting impression on state policy and politics? Very little."[9]

Liberal New Dealers longed for more sweeping change and lamented their inability to goad the president into additional action. They envisioned a wholesale purge of the Democratic party and the creation of a new organization embodying fully the principles of liberalism. They could not abide Roosevelt's toleration of the political conservatives and unethical bosses who composed part of the New Deal coalition. They sought racial equality, constraints upon the southern landholding class, and federal intrusion to curb the power of urban real estate interests on behalf of the inveterate poor. Yet to do these things would be to attempt changes well beyond the desires of most Americans. People pursuing remunerative jobs and the economic security of the middle class approved of government aiding the victims of an unfortunate economic crisis but had no interest in an economic system that would limit opportunity. The fear that the New Deal would lead to such thoroughgoing change explains the seemingly irrational hatred of Roosevelt by the economic elite. But, as historian Barry Karl has noted, "it was characteristic of Roosevelt's presidency that he never went as far as his detractors feared or his followers hoped."[10]

The New Deal achieved much that was good and left much undone. Roosevelt's programs were defined by the confluence of forces that circumscribed his admittedly limited reform agenda—hostile judiciary; powerful congressional opponents, some of whom entered into alliances of convenience with New Dealers and some of whom awaited the opportunity to build on their opposition; the political impotence of much of the populace; the pugnacious independence of local and state authorities; the strength of people's attachment to traditional values and institutions; and the basic conservatism of American culture. Obeisance to local custom and the decision to avoid tampering with the fabric of American society allowed much injustice to survive while shortchanging blacks, women, small farmers, and the "unworthy" poor. Those who criticized Franklin Roosevelt for an unwillingness to challenge racial, economic, and gender inequality misunderstood either the nature of his electoral mandate or the difference between reform and revolution—or both.

If the New Deal preserved more than it changed, that is understandable in a society whose people have consistently chosen freedom over equality. Americans traditionally have eschewed expanded government, no matter how efficiently managed or honestly administered, that imposed restraints on personal success—even though such limitations redressed legitimate grievances or righted imbalances. Parity, most Americans believed, should not be purchased with the loss of liberty. But although the American dream has always entailed individual success with a minimum of state interference, the profound shock of capitalism's near demise in the 1930s undermined numerous previously unquestioned beliefs. The inability of capitalism's "invisible hand" to stabilize the market and the failure of the private sector to restore prosperity enhanced the consideration of stronger executive leadership and centralized planning. Yet with the collapse of democratic governments and their replacement by totalitarian regimes, Americans were keenly sensitive to any threats to liberty. New Deal programs, frequently path breaking in their delivery of federal resources outside normal channels, also retained a strong commitment to local government and community control while promising only temporary disruptions prior to the return of economic stability. Reconciling the necessary authority at the federal level to meet nationwide crises with the local autonomy desirable to safeguard freedom has always been one of the salient challenges to American democracy. Even after New Deal refinements, the search for the proper balance continues.

Notes

1. Otis L. Graham, Jr., and Meghan Robinson Wander, eds., *Franklin D. Roosevelt, His Life and Times: An Encyclopedic View* (Boston: G. K. Hall, 1985), p. 285 (first quotation); Harvard Sitkoff, "Introduction," in Sitkoff, *Fifty Years Later,* p. 5 (second quotation).

2. Richard S. Kirkendall, "The New Deal as Watershed: The Recent Literature," *Journal of American History* 54 (March 1968), p. 847 (quotation).

3. Graham and Wander, *Franklin D. Roosevelt, His Life and Times,* p. 228 (quotation).

4. Leuchtenburg, "The Achievement of the New Deal," p. 220 (first quotation); Patterson, *America's Struggle against Poverty, 1900–1980,* p. 56 (second quotation).

5. Louchheim, *The Making of the New Deal: The Insiders Speak,* p. 15 (quotation).

6. John Braeman, "The New Deal: The Collapse of the Liberal Consensus," *Canadian Review of American Studies* 20 (Summer 1989), p. 77.

7. David Burner, *The Politics of Provincialism: The Democratic Party in Transition, 1918–1932* (New York: Alfred A. Knopf, 1968).

8. Mark Leff, *The Limits of Symbolic Reform,* p. 287 (quotation).

9. James T. Patterson, *The New Deal and the States: Federalism in Transition* (Princeton: Princeton University Press, 1969), p. 202.

10. Barry D. Karl, *The Uneasy State: The United States from 1915 to 1945* (Chicago: University of Chicago Press, 1983), p. 124.

POSTSCRIPT

Did the New Deal Prolong the Great Depression?

Professor Folsom argues that the New Deal prolonged a depression that was started in the late 1920s. Both the Hoover and Roosevelt administrations, in his view, abandoned free market economics when it passed the Smoot–Hawley Tariff Act in 1930 that created high tariffs on 3,218 goods American industries needed for their production, increased prices to the American consumer and prevented European countries from paying off their debts. Meanwhile the Federal Reserve System continued to raise interest rates and that made it harder for businesses to borrow money. Folsom also challenges the notion that underconsumption and overproduction of consumer goods was a major problem into the 1920s. He then goes on to argue that the New Deal itself with its shortsighted programs increased the size and power of the federal government that prevented the country from ending the depression more quickly.

Folsom's analysis can be faulted on several grounds. For example, he underestimates the enormity of the economic crisis facing the country on the eve of Roosevelt's inauguration. Bank failures were rampant, farmers declared "farm holidays" and destroyed crops to keep up prices, and an assassin tried to kill the president-elect in Miami. As Roosevelt often quipped, "People don't eat in the long run, they eat every day." His immediate response to the crisis was the "100 days" New Deal recovery programs.

Folsom's critique is based on the conservative assumptions of the well-known free-market advocates Milton Friedman and Anna Jacobson Schwartz, who argue in *A Monetary History of the United States, 1867–1960* (Princeton University Press, 1963) that the Great Depression was a government failure, brought on primarily by Federal Reserve policies that abruptly cut the money supply. This view runs counter to those of Peter Temin, *Did Monetary Forces Cause the Depression?* (Norton, 1976); Michael A. Bernstein, *The Great Depression: Delayed Recovery and Economic Change in America* (Cambridge University Press, 1987); and the readable and lively account of John Kenneth Galbraith, *The Great Crash* (Houghton Mifflin, 1955), which argue that the crash exposed various structural weaknesses in the economy that caused the depression.

Folsom also argues that unemployment was higher and industrial production was lower throughout the decade of the 1930s as compared with the nations of Western Europe. He goes even further than almost all historians and economists who believe that it was World War II and not the New Deal that got us out of the Great Depression. He uses the arguments of economist Robert Higgs who rejects the explanation that the massive deficit spending during the war that decreased unemployment and increased savings led to the economic recovery after the war. According to Higgs, FDR's probusiness policy during the war and carried on by his successor President Harry Truman was the primary reason for the nation's recovery. Folsom's critique in large measure is based upon the arguments used by Roosevelt's Republican opponents in the 1930s. A number of books in the past two decades have given the free market argument against the New Deal. See Gary Dean Best, *Pride, Prejudice and Politics: Roosevelt versus Recovery, 1933–1938* (Praeger, 1990); Robert Eden, ed., *The New Deal and Its Legacy: Critique and Reappraisal* (Greenwood Press, 1989); and Jim Powell, *FDR's Folly: How Roosevelt and His New deal Prolonged the Great Depression* (Crown Forum, 2003). Wall Street Journal writer Amity Shlaes wrote *The Forgotten Man* (Harper Collins, 2007), a highly publicized and widely reviewed controversial critique of New Deal programs. Finally Robert Higgs has a short concise essay criticizing the New Deal among other liberal programs in *Against Leviathan: Government Power and a Free Society* (The Independent Institute, 2004). See also Higgs' important essay used by Folsom, "Regime Uncertainty: Why the Great Depression Lasted So Long and Why Prosperity Resumed after the War," *Independent Review*, vol. 1 (Spring, 1997).

Historian Roger Biles argues that the New Deal was a nonrevolution compared to the economic and political changes that were taking place in communist Russia, fascist Italy, and Nazi Germany. The New Deal, in his view, was not so new. Social insurance appeared earlier in several states, notably Wisconsin. The economic planning embodied in the National Industrial Recovery Act extends back to President Wilson's World War I War Industries Board. The use of the federal government to aid farmers was begun with President Wilson's Farm Credit Act and continued during the Harding, Coolidge, and Hoover administrations.

Although the recovery doesn't come about until World War II, Biles admits that the New Deal changed the relationship between the federal government and the people. The New Deal stabilized the banking industry and stock exchange. It ameliorated the relationship of workers with business and its support of the Wagner Act and the Fair Standard labor Act. Social Security provided a safety net for the aged, the unemployed, and the disabled. In politics, urbanization and immigration cemented a new Democratic coalition in 1936 with the conservative South around common economic interests until the 1980s when racial issues and the maturing of a new suburban middle class fractured the Democratic majority.

Biles' analysis basically agrees with the British historian Anthony J. Badger who argues in *The New Deal* (Hill and Wang, 1989) that the New Deal was a "holding operation" until the Second World War created the "political economy of modern America." Both Biles and Badger argue that once the immediate crisis of 1933 subsided, the opposition to the New Deal came from big business, conservative congressmen, and local governments who resisted the increasing power of the federal government. As the Office of War Information told Roosevelt, the American people's postwar aspirations were "compounded largely of 1929 values and the economics of the 1920s, leavened with a handover from the makeshift controls of the war."

The most recent annotated bibliography is Robert F. Himmelberg, *The Great Depression and the New Deal* (Greenwood Press, 2001). Two important collections of recent writings are David E. Hamilton, ed., *The New Deal* (Houghton Mifflin, 1999); and Colin Gordon, ed., *Major Problems in American History, 1920–1945* (Houghton Mifflin, 1999). Finally, Steve Fraser and Gary Gerstle edited a series of social and economic essays, which they present in *The Rise and Fall of the New Deal Order, 1930–1980* (Princeton University Press, 1989).

Two of the most recent studies sympathetic to the New Deal are David M. Kennedy, *Freedom from Fear: The American People in Depression and War, 1929–1945* (Oxford University Press, 1999); and George McJimsey, *The Presidency of Franklin Delano Roosevelt* (University Press of Kansas, 2000). Out of vogue but still worth reading are the pro-Roosevelt studies of the New Deal by William Leuchtenburg, *Franklin D. Roosevelt and the New Deal* (Harper and Row, 1963) and his interpretative essays written over 30 years in *The FDR Years: On Roosevelt and His Legacy* (Columbia University Press, 1985). See also the beautifully written but never to be completed second and third volumes of Arthur M. Schlesinger, Jr.'s *The Coming of the New Deal* (Houghton Mifflin, 1959) and *The Politics of Upheaval* (Houghton Mifflin, 1960), which advance the interpretation of the first and second New Deal, found in most American history survey textbooks.

Most presidential polls rank FDR in the top three alongside Lincoln and Washington. For a recent example, see Arthur M. Schlesinger, Jr., "Rating the Presidents: Washington to Clinton," *Political Science Quarterly*, vol. 112 (1997).

ISSUE 12

Did President Roosevelt Deliberately Withhold Information About the Attack on Pearl Harbor from the American Commanders?

YES: Robert A. Theobald, from *The Final Secret of Pearl Harbor: The Washington Contribution to the Japanese Attack* (Devin-Adair, 1954)

NO: Roberta Wohlstetter, from *Pearl Harbor: Warning and Decision* (Stanford University Press, 1967)

ISSUE SUMMARY

YES: Retired rear admiral Robert A. Theobald argues that President Franklin D. Roosevelt deliberately withheld information from the commanders at Pearl Harbor in order to encourage the Japanese to make a surprise attack on the weak U.S. Pacific Fleet.

NO: Historian Roberta Wohlstetter contends that even though naval intelligence broke the Japanese code, conflicting signals and the lack of a central agency coordinating U.S. intelligence information made it impossible to predict the Pearl Harbor attack.

In 1899 and 1900 Secretary of State John Hay enunciated two notes, known as the Open Door policy. The first pronouncement attempted to provide equal access to commercial rights in China for all nations. The second note called on all countries to respect China's "territorial and administrative" integrity. For the next 40 years the open door was restated by every president from Theodore Roosevelt to Franklin Roosevelt for two reasons: (1) to prevent China from being taken over by Japan, and (2) to preserve the balance of power in the world. The Open Door policy appeared to work during World War I and the 1920s.

The Nine-Power Treaty of 1922 restated the Open Door principles, and its signatories agreed to assist China in forming a stable government. Japan supported the agreements because the world economy was reasonably stable. But the worldwide depression had a major effect on the foreign policies of all nations. Japan decided that she wanted to extend her influence politically as well as economically in Asia. On the night of September 18, 1931, an explosion, probably staged by Japanese militarists, damaged the Japanese-controlled South Manchurian Railroad. Japanese troops not only overran Chinese troops stationed in South Manchuria but within five months established the puppet state of Manchukuo. When the League of Nations condemned Japan's actions, the Japanese gave their two-year's notice and withdrew from the league. A turn for the worse came for the Chinese on July 7, 1937, when a shooting incident at the Marco Polo Bridge between Chinese and Japanese troops led to a full-scale war on China's mainland. President Franklin Roosevelt took a strong verbal stand in a speech he delivered on October 5, 1937, demanding that nations stirring up "international anarchy" should be quarantined.

Roosevelt aided the Chinese with nonembargoed, nonmilitary goods when he found a loophole in the neutrality laws. Japan's goal to establish a "new order in East Asia" was furthered by the outbreak of World War II in Europe in the fall of 1939, and the ease with which the German army overran and defeated France the following spring. In September 1940 Japanese forces occupied northern French Indochina (later known as Vietnam). Although Roosevelt was unable to stop Japan's military expansionism, he did jar them with economic sanctions. When the Japanese occupied southern Indochina on July 25, 1941, Roosevelt again jolted the Japanese government by issuing an order freezing all Japanese assets in the United States, which created major problems. Japan had only 12 to 18 months of oil in reserves for military use. A military statement had developed in the war with China in part because the United States was funneling economic and military aid to her ally. Consequently, Japan sought an accommodation with the United States in the fall of 1941. Japan tried to negotiate two plans that would have resulted in a partial withdrawal from Indochina and the establishment of a coalition government in China proper that would be partially controlled by the Japanese and would take place once the war stopped. In return, America would resume trade with Japan prior to the July 26 freezing of Japanese assets.

Because American cryptologists had broken the Japanese diplomatic code for a second time in the summer of 1941, American policymakers knew that these were Japan's final proposals. Secretary of State Cordell Hull sent the Japanese a note on November 26 that restated America's Open Door policy and asked "the government of Japan [to] withdraw all military naval, air, and police forces from China and from Indochina." When Japan rejected the proposal both sides realized this meant war. Where or when was the question. Japan's surprise December 7 attack on Pearl Harbor provided the answer.

In the following selection, Robert A. Theobald argues that President Roosevelt deliberately withheld information from the Hawaiian army and naval commanders at Pearl Harbor in order to encourage the Japanese to make a surprise attack on the weak Pacific Fleet. In the second selection, Roberta Wohlstetter maintains that even though naval intelligence broke the Japanese code, conflicting signals made it impossible to predict the Pearl Harbor attack.

YES

Robert A. Theobald

The Final Secret of Pearl Harbor

Having been present at Pearl Harbor on December 7, 1941, and having appeared with Admiral Husband E. Kimmel when that officer testified before the Roberts Commission,[1] the author has ever since sought a full understanding of the background that made that day possible. For many years, he gathered and pieced together the available evidence which appeared to shed light upon the Washington happenings concerned with that attack. These studies produced very definite conclusions regarding the manner in which our country's strategy had been shaped to entice the Japanese to attack Pearl Harbor, and the efforts that have since been made to keep these facts from the knowledge of the American People.

For over three years, the thirty-nine-volume set which comprises the Record of Proceedings of all the Pearl Harbor Investigations has been available to the author. Serious study of these volumes has caused many revisions of errors in detail, but it has served to divest the writer's mind of all doubt regarding the soundness of his basic conclusions.

It is firmly believed that those in Washington who knew the facts, decided from the first that considerations of patriotism and loyalty to their wartime Commander-in-Chief required that a veil of secrecy should be drawn about the President's handling of the situation which culminated in the Pearl Harbor attack.

While there was great justification for this secrecy during the continuance of the war, the reasons for it no longer exist. The war is finished. President Roosevelt and his administration are now history. Dictates of patriotism requiring secrecy regarding a line of national conduct in order to preserve it for possible future repetition do not apply in this case because, in this atomic age, facilitating an enemy's surprise attack, as a method of initiating a war, is unthinkable. Our Pearl Harbor losses would preclude that course of action in the future without consideration of the increased destructiveness of present and future weapons. Finally, loyalty to their late President in the matter of Pearl Harbor would be better served today, if his friends would discard their policy of secrecy in favor of full publicity.

Another consideration which today strongly favors a complete understanding of the whole Pearl Harbor story, is the thought of justice to the professional reputations of the Hawaiian Commanders, Admiral Kimmel and General Short—a justice which is long overdue.

Throughout the war, maintenance of the national morale at the highest possible level demanded complete public confidence in the President and his principal military advisers. During that time, the public could not be given cause to assign a tithe of blame for the Pearl Harbor attack to Washington. And so, dating from the report of the Roberts Commission, most of the responsibility for Pearl Harbor has been placed upon the two Hawaiian Commanders. This carefully executed plan which diverted all suspicion from Washington contributed its full measure to the successful conduct of the war.

The time has come when full publicity should be given to the Washington contribution to the Pearl Harbor attack, in order that the judgment of the American people may assign to Admiral Kimmel and General Short no more than their just and proper share of the responsibility for that tragic day.

Manifestly, many readers will be reluctant to agree with the main conclusions which have been reached in this study. In recognition of this fact, the normal sequence of deductive reasoning is discarded in favor of the order used in a legal presentation. The case is stated at the outset, and the evidence is then marshalled and discussed. The reader is thus enabled to weigh each fact, as it is presented, against the conclusions, which have been firmly implanted in the mind of the author by the summation of these facts.

The sole purpose of the subject matter contained herein is a searching for the truth, and it is hoped that the absence of any ulterior motive is apparent throughout. Comments of a critical character concerning the official actions of officers frequently intersperse the pages which follow. No criticism of the officer is intended. Those officers were obeying orders, under circumstances which were professionally most trying to them. Such comments are necessary to a full understanding of the discussion of the moment, however, but there is no intention to impugn the motives of any individual. Patriotism and loyalty were the wellsprings of those motives. . . .

Main Deduction: President Roosevelt Circumvents American Pacifism

In the spring of 1940, Denmark, Norway, Holland, Belgium, and France were conquered by Germany, and throughout the remainder of that year Great Britain's situation was so desperate that many expected her collapse early in the ensuing year. Fortunately, however, the Axis powers turned East in 1941 to conquer Greece and to attack Russia.

There is every reason to believe that when France was overcome President Roosevelt became convinced the United States must fight beside Great Britain, while the latter was still an active belligerent, or later sustain the fight alone, as the last democratic stronghold in a Nazi world. Never, however, had the country been less prepared for war, both psychologically and physically. Isolationism was a dominant philosophy throughout the land, and the armed forces were weak and consequently unready.

The United States not only had to become an active participant in democracy's fight as quickly as possible, but a people, completely united in support of the war effort, had to be brought into the arena. But, how could the country be made to fight? Only a cataclysmic happening could move Congress to enact a declaration of war; and that action would not guarantee that the nation's response would be the completely united support which victory has always demanded. This was the President's problem, and his solution was based upon the simple fact that, while it takes two to make a fight, either one may start it.

As the people of this country were so strongly opposed to war, one of the Axis powers must be forced to involve the United States, and in such a way as to arouse the American people to wholehearted belief in the necessity of fighting. This would require drastic action, and the decision was unquestionably a difficult one for the President to make.

In this connection, it should be remembered that Japan, Germany, and Italy signed the Tripartite Treaty on September 28, 1940, by which the three nations agreed to make common cause against any nation, not then a participant in the European war or the Sino-Japanese conflict, which attacked one of the signatories.

Thereafter, the fact that war with Japan meant war with Germany and Italy played an important part in President Roosevelt's diplomatic strategy. Throughout the approach to war and during the fighting, the primary U.S. objective was the defeat of Germany.

To implement the solution of his problem, the President: (1) instituted a successful campaign to correct the Nation's military unpreparedness; (2) offered Germany repeated provocations, by violations of neutrality and diplomatic usage; (3) applied ever-increasing diplomatic-economic pressure upon Japan, which reached its sustained climax on July 25, 1941, when the United States, Great Britain, and the Netherlands stopped their trade with Japan and subjected her to almost complete economic encirclement; (4) made mutual commitments with the British Prime Minister at Newfoundland in August, 1941, which promised mutual support in the event that the United States, Great Britain, or a third country not then at war were attacked by Japan in the Pacific; (5) terminated the Washington conference with the note of November 26, 1941, which gave Japan no choice but surrender or war; (6) retained a weak Pacific Fleet in Hawaiian waters, despite contrary naval advice, where it served only one diplomatic purpose, an invitation to a Japanese surprise attack; (7) furthered that surprise by causing the Hawaiian Commanders to be denied invaluable information from decoded Japanese dispatches [or "Magic"] concerning the rapid approach of the war and the strong probability that the attack would be directed at Pearl Harbor.

This denial of information was a vital feature of enticing a Japanese surprise attack upon Pearl Harbor. If Admiral Kimmel and General Short had been given the knowledge possessed by the Washington authorities, the Hawaiian Commands would have been alerted against an overseas attack. The Pacific Fleet would have kept the sea during the first days of December, 1941, until the issue of peace or war had been decided. With the highly effective Japanese espionage in Hawaii, this would have caused Tokyo to cancel the surprise attack.

The problem which faced Lincoln during March of 1861 was identical in principle—to unite the sentiment of the North behind the policy of compelling the seceded Southern states by force of arms to return to the Union. For a month after his inauguration, he made no move, and then South Carolina's insistent demands for the surrender of Fort Sumter gave him the answer to his problem. He refused to surrender the fort, and dispatched a fleet to reprovision it. South Carolina then fired the first shots of the Civil War. Pearl Harbor was President Roosevelt's Fort Sumter.

Diplomatically, President Roosevelt's strategy of forcing Japan to war by unremitting and ever-increasing diplomatic-economic pressure, and by simultaneously holding our Fleet in Hawaii as an invitation to a surprise attack, was a complete success. Militarily, our ship and personnel losses mark December 7, 1941 as the day of tragic defeat. One is forced to conclude that the anxiety to have Japan, beyond all possibility of dispute, commit the first act of war, caused the President and his civilian advisers to disregard the military advice which would somewhat have cushioned the blow. The President, before the event, probably envisaged a *Panay* incident[2] of somewhat larger proportions. Despite the fact that the attack laid the foundation for complete victory, a terrific price was paid, as the following account of the ship, plane, and personnel losses discloses.

The Pearl Harbor Losses: Facts and Figures

The Japanese clearly intended that their entire surprise attack should be delivered against military objectives. The first waves of the attack were delivered against the airfields on the Island of Oahu—Army, Navy, and Marine Corps— to reduce the air-borne opposition as much as possible. The main attacks began 15 minutes after these preliminary attacks, and were primarily directed against the capital ships in Pearl Harbor. Damage inflicted upon smaller vessels was clearly the incidental consequence of the main operation. Very few planes dropped their bombs upon the city of Honolulu. Three planes did so in the late phases of the attack, but their last-minute changes of course indicated that this was done because those particular pilots did not care to encounter the severe anti-aircraft fire that was then bursting over their main target area.

In December, 1941, the capital ships of the Pacific Fleet numbered twelve: 9 Battleships; 3 Carriers. Of these, eight Battleships but none of the Carriers were present in Pearl Harbor at the time of the Japanese attack: the Battleship *Colorado* was in the Bremerton Navy Yard; the Carrier *Enterprise* was in a Task Force returning from Wake; the *Lexington* was in a Task Force ferrying planes to Midway; the *Saratoga* was on the West Coast, having just completed a Navy Yard overhaul.

The results of the Japanese air attacks upon the U.S. Pacific Fleet in Pearl Harbor on December 7, 1941, were as follows:

Battleships:

Arizona: total loss, as her forward magazines blew up;

Oklahoma: total loss, capsized and sank in harbor—later raised solely to clear harbor of the obstruction and resunk off Oahu;

California, West Virginia: sank in upright position at their berths with quarterdecks awash—much later raised, repaired, and returned to active war service;

Nevada: beached while standing out of the harbor, to prevent sinking in deep water after extensive bomb damage—repaired and returned to active war service;

Pennsylvania, Maryland, and Tennessee: all received damage but of a less severe character.

Smaller Ships:

Cruisers: Helena, Honolulu, and *Raleigh* were all damaged, but were repaired and returned to active war service;

Destroyers: Two damaged beyond repair; two others damaged but repaired and returned to active war service;

Auxiliary Vessels: 1 Seaplane Tender, 1 Repair Ship, both severely damaged but repaired and returned to active war service;

Target Ship: Utah, former battleship, sank at her berth.

The Japanese attacks upon the various Oahu airfields resulted in the following U.S. plane losses: Navy 80; Army 97.

U.S. military personnel casualties were: Navy, including Marine Corps, 3077 officers and enlisted men killed, 876 wounded; Army, including the Army Air Corps, 226 officers and enlisted men killed, 396 wounded. Total: 4575.

The Japanese losses were 48 planes shot down and three midget submarines destroyed. These vessels displaced 45 tons and were of little, if any, military value.

The Final Summation

Review of the American Moves Which Led to the Japanese Attack

Our Main Deduction is that President Roosevelt forced Japan to war by unrelenting diplomatic-economic pressure, and enticed that country to initiate hostilities with a surprise attack by holding the Pacific Fleet in Hawaiian waters as an invitation to that attack.

The evidence shows how surely the President moved toward war after June, 1940. His conversation with Admiral Richardson in October, 1940, indicated his conviction that it would be impossible without a stunning incident to obtain a declaration of war from Congress.

Despite the conditions of undeclared war which existed in the Atlantic during the latter half of 1941, it had long been clear that Germany did not intend to contribute to the creation of a state of formal war between her and the United States. The Tripartite Treaty of September, 1940, however, supplied the President with the answer. Under that treaty, war with Japan meant war with Germany and Italy.

The highlights of the ever-increasing pressure upon Japan were:

1. the extension of financial and military aid to China in concert with Great Britain and the Netherlands, which began early in 1941;
2. the stoppage of Philippine exports to Japan by Executive Order on May 29, 1941;
3. the freezing of Japanese assets and the interdiction of all trade with Japan by the United States, Great Britain, and the Netherlands on July 25, 1941;
4. President Roosevelt's very frank statements of policy to Ambassador Nomura in their conference of August 17, 1941;
5. the termination of the Washington conference by the American note of November 26, 1941, which brought the war to the United States as the President so clearly intended it would.

That the Pearl Harbor attack was in accord with President Roosevelt's plans is attested by the following array of facts:

1. President Roosevelt and his military and naval advisers were well aware that Japan invariably started her wars with a surprise attack synchronized closely with her delivery of the Declaration of War;
2. In October, 1940, the President stated that, if war broke out in the Pacific, Japan would commit the overt act which would bring the United States into the war;
3. The Pacific Fleet, against contrary naval advice, was retained in Hawaii by order of the President for the alleged reason that the Fleet, so located, would exert a restrictive effect upon Japanese aggressions in the Far East;
4. The Fleet in Hawaii was neither powerful enough nor in the necessary strategic position to influence Japan's diplomatic decisions, which could only be accomplished by the stationing of an adequate naval force in Far Eastern waters;
5. Before that Fleet could operate at any distance from Pearl Harbor, its train (tankers, supply and repair vessels) would have had to be tremendously increased in strength—facts that would not escape the notice of the experienced Japanese spies in Hawaii;
6. President Roosevelt gave unmistakable evidence, in March, 1941, that he was not greatly concerned with the Pacific Fleet's effects upon Japanese diplomatic decisions, when he authorized the weakening of that Fleet, already inferior to that of Japan, by the detachment of 3 battleships, 1 aircraft carrier, 4 light cruisers, and 18 destroyers for duty in the Atlantic—a movement which would immediately be detected by Japanese espionage in Hawaii and Panama Canal Zone;
7. The successful crippling of the Pacific Fleet was the only surprise operation which promised the Japanese Navy sufficiently large results to justify the risk of heavy losses from land-based air attacks if the surprise failed;
8. Such an operation against the Fleet in Hawaii was attended with far greater chances of success, especially from the surprise standpoint, and far less risk of heavy losses than a similar attack against that Fleet based in U.S. West Coast ports;

9. The retention of the Fleet in Hawaii, especially after its reduction in strength in March, 1941, could serve only one possible purpose, an invitation to a surprise Japanese attack;
10. The denial to the Hawaiian Commanders of all knowledge of Magic was vital to the plan for enticing Japan to deliver a surprise attack upon the Fleet in Pearl Harbor, because, as late as Saturday, December 6, Admiral Kimmel could have caused that attack to be cancelled by taking his Fleet to sea and disappearing beyond land-based human ken.

Review of the Situation Known to Washington Before the Attack

From the beginning of the Washington conference in November, 1941, President Roosevelt and his advisers had repeated evidence that this was Japan's last and supreme effort to break the economic encirclement by peaceful means.

Throughout the negotiations, the Japanese secret dispatches stressed a "deadline date," after which "things were automatically going to happen."

Automatic events which were to follow the breakdown of such vital negotiations could only be acts of war, clear evidence that Japan intended to deliver a surprise attack to initiate the hostilities.

The fact that surprise was essential to the Japanese plans was repeatedly emphasized, on and after November 28, by the Tokyo dispatches and by telephone instructions to the two Ambassadors, cautioning them to keep alive the appearance of continuing negotiation.

Everyone familiar with Japanese military history knew that her first acts of war against China in 1894 and Russia in 1904 had been surprise attacks against the main fleets of those countries.

The only American Naval Force in the Pacific that was worth the risk of such an operation was the Fleet in Hawaiian waters.

The President and his military naval advisers well knew, on October 9, from the Tokyo dispatch to Honolulu of September 24, that Japan intended to plan a surprise air attack on the American Fleet in Pearl Harbor, and had daily evidence from the late decodes of certain Tokyo-Honolulu dispatches during the period, December 3–6 inclusive, that the planned attack was soon to occur.

On November 26, the recipients of Magic all had positive information from the Tokyo dispatch to Hong Kong of November 14 that Japan intended war with the United States and Great Britain if the Washington negotiations should fail.

The Tokyo dispatch to the Washington Embassy of November 28 definitely stated that the Japanese Government considered that the American note of the 26th had terminated all possibility of further negotiations.

The Tokyo-Berlin messages dated November 30 instructed the Japanese Ambassador to inform Hitler and von Ribbentrop that war between Japan and the Anglo-Saxon nations would come sooner than anyone expected.

The Japanese code-destruction messages of December 1 and 2 meant that war was extremely close at hand.

With the distribution of the Pilot Message at 3:00 P.M. on Saturday, December 6, the picture was complete for President Roosevelt and the other recipients of Magic, both in Washington and Manila. It said that the answer to the American note was about to arrive in the Embassy, that it was very lengthy, and that its delivery to the U.S. Government was to be especially timed. That timed delivery could only have meant that the answer was a Declaration of War, synchronized with a surprise attack. No other deduction was tenable.

The Saturday receipt of this definite information strongly supported the existing estimates in the War and Navy Departments, that the Japanese surprise attack would be delivered on a Sunday, and marked the morrow, Sunday, December 7, as the day. All this, beyond doubt, was known to President Roosevelt, General Marshall, and Admiral Stark at about 3:00 P.M. on that Saturday, Washington time, 21 hours before the next sunrise in Hawaii.

In obedience to the basic dictates of the Military Art, the information contained in the Pilot Message and the unmistakable implications thereof should have been transmitted to Admiral Kimmel and General Short at once. There was no military consideration that would warrant or tolerate an instant's delay in getting this word to those officers. There cannot be the slightest doubt that General Marshall and Admiral Stark would have had this done, if they had not been restrained from doing so by the orders of President Roosevelt. In the situation which then existed for them, no officer of even limited experience, if free to act, could possibly decide otherwise.

The fighting words in the selected passages of the 13-part message received on that same Saturday were merely additional evidence that this was a Declaration of War. The 14th part received early Sunday morning was further confirmation of that fact.

The 1:00 P.M. Washington delivery, ordered by the time-of-delivery dispatch, clearly indicated Pearl Harbor as the objective of the surprise attack, the final link in the long chain of evidence to that effect.

There Would Have Been No Pearl Harbor If Magic Had Not Been Denied to the Hawaiian Commanders

The recurrent fact of the true Pearl Harbor story has been the repeated withholding of information from Admiral Kimmel and General Short. If the War and Navy Departments had been free to follow the dictates of the Art of War, the following is the minimum of information and orders those officers would have received:

The Tokyo-Honolulu dispatches regarding the exact berthing of U.S. ships in Pearl Harbor and, in that connection, a reminder that Japan invariably started her wars with a surprise attack on the new enemy's Main Fleet; the dispatches concerning the Washington Conference and the deadline date after which things were automatically going to happen—evidence that this was Japan's last effort to solve U.S.-Japanese differences by peaceful means and the strong intimation of the surprise attack; the Tokyo-Hong Kong dispatch of November 14, which told of Japan's intentions to initiate war with the two Anglo-Saxon powers if the Washington negotiations failed; the Tokyo-Washington dispatch of November 28, which stated that the American note of November 26 had terminated those negotiations; the Pilot Message of December 6, which told that the Declaration of War was about to arrive in Washington, and that its delivery to the U.S. Government was to be especially timed, an essential feature for synchronizing the surprise attack with that delivery.

Not later than November 28, the War and Navy Departments should have ordered the Hawaiian Commanders to place the Joint Army-Navy Coastal Frontier Defense Plans in effect, and to unify their Commands; the Navy Department should have ordered the mobilization of the Naval Establishment.

On November 28, the Chief of Naval Operations should have ordered Admiral Kimmel to recall the *Enterprise* from the Wake operation, and a few days later should have directed the cancellation of the contemplated sending of the *Lexington* to Midway.

. . . [N]ot one word of this information and none of the foregoing orders were sent to Hawaii.

General Marshall Looks Ahead, but Admiral Stark Lets the Cat Out of the Bag

Everything that happened in Washington on Saturday and Sunday, December 6 and 7, supports the belief that President Roosevelt had directed that no message be sent to the Hawaiian Commanders before noon on Sunday, Washington time.

General Marshall apparently appreciated that failure to act on the Declaration of War message and its timed delivery was going to be very difficult to explain on the witness stand when the future inevitable investigation into the incidents of those days took place. His avoidance of contact with the messages after the Pilot message until 11:25 on Sunday morning was unquestionably prompted by these thoughts. Otherwise, he would undoubtedly have been in his office by 8:00 A.M. on that fateful day.

Admiral Stark, on the other hand, did arrive in his office at 9:25 A.M. on Sunday, and at once accepted delivery of the full Declaration of War message. Against the advice of his assistants, he refused to inform Admiral Kimmel of its receipt. Forty minutes later, he knew that the 14-part message was to be delivered to the U.S. Government at 1:00 P.M., Washington time, which was 7:30 A.M., Hawaiian time, as was pointed out to him at once. Again, despite the urging of certain of his aides, he refused to send word to Admiral Kimmel.

Never before in recorded history had a field commander been denied information that his country would be at war in a matter of hours, and that everything pointed to a surprise attack upon his forces shortly after sunrise. No Naval Officer, on his own initiative, would ever make such a decision as Admiral Stark thus did.

That fact and Admiral Stark's decisions on that Sunday morning, even if they had not been supported by the wealth of earlier evidence, would reveal, beyond question, the basic truth of the Pearl Harbor story, namely that these Sunday messages and so many earlier ones, of vital import to Admiral Kimmel's exercise of his command, were not sent because Admiral Stark had orders from the President, which prohibited that action.

This deduction is fully supported by the Admiral's statement to the press in August, 1945, that all he did during the pre-Pearl Harbor days was done on order of higher authority, which can only mean President Roosevelt. The most arresting thing he did, during that time, was to withhold information from Admiral Kimmel.

President Roosevelt's Strategy Accomplishes Its Purpose

Thus, by holding a weak Pacific Fleet in Hawaii as an invitation to a surprise attack, and by denying the Commander of that Fleet the information which might cause him to render that attack impossible, President Roosevelt brought war to the United States on December 7, 1941. He took a fully aroused nation into the fight because none of its people suspected how the Japanese surprise attack fitted into their President's plans. Disastrous as it was from a naval standpoint, the Pearl Harbor attack proved to be the diplomatic prelude to the complete defeat of the Axis Powers.

As each reader will make up his own mind regarding the various questions raised by President Roosevelt's solution to his problem, nothing would be gained by an ethical analysis of that solution.

Notes

1. Admiral Kimmel had asked the author to act as his counsel before the Roberts Commission, but the Admiral was not allowed counsel. Nevertheless, although his status before the Commission was anomalous, the author did accompany the Admiral whenever the latter testified before that body, and late on the first day of that testimony was sworn as a witness. During the discussion connected with this swearing, the following exchange occurred:

   Justice Roberts: "So it is understood that you are not acting as counsel."
   Admiral Theobald: "No, sir."
   General McCoy: "The admiral is not on trial, of course."
   Justice Roberts: "No, this is not a trial of the admiral, in any sense."

   It has always been difficult to understand Justice Roberts' statement that Admiral Kimmel was not on trial. The Commission came into being to investigate the surprise attack upon the Fleet which he had commanded at the time, and it was generally recognized that the result of the inquiry would be the severe arraignments of Admiral Kimmel and General Short, which did constitute the principal findings of the Commission; findings which were given wide publicity at the earliest possible moment.

2. U.S.S. *Panay*, an American gunboat, sunk by Japanese bombing planes on the Yangtze River on December 12, 1937.

Roberta Wohlstetter

 **NO**

Surprise

If our intelligence system and all our other channels of information failed to produce an accurate image of Japanese intentions and capabilities, it was not for want of the relevant materials. Never before have we had so complete an intelligence picture of the enemy. And perhaps never again will we have such a magnificent collection of sources at our disposal.

Retrospect

To review these sources briefly, an American cryptanalyst, Col. William F. Friedman, had broken the top-priority Japanese diplomatic code, which enabled us to listen to a large proportion of the privileged communications between Tokyo and the major Japanese embassies throughout the world. Not only did we know in advance how the Japanese ambassadors in Washington were advised, and how much they were instructed to say, but we also were listening to top-secret messages on the Tokyo-Berlin and Tokyo-Rome circuits, which gave us information vital for conduct of the war in the Atlantic and Europe. In the Far East this source provided minute details on movements connected with the Japanese program of expansion into Southeast Asia.

Besides the strictly diplomatic codes, our cryptanalysts also had some success in reading codes used by Japanese agents in major American and foreign ports. Those who were on the distribution list for MAGIC had access to much of what these agents were reporting to Tokyo and what Tokyo was demanding of them in the Panama Canal Zone, in cities along the east and west coasts of the Americas from northern Canada as far south as Brazil, and in ports throughout the Far East, including the Philippines and the Hawaiian Islands. They could determine what installations, what troop and ship movements, and what alert and defense measures were of interest to Tokyo at these points on the globe, as well as approximately how much correct information her agents were sending her.

Our naval leaders also had at their disposal the results of radio traffic analysis. While before the war our naval radio experts could not read the content of any Japanese naval or military coded messages, they were able to deduce from a study of intercepted ship call signs the composition and location of the Japanese Fleet units. After a change in call signs, they might lose

Excerpts from *Pearl Harbor: Warning and Decision* by Roberta Wohlstetter, (University Press, 1962) pp. 382–396. Copyright © 1962 by the Board of Trustees of the Leland Stanford, Jr. University. Reprinted by permission of Stanford University Press and the Roberta and Albert Wohlstetter estate. www.sup.org

sight of some units, and units that went into port in home waters were also lost because the ships in port used frequencies that our radios were unable to intercept. Most of the time, however, our traffic analysts had the various Japanese Fleet units accurately pinpointed on our naval maps.

Extremely competent on-the-spot economic and political analysis was furnished by Ambassador Grew and his staff in Tokyo. Ambassador Grew was himself a most sensitive and accurate observer, as evidenced by his dispatches to the State Department. His observations were supported and supplemented with military detail by frequent reports from American naval attachés and observers in key Far Eastern ports. Navy Intelligence had men with radio equipment located along the coast of China, for example, who reported the convoy movements toward Indochina. There were also naval observers stationed in various high-tension areas in Thailand and Indochina who could fill in the local outlines of Japanese political intrigue and military planning. In Tokyo and other Japanese cities, it is true, Japanese censorship grew more and more rigid during 1941, until Ambassador Grew felt it necessary to disclaim any responsibility for noting or reporting overt military evidence of an imminent outbreak of war. This careful Japanese censorship naturally cut down visual confirmation of the decoded information but very probably never achieved the opaqueness of Russia's Iron Curtain.

During this period the data and interpretations of British intelligence were also available to American officers in Washington and the Far East, though the British and Americans tended to distrust each other's privileged information.

In addition to secret sources, there were some excellent public ones. Foreign correspondents for *The New York Times, The Herald Tribune*, and *The Washington Post* were stationed in Tokyo and Shanghai and in Canberra, Australia. Their reporting as well as their predictions on the Japanese political scene were on a very high level. Frequently their access to news was more rapid and their judgment of its significance as reliable as that of our Intelligence officers. This was certainly the case for 1940 and most of 1941. For the last few weeks before the Pearl Harbor strike, however, the public newspaper accounts were not very useful. It was necessary to have secret information in order to know what was happening. Both Tokyo and Washington exercised very tight control over leaks during this crucial period, and the newsmen accordingly had to limit their accounts to speculation and notices of diplomatic meetings with no exact indication of the content of the diplomatic exchanges.

The Japanese press was another important public source. During 1941 it proclaimed with increasing shrillness the Japanese government's determination to pursue its program of expansion into Southeast Asia and the desire of the military to clear the Far East of British and American colonial exploitation. This particular source was rife with explicit signals of aggressive intent.

Finally, an essential part of the intelligence picture for 1941 was both public and privileged information on American policy and activities in the Far East. During the year the pattern of action and interaction between the Japanese and American governments grew more and more complex. At the last, it became especially important for anyone charged with the responsibility of ordering an alert to know what moves the American government was going to make with respect to Japan, as well as to try to guess what Japan's next move would be, since Japan's next move would respond in part to ours. Unfortunately our military leaders, and especially our Intelligence officers, were sometimes as surprised as the Japanese at the moves of the White House and the State Department. They usually had more orderly anticipations about Japanese policy and conduct than they had about America's. On the other hand, it was also true that State Department and White House officials were handicapped in judging Japanese intentions and estimates of risk by an inadequate picture of our own military vulnerability.

All of the public and private sources of information mentioned were available to America's political and military leaders in 1941. It is only fair to remark, however, that no single person or agency ever had at any given moment all the signals existing in this vast information network. The signals lay scattered in a number of different agencies; some were decoded, some were not; some traveled through rapid channels of communication, some were blocked by technical or procedural delays; some never reached a center of decision. But it is legitimate to review again the general sort of picture that emerged during the first week of December from the signals readily at hand. Anyone close to President Roosevelt was likely to have before him the following significant fragments.

There was first of all a picture of gathering troop and ship movements down the China coast and into Indochina. The large dimensions of this movement to the south were established publicly and visually as well as by analysis of ship call signs. Two changes in Japanese naval call signs—one on November 1 and another on December 1—had also been evaluated by Naval Intelligence as extremely unusual and as signs of major preparations for some sort of Japanese offensive. The two changes had interfered with the speed of American radio traffic analysis. Thousands of interceptions after December 1 were necessary before the new call signs could be read. Partly for this reason American radio analysts disagreed about the locations of the Japanese carriers. One group held that all the carriers were near Japan because they had not been able to identify a carrier call sign since the middle of November. Another group believed that they had located one carrier division in the Marshalls. The probability seemed to be that the carriers, wherever they were, had gone into radio silence; and past experience led the analysts to believe that they were therefore in waters near the Japanese homeland, where they could communicate with each other on wavelengths that we could not intercept. However, our inability to locate the carriers exactly, combined with the two changes in call signs, was itself a danger signal.

Our best secret source, MAGIC, was confirming the aggressive intentions of the new military cabinet in Tokyo, which had replaced the last moderate cabinet on October 17. In particular, MAGIC provided details of some of the preparations for the move into Southeast Asia. Running counter to this were increased troop shipments to the Manchurian border in October. (The intelligence picture is never clear-cut.) But withdrawals had begun toward the end of that month. MAGIC also carried explicit instructions to the Japanese ambassadors in Washington to pursue diplomatic negotiations with the United States with increasing energy, but at the same time it announced a deadline for the favorable conclusion of the negotiations, first for November 25, later postponed until November 29. In case of diplomatic failure by that date, the Japanese ambassadors were told, Japanese patience would be exhausted, Japan was determined to pursue her Greater East Asia policy, and on November 29 "things" would automatically begin to happen.

On November 26 Secretary Hull rejected Japan's latest bid for American approval of her policies in China and Indochina. MAGIC had repeatedly characterized this Japanese overture as the "last," and it now revealed the ambassadors' reaction of consternation and despair over the American refusal and also their country's characterization of the American Ten Point Note as an "ultimatum."

On the basis of this collection of signals, Army and Navy Intelligence experts in Washington tentatively placed D-day *for the Japanese Southeastern campaign* during the week end of November 30, and when this failed to materialize, during the week end of December 7. They also compiled an accurate list of probable British and Dutch targets and included the Philippines and Guam as possible American targets.

Also available in this mass of information, but long forgotten, was a rumor reported by Ambassador Grew in January, 1941. It came from what was regarded as a not-very-reliable source, the Peruvian embassy, and stated that the Japanese were preparing a surprise air attack on Pearl Harbor. Curiously the date of the report is coincident roughly with what we now know to have been the date of inception of Yamamoto's plan; but the coincidence is fairly pure. The rumor was traced to a Japanese cook in the Embassy who had been reading a novel that began with an attack on Pearl Harbor. Consequently everyone concerned, including Ambassador Grew, labeled the rumor as quite fantastic and the plan as absurdly impossible. American judgment was consistent with Japanese judgment at this time, since Yamamoto's plan was in direct contradiction to Japanese naval tactical doctrine.

Perspective

On the basis of this rapid recapitulation of the highlights in the signal picture, it is apparent that our decisionmakers had at hand an impressive amount of information on the enemy. They did not have the complete list of targets, since none of the last-minute estimates included Pearl Harbor. They did not know the exact hour and date for opening the attack. They did not have an accurate knowledge of Japanese capabilities or of Japanese ability to accept very high risks. The crucial question then, we repeat, is, If we could enumerate accurately the British and Dutch targets and give credence to a Japanese attack against them either on November 30 or December 7, why were we not expecting a specific danger to *ourselves?* And by the word "expecting," we mean expecting in the sense of taking specific alert actions to meet the contingencies of attack by land, sea, or air.

There are several answers to this question. . . . First of all, it is much easier *after* the event to sort the relevant from the irrelevant signals. After the event, of course, a signal is always crystal clear; we can now see what disaster it was signaling, since the disaster has occurred. But before the event it is obscure and pregnant with conflicting meanings. It comes to the observer embedded in an atmosphere of "noise," i.e., in the company of all sorts of information that is useless and irrelevant for predicting the particular disaster. For example, in Washington, Pearl Harbor signals were competing with a vast number of signals from the European theater. These European signals announced danger more frequently and more specifically than any coming from the Far East. The Far Eastern signals were also arriving at a center of decision where they had to compete with the prevailing belief that an unprotected offensive force acts as a deterrent rather than a target. In Honolulu they were competing not with signals from the European theater, but rather with a large number of signals announcing Japanese intentions and preparations to attack Soviet Russia rather than to move southward; here they were also competing with expectations of local sabotage prepared by previous alert situations.

In short, we failed to anticipate Pearl Harbor not for want of the relevant materials, but because of a plethora of irrelevant ones. Much of the appearance of wanton neglect that emerged in various investigations of the disaster resulted from the unconscious suppression of vast congeries of signs pointing in every direction except Pearl Harbor. It was difficult later to recall these signs since they had led nowhere. Signals that are characterized today as absolutely unequivocal warnings of surprise air attack on Pearl Harbor become, on analysis in the context of December, 1941, not merely ambiguous but occasionally inconsistent with such an attack. To recall one of the most controversial and publicized examples, the winds code, both General Short and Admiral Kimmel testified that if they had had this information, they would have been prepared on the morning of December 7 for an air attack from without. The messages establishing the winds code are often described in the Pearl Harbor literature as Tokyo's declaration of war against America. If they indeed amounted to such a declaration, obviously the failure to inform Honolulu of this vital news would have been criminal negligence. On examination, however, the messages proved to be instructions for code communication after normal commercial channels had been cut. In one message the recipient was instructed on receipt of an execute to destroy all remaining codes in his possession. In another version the recipient was warned that the execute would be sent out "when relations are becoming dangerous" between Japan and three other countries. There was a different code term for each country: England, America, and the Soviet Union.

There is no evidence that an authentic execute of either message was ever intercepted by the United States before December 7. The message ordering code destruction was in any case superseded by a much more explicit code-destruction order from Tokyo that was intercepted on December 2 and translated on December 3. After December 2, the receipt of a winds-code execute for code destruction would therefore have added nothing new to our information, and code destruction in itself cannot be taken as an unambiguous substitute for a formal declaration of war. During the first week of December the United States ordered all American consulates in the Far East to destroy all American codes, yet no one has attempted to prove that this order was equivalent to an American declaration of war against Japan. As for the other winds-code message, provided an execute had been received warning that relations were dangerous between Japan and the United States, there would still have been no way on the basis of this signal alone to determine whether Tokyo was signaling Japanese intent to attack the United States or Japanese fear of an American surprise attack (in reprisal for Japanese aggressive moves against American allies in the Far East). It was only after the event that "dangerous relations" could be interpreted as "surprise air attack on Pearl Harbor."

There is a difference, then, between having a signal available somewhere in the heap of irrelevancies, and perceiving it as a warning; and there is also a difference between perceiving it as a warning, and acting or getting action on it. These distinctions, simple as they are, illuminate the obscurity shrouding this moment in history.

Many instances of these distinctions have been examined in the course of this study. We shall recall a few of the most dramatic now. To illustrate the difference between having and perceiving a signal, let us [look at] Colonel Fielder. . . . Though he was an untrained and inexperienced Intelligence officer, he headed Army Intelligence at Pearl Harbor at the time of the attack. He had been on the job for only four months, and he regarded as quite satisfactory his sources of information and his contacts with the Navy locally and with Army Intelligence in Washington. Evidently he was unaware that Army Intelligence in Washington was not allowed to send him any "action" or policy information, and he was therefore not especially concerned about trying to read beyond the obvious meaning of any given communication that came under his eyes. Colonel Bratton, head of Army Far Eastern Intelligence in Washington, however, had a somewhat more realistic view of the extent of Colonial Fielder's knowledge. At the end of November, Colonel Bratton had learned about the winds-code setup and was also apprised that the naval traffic analysis unit under Commander Rochefort in Honolulu was monitoring 24 hours a day for an execute. He was understandably worried about the lack of communication between this unit and Colonel Fielder's office, and by December 5 he finally felt that the matter was urgent enough to warrant sending a message directly to Colonel Fielder about the winds code. Now any information on the winds code, since it belonged to the highest classification of secret information, and since it was therefore automatically evaluated as "action" information, could not be sent through normal G-2 channels. Colonel Bratton had to figure out another way to get the information to Colonel Fielder. He sent this message: "Contact Commander Rochefort immediately thru Commandant Fourteenth Naval District regarding broadcasts from Tokyo reference weather." Signal Corps records establish that Colonel Fielder received this message. How did he react to it? He filed it. According to his testimony in 1945, it made no impression on him and he did not attempt to see Rochefort. He could not sense any urgency behind the lines because he was not expecting immediate trouble, and his expectations determined what he read. A warning signal was available to him, but he did not perceive it.

Colonel Fielder's lack of experience may make this example seem to be an exception. So let us recall the performance of Captain Wilkinson, the naval officer who headed the Office of Naval Intelligence in Washington in the fall of 1941 and who is unanimously acclaimed for a distinguished and brilliant career. His treatment of a now-famous Pearl Harbor signal does not sound much different in the telling. After the event, the signal in question was labeled "the bomb-plot message." It originated in Tokyo on September 24 and was sent to an agent in Honolulu. It requested the agent to divide Pearl Harbor into five areas and to make his future reports on ships in harbor with reference to those areas. Tokyo was especially interested in the locations of battleships, destroyers, and carriers, and also in any information on the mooring of more than one ship at a single dock.

This message was decoded and translated on October 9 and shortly thereafter distributed to Army, Navy, and State Department recipients of MAGIC. Commander Kramer, a naval expert on MAGIC, had marked the message with an asterisk, signifying that he thought it to be of particular interest. But what was its interest? Both he and Wilkinson agreed that it illustrated the "nicety" of Japanese intelligence, the incredible zeal and efficiency with which they collected detail. The division into areas was interpreted as a device for shortening the reports. Admiral Stark was similarly impressed with Japanese efficiency, and no one felt it necessary to forward the message to Admiral Kimmel. No one read into it a specific danger to ships anchored in Pearl Harbor. At the time, this was a reasonable estimate, since somewhat similar requests for information were going to Japanese agents in Panama, Vancouver, Portland, San Diego, San Francisco, and other places. It should be observed, however, that the estimate was reasonable only on the basis of a very rough check on the quantity of espionage messages passing between Tokyo and these American ports. No one in Far Eastern Intelligence had subjected the messages to any more refined analysis. An observer assigned to such a job would have been able to record an increase in the frequency and specificity of Tokyo's requests concerning Manila and Pearl Harbor in the last weeks before the outbreak of war, and he would have noted that Tokyo was not displaying the same interest in other American ports. These observations, while not significant in isolation, might have been useful in the general signal picture.

There is no need, however, to confine our examples to Intelligence personnel. Indeed, the crucial areas where the signals failed to communicate a warning were in the operational branches of the armed services. Let us take Admiral Kimmel and his reaction to the information that the Japanese were destroying most of their codes in major Far Eastern consulates and also in London and Washington. Since the Pearl Harbor attack, this information has frequently been characterized by military experts who were not stationed in Honolulu as an "unmistakable tip-off." As Admiral Ingersoll explained at the congressional hearings, with the lucidity characteristic of statements after the event:

> If you rupture diplomatic negotiations you do not necessarily have to burn your codes. The diplomats go home and they can pack up their codes with their dolls and take them home. Also, when you rupture diplomatic negotiations, you do not rupture consular relations. The consuls stay on.

Now, in this particular set of dispatches that did not mean a rupture of diplomatic negotiations, it meant war, and that information was sent out to the fleets as soon as we got it. . . .[1]

The phrase "it meant war" was, of course, pretty vague; war in Manila, Hong Kong, Singapore, and Batavia is not war 5000 miles away in Pearl Harbor. Before the event, for Admiral Kimmel, code burning in major Japanese consulates in the Far East may have "meant war," but it did not signal danger of an air attack on Pearl Harbor. In the first place, the information that he received was not the original MAGIC. He learned from Washington that Japanese consulates were burning "almost all" of their codes, not all of them, and Honolulu was not included on the list. He knew from a local source that the Japanese consulate in Honolulu was burning secret papers (not necessarily codes), and this back yard burning had happened three or four times during the year. In July, 1941, Kimmel had been informed that the Japanese consulates in lands neighboring Indochina had destroyed codes, and he interpreted the code burning in December as a similar attempt to protect codes in case the Americans or their British and Dutch allies tried to seize the consulates in reprisal for the southern advance. This also was a reasonable interpretation at the time, though not an especially keen one.

Indeed, at the time there was a good deal of evidence available to support all the wrong interpretations of last-minute signals, and the interpretations appeared wrong only *after* the event. There was, for example, a good deal of evidence to support the hypothesis that Japan would attack the Soviet Union from the east while the Russian Army was heavily engaged in the west. Admiral Turner, head of Navy War Plans in Washington, was an enthusiastic adherent of this view and argued the high probability of a Japanese attack on Russia up until the last week in November, when he had to concede that most of Japan's men and supplies were moving south. Richard Sorge, the expert Soviet spy who had direct access to the Japanese Cabinet, had correctly predicted the southern move as early as July, 1941, but even he was deeply alarmed during September and early October by the large number of troop movements to the Manchurian border. He feared that his July advice to the Soviet Union had been in error, and his alarm ultimately led to his capture on October 14. For at this time he increased his radio messages to Moscow to the point where it was possible for the Japanese police to pinpoint the source of the broadcasts.

It is important to emphasize here that most of the men that we have cited in our examples, such as Captain Wilkinson and Admirals Turner and Kimmel—these men and their colleagues who were involved in the Pearl Harbor disaster—were as efficient and loyal a group of men as one could find. Some of them were exceptionally able and dedicated. The fact of surprise at Pearl Harbor has never been persuasively explained by accusing the participants, individually or in groups, of conspiracy or negligence or stupidity. What these examples illustrate is rather the very human tendency to pay attention to the signals that support current expectations about enemy behavior. If no one is listening for signals of an attack against a highly improbable target, then it is very difficult for the signals to be heard.

For every signal that came into the information net in 1941 there were usually several plausible alternative explanations, and it is not surprising that our observers and analysts were inclined to select the explanations that fitted the popular hypotheses. They sometimes set down new contradictory evidence side by side with existing hypotheses, and they also sometimes held two contradictory beliefs at the same time. We have seen this happen in G-2 estimates for the fall of 1941. Apparently human beings have a stubborn attachment to old beliefs and an equally stubborn resistance to new material that will upset them.

Besides the tendency to select whatever was in accord with one's expectations, there were many other blocks to perception that prevented our analysts from making the correct interpretation. We have just mentioned the masses of conflicting evidence that supported alternative and equally reasonable hypotheses. This is the phenomenon of noise in which a signal is embedded. Even at its normal level, noise presents problems in distraction; but in addition to the natural clatter of useless information and competing signals, in 1941 a number of factors combined to raise the usual noise level. First of all, it had been raised, especially in Honolulu, by the background of previous alert situations and false alarms. Earlier alerts, as we have seen, had centered attention on local sabotage and on signals supporting the hypothesis of a probable Japanese attack on Russia. Second, in both Honolulu and Washington, individual reactions to danger had been numbed, or at least dulled, by the continuous international tension.

A third factor that served to increase the natural noise level was the positive effort made by the enemy to keep the relevant signals quiet. The Japanese security system was an important and successful block to perception. It was able to keep the strictest cloak of secrecy around the Pearl Harbor attack and to limit knowledge only to those closely associated with the details of military and naval planning. In the Japanese Cabinet only the Navy Minister and the Army Minister (who was also Prime Minister) knew of the plan before the task force left its final port of departure.

In addition to keeping certain signals quiet, the enemy tried to create noise, and sent false signals into our information system by carrying on elaborate "spoofs." False radio traffic made us believe that certain ships were maneuvering near the mainland of Japan. The Japanese also sent to individual commanders false war plans for Chinese targets, which were changed only at the last moment to bring them into line with the Southeastern movement.

A fifth barrier to accurate perception was the fact that the relevant signals were subject to change, often very sudden change. This was true even of the so-called static intelligence, which included data on capabilities and the composition of military forces. In the case of our 1941 estimates of the infeasibility of torpedo attacks in the shallow waters of Pearl Harbor, or the underestimation of the range and performance of the Japanese Zero, the changes happened too quickly to appear in an intelligence estimate.

Sixth, our own security system sometimes prevented the communication of signals. It confronted our officers with the problem of trying to keep information from the enemy without keeping it from each other, and, as in the case of MAGIC, they were not always successful. As we have seen, only a very few key individuals saw these secret messages, and they saw them only briefly. They had no opportunity or time to make a critical review of the material, and each one assumed that others who had seen it would arrive at identical interpretations. Exactly who those "others" were was not quite clear to any recipient. Admiral Stark, for example, thought Admiral Kimmel was reading all of MAGIC. Those who were not on the list of recipients, but who had learned somehow of the existence of the decodes, were sure that they contained military as well as diplomatic information and believed that the contents were much fuller and more precise than they actually were. The effect of carefully limiting the reading and discussion of MAGIC, which was certainly necessary to safeguard the secret of our knowledge of the code, was thus to reduce this group of signals to the point where they were scarcely heard.

To these barriers of noise and security we must add the fact that the necessarily precarious character of intelligence information and predictions was reflected in the wording of instructions to take action. The warning messages were somewhat vague and ambiguous. Enemy moves are often subject to reversal on short notice, and this was true for the Japanese. They had plans for canceling their attacks on American possessions in the Pacific up to 24 hours before the time set for attack. A full alert in the Hawaiian Islands, for example, was one condition that might have caused the Pearl Harbor task force to return to Japan on December 5 or 6. The fact that intelligence predictions must be based on moves that are almost always reversible makes understandable the reluctance of the intelligence analyst to make bold assertions. Even if he is willing to risk his reputation on a firm prediction of attack at a definite time and place, no commander will in turn lightly risk the penalties and costs of a full alert. In December, 1941, a full alert required shooting down any unidentified aircraft sighted over the Hawaiian Islands. Yet this might have been interpreted by Japan as the first overt act. At least that was one consideration that influenced General Short to order his lowest degree of alert. While the cautious phrasing in the messages to the theater is certainly understandable, it nevertheless constituted another block on the road to perception. The sentences in the final theater warnings—"A surprise aggressive move in any direction is a possibility" and "Japanese future action unpredictable but hostile action possible at any moment"—could scarcely have been expected to inform the theater commanders of any change in their strategic situation.

Last but not least we must also mention the blocks to perception and communication inherent in any large bureaucratic organization, and those that stemmed from intraservice and interservice rivalries. The most glaring example of rivalry in the Pearl Harbor case was that between Naval War Plans and Naval Intelligence. A general prejudice against intellectuals and specialists, not confined to the military but unfortunately widely held in America, also made it difficult for intelligence experts to be heard. McCollum, Bratton, Sadtler, and a few others who felt that the signal picture was ominous enough to warrant more urgent warnings had no power to influence decision. The Far Eastern code analysts, for example, were believed to be too immersed in the "Oriental point of view." Low budgets for American Intelligence departments reflected the low prestige of this activity, whereas in England, Germany, and Japan, 1941 budgets reached a height that was regarded by the American Congress as quite beyond reason.

⋯◈⋯

In view of all these limitations to perception and communication, is the fact of surprise at Pearl Harbor, then, really so surprising? Even with these limitations explicitly recognized, there remains the step between perception and action. Let us assume that the first hurdle has been crossed: An available signal has been perceived as an indication of imminent danger. Then how do we resolve the next questions: What specific danger is the signal trying to communicate, and what specific action or preparation should follow?

On November 27, General MacArthur had received a war warning very similar to the one received by General Short in Honolulu. MacArthur's response had been promptly translated into orders designed to protect his bombers from possible air attack from Formosan land bases. But the orders were carried out very slowly. By December 8, Philippine time, only half of the bombers ordered to the south had left the Manila area, and reconnaissance over Formosa had not been undertaken. There was no sense of urgency in preparing for a Japanese air attack, partly because our intelligence estimates had calculated that the Japanese aircraft did not have sufficient range to bomb Manila from Formosa.

The information that Pearl Harbor had been attacked arrived at Manila early in the morning of December 8, giving the Philippine forces some 9 or 10 hours to prepare for an attack. But did an air attack on Pearl Harbor necessarily mean that the Japanese would strike from the air at the Philippines? Did they have enough equipment to mount both air attacks successfully? Would they come from Formosa or from carriers? Intelligence had indicated that they would have to come from carriers, yet the carriers were evidently off Hawaii. MacArthur's headquarters also pointed out that there had been no formal declaration of war against Japan by the United States. Therefore approval could not be granted for a counterattack on Formosan bases. Furthermore there were technical disagreements among airmen as to whether a counterattack should be mounted without advance photographic reconnaissance. While Brereton was arranging permission to undertake photographic reconnaissance, there was further disagreement about what to do with the aircraft in the meantime. Should they be sent aloft or should they be dispersed to avoid destruction in case the Japanese reached the airfields? When the Japanese bombers arrived shortly after noon, they found all the American aircraft wingtip to wingtip on the ground. Even the signal of an actual attack on Pearl Harbor was not an unambiguous signal of an attack on the Philippines, and it did not make clear what response was best.

Note

1. *Hearings*, Part 9, p. 4226.

POSTSCRIPT

Did President Roosevelt Deliberately Withhold Information About the Attack on Pearl Harbor from the American Commanders?

Theobald was an eyewitness to the Pearl Harbor attack. In his selection, he defends his former boss, Admiral Husband E. Kimmel of the U.S. Pacific Fleet, from responsibility for the fleet's lack of preparation prior to Japan's surprise attack. Theobald argues that President Roosevelt and his chief military aides deliberately withheld from Kimmel information that they had received from intelligence intercepts going to Japanese diplomats that the Japanese navy was going to attack Pearl Harbor on December 7. Why would Roosevelt do such a thing? Because, says Theobald, Roosevelt wanted to enter the war against Germany and Japan, but he could not mobilize a reluctant public for war unless the United States was attacked first. Disastrous as it was from a naval standpoint, says Theobald, "the Pearl Harbor attack proved to be the diplomatic prelude to the complete defeat of the Axis Powers."

Theobald wrote *The Final Secret of Pearl Harbor* in the 1950s at the height of the battle between the internationalist historians, who defended Roosevelt's policies toward Germany and Japan, and the revisionists, who believed that Roosevelt unnecessarily and deliberately deceived the American public by enticing the Japanese to attack Pearl Harbor. Both groups held different assumptions about the nature of America's foreign policy before World War II. Internationalists believed that Germany and Japan constituted threats to world peace and the overall balance of power and that they had to be defeated with or without active U.S. participation in the war. Revisionist historians believed that Germany and Japan did not threaten America's security even if they con-trolled Europe and Asia. For the best defenses of President Roosevelt's foreign policies, see Robert Dallek, *Franklin Roosevelt and American Foreign Policy, 1932–1945* (Oxford University Press, 1979); and Waldo H. Heinrichs, *Threshold of War: Franklin D. Roosevelt and American Entry Into World War II* (Oxford Univer-sity Press, 1988). Early revisionist studies of Roosevelt are summarized in Harry Elmer Barnes, ed., *Perpetual War for Perpetual Peace: A Critical Examination of the Foreign Policy of Franklin D. Roosevelt and Its Aftermath* (Caxton, 1953). Later criticisms include John T. Toland, *Infamy: Pearl Harbor and Its Aftermath* (Doubleday, 1982); and *Wind Over Sand: The Diplomacy of Franklin Roosevelt* (University of Georgia Press, 1988).

Theobald's account raises a number of questions. Did Roosevelt shift 3 battleships, 1 aircraft carrier, 4 light cruisers, and 18 destroyers for duty (in mention)? Or was Roosevelt, who knew that their intelligence agents would be aware of the maneuvers, trying to entice the Japanese to attack Pearl Harbor? What about Theobald's charge that the commanders at Pearl Harbor were deliberately denied information about Japan's plans so that the Japanese Navy would be tempted to attack the fleet? If this is true, why wasn't Roosevelt tried as a war criminal (after his death)? Furthermore, if the president wanted to use the attack to get America into the war, why would he destroy most of his Pacific task force? Perhaps Gordon W. Prange is correct to reject revisionist historians in his massive, well-documented account *At Dawn We Slept: The Untold Story of Pearl Harbor* (McGraw-Hill, 1981). Prange faults the commanders at Pearl Harbor: Lieutenant General Walter C. Short, for example, was so obsessed with sabotage that ammunition was not available when the attack came. Short also failed to use radar and ignored Washington's orders to undertake reconnaissance.

Although most revisionists will disagree with her, Wohlstetter's analysis of the decision-making process provides an alternative to both the revisionist conspiratorial views of Roosevelt and his staunchest defenders. Wohlstetter makes several telling points. First, the intelligence community was organizationally divided between army and navy intelligence units in Washington, D.C., and Hawaii, so there was no systematic analysis of the decrypted diplomatic messages collectively known as MAGIC by the War Department's Signal Intelligence Service (SIS). Second, because of the abundance of information from public and private sources as well as from diplomatic intelligence intercepts, it was difficult to sort through the noise level and separate relevant materials from irrelevant materials. Third, the Japanese themselves provided misleading signals so that American observers would think the fleet was home—near the Marshall Islands. Fourth, even though President Roosevelt knew that war was coming with Japan, he thought the attack might be against Russia in Siberia, with its oil reserves, or in Southeast Asia against the British and Dutch possessions, especially Indonesia, with its important supply of rubber. Finally, Wohlstetter contends that even with an eight-hour warning, America's leaders in the Philippines were immobilized by bureaucratic indecisiveness and that Japanese planes destroyed most of the American aircraft at Clark Field because the planes were not moved to hidden areas.

The starting points for further study on Pearl Harbor are Hans Trefouse, *Pearl Harbor: The Continuing Controversy* (Krieger, 1982); and Akira Iriye, *Pearl Harbor and the Coming of the Pacific War: A Brief History with Documents and Essays* (St. Martin's Press, LLC, 1999). On Pearl Harbor itself see Gordon Prange, *Pearl Harbor: The Verdict of History* (McGraw-Hill, 1986). A trenchant analysis with a comprehensive bibliography of the whole period is Justus D. Doenecke and John E. Wiltz, *From Isolation to War: 1931–1941*, 2nd ed. (Harlan Davidson, 1991). For a discussion of early interpretations, see Wayne S. Cole, "American Entry Into World War II: A Historiographical Appraisal," *Mississippi Valley Historical Review* (March 1957). For a more recent evaluation, see J. Gary Clifford, "Both Ends of the Telescope: New Perspectives on F.D.R. and American Entry into World War II," *Diplomatic History* (Spring 1989).

Internet References . . .

Remembering Jim Crow

Created as a companion to a National Public Radio (NPR) documentary on seg-regation in the South, this Web site presents legal, social, and cultural aspects of segregation, black community, and black resistance to the Jim Crow way of life.

http://americanradioworks.publicradio.org/features/remembering/

Brown@50: Fulfilling the Promise

This site provides links to relevant court cases both north and south since *Plessy v. Ferguson* (1896) as well as journal articles.

http://www.brownat50.org/

Civil Rights in Mississippi Digital Archive

University of Southern Mississippi Libraries and Center for Oral History contains collections of documents addressing the civil rights movement in Mississippi.

http://www.lib.usm.edu/legacy/spcol/crda/

CWIHP: Cold War International History Project

Scholarship on the Cold War has been written primarily by Westerners without access to sources in Soviet archives. This extensive collection seeks to remedy the gap in Cold War historiography by presenting sources from the former Com-munist bloc.

http://www.wilsoncenter.org/index.cfm?fuseaction=topics.home&topic_id=14

Central Intelligence Agency (CIA) Electronic Reading Room

The CIA has digitized thousands of formerly secret documents declassified to comply with Freedom of Information Act requests. Keyword search capabilities are provided for the complete Web site. In addition, there are eight collections designated as "frequently requested records" that total nearly 8,000 documents. These collections cover a number of Cold War topics.

http://www.foia.cia.gov/default.asp

Vietnam Center and Archive

This massive Web site furnishes several large collections. The "Oral History Project" presents full transcriptions of more than 475 audio oral histories con-ducted with U.S. men and women who served in Vietnam. The "Virtual Vietnam Archive" offers more than 408,000 pages from more than 270,000 documents regarding the Vietnam War.

http://Vietnam.ttu.edu/

Teach Women's History Project

These teaching and reference materials focus on the women's rights movement of the past 50 years and its opposing forces.

http://www.feminist.org/research/teachersguide/teach1.html

National Council for Science and the Environment

The National Council for Science and the Environment (NCSE) has been working since 1990 to improve the scientific basis for environmental decision making. NCSE is supported by almost 500 academic, scientific, environmental, and busi-ness organizations.

http://www.cnie.org

The Cold War and Beyond

World War II ended in 1945, but the peace that everyone had hoped for never came. By 1947 a "Cold War" between the Western powers and the Russians was in full swing. Three years later, American soldiers were fighting a hot war of "containment" against communist expansion in Korea. By 1968, President Lyndon Johnson had escalated America's participation in the Vietnam War and then tried to negotiate peace, which was accomplished by President Nixon in January 1973.

From 1950 to 1974, most white American families were economically well-off. Many veterans had attended college under the G.I. bill, moved to the suburbs and worked in white collar jobs. The nuclear family was frozen in a state described by one historian as "domestic containment." Ideally, Dad went to work, Mom stayed home, and the kids went to school. But fissures developed in the 1950s that affected African Americans who were segregated from the suburbs and most white collar jobs; women who questioned the role of stay-at-home mom; and children who felt alienated from the cultural values of their family. The first sign was the emergence of rock and roll and its white icon Elvis Presley. Was the music revolt the traditional acting out of children against their parents, or did it reflect a real change in values that would culminate in political protests and the establishment of a counterculture in the 1960s?

Did rock and roll reflect a real change in values and lead to the counterculture protests of the 1960s? Did the Brown *decision*, which outlawed "separate but equal" schools, pave the way for the elimination of a segregated society? Did the women's liberation movement destroy the traditional American family, or did it provide opportunities for women to become physicians, lawyers, and CEOs of large corporations? Finally did the industrialization of the economy of the 1970s destroy the blue collar working class New Deal Democrats and create a more affluent middle-class of Reagan Republican voters? Or is America a declining power with a major wealth gap between upper middle class and the working poor?

- Was President Truman Responsible for the Cold War?
- Was Rock and Roll Responsible for Dismantling America's Traditional Family, Sexual, and Racial Customs in the 1950s and 1960s?
- Did President John F. Kennedy Demonstrate a Strong Commitment to Civil Rights?
- Did President Nixon Negotiate a "Peace With Honor" in Vietnam in 1973?
- Has the Women's Movement of the 1970s Failed to Liberate American Women?
- Is the United States a Declining Power?

ISSUE 13

Was President Truman Responsible for the Cold War?

YES: Arnold A. Offner, from "Another Such Victory": President Truman, American Foreign Policy, and the Cold War, *Diplomatic History* (Spring 1999)

NO: John Lewis Gaddis, from *We Now Know: Rethinking Cold War History* (Oxford University Press, 1997)

ISSUE SUMMARY

YES: Arnold A. Offner argues that President Harry S. Truman was a parochial nationalist whose limited vision of foreign affairs precluded negotiations with the Russians over cold war issues.

NO: John Lewis Gaddis argues that after a half century of scholarship, Joseph Stalin was uncompromising and primarily responsible for the cold war.

Less than a month before the war ended in Europe the most powerful man in the world, President Franklin Delano Roosevelt, died suddenly from a brain embolism. A nervous, impetuous, and an inexperienced Vice President Harry S. Truman became the president. Historians disagree whether Truman reversed Roosevelt's relationship with Stalin or whether the similarities in policy were negated by Truman's blunt negotiating style compared with FDR's suave, calm approach. But disagreements emerged over issues such as control over the atomic bomb, Germany, Poland, and the economic reconstruction of Europe.

The question of Germany was paramount. During the war it was agreed that Germany would be temporarily divided into zones of occupation with the United States, Great Britain, and the newly liberated France controlling the Western half of Germany while the Russians were in charge of the Eastern half. Berlin, which was 90 miles inside of the Russian zone, would also be divided into zones of occupation. Arguments developed over boundaries, reparations and transfers of industrial equipment and agricultural foodstuffs between zones. In May, 1946, the Americans began treating the western zones as a separate economic unit because the Russians were transferring the food from their zone back to the Soviet Union. In September, 1946, Secretary of State James Byrnes announced that the Americans would continue to occupy their half of Germany indefinitely with military troops. By 1948, a separate democratic

West German government was established. The Russians protested by blocking ground access to the western zones of Berlin. But the Americans continued to supply the West Berliners with supplies through an airlift. After 10 months, because of the bad publicity, the Russians abandoned the Berlin blockade and created a separate communist East German government.

Roosevelt and Churchill had conceded Russian control over Eastern Europe during the World War II Conferences. The question was how much control. Stalin was not going to allow anti-Communist governments to be established in these countries. He had no understanding of how free elections were held. Consequently, when the cold war intensified in 1947 and 1948, Russian-dominated Communist governments were established in Hungary, Poland, and Czechoslovakia.

In February 1946, Stalin delivered a major speech declaring the incompatibility of the two systems of Communism and Capitalism. The next month, Winston Churchill, now a retired politician, delivered his famous speech at a commencement in Fulton, Missouri, with the Truman administration's consent in which he complained about the "iron curtain" that Russia was imposing on Eastern Europe. At the same time, George Kennan, a bright multilinguist American diplomat who spent years in Germany and Russia and would become the head of Truman's policy planning staff, wrote a series of telegrams and articles which set the tone for the specific policies the Truman administration would undertake. Kennan had coined the phrase "containment," a word that would be used to describe America's foreign policy from Truman to the first President Bush. Containment would assume various meanings and would be extended to other areas of the globe besides Europe in ways Kennan claims were a misuse of what his original intentions were. Nevertheless the Truman administration took steps to stop further Russian expansionism.

In 1947, a series of steps were undertaken both to "contain" Russian expansionism and to rebuild the economies of Europe. On March 12, in an address before a Republican-controlled Congress, Truman argued in somewhat inflated rhetoric that "it must be the policy of the United States to support free peoples who are resisting attempted subjugation by armed minorities or by outside pressures." In the same speech in what became known as the "Truman Doctrine," the President requested and received $400 million economic and military assistance to Greece and Turkey. Almost as an afterthought, American military personnel were sent to oversee the reconstruction effort, a precedent that would later be used to send advisers to Vietnam.

In June 1947, Secretary of State George C. Marshall announced a plan to provide economic assistance to all European nations. This included the Soviet Union, who rejected the program and formed its own economic recovery group. In April 1948, Congress approved the creation of the Economic Cooperation Administration, the agency that would administer the program. The Marshall Plan would be remembered as America's most successful foreign aid program, where a billion dollars were channeled to the Western European nations. By 1950, industrial production had increased 64 percent since the end of the war, while the communist parties declined in membership and influence.

When did the cold war begin? Was it inevitable? Or should one side take most of the blame?

YES

Arnold A. Offner

"Another Such Victory": President Truman, American Foreign Policy, and the Cold War

As the twenty-first century nears, President Harry S. Truman's reputation stands high. This is especially true regarding his stewardship of foreign policy although, ironically, he entered the Oval Office in 1945 untutored in world affairs, and during his last year in the White House, Republicans accused his administration of having surrendered fifteen countries and five hundred million people to communism and sending twenty thousand Americans to their "burial ground" in Korea. Near the end of his term, Truman's public "favorable" rating had plummeted to 23 percent.

Within a decade, however, historians rated Truman a "near great" president, crediting his administration with reconstructing Western Europe and Japan, resisting Soviet or Communist aggression from Greece to Korea, and forging collective security through NATO. In the 1970s the "plain speaking" Truman became a popular culture hero. Recently, biographers have depicted him as the allegory of American life, an ordinary man whose extraordinary character led him to triumph over adversity from childhood through the presidency, and even posited a symbiotic relationship between "His Odyssey" from Independence to the White House and America's rise to triumphant superpower status. Melvyn P. Leffler, in his *A Preponderance of Power,* has judged Truman to have been neither a naif nor an idealist but a realist who understood the uses of power and whose administration, despite serious, costly errors, prudently preserved America's national security against real or perceived Soviet threats.

Collapse of the Soviet Union and Europe's other Communist states, whose archives have confirmed Truman's belief in 1945 that their regimes governed largely by "clubs, pistols and concentration camps," has further raised the former president's standing. This has encouraged John Lewis Gaddis and others to shift their focus to Stalin's murderous domestic rule as the key determinant of Soviet foreign policy and the Cold War. As Gaddis has contended, Stalin was heir to Ivan the Terrible and Peter the Great, responsible for more state-sanctioned murders than Adolf Hitler, and treated world politics as an extension of domestic politics: a zero sum game in which his gaining security meant depriving all others of it. For Gaddis and others, that is largely the answer to the question of whether Stalin sought or caused the Cold War.

From *Diplomatic History,* vol. 32, no. 2, Spring 1999, pp. 127–143, 153–155 (excerpts). Copyright © 1999 by Society for Historians of American Foreign Relations. Reprinted by permission of Wiley-Blackwell Publishing.

But as Walter LaFeber has said, to dismiss Stalin's policies as the work of a paranoid is greatly to oversimplify the Cold War. Indeed, historians of Stalin's era seem to be of the preponderant view that he pursued a cautious but brutal realpolitik. He aimed to restore Russia's 1941 boundaries, establish a sphere of influence in border states, provide security against a recovered Germany or Japan or hostile capitalist states, and gain compensation, notably reparations, for the ravages of war. Stalin calculated forces, recognized America's superior industrial and military power, put Soviet state interests ahead of Marxist–Leninist ideology, and pursued pragmatic or opportunistic policies in critical areas such as Germany, China, and Korea.

Thus, the time seems ripe, given our increased knowledge of Soviet policies, to reconsider President Truman's role in the Cold War. As Thomas G. Paterson has written, the president stands at the pinnacle of the diplomatic-military establishment, has great capacity to set the foreign policy agenda and to mold public opinion, and his importance, especially in Truman's case, cannot be denied. But contrary to prevailing views, I believe that his policymaking was shaped by his parochial and nationalistic heritage. This was reflected in his uncritical belief in the superiority of American values and political-economic interests and his conviction that the Soviet Union and communism were the root cause of international strife. Truman's parochialism also caused him to disregard contrary views, to engage in simplistic analogizing, and to show little ability to comprehend the basis for other nations' policies. Consequently, his foreign policy leadership intensified Soviet–American conflict, hastened the division of Europe, and brought tragic intervention in Asian civil wars.

In short, Truman lacked the qualities of the creative or great leader who, as James MacGregor Burns has written, must broaden the environment in which he and his citizenry operate and widen the channels in which choices are made and events flow. Truman, to the contrary, narrowed Americans' perception of their world political environment and the channels for policy choices and created a rigid framework in which the United States waged long-term, extremely costly global cold war. Indeed, before we celebrate America's victory in this contest we might recall that after King Pyrrhus's Greek forces defeated the Romans at the battle of Asculum in 280 B.C., he reflected that "another such victory, and we are undone."

II

Truman's parochialism and nationalism, and significant insecurity, were rooted in his background, despite his claim to have had a bucolic childhood of happy family, farm life, and Baptist religiosity. In fact, young Harry's poor eyesight, extended illness, and "sissy" piano playing alienated him from both his peers and his feisty father and fostered ambivalence in him toward powerful men. On the one hand, Truman deferred to "Boss" Thomas Pendergast, his dishonest political benefactor, and to Secretaries of State George Marshall and Dean Acheson, whose manner and firm viewpoints he found reassuring. On the other hand, he denounced those whose style or ways of thinking were unfamiliar. This included the State Department's "striped pants boys," the military's "brass hats" and "prima donnas," political "fakirs" [*sic*] such as Teddy and Franklin Roosevelt, and "professional liberals." For Truman, Charles de Gaulle, Josef Stalin, Ernest Bevin, and Douglas MacArthur were each, at one time or another, a "son of a bitch."

Truman's need to demonstrate his authority underlay his upbraiding of both Soviet Foreign Minister Vyacheslav Molotov in April 1945 for Russia's alleged failure to keep its agreements and his secretary of state, James Byrnes, for allegedly exceeding his authority at the Moscow Conference of Foreign Ministers (CFM) that December. Truman naively likened Stalin to Pendergast, who, like Harry's father, always kept his word, but then took great umbrage at the thought that the Soviet leader had broken his word over Poland, Iran, or Germany. Truman also blamed MacArthur for misleading him at their Wake Island meeting in 1950 about Chinese intentions in the Korean War, but this was equally Truman self-deception.

Truman's self-tutelage in history derived largely from didactic biographies of "great men" and empires. This enhanced his vision of the globe but provided little sense of complexity or ambiguity and instilled exaggerated belief that current events had exact historical analogues that provided the key to contemporary policy. The new president was "amazed" that the Yalta accords were so "hazy" and fraught with "new meanings" at every reading, which probably contributed to his "lackluster" adherence to them. Shortly, Truman uncritically applied analogues about 1930s appeasement of Nazi Germany to diplomacy with the Soviet Union and crises in Iran, Greece, Turkey, and Korea.

Further, young Harry's Bible reading and church going did not inspire an abiding religiosity or system of morals so much as a conviction that the world was filled with "liars and hypocrites," terms he readily applied to his presidential critics, and a stern belief, as he wrote in 1945, that "punishment always followed transgression," a maxim that he applied to North Korea and the People's Republic of China (PRC).

Truman's early writings disdained non-Americans and minorities ("Chink doctor," "dago," "nigger," "Jew clerk," and "bohunks and Rooshans"), and in 1940 he proposed to deport "disloyal inhabitants." As president in 1945 he questioned the loyalty of "hyphenate" Americans, and in 1947 he signed Executive Order 9835, creating an unprecedented "loyalty" program that jettisoned basic legal procedural safeguards and virtually included a presumption of guilt.

Truman's command of men and bravery under fire in World War I were exemplary but not broadening. He deplored Europe's politics, mores, and food and sought only to return to "God's country." He intended never to revisit Europe: "I've nearly promised old Miss Liberty that she'll have to turn around to see me again," he wrote in 1918, and in 1945 he went reluctantly to Potsdam to his first and only European summit.

Nonetheless, Truman identified with Wilsonian internationalism, especially the League of Nations, and as a senator he supported President Franklin Roosevelt on the World Court, neutrality revision, rearmament, and Lend Lease for Britain and Russia. He rightfully said "I am no appeaser." But his internationalism reflected unquestioned faith in American moral superiority, and his foreign policy proposals largely comprised military preparedness. He was indifferent to the plight of Republican Spain and too quickly blamed international conflict on "outlaws," "savages," and "totalitarians." After Germany invaded the Soviet Union in 1941, he hastily remarked that they should be left to destroy one another—although he opposed Germany's winning—and he likened Russian leaders to "Hitler and Al Capone" and soon inveighed against the "twin blights—atheism and communism." Hence, while Truman supported the fledgling United Nations and the liberalization of world trade, the man who became president in April 1945 was less an incipient internationalist than a parochial nationalist given to excessive fear that appeasement, lack of preparedness, and enemies at home and abroad would thwart America's mission (the "Lord's will") to "win the peace" on its terms.

President Truman inherited an expedient wartime alliance that stood on shaky ground at Yalta in February 1945 and grew more strained over Soviet control in Romania and Poland and U.S. surrender talks with German officials at Bern that aroused Stalin's fears of a separate peace. Truman lamented that "they didn't tell me anything about what was going on." He also had to depend on advisers whose views ranged from Ambassador Averell Harriman's belief that it was time to halt the Russians' "barbarian invasion" of Europe to counsel from FDR emissaries Joseph Davies and Harry Hopkins to try to preserve long-term accord. Truman's desire to appear decisive by making quick decisions and his instinct to be "tough" spurred his belief that he could get "85 percent" from the Russians on important matters and that they could go along or "go to hell."

Initially, the president's abrupt style and conflicting advice produced inconsistent policy. His mid-April call for a "new" government in Poland and his "one-two to the jaw" interview with Molotov brought only a sharp reply from Stalin, after which the United States recognized a predominantly Communist Polish government. In May, Truman approved "getting tough" with the Russians by suddenly curtailing Lend Lease shipments, but Anglo-Soviet protests caused him to countermand the cutoffs. He then refused Prime Minister Winston Churchill's proposal to keep Anglo-American troops advanced beyond their agreed occupation zones to bargain in Germany and soon wrote that he was "anxious to keep all my engagements with the Russians because they are touchy and suspicious of us."

Still, Truman determined to have his way with the Russians, especially in Germany. Tutored in part by Secretary of War Henry L. Stimson, he embraced the emergent War-State Department position that Germany was key to the balance of power in Europe and required some reconstruction because a "poor house" standard of living there meant the same for Europe, and might cause a repeat of the tragic Treaty of Versailles history. Truman replaced Roosevelt's reparations negotiator, Isador Lubin, with conservative oil entrepreneur Edwin Pauley, who brushed off both Soviet claims to Yalta's $20 billion in reparations and State Department estimates that Germany could pay $12–14 billion. Truman also said that when he met with Churchill and Stalin he wanted "all the bargaining power—all the cards in my hands, and the plan on Germany is one of them."

The other card was the atomic bomb, which inspired Truman and Byrnes to think that they could win their way in Europe and Asia. Byrnes told the president in April that the bomb might allow them to "dictate our terms" at the war's end and in May indicated his belief that it would make the Russians more "manageable." Stimson counseled Truman that America's industrial strength and unique weapon comprised a "royal straight flush and we mustn't be a fool about how we play it," that it would be "dominant" in any dispute with Russia over Manchuria, and a "weapon" or "master card" in America's hand in its "big stakes" diplomacy with the Russians.

The president readily analogized diplomacy with his poker playing and, as Martin J. Sherwin has shown, believed that use of his atomic "ace-in-the-hole" would allow him to wrest concessions from Stalin. Truman had incentive to delay a summit meeting until the bomb was ready and to take no steps to obviate its use. In late spring he passed over proposals to modify unconditional surrender that sought to induce Japan's quick capitulation, and he would not give the Japanese or Russians notice of the atomic bomb.

Truman set sail for Potsdam highly disposed to atomic diplomacy, albeit not "blackmail." His nationalist perspective shaped his thinking. He aimed to advance American interests only: "win, lose, or draw—and we must win." En route, he approved Pauley's policy to give "first charge" priority to German occupation and maintenance costs over reparations. "Santa Claus is dead," Truman wrote, and the United States would never again "pay reparations, feed the world, and get nothing for it but a nose thumbing." Further, after Stimson brought word on 16 July of the successful atomic test in New Mexico and urged an early warning and offer to retain the Emperor as means to induce Japan's rapid surrender, Truman and Byrnes refused. That ended the last, brief chance at atomic restraint.

After meeting Stalin on 17 July, Truman wrote that he was unfazed by the Russian's "dynamite" agenda because "I have some dynamite too which I'm not exploding now." The following day he asserted that the "Japs will fold up" before Russia entered the Pacific war, specifically "when Manhattan appears over their homeland." Truman agreed with Byrnes that use of the bomb would permit them to "out-maneuver Stalin on China," that is, negate the Yalta concessions in Manchuria and guarantee that Russia would "not get in so much on the kill" of Japan or its occupation. Assured by 24 July that the bomb would be ready before Russia's entry, the president had to be persuaded even to hint to Stalin that he had a new weapon and afterward exulted in the mistaken belief that the Russian leader had not caught on to the bomb. Truman then hastened to issue the Potsdam Declaration without Soviet signature on 26 July and signed his "release when ready" order on the bombs on the 31st.

News of the bomb's power also greatly reinforced Truman's confidence to allow Byrnes to press European negotiations to impasse by refusing the Russians access to the Ruhr, rejecting even their low bid for $4 billion in industrial reparations, and withdrawing the Yalta accords. Convinced that the New Mexico atomic test would allow the United States to "control" events, Byrnes pushed his famous 30 July tripartite ultimatum on German zonal reparations, Poland's de facto control over its new western border (including Silesia) with Germany, and Italy's membership in the UN. "Mr. Stalin is stallin'," Truman wrote hours before the American-set deadline on 31 July, but that was useless because "I have an ace in the hole and another one showing," aces that he knew would soon fall upon Japan.

Truman won his hand, as Stalin acceded to zonal reparations. But Truman's victory was fraught with more long-term consequences than he envisioned. He had not only equated his desire to prevent use of taxpayer dollars to help sustain occupied Germany with the Russians' vital need for reparations, but also given them reason to think, as Norman Naimark has written, that the Americans were deaf to their quest for a "paltry" $10 billion or less to compensate for Germany's having ravaged their nation. Further, America's insistence on zonal reparations would impede development of common economic policy for all of Germany and increase likelihood of its East–West division.

In addition, use of two atomic bombs on Hiroshima and Nagasaki—the second was not militarily necessary—showed that for Truman and Byrnes, the prospect of political gain in Europe and Asia precluded serious thought not to use the bombs. And this may have led the Russians to conclude that the bombs were directed against them, or their ability to achieve their strategic interests. But Stalin would not be pressured; he was determined to pursue a Russian atomic bomb.

Shortly, Truman backed Byrnes's "bomb in his pocket" diplomacy at the London CFM, which deadlocked over Russian control in Eastern Europe and American control in Japan. Truman told Byrnes to "stick to his guns" and tell the Russians "to go to hell." The president then agreed with "ultranationalist" advisers who opposed international atomic accord by drawing misleading analogies about interwar disarmament and "appeasement" and by insisting that America's technological-industrial genius assured permanent atomic supremacy. Truman held that America was the world's atomic "trustee"; that it had to preserve the bomb's "secret"; and that no nation would give up the "locks and bolts" necessary to protect its "house" from "outlaws." The atomic arms race was on, he said in the fall of 1945, and other nations had to "catch up on their own hook."

In the spring of 1946, Truman undercut the Dean Acheson-David Lilienthal plan for international control and development of atomic resources by appointing as chief negotiator Bernard Baruch, whose emphasis on close inspections, sanctions, no veto, and indefinite American atomic monopoly virtually assured Russian refusal. Despite Acheson's protests, Truman analogized that "if Harry Stimson had been backed up in Manchuria [in 1931] there would have been no war." And as deadlock neared in July 1946, the president told Baruch to "stand pat."

Ultimately the UN commission weighing the Baruch Plan approved it on 31 December 1946. But the prospect of a Soviet veto in the Security Council precluded its adoption. Admittedly, Stalin's belief that he could not deal with the United States on an equal basis until he had the bomb and Soviet insistence on retention of their veto power and national control of resources and facilities may have precluded atomic accord in 1946. Still, Baruch insisted that the United States could get its way because it had an atomic monopoly, and American military officials sought to preserve a nuclear monopoly as long as possible and to develop a strategy based on air power and atomic weapons. As

David Holloway has written, neither Truman nor Stalin "saw the bomb as a common danger to the human race."

Meanwhile, Byrnes's diplomacy in Moscow in December 1945 had produced Yalta-style accords on a European peace treaty process, Russian predominance in Bulgaria and Romania and American primacy in China and Japan, and compromise over Korea, with Soviet disputes with Iran and Turkey set aside. But conservative critics cried "appeasement," and in his famous but disputed letter of 5 January 1946, an anxious president charged that Byrnes had kept him "completely in the dark"; denounced Russian "outrage[s]" in the Baltic, Germany, Poland, and Iran and intent to invade Turkey; and said that the Russians understood only an "iron fist" and "divisions" and that he was tired of "babying" them. In fact, Truman knew of most of Byrnes's positions; they had hardly "babied" Russia since Potsdam; and no Russian attack was imminent. The letter reflected Truman's new "get tough" policy, or personal cold war declaration, which, it must be emphasized, came six weeks before George Kennan's Long Telegram and Churchill's Iron Curtain speech.

Strong American protests in 1946 caused the Russians to withdraw their troops from Iran and their claims to joint defense of the Turkish Straits. In the latter case, Truman said he was ready to follow his policy of military response "to the end" to determine if Russia intended "world conquest." Once again he had taken an exaggerated, nationalist stance. No one expected a Russian military advance; America's action rested on its plans to integrate Turkey into its strategic planning and to use it as a base of operations against Russia in event of war. And in September, Truman approved announcement of a Mediterranean command that led to the United States becoming the dominant naval power there by year's end.

Meanwhile, Truman ignored Secretary of Commerce Henry Wallace's lengthy memoranda during March–September 1946 that sought to promote economic ties with Russia and questioned America's atomic policies and global military expansiveness. The president then fired Wallace after he publicly challenged Byrnes's speech on 6 September in Stuttgart propounding West German reconstruction and continued American military presence there. The firing was reasonable, but not the rage at Wallace as "a real Commy" and at "parlor pinks and soprano-voiced men" as a "national danger" and "sabotage front" for Stalin.

Equally without reason was Truman's face value acceptance of White House special counsel Clark Clifford's "Russian Report" of September 1946 and accompanying "Last Will of Peter the Great." Clifford's report rested on a hasty compilation of apocalyptic projections of Soviet aim to conquer the world by military force and subversion, and he argued that the United States had to prepare for total war. He wrote in the "black and white" terms that he knew Truman would like and aimed to justify a vast global military upgrade and silence political critics on the left and right. Tsar Peter's will was an old forgery purporting to show that he had a similar design to conquer Eurasia. Truman may have found the report so "hot" that he confined it to his White House safe, but he believed the report and the will and soon was persisting that the governments of the czars, Stalin, and Hitler were all the same. Later he told a mild critic of American policy to read Tsar Peter's will to learn where Russian leaders got their "fixed ideas."

It was a short step, Clifford recalled, from the Russian Report to Truman's epochal request in March 1947 for military aid to Greece and Turkey to help "free peoples" fight totalitarianism. Truman vastly overstated the global-ideological aspects of Soviet–American conflict. Perhaps he sought to fire "the opening gun" to rouse the public and a fiscally conservative Republican Congress to national security expenditures. But he also said that this was "only the beginning" of the "U.S. going into European politics," that the Russians had broken every agreement since Potsdam and would now get only "one language" from him. He added in the fall of 1947 that "if Russia gets Greece and Turkey," it would get Italy and France, the iron curtain would extend to western Ireland, and the United States would have to "come home and prepare for war."

Truman's fears were excessive. Stalin never challenged the Truman Doctrine or Western primacy in Turkey, now under U.S. military tutelage, and Greece. He provided almost no aid to the Greek rebels and told Yugoslavia's leaders in early 1948 to halt their aid because the United States would never allow the Greek Communists to win and break Anglo-American control in the Mediterranean. When Marshal Josip Broz Tito balked, Stalin withdrew his advisers from Yugoslavia and expelled that nation from the Cominform. Tito finally closed his borders to the Greek rebels in July 1949.

Perhaps U.S. officials feared that Britain's retreat from Greece might allow Russia to penetrate the Mediterranean, or that if Greek Communists overthrew the reactionary Greek regime (Turkey was not threatened) they might align Athens with Moscow. Still, the Truman administration's costly policy never addressed the causes of Greece's civil war; instead, it substituted military "annihilation of the enemy for the reform of the social and economic conditions" that had brought civil war. Equally important, Truman's rhetorical division of the world into "free" versus "totalitarian" states, as Gaddis once said, created an "ideological straitjacket" for American foreign policy and an unfortunate model for later interventions, such as in Korea—"the Greece of the Far East," as Truman would say—and in French Indochina.

The Truman Doctrine led to the Marshall Plan in June 1947, but they were not "two halves of the same walnut," as Truman claimed. State Department officials who drew up the European Recovery Plan (ERP) differentiated it from what they viewed as his doctrine's implications for "economic and ultimately military warfare." The Soviets likened the Truman Doctrine to retail purchase of separate nations and the Marshall Plan to wholesale purchase of Europe.

The Soviet view was narrow, although initially they had interest in participating and perhaps even harbored dreams that the United States would proffer a generous Lend Lease-style arrangement. But as the British quickly saw, Soviet participation was precluded by American-imposed financial and economic controls and, as Michael J. Hogan has written, by the integrated, continental approach to aid rather than a nation-by-nation basis that would have benefited war-devastated Russia. Indeed, in direct talks in Paris, U.S. officials refused concessions, focused on resources to come from Russia and East Europe, and insisted on German contributions to the ERP ahead of reparations payments or a peace treaty—and then expressed widespread relief when the Soviets rejected the ERP for themselves and East Europe.

The Marshall Plan proved to be a very successful geostrategic venture. It helped to spur American–European trade and Western European recovery, bring France into camp with Germany and satisfy French economic and security claims, and revive estern Germany industrially without unleashing the 1930s-style "German colossus" that Truman's aides feared. The Marshall Plan was also intended to contain the Soviets economically, forestall German–Soviet bilateral deals, and provide America with access to its allies' domestic and colonial resources. Finally, as the British said, the Truman administration sought an integrated Europe resembling the United States, "God's own country."

The Marshall Plan's excellent return on investment, however, may have cost far more than the $13 billion expended. "The world is definitely split in two," Undersecretary of State Robert Lovett said in August 1947, while Kennan forewarned that for defensive reasons the Soviets would "clamp down completely on Czechoslovakia" to strengthen their hold on Eastern Europe. Indeed, the most recent evidence indicates that Stalin viewed the Marshall Plan as a "watershed" event, signaling an American effort to predominate over all of Europe. This spurred the Soviets into a comprehensive strategy shift. They now rigged the elections in Hungary, proffered Andrei Zhdanov's "two camps" approach to world policy, created the Cominform, and blessed the Communist coup in Czechoslovakia in February 1948. Truman, in turn, concluded that the Western world confronted the same situation it had a decade earlier with Nazi Germany, and his bristling St. Patrick's Day speeches in March 1948 placed sole onus for the Cold War on the Soviet Union. Subsequently, Anglo-American talks at the Pentagon would culminate in NATO in April 1949.

Meanwhile, the U.S. decision to make western Germany the cornerstone of the ERP virtually precluded negotiations to reunify the country. In fact, when Secretary of State Marshall proposed during a CFM meeting in the spring of 1947 to offer current production reparations to the Russians to induce agreement to unify Germany, the president sternly refused. Marshall complained of lack of "elbow room" to negotiate. But Truman would not yield, and by the time of the next CFM in late 1947 the secretary showed no interest in Russian reparations or Ruhr access. Despite America's public position, Ambassador to Moscow Walter Bedell Smith wrote, "we really do not want nor intend to accept German unification on any terms that the Russians might agree to, even though they seemed to meet most of our requirements."

The Americans were by then onto their London Conference program to create a West German state and, as Stalin said in February 1948, "The West will make Western Germany their own, and we shall turn Eastern Germany into our own state." In June, the Soviet dictator initiated the Berlin blockade to try to forestall the West's program, but Truman determined to "stay, period." He believed that to withdraw from Berlin would seriously undermine U.S. influence in Europe and the ERP and destroy his presidential standing, and he remained determined to avert military confrontation.

But Truman saw no connection between the London program and the blockade, as Carolyn Eisenberg has written. Further, his belief that "there is nothing to negotiate" and accord with General Lucius Clay's view that to withdraw from Berlin meant "we have lost everything we are fighting for" exaggerated the intent of Stalin's maneuver and diminished even slim chances for compromise on Germany, including Kennan's "Plan A" for a unified, neutralized state with American and Soviet forces withdrawn to its periphery. As Marshall said in August 1948, there would be "no abandonment of our position" on West Germany.

Eventually, Truman and the airlift prevailed over Stalin, who gave in to a face-saving CFM in May 1949 that ended the blockade, with nothing else agreed. The new secretary of state, Acheson, said that the United States intended to create a West German government "come hell or high water" and that Germany could be unified only by consolidating the East into the West on the basis of its incipient Bonn Constitution. Likewise Truman said in June 1949 that he would not sacrifice West Germany's basic freedoms to gain "nominal political unity."

Long convinced that the United States was locked in "a struggle with the USSR for Germany," the president showed no interest when Stalin made his most comprehensive offer on 10 March 1952, proposing a Big Four meeting to draft a peace treaty for a united, neutral, defensively rearmed Germany free of foreign troops. Whether Stalin was seeking a settlement to reduce great power conflict over a divided Germany has been debated. His note came only after the United States and its allies were near contractual accord on West German sovereignty and Acheson had just negotiated his "grand slam" providing for German forces to enter a proposed European Defense Community (EDC) linked to NATO. Acheson held that Stalin had thrown a "golden apple" of discord over the iron curtain to forestall a sovereign, industrially strong, and rearmed West Germany joining an American-led alliance system.

Truman gave full sway to Acheson, who hesitated to reject Stalin's offer out of hand. But he insisted that the allies "drive ahead" with the German contractuals and EDC. He also got support from West German Chancellor Konrad Adenauer to shape uniform allied replies, with conditions, such as UN-supervised elections in all of Germany prior to negotiations and unified Germany's right to join any "defensive European community," that he knew Stalin would reject. Further, although Truman and Acheson had just coaxed Kennan to become ambassador to Moscow, they never asked his advice or gave him a policy clue despite meeting with him three times in April. This confirmed Kennan's view that "we had no interest in discussing the German problem with the Soviet Government in any manner whatsoever."

Stalin, meanwhile, told East German leaders in April 1952 that the West would never accept any proposal they made and that it was time to "organize your own state" and protect its border. The United States won the so-called battle of the notes, although exchanges continued. But the allies concluded the German contractuals and the EDC in late May. And when the French then reverted to proposing a four power meeting on Germany, Acheson said that four power control was long past. He then shaped the note so that it "puts onus on Sovs sufficiently to make it unlikely that Sovs will agree to mtg on terms proposed." He was right, and in September the note writing drew to its anticlimactic closure.

Prospect for accord based on Stalin's note was remote, but not just because Stalin wanted, as Vojtech Mastny has written, either a unified "pro-Soviet though not necessarily communist" Germany or a full-fledged East German satellite. Truman had no interest in a unified, neutral, or demilitarized Germany and now believed that a rearmed FRG was as vital to NATO as West Germany was to ERR German unity was possible only on the basis of West over East. Thus, Ambassador Kennan said after talking to U.S. officials linked to NATO in the fall of 1952 that they saw no reason to withdraw U.S. forces from Germany "at any time within the foreseeable future under any conceivable agreement with Russia." This meant that the "split of Germany and Europe" would continue. And it did, for the next forty years. . . .

⋅❦⋅

No one leader or nation caused the Cold War. The Second World War generated inevitable Soviet–American conflict as two nations with entirely different political-economic systems confronted each other on two war-torn continents. The Truman administration would seek to fashion a world order friendly to American political and economic interests, to achieve maximum national security by preventing any nation from severing U.S. ties to its traditional allies and vital areas of trade and resources, and to avoid 1930s-style "appeasement." Truman creditably favored creation of the UN, fostered foreign aid and reconstruction, and wished to avert war, and, after he recognized his "overreach" in Korea, he sought to return to the status quo ante.

Nonetheless, from the Potsdam Conference through the Korean War, the president contributed significantly to the growing Cold War and militarization of American foreign policy. He assumed that America's economic-military-moral superiority assured that he could order the world on its terms, and he ascribed only dark motives to nations or leaders who resisted America's will. Monopoly control of the atomic bomb heightened this sense of righteous power and impelled his use of atomic bombs partly to outmaneuver the Russians in China and over Japan. Truman also drew confidence from the bombs that he could deny the Soviets any fixed sum of German reparations despite their feasibility, the Yalta accords, and the apparent disregard of Russia's claim to compensation for its wartime suffering. American-imposed zonal reparations policy only increased the East–West divide and diminished prospects to reunite Germany, although Stalin evidently remained open to the idea of a united and neutralized Germany until 1949 and conceivably as late as 1952. But Truman, as Marshall learned in the spring of 1947, had little interest in negotiating such an arrangement, and his administration's decision that year to make western Germany the cornerstone of the Marshall Plan and Western Europe's reconstruction virtually precluded German unification except by melding East into West. Formation of NATO and insistence that a unified Germany be free to join a Western military alliance reinforced division of Germany and Europe.

It is clear that Truman's insecurity with regard to diplomacy and world politics led him to seek to give the appearance of acting decisively and reinforced his penchant to view conflict in black and white terms and to divide nations into free or totalitarian societies. He shied from weighing the complexities of historic national conflicts and local or regional politics. Instead, he attributed nearly every diplomatic crisis or civil war—in Germany, Iran, Turkey, Greece, and Czechoslovakia—to Soviet machination and insisted that the Russians had broken every agreement and were bent on "world conquest." To determine his response he was quick to reach for an analogy, usually the failure of the Western powers to resist Germany and Japan in the 1930s, and to conclude that henceforth he would speak to the Russians in the only language that he thought they understood: "divisions." This style of leadership and diplomacy closed off both advocates and prospects for more patiently negotiated and more nuanced or creative courses of action.

Truman also viscerally loathed the Chinese Communists, could not comprehend Asian nationalism, demonized Asian opponents, and caused the United States to align itself with corrupt regimes. He was unable to view China's civil war apart from Soviet–American conflict. He brushed off criticism of America's intervention on behalf of the frightful GMD, refused to open channels of communication with the emergent PRC, and permitted the American-armed, Taiwan-based GMD to wage counterrevolutionary war against China's new government, whose sovereignty or legitimacy he never accepted. The Korean War then overtook his administration. The president decided to preserve South Korea's independence but set an unfortunate if not tragic precedent by refusing to seek formal congressional sanction for war. His decision to punish North Korea and implement "rollback," and his disdain for the PRC and its concerns before and after it entered the war, brought unnecessary, untold destruction and suffering to Asians and Americans and proved fatal to his presidency. Still, in his undelivered farewell address Truman insisted that "Russia was at the root" of every problem from Europe to Asia, and that "Trumanism" had saved countless countries from Soviet invasion and "knocked the socks off the communists" in Korea.

In conclusion, it seems clear that despite Truman's pride in his knowledge of the past, he lacked insight into the history unfolding around him. He often could not see beyond his immediate decision or visualize alternatives, and he seemed oblivious to the implications of his words or actions. More often than not he narrowed rather than broadened the options that he presented to the American citizenry, the environment of American politics, and the channels through which Cold War politics flowed. Throughout his presidency, Truman remained a parochial nationalist who lacked the leadership to move America away from conflict and toward detente. Instead, he promoted an ideology and politics of Cold War confrontation that became the modus operandi of successor administrations and the United States for the next two generations.

John Lewis Gaddis  **NO**

We Now Know:
Rethinking Cold War History

[Joseph] Stalin appears to have relished his role, along with [Franklin D.] Roosevelt and [Winston] Churchill, as one of the wartime Big Three. Such evidence as has surfaced from Soviet archives suggests that he received reassuring reports about Washington's intentions: "Roosevelt is more friendly to us than any other prominent American," Ambassador Litvinov commented in June 1943, "and it is quite obvious that he wishes to cooperate with us." Whoever was in the White House, Litvinov's successor Andrei Gromyko predicted a year later, the Soviet Union and the United States would "manage to find common issues for the solution of . . . problems emerging in the future and of interest to both countries." Even if Stalin's long-range thinking about security did clash with that of his Anglo-American allies, common military purposes provided the strongest possible inducements to smooth over such differences. It is worth asking why this *practice* of wartime cooperation did not become a *habit* that would extend into the postwar era.

The principal reason, it now appears, was Stalin's insistence on equating security with territory. Western diplomats had been surprised, upon arriving in Moscow soon after the German attack in the summer of 1941, to find the Soviet leader already demanding a postwar settlement that would retain what his pact with Hitler had yielded: the Baltic states, together with portions of Finland, Poland, and Romania. Stalin showed no sense of shame or even embarrassment about this, no awareness that the *methods* by which he had obtained these concessions could conceivably render them illegitimate in the eyes of anyone else. When it came to territorial aspirations, he made no distinction between adversaries and allies: what one had provided the other was expected to endorse. . . .

On the surface, this strategy succeeded. After strong initial objections, Roosevelt and Churchill did eventually acknowledge the Soviet Union's right to the expanded borders it claimed; they also made it clear that they would not oppose the installation of "friendly" governments in adjoining states. This meant accepting a Soviet sphere of influence from the Baltic to the Adriatic, a concession not easily reconciled with the Atlantic Charter. But the authors of that document saw no feasible way to avoid that outcome: military necessity required continued Soviet cooperation against the Germans. Nor were they themselves prepared to relinquish spheres of influence in Western Europe and the Mediterranean, the Middle East, Latin America, and East Asia. Self-determination was a sufficiently malleable concept that each of the Big Three could have endorsed, without sleepless nights, what the Soviet government had said about the Atlantic Charter: "practical application of these principles will necessarily adapt itself to the circumstances, needs, and historic peculiarities of particular countries."

That, though, was precisely the problem. For unlike Stalin, Roosevelt and Churchill would have to defend their decisions before domestic constituencies. The *manner* in which Soviet influence expanded was therefore, for them, of no small significance. Stalin showed little understanding of this. Having no experience himself with democratic procedures, he dismissed requests that he respect democratic proprieties. "[S]ome propaganda work should be done," he advised Roosevelt at the Tehran conference after the president had hinted that the American public would welcome a plebiscite in the Baltic States. "It is all nonsense!" Stalin complained to [Soviet Foreign Minister V. M.] Molotov. "[Roosevelt] is their military leader and commander in chief. Who would dare object to him?" When at Yalta F.D.R. stressed the need for the first Polish election to be as pure as "Caesar's wife," Stalin responded with a joke: "They said that about her, but in fact she had her sins." Molotov warned his boss, on that occasion, that the Americans' insistence on free elections elsewhere in Eastern Europe was "going too far." "Don't worry," he recalls Stalin as replying, "work it out. We can deal with it in our own way later. The point is the correlation of forces."

The Soviet leader was, in one sense, right. Military strength would determine what happened in that part of the world, not the enunciation of lofty principles. But unilateral methods carried long-term costs Stalin did not foresee: the most significant of these was to ruin whatever prospects existed for a Soviet sphere of influence the East Europeans themselves might have accepted. This possibility was not as far-fetched as it would later seem. . . . [Stalin] would, after all, approve such a compromise as the basis for a permanent settlement with Finland. He would initially allow free elections in Hungary, Czechoslovakia, and the Soviet occupation zone in Germany. He may even have *anticipated an enthusiastic response* as he took over Eastern Europe. "He was, I think, surprised and hurt," [W. Averell] Harriman [one of Roosevelt's closest advisors] recalled, "when the Red Army was not welcomed in all the neighboring countries as an army of liberation." "We still had our hopes," [Nikita] Khrushchev remembered, that "after the catastrophe of World War II, Europe, too, might become Soviet. Everyone would take the path from capitalism to socialism." It could be that there was another form of romanticism at work here, quite apart from Stalin's affinity for fellow authoritarians: that he was unrealistic enough to expect ideological solidarity and gratitude for liberation to override old fears of Russian expansionism as well as remaining manifestations of nationalism among the Soviet Union's neighbors, perhaps as easily as he himself had overridden the latter—or so it then appeared—within the multinational empire that was the Soviet Union itself.

If the Red Army could have been welcomed in Poland and the rest of the countries it liberated with the same enthusiasm American, British, and Free French forces encountered when they landed in Italy and France in 1943 and

1944, then some kind of Czech–Finnish compromise might have been feasible. Whatever Stalin's expectations, though, this did not happen. That non-event, in turn, removed any possibility of a division of Europe all members of the Grand Alliance could have endorsed. It ensured that an American sphere of influence would arise there largely by consent, but that its Soviet counterpart could sustain itself only by coercion. The resulting asymmetry would account, more than anything else, for the origins, escalation, and ultimate outcome of the Cold War.

❦

. . . It has long been clear that, in addition to having had an authoritarian vision, Stalin also had an imperial one, which he proceeded to implement in at least as single-minded a way [as the American]. No comparably influential builder of empire came close to wielding power for so long, or with such striking results, on the Western side.

It was, of course, a matter of some awkwardness that Stalin came out of a revolutionary movement that had vowed to smash, not just tsarist imperialism, but all forms of imperialism throughout the world. The Soviet leader constructed his own logic, though, and throughout his career he devoted a surprising amount of attention to showing how a revolution and an empire might coexist. . . .

Stalin's fusion of Marxist internationalism with tsarist imperialism could only reinforce his tendency, in place well before World War II, to equate the advance of world revolution with the expanding influence of the Soviet state. He applied that linkage quite impartially: a major benefit of the 1939 pact with Hitler had been that it regained territories lost as a result of the Bolshevik Revolution and the World War I settlement. But Stalin's conflation of imperialism with ideology also explains the importance he attached, following the German attack in 1941, to having his new Anglo-American allies confirm these arrangements. He had similar goals in East Asia when he insisted on bringing the Soviet Union back to the position Russia had occupied in Manchuria prior to the Russo-Japanese War: this he finally achieved at the 1945 Yalta Conference in return for promising to enter the war against Japan. "My task as minister of foreign affairs was to expand the borders of our Fatherland," Molotov recalled proudly many years later. "And it seems that Stalin and I coped with this task quite well." . . .

❦

From the West's standpoint, the critical question was how far Moscow's influence would extend *beyond* whatever Soviet frontiers turned out to be at the end of the war. Stalin had suggested to Milovan Djilas that the Soviet Union would impose its own social system as far as its armies could reach, but he was also very cautious. Keenly aware of the military power the United States and its allies had accumulated, Stalin was determined to do nothing that might involve the USSR in another devastating war until it had recovered sufficiently to be certain of winning it. "I do not wish to begin the Third World War over the Trieste question," he explained to disappointed Yugoslavs, whom he ordered to evacuate that territory in June 1945. Five years later, he would justify his decision not to intervene in the Korean War on the grounds that "the Second World War ended not long ago, and we are not ready for the Third World War." Just how far the expansion of Soviet influence would proceed depended, therefore, upon a careful balancing of opportunities against risks. . . .

Who or what was it, though, that set the limits? Did Stalin have a fixed list of countries he thought it necessary to dominate? Was he prepared to stop in the face of resistance within those countries to "squeezing out the capitalist order"? Or would expansion cease only when confronted with opposition from the remaining capitalist states, so that further advances risked war at a time when the Soviet Union was ill-prepared for it?

Stalin had been very precise about where he wanted Soviet boundaries changed; he was much less so on how far Moscow's sphere of influence was to extend. He insisted on having "friendly" countries around the periphery of the USSR, but he failed to specify how many would have to meet this standard. He called during the war for dismembering Germany, but by the end of it was denying that he had ever done so: that country would be temporarily divided, he told leading German communists in June 1945, and they themselves would eventually bring about its reunification. He never gave up on the idea of an eventual world revolution, but he expected this to result—as his comments to the Germans suggested—from an expansion of influence emanating from the Soviet Union itself. "[F]or the Kremlin," a well-placed spymaster recalled, "the mission of communism was primarily to consolidate the might of the Soviet state. Only military strength and domination of the countries on our borders could ensure us a superpower role."

But Stalin provided no indication—surely because he himself did not know—of how rapidly, or under what circumstances, this process would take place. He was certainly prepared to stop in the face of resistance from the West: at no point was he willing to challenge the Americans or even the British where they made their interests clear. . . . He quickly backed down when confronted with Anglo-American objections to his ambitions in Iran in the spring of 1946, as he did later that year after demanding Soviet bases in the Turkish Straits. This pattern of advance followed by retreat had shown up in the purges of the 1930s, which Stalin halted when the external threat from Germany became too great to ignore, and it would reappear with the Berlin Blockade and the Korean War, both situations in which the Soviet Union would show great caution after provoking an unexpectedly strong American response.

What all of this suggests, though, is not that Stalin had limited ambitions, only that he had no timetable for achieving them. Molotov retrospectively confirmed this: "Our ideology stands for offensive operations when possible, and if not, we wait." Given this combination of appetite with aversion to risk, one cannot help but wonder what would have happened had the West tried containment earlier. To the extent that it bears partial responsibility for the coming of the Cold War, the historian Vojtech Mastny has argued, that responsibility lies in its failure to do just that. . . .

Stalin's policy, then, was one of imperial expansion and consolidation differing from that of earlier empires only in the determination with which he pursued it, in the instruments of coercion with which he maintained it, and in the ostensibly anti-imperial justifications he put forward in support of it. It is a testimony to his skill, if not to his morality, that he was able to achieve so many of his imperial ambitions at a time when the tides of history were running against the idea of imperial domination—as colonial offices in London, Paris, Lisbon, and The Hague were finding out—and when his own country was recovering from one of the most brutal invasions in recorded history. The fact that Stalin was able to *expand* his empire when others were contracting and while the Soviet Union was as weak as it was, requires explanation. Why did opposition to this process, within and outside Europe, take so long to develop?

One reason was that the colossal sacrifices the Soviet Union had made during the war against the Axis had, in effect, "purified" its reputation: the USSR and its leader had "earned" the right to throw their weight around, or so it seemed. Western governments found it difficult to switch quickly from viewing the Soviet Union as a glorious wartime ally to portraying it as a new and dangerous adversary. President Harry S. Truman and his future Secretary of State Dean Acheson—neither of them sympathetic in the slightest to communism—nontheless tended to give the Soviet Union the benefit of the doubt well into the early postwar era. . . .

Resistance to Stalin's imperialism also developed slowly because Marxism–Leninism at the time had such widespread appeal. It is difficult now to recapture the admiration revolutionaries outside the Soviet Union felt for that country before they came to know it well. . . . Because the Bolsheviks themselves had overcome one empire and had made a career of condemning others, it would take decades for people who were struggling to overthrow British, French, Dutch, or Portuguese colonialism to see that there could also be such a thing as Soviet imperialism. European communists—notably the Yugoslavs—saw this much earlier, but even to most of them it had not been apparent at the end of the war.

Still another explanation for the initial lack of resistance to Soviet expansionism was the fact that its repressive character did not become immediately apparent to all who were subjected to it. . . .

One has the impression that Stalin and the Eastern Europeans got to know one another only gradually. The Kremlin leader was slow to recognize that Soviet authority would not be welcomed everywhere beyond Soviet borders; but as he did come to see this, he became all the more determined to impose it everywhere. The Eastern Europeans were slow to recognize how confining incorporation within a Soviet sphere was going to be; but as they did come to see this, they became all the more determined to resist it, even if only by withholding, in a passive but sullen manner, the consent any regime needs to establish itself by means other than coercion. Stalin's efforts to consolidate his empire therefore made it at once more repressive and less secure. Meanwhile, an alternative vision of postwar Europe was emerging from the other great empire that established itself in the wake of

World War II, that of the United States, and this too gave Stalin grounds for concern. . . .

⊷⧉⊶

What is there new to say about the old question of responsibility for the Cold War? Who actually started it? Could it have been averted? Here I think the "new" history is bringing us back to an old answer: that *as long as Stalin was running the Soviet Union, a cold war was unavoidable.*

History is always the product of determined and contingent events: it is up to historians to find the proper balance between them. The Cold War could hardly have happened if there had not been a United States and a Soviet Union, if both had not emerged victorious from World War II, if they had not had conflicting visions of how to organize the postwar world. But these long-term trends did not in themselves *ensure* such a contest, because there is always room for the unexpected to undo what might appear to be inevitable. *Nothing* is ever completely predetermined, as real triceratops and other dinosaurs discovered 65 million years ago when the most recent large asteroid or comet or whatever it was hit the earth and wiped them out.

Individuals, not asteroids, more often personify contingency in history. Who can specify in advance—or unravel afterwards—the particular intersection of genetics, environment, and culture that makes each person unique? Who can foresee what weird conjunctions of design and circumstance may cause a very few individuals to rise so high as to shape great events, and so come to the attention of historians? Such people may set their sights on getting to the top, but an assassin, or a bacillus, or even a carelessly driven taxicab can always be lurking along the way. How entire countries fall into the hands of malevolent geniuses like Hitler and Stalin remains as unfathomable in the "new" Cold War history as in the "old."

Once leaders like these do gain power, however, certain things become highly probable. It is only to be expected that in an authoritarian state the chief authoritarian's personality will weigh much more heavily than those of democratic leaders, who have to share power. And whether because of social alienation, technological innovation, or economic desperation, the first half of the twentieth century was particularly susceptible to great authoritarians and all that resulted from their ascendancy. It is hardly possible to imagine Nazi Germany or the world war it caused without Hitler. I find it increasingly difficult, given what we know now, to imagine the Soviet Union or the Cold War without Stalin.

For the more we learn, the less sense it makes to distinguish Stalin's foreign policies from his domestic practices or even his personal behavior. Scientists have shown the natural world to be filled with examples of what they call "self-similarity across scale": patterns that persist whether one views them microscopically, macroscopically, or anywhere in between. Stalin was like that: he functioned in much the same manner whether operating within the international system, within his alliances, within his country, within his party, within his personal entourage, or even within his family. The Soviet leader waged cold wars on all of these fronts. The Cold War we came to know was only one of many from *his* point of view.

Nor did Stalin's influence diminish as quickly as that of most dictators after their deaths. He built a *system* sufficiently durable to survive not only his own demise but his successors' fitful and half-hearted efforts at "de-Stalinization." They were themselves its creatures, and they continued to work within it because they knew no other method of governing. Not until [Mikhail] Gorbachev was a Soviet leader fully prepared to dismantle Stalin's structural legacy. It tells us a lot that as it disappeared, so too did the Cold War and ultimately the Soviet Union itself.

This argument by no means absolves the United States and its allies of a considerable responsibility for how the Cold War was fought—hardly a surprising conclusion since they in fact won it. Nor is it to deny the feckless stupidity with which the Americans fell into peripheral conflicts like Vietnam, or their exorbitant expenditures on unusable weaponry: these certainly caused the Cold War to cost much more in money and lives than it otherwise might have. Nor is it to claim moral superiority for Western statesmen. None was as bad as Stalin—or Mao—but the Cold War left no leader uncorrupted: the wielding of great power, even in the best of times, rarely does.

It is the case, though, that if one applies the always useful test of counterfactual history—drop a key variable and speculate as to what difference this might have made—Stalin's centrality to the origins of the Cold War becomes quite clear. For all of their importance, one could have removed Roosevelt, Churchill, Truman, Bevin, Marshall, or Acheson, and a cold war would still have probably followed the world war. If one could have eliminated Stalin, alternative paths become quite conceivable. For with the possible exception of Mao, no twentieth-century leader imprinted himself upon his country as thoroughly and with such lasting effect as Stalin did. And given his personal propensity for cold wars—a tendency firmly rooted long before he had even heard of Harry Truman—once Stalin wound up at the top in Moscow and once it was clear his state would survive the war, then it looks equally clear that there was going to be a Cold War whatever the west did. Who then was responsible? The answer, I think, is authoritarianism in general, and Stalin in particular.

POSTSCRIPT

Was President Truman Responsible for the Cold War?

Offner takes issue with President Truman's recent biographers, Robert H. Ferrell, *Harry S. Truman: A Life* (University of Missouri Press, 1994); Alonzo L. Hamby, *Man of the People: A Life of Harry S. Truman* (Oxford, 1995); and especially David McCullough's bestseller, *Truman* (Simon & Schuster, 1992), all of whom rank Truman among the near-great presidents. All of the most recent polls of presidents place Truman among the ten greatest. Offner calls Truman a "parochial nationalist." His outlook on foreign policy was ethnocentric in spite of his command in combat in a Missouri national guard unit in World War One. He deplored Europe's politics, customs and food. In his early writings, he expressed disdain for "chinks," "dagos," "niggers," "Jew clerks," "bohunks" and "Rooshans."

Brash and impulsive in temperament, Offner accuses Truman of making rash and quick decisions to cover over his insecurities. Truman, he says, often relied on strong personalities such as Boss Tom Pendergast, who pushed Truman up the ladder of Missouri politics and General George Marshall and career diplomat Dean Acheson among others who helped formulate "the containment policy" in 1946 to prevent the Russians from imposing an iron curtain around all of Europe.

Offner also charges the Truman administration of practicing "Atomic diplomacy" at the end of the war, when we were the sole possessor of the A-bomb, to make the Russians more manageable in Europe. He also argues that the Truman doctrine, the Marshall plan, refusing to compromise on the German questions, and the formation of the North Atlantic Treaty Organization (NATO) run roughshod over a country who suffered many more military losses and severe damage to its economy and physical infrastructure.

In his attempt to place most of the blame for the cold war on Truman, Offner overstates his case. He calls Truman a parochial nationalist, yet the former President, though not formerly educated, read widely biographies of great leaders and military history. He also, as Offner admits, performed heroically as an officer in a Missouri national guard unit in combat and as a United States Senator supported FDR's foreign policy "on the World Court, neutrality revision, rearmament and Lend Lease for Britain and Russian before America's Entrance into World War Two."

Offner also downplays the uncertainties facing American foreign policy at the end of the war. For example, FDR had hoped that a revised international organization such as the United Nations might succeed in preventing future world wars because it would be stronger and supported by the major powers than the failed League of Nations.

Offner plays up Truman's insecurities which was true, but then accuses him of making both rash decisions and relying on strong foreign policy advisers such as George Kennan, George Marshall, and Dean Acheson. But why wouldn't Truman be insecure? He was chosen as vice president in 1944 to replace the controversial Henry Wallace because he came from Missouri, a border state that made him acceptable to southern conservative democrats, yet with a voting record that supported FDR's New Deal liberal domestic programs.

When he became president after Roosevelt's sudden death on April 12, 1945, Truman knew very little of the intricacies of Roosevelt's agreements with Churchill and Stalin. In fact, both Henry Stimson, the Secretary of Defense and Senator James Byrnes both claim to have informed Truman about the "Manhattan Project's" development of atomic bombs which would be ready for use in the summer of 1945.

Professor John Gaddis accepts the fact that Truman was insecure. He also believes that for all of 1945 up to early 1946, the Truman administration was responding to the political and economic uncertainties of the post-World War Two environment. While the United States took the lead in creating the World Bank and the International Monetary Fund to supply money for rebuilding Europe's destroyed infrastructure, these institutions were woefully inadequate to the task. It was also unclear whether the United States was going to re-enter its own recession as had occurred at the end of the First World War which turned into the great depression of the 1930s.

Gaddis believes that the United States created its Western European empire by invitation through the implementation of the Truman Doctrine, the Marshall Plan, the rebuilding of West Germany, and the formation of NATO. On the other hand, Russia created its empire by force. Starting in Romania in 1945 and in Poland and Hungary in 1947 and ending with the murder or suicide of the Masuryk government in Czechoslovakia in 1948, the Russians imposed totalitarian governments on its citizens.

Gaddis places most of the blame for the cold war on Stalin, an authoritarian imperialist who "equated world revolution with the expanding influence of the Soviet state." Truman was constrained by the democratic electoral system of checks and balances and a Republican-controlled Congress from 1946 to 1948. But Stalin had no such constraints. He purged all his real and potential revolutionary opponents in the 1930s and also the late 1940s and pursued foreign policy objectives as a romantic revolutionary. What limits did Stalin have? Gaddis said Stalin was precisely where he wanted Soviet boundaries changed but was imprecise about how far Moscow's sphere of influence would extend without confronting Western resistance.

In summary, if Gorbachev was the Soviet leader in 1945, there may have been alternate paths to the cold war. But with Stalin in charge, says Gaddis, "there was going to be a cold war whatever the West did."

Gaddis' interpretation goes too far in blaming most of the cold war on Stalin. He argues that new sources from the former USSR and the Eastern European countries demonstrate the control that Stalin exerted. But as Tony Judt points out, these sources are quite limited and they do not tell us about the operations of the Politburo and the twelve men who along with Stalin made decisions. See Tony Judt, "Why the Cold War Worked," *The New York Review of Books* (October 9, 1997) and "A Story Still to be Told," *The New York Review of Books* (March 23, 2006) for critical reviews of Gaddis' *We Now Know: Rethinking Cold War History* (Oxford University Press, 1997) and *The Cold War: A New History* (Penguin Press, 2005). The best critiques of Gaddis are three of his earlier books, *The United States and the Origins of the Cold War, 1941–1947* (Columbia University Press, 1972); *Russia, the Soviet Union and the United States: An Interpretative History*, 2nd ed. (McGraw Hill, 1990); and *Strategies of Containment: A Critical Appraisal of America's Postwar Foreign Policy* (Oxford, 1978).

The literature on the cold war is enormous. Students who wish to study the cold war in greater detail should consult *Containment: Documents on American Policy and Strategy, 1945–1950* edited by Thomas H. Etzold and John Lewis Gaddis (Columbia University Press, 1978). Another comprehensive work is Melvyn P. Leffler, *A Preponderance of Power: National Security, the Truman Administration, and the Cold War* (Stanford University Press, 1992). The two best readers to excerpt the various viewpoints on the cold war are Thomas G. Paterson and Robert J. McMahon, eds., *The Origins of the Cold War,* 3rd ed. (D. C. Heath, 1991) and Melvyn P. Leffler and David S. Painter, eds., *Origins of the Cold War: An International History* (Routledge, 1994). Finally David Reynolds has edited a series of essays in *The Origins of the Cold War: International Perspectives* (Yale University Press, 1994).

Bibliographies are contained in all the previous books. The most up-to-date is Melvin P. Leffler, "Cold War and Global Hegemony, 1945–1991," *OAH Magazine of History* (March 2005). Gaddis' argument with the revisionists is nicely summarized in Karen J. Winkler, "Scholars Refight the Cold War," *The Chronicle of Higher Education* (March 2, 1994), pp. 8–10.

ISSUE 14

Was Rock and Roll Responsible for Dismantling America's Traditional Family, Sexual, and Racial Customs in the 1950s and 1960s?

YES: Jody Pennington, from "Don't Knock the Rock: Race, Business, and Society in the Rise of Rock and Roll," in Dale Carter, ed., *Cracking the Ike Age: Aspects of Fifties America* (Aarhus University Press, 1992)

NO: J. Ronald Oakley, from *God's Country: America in the Fifties* (Dembner Books, 1986, 1990)

ISSUE SUMMARY

YES: Professor Jody Pennington believes that the emergence of rock and roll in the 1950s along with new forms of consumerism expressed "the inner conflict between conservative and rebellious forces for high school teenagers who wanted to rebel against their parents yet still grow up to be them."

NO: Writer J. Ronald Oakley argues that although the lifestyles of youth departed from their parents, their basic ideas and attitudes were still the conservative ones that mirrored the conservativism of the affluent age in which they grew up.

Most Americans assume that rock and roll has dominated American popular music since the 1950s, but this is not true. The phrase "rhythm and blues" was coined by the first white rock and roll Cleveland disc jockey Alan Freed who, when he went national, was pushed by a lawsuit in 1954 to abandon the name of his show from "The Moondog House" to "Rock 'n' Roll Party." A black euphemism for sexual intercourse, "rock 'n' roll" had appeared as early as 1922 in a blues song and was constantly used by black singers into the early 1950s. It's not clear whether DJ Freed consciously made the name change to cultivate a broader audience, but that is precisely what happened.

Rock and roll was a fashion of rhythm and blues, black gospel, and country-western music. It combined black and white music, which explains why so many of the early rock singers came from the south and recorded their hit songs in New Orleans or Memphis. Between 1953 and 1955, the first true rockers—Fats

Domino, Chuck Berry, and Little Richard—were African-American. Fats Domino came from New Orleans, sang from his piano, and sold over 65 million records between 1949 and 1960, including "Ain't That a Shame," "I'm Walking," and "Blueberry Hill." Even more influential because of his electric guitar riffs, body and leg gyrations, and songs full of wit and clever wordplay was Chuck Berry, whose lifestyle (he did two stints in prison) and songs ("Maybellene," "Johnny B. Good," and "Roll Over Beethoven") influenced two generations of rockers, including sixties British rock bands the Beatles and the Rolling Stones. Another rocker, Little Richard, known as "the Georgia Peach," became famous as much for his flamboyant style of dress with his towering hair and multicolored clothes that reflected a teasing sexuality. He created a string of hits—"Tutti Frutti," "Long Tall Sally," and "Good Golly Miss Molly"—which were recorded as cover records by white artists like Pat Boone. Little Richard scared the hell out of the parents from white middle-class America.

More threatening to middle-class white American parents was Elvis Presley, the king of rock and roll, and the most influential pop icon in the history of America, but Elvis was not the inventor of rock and roll. His voice was average, and his songs (written by others) were often mediocre. But his rugged good looks and his sexy gyrations on the stage threw young girls into spasms. Most importantly, he was white. More than 30 years after his death, Elvis still defines the age of rock and roll. He continues to sell records, which number over a billion.

Presley was the first star to take advantage of the new teenage consumer market. By the middle 1950s there were 16.5 million teenagers, half in high school and the other half in college or the work force, who possessed a lot of disposable income, available via allowances or part-time jobs. Suburban teenagers had their own rooms replete with radios and record players. "By the end of 1957," says Professor Altschuler, "seventy-eight Elvis Presley items had grossed $55 million."

There is little argument that a new generation of teenagers had emerged in the fifties. Historians can trace the adolescent generations to the early twentieth century. The gap between parent and child always existed, but the new value system that set apart the two generations might have occurred earlier had the great depression and World War II not intervened. Television shows were geared to the very young and the parents. Radio had lost its nightly sitcoms to television and switched to news and music formats. Teenagers were tired of croon and woon ballads that did not address their feelings. New DJs emerged, who played the rock and roll songs for teenagers who sat in their rooms pretending to do their homework.

Was rock and roll responsible for the revolution in values that took place in the 1960s? Professor Jody Pennington believes that the emergence of rock and roll in the 1950s along with new forms of consumerism expressed "the inner conflict between conservative and rebellious forces for high school teenagers who wanted to rebel against their parents yet still grow up to be them." J. Ronald Oakley disagrees. "Although their lifestyle had departed from the conventions of their elders," Oakley believes "their basic ideas and attitudes were still the conservative ones that mirrored the conservativism of the affluent age in which they grew up."

Jody Pennington

Don't Knock the Rock: Race, Business, and Society in the Rise of Rock and Roll

Forty Miles of Bad Road

From the beginning, rock 'n' roll was geared for movement, for dancing: it sounded best in a car, cruising down the highway or cutting down the boulevard. You could buy the record and play it at home above the din of parents yelling 'turn that crap down!' or 'you call that music?' But that was never the same as hearing it suddenly on the car radio (even if for the tenth time in the same day) when some cool disc jockey dropped the needle in the groove. The music was everywhere: blaring out of every apartment, a radio in every car, turned on all the time. In 1956, the year rock 'n' roll peaked, it was the perfect accompaniment for bombing around in a '49 Ford or a new '55 Chevy: raked and flamed, decked and lowered, chopped and channeled with fins and tails on a Saturday night; burning rubber zero to sixty to the first red light and then on to the next, looking for another chump with overhead cams, a 4.56 rear end to cut out.

Cars and kids came together in the 1950s, and rock 'n' roll was best man at the wedding. This was the latest generation of American Huck Finns running from routine and convention. Their rivers were the roads, highways, boulevards, avenues, and streets of America's big cities and small towns. Their rafts were their cars, and their Nigger Jim was the latest hit on the radio. The night was all beginning and without end.

Mobility meant escape: from the rigidity of home, from high school, from authority. Suburban mothers abhorred deviant behavior in their children and had little patience with wild rock 'n' rollers who threatened their own interests or the creeds and symbols they cherished. Dad wanted stability and order on the home front so he could go about his daily bread-winning tasks. Parents restrained their kids with 'restriction', a form of Levittown house arrest meant to quash any interest in music, dancing, motorcycles, souped-up cars, violence, and sex.

Rock 'n' roll reflected the interests and needs of its young public; it moved them. This raucous new music appeared in young people's lives at the crucial

From *Cracking the Ike Age: Aspects of Fifties America* by Dale Carter (Aarhus University Press, 1992), pp. 214–215, 216–219, 221–228, 229–230, 231, 232–233. Copyright © 1992 by Jody Pennington. Reprinted by permission of Jody Pennington and Aarhus University Press.

intersection of the dependency of puberty and the autonomy of the post-teen years. To millions at this age, sitting with the family around the tube watching Milton Berle or Sid Caesar was a drag. Instead they kept to themselves in their own rooms, listening to the hi-fi or radio, with posters of Little Richard, Elvis, and Buddy Holly on the wall; or they went to concerts or dated or hung out with friends at diners and juke joints. Whatever they did, they got away from parents; wherever they went, rock 'n' roll was there: reinforcing and enhancing the sensation of independence. Mom and Dad stayed home, secure in their own opinions, values, and standards of conduct. They knew bikers, greasers, and rock 'n' rollers who flouted them were ignorant or wicked.

The attitudes embodied by the music were rebellious and provocative. That in itself was nothing new. Jitterbuggers in the 1930s had had their music labeled 'syncopated savagery'. Now as parents, twenty years later, these former savages were shocked at how seriously their offspring took rock 'n' roll. Parents saw in rock 'n' roll a destructive force, not just a symptom of awkward adolescence. Partly because the kids of the postwar era had wealth like none before them, however, the generational conflict sharpened as never before. As Greil Marcus would later write: 'it's a sad fact that most of those over thirty cannot be a part of it [rock 'n' roll], and it cannot be a part of them.' Who, then, were these parents, these over-thirty enemies of rock 'n' roll?

Squaresville

Following their victory over fascist Germany and Japan, returning vets felt like national heroes. It was now time to earn a little money, have a family, and prosper. Commuting along the paved highways of the golden fifties in MG-TCs, ex-GIs basked perkily in the suburban afterglow of battlefield heroism. The world was theirs for the conquering: a promotion here, a new house there; a barbecue grill, 2.5 kids who would some day go to college, a wife at home enjoying—or enduring—what Betty Friedan would later call the feminine mystique. Heroes made good neighbors: conservative, a bit artificial, and stiff. Jumpy at the mention of Alger Hiss and Whittaker Chambers, communist spies and Congressional committees, good Americans wore loyalty oaths on their sleeves . . .

High school: educational institution and model of life. A world all its own, filled with pep rallies and glee clubs, dress codes and demerits, school papers and assembly programs, field trips and drill teams; a complex of hall passes and phi-deltas, cheerleaders and team spirit, Big-Man-on-Campus and jocks, clicks and outsiders; a realm where one dressed for success in letter jackets, chinos, and penny loafers. Students were groomed to compete in the toughest of schools: popularity. You were either neat or gross, peachy keen or spastic. Lose in this game and you were a creep, a turkey, a *nothing*.

In many small towns and city neighborhoods, school was the focus of students' social lives. They were whipped into enthusiastic abandon by the marching band and wooed by the majorettes at the Friday night football games in the fall under stadium lights or wowed by the cheerleaders at basketball games. There were hockey games, track meets, and the wrestling team, as well as a plethora of cultural activities, from car washes and banquets to brownie sells and parades. To cap it off there were the high school balls: Homecoming, the sock hops, and the Senior Prom, the culmination of four exciting, memorable years. Amidst all this there was still time for classes. Governed by the conservative norms and mores of the middle class, these were simulations of 'real life' designed to transfigure zitty-faced kids into government or company employees, replicas of what William H. Whyte's 1956 volume dubbed *The Organization Man*. Character was molded by disciplinary measures like restrictions and demerits, but the emphasis was always on the individual. American high schools in the 1950s churned out good citizens: members of the Key Club or the Beta Club, trained in the habits of good citizenship; good employees: members of VICA, prepared to enter the world of work, or DECCA, the future marketing leaders of America; and good wives: members of the Future Home-makers of America, a credit to their sex. Still bolstered by the legacy of McCarthyism, moreover, schools had little problem dishing out their version of the 'American Way'. More than any other age-group, teenagers felt under pressure to conform and to become achievers in a society preoccupied with belonging and success.

Off campus, teenagers were flooded with enticements to consume. If they turned on the television or the radio, flipped through a magazine, or went to the movies, they found themselves barraged with endless images of a stimulating world, one which appeared as the virtual antithesis of high school's drab halls, lockers, and desks. Hedonism beckoned, and teenagers from middle-class families responded with indulgence: girls filled their hope chests with the basics for a good marriage; boys filled the tanks of their cars. They bought radios, cameras, hoola-hoops, frisbees, pogo sticks, television sets, swim suits, clothes, i.d. bracelets, deo, 'greasy kid stuff—anything that brought them pleasure.

Rock 'n' roll hit this world like a bomb. The ultimate safety valve, the ultimate escape for anyone destined for a nine-to-five office job, it was music for the moment (it barely lasted longer). For two or three minutes anybody could be a rebel: speed the car up, hang an arm out the window, cop an attitude, moon a cop, *anything*. The best tracks could obliterate time, creating a world you could vanish into, lose yourself in, and then return from with the help of the disc jockey's patter. Maybe the nine-to-five world could serve as a means to an end: consumption. But it couldn't give life a purpose.

Rock 'n' roll fit perfectly into the conflict between the new patterns of the consumer society and the traditional Puritan work ethic of abstinence and industriousness. For these well-to-do teenagers the day was divided between the two worlds: in the classroom teachers propagated the traditional values; in their free time teenagers lived a life of impulse shopping. Just as the stop-and-jerk pace of Chuck Berry's 'Sweet Little Sixteen' swings the young girl from pretty young wild thing to Daddy's little girl, so their lives oscillated between obedience and indulgence. Through the works of writers like Jerry Leiber and Mike Stoller (who wrote 'Hound Dog' and 'Jailhouse Rock' for Elvis Presley, and all the Coasters' hits); Felice and Boudleaux Bryant (who penned hits for the Everly Brothers); and especially rock 'n' roll poet laureate Chuck Berry, rock 'n' roll spoke to these teenagers: it dealt with their problems and frustrations, their dancing and dates, their likes, dislikes, and obsessions.

That'll Be the Day

As much medium as message, rock 'n' roll was one of the first strokes of cultural self-awareness to blossom in the 1950s. Maybe the lyrics were sometimes as trite or nonsensical as Tin Pan Alley's, maybe white kids had problems understanding the singing, but rock 'n' roll—with its solid backbeat and driving eighth-note rhythm—fit the pace and rhythm of a world which had grown modern during the war and which was now coming to grips with its modernity: coast-to-coast broadcasts, transatlantic jet flights, super highways, fast cars, transistors, the Bomb, roller derbies, instant coffee, Sputnik, desegregation, *Playboy*, the rat race, frisbees, and Sugar Ray Robinson. Let Mom and Pop Suburbia condemn the noise and the meaningless babble, let them fox-trot and cha-cha to Frank Sinatra and Rosemary Clooney: what a slow burn! For Junior, it was slow dancing with a rise in his Levis and a tale to take back to the guys: get much?

From the start rock 'n' roll had its prophets of doom: 'it'll never last' went the wisdom of schmaltz, and it seemed sound enough. This was, after all, *Leave it to Beaver-land*: fads came, fads went. In fact, rock 'n' roll never dominated the charts or musical tastes. As Charlie Gillet points out in *The Sound of the City*, even during its heyday 'from 1955 through 1959, just under half of the top ten hits . . . could be classified as rock 'n' roll'. During those years, according to Serge Denisoff, rock 'n' roll 'did not constitute all of popular music, and even in the heyday of Elvis Presley not all teenagers were into his music, as many rock histories seem to imply'. Nonetheless rock 'n' roll endured. It was exclusive and well-guarded, with a strong sense of awareness that the music was something special; it was almost elitist in its sense of being reserved for those hip enough to *dig it*. Rock 'n' roll was a fever, a craze; and a lot of kids in the 1950s were on the edge of a fighting mood: 'Your ass is grass! Get bent! You're cruisin' for a bruisin'! Don't give me any grief.' Rock 'n' roll caught the mood—'Blue Suede Shoes', 'That'll Be the Day', 'Too Much Monkey Business', 'Hound Dog', 'Rip it Up'. Chuck Berry summed up the new generation's disdain for the older: 'Roll Over Beethoven.'

Rock 'n' roll alone did not induce the new teenage behavioral patterns in the 1950s. Prosperity, new forms of distribution, the portable radio, and television made their presence felt. Still, something in the music sparked fires where cinders glowed. Rock 'n' roll was the matrix inside which middle-class teenagers played out fantasies of rebellion within the context of family, home, and future career. With rock 'n' roll's distribution through radio, television, and film, these kids became the standard image of teenagers' lives and values for the entire social spectrum. With the appearance of Elvis, *they*—white, American, middle-class teenagers—could dream of performing the music as well. Elvis expressed the inner conflict between conservative and rebellious forces for high school teenagers who wanted to rebel against their parents yet still grow up to be them.

Graceland

If rock 'n' roll was the dominant music of white teenagers during the second half of the 1950s, then the key was the King: Elvis Presley. An outsider and a success, he summed up and incarnated the contradictions of the teenager's world. He was one of them: white and young. He had rejected the adult world and sneered his way to the pinnacle of stardom. Elvis not only got the Cadillac; Elvis was bigger and better than a Cadillac. In his music, in his stage act, in his voice, he demanded—and got—respect. As Peter Wicke puts it, he 'embodied the uncertain and consuming desire of American high school teenagers in the fifties, the desire somehow to escape the oppressive ordinariness which surrounded them without having to pay the bitter price of conformity. His quick success seemed to be the proof that, in principle, escape was possible'.

For parents and high school principals in an era when these words still meant something, Elvis Presley was sinful and wicked. He set a bad example. He was a hood, with his long sideburns, ducktail haircut, and curled upper lip. His blatant sexuality, aggressiveness, and bumping and grinding troubled adults. Inside the music industry, though, Elvis was King. From late April 1956, when 'Heartbreak Hotel' dethroned Nelson Riddle's 'Lisbon Antigua' and Les Baxter's 'The Poor People of Paris' at the top of the charts (remaining there for eight weeks), to his late March 1958 induction into the U.S. Army, Elvis ruled the hit parade. He had the number one single in no less than fifty-five out of one hundred and four weeks: 'I Want You, I Need You, I Love You'; 'Don't Be Cruel' and 'Hound Dog' (eleven weeks at number one); 'Love Me Tender' (five weeks); 'Too Much' (three weeks); 'All Shook Up' (nine weeks); 'Teddy Bear' and 'Jailhouse Rock' (seven weeks); and 'Don't' (five weeks).

Although his manager, 'Colonel' Tom Parker, and his record label, RCA, orchestrated his ascent to the top of the pop world, Elvis himself ultimately deserves credit. He had the charisma, the style, the personality, the voice, and (in contrast to Jerry Lee Lewis, who still hasn't lost his rough edges) he could adapt. Elvis had it all. As Greil Marcus would write: 'The version of the American dream that is Elvis's performance is blown up again and again, to contain more history, more people, more music, more hopes; the air gets thin but the bubble does not burst, nor will it ever. This is America when it has outstripped itself, in all of its extravagance.' . . .

The poverty and rural attitudes that were a part of life in the postwar South influenced the course of rock 'n' roll's development. Although the population of the Deep South had shifted during the twentieth century from ninety per cent rural to more than fifty per cent urban, transplanted bumpkins like the Presleys, who had themselves only recently moved to Memphis from Tupelo, Mississippi, stayed 'country'. They did so, moreover, in spite of an increase in their standard of living. (The New Deal and World War Two had been important stimuli to economic growth in the South, but by the 1950s the region's average per capita income was still only half that of the national average). Like country truck driver Elvis, rock 'n' roll reflected this migration from the farm to the city. Elvis's first single had a blues number on the A-side and a country song on the flip side. Bill Haley had his roots in Texas and Oklahoma country swing in the tradition of Bob Wills. Jerry Lee (as well as Elvis and the other Sun label stars) had his roots in country swing and white gospel. The Everly Brothers had theirs in bluegrass and the country duet singing of Charlie and Ira Louvin and the Delmore Brothers.

Both the R&B and the country elements of rock 'n' roll have origins in the folk music traditions of the outsiders and outcasts of twentieth century America: on the one hand, the African-Americans who picked the cotton; on the other, the so-called 'white trash' who worked it through the cotton mills. The folk blues, typically in a first-person voice, express the experience of African-Americans living in the South during the first half of the twentieth century. The vocabulary is minimal and filled with images of traveling and country roads, field workers and prisoners. Although the dialect and diction are slightly different, the lyrics of country music deal with the realities of rural and city life in the South and the West, again in simple, straightforward language that incorporates the colloquialisms of these regions. Images of truck stops and sunsets, honky-tonks and fields, gamblers and drinkers, cheating and working tell the sentimental stories of taxing, emotional circumstances. The lyrics, sentiments, and, frequently, religious undertones common to both country blues and country and western reflected the inanity of segregation: Southerners of any race had more in common with each other than with anyone from other regions of the USA. Both forms feature expressive vocals: on the one hand, the sharp, nasal sound of country; on the other, the minor pentatonic sound of the blues. An original American sound was heard in the meeting of the two: first in minstrels and then in the songs of Stephen Foster, who was influenced not only by the minstrels but by the music of the African-American churches as well. Generations later, rock 'n' roll would emerge as a sort of electrified Stephen Foster in the unlikely form of Bill Haley.

Although both blues and country had long been commercialized when they merged in the guise of rock 'n' roll, Decca was taking a chance on Haley. And while the label enjoyed great success—at his first session with Decca, Haley recorded both 'Rock Around the Clock' and 'Shake, Rattle and Roll'—taking chances was not the norm for the majors. Their standard operating procedure had long been to chum out 'cover versions' of songs that had already been recorded by someone else. In the 1950s, however, the majors gave cover versions a new twist. Just as in the 1920s Paul Whiteman's orchestra had set out, in his words, to 'make a lady' if hot jazz, so thirty years later the industry recast R&B in an all-white form: performed by whites (such as Steve Lawrence, Andy Williams, Pat Boone, or the Fontane Sisters), recorded by whites, sold by whites, bought by whites, and profited form by whites. (Otherwise rejecting African-American music, the majors would at best record socalled 'black sepias' like Nat King Cole, who appealed to the white mainstream with sentimental, melodramatic crooning.)

As part of this tactic, the majors thus recorded white artists covering R&B tunes originally cut by African-American artists for the independent lablels or 'indies'. These white versions were arranged and perfomed to sound like banal pop music, with a unique beat but always in a simple 'sing-along' form that would be music to white ears. Working on assumptions derived from European classical music traditions, producers like Mitch Miller considered their cover versions to be an improvement on the originals, which they thought sounded like primitive jungle music: harsh, low-down, and dirty. Such assumptions were broadly shared by the white record-buying public. In mainstream America,

Bill Haley was thought of as having introduced a new music, a new rhythm; hardly anyone bothered to mention that 'his sound came from the music of the black population, a people whose "great sense of rhythm" had always been admired, but who, white America insisted, otherwise had nothing non-physical to contribute'.

A Choice of Colors

Cultural interaction between African-Americans and the white majority was never strictly a matter of black *or* white. An irreducible component of South-ern culture was the mutual influence of the races upon one another. At shows in towns like Macon, Georgia, white kids would sneak in (behind the backs of their parents and white authorities) and slip upstairs to see the African-American kids down on the floor. At first, the white kids would just sit and watch. In the end, however, they were bound to come down and dance. When some young white performers—like Jerry Lee Lewis, sneaking into the 'nigra' clubs in Ferriday, Louisiana, with his cousin Jimmy Lee Swaggart to hear artists like B.B. King—took the music at face value, they helped transform popular music and thereby American youth culture.

Sometimes these Southern rockers covered R&B hits, but more often they brought elements of R&B into their own tunes. Instead of adapting African-American styles to white tastes, they tried to imitate the originals as closely as they could, as when Elvis covered Big Mama Thornton's 'Hound Dog'. Perhaps the swing disappeared in these white attempts at R&B: simplified in rock 'n' roll to a more rigid, basic rhythm under the influence of Hank Williams and the hard-driving style of country pickers like Merle Travis, Joe Maphis, and James Burton. Still, rock 'n' roll was noisy and aggressive because these musicians had been singing and playing that way all along. The rock 'n' roll played by their native sons, rockabilly, frightened white Southerners most. Long in touch with African-American music, these musicians had sufficient spirit to sell records in the R&B, country, and pop markets. Since they were white, moreover, they could get away with it to such a degree that by 1956 even genuine R&B records started to gain acceptance in the mainstream pop market, much to the horror of many white Southerners.

It was no surprise, therefore, that 'the most extreme and bizarre expres-sions of antagonism towards rock 'n' roll tended to take place in the South. In April 1956, the *New York Times* reported several attempts by white Southern church groups to have rock 'n' roll suppressed. The whole movement towards rock 'n' roll, the church groups revealed, was part of a plot by the NAACP to corrupt white Southern youth'. A stepchild of R&B, the music was known dis-missively in the South during those years as 'nigger music'. Rock 'n' roll was music played by and for *niggers* (African-American or white): Little Richard, Fats Domino, and Chuck Berry; Elvis Presley, Jerry Lee Lewis, Carl Perkins, and Buddy Holly. Renegade rednecks in the best Southern tradition, the white rock 'n' rollers were the very stuff of Southern nightmares. For although white Southerners deemed African-Americans rarely capable of attaining the same level of rectitude, white descent into blackness had to be averted. For decades

Southern whites had drawn arms against an unseen enemy, evincing a distrust of both mulattoes (who *looked* white) and whites who behaved 'black'. Whites who, like the Southern rock 'n' rollers, strayed too close to African-Americans were known as 'white niggers': genetically white but 'black' in their behavior. The music they played, rock 'n' roll, which sounded like R&B, was the 'jungle music' of burr–heads, blue–skins, tar-pots, spies, jigaboos, darkies, and shines.

The white South's image of African-Americans in the 1950s was much as it had been since the turn of the century. Generations had grown up believing Booker T. Washington to have spoken for all African-Americans and spoken the truth: that they were content to 'cast down their buckets' where they were, chop cotton, lay rails, and work, work, work until Saturday night. By the 1950s, Booker T. was long dead, but in white minds Sambo continued to shuffle contentedly along, bucket in hand. Even while insisting that 'our Nigras are good Nigras', white Southerners had nonetheless devised dogmas and institutions that assured the greatest possible distance between the races. Known collectively as Jim Crow, these had consisted of both legal and extralegal means designed to keep African-Americans in their place and to compel them to behave 'properly' in the presence of whites. The legal measures—the poll tax, stiff residency requirements, literacy tests, and 'grandfather clauses'—kept African-Americans away from the polls and thus ensured the stability of a caste system which governed all aspects of African-American life. Extralegal steps helped guarantee the invisibility of most African-Americans and made those who were visible the Sambos whites needed to see: gullible children in grown-up bodies who slapped their knees, jumped, and turned, and whom whites could allow to run free within their own world without constant guidance after work on Saturday—as long as they showed up at work on Monday morning.

The white South's ability to sustain the system was, of course, challenged on a city bus in Montgomery, Alabama, on 1 December 1955, when Rosa Parks refused to yield her seat to a white man. Although it took years to secure its greatest gains (after Montgomery there was a lull), with Martin Luther King, Jr. more than rising to the occasion the civil rights movement was in the ascendant.

From the Station to the Train

By the time of the civil rights movement, another movement, primarily geographical and cultural rather than social and political, had long since begun: the exodus of millions of African-Americans from the countryside to the nation's cities. Prompted partly by the decline and subsequent mechanization of Southern agriculture, partly by the attraction of often military-spawned jobs, and partly by the dream of a better life beyond Jim Crow, this vast folk migration took hundreds of thousands to Northern industrial cities like New York, Chicago, and Detroit and, to a lesser degree, Southern cities like Memphis and New Orleans. Between 1860 and 1960 the African-American share of the total Southern population dwindled from almost fifty per cent to twenty-nine per cent.

Musical forms born and raised in the South—the blues, jazz, gospel, R&B, and soul—also traveled. On the road, gospel waited alongside the blues in bus depots; jazz and R&B rode together on trains. The movement to the cities helped turn the blue note electric, and African-American radio stations pumped it out. By the early 1950s, R&B stations dotted the urban landscape. Fans had only to turn their tuning knobs to hear the dance blues of singers like Amos Milburn, Roy Brown, Fats Domino, and Lloyd Price, and the 'hot' style of disc jockeys like Hamp Swain in Macon, Georgia, Zenas 'Big Daddy' Sears and 'Jockey Jack' Gibson in Atlanta, and 'Sugar Daddy' in Birmingham. Meanwhile, Alan Freed at WINS in New York set a precedent for white disc jockeys playing R&B; those who followed his lead included Al Benson in Chicago, Hunter Hancock in Los Angeles, and 'Poppa Stoppa' in New Orleans.

These and other artists and disc jockeys gave a voice to a nation of wanderers looking for home: a tricky concept, as James Brown once pointed out, for a people who had been told to move along for a century and a half. Newly-urbanized African-Americans faced a world very different from the one they had known before, but when it came to the question of color, they found themselves on familiar ground. Not surprisingly, when confronted by the racial prejudice of the North and West, they survived just as they and their predecessors had done in the South: by building up their community, families, clubs, and churches. Whether in the North or South, then, home was cut off from white society. White people may have heard R&B as it made its way across the air waves. What their ears didn't hear, what their eyes didn't see, what they wanted neither to hear nor to see, was the distinct *community* which it addressed, a largely self-contained world created by American apartheid: the chitlin' circuit. . . .

Gospel music spoke for and sustained a distinct community, retaining collective and communal features which expressed something of the suppression which so many in that community had experienced. It also helped to transform that community. It did so partly through its influence on rhythm and blues.

Boogie at Midnight

Cacophonous vocals shouted explicit lyrics; loud saxophones, pianos, and guitars honked, rolled, and wailed while drums banged out the heavy rhythm; delirious artists expressed emotions and ideas which exhilarated their audience. Until 1949, when Jerry Wexler gave it the more sophisticated name 'rhythm and blues' while writing for *Billboard,* the white music industry branded all this 'race music'. The lines between urban blues and R&B were tenuous (as are all popular musical categories), and the early R&B charts looked like a blues who's-who: John Lee Hooker's 'Boogie Chillen', Lonnie Johnson's 'Tomorrow Night', shouter Wynonie Harris's 'Good Rockin' Tonight', as well as tunes by Howlin' Wolf, Charles Brown, Muddy Waters, Bull Moose Jackson, and Ivory Joe Hunter.

R&B was updated and mellowed as the influence of gospel smoothed over its rougher edges. Technology played a crucial part. Although different radio stations programmed specific genres, listeners were not so constrained; as a result gospel singles crossed over to the R&B charts: in 1950, for example, the Five Blind Boys' 'Our Father' was chasing Wynonie Harris's 'I Like My Baby's Pudding' up the charts. Quartet singing, long a crossover area for artists like the Mills Brothers and the Ink Spots, was the springboard for the 'bird groups' (the Ravens and the Orioles), who in turn inspired groups like the Clovers and the Dominoes. Founded in 1950 by Billy Ward, the Dominoes built their sound around the gospel-style vocals of Clyde McPhatter. Race restricted the success of songs like 'Do Something for Me' and 'Have Mercy Baby' to the R&B charts, until the appearance of rock 'n' roll enabled an R&B group, Frankie Lymon and the Teenagers, to hit the charts for sixteen weeks in 1956, peaking at number six, with 'Why Do Fools Fall in Love?' The original did better than the cover versions by the Diamonds and Gale Storm. The Platters, who had charted in 1955 with 'Only You' released three Top Ten pop and R&B hits in 1956. Many of the R&B acts that followed went on to become rock 'n' roll, rather than soul, stars. Imperial artist Fats Domino rode 'Blueberry Hill' and 'I'm in Love Again' into the Top Ten. Two other 'R&B' artists, Chuck Berry and Little Richard, hit the charts with 'Maybellene', 'School Days', and 'Sweet Little Sixteen'; and 'Tutti-Frutti', 'Long Tall Sally', and 'Rip it Up', respectively.

White listeners started to develop a better feeling for the music: they heard R&B differently. As it became familiar, it became acceptable on its own terms. In its initial cross over into white culture, R&B attracted a cult following among college and high school students. Its rhythm and forbidden thrills, though still contrasting sharply with the milquetoast sounds of Perry Como and company, had been made more palatable by gospel. White R&B fans could now accept the real thing, not covers.

Even though more and more people came to prefer R&B, the majors could not and did not start promoting the product; they seemed scarcely aware of the market. The indies—often using singers with regional appeal in a regional market—detected the trend more quickly. Largely through their efforts, some juke boxes began stocking R&B records, while white dance bands started to incorporate R&B hits in their sets. Whether through the efforts of the majors or the indies, singers and musicians like Chuck Berry, Bo Diddley, and Little Richard found themselves able to play African-American music *as* African-American music: no crooning sepia nonsense. Racial barriers were dissolving as sons of slaves and sons of Pilgrims broke sonic barriers to create the sound of rebellion and deliverance: rock 'n' roll.

Whatever their race, these artists were dependent upon the various media to get their music to the widest possible audience. The people who played rock 'n' roll could not have known they were making history, but they did know they were on to something new, something that broke with musical traditions. These early rock 'n' rollers were no navel-gazers: they were carnival sideshow entertainers with a product to sell and a get-rich-quick scheme: a number one record. The world of rock 'n' roll was not only a cultural and social expression but also a commercial network of musical commodities—singles and albums—which had to be recorded, distributed, and promoted.

Have You Heard the News?

The music industry has survived despite the appearance of successive new media that at one time or another seemed capable of subjugating it. Radio initially made the need to buy records appear obsolete—until swing music became so popular in the 1930s that a rush on records ensued. Later, television appeared to threaten the industry. Again, however, it endured (most recently by becoming a part of television through MTV). Recorded music has survived because of its unique ability to create an emotional bond between the listener and recorded sound. Everything else—the technology, the marketing, the profits—have resulted from that bond and its basic power.

During and after World War Two, the record industry, radio, and television all experienced changes that together radically altered the modes of musical production: new recording techniques and small-group recording budgets; new companies and a redefinition of the target audience; reductions in record prices; and a new affiliation with broadcast radio. The shift from 78 revolutions per minute to the 33⅓ and 45 rpm speeds, a change in the sizes of records, the substitution of shellac by vinyl, and television's influence on radio station programming—each had an impact on the industry. Although its story cannot be reduced solely to technical innovations, rock 'n' roll did evolve out of and along with the technology of these media. What was new about rock 'n' roll was its relationship with the means of mass communication: record, radio, television, and film. American rock 'n' roll depended on the existence of these media and accepted them without compromise as a condition of artistic creativity.

This Year's Model

Notable technological improvements associated with the introduction of magnetic tape resulted in recording techniques which were not only inexpensive but which made both overdubbing (with remarkably improved microphones) and the correcting of mistakes possible. One pioneer was guitarist Les Paul, who by 1947 had started making 'sound-on-sound' recordings. Real multitrack recording was first used in 1954. Employing just two tracks, it was far from today's sixty-four track digital studios; the basic principle of studio music production—sound-on-sound—nevertheless remains unaltered. Multitrack technology was to influence both the sound and the structure of rock music, since a producer could now assemble the music from individually recorded parts in a final mix instead of reproducing a single take of a song: records no longer needed to be exact copies of live performances, rendering the large rooms previously employed for recording big band orchestras unnecessary. . . .

When the majors finally realized that rock 'n' roll was here to stay, they restructured their A&R departments and hired men who had a better feel for the sound and who understood the new standards. From this point on, the A&R men from the majors picked from the same flock of producers, song writers, arrangers, and session men as the indies.

The most conspicuous technological innovation triggered the 'Battle of the Speeds'. By 1948 CBS engineer Peter Goldmark had perfected the high fidelity long-playing record (LP), which reduced the playing speed from 78 to 33⅓ rpm. With their low noise characteristics and extended duration, LPs transformed not only recording studios and the contents of records themselves, but also the industry's hierarchy, as Columbia first stole the lead on RCA only to see the latter respond with 45 rpm singles. The ascent of rock 'n' roll paralleled that of the 45 rpm single (along with the portable radio). Until the emergence of rock 'n' roll, and especially Elvis Presley, the 45 rpm single's role in popular music had been minimal. Aimed at the new teenage market and priced within reach of teenagers' pocket money, however, its popularity rose quickly.

Until rock 'n' roll appeared in the 1950s, radio programming had changed very little since the 1930s, when the friendly, conversational microphone styles of Al Jarvis at KFWB in Los Angeles, Martin Block at WNEW in New York, and Arthur Godfrey had first raised announcers to the status of 'personalities', who received as much attention from their listeners as the music they played. Jarvis pioneered the 'Make Believe Ballroom' format, which simulated the atmosphere of a ballroom through the use of real or contrived conversations with the performers and dancers. Block's use of this framework would engender *Your Hit Parade* and *Lucky Lager Dance Time*. Godfrey's irreverent style helped make the radio disc jockey someone not to be treated lightly; his early morning show attracted many listeners and thus numerous sponsors. Such sponsorship represented a commercialization of radio that would have profound consequences. When the American Tobacco Company started sponsoring *The Lucky Strike Hit Parade* nationwide, records began to be ranked according to their popularity. Air play became the most effective type of direct marketing. By the end of World War Two most singers, musicians, record companies, and sheet music publishers had become aware of the interaction between sales and air play. Record sales and taste trends increasingly engendered and reflected one another: each at once parasite on and host for the other; both having a symbiotic relationship with the charts (particularly *Billboard*'s). A song could become a hit because a lot of people liked it and bought the record, and a lot of people liked a song and bought the record because it was a hit.

Since television during the 1950s rapidly took over the family entertainment role once held by radio, and since programs like *Monitor* (a weekend program of interviews, satire, and news features) proved failures, radio programming other than news broadcasts returned to the hands of station owners, who responded to the challenge of television by converting their stations to a 'Top-Forty' format in order to survive. Top-Forty programs shaped teenagers' perceptions of rock 'n' roll: music was ranked, and hits were important. Cheap, battery-driven portable radios made possible by transistor technology came on the market in 1954. Rock 'n' roll developed within a technological milieu increasingly beyond parental control. Teenagers' relative independence in deciding what they liked and what they wanted to listen to resulted in an age-specific audience, and rock 'n' roll developed on its audience's terms. . . . Between 1954 and 1959 the record industry increased its sales from $213,000,000 to $603,000,000. A large proportion of the increase in sales accrued to the indies, who made their break into the market by providing assorted kinds of rock 'n' roll. After the majors had dropped their 'race' and 'new jazz' artists during World War Two, the indies had moved into the 'race' market and begun recording rhythm and blues. In 1954 they extended their market to white kids as they developed distribution networks sufficient to give them as good a chance of having a hit with a new record as any of the majors; once they saw the possibilities of profit in rock 'n' roll, they recorded almost anybody singing almost anything and put all their energy and money into promoting those records that seemed to stand a chance. The independents doubled their number of Top Ten hits between 1955 and 1956, then doubled them again by 1957. They succeeded in spotting and responding to the grass-roots signs of rock 'n' roll's popularity partly because, unlike the majors, the indies often signed singers with regional or local appeal. . . . Although lacking the sales figures, budgets, and distribution facilities of the major music publishers, record companies, and radio networks, the indies nevertheless changed the direction of popular music and the structure of the record industry.

The indies had produced twice as many hits by the end of the decade as the majors, yet the struggle for survival never eased up. Few would survive the 1960s. Plagued by competition from bootleggers (who pirated copies of their hits) and always fighting to collect from their distributors, indie labels still had to pay 'consultancy fees' to disc jockeys, and the monthly overheads of staff and offices, on top of the costs of pressings. Sometimes their wisest move was to license a likely hit to larger companies like Mercury, ABC, or Dot (all of whom formed fruitful relationships with independent producers).

Through their influence over distribution networks, the majors effectively controlled most record stores, juke boxes, sheet music sales, and radio airplay. Slow to realize the closing of the American racial gap which accompanied and followed World War Two, the majors thus adopted a conservative strategy, deploying their sizeable resources to fight for the success of their established performers, mostly older artists from the dance band era still under five year contracts. The singers who operated under such contracts had to be musical chameleons and appeal to just about anyone (unlike rock 'n' roll madmen like Little Richard and Jerry Lee Lewis who were, by contrast, anything but malleable). The majors used their contract singers for the cover versions recorded, released, and promoted hot on the tail of R&B hits. The majors did renovate their commercial policy by releasing singles more quickly, while strengthening their promotion work by marketing from coast to coast. Confident in their market domination, however, they underestimated the ways in which a few radio disc jockeys who appreciated the power of rhythm and blues (such as Danny 'Cat Man' Stiles, Hal Jackson, and George 'Hound Dog' Lorenz) could penetrate the cracks of segregation and discrimination by playing it to anyone who would listen.

The majors slowly came to understand teenage record buyers, drop their traditional sales categories of popular music and rhythm and blues, and call anything that appealed to teenage record buyers 'rock 'n' roll'. When the majors finally acted, rock 'n' roll devolved into teenybopper music, designed for and chiefly bought by people between the ages of nine and twenty four, who determined what the record charts looked like by the manner in which they spent their own or their parents' money. When some seventeen-year-old Peggy Sue bought the latest hit single by the King, she cared little about the technology or money that had gone into its production and had little interest in knowing that she was dancing to a product made to be marketed and consumed for profit. She simply bought a record she *liked*. Her reasons for picking this particular record were, of course, influenced by many things—her age, gender, race, and social background as well as the forces of advertising and peer group pressure—which may have had little to do with the song itself. Later, as she grew older, the music would nevertheless bring back memories of those halcyon days and the experiences she and her friends had shared with a rock 'n' roll backdrop.

As the music industry itself matured, styles would change: from heavy to folk, from country to soft, from bubble gum to disco, from glitter to glam; all, however, were variations on the basic rock 'n' roll theme, products of industry attempts to sustain old or develop new markets, while kids tried to find a new sound that fit their world and their experiences. Musicians starting out as kids looking for new sounds came into the industry and developed new styles in the lacuna between the industry's creating and following trends. As a result, the various genres of rock music through the ages—and especially the records that came with them—had (and continue to have) one thing in common: what James Von Schilling has called the ability to 'capture in time a unique combination of music, performance, and artistry and then enable us to make this "timepiece" part of our personal experience'.

Afterword: Funeral Dirge
American Pie

Legend has it that rock 'n' roll died. Estimates of the precise date differ, but most agree that at some point in the late 1950s rock 'n' roll passed away, only to be reborn as 'rock' in 1964 when the Beatles arrived in New York and Dylan went electric. . . .

God's Country: America in the Fifties

Generation in a Spotlight

As the 1950s opened, America's adolescents were basically a conservative, unrebellious lot. Although the word *teenager* had come into widespread circulation in the 1940s to describe this distinct age group mired in the limbo between puberty and adulthood, the teenagers of the early fifties had not yet developed a distinct subculture. They had few rights and little money of their own, wore basically the same kind of clothing their parents wore, watched the same television shows, went to the same movies, used the same slang, and listened to the same romantic music sung by Perry Como, Frank Sinatra, and other middle-aged or nearly middle-aged artists. Their idols were Joe DiMaggio, General MacArthur, and other prominent members of the older generation. In spite of what they learned from older kids and from the underground pornography that circulated on school playgrounds, they were amazingly naive about sex, believing well into their high school years that French kissing could cause pregnancy or that the douche, coitus interruptus, and chance could effectively prevent it. Heavy petting was the limit for most couples, and for those who went "all the way" there were often strong guilt feelings and, for the girl at least, the risk of a bad reputation. Rebellion against authority, insofar as it occurred, consisted primarily of harmless pranks against unpopular adult neighbors or teachers, occasional vandalism (especially on Halloween night), smoking cigarettes or drinking beer, and the decades-old practice of mooning. Although most families had the inevitable clashes of opinion between parents and offspring, there were few signs of a "generation gap" or of rebellion against the conventions of the adult world.

But all of this began to change in the early fifties, and by the middle of the decade the appearance of a distinct youth subculture was causing parents and the media to agonize over the scandalous behavior and rebellious nature of the nation's young people. The causes of the emergence of this subculture are not hard to find. One was the demographic revolution of the postwar years that was increasing the influence of the young by producing so many of

From *God's Country: America in the Fifties* (Barricade Books, 1990), pp. 267–271, 274–276, 279–290. Copyright © 1990 by J. Ronald Oakley. Reprinted by permission of Barricade Books.

them in such a short period of time. Another was the affluence of the period, an affluence shared with the young through allowances from their parents or through part-time jobs. As teenagers acquired their own money, they were able to pursue their own life-style, and now American business and advertisers geared up to promote and exploit a gigantic youth consumer market featuring products designed especially for them. Then there were the effects of progressive education and Spockian child-rearing practices, for while neither was quite as permissive or indulgent toward the young as the critics claimed, they did emphasize the treatment of adolescents as unique people who should be given the freedom to develop their own personality and talents. Another factor was television and movies, which had the power to raise up new fads, new heroes, and new values and to spread them to young people from New York to Los Angeles. And finally, there was rock 'n' roll, which grew from several strains in American music and emerged at mid-decade as the theme song of the youth rebellion and as a major molder and reflector of their values.

One of the earliest landmarks in the history of the youth rebellion came in 1951 with the publication of J. D. Salinger's *The Catcher in the Rye*. Infinitely more complex than most of its young readers or older detractors perceived, this novel featured the actions and thoughts of one Holden Caulfield, a sixteen-year-old veteran of several private schools, who roams around New York City in his own private rebellion from home and school. In colloquial language laced with obscenities absent from most novels of the day, Holden tells the reader of his rejection of the phoniness and corruption of the adult world, of how parents, teachers, ministers, actors, nightclub pianists and singers, old grads, and others lie to themselves and to the young about what the world is really like. *The Catcher in the Rye* was popular throughout the fifties with high school and college students, for while young people might not understand all that Salinger was trying to say, they did identify with his cynical rejection of the adult world and adult values. The book was made even more popular by the attempts of school boards, libraries, and state legislatures to ban it. It was one of the first books, if not the first, to perceive the existence of a generation gap in the supposedly happy, family-oriented society of the early 1950s.

Still another sign of the changes occurring in the nation's youth was the rise of juvenile delinquency. Between 1948 and 1953 the number of juveniles brought into court and charged with crimes increased by 45 percent, and it was estimated that for every juvenile criminal brought into court there were at least five who had not been caught. It was especially disturbing that juvenile crimes were committed by organized gangs that roamed—and seemed to control—the streets of many of the larger cities. Street gangs had existed before in American history, but in the fifties they were larger, more violent, and more widespread than ever before. Thanks to modern communications, they tended to dress alike, to use the same jargon, and share the same values all across the country. And they were not just in America—they appeared in England (Teddy Boys), Sweden ("Skinn-Nuttar" or leather jackets), and other industrial countries across the globe. The youth rebellion, including the criminal fringe that made up part of it, was international.

Learning about these gangs in their newspapers and weekly magazines, Americans were horrified by what they read and by how often they read it. It seemed that hardly a week went by without the occurrence of shocking crimes committed by teenagers or even younger children who did not seem to know the difference between good and bad—or worse, deliberately chose the bad over the good. Sporting colorful names like Dragons, Cobras, Rovers, and Jesters, they carried all kinds of weapons—zip guns, pistols, rifles, knives, chains, shotguns, brass knuckles, broken bottles, razors, lead pipes, molotov cocktails, machetes, and lye and other chemicals. They drank alcoholic beverages, smoked reefers, took heroin and other drugs, had their own twisted code of honor, and organized well-planned attacks on other gangs or innocent victims. They also had their own jargon, borrowed from the criminal underworld and spoken by gangs from coast to coast: *dig, duke, gig, jap, jazz, rumble, turf, cool, chick, pusher, reefer,* and hundreds of other slang terms.

To a nation accustomed to believing in the essential goodness of its young people, the behavior of these delinquent gangs was puzzling and frightening. They seemed to pursue violence for the pure joy of violence and to delight in sadistic actions toward other gangs or innocent victims. They engaged in shootings, stabbings, individual and gang rapes, senseless beatings, and unspeakable tortures. They extorted "protection" money from frightened merchants, sprayed crowds in streets or restaurants or subways with rifle fire, doused people with gasoline and set them ablaze, firebombed bars and nightclubs, stole automobiles, vandalized apartments and public buildings, and fought vicious gang wars over girls or invasion of turf or to avenge some real or imagined slight. They often terrorized and vandalized schools and assaulted teachers and students, leading the *New York Daily News* in 1954 to describe "rowdyism, riot, and revolt," as the new three Rs in New York's public schools.

It was particularly disturbing that these young hoodlums often showed no remorse for their actions, recounting with delight to police or social workers the details of a rape, murder, or torture in which they had been involved. One eighteen-year-old who had participated in the torture and murder of an innocent young man in a public park told police that "last night was a supreme adventure for me." Describing his role in the killing of another gang member, one young man told police that "he was laying on the ground looking up at us. I kicked him on the jaw or someplace; then I kicked him in the stomach. That was the least I could do, was kick 'im." In another incident a gang member described his part in a stabbing by saying: "I stabbed him with a bread knife. You know, I was drunk, so I just stabbed him. [Laughs] He was screaming like a dog."

The rise of juvenile delinquency, and especially its organized forms in the street gangs of the major cities, caused agonizing soul-searching among anxious parents, school authorities, psychologists, and other experts on adolescent and criminal behavior. Parents of delinquents anxiously asked, "What did we do wrong?" and many admitted to school, police, and court authorities that they could not control their children. The experts came up with a whole range of explanations of juvenile criminality, blaming it on poverty, slum conditions, permissive parents, lack of religious and moral training, television, movies, comic books, racism, parents who were too busy working or pursuing their own pleasures to rear their children properly, the high divorce rate with the resulting broken homes, anxiety over the draft, and decline of parental discipline and control. Early in the decade most authorities tended to blame it on the problems of poverty and slum living, but as the decade wore on, it became very clear that many of the delinquents were from middle- and upper-class families that provided a good environment for their children. So then it was blamed on society or on simple "thrill seeking" by bored, pampered, and jaded youths. As the problem worsened, many were inclined to agree with Baltimore psychologist Robert Linder, who claimed that the young people of the day were suffering from a form of collective mental illness. "The youth of the world today," he told a Los Angeles audience in 1954, "is touched with madness, literally sick with an aberrant condition of mind formerly confined to a few distressed souls but now epidemic over the earth."

Whatever the causes of juvenile delinquency, and they were certainly multiple and complex, it was obvious that delinquent and criminal acts by individual adolescents and organized gangs were increasing every year and were making the streets of many large cities dangerous for law-abiding citizens. And while many people thought of the problem as one that plagued primarily the slums of the big cities of the Northeast or California, it soon became clear that it was spreading to large cities all across the country, to the new suburbs, to the rural areas which were so accessible now to middle-class teenagers with automobiles, and to the South, which had often prided itself on not having the problems of the big northern cities. In 1954 *New York Times* education editor Benjamin Fine wrote a much-discussed book on the problem, *1,000,000 Delinquents*, which correctly predicted that during the next year 1 million adolescents would get into serious trouble that would bring them into the courtroom. In that same year *Newsweek* published an article entitled "Our Vicious Young Hoodlums: Is There Any Hope?" By now, many people thought that there was none and found themselves in the unusual position of being afraid of their own children.

By the midfifties Americans had become so saturated with stories of juvenile delinquency that there was a tendency among many to stereotype all teenagers as bad, especially if they adopted the clothing, ducktail haircuts, or language of gangs. But the truth was that few teenagers were juvenile delinquents or gang members, very few used drugs (except for alcohol), and very few ever got into trouble with the police. And many teenagers resented the stereotyped image the adult world had of them. As one seventeen-year-old high school girl said in 1955, "I've never set a fire, robbed a gas station, or beaten a defenseless old man. In fact, I don't even know anyone who has. . . . I wish someone would think of the 95% of us who *aren't* delinquents. Because we're here, too." The young woman was correct, of course, for most teenagers were not delinquents. But they were changing in ways that were disturbing even the parents of "good" teens, and one of the major causes of these changes was the rise of a new musical form, rock 'n' roll. . . .

Born in the small town of Fairmount, Indiana, on February 8, 1931, James Dean led a life much like that of the troubled youth he later came to portray in his movies. His mother died when he was nine, and he was reared on the farm of his aunt and uncle with only brief glimpses of his father. A confused adolescent, he went to California after his graduation from high school, attended Santa Monica City College and UCLA, and played some small parts in movies before going back to New York to study acting in 1951. In 1954 he came back to Hollywood as an admirer of Marlon Brando, motorcycles, and fast cars. He quickly earned a reputation as a lazy, undisciplined, ill-mannered star who often stayed out all night long and then showed up on the set too tired to do good work. His first major film, *East of Eden* (1955), brought him instant fame through his portrayal of the sensitive son suffering from the fear that his father does not love him, but his rise as a teenage idol came later in the year through his performance as a misunderstood and rebellious teenager in *Rebel Without a Cause*. Costarring Natalie Wood and Sal Mineo, the film was released to the theaters in the fall of 1955, only two weeks after Dean's tragic death in a high-speed wreck between his Porsche and a Ford on a lonely California highway. By the time the just-completed *Giant* was released, in November of 1956, an astonishing cult had sprung up around the young star and his death, so senseless, at the age of twenty-four.

The legends that grew up around James Dean were the greatest since the death of Rudolph Valentino. Young people saw Dean as the embodiment of their restlessness, confusion, and rejections, as a rebel fighting, like them, against the rules and conformity the adult world was trying to impose upon them. But while Valentino and most other movie legends had appealed as sex symbols. Dean appealed to an age group—to young males and females between fourteen and twenty-four. Young males saw him as a symbol of their own rebellious and troubled nature, while young girls saw him as an attractive, sensual male who needed mothering as much as sexual love. Although Dean was a good actor with great promise, his acting reputation was exaggerated beyond all reality by the myths and legends that shrouded his life and acting career after his premature death.

Within a few weeks after Dean's death, Warner Brothers was swamped with hundreds of letters. Their number rose to 3,000 a month by January of 1956 and to 7,000 a month by July, some with money enclosed for a picture of the dead star. The fan magazines played the Dean legend for all it was worth, publishing thousands of pictures and stories. In these magazines and across the national teenage grapevine, the rumors flew: that he was not really dead, that he had been so disfigured from the wreck that he had gone into hiding or been sent to a sanatorium, that he was just a vegetable in a secret hospital room known only to his close friends, that he had talked to some of his fans from beyond his grave, and that his tomb in Fairmount, Indiana, had been emptied by grave robbers or by Dean's own miraculous resurrection. Several records appeared—"Tribute to James Dean," "The Ballad of James Dean," "His Name Was Dean." "The Story of James Dean," "Jimmy Jimmy," and "We'll Never Forget You." Dozens of biographies and other literary tributes were rushed to the market, along with the inevitable movie,

The James Dean Story. When the wreckage of his car was put on display in Los Angeles, over 800,000 people paid to view it. The adulation swept teens all across America and even in Europe. In England, a young man legally changed his name to James Dean, copied his clothing and mannerisms, went to America twice to visit the real Dean's family and grave, and claimed to have seen *Rebel Without a Cause* over 400 times. As *Look* magazine observed, the subject of this almost psychopathic adulation was "a 24-year old who did not live long enough to find out what he had done and was in too much of a hurry to find out who he was."

Along with *The Wild One*, a 1954 film starring Marlon Brando as the leader of a motorcycle gang, *The Blackboard Jungle* and the films of James Dean helped to spawn a series of films aimed specifically at young people. In addition to the films of Elvis Presley and other teen idols, the second half of the fifties saw a spate of second-rate rock movies—*Rock Around the Clock, Don't Knock the Rock, Rock Pretty Baby, Rock Around the World,* and *Let's Rock*—and a series of shallow, trashy movies about young people and delinquency, such as *Girls in Prison, Eighteen and Anxious, Reform School Girl, Hot Rod Rumble,* and *High School Confidential*. For better or worse—mostly worse—teenagers were getting their own movies as well as their own music.

In 1955 teenagers had their music, their movies, their idols—dead and alive—but as yet they had no one who combined all three of these and served as a focal point for their growing consciousness as a subculture. But he was waiting in the wings, for in that year a young performer with a regional reputation was making records and gaining a wide following among teenagers, especially young girls, with live performances in southern cities that were often punctuated by desperate attempts by the police to prevent these screaming fans from rushing the stage to tear off his clothes. He was a James Dean fan, who had seen *Rebel Without a Cause* several times, could recite the script by heart, and had been wearing tight pants, leather jackets, and a ducktail haircut with long sideburns for several years. In 1956 he would burst on the national entertainment stage and proceed to become one of the most popular and influential musical performers of all time, rivaling Rudy Vallee, Bing Crosby, Frank Sinatra, and other singers before him. His name was Elvis Presley, and he was destined to claim the title of King of Rock 'n' Roll. . . .

Record sales soared with the coming of rock 'n' roll. Aided by the affluence of the time, the invention of the 45 rpm and 33⅓ rpm records, and the introduction of high fidelity, record sales had steadily climbed from 109 million in 1945 to 189 million in 1950 and to 219 million in 1953, then with the arrival of rock 'n' roll rose to 277 million in 1955 and to 600 million in 1960. In 1956 alone, RCA Victor sold over 13.5 million Elvis Presley singles and 3.75 million Presley albums. By 1957, the new 45s and 33⅓s had driven the 78s out of production. Teenagers bought most of the inexpensive and convenient 45s and most of the long-playing rock 'n' roll albums, whereas adults bought most of the long-playing albums of traditional popular music, jazz, and classical music. While in 1950 the average record buyer was likely to be in his early twenties, by 1958, 70 percent of all the records sold in the United States were purchased by teenagers. Most of the popular singles were purchased by girls between the ages of thirteen and nineteen, the group most receptive, as one critic said, to "little wide-eyed wishes for ideal love and perfect lovers, little songs of frustration at not finding them." Thanks to these revolutions in the musical world, record sales, which had stood at only $7.5 million in 1940, had risen to a healthy $521 million in 1960.

Why was rock 'n' roll so popular? One of the reasons, of course, was that it was written and performed by young people and was centered upon what was important to them: love, going steady, jealousy, high school, sex, dancing, clothing, automobiles, and all the other joys and problems of being young. The lyrics were just as silly, sentimental, and idealistic as the music of the crooners of the first half of the decade, but it was written just for the young and the singing styles, beat, electrical amplification, and volume of the music was much more dynamic than that of the earlier period. Teens were attracted to its celebration of sexuality, expressed in the more explicit lyrics, driving tempo, movements of the rock 'n' roll performers, and in new dances at high school hops and private parties. Perhaps Jeff Greenfield, a member of this first generation of rock 'n' roll fans, expressed it best in his *No Peace, No Place.* "Each night, sprawled on my bed on Manhattan's Upper West Side, I would listen to the world that Alan Freed created. To a twelve- or thirteen-year-old, it was a world of unbearable sexuality and celebration: a world of citizens under sixteen, in a constant state of joy or sweet sorrow. . . . New to sexual sensations, driven by the impulses that every new adolescent generation knows, we were the first to have a music rooted in uncoated sexuality." And very importantly, rock 'n' roll gave young people a sense of cohesion, of unity, all across the nation. It was *their* music, written for them and for them only, about their world, a world that adults could not share and did not understand. As such, it was one of the major harbingers of the generation gap.

It was not long after teenagers acquired their own music and movies that they also acquired their own television show. *American Bandstand* began as a local television show in Philadelphia in 1952, and in August of 1957 it premiered as a network show on ABC over sixty-seven stations across the country, from 3:00 to 4:30 in the afternoon, with twenty-six-year-old Dick Clark as the host. The first network show featured songs by Jerry Lee Lewis, the Coasters, and other top rock 'n' roll artists, and guest star Billy Williams singing "I'm Gonna Sit Right Down and Write Myself a Letter." Some of the early reviews of the show were not complimentary. According to *Billboard,* "The bulk of the ninety minutes was devoted to colorless juveniles trudging through early American dances like the Lindy and the Box Step to recorded tunes of the day. If this is the wholesome answer to the 'detractors' of rock 'n' roll, bring on the rotating pelvises." But by the end of 1958 the show was reaching over 20 million viewers over 105 stations, and had spawned dozens of imitations on local stations. This was a show about teens, and its consistent high rating and longevity proved that they liked it, regardless of what adults said about it.

American Bandstand had a great influence on popular music and on America's teenagers. Clark's good looks, neat clothing, and civilized manner helped reassure American parents that rock 'n' roll was not a barbarian invasion that was turning the young into juvenile delinquents. All the dancers on the show in the fifties were white, adhered to a strict dress code (coats and ties for boys, dresses and skirts and blouses for girls, and no jeans, T-shirts, or tight sweaters), and followed a strict language code that even prohibited the use of the term "going steady." One of Clark's most embarrassing moments on the show came when a young girl told him that the pin she was wearing was a "virgin pin." Stars with unsavory reputations were not allowed on the show, so when the news of Jerry Lee Lewis's marriage to his thirteen-year-old cousin broke, Clark joined other disc jockeys and promotors across the country in canceling all future appearances of the pioneer rock 'n' roll star. The show also featured the biggest stars of the day and helped launch the careers of Connie Francis, Fabian, Frankie Avalon, and several other singers. The new dances performed on the show—such as "the stroll," "the shake," and "the walk"—were soon copied all across the country. Teenagers everywhere also imitated the slang and the dress of this very influential show and brought the records its regulars danced to. The success of this dance show brought popularity and wealth to its host, who freely admitted that "I dance very poorly," yet became a millionaire by the age of thirty.

The rise of rock 'n' roll, teen movies, teen television shows, and teen magazines helped create the teen idol. Many of the idols were singers, like Elvis Presley, Rick Nelson, Frankie Avalon, Bobby Darin, Fabian, Pat Boone, Connie Francis, and Annette Funicello. Others were movie or television actors, like James Dean and Marlon Brando, though, of course, many of the singers also went on to movie careers which might be called, at best, undistinguished. Most of the idols were teenagers themselves or in their twenties, and it is important to note here that while earlier generations had tended to create idols much older than themselves—like Bing Crosby, Perry Como, and Clark Gable—the teenagers of the late fifties made idols of people from their own generation. And although clean-cut starts like Ricky Nelson or Frankie Avalon were chosen as idols, many young people also idolized Brando and Dean, who seemed so much like them in their agonizing over the problems of life. The inclination of the young to idolize those who portrayed problem youth was puzzling and disturbing to parents who wanted their children to grow up to be clean-cut, middle-class kids who went to church, obeyed their parents and other authorities, drank nothing harder than a soft drink, had no sexual experience before marriage, saved and studied for college, hung around soda shops rather than pool rooms, and after college went into a respectable career with a good income and a secure future. In short, they wanted their children to be like Pat Boone.

Born in Jacksonville, Florida, in 1934, Boone rose to fame while still a college student by winning first place on Ted Mack's *Original Amateur Hour* and *Arthur Godfrey's Talent Scouts* in 1954. He became a regular on Godfrey's morning show, and then began a career as a singer, movie star (*Bernadine* and *April Love*, both in 1957), and television star with his own show (*Pat Boone Chevy Showroom*). Many of his recordings were covers of original black songs like "Tutti-Frutti" and "Ain't That a Shame," and traditional romantic tunes such as "Friendly Persuasion," "April Love," and "Love Letters in the Sand." Boone was an all-American boy, a dedicated Christian and family man who had not been spoiled by his success, although at the age of twenty-four he was already popular and wealthy, earning $750,000 annually. He had an attractive wife, four pretty daughters, a baccalaureate degree from Columbia University, a love of milk and ice cream, and a severe distaste for strong drink, tobacco, and anything else immoral. He attracted wide publicity in 1958 when he refused to kiss Shirley Jones in the movie *April Love*, saying that "I've always been taught that when you get married, you forget about kissing other women." However, after talking it over with his wife, he agreed to do the kissing scene, although "she would prefer to keep that part of our lives solely to ourselves." This old-fashioned wholesomeness enabled him to hit the best-seller list in 1958 with *Twist Twelve and Twenty,* a moral and social guide for teenagers that reflected Boone's conservative view of sex and his deeply religious outlook on life. Some teenagers found Boone hopelessly "square," but many others admired his moral rectitude. He was immensely popular in the fifties, perhaps second only to Elvis.

In spite of the existence of clean-cut white performers like Pat Boone, much of the adult world was against the new rock 'n' roll. Many musicians and music critics condemned it on musical grounds, disliking its primitive beat, electrical amplification, witless and repetitive lyrics, loudness, and screams. But most adults opposed it for other reasons. Many objected to its suggestive lyrics and claimed that it fomented rebellion against parents and other authorities, bred immorality, inflamed teenagers to riot, and was unchristian and unpatriotic. They agreed with Frank Sinatra, who called it "the martial music of every sideburned delinquent on the face of the earth." Others objected to its racial background and content, even claiming, as many southerners did, that rock 'n' roll was a plot jointly sponsored by the Kremlin and the NAACP, and that rock musicians and disc jockeys were dope addicts, communists, integrationists, atheists, and sex fiends. To many whites, North and South, it was "nigger music," and as such was designed to tear down the barriers of segregation and bring about sexual promiscuity, intermarriage, and a decline in the morals of young whites.

The fears of parents and other adults were fed by the isolated incidents of rioting that accompanied rock 'n' roll concerts in Boston, Washington, D.C., and several other cities. As a result of these headline-getting events, rock 'n' roll concerts were banned in many cities or else accompanied by heavy police security and strict regulations as to what the performers could do or say on stage. In many cities, city councils and other local groups also tried to ban rock 'n' roll from record stores or jukeboxes. In San Antonio, Texas, the city council even went so far as to ban the music from the jukeboxes of public swimming pools, claiming that it "attracted undesirable elements given to practicing their gyrations in abbreviated bathing suits." A disc jockey in Buffalo was fired when he played an Elvis Presley record, and across the country disc jockeys were similarly punished for playing the new music or were pressured into boycotting it. Some disc jockeys broke rock 'n' roll records on the air, while radio station WLEV in Erie, Pennsylvania, loaded over 7,000 rock 'n' roll records into a rented hearse and led a funeral procession to Erie Harbor, where the records were "buried at sea." Ministers preached against it, claiming, like the Rev. John Carroll in Boston, that the music corrupted young people and that "rock and roll inflames and excites youth like jungle tom-toms readying warriors for battle," and many churches held public burnings of rock 'n' roll records. Some were even willing to resort to the ugliest kinds of violence to try to stem the advance of rock music. On April 23, 1956, in Birmingham, Alabama, where the White Citizens' Council had succeeded in removing all rock 'n' roll records from jukeboxes, five men connected with the council rushed the stage of the city auditorium and assaulted black ballad singer Nat King Cole, who was badly bruised before the police stopped the attack.

The debate over rock 'n' roll continued through the end of the decade, carried on in the press, over radio and television, in teachers' meetings, pulpits, and city council meeting rooms. By 1960 the debate had begun to die down, with parents coming to see that the music was not going to fade away, that it had not made delinquents of their children, and that all the other dire predictions had not come to pass, either. Some even began to admit grudgingly that they liked some of it, though they wished that it were not played so loudly. Some of the older professional musicians had also come to defend it—Benny Goodman, Sammy Kaye, Paul Whiteman, and Duke Ellington had kind words for the new music from the very beginning, and Whiteman and Kaye publicly recalled that most new musical forms, including their own swing music, had been condemned when it first appeared. And in the May 1959 issue of *Harper's*, critic Arnold Shaw noted that "perhaps it should be added (although it should be self-evident) that just as hot jazz of the twenties (then anathema to our grandparents) did not destroy our parents, and swing (anathema to our parents) did not destroy us, it is quite unlikely that rock 'n' roll will destroy our children."

The spectacular rise of rock 'n' roll should not obscure the fact that the older music continued to thrive. In 1957, when rock 'n' roll claimed seven of the top ten records of the year, the number one song was "Tammy," recorded by both Debbie Reynolds and the Ames Brothers, and Perry Como remained a favorite of young and old throughout the decade. In a 1956 poll by *Woman's Home Companion*, teenage boys and girls chose Como as the best male vocalist, with Presley, Boone, and Sinatra trailing behind. Johnny Mathis, Paul Anka, Pat Boone, Bobby Darin, the Everly Brothers, and many other teen idols also continued to sing fairly traditional love songs, and in the late fifties, building on a tradition established early in the decade by the Weavers, the Kingston Trio brought a revival of folk music to college students with a touch of rock and protest in songs like "Tom Dooley," "Tijuana Jail," and "A Worried Man," paving the way for the folk music explosion in the early 1960s. Rock music dominated from 1956 to 1960, but it did not completely push the older music aside.

In addition to obtaining their own music, movies, television shows, and idols, teenagers of the fifties also acquired their own fashions, and here they followed the trend toward casual dress that was characterizing the rest of society. The favorite dress of high school boys was denim jeans with rolled-up cuffs, sport shirts, baggy pegged pants, pleated rogue trousers with a white side stripe, slacks with buckles in the back, V-neck sweaters, button-down striped shirts, blazers, white bucks, and loafers. In 1955 they also joined older males on college campuses and executive offices in the pink revolution, donning pink shirts, pink striped or polka dot ties, and colonel string ties. Hair styles ranged from the popular flat top or crew cut to the Apache or ducktail (banned at some high schools). "Greasers" of course shunned the Ivy League and pink attire as too effeminate, sticking to their T-shirts (often with sleeves rolled up to hold a cigarette pack), jeans, leather jackets, and ducktails. For girls, the fashions ranged from rolled-up jeans to casual blouses or men's shirts, full dresses with crinolines, skirts and sweaters, blazers, occasional experiments with the tube dress and sack dress and other disasters foisted upon older women by fashion designers, short shorts (with rolled-up cuffs) that got progressively shorter as the decade wore on, two-piece bathing suits (few were bold enough to wear the bikini, imported from France in the late forties), brown and white saddle shoes and loafers, and hair styles from the poodle to the ponytail. Couples who were going steady wore one another's class rings, identification tags, and necklaces or bracelets, and often adopted a unisex look by wearing matching sweaters, blazers, and shirts.

Like the generations before them, the teenagers of the fifties also had their slang. Much of it was concerned, of course, with the great passion of teens, cars. Cars were *wheels*, tires were *skins*, racing from a standing start was called a *drag*, the bumper was *nerf-bar*, a special kind of exhaust system was called *duals*, and a car specially modified for more engine power was a *hot rod* or *souped up car* or *bomb*. A drive-in movie was a *passion pit*, anything or anyone considered dull was a *drag,* and a really dull person was a *square* or a *nosebleed*. An admirable or poised individual or anything worthy of admiration or approval was *cool* or *neat* or *smooth,* someone who panicked or lost his *cool* was accused of *clutching*, and people admonished not to worry were told to *hang loose*. Teenagers also borrowed lingo from the jazz and beatnik world, such as *dig, hip, cat, bread,* and *chick*. A cutting, sarcastic laugh at someone's bad joke was expressed by a *hardeeharhar*. And teenagers also shared the jargon of the rest of society—*big deal, the royal screw or royal shaft, up the creek without a paddle, forty lashes with a wet noodle, wild, wicked, crazy, classy, horny, BMOC, looking for action, bad news, out to lunch, gross, fink, loser, creep, dumb cluck, doing the deed, going all the way,* or *coming across.* Many of these colloquialisms were borrowed from earlier generations, sometimes with modifications in meaning, while some had been regionalisms that now became national through the great homogenizing power of television.

By the mid-1950s there were 16.5 million teenagers in the United States. About half of them were crowding the nation's secondary schools, while the rest had entered college or the work world. Wherever they were, they had become, as Gereon Zimmerman would write in *Look* magazine, a "Generation in a Searchlight," a constant subject of media attention and a constant source of anxiety for their parents and the rest of the adult world. As Zimmerman observed, "No other generation has had so such attention, so much admonition, so many statistics."

Zimmerman might also have added that no other young generation had had so much money. One of the most revolutionary aspects of the teenage generation was its effects on the American economy, for by the midfifties teenagers made up a very lucrative consumer market for American manufacturers. By mid-decade teenagers of this affluent era were viewing as necessities goods that their parents, reared during the depression, still saw as luxuries, such as automobiles, televisions, record players, cameras, and the like. By the midfifties, teenagers were buying 43 percent of all records, 44 percent of all cameras, 39 percent of all new radios, 9 percent of all new cars, and 53 percent of movie tickets. By 1959, the amount of money spent on teenagers by themselves and by their parents had reached the staggering total of $10 billion a year. Teenagers were spending around $75 million annually on single popular records, $40 million on lipstick, $25 million on deodorant, $9 million on home permanents, and over $837 million on school clothes for teenage girls. Many teenagers had their own charge accounts at local stores and charge cards issued especially for them, such as Starlet Charge Account, Campus Deb Account, and the 14 to 21 Club. Like their parents, teenagers were being led by the affluence and advertising of the age to desire an ever-increasing diet of consumer goods and services and to buy them even if they had to charge them against future earnings.

Many adults had a distorted image of this affluent young generation, focusing too much on its delinquency, rock 'n' roll, unconventional hair styles and clothing, and dating and sexual practices. Only a very small percentage were delinquents or problem-ridden adolescents. Most were reasonably well-groomed, well-behaved, and active in school and extracurricular functions. Most were interested in sports, automobiles, movies, rock 'n' roll, dating, dancing, hobbies, radio, and television. Their major worries were the typical problems of youth in an affluent age: problems with their parents, their popularity with other teens, their looks and complexions, proper dating behavior, sex, first dates, first kisses, love, bad breath, body odors, posture, body build, friends, schoolwork, college, future careers, money, religion, and the draft.

These teenagers that parents worried so much about were remarkably conservative. Survey after survey of young people in the fifties found that over half of them—and sometimes even larger percentages—believed that censorship of printed materials and movies was justified, that politics was beyond their understanding and was just a dirty game, that most people did not have the ability to make important decisions about what was good for them, that masturbation was shameful and perhaps harmful, that women should not hold public office, and that the theory of evolution was suspect and even dangerous. Like their parents, they were also very religious as a group, tending to believe in the divine inspiration of the Bible, heaven and hell, and a God who answered the prayers of the faithful. They were suspicious of radical groups and were willing to deny them the right to assemble in meetings and to disseminate their ideas, and they saw nothing wrong with denying accused criminals basic constitutional rights, such as the right to know their accuser, to be free from unreasonable search or seizure of their property, or to refuse to testify against themselves. Teenagers were also very conformist: They were very concerned about what their friends thought of their dress, behavior, and ideas, and they tried very hard to be part of the group and not be labeled an oddball or individualist. In short, in this age of corporation man, the country also had corporation teen.

Most teens were also conservative in their approach to dating, sex, and marriage. Religious views, social and peer pressure, and fear of pregnancy all combined to create this conservatism and to ensure that most teens kept their virginity until marriage or at least until the early college years, though heavy petting was certainly prevalent among couples who were engaged or "going steady," a practice reflecting society's emphasis on monogamy. These conservative attitudes toward sexual behavior were reinforced by the authorities teenagers looked to for guidance—parents, teachers, ministers, advice to the lovelorn columnists like Dear Abby and Ann Landers (both of whom began their columns in the midfifties), and books on teenage etiquette by Allen Ludden, Pat Boone, and *Seventeen* magazine. In his book for young men, *Plain Talk for Men Under 21,* Ludden devoted an entire chapter to such things as "That Good Night Kiss"—discussing whether to, how to, and the significance of it if you did. And in the very popular *The Seventeen Book of Young Living* (1957), Enid Haupt, the editor and publisher of *Seventeen* magazine, advised young girls to "keep your first and all your romances on a beyond reproach level" and to save themselves for the one right man in their lives. Acknowledging that "it isn't easy to say no to a persuasive and charming boy," she offered one answer for all potentially compromising situations: "'No, please take me home. Now.'"

The conservatism of the young would continue over into the college-age population, where it would remain entrenched for the rest of the fifties. The decade witnessed a boom in higher education, as rising prosperity. G.I. benefits, increasing governmental and private financial aid, fear of the draft, and a growing cultural emphasis on higher education all contributed to a great increase in the number of college students, faculty, programs, and buildings. The boom occurred at all levels—undergraduate, graduate, professional, and in the burgeoning junior- and community-college movement. The number of students, which had stood at 1.5 million in 1940 and 2.3 million in 1950, steadily rose in the decade and reached 3.6 million in 1960, and while the population of the country grew by 8 percent in the decade, the college population grew by 40 percent. By the end of the decade, almost 40 percent of the eighteen-to-twenty-one-year-old age group was attending some institution of higher education.

The conservatism of the college students of the 1950s led them to be called the Silent Generation. Why was it so silent? One of the most important reasons was that it mirrored the conservatism of the society at large, a society caught up in the materialistic and Cold War mentality of the decade. Like their elders, students were seeking the good life rather than the examined one, and as the Great Fear spread to the campuses, many were afraid of acquiring a radical reputation that might jeopardize their scholarships and their future careers in private industry, government service, or the military. Many were veterans, and their military experience, especially for those who had served in Korea, had tended to confirm their conservatism. Many others were in college in order to evade or at least defer the draft, and did not want to do or say anything that might endanger their deferred status. And finally, most students were white and drawn from the middle and upper-middle classes of society. The doors of higher education were still closed to most minority groups and to the economically and socially disadvantaged—groups who might have brought questioning or even radical attitudes into the field of higher education had they been part of it. It is not surprising then that most college students were hardworking, conservative, and career-oriented, truly deserving of their Silent Generation label.

The conservatism of the college generation prevailed throughout the decade. In a study of the college generation in 1951, *Time* magazine noted that "the most startling thing about the younger generation is its silence. . . . It does not issue manifestoes, make speeches, or carry posters." Most students, *Time* found, were worried about the Korean War and its effects on their plans for careers and marriage, but they pushed these fears into the background and concentrated on earning good grades and landing a good job. They were serious and hardworking, in rebellion against nothing, and had no real heroes or villains. Born during the depression years, they were primarily interested in a good job and security, and they did not want to do or say anything that would jeopardize these goals. "Today's generation," *Time* concluded, "either through fear, passivity, or conviction, is ready to conform."

Soon after the end of the Korean War, *Newsweek* studied college students in seven institutions, and its findings were little different from those of *Time* two years before. In "U.S. Campus Kids of 1953: Unkiddable and Unbeatable," *Newsweek* reported that students were hardworking, ambitious conformists who looked forward to secure jobs and a happy married life. Going steady was more popular then ever before, a sign of the period's emphasis on marriage and of young people's desire for the security that a going-steady relationship brought. Most students, *Newsweek* found, were not very interested in politics or international affairs, and they avoided being linked with unpopular causes. One Vassar girl told the magazine, "We're a cautious generation. We aren't buying any ideas we're not sure of." Another said that "you want to be popular, so naturally you don't express any screwy ideas. To be popular you have to conform." And a Princeton senior said that "the world doesn't owe me a living—but it owes me a job." *Newsweek* also saw a renewed interest in religion, as reflected in increasing enrollments in religion courses and frequent "religious emphasis weeks." The magazine found much to admire in the hardworking materialistic class of 1953, although it did concede that "they might seem dull in comparison with less troubled eras."

Similar collegiate characteristics were reported in a 1955 study by David Riesman, who found that students were ambitious, very sure of what they wanted to do, but also very unadventurous—they wanted secure positions in big companies and were already concerned about retirement plans. As one Princeton senior saw it, "Why struggle on my own, when I can enjoy the big psychological income of being a member of a big outfit?" Most males had already decided that they wanted middle-management jobs—they did not want to rise to the presidential or vice-presidential level because that would require too much drive, take time away from their family life and leisure time, and force them to live in a big city. Most had already decided upon the kind of girl they would marry, how many kids they would have, and which civic clubs and other organizations they would join—and they would be joiners, for they liked the gregarious life and knew it would help their careers. They wanted educated wives who would be intellectually stimulating, yet they wanted them to be dutiful and obedient and to stay at home and raise the kids. Many said they wanted as many as four or five kids, because they felt that a large family would bring happiness, security, contentment. One Harvard senior said that "I'd like six kids. I don't know why I say that—it seems like a minimum production goal." They did not know or care much about politics, but they did like Ike and said that they would probably be Republicans because corporation life dictated that they should be.

These attitudes still seemed to prevail in 1957, when *The Nation* surveyed college and university professors about what their students were reading and thinking. Most reported that their students still read the standard authors—Hemingway, Wolfe, Lawrence, Orwell, Huxley, Faulkner, and Steinbeck—but shied away from fiction or nonfiction that dealt with economic, social, or political protest. One professor lamented that "the only young novelist I have heard praised vociferously is J. D. Salinger, for his discovery of childhood," and complained that "when a liberal and speculative voice is heard in the classroom, it is more likely than not to be the professor's, despite whatever caution the years may have taught him." The director of the Writing Program at Stanford University claimed that students were "hard to smoke out. Sometimes a professor is baited into protest by the rows and circles of their closed, watchful, apparently apathetic faces, and says in effect, 'My God, *feel* something! Get enthusiastic about something, plunge, go boom, look alive!'" A Yale English professor complained that "the present campus indifference to either politics or reform or rebellion is monumental." And most agreed with a University of Michigan professor's claim that to the student of 1957, "college has ceased to be a brightly lighted stage where he discovers who he is. It is rather a processing-chamber where, with touching submissiveness, he accepts the remarks of lecturers and the hard sentences of textbooks as directives that will lead him to a job."

What did the members of the Silent Generation do when they were not studying, planning what company they intended to find a safe niche in, deciding what kind of mate they would marry or how many kids they would have, or planning for retirement? They played sports, drank beer, ate pizzas and hamburgers, went to football games and movies, participated in panty raids, dated, dreamed of the opposite sex, read novels and magazines, watched television, and listened to recordings of jazz, classical music, or the popular crooners of the day. For most, the hottest issues on campus were what to do about a losing football coach or who should be elected homecoming queen or student body president. Both sexes wore conservative preppy clothes, and at many coeducational institutions women were forbidden to wear jeans or shorts to class. Those who could afford to joined one of the fast-growing number of fraternities or sororities in order to party, find identity and security, and form friendships that might later be useful in the business world they hoped to enter after graduation. College students were, indeed, an unrebellious lot.

By the late fifties America's teenagers had acquired a distinct subculture of their own. They had their own money, music, movies, television shows, idols, clothing, and slang. In contrast to previous generations, they were more affluent, better educated, talked more openly about sex, had greater mobility through the widespread ownership of automobiles by their parents or themselves, demanded and received more personal freedom, had more conflicts with their parents, and were the subject of more media and parental concern. But they were not yet in rebellion, for although their life-style had departed from the conventions of their elders, their basic ideas and attitudes were still the conservative ones that mirrored the conservatism of the affluent age in which they grew up.

Still, their parents were worried. As *Look* magazine reported in 1958 in an article entitled "What Parents Say About Teenagers," "many parents are in a state of confusion or despair about their teenagers. And they don't exactly know what to do about it. They would like to sit down with their children and talk over their mutual problems, but often this desire is thwarted by the teenagers themselves." The much-heralded generation gap was coming into view. In the next decade, when the junior high and senior high school students of the fifties crowded the colleges, marched in civil rights demonstrations, protested the Vietnam War, and engaged in unconventional sexual and drug practices, it would take on the temper of a revolution.

POSTSCRIPT

Was Rock and Roll Responsible for Dismantling America's Traditional Family, Sexual, and Racial Customs in the 1950s and 1960s?

Between 1958 and 1963, rock and roll as a distinct form of music nearly disappeared. There were several reasons for this. First were the congressional investigations of 1959–1961 into payoffs to DJs to push certain records on their shows. "Payola" ruined the careers of a number of rock DJs, including Alan Freed, the original rock DJ, who lost his two major jobs in New York, was hounded by the IRS for back taxes, and succumbed to alcoholism in 1965. But Dick Clark of "American Bandstand" fame, was protected by the music establishment even though he became a multimillionaire with interests in a number of record companies whose songs he featured on his own show.

Second, payola McCarthyism receded in the early sixties as a result of rock and roll being fused into the mainstream of American popular music. Religious preachers appeared less worried about rock's perversion of the country's sexual moral values, southerners lost the fear of rock's racial mongrelization, and American parents no longer associated rock music with subversives, communists, and other radicals. How could they, when Elvis Presley cut his hair, was drafted into the army, and sang ballads and religious songs that were often integrated into his two dozen forgettable movies? By the time Presley's manager finished reshaping the King's image, Elvis looked more like Pat Boone, a clean-cut handsome wide-toothed singer who "covered" Little Richard's songs for white audiences in the early rock period. At the same time, Dick Clark turned his Philadelphia-based show, "American Bandstand," into an afternoon phenomenon that featured well-groomed teenagers dancing to the latest songs.

In 1963, serious rock was replaced by folk music. Greenwich Village, in the heart of downtown New York City, was its epicenter, Bob Dylan was its creator by writing new folk songs instead of retreading old ones, and the group Peter, Paul, and Mary popularized the music into commercial success. At the same time, folk music became anthems for the civil rights and anti-war protest movements.

Meanwhile, a sixties rock revival came from two sources. First was the British invasion, symbolized by the arrival of the Beatles in 1963, followed by other groups, such as the Rolling Stones, who traced their roots to the early guitar riffs of Chuck Berry. Having come from working-class backgrounds in

Liverpool, the Beatles grew up in an environment that challenged authority and poked fun at some of the hypocrisy of middle-class values. Their later songs influenced the protest movements in the United States.

A second source of revival for protest rock music came from the counterculture movement in San Francisco. Bands such as the Grateful Dead and Jefferson Airplane brought "underground" rock to the forefront. Soon, even the Beatles were imitating the San Francisco underground with their classic album, "Sgt. Pepper's Lonely Hearts Club Band," a style that, according to one writer, combined "a peculiar blend of radical political rhetoric, of allusions to the drug culture, and of the excited sense of imminent, apocalyptic liberation."

Two events in 1969 symbolized the high and low points of sixties rock. In August, 500,000 people converged on a farm in upstate New York for a three-day rock festival. Woodstock became a legendary symbol. There was scant political protest. Music was the common bond that united people sitting in the rain-filled mud, sharing food and drugs while drowning out the fears of participating in an endless war. In December, all the good will of Woodstock was destroyed at a free Rolling Stones concert in Altamont, California. Four people died, one of whom was clubbed, stabbed, and kicked to death by the Hell's Angels, hired as body guards for the Stones on the advice of the Grateful Dead.

Would the sixties "new left" and counterculture movements have taken place without the emergence of rock and roll in the 1950s? Did rock help to reshape America's values, or was it all one big commercial hustle?

The two best overviews of the early history of rock and roll are Glenn C. Altschuler, *All Shook Up: How Rock and Roll Changed America* (Oxford University Press, 2003) and James Miller, *Flowers in the Dustbin: The Rise of Rock and Roll, 1947–1977* (Simon & Schuster, 1999). Four excellent overviews of the 1950s are Douglas T. Miller and Marion Nowak, *The Fifties: The Way We Really Were* (Doubleday, 1975); J. Ronald Oakley, *God's Country: America in the Fifties* (Dembner Books, 1985–1990); David Halberstam, *The Fifties* (Villard, 1993); and William L. O'Neill, *American High: The Years of Confidence, 1945–1960* (Simon & Schuster, 1986). Earlier, O'Neill wrote *Coming Apart: An Informal History of the 1960s* (Times Books, 1971), a classic treatment of the 1960s replete with vignettes that still hold up. David Marcus examines the impact of the 1950s and 1960s upon present-day politics and pop culture in *Happy Days and Wonder Years: The Fifties and Sixties in Contemporary Cultural Politics* (Rutgers University Press, 2004). Between 2000 and 2005, Greenhaven Press has published three readers with great selections on *The 1950s*, *The 1960s*, and *The 1960s: Examining Pop Culture*.

ISSUE 15

Did President John F. Kennedy Demonstrate a Strong Commitment to Civil Rights?

YES: Carl M. Brauer, from *John F. Kennedy and the Second Reconstruction* (Columbia University Press, 1977)

NO: Nick Bryant, from *The Bystander: John F. Kennedy and the Struggle for Black Equality* (Basic Books, 2006)

ISSUE SUMMARY

YES: Carl M. Brauer asserts that President John F. Kennedy carried out an unambiguous commitment to civil rights that far exceeded anything his immediate predecessors had done and which included efforts to end discrimination in voting, education, hiring practices, public facilities, and housing.

NO: Nick Bryant claims that President Kennedy took an overly cautious approach to civil rights matters to avoid a confrontation with white southern Democrats in Congress and relied too heavily on symbolic, largely cosmetic changes that left him with a meager legacy of civil rights accomplishments.

T he image is one that is indelibly etched in the memory of virtually every American old enough to realize the monumental significance of the scene they were witnessing. Martin Luther King, Jr., the most prominent spokesman of the civil rights movement, stood at a podium and proclaimed to his audience, "I have a dream." For many Americans, black and white, King's speech at the March on Washington was the symbolic climax of the civil rights movement. The Civil Rights Act of 1964 and the Voting Rights Act of 1965 were merely denouement.

Actually, there was more that was symbolic at the March on Washington than King's electrifying oration. The call for the march had been issued by A. Philip Randolph, a long-time civil rights activist, who had threatened in 1941 to stage a similar protest march to bring attention to the economic inequality suffered by African Americans. Randolph's presence at the head of this march in 1963 reflected a realization of *his* dream. Moreover, several of the speakers that day paid homage to W. E. B. Du Bois, the godfather of the twentieth-century black protest movement in the United States, who had died the previous day (at the age of 95) in Ghana, West Africa, an embittered exile from the land of his birth.

For generations, African Americans had endured an enforced second-class citizenship in a nation circumscribed by Jim Crow. But in the 1940s and 1950s, following constitutional victories spearheaded by the National Association for the Advancement of Colored People (NAACP) in the areas of housing, voting, and education, black Americans awakened to the possibilities for change in their status. These victories coincided with the rise of independent nations in Africa, led by black leaders such as Kwame Nkrumah, which encouraged pride in the African homeland among many black Americans. Finally, the nonviolent direct action movement, pioneered by interracial organizations such as the Congress of Racial Equality (CORE) and individuals like Randolph, King, Ella Baker, James Farmer, and Fannie Lou Hamer, issued a clarion call to African Americans and their white supporters that full equality was around the corner.

Despite his idealistic predictions of the future, King's vision of a color blind society liberated from the harsh realities of prejudice and discrimination faced serious barriers, not the least of which was a federal government whose leaders offered an ambiguous response to the African American freedom struggle. President Harry S. Truman, despite the southern orientation of his own family background, insisted that "we shall not finally achieve the ideals for which this nation was founded so long as any American suffers discrimination as a result of his race," but Truman did not mount a campaign to eliminate racial segregation. Furthermore, he expressed some reluctance about anti-poll tax legislation in Congress. Truman's successor, Dwight D. Eisenhower, signed the Civil Rights Acts of 1957 and 1960 and appointed Earl Warren as Chief Justice of the United States Supreme Court, marking a liberal, activist direction for the highest judicial tribunal in the country, but Eisenhower also avoided any public expression of support for the *Brown v. Board of Education of Topeka* decision and only reluctantly deployed members of the 101st Airborne Division to Arkansas to oversee the desegregation of Little Rock's Central High School in 1957. John Kennedy campaigned for the presidency in 1960 on behalf of a strong civil rights platform and benefited from the support of African American voters, but his record of accomplishment on this issue was irritatingly slow to many blacks.

What was John Kennedy's legacy in the realm of civil rights for African Americans? Did his actions match his campaign rhetoric? Was he able to improve appreciably the status of black Americans during his short time in office? These questions are addressed in te essays that follow.

Carl Brauer offers a very positive portrayal of Kennedy as a civil rights advocate. According to Brauer, JFK's activism in the field of civil rights far exceeded that of his predecessors and included broad-based efforts to end racial discrimination in the United States.

Nick Bryant, on the other hand, is far more critical of Kennedy's performance. Bryant believes that President Kennedy abdicated a responsibility to lead and that by the time of his assassination, Kennedy possessed only a meager record of accomplishment in the field of civil rights.

YES

Carl M. Brauer

John F. Kennedy and the Second Reconstruction

President Kennedy's murder stunned the nation. There are probably few adults today who cannot recall the exact circumstances of their hearing the news on November 22, 1963. Across the country people wept openly in the streets, and millions attended hurriedly called memorial services. Normal activities slowed and even ceased as a vast audience sat mesmerized in front of their television sets which broadcast little for three days other than films of Kennedy's career, eulogies, news about the assassination, and then, finally, his deeply moving funeral. Outside the United States the reaction to Kennedy's death often reached equal intensity.

The enormous impact of his death can be explained by a number of factors. Assassinations had become rare in American life; the last murder of a President (McKinley) had occurred sixty-two years before. Yet, even had Kennedy died suddenly of natural causes, the public reaction would have been great. Kennedy had been the picture of youth and vitality. He had two small children and a glamorous young wife. He belonged to a large, wealthy, and closely knit family, many of those members could be individually identified by the public. Indeed, the Kennedy family had a special aura, almost royal in aspect, which captivated the popular imagination. Over and above all this, Kennedy had become identified with hopes for peace and social and economic progress. In an age when humanity's very survival appeared to be at stake, the unexpected, violent death of the person who seemed to represent its best chances for the future shocked and frightened many millions of people.

White Southerners, many of whom had come to resent Kennedy's civil rights advocacy, nevertheless generally grieved his death. It was true that in a number of segregated school rooms in the South white children applauded word of Kennedy's death, but authorities went to great lengths to hide these displays of passion, which they considered shameful. White Southerners, segregationist or not, for the most part mourned the President's passing along with the rest of the country. "I thought it was terrible, I didn't think a thing like this could happen in this country," Bull Connor said. James Gray of Albany called the assassination "a stunning shock." "Our politics were miles apart, and getting further all the time. But we remained good friends," he went on. The day of the funeral many Southern government offices, schools, and businesses

From *John F. Kennedy and the Second Reconstruction* by Carl M. Brauer (Columbia University Press, 1977), pp. 311–320. Copyright © 1977 by Carl M. Brauer. Reprinted by permission of the author. www.carlbrauer.com.

closed down just as in the rest of the country. Over 1,200 people attended a memorial service at Ole Miss. More than 2,000, including the Governor-elect and many state officials, crowded into an interfaith service in the cathedral in Jackson, Mississippi. It became one of the most integrated gatherings in Mississippi history to that time. George Wallace described his attendance at Kennedy's funeral as "one of the saddest tasks I have ever performed."

Two public opinion studies completed soon after the assassination suggest that black Americans were particularly troubled by Kennedy's death. A national survey asked people to compare their own reactions with those of other people. Overall, 30 percent believed that they were more upset than "most people," but 49 percent of blacks thought they were more upset. Two-thirds of blacks, as compared to 38 percent of all respondents, agreed with the statement that they were "so confused and upset, they didn't know what to feel." Furthermore, half of the blacks surveyed, compared with one-fifth of the total sample, "worried how this might affect my own life, job and future." A study of 1,348 Detroit schoolchildren, 1,006 white and 342 black, produced complementary findings. Its director reported that Negro children were considerably more distraught and anxious. Many of them expressed concern about "how my folks will now get along," and 81 percent of black children, compared to 69 percent of white, said that they "felt the loss of someone very close and dear." Seventy percent of the black youngsters and 55 percent of the white "worried about how the U.S. would get along without its leader."

Kennedy's death hit many civil rights activists especially hard. "Nothing had ever affected me as deeply as President Kennedy's death, not even the news that Martin had been stabbed in Harlem," Coretta King wrote in 1969. The assassination confirmed her husband's private fears that America was a "sick society." Anne Moody, a courageous black activist who had virtually been run out of her native Mississippi, was working in a New Orleans restaurant on the day Kennedy was killed. In her poignant memoir, *Coming of Age in Mississippi,* she recalled losing consciousness momentarily when she heard the news. She and the other black employees were afraid to contemplate what Kennedy's death might mean to Negroes. After entering the dining room, her shock and fear turned to anger. "When I turned around and looked at all those white faces—all of those Southern white faces—fire was in my eyes. I felt like racing up and down the tables, smashing food into their faces, breaking dishes over their heads, and all the time I would shout and yell MURDERERS! MURDERERS! MURDERERS!" Later, on the streetcar, she looked to see the expressions on the faces of blacks. "I knew they must feel as though they had lost their best friend—one who was in a position to help determine their destiny. To most Negroes, especially to me, the President had made 'Real Freedom' a hope." Addressing a dinner in New York on November 26, Fred Shuttlesworth, the black leader from Birmingham, began by paying tribute to Kennedy. "It would be impossible to think or speak of the Negro revolt—which has become in truth an American Revolution—and its impact upon our American Society at this time or even in the future, without saluting our martyred President, John Fitzgerald Kennedy, whose understanding, skill and determination of purpose helped in a positive way, to lay the groundwork for a better system of democracy than that which we now know," he said. "The dedication to freedom and desire for justice found in Negro leadership and the passionate yearnings of the oppressed masses in this country were matched by his own courage of convictions, grasp of the needs of the hour, and his devotion to making the U.S. Constitution become meaningful to all its citizens."

Kennedy's death probably frightened blacks, in part because his successor, Lyndon B. Johnson, came from Texas and bore the identity—indeed stigma—of a white Southerner. Johnson, however, took pride in having gotten the 1957 Civil Rights Act through Congress. As Vice President, he had endeavored to erase his image as the candidate of the white South and had actively cultivated Negro support. Within ten days of assuming the Presidency, moreover, he publicly committed himself to fulfilling Kennedy's civil rights program. "We have talked long enough in this country about equal rights. We have talked for 100 years or more. It is time now to write the next chapter and to write it in books of law," the new President told a joint session of Congress on November 27. Early passage of the pending civil rights legislation, he declared, would be the most fitting memorial to President Kennedy. After a prolonged struggle, which included the successful invoking of cloture, Congress heeded Johnson's plea in June. Before Johnson left the White House in January 1969, he had guided additional pieces of important civil rights legislation through Congress, had secured enactment of a variety of other pieces of social and economic legislation which had a bearing on the lives of many blacks, and had established his own substantial record of executive action and moral leadership in the field of civil rights. In concrete accomplishments, Johnson eventually outstripped his predecessor's civil rights record. It is clear, however, that the foundations for Johnson's record—in Congress, through executive action, and through Presidential leadership—were laid by Kennedy.

In the quarter century before Kennedy became President, his predecessors initiated a number of measures to advance civil rights, but Kennedy's activism in this regard far surpassed any of theirs. Franklin D. Roosevelt tolerated civil rights advocacy among his lieutenants, although he cautiously refrained from using the Presidency or his own enormous personal prestige to promote equal treatment of blacks. Under considerable pressure from militant blacks on the eve of American entrance into World War II, Roosevelt created the Fair Employment Practices Commission, but invested it with meager enforcement powers. Harry S. Truman pioneered in the employment of Presidential power on behalf of racial progress, ordering the desegregation of the military, speaking out against the ill-treatment of blacks, and creating a blue-ribbon committee on civil rights. Overall, however, civil rights played a relatively minor role in his administration, with issues of foreign policy, the economy, and internal security predominating. An uncooperative Congress, meanwhile, blocked his legislative recommendations on civil rights. Dwight D. Eisenhower proceeded down the trails of executive action Truman had blazed, but displayed little enthusiasm for the task. His heart never belonged to the civil rights cause, and Eisenhower generally played a passive role in the gains that did occur during his Presidency, including the *Brown* decision and its follow-up, and the enactment of civil rights legislation in 1957 and 1960. Kennedy, by contrast, turned Truman's trails into wide avenues. He used his executive powers broadly, promoting an end to racial discrimination in voting, schools, the federal government, jobs, public facilities, and housing. He committed the moral authority of the President to racial justice in the most clear-cut terms ever. And he proposed and made significant progress toward securing the most important piece of civil rights legislation in a century. Under Kennedy, civil rights became a focal point of public policy and political debate. Moreover, so unambiguous had Kennedy's commitment to civil rights been that it is hard to imagine any Vice President who succeeded him in November 1963, reversing it.

Kennedy's motives for proceeding as he did on the civil rights issue were complex, but for the sake of understanding may be divided into three types: political, attitudinal or intellectual, and personal. Naturally his actions at different times derived from different combinations of these and to different degrees. For example, politics dominated during the 1960 campaign, but when the Birmingham crisis erupted, factors of attitude and personality were most important. In addition, each kind of motive changed intrinsically over time; his political needs as a newly elected President, for instance, differed somewhat from the requirements of candidacy. Likewise his view of Reconstruction underwent a significant change. Looking briefly at each of these motives in isolation helps clarify Kennedy's actions and effects.

Kennedy was a consummate politician. As a Senator ambitious for the Presidency, he curried the favor of civil rights proponents and opponents. In the end he succeeded in winning critical support from both sides without trading away basic principle. He promised new Presidential leadership but assured the white South that he would not be vindictive. Once elected, he had to contend with a Congress in which the Southern wing of his party possessed disproportionate power. Consequently, he did not immediately carry through on his promise of civil rights legislation and compromised on his executive action program. Nevertheless, that program marked a significant break with the past, achieved some meaningful results, and, perhaps most important, raised the hopes of black people. Indeed, higher black expectations led ultimately to Kennedy's changing his approach in June 1963. The task of getting his proposed legislation enacted in turn presented a challenge to his political leadership, which he rose to meet. He rallied important segments of the public to his cause, and in time won several key Congressional skirmishes. Simultaneously, as a candidate for reelection, he began to mend his Southern fences preparatory to his next and expectedly last campaign. To the end, he neither abandoned nor excoriated the white South. Black voters, it appeared, had meanwhile given him nearly complete allegiance.

Certain ideas guided Kennedy. As an American nationalist, he was troubled by the damage racial intolerance was inflicting upon his country's image abroad, particularly in the Third World where he hoped to expand American influence. As a student of American history, on the other hand, he for a long time accepted a simplistic though widely held view of Reconstruction as a vindictive reign of terror and corruption which the North had visited upon the South. This perspective helped smooth his relations with Southern officeholders.

Eventually, confrontations with ardent segregationists led him to question his former assumptions about the first Reconstruction and eased the way toward his launching a second, though he never advocated punishing the region. In addition, Kennedy worried about the damaging effects racial discrimination had on the nation's economy and on the health and education of its citizens. He shared the modern liberal's faith that the central government, led by an active President, could and should solve pressing social problems, of which racial discrimination was a leading one. Finally, Kennedy believed that all citizens should receive the same treatment regardless of race. Racial discrimination offended him intellectually. Hence, he shared with the civil rights movement a fundamental belief.

Personal factors also shaped Kennedy's handling of civil rights. His grace and style charmed black delegates in personal meetings. Sensitivity and empathy contributed to his making symbolic gestures of significance, such as calling Coretta King, and permitted him to comprehend, on more than an intellectual level, the struggle for equal rights. Finally, Kennedy needed to feel that he was leading rather than being swept along by events. As President, he was uncomfortable playing a passive role. Therefore, when in the spring of 1963 he perceived that he was losing the reins of leadership, he boldly reached out to grasp them once again.

Kennedy's exercise of leadership probably helped instill in many potential civil rights activists a confidence and daring that they would not otherwise have had. In this regard it might be recalled that James Meredith applied to Ole Miss the day, Kennedy was inaugurated and that for Anne Moody, Kennedy had made "'Real Freedom' a hope." Indeed, the spirit Kennedy conveyed may well have made possible the eruption of social protest to which he in turn responded. Certainly Kennedy did not create the civil rights movement, but he did affect its course. Some of the things that occurred during his years as President probably would have occurred in any case. Most definitely the Freedom Rides would have taken place and undoubtedly there would have been some other direct challenges to segregation. But what would have happened had Richard Nixon been elected President? Would he have sent marshals to Montgomery, would a Voter Education Project have been created, would the Justice Department have dramatically stepped up enforcement under the guidance of someone like Robert Kennedy, would thousands of blacks have demonstrated in Birmingham, and, most important, if they had, would Nixon have responded by proposing and working for enactment of sweeping civil rights legislation?

Those conservative critics who in 1963 charged Kennedy with encouraging massive law-breaking were in a sense not so wide of the mark. Kennedy, of course, never urged blacks to march in the streets, but he did foster an atmosphere where protests against the status quo could occur. He created that atmosphere through symbolic acts such as phoning Coretta King, appointing Thurgood Marshall to the federal bench, and opening the White House to blacks, and through more substantive deeds such as establishing a close working relationship between the Justice Department and the civil rights movement, sending marshals to Montgomery and Oxford, and using the executive powers of his office to combat discrimination. He also contributed to it in a general way, for in his campaign and in office, he represented change, not continuity; the future, not the past.

One could well draw up a balance sheet of Kennedy's civil rights record. On the minus side, one might list the appointment of segregationist judges in the South, the delay in the housing order followed by the promulgation of the narrowest possible one, as well as numerous instances of executive cautiousness. Kennedy could be faulted for not making even more high-level appointments of blacks than he did, especially to the White House staff, and for failing to remove barriers to effective criminal enforcement that existed within the federal government, specifically within the FBI. One might also want to add the fact that Kennedy did not win enactment of his proposed legislation. Yet, to blame the murdered Kennedy for that implies a certain callousness.

The plus side of the ledger would be considerably longer. It would include a large number of executive actions, such as the appointment of blacks to high offices and the gains in federal employment generally. In the upper civil service ranks, black employment increased 88 percent from June 1961 to June 1963, as compared to an overall increase at these levels of under 23 percent. High on the list would belong the many accomplishments relating to law enforcement, including the use of marshals to prevent mob rule in Montgomery, the application of legal pressure to bring about desegregation of transportation terminals, and the persistent implementation of court orders to effect desegregation at the universities of Mississippi and Alabama. Between Robert Kennedy's swearing in and his resignation in the summer of 1964, the number of voting rights suits increased from ten to sixty-nine, including statewide cases in Mississippi and Louisiana. The administration also scored some gains by promoting voluntary action. For example, partly as a result of Justice Department efforts, between May and December 1963, some voluntary desegregation of public accommodations took place in 356 out of 566 cities in the South and border states; biracial committees were established in at least 185 of these cities. Because the administration played a role in the creation of the Voter Education Project, it might be afforded partial credit for its accomplishments. By April 1964, the VEP had registered nearly 580,000 new voters in the South. President Kennedy's proposal of a broad civil rights bill in 1963 and his preliminary successes in getting that bill through Congress would also deserve places on the plus side of the ledger. Finally, Kennedy's exercise of moral leadership, through rhetorical advocacy and through personal example, would certainly merit inclusion in the positive column.

A balance sheet does not convey Kennedy's full importance, however. Kennedy was significant not only for what he did, but for what he started. His Presidency marked a profound change from the inertia that had generally characterized the past. In a tragically foreshortened term of less than three years, he instituted a vigorous and far-reaching effort to eliminate racial discrimination in American life. Operating within the bounds of a democratic political system, Kennedy both encouraged and responded to black aspirations and led the nation into its Second Reconstruction.

The Bystander: John F. Kennedy and the Struggle for Black Equality

Had Kennedy lived, he would almost certainly have secured passage of the 1964 Civil Rights Act. The key to the passage of the bill, after all, was the support of moderate Republicans, and Kennedy had already received firm assurances from Senate Minority Leader Everett Dirksen that they would stand with the president. "This program was on its way before November 22," Dirksen commented after its passage. "Its time had come." Senate Majority Leader Mike Mansfield agreed that the civil rights bill would still have passed, but "might have taken a little longer"—a reference perhaps to Kennedy's deficiencies as a legislative strategist as well as the skills with which [Lyndon] Johnson had transformed national grief over Kennedy's murder into support for the civil rights bill. But Kennedy had proposed the legislation, and he deserved much of the credit when it became law.

At the time of his death, however, Kennedy had only a small record of accomplishments in civil rights. Progress had been agonizingly slow in voting rights and employment reform, the areas where his administration had devoted most of its energy. By 1963, black registration had increased from five percent to just 8.3 percent of eligible voters in the 100 counties targeted by the Justice Department. Between 1961 and 1964, the number of blacks employed by the federal government had inched from 12.9 percent to 13.2 percent. The Plans for Progress, meanwhile, remained an embarrassment. Between May 1961 and January 1963, black employment in participating companies rose from 5 percent to 5.1 percent. The black share of white-collar jobs showed only a negligible gain, from 1.5 percent to 1.6 percent. Even so, the president continued to encourage new firms to sign up. In other areas of policy, too, the picture was much the same. The long-delayed housing order had proved to be a glaring failure in practice. After Kennedy's death, Robert Weaver estimated the order had covered less than three percent of existing housing. Most African diplomats continued to look on Washington as a hardship posting, because of their difficulties in finding adequate housing.

The administration had also adhered to a distinctly southern timetable in the implementation of *Brown*. By 1963, one hundred and sixty-six school

From *The Bystander: John F. Kennedy and the Struggle for Black Equality* by Nick Bryant (Basic Books, 2006), pp. 462–470, 471–473 (notes omitted). Copyright © 2006 by Nick Bryant. Reprinted by permission of Basic Books, a member of Perseus Books Group.

districts had been integrated, compared to just seventeen in 1960. But in Mississippi, Alabama, and South Carolina, not a single school district had been entirely desegregated. Georgia and Louisiana could claim just one. King estimated that if integration continued at the current pace, it would take until 2054 for southern schools to be completely desegregated. After all, by 1964 just one in a hundred black schoolchildren attended integrated schools in the south.

The Kennedy administration had made greater strides in less readily quantifiable areas. The White House became more welcoming to blacks, which in turn encouraged greater racial integration in much of American society. Kennedy's ease in the company of blacks, combined with his public denunciations of the capital's all-white gentlemen's clubs, helped to establish an unwritten code of racial acceptance. Washington hostesses adorned their cocktail and dinner parties with more black faces. It was now unthinkable to plan a major national event without guaranteeing the participation of blacks. Through his own powerful personal example, Kennedy had made it unfashionable to be racist. Up until the summer of 1963, it was arguably his greatest contribution to the struggle for equality.

Kennedy's inclusiveness represented a genuine paradigm shift in American racial politics. Franklin Delano Roosevelt, a far more aloof politician, had earned the love of blacks through his success in ameliorating black poverty. Kennedy offered blacks something quite different, but no less empowering: a sense of acceptance. As his consistently high poll numbers among blacks demonstrated, and the thousands of black mourners at his funeral confirmed, many blacks felt a tremendously powerful connection to Kennedy. Some considered him to be the Great Emancipator of the twentieth century.

Of course, Kennedy's symbolic approach to the race problem meant that many of the changes he ushered in were largely cosmetic. And often they were restricted to the capital—where segregation had troubled him since his earliest days in Congress. Kennedy certainly had a keen eye for racial detail—as he demonstrated on his first day in office when he complained that the Coast Guard Academy honor guard did not include any blacks. But the episode was also emblematic of Kennedy's tendency to respond to examples of racial inequity that were directly in front of him, while he ignored the broader problems that fell outside of his limited range of vision. Far too often, Kennedy was content as long as problems simply disappeared from view. Sometimes, it was what he saw with his own eyes that disturbed him—as with the whites-only gentlemen's clubs in Washington. Other times, he wanted to hide segregation from the sight of others—African diplomats, the Kremlin, newspaper photographers.

Perhaps not surprisingly, given his privileged upbringing, Kennedy identified far more easily with middle-class blacks, who were more concentrated in the North, than with the far poorer blacks who populated the South. Middle-class blacks had already achieved a degree of financial success and longed primarily for social acceptance—something Kennedy could bestow through his highly publicized gestures of black outreach. Southern blacks still needed basic civil rights—access to jobs, education, voting booths. These demands were far harder to fulfill—particularly because in many cases whites would have to pay the price for black advancement. And so Kennedy shied away from more controversial policy areas, such as schooling and public accommodations, which would be successfully implemented only with substantial white support. Instead, Kennedy steered his administration toward areas such as voting rights and employment reform, which emphasized black self-improvement and self-empowerment.

When it came to emotionally charged issues, such as school integration, Kennedy always advocated piecemeal reform. But his timetable was completely misaligned with that of the black leadership. In 1961, black leaders were initially prepared to accept the administration's nonlegislative strategy but expected other civil rights reforms to come at a quicker pace. By 1963, civil rights activists demanded "Freedom Now," and adopted more militant tactics in the hope of spurring the administration to act more quickly.

What if Kennedy had moved faster? In 1961, his administration could have dealt with many black demands—such as accelerated school integration, fair housing, greater employment opportunities, and greater presidential leadership on race—with only a relatively mild readjustment of policies. Had the administration released the housing order at an earlier date, pushed for a more active PCEEO [President's Committee on Equal Employment Opportunity], launched a greater number of voting rights suits, or sought to enforce the ICC ruling on interstate travel, it probably could have channeled the civil rights movement in a more peaceful direction. Instead, the most violent clashes—the Freedom Rides, Ole Miss, and the Birmingham crisis—all ignited as a result of the frustration of protesters, who wanted to jolt the administration into action. Had Kennedy done more, earlier, then many of these crises—along with the southern backlash they provoked—might have been averted.

Certainly, the race crisis would not have melted away—after all, the civil rights movement was trying to reverse the effects of an American institution that had endured for over 250 years. But bolder federal policies would almost certainly have had a calming effect and could have led to a sincere collaboration between black activists and white policymakers. When civil rights rose to the top of the presidential agenda in the summer of 1963, Kennedy finally helped to engineer a multipronged assault on southern segregation and northern discrimination that blacks had been demanding since the end of World War II. But it was too late for black leaders. Even Kennedy's civil rights bill, the boldest proposals ever put by a president before Congress, was not enough to satisfy black demands. Civil rights leaders attacked the administration for the absence of stronger Part III powers and a commitment to create a fair employment practices committee. And they raised the stakes far higher—now they called for quotas, affirmative action, reparations, and other compensatory governmental programs. Kennedy had lost so much credibility through his years of equivocation that there was now little he could do to appease black activists.

After Kennedy's death, black leaders plotted more aggressive protest campaigns. They did so partly to safeguard their own leadership positions within an increasingly radicalized movement but mainly to maintain pressure on the federal government. In 1964, CORE, SNCC, the SCLC, and the NAACP joined forces to mount the Mississippi Freedom Summer Project, a voter registration campaign that resulted in another upsurge of racial violence. Segregationists firebombed thirty buildings and razed twelve churches. A thousand protesters were arrested by police, and civil rights activists James Chaney, Andrew Goodman, and Michael Schwerner were murdered. In January 1965, the SCLC launched a bold new voting rights campaign in Selma, in hopes of provoking a violent white backlash. Martin Luther King intended to "arouse the federal government," as he put it, into proposing new voting rights legislation. King was merely applying the central lesson that black activists had learned during the Kennedy years: that provoking racist violence was the best way to secure presidential attention.

By the mid-1960s, the movement had gained such momentum that it was now largely beyond presidential control. Legislative remedies held only limited value. On August 6, 1965, Johnson signed the Voting Rights Act into law. Five days later, rioting erupted in the Watts section of Los Angeles, during which thirty-four people were killed, hundreds injured, and almost 4,000 people arrested. In the years after Kennedy's death, there was an explosion of racial violence on the streets of the country's worst black slums—Rochester, Harlem, and Philadelphia erupted in 1964, and later Washington, Baltimore, San Francisco, Detroit, Cleveland, and Chicago.

In July 1967, President Johnson appointed a commission headed by Illinois Governor Otto Kerner to investigate the racial disorders in American cities. The Kerner Commission, as it became known, reported back the following year. The commissioners discussed urban violence—and the sense of disillusionment from which it sprang—in the context of broader national trends. They pointed out that the great judicial and legislative victories of the civil rights era had produced a new form of resentment as blacks realized that it would take far more comprehensive reforms to ensure genuine black equality. They also cited the "white terrorism directed against nonviolent protesters" as a precipitating factor in the riots, along with a prevailing sense of alienation and powerlessness among young black Americans, which had led many to believe that there was no effective alternative to violence. In many communities, the commissioners also noted, the police had come to symbolize "white power, white racism, and white repression." Every one of these trends cited in the report had been in evidence at various stages of the Kennedy presidency— from police brutality to white terrorism. But the Kennedy administration had done little to address these underlying problems. If anything, it had exacerbated them through its own inaction.

･◌･

There are a number of explanations—political and temperamental—for Kennedy's distracted and often excessively and unnecessarily cautious approach to the civil rights agenda. But perhaps the most obvious explanation lies in Kennedy's own successes as a lawmaker and as a political candidate. From his very first congressional campaign, Kennedy had learned how to gain electoral advantage through manipulation—sometimes cynical, sometimes sincere—of black opinion. He had drawn on the same skills during his years in Congress—had it not been for his adroit, and at times brilliant, handling of civil rights, Kennedy would never have risen so fast in the 1950s. Throughout his political career, up until and including his 1960 presidential campaign, Kennedy had reached out to black voters (as well as white liberal sympathizers) through symbolic gestures and tokenistic measures.

Kennedy believed he could enjoy much the same political success as president—and to some extent, he was right. At the very moment that SNCC activists were formulating their Montgomery Battle Plan, Kennedy enjoyed black approval ratings above eighty percent. Kennedy had good reason to believe that his policies were in step with the expectations of blacks nationwide. His sense that black activists such as King and Wilkins had gone beyond the constituency they claimed to represent was not entirely unjustified.

But over the long term, Kennedy's reliance on opinion polls proved to be politically myopic. High black approval ratings validated lackluster policies. Kennedy marginalized advisers like Harris Wofford and Louis Martin who tried to draw attention to the disaffection of black leaders and civil rights activists. He kept his distance from those who tried to confront him with less rosy assessments of the race problem—including members of the Civil Rights Commission. When criticized, Kennedy would lurch to the defensive. All too often, he would justify any perceived complacency by comparing his record on civil rights to that of his predecessors. But given the turbulent and rapidly changing political climate of the early 1960s, and the heightened expectations of civil rights activists, the comparison was meaningless.

There were other reasons for Kennedy's shortcomings when it came to civil rights. He was temperamentally averse to confrontation, which partly explained his preference for voluntary solutions to intractable problems of segregation and discrimination. He was chronically unwilling to endorse punitive action, particularly in the realm of employment reform and school integration.

Kennedy's convivial leadership style also meant that he was unwilling to do anything that would antagonize members of the Southern Caucus—he was afraid of souring his cordial personal relationships by conducting what he considered pointless arguments over race. He was endlessly ingratiating even when it came to negotiating with diehard segregationists—a tendency that proved particularly disastrous at the height of the Ole Miss crisis.

Kennedy could have accomplished a great deal by taking on the Southern Caucus early in his presidency. Had he done so, and thereby exposed their diminishing political power, radical figures such as George Wallace and Ross Barnett would never have had the confidence to defy the federal government so brazenly. But Kennedy's deference toward southern lawmakers emboldened diehard segregationists. It contributed to a culture of impunity in the Deep South, in which the most virulent proponents of segregation—Wallace, Barnett, and their ilk—were able to commit flagrant violations of basic civil rights on behalf of their shrinking constituency.

Kennedy was also emotionally limited—in many ways a product of his highly regimented Boston family and the exclusive schools he had attended. He took great pride in his coolness under pressure, and this detachment came to define his style of presidential leadership. At times, such as the Cuban missile crisis, it was a tremendous asset. But when it came to civil rights, it meant that he was notoriously unresponsive even when confronted by the most heinous acts of racial violence. Images that affected most Americans on a visceral level—from the Birmingham photograph to Martin Luther King's "I Have a Dream" speech—elicited purely pragmatic responses from the president.

Kennedy's extraordinary personal charisma and the idealistic promise of his young administration often masked his cynicism and conservatism. His restless campaign rhetoric had created the false impression that he intended to usher in an era of fervent reform. The reality was less stirring. Kennedy could be an inspiring speaker, but he was no political visionary. As his congressional record demonstrated, he was an incrementalist with only limited ambitions in domestic policy. The Kennedy campaign had invented the phrase "New Frontier" specifically to tap into the deep well of American nostalgia for the presidency of Franklin Delano Roosevelt. But when it came to civil rights Kennedy had no intention of offering the nation a genuinely new deal.

Kennedy had immense skill when it came to crafting his own image. But he was largely unwilling to lend this skill to the cause of civil rights. As the columnist James Reston once so aptly pointed out, Kennedy was much better at dramatizing himself than the issues. In the spring of 1963, when a delegation from the ADA [Americans for Democratic Action] suggested a series of fireside chats to help defuse the civil rights crisis, Kennedy demurred on the grounds that he did not have Roosevelt's voice. The response spoke less of humility than of Kennedy's timid governing philosophy.

Kennedy compounded his deficiencies by surrounding himself with advisers who reinforced his instinctively conservative nature. Political operatives like Kenneth O'Donnell and Larry O'Brien shared not only Kennedy's cautious political instincts but also his contempt for moralizing liberals. During the summer of 1963, Kennedy started to rely more and more on the advice of his brother and Burke Marshall, who were pushing him to embrace reform. Nonetheless, O'Donnell and O'Brien repeatedly tried to restrain him.

By the time of his death, Kennedy had unquestionably become more sympathetic to the plight of black Americans. He had grown in office. He had started to question the version of southern history that had underpinned much of his thinking on federal power and had grown increasingly impatient with die-hard segregationists, who seemed ever more irrational to Kennedy and in some cases even deranged. He also showed some signs of increased emotional engagement—evident in his extemporaneous remarks during his nationwide television address on June 11, and his response to the death of Medgar Evers.

But Kennedy never seemed able to sustain this level of empathy for the black cause. Days after he invited Myrlie Evers to the White House, Kennedy spoke scornfully of how the black demonstrators who were arriving in the capital might "shit" on the Washington monument. He vacillated in much the same way in the aftermath of the Birmingham bombing. He released a fiercely worded statement on the Monday after the bomb attack but failed even to mention the murders when he addressed the nation the very next evening.

Martin Luther King was right to draw attention to Kennedy's "schizophrenic tendency" when it came to civil rights. There was, however, something of a pattern to Kennedy's fluctuations. He tended to be cold and calculating when organized civil rights protesters tried to pressure him into taking a political stand. He was much more sympathetic to individuals who had suffered directly from the violent outrages of segregation. He offered no public support to King and the Birmingham protesters in April 1963, for instance, but hastened to offer private reassurances to Coretta King over the telephone. That same month, Kennedy publicly criticized the CRC for its interim report on the racial crisis in Mississippi but made a point of calling to the attention of journalists his revulsion at the murder of William Moore. The CRC was an abstract political entity that both criticized Kennedy and demanded of him an overtly political response. Moore's protest, by contrast, was far more understated. While he had also sought to focus attention on Mississippi, Moore did so by making a solitary march toward Jackson, with only a simple placard: "Equal Rights for All (Mississippi or Bust)." Because little in Moore's actions challenged Kennedy or his administration directly, the president was able to respond in purely human terms to this appalling murder.

Perhaps there is something more to Kennedy's pattern of response. At times, it seemed almost as if Kennedy found in these individual victims a means of expiating his guilt for his failure to speak and act more forcefully on the public stage. From his earliest days as a congressman, Kennedy had been personally committed to the cause of black equality—but he constantly made excuses for failing to push for it politically. Perhaps on some level, Kennedy wanted to be something more than he was—a stronger president, a more virtuous man.

Civil rights could certainly bring out the best in Kennedy—his personal warmth, his lack of prejudice, his gallantry, his natural skill as a speaker, and—belatedly—his extraordinary ability to inspire. But the issue also brought out the weaker side of his personality—his indecisiveness, his political cautiousness, his instinctive defensiveness in the face of criticism, and, above all, his lack of moral conviction.

In the final summer of his life, Kennedy seemed to be trying to resurrect the nobler ideals that motivated him in the early years of his career, when his views on civil rights were less corrupted by politics. But would that dedication have endured into his second term? Perhaps. By the time of his assassination, Kennedy had considerable support for civil rights reform throughout the country. And he was beginning to experiment with this new southern strategy, which had already shown early promise. But it is all too easy to imagine a real retrenchment. Throughout his political career, Kennedy had been willing—even eager—to abandon the cause of reform when he sensed it might lead to any sort of unpleasant confrontation. There is no way, of course, to know what Kennedy would have done in the next five years of his presidency. But his political history demonstrates that, at least when it came to civil rights, he almost always allowed the voice of political expedience to drown out the better angels of his nature. . . .

⊷❦⊶

John Kennedy had never set out—as a legislator or as president—to dramatically overhaul race relations in the American South. For him, the defining struggle of the postwar era was not civil rights but the Cold War, and he not unreasonably believed that his presidency would be judged by his handling of the threat from the Soviet Union. From the outset of his career, Kennedy was primarily interested in foreign relations, and as president during the hottest years of the Cold War, he trained his gaze on Moscow far more often than on Birmingham or Atlanta. Consequently, Kennedy was almost perpetually distracted from civil rights issues. Even on the day of the momentous March on Washington, Kennedy spent more time chairing discussions on South Vietnam than he did with King and other march leaders.

But Kennedy's approach to civil rights was also deeply intertwined with his foreign policy. To a large extent, Kennedy's early interest in the problem of segregation derived from his fear that it would embarrass the United States on the international stage and provide the Soviets with a crucial propaganda tool in their battle for supremacy in the developing world. Kennedy spoke out vocally against segregation in many of his early speeches specifically for this reason, and his early presidential efforts to promote integration in both the federal government and the clubs and restaurants of the capital were all part of the broader Cold War strategy.

Because his anticommunism drove so much of his thinking about civil rights, however, Kennedy could also quickly turn against the black cause when it suited the exigencies of international politics. During the Freedom Rides, Kennedy was almost paralyzed by his fear of handing Khrushchev, a public relations victory, which partly explained why his personal role during the first civil rights crisis of his presidency was so very limited. He later infuriated civil rights leaders when it became clear that his early support for black nationalist movements in Africa had given way to purely strategic geopolitical considerations. Even in the final year of his presidency, Kennedy continued to refer to civil rights in the context of the Cold War. But the rhetoric began to sound hollow. Transfixed by the fierce spiritual energy of Martin Luther King, a new generation of black Americans needed a president who spoke with the same kind of moral force.

Kennedy was all too often tone deaf when it came to civil rights. He was never able to provide the kind of principled leadership that black activists so desperately needed. Instead, the president leaned heavily on his highly effective strategy of association—a strategy that his successors quickly learned to imitate. The Kennedy administration taught Washington an ugly political lesson: that politicians could win black support through grand symbolic gestures, which obviated the need for trolly substantive reforms.

Kennedy's strategy ultimately transformed the politics of race in America. Lyndon Johnson pressed for fresh civil rights legislation, but he also acutely understood the value of symbolic change. He awarded Roy Wilkins, Whitney Young, and A. Philip Randolph the Presidential Medal of Freedom, elevated Thurgood Marshall to the Supreme Court, and made Robert Weaver the head of the Department of Housing and Urban Development (HUD). Jimmy Carter relied more heavily on this tactic. In the absence of a forceful civil rights program, he appointed Andrew Young as his ambassador to the United Nations, made a pilgrimage to Martin Luther King's tomb at the Ebenezer Baptist Church in Atlanta, and even had a White House adviser who was nicknamed the "Secretary for Symbolism." The strategy also worked in reverse, of course. When Richard Nixon wanted to court the George Wallace constituency during the 1972 election campaign, he asked Alexander Haig, his chief of staff, to explore of possibility of securing federal funding for a statute of Robert E. Lee and a memorial to Confederate soldiers. Kennedy had demonstrated that racial politics could be played out at the level of spectacle—it was far less dangerous than a serious battle of ideas.

Kennedy had become president at a turning point in American history. By the end of the 1950s, many segregationists had come to accept the vulnerability of their position. Southern blacks looked forward to the day—just around the corner it seemed—when they would finally enjoy first class citizenship. An optimistic civil rights movement remained resolutely committed to the idea of nonviolent, peaceful change. A majority of Americans were favorably disposed toward racial reform.

At the time of his presidential victory, Kennedy had a unique opportunity to secure a peaceful transition toward a more integrated and equitable society. Instead, Kennedy stood aside. The battle for the revision of Rule XXII in 1960, the New Orleans school crisis, the Freedom Rides, the Battle of Ole Miss, D-Day in Birmingham—all were opportunities for Kennedy to hasten the downfall of southern segregation. But up until the Birmingham riot in 1963, when the crisis in race relations finally threatened to overwhelm the country, Kennedy abdicated his responsibility to lead the great social revolution of his age. And by then it was too late. At the time of his death, America was already moving inexorably toward what the Kerner Commission would later vividly describe as "two societies, one black, one white—separate and unequal." For far too long, Kennedy had remained a bystander.

POSTSCRIPT

Did President John F. Kennedy Demonstrate a Strong Commitment to Civil Rights?

Writing against the backdrop of John Kennedy's assassination in Dallas on November 22, 1963, the first generation of biographers of the 37th President of the United States tended to write glowingly of the fallen leader's accomplishments. The earliest full-length assessments came from the President's inner circle. They include Arthur Schlesinger, Jr., *A Thousand Days: John F. Kennedy in the White House* (Houghton Mifflin, 1965); Theodore C. Sorensen, *Kennedy* (Harper and Row, 1965); and Kenneth P. O'Donnell and David F. Powers, with Joe McCarthy, *"Johnny, We Hardly Knew Ye": Memories of John Fitzgerald Kennedy* (Little, Brown, 1970). More critical appraisals can be found in Henry Fairlie, *The Kennedy Promise: The Politics of Expectation* (Doubleday, 1973); Garry Wills, *The Kennedy Imprisonment: A Meditation on Power* (Little, Brown, 1982); and Richard Reeves, *President Kennedy: Profile of Power* (Simon & Schuster, 1993). Newer, balanced studies include Robert Dallek, *An Unfinished Life: John F. Kennedy, 1917–1963* (Little, Brown, 2003) and David Burner, *John F. Kennedy and a New Generation* (2nd ed.; Pearson Longman, 2005). For additional works that treat JFK's civil rights record, see Burke Marshall, *Federalism and Civil Rights* (Columbia University Press, 1964); Harris Wofford, *Of Kennedys and Kings* (Farrar, Strauss & Giroux, 1980); Irving Bernstein, *Promises Kept: John F. Kennedy's New Frontier* (Oxford University Press, 1991), especially chapters 2 and 3; and Mark Stern, *Calculating Visions: Kennedy, Johnson, and Civil Rights* (Rutgers University Press, 1992). Important insights also can be gleaned from John Hart, "Kennedy, Congress, and Civil Rights," *Journal of American Studies* 13 (August 1979): 165–178; and Robert E. Gilbert, "John F. Kennedy and Civil Rights for Black Americans," *Presidential Studies Quarterly* 12 (Summer 1982): 386–399.

The literature on the civil rights movement is extensive. August Meier, Elliott Rudwick, and Francis L. Broderick, eds., *Black Protest Thought in the Twentieth Century* (2nd ed.; Bobbs-Merrill, 1971) present a collection of documents that places the activities of the 1950s and 1960s in a larger framework. The reflections of many of the participants of the movement are included in Howell Raines, *My Soul Is Rested: The Story of the Civil Rights Movement in the Deep South* (G. P. Putnam, 1977). August Meier's contemporary assessment, "On the Role of Martin Luther King," *Crisis* (1965), in many ways remains the most insightful analysis of King's leadership. More detailed studies include David J. Garrow's Pulitzer-Prize winning *Bearing the Cross: Martin Luther King, Jr., and the Southern Christian Leadership Conference* (William Morrow, 1986); and Harvard Sitkoff, *King: Pilgrimage to the Mountaintop* (Hill and Wang, 2008).

Taylor Branch's award-winning trilogy *America in the King Years* (Simon & Schuster, 1988, 1998, 2006) is a wonderful read.

The black nationalist critique of King and the nonviolent direct action campaign is effectively presented in Malcolm X (with Alex Haley), *The Autobiography of Malcolm X* (Grove Press, 1964); and Peter Goldman, *The Death and Life of Malcolm X* (Harper and Row, 1974). James H. Cone's *Martin & Malcolm & America: A Dream or a Nightmare* (Orbis, 1991) is a valuable analysis that emphasizes the convergence of these two leaders' ideas.

For an understanding of the major civil rights organizations in the 1960s, see August Meier and Elliott Rudwick, *CORE: A Study in the Civil Rights Movement, 1942–1968* (Oxford University Press, 1973); Clayborne Carson, *In Struggle: SNCC and the Black Awakening of the 1960s* (Harvard University Press, 1981); Adam Fairclough, *To Redeem the Soul of America: The Southern Christian Leadership Conference and Martin Luther King, Jr.* (University of Georgia Press, 1987); and Patricia Sullivan, *Lift Every Voice: The NAACP and the Making of the Civil Rights Movement* (New Press, 2009). Finally, the texture of the civil rights movement is captured brilliantly in Henry Hampton's documentary series "Eyes on the Prize."

ISSUE 16

Did President Nixon Negotiate a "Peace with Honor" in Vietnam in 1973?

YES: Richard Nixon, from *The Real War* (Warner Books, 1980)

NO: Larry Berman, from *No Peace, No Honor: Nixon, Kissinger, and Betrayal in Vietnam* (The Free Press, 2001)

ISSUE SUMMARY

YES: Former president Richard Nixon believes that the South Vietnamese government would not have lost the war to North Vietnam in 1975 if Congress had not cut off aid.

NO: According to Professor Larry Berman, President Nixon knew that the Paris Peace Accords of January 1973 were flawed, but he intended to bomb North Vietnamese troops to prevent the collapse of South Vietnam until he left office.

$\mathbf{A}$t the end of World War II, imperialism was coming to a close in Asia and anti-imperialist movements emerged all over Asia and Africa, often producing chaos. The United States faced a dilemma. On the one hand, America was a nation conceived in revolution and was sympathetic to the struggles of the Third World nations. On the other hand, the United States was afraid that many of the revolutionary leaders were Communists who would place their countries under the control of the expanding empire of the Soviet Union. By the late 1940s, the Truman administration decided that it was necessary to stop the spread of communism. The policy that resulted was known as "containment."

The first true military test of the "containment" doctrine came soon. Korea, previously controlled by Japan, had been temporarily divided at the 38th Parallel at the end of World War II. Communists gained control of North Korea while anticommunist revolutionaries established a government in South Korea. When neither side would agree to a unified government, the temporary division became permanent. After North Korea attacked South Korea in late June 1950, President Truman led the nation into an undeclared war under United Nations auspices. The Korean War lasted 3 years and was fought to a stalemate.

Vietnam provided the second test of the "containment" doctrine in Asia. Vietnam had been a French protectorate from 1885 until Japan took control during World War II. Shortly before the war ended, the Japanese gave Vietnam its independence but the French were determined to reestablish their influence in the area. Conflicts emerged between the French-led nationalist forces of South Vietnam and the Communist-dominated provisional government of the Democratic Republic of Vietnam established in Hanoi in August 1945. Ho Chi Minh was the president of the DRV. An avowed Communist since the 1920s, Ho had also become the major nationalist figure in Vietnam and managed to tie together the Communist and nationalist movements in Vietnam.

A full-scale war broke out in 1946 between the Communist government of North Vietnam and the French-dominated country of South Vietnam. The war lasted 8 years. After the Communists had inflicted a disastrous defeat on the French at the battle of Dienbienphu in May 1954, the latter decided to pull out. At the Geneva Conference the following summer, Vietnam was divided at the 17th Parallel pending elections.

The United States involvement in Vietnam came after the French withdrew. In 1955, the Republican President Dwight Eisenhower refused to recognize the Geneva Accords but supported the establishment of the South Vietnamese government. Its leader was Ngo Dinh Diem. In 1956 Diem, with United States approval, refused to hold elections that would have provided a unified government for Vietnam in accordance with the Geneva agreement. The Communists in the South responded by again taking up the armed struggle. The war continued unabated for another 19 years.

Both President Eisenhower and his Democratic successor, John F. Kennedy, were anxious to prevent South Vietnam from being taken over by the Communists. Economic assistance and military aid were given to the South Vietnamese government. A major problem for President Kennedy lay in the unpopularity of the South Vietnamese government. He supported the overthrow of the Diem regime (though not his murder) in October 1963, and hoped that the successor government would establish an alternative to communism. It didn't work. Kennedy himself was assassinated 3 weeks later. His successor Lyndon Johnson changed the character of American policy in Vietnam by escalating the air war and increasing the number of ground forces from 21,000 in 1965, to a full fighting force of 550,000 at its peak in 1968.

The next president, Richard Nixon, adopted a new policy of "Vietnamization" of the war. Military aid to the Republic of South Vietnam was increased to ensure the defeat of the Communists. At the same time, American troops were gradually withdrawn from Vietnam. The bombing raids in the fall and winter of 1972 probably convinced the North Vietnamese to negotiate a peace settlement. In the first selection, Nixon argues that South Vietnam had defeated the Communists by the time of the cease-fire in January 1973 and that the victory was short-lived because after North Vietnam violated the accords in 1975, the United States Congress refused to give South Vietnam the aid that would have prevented its fall to the communists. Professor Larry Berman argues there was no peace and no honor. President Nixon knew the Paris Peace Accords were flawed, but once he got the prisoners of war home, when the cease-fire collapsed, he intended to bomb North Vietnam to prevent the collapse of South Vietnam until he left office.

YES

Richard Nixon

The Vietnam Syndrome

The final chapters have yet to be written on the war in Vietnam. It was a traumatizing experience for Americans, a brutalizing experience for the Vietnamese, an exploitable opportunity for the Soviets. It was also one of the crucial battles of World War III. . . .

Vietnam was partitioned in 1954, with a communist government in the North under Ho Chi Minh and a noncommunist government in the South with its capital in Saigon. Between the two was a demilitarized buffer zone—the DMZ. Soon Ho's government in Hanoi was infiltrating large numbers of agents into the South, where they worked with guerrilla forces to set up networks of subversion and terrorism designed to undermine the Saigon government.

The interim premier of South Vietnam, Ngo Dinh Diem, became its first president In 1955. He proved to be a strong and effective leader, particularly in containing the communist guerrilla forces that were directly supported by the North in violation of the 1954 Partition Agreement. The Eisenhower administration provided generous economic assistance and some military aid and technical advisers, but Eisenhower rejected proposals to commit American combat forces.

Large-scale infiltration from the North began in 1959, and by 1961 the communists had made substantial gains. Sir Robert Thompson arrived in Vietnam that year to head the British Advisory Mission. Thompson had been Secretary of Defense of the Malayan Federation when the communist insurgency had been defeated there. He and the CIA people on the scene understood the importance of local political realities in guerrilla war. In putting down the rebellion in Malaya over the course of twelve years, from 1948 to 1960, the British had learned that local, low-level aggression was best countered by local, low-level defense. Britain had used only 30,000 troops in Malaya, but had also employed 60,000 police and 250,000 in a home guard.

With the excellent advice he was getting, Diem was able to reverse the momentum of the war and put the communists on the defensive. Just as the war in Malaya had been won, the war in Vietnam was being won in the early 1960s. But then three critical events occurred that eventually turned the promise of victory into the fact of defeat.

The first took place far from Vietnam, in Cuba, in 1961: the Bay of Pigs invasion. That disastrous failure prompted President John F. Kennedy to order a postmortem, and General Maxwell Taylor was chosen to conduct it. He concluded that the CIA was not equipped to handle large-scale paramilitary operations and decided that the American effort in Vietnam fit into this category. He therefore recommended that control of it be handed over to the Pentagon, a decision that proved to have enormous consequences. The political sophistication and on-the-spot "feel" for local conditions that the CIA possessed went out the window, as people who saw the world through technological lenses took over the main operational responsibility for the war.

Another key turning point came the next year, in 1962, in Laos. At a press conference two months after his inauguration Kennedy had correctly declared that a communist attempt to take over Laos "quite obviously affects the security of the United States." He also said, "We will not be provoked, trapped, or drawn into this or any other situation; but I know that every American will want his country to honor its obligations." At the Geneva Conference in July 1962 fifteen countries signed an agreement in which those with military forces in Laos pledged to withdraw them and all agreed to stop any paramilitary assistance. All the countries complied except one: North Vietnam. North Vietnam never took any serious steps to remove its 7,000-man contingent from Laos—only 40 men were recorded as leaving—and the United States was therefore eventually forced to resume covert aid to Laos to prevent the North Vietnamese from taking over the country.

North Vietnam's obstinacy in keeping its forces in Laos—which had increased to 70,000 by 1972—created an extremely difficult situation for the South Vietnamese. The communists used the sparsely inhabited highlands of eastern Laos, and also of Cambodia, as a route for supplying their forces in South Vietnam. These areas also gave them a privileged sanctuary from which to strike, enabling them to concentrate overwhelmingly superior forces against a single local target and then slip back across the border before reinforcements could be brought in. The "Ho Chi Minh Trail" through Laos enabled the communists to do an end run around the demilitarized zone between North and South and to strike where the defenders were least prepared.

If South Vietnam had only had to contend with invasion and infiltration from the North across the forty-mile-long DMZ, it could have done so without the assistance of American forces. In the Korean War the enemy had had to attack directly across the border; North Korea could hardly use the ocean on either side of South Korea as a "privileged sanctuary" from which to launch attacks. But Hanoi was able to use sanctuaries in Laos and Cambodia as staging grounds for its assault on South Vietnam. In addition to making hit-and-run tactics possible, these lengthened the border the South had to defend from 40 to 640 miles, not counting indentations. Along these 640 miles there were few natural boundaries. The North Vietnamese were free to pick and choose their points of attack, always waiting until they had an overwhelming local advantage, in accordance with the strategy of guerrilla warfare. Our failure to prevent North Vietnam from establishing the Ho Chi Minh Trail along Laos' eastern border in 1962 had an enormous effect on the subsequent events in the war.

The third key event that set the course of the war was the assassination of Diem. Diem was a strong leader whose nationalist credentials were as solid as Ho Chi Minh's. He faced the difficult task of forging a nation while waging a war. In the manner of postcolonial leaders, he ran a regime that drew its inspiration partly from European parliamentary models, partly from traditional Asian models, and partly from necessity. It worked for Vietnam, but it offended American purists, those who inspect the world with white gloves and disdain association with any but the spotless. Unfortunately for Diem, the American press corps in Vietnam wore white gloves, and although the North was not open to their inspection, the South was. Diem himself had premonitions of the fatal difference this might make when he told Sir Robert Thompson in 1962, "Only the American press can lose this war."

South Vietnam under Diem was substantially free, but, by American standards, not completely free. Responsible reporting seeks to keep events in proportion. The mark of irresponsible reporting is that it blows them out of proportion. It achieves drama by exaggeration, and its purpose is not truth but drama. The shortcomings of Diem's regime, like other aspects of the war, were blown grossly out of proportion.

"The camera," it has been pointed out, "has a more limited view even than the cameraman and argues always from the particular to the general." On June 11, 1963, the camera provided a very narrow view for the television audience in the United States. On that day, in a ritual carefully arranged for the camera, a Buddhist monk in South Vietnam doused himself with gasoline and set himself on fire. That picture, selectively chosen, seared a single word into the minds of many Americans: repression. The camera's focus on this one monk's act of self-immolation did not reveal the larger reality of South Vietnam; it obscured it. Even more thoroughly obscured from the television audience's view were the conditions inside North Vietnam, where unfriendly newsmen were not allowed.

Recently, in the Soviet Union, a Crimean Tartar set himself on fire to protest the thirty-five-year exile of his people from their ancestral homeland. A picture of this did not make the network news; it did not even make the front pages; I saw a story about it, with no pictures, buried on page twenty-one of the Los Angeles *Times*.

Communist regimes bury their mistakes; we advertise ours. During the war in Vietnam a lot of well-intentioned Americans got taken in by our well-advertised mistakes.

Some Buddhist temples in Vietnam were, in effect, headquarters of political opposition, and some Buddhist sects were more political than religious. The fact that Diem was a devout Catholic made him an ideal candidate to be painted as a repressor of Buddhists. They also played very skillful political theater; the "burning Buddhist" incident was an especially grisly form. But the press played up the Buddhists as oppressed holy people, and the world placed the blame on their target, Diem. The press has a way of focusing on one aspect of a complex situation as "the" story; in Vietnam in 1963 "the" story was "repression."

President Kennedy grew increasingly, unhappy at being allied with what was being portrayed as a brutal, oppressive government. Apparently without seriously considering the long-term consequences, the United States began putting some distance between itself and Diem.

On November 1, 1963, Diem was overthrown in a coup and assassinated. Charges that the U.S. government was directly involved may be untrue and unfair. However, the most charitable interpretation of the Kennedy administration's part in this affair is that it greased the skids for Diem's downfall and did nothing to prevent his murder. It was a sordid episode in American foreign policy. Diem's fall was followed by political instability and chaos in South Vietnam, and the event had repercussions all over Asia as well. President Ayub Khan of Pakistan told me a few months later, "Diem's murder meant three things to many Asian leaders: that it is dangerous to be a friend of the United States; that it pays to be neutral; and that sometimes it helps to be an enemy."

The months of pressure and intrigue preceding the coup had paralyzed the Diem administration and allowed the communists to gain the initiative in the war. Once Diem was disposed of, the gates of the Presidential Palace became a revolving door. Whatever his faults, Diem had represented "legitimacy." With the symbol of legitimacy gone, power in South Vietnam was up for grabs. Coup followed coup for the next two years until Nguyen Van Thieu and Nguyen Cao Ky took over in 1965. The guerrilla forces had taken advantage of this chaotic situation and gained a great deal of strength in the interim.

President Kennedy had sent 16,000 American troops to Vietnam to serve as combat "advisers" to the regular South Vietnam units, but after Diem's assassination the situation continued to deteriorate. In 1964 Hanoi sent in troops in order to be in a position to take over power when the government of South Vietnam fell. By 1965 South Vietnam was on the verge of collapse. In order to prevent the conquest by the North, President Johnson, in February started bombing of the North, and in March the first independent American combat units landed in Danang. As our involvement deepened, reaching a level of 550,000 troops by the time Johnson left office, fatal flaws in the American approach became manifest.

In World War II we won basically by out producing the other side. We built more and better weapons, and we were able to bombard the enemy with so many of them that he was forced to give up. Overwhelming firepower, unparalleled logistical capabilities, and the massive military operations that our talent for organization made possible were the keys to our success. But in World War II we were fighting a conventional war against a conventional enemy. We also were fighting a total war, and therefore, like the enemy, we had no qualms about the carnage we caused. Even before Hiroshima an estimated 35,000 people were killed in the Allied firebombing of Dresden; more than 80,000 perished in the two-day incendiary bombing of Tokyo a month later.

Vietnam, like Korea, was a limited war. The United States plunged in too impulsively in the 1960s, and then behaved too indecisively. We tried to wage a conventional war against an enemy who was fighting an unconventional war. We tried to mold the South Vietnamese Army into a large-scale conventional force while the principal threat was still from guerrilla forces, which called for the sort of smaller-unit, local-force response that had proved so successful in Malaya. American military policy-makers tended to downplay the subtler political and psychological aspects of guerrilla war, trying instead to win by throwing massive quantities of men and arms at the objective. And then, the impact even of this was diluted by increasing American pressure gradually rather than suddenly, thus giving the enemy time to adapt. Eisenhower, who refrained from publicly criticizing the conduct of the war, privately fumed about the gradualism. He once commented to me: "If the enemy holds a hill with a battalion, give me two battalions and I'll take it, but at great cost in casualties. Give me a division and I'll take it without a fight."

In Vietnam during that period we were not subtle enough in waging the guerrilla war; were too subtle in waging the conventional war. We were too patronizing, even contemptuous, toward our ally, and too solicitous of our enemy. Vietnamese morale was sapped by "Americanization"of the war; American morale was sapped by perpetuation of the war.

Democracies are not well equipped to fight prolonged wars. A democracy fights well after its morale is galvanized by an enemy attack and it gears up its war production. A totalitarian power can coerce its population into fighting indefinitely. But a democracy fights well only as long as public opinion supports the war, and public opinion will not continue to support a war that drags on without tangible signs of progress. This is doubly true when the war is being fought half a world away. Twenty-five years ago the ancient Chinese strategist Sun Tzu wrote, "There has never been a protracted war from which a country had benefited. . . . What is essential in war," he went on, "is victory not prolonged operations." Victory was what the American people were not getting.

We Americans are a do-it-yourself people. During that period we failed to understand that we could not win the war for the South Vietnamese: that, in the final analysis, the South Vietnamese would have to win it for themselves. The United States bulled its way into Vietnam and tried to run the war our way instead of recognizing that our mission should have been to help the South Vietnamese build up their forces so that they could win the war.

When I was talking with an Asian leader before I became President, he graphically pointed out the weakness in what was then the American policy toward South Vietnam: "When you are trying to assist another nation in defending its freedom, U.S. policy should be to help them fight the war but not to fight it for them." This was exactly where we had been going wrong in Vietnam. As South Vietnam's Vice President Ky later said, "You captured our war."

When I took office in 1969 it was obvious the American strategy in Vietnam needed drastic revision. My administration was committed to formulating a strategy that would end American involvement in the war and enable South Vietnam to win.

Our goals were to:

—Reverse the "Americanization" of the war that had occurred from 1965 to 1968 and concentrate instead on Vietnamization.
—Give more priority to pacification so that the South Vietnamese could be better able to extend their control over the countryside.
—Reduce the invasion threat by destroying enemy sanctuaries and supply lines in Cambodia and Laos.
—Withdraw the half million American troops from Vietnam in a way that would not bring about a collapse in the South.

—Negotiate a cease-fire and a peace treaty.

—Demonstrate our willingness and determination to stand by our ally if the peace agreement was violated by Hanoi, and assure South Vietnam that it would continue to receive our military aid as Hanoi did from its allies, the Soviet Union and, to a lesser extent, China.

En route to Vietnam for my first visit as President, I held a press conference in Guam on July 25, 1969, at which I enunciated what has become known as the Nixon Doctrine. At the heart of the Nixon Doctrine is the premise that countries threatened by communist aggression must take the primary responsibility for their own defense. This does not mean that U.S. forces have no military role; what it does mean is that threatened countries have to be willing to bear the primary burden of supplying the manpower. We were already putting the Nixon Doctrine into effect in Vietnam by concentrating on Vietnamization. This meant, as Secretary of Defense Melvin Laird put it, helping South Vietnam develop "a stronger administration, a stronger economy, stronger military forces and stronger police for internal security."

The most important aspect of Vietnamization was the development of South Vietnam's army into a strong, independent fighting force capable of holding its own against the communists—both the guerrilla forces and the main-force units from the north that were then waging conventional war.

In October 1969 I sent Sir Robert Thompson to Vietnam as my special adviser, with instructions to give me a candid, first-hand, independent evaluation of the situation. He reported that he was able to walk safely through many villages that had been under Vietcong control for years. He was so impressed with the progress that had been made that he thought we were in "a winning position" to conclude a just peace if we were willing to follow through with the efforts we were making.

After giving sharply increased emphasis to Vietnamization and pacification, the first order of military business was to hit at the enemy sanctuaries and supply lines in Laos and Cambodia. . . .

Cambodia

In March 1969, in response to a major new offensive that the North Vietnamese had launched against our forces in South Vietnam, I ordered the bombing of enemy-occupied base areas in Cambodia. The bombing was not publicly announced because of our concern that if it were, Sihanouk would be forced to object to it. However, even after it was disclosed by leaks to the New York *Times* in April, Sihanouk did not object. On the contrary, in May 1969, two months after the bombing had started, he said, "Cambodia only protests against the destruction of the property and lives of Cambodians. . . . If there is a buffalo or any Cambodian killed, I will be informed immediately . . . (and) I will protest."

In June 1969, Sihanouk said at a press conference that one of Cambodia's northeast provinces was "practically North Vietnamese territory," and the next month he invited me to visit Cambodia to mark the improvement of relations between our two countries. But Sihanouk's tilt toward the United States did not satisfy Cambodian public opinion. The Cambodians strongly objected to North Vietnam's violation of their sovereignty. In a series of rapidly moving events in March 1970, demonstrations against North Vietnamese occupation of Cambodian territory led to the sacking of the North Vietnamese and Vietcong embassies in Phnom Penh. Within a matter of days the North Vietnamese were given forty-eight hours' notice to vacate the country. Tiring of Sihanouk's careful balancing act, the Cambodian Parliament voted unanimously to depose him. . . .

Throughout April we showed restraint while the Vietnamese communist forces ran rampant through Cambodia. Our total military aid delivered to Cambodia consisted of 3,000 rifles provided covertly. The communists did not show similar restraint; they made it clear that their sole objective was domination of Cambodia.

Finally, on April 30, I announced our decision to counter the communist offensive by attacking North Vietnamese-occupied base areas in Cambodia bordering on South Vietnam. Our principal purpose was to undercut the North Vietnamese invasion of that country so that Vietnamization and plans for the withdrawal of American troops could continue in South Vietnam. A secondary purpose was to relieve the military pressure exerted on Cambodia by the North Vietnamese forces that were rapidly overrunning it. The North Vietnamese had been occupying parts of eastern Cambodia for over five years and returned there after we left; in contrast we limited our stay to two months and advanced only to a depth of twenty-one miles. It is obvious to any unbiased observer who the aggressor was. . . .

The joint operations by the U.S. Army and ARVN wiped out huge stores of North Vietnamese equipment—15 million rounds of ammunition (a full year's supply), 14 million pounds of rice (four months' supply), 23,000 weapons (enough for seventy-four full-strength North Vietnamese battalions), and much more.

Thanks to this and the following year's Lam Son operation in Laos by the South Vietnamese forces, Hanoi was unable to stockpile enough supplies for a full-scale attack on South Vietnam until two years later—in 1972. Valuable time had been won with which to complete the task of Vietnamization. And even when the 1972 offensive came, it was weakest and easiest to contain from the direction of the sanctuaries in Cambodia, a testimony to the effectiveness of our measures. . . .

The 1972 Invasion

The American and South Vietnamese operations in Cambodia and Laos in 1970 and 1971 successfully prevented major North Vietnamese and Vietcong offensives in South Vietnam during those years and made it possible for the United States to continue to withdraw its forces on schedule.

By the spring of 1972 Hanoi recognized that it could not conquer South Vietnam through guerrilla war tactics, even with the help of conventional units, and that it could not win the support of the South Vietnamese people. There was no creditable way for Hanoi to claim any longer that the war in the South was a civil war between the Saigon government and the Vietcong, so North Vietnam dropped the facade of "civil war" and launched a full-scale conventional invasion of the South. Fourteen divisions and twenty-six independent regiments invaded the South. This left only one division and four independent regiments in Laos and no regular ground forces at all in North Vietnam.

As Sir Robert Thompson put it, "It was a sign of the times that this Korean-type communist invasion, which twenty years before would have prompted united Western action and ten years before a Kennedy crusade, immediately put in doubt American resolve and probably won the Wisconsin primary for Senator George McGovern."

U.S. mining of Haiphong Harbor and the use of our airpower against targets in North Vietnam helped save the day, but the fighting on the ground was done exclusively by South Vietnamese forces. North Vietnam lost an estimated 130,000, killed and disabled. The invasion was a failure. . . .

[Our] actions in 1972 strengthened rather than weakened our new relationship with the Soviets and the Chinese. They both could see that we had power, the will to use it, and the skill to use it effectively. This meant that we were worth talking to. We could be a reliable friend or a dangerous enemy. This did not mean that they could publicly abandon their communist allies in Hanoi. However, their support for Hanoi noticeably cooled, which increased the incentive for Hanoi's leaders to make a peace agreement.

As a result of their decisive defeat in the 1972 offensive and their growing concern about the reliability of their Soviet and Chinese allies, the North Vietnamese finally began to negotiate seriously. But they were as stubborn at the conference table as they were on the battlefield. They wanted victory more than they wanted peace. Despite the overwhelming defeat of the peace-at-any-price candidate in the U.S. November elections, they continued to balk at our minimum terms.

On December 14 I made the decision to renew and increase the bombing of military targets in North Vietnam. The bombing began on December 18. It was a necessary step, and it proved to be the right decision. Although it was a very difficult choice, the realities of war, and not the wishful thinking of the ill-informed, demanded this action. The bombing broke the deadlock in negotiations. The North Vietnamese returned to the negotiating table, and on January 23, 1973, the long-waited peace agreement was finally achieved.

After their decisive defeat on the ground by South Vietnamese forces in the spring offensive and the destruction of their war-making capabilities by the December bombing, the North Vietnamese knew that militarily they were up against almost impossible odds. As the South Vietnamese economy continued to prosper far more than that of the North, Hanoi's communist ideology had less and less appeal. Thieu's Land to the Tiller program, for example, had reduced tenancy from 60 to 7 percent by 1973, a truly revolutionary development that undercut the communists' argument that the government allied itself with the rich and oppressed the people. Also, the North Vietnamese knew that both the Soviets and the Chinese had a stake in their new relationship with us and might not be willing to endanger that relationship by providing military supplies in excess of those allowed by the Paris peace agreement of January 1973.

From Victory to Defeat

We had won the war militarily and politically in Vietnam. But defeat was snatched from the jaws of victory because we lost the war politically in the United States. The peace that was finally won in January 1973 could have been enforced and South Vietnam could be a free nation today. But in a spasm of shortsightedness and spite, the United States threw away what it had gained at such enormous cost. . . .

On January 2, 1973, the House Democratic Caucus voted 154-75 to cut off all funds for Indochina military operations as soon as arrangements were made for the safe withdrawal of U.S. troops and the return of our prisoners of war. Two days later a similar resolution was passed by the Senate Democratic Caucus, 36-12. This, it should be noted, was before Watergate began to weaken my own position as President, and only three months before withdrawal of American forces was completed, and the last of the 550,000 American troops that were in Vietnam when I took office in 1969 were brought back. . . .

If the peace agreement was to have any chance to be effective, it was essential that Hanoi be deterred from breaking it. In a private letter to Thieu I had stated that "if Hanoi fails to abide by the terms of this agreement, it is my intention to take swift and severe retaliatory action." At a news conference on March 15, with regard to North Vietnamese infiltration into South Vietnam and violation of the agreement, I stated, "I would only suggest that based on my actions over the past four years, the North Vietnamese should not lightly disregard such expressions of concern, when they are made with regard to a violation."

In April, May, and June of 1973, with my authority weakened by the Watergate crisis, retaliatory action was threatened but not taken. Then Congress passed a bill setting August 15 as the date for termination of U.S. bombing in Cambodia and requiring congressional approval for the funding of U.S. military action in any part of Indochina. The effect of this bill was to deny the President the means to enforce the Vietnam peace agreement by retaliating against Hanoi for violations.

Once Congress had removed the possibility of military action against breaches of the peace agreement, I knew I had only words with which to threaten. The communists knew it too. By means of the bombing cutoff and the War Powers resolution passed in November 1973, Congress denied to me and to my successor, President Ford, the means with which to enforce the Paris agreement at a time when the North Vietnamese were openly and flagrantly violating it. It is truly remarkable that, for two years after the signing of the peace agreement in January 1973, the South Vietnamese held their own against the well-supplied North, without American personnel support either in the air or on the ground and with dwindling supplies.

Throughout 1974 the Russians poured huge amounts of ammunition, weaponry, and military supplies into North Vietnam, and the North in turn poured them into the South. In March 1974 Hanoi was estimated to have 185,000 men, 500 to 700 tanks, and 24 regiments of antiaircraft troops in the South. With the threat of American air power gone, the North Vietnamese built new roads and pipelines to move their armies and supplies about. At the same time, that the Soviet Union was arming Hanoi for the final assault, the United States Congress was sharply curtailing the flow of aid to South Vietnam. U.S. aid to South Vietnam was halved in 1974 and cut by another third in 1975. The United States ambassador to South Vietnam, Graham Martin, warned the Senate foreign Relations Committee that such cuts in military aid would "seriously tempt the North to gamble on an all-out military offensive." His warning was tragically prophetic.

The original plan of the North Vietnamese was to launch their final offensive in 1976. But then they stepped up their timetable. At the start of 1975 Phuoc Long province fell to the communists, the first province South Vietnam had lost completely since 1954. There was relatively little reaction in the United States. Hanoi decided to make larger attacks in 1975 in preparation for the final offensive in 1926. On March 11, Ban Me Thout fell, and on the same day the U.S. House of Representatives refused to fund a $300 million supplemental military aid package that President Ford had proposed. Together with the earlier cutback of aid, this had a devastating effect on the morale of the South Vietnamese, as well as denying them the means with which to defend themselves; they were desperately short of military supplies and dependent for them on the United States. It also gave a tremendous psychological boost to the North. The North threw all of its remaining troops into the battle. Thieu tried to regroup his undersupplied forces in more defensible perimeters, and the hastily executed maneuver turned into a rout. By the end of April it was all over. Saigon became Ho Chi Minh City.

Hanoi had suffered an overwhelming defeat when it launched a conventional attack on the South in 1972. Then the North Vietnamese had been stopped on the ground by the South Vietnamese, while bombing by our air force and mining by our navy crippled their efforts to resupply their forces in the South. B-52 strikes could have had a devastating effect on the large troop concentrations that Hanoi used in its final offensive, but in 1975 Hanoi did not have to reckon with our air and naval forces, and thanks to ample Soviet military aid they had overwhelming advantages in tanks and artillery over South Vietnam's ground forces. After North Vietnam's victory General Dung, Hanoi's field commander in charge of the final offensive, remarked that "The reduction of U.S. aid made it impossible for the puppet troops to carry out their combat plans and build up their forces. . . . Thieu was then forced to fight a poor man's war. Enemy firepower had decreased by nearly 60 percent because of bomb and ammunition shortages. Its mobility was also reduced by half due to lack of aircraft, vehicles and fuel."

Our defeat in Vietnam can be blamed in part on the Soviets because they provided arms to Hanoi in violation of the peace agreement, giving the North an enormous advantage over the South in the final offensive in the spring of 1975. It can be blamed in part on the tactical and strategic mistakes made by President Thieu and his generals. It is grossly unfair to put the blame on South Vietnam's fighting men, the great majority of whom fought bravely and well against overwhelming odds. A major part of the blame must fall on the shoulders of those members of the Congress who were responsible for denying to the President, first me and then President Ford, the power to enforce the peace agreements, and for refusing to provide the military aid that South Vietnamese needed in order to meet the North Vietnamese offensive on equal terms.

But Congress was in part the prisoner of events. The leaders of the United States in the crucial years of the early and mid-1960s failed to come up with a strategy that would produce victory. Instead, first they undermined a strong regime, and then simply poured more and more U.S. troops and materiel into South Vietnam in an ineffective effort to shore up the weaker regimes that followed. They misled the public by insisting we were winning the war and thereby prepared the way for defeatism and demagoguery later on. The American people could not be expected to continue indefinitely to support a war in which they were told victory was around the corner, but which required greater and greater effort without any obvious signs of improvement.

By following the strategy I initiated in 1969, we and the South Vietnamese were able to win the war militarily by the time of the Paris accords of January 27, 1973. The 550,000 American troops that were in Vietnam when I came into office in 1969 had been withdrawn and South Vietnam was able to defend itself—if we supplied the arms the Paris accords allowed.

But the public had been so misinformed and misled by unwise government actions and the shallow, inflammatory treatment of events by the media that morale within the United States collapsed just when the North was overwhelmingly defeated on the battlefield. We won a victory after a long hard struggle, but then we threw it away. The communists had grasped what strategic analyst Brian Crozier said is the central point of revolutionary war: "that it is won or lost on the home front." The war-making capacity of North Vietnam had been virtually destroyed by the bombings in December of 1972, and we had the means to make and enforce a just peace, a peace with honor. But we were denied these means when Congress prohibited military operations in or over Indochina and cut back drastically on the aid South Vietnam needed to defend itself. In the final analysis, a major part of the blame must be borne by those who encouraged or participated in the fateful decisions that got us into the war in the 1960's, and who then by their later actions sabotaged our efforts to get us out in an acceptable way in the 1970's.

By inaction at the crucial moment, the United States undermined an ally and abandoned him to his fate. The effect on the millions of Cambodians, Laotians, and South Vietnamese who relied on us and have now paid the price of communist reprisals is bad enough. But the cost in terms of raising doubts among our allies as to America's reliability, and in terms of the encouragement it gives to our potential enemies to engage in aggression against our friends in other parts of the world, will be devastating for U.S. policy for decades to come. . . .

Larry Berman

 **NO**

No Peace, No Honor: Nixon, Kissinger, and Betrayal in Vietnam

To date, there have been two quite different explanations for the failure of the Paris Accords and the subsequent end of the country known as South Vietnam.

Richard Nixon and Henry Kissinger have always maintained that they won the war and that Congress lost the peace. The treaty itself, they said, although not perfect, was sound enough to have allowed for a political solution if North Vietnam had not so blatantly violated it. North and South Vietnam could have remained separate countries. When the North did violate the agreement, Watergate prevented the president from backing up his secret guarantees to President Thieu. Kissinger goes even further, insisting there was nothing secret about the promises Nixon made to Thieu. In any case, by mid-1973 Nixon was waging a constitutional battle with Congress over executive privilege and abuse of powers; he could hardly start a new battle over war powers to defend South Vietnam. "By 1973, we had achieved our political objective: South Vietnam's independence had been secured," Nixon later told Monica Crowley, former foreign policy assistant and confidante, "But by 1975, the Congress destroyed our ability to enforce the Paris agreement and left our allies vulnerable to Hanoi's invading forces. If I sound like I'm blaming Congress, I am."

Kissinger has put it this way: "Our tragedy was our domestic situation. . . .

In April [1973], Watergate blew up, and we were castrated. . . . The second tragedy was that we were not permitted to enforce the agreement. . . . I think it's reasonable to assume he [Nixon] would have bombed the hell out of them during April."

The other explanation for the failure of the Paris Accords is known as the "decent interval." This explanation is far less charitable to Nixon or Kissinger because it is premised on the assumption that by January 1973, U.S. leaders cared only about securing the release of American POWs and getting some type of accounting on MIAs, especially in Laos. The political future of South Vietnam would be left for the Vietnamese to decide; we just did not want the communists to triumph too quickly. Kissinger knew that Hanoi would eventually win. By signing the peace agreement, Hanoi was not abandoning its long-term objective, merely giving the U.S. a fig leaf with which to exit. In his book *Decent Interval,* Frank Snepp wrote: "The Paris Agreement was thus a cop-out of sorts, an American one. The only thing it definitely guaranteed was an American withdrawal from Vietnam, for that depended on American action alone. The rest of the issues that had sparked the war and kept it alive were left essentially unresolved—and irresolvable."

Kissinger was asked by the assistant to the president, John Ehrlichman, "How long do you figure the South Vietnamese can survive under this agreement?" Ehrlichman reported that Kissinger answered, "I think that if they're lucky they can hold out for a year and a half." When Kissinger's assistant John Negroponte opined that the agreement was not in the best interests of South Vietnam, Kissinger asked him, "Do you want us to stay there forever?"

Nixon yearned to be remembered by history as a great foreign policy president; he needed a noncommunist South Vietnam on that ledger in order to sustain a legacy that already included détente with the Soviets and an opening with China. If South Vietnam was going down the tubes, it could not be on Nixon's watch. "What really matters now is how it all comes out," Nixon wrote in his diary in April 1972. "Both Haldeman and Henry seem to have an idea—which I think is mistaken—that even if we fail in Vietnam we can survive politically. I have no illusions whatsoever on that score, however. The US will not have a credible policy if we fail, and I will have to assume responsibility for that development."

⚜

No Peace, No Honor draws on recently declassified records to show that the true picture is worse than either of these perspectives suggests. The reality was the opposite of the decent interval hypothesis and far beyond Nixon's and Kissinger's claims. The record shows that the United States *expected* that the signed treaty would be immediately violated and that this would trigger a brutal military response. Permanent war (air war, not ground operations) at acceptable cost was what Nixon and Kissinger anticipated from the so-called peace agreement. They believed that the only way the American public would accept it was if there was a signed agreement. Nixon recognized that winning the peace, like the war, would be impossible to achieve, but he planned for indefinite stalemate by using the B-52s to prop up the government of South Vietnam until the end of his presidency. Just as the Tonkin Gulf Resolution provided a pretext for an American engagement in South Vietnam, the Paris Accords were intended to fulfill a similar role for remaining permanently engaged in Vietnam. Watergate derailed the plan.

The declassified record shows that the South Vietnamese, North Vietnamese, and the United States disregarded key elements of the treaty because all perceived it was in their interest to do so. No one took the agreement seriously because each party viewed it as a means for securing something unstated. For the United States, as part of the Nixon Doctrine, it was a means of remaining permanently involved in Southeast Asia; for the North Vietnamese, it was the means for eventual conquest and unification of Vietnam; for the South Vietnamese, it was a means for securing continued support from the United States.

The truth has remained buried for so long because Richard Nixon and Henry Kissinger did everything possible to deny any independent access to the historical record. As witnesses to history, they used many classified top-secret documents in writing their respective memoirs but later made sure that everyone else would have great difficulty accessing the same records. They have limited access to personal papers, telephone records, and other primary source materials that would allow for any independent assessments of the record pertaining to the evolution of negotiating strategies and compromises that were raised at different stages of the protracted process. The late Admiral Elmo "Bud" Zumwalt, Jr., former chief of naval operations, said that "Kissinger's method of writing history is similar to that of communist historians who took justifications from the present moment and projected backwards, fact by fact, in accounting for their country's past. Under this method, nothing really was as it happened." This is how the administration's history of "peace with honor" was written.

The personal papers of Henry Kissinger are deposited in the Library of Congress with a deed of gift restricting access until five years after his death. For years we have been denied access to the full transcripts of Kissinger's negotiations. Verbatim hand-written transcripts of the secret meetings in Paris were kept by Kissinger's assistants, Tony Lake, Winston Lord, and John Negroponte. Negroponte gave a complete set of these meeting notes to Kissinger for writing his memoirs, but they were never returned. In his deposition to the Kerry Committee investigation, which examined virtually all aspects of the MIA issue and gave special attention to the Paris negotiations, Winston Lord stated that there were "verbatim transcripts of every meeting with the Vietnamese. I'm talking now about the secret meetings, because I took, particularly toward the beginning, and we got some help at the end, the notes as did Negroponte or Smyser or Rodman and so on." Only now have notes of these secret back-channel meetings become available. Furthermore, the North Vietnamese have published their own narrative translation of the Kissinger-Tho negotiations.

This is the story of a peace negotiation that began with Lyndon Johnson in 1968 and ended with the fall of South Vietnam in 1975. Many secret meetings were involved. The principal sources include transcript-like narratives of documents from Hanoi archives that have been translated by Luu Van Loi and Nguyen Anh Vu and published as *Le Duc Tho-Kissinger Negotiations in Paris;* declassified meeting transcripts from a congressional investigation of MIAs in Southeast Asia; declassified meeting notes from the papers of Tony Lake and memoranda of conversations from recently declassified materials in the National Archives or presidential libraries. These three have been triangulated to connect minutes as well as linkages between events. In many cases, I have been able to fill in classified sections through materials in back-channel cables from Kissinger to Ambassador Ellsworth Bunker or President Nixon.

Here, then, is the emerging story of what Nixon called "peace with honor" but was, in fact, neither. This story of diplomatic deception and public betrayal has come to the light only because of the release of documents and tapes that Richard Nixon and Henry Kissinger sought to bury for as long as possible. Prior to these declassifications, we knew only what Nixon or Kissinger wanted us to know about the making of war and shaping of the so-called honorable peace in Vietnam. . . .

⋅◈⋅

It has been over thirty years since the United States and Vietnam began talks intended to end the Vietnam War. The Paris Peace Talks began on May 13, 1968, under the crystal chandeliers in the ballroom of the old Majestic Hotel on Avenue Kleber and did not end until January 27, 1973, with the signing of the Agreement on Ending the War and Restoring Peace in Vietnam at the International Conference Center in Paris. Despite the agreement, not a moment of peace ever came to Vietnam. This book uses a cache of recently declassified documents to offer a new perspective on why the country known as South Vietnam ceased to exist after April 1975.

Since the very first days of his presidency in January 1969, Richard Nixon had sought an "honorable peace" in Vietnam. In January 1973 he characterized the Paris agreement as having achieved those lofty goals: "Now that we have achieved an honorable agreement, let us be proud that America did not settle for a peace that would have betrayed our allies, that would have abandoned our prisoners of war, or that would have ended the war for us, but would have continued the war for the 50 million people of Indochina."

A speakers' kit assembled within the White House on the evening of the president's announcement of the cease-fire described the final document as "a vindication of the wisdom of the President's policy in holding out for an honorable peace—and his refusal to accept a disguised and dishonorable defeat. Had it not been for the President's courage—during four years of unprecedented vilification and attack—the United States would not today be honorably ending her involvement in the war, but would be suffering the consequences of dishonor and defeat. . . . The difference between what the President has achieved and what his opponents wanted, is the difference between peace with honor, and the false peace of an American surrender."

A White Paper drafted for distribution to members of Congress offered more barbed attacks on his critics.

> For four agonizing years, Richard Nixon has stood virtually alone in the nation's capital while little, petty men flayed him over American involvement in Indochina. For four years, he has been the victim of the most vicious personal attacks. Day and night, America's predominantly liberal national media hammered at Mr. Nixon, slicing from all sides, attacking, hitting, and cutting. The intellectual establishment—those whose writings entered America into the Vietnam war—pompously postured from their ivy hideaways, using their inordinate power to influence public opinion. . . . No President has been under more constant and unremitting harassment by men who should drop to their knees each night to thank the Almighty that they do not have to make the same decisions that Richard Nixon did. Standing with the President in all those years were a handful of reporters and number of newspapers—nearly all outside of Washington. There were also the

courageous men of Congress who would stand firm beside the President. But most importantly there were the millions upon millions of quite ordinary Americans—the great *Silent Majority* of citizens—who saw our country through a period where the shock troops of leftist public opinion daily propagandized against the President of the United States. *They were people of character and steel.*

Meanwhile, the North Vietnam heralded the Paris agreement as a great victory. Radio Hanoi, in domestic and foreign broadcasts, confined itself for several days to reading and rereading the Paris text and protocols. From the premier's office in Hanoi came the declaration that the national flag of the Democratic Republic of Vietnam (DRV) should be flown throughout the country for eight days, from the moment the cease-fire went into effect on January 28 through February 4. For three days and nights, Hanoi's streets were filled with crowds of people celebrating the fact that in 60 days there would be no foreign troops in Vietnam.

The *Nhan Dan* editorial of January 28, titled "The Great Historic Victory of Our Vietnamese People," observed, "Today, 28 January, the war has ended completely in both zones of our country. The United States and other countries have pledged to respect our country's independence, sovereignty, reunification, and territorial integrity. The United States will withdraw all U.S. troops and the troops of other foreign countries and their advisors and military personnel, dismantle U.S. military bases in the southern part of our country and respect our southern people's right to self-determination and other democratic freedoms."

Premier Pham Van Dong was more forthcoming to American broadcaster Walter Cronkite that "the Paris Agreement marked an important victory of our people in their resistance against U.S. aggression, for national salvation. For us, its terms were satisfactory. . . . The Paris agreement paved the way for our great victory in the Spring of 1975 which put an end to more than a century of colonial and neo-colonial domination over our country and restored the independence, freedom and unity of our homeland."

Perhaps the most honest response came from a young North Vietnamese cadre by the name of Man Duc Xuyen, living in Ha Bac province in North Vietnam. In a postcard, he extended Tet New Year wishes to his family. "Dear father, mother and family," the letter began. "When we have liberated South Viet-Nam and have unified the country, I will return."

Only in South Vietnam was there no joy or celebration over the signing of the Paris agreement. By the terms of the deal, over 150,000 North Vietnamese troops remained in the South, whereas the United States, over the course of Nixon's presidency, had unilaterally withdrawn over 500,000 of its own troops. President Nguyen Van Thieu and his fellow countrymen understood that the diplomatic battle had been won by Le Duc Tho. President Thieu was agreeing to nothing more than a protocol for American disengagement. True, President Nixon had guaranteed brutal retaliation if the North resumed any aggression. But could these guarantees be trusted? The fate of his country depended on them. Twenty-eight months later, South Vietnam would disappear. . . .

James Reston wrote on March 18 that, "once the withdrawal of American prisoners and troops is complete—and it will be within a few weeks—there will be an interesting legal question: what legal authority would the President then have to order American men and bombers back into battle?" The administration was quick to respond. Secretary of Defense Richardson stated that the president retained "residual authority" to bomb in order to maintain the peace and that such bombing was merely a "mopping up exercise." He provided an elaboration on this crucial point: "If he had the authority up to the moment the documents were signed, he has the authority in the following weeks to see that those agreements are lived up to."

But there would be no strikes in March after all. Nixon decided he did not want to jeopardize the return of the final group of American POWs, which finally occurred on March 29, 1973.

By April 1973 Nixon and Kissinger were again considering bombing Khe Sanh. On April 16, Bunker tried to talk Kissinger and Nixon out of it because it would "effectively destroy the cease-fire. I question whether the ICCS would survive bombing attacks in SVN or Laos. . . . Our resuming the bombing of SVN or Laos would also destroy the cease-fire in the minds of the South Vietnamese." Besides, in Bunker's view, the rainy season was about to start and there was no need to restart the bombing in South Vietnam. "In fact, the communists may regard this infiltration effort as compensating for our Enhance and Enhance Plus."

On April 17, Bunker backed off a bit: "I have no problem with 'massive strikes' in Laos and Cambodia. . . . I question the effectiveness of bombing the Trail in Laos and the advisability of bombing either the Trail or Khe Sanh before your meeting with Le Duc Tho." (Kissinger was scheduled to meet again with Le Duc Tho in order to hammer out problems in the agreement.) Kissinger cabled right back with his long-held belief that "it is our judgment that the North Vietnamese will break the cease-fire whenever and however it suits their purpose. They need no provocation. We are therefore considering massive strikes in Laos [to] leave no doubt as to their chances of getting away with flagrant disregard of the agreements."

❧

Five days before he had been sworn in for his second term as the nation's thirty-seventh president, Nixon had written in his diary, "It is ironic that the day the news came out stopping the bombing of North Vietnam, the Watergate Four plead guilty." Unbeknown to anyone, as Henry Kissinger was negotiating with Le Duc Tho in Paris, "Watergate was changing from amber to red," recalled Admiral Zumwalt. "The private commitments made by Nixon to Thieu were unraveling alongside Nixon's presidency."

More than a private commitment was at stake; a secret plan was being overtaken by events. By April 30, Nixon had told the country that he accepted responsibility for the Watergate incident, but he also denied any personal involvement in either the break-in or cover-up. He said that he had been misled by subordinates who had made an "effort to conceal the facts." Nixon announced the nomination of Elliot Richardson as attorney general and that Richardson would have authority to appoint a special prosecutor. The White House also announced that the president had accepted the resignations of Ehrlichman, Haldeman, Attorney General Richard Kleindienst, and the president's counsel, John Dean. As Kissinger later told Stanley Karnow, "After June 1973 I did not believe that the cease-fire would hold. I certainly did not after July 1973. Watergate was in full strength. We had intelligence documents from North Vietnam decoded that Nixon could not honor his pledge and do what he had done in 1972 because of domestic situations."

Watergate would have another effect. Kissinger later stated that this was a "different Nixon. He approached the problems of the violations in a curiously desultory fashion. He drifted. He did not hone in on the decision in the single-minded, almost possessed manner that was his hallmark. The rhetoric might be there, but accompanied this time with excuses for inaction. In retrospect, we know that by March, Watergate was boiling."

There is no question now, nor was there then, that Watergate sapped any resolve that Nixon may have had to bomb again. For decades, Henry Kissinger has used that fact to justify his argument that the administration—including himself—never intended to abandon South Vietnam. Yet something is hard to swallow in that argument. Nixon, the die-hard anticommunist, may have convinced himself that the American people would support South Vietnam in the face of the new—and newly illegal—Northern aggression no matter what. But most Americans were weary of the war, and the public no longer held the same zeal for anticommunism that it had had in the late 1940s and 1950s.

Could Kissinger, the realist, the pragmatist, have failed to see this? Indeed, two newly released records of conversations at meetings suggest a more devious plan. The first, a meeting with Lee Quan Yew, prime minister of Singapore, on August 4, 1973, reveals, in Kissinger's own words, the belief that bombing was the only way to make certain that the South would not fall.

The secret meeting occurred in the Captain's Conference Room of the New York Port Authority Policy Building at Kennedy Airport. The euphoria of January's peace with honor was now a distant memory. Lee had just returned from meeting Nha.

Kissinger told Lee that "[Nha] dislikes me intensely!"

"That is not important—personal likes and dislikes. The important thing is the job to be done. I told him it would be useful if Thieu met me. He said, 'why not just meet me?'"

"What is your impression of Nha?" asked Kissinger.

"He is bright, ambitious. With full confidence that what he says will carry weight with the President," said Lee.

"That is true. He is also immature. Emotional," concluded Kissinger.

But Kissinger had come to talk about Watergate and Vietnam, not Mr. Nha. "Our objectives are still the same. We have suffered a tragedy because of Watergate. . . . We were going to bomb North Vietnam for a week, then go to Russia, then meet with Le Duc Tho. Congress has made it impossible." Then Kissinger made the tell-tale confession of his dashed hopes: "In May and June I drew the conclusion that the North Vietnamese were resigning themselves to a long pull of 5-to-6 years. . . . And it would have been a certainty if we had given them one blow." In other words, a little bombing now might have slowed them down, which would be a decent interval before losing the South. Nixon and Kissinger would not be directly tied to it.

One more blow was a far more realistic expectation on Kissinger's part. Kissinger told Lee that "the last three months were the most difficult period for us. We couldn't say anything because we could never be sure what some junior aide would say next. But as soon as the hearings are over, we will go on the counter-offensive. We are already in the process. While we are in these difficulties, we have to stay cool. But we won't give up our foreign policy. We will regain the initiative. In Southeast Asia, we haven't gone through all this for four years to abandon it. Sixty-one percent voted in November 1972 not to abandon Southeast Asia. It was a clear issue."

The meeting ended with Lee Kuan Yew's saying how important it was that South Vietnam survive through 1976. "My concern is to have it last through 1976 so that you will have a strong President. If it falls, you will have a new President who says, 'that's what tore American society apart.'"

Kissinger must have been reassured, because he told Lee, "You are an asset to us in that part of the world and we have no interest in destroying you. We won't leave any documents around. They stay in my office."

A little more than a month later, on September 26, Kissinger met with Nguyen Phu Duc in the Waldorf Towers in New York. Kissinger was now secretary of state, and Duc asked Kissinger what the United States planned to do with respect to the North's violations of the Paris Accord. "If it were not for domestic difficulties, we would have bombed them. This is now impossible. Your brothers in the North only understand brutality," said Kissinger. The secretary then spoke about how the Congress had acted "irresponsibly" by cutting off support for bombing, but North Vietnamese "suspiciousness is playing into our hands. They don't completely understand the restrictions placed on us by Congress. President Nixon has fooled them so often that they are probably more concerned that you believe. It is important that you show confidence and behave strongly." He ended with a joke: "Treat them like you treat me."

The conversation then got much more revealing. Kissinger made a startling admission: "I came away from the January negotiations with the feeling that we would have to bomb the North Vietnamese again in early April or May." He did not say, "If the North violated the accord, we would bomb." He confirmed what Haig had told Phouma, what Nixon had said to Thieu and what Zumwalt had concluded in November 1972 at the JCS meeting: it was a sham peace held together with a plan to deceive the American public with the rhetoric of American honor. He knew the North would cheat and was planning on resuming the bombing.

As Kissinger toasted Le Duc Tho with words of peace in January 1973, and as Richard Nixon addressed the nation with news of an honorable peace in Vietnam, both men knew that as soon as the last American POW was home, the bombing would be renewed. For Nixon, the bombing would continue right through 1976, and for Kissinger, just long enough to pick up his Nobel Peace Prize.

Writing in the *Wall Street Journal* on April 27, 1975, William Buckley noted that Watergate had derailed the president's plan to pulverize Hanoi and that Nixon at the time was too emotionally unstable to renew the bombing: "What would Nixon, under Kissinger's prodding, have done, if his reactions had been healthy, when only a few weeks after the Paris Accord was executed, North Vietnam began its blatant disregard of it. My own information is that it was planned, sometime in April, to pulverize Hanoi and Haiphong," wrote Buckley. Indeed, the plans were made even earlier.

One final question remains: Would even short-term bombing support for the South have been accepted by the public? In interviewing done on the day of the Vietnam agreement, a Gallup Poll asked the following questions:

- "When United States troops are withdrawn from Vietnam, do you think a strong enough government can be maintained in South Vietnam to withstand Communist political pressure, or not?" Fifty-four percent believed that government in the South would not survive; 27 percent believed South Vietnam would last; 19 percent had no opinion.
- "After United States troops are withdrawn from Vietnam, do you think North Vietnam in the next few years is likely to try to take over South Vietnam again, or not?" Seventy percent thought that the North would try to take over the South, 16 percent thought no, and 14 percent had no opinion.
- "Suppose when the United States troops are withdrawn, North Vietnam does try to take over South Vietnam again, do you think the United States should send war materials to South Vietnam, or not?" Fifty percent believed the U.S. should not send war materials, while 38 percent said yes, and 12 percent had no opinion.
- "If North Vietnam does try to take over South Vietnam again, do you think the United States should bomb North Vietnam, or not?" Seventy-one percent said no to bombing, while 17 percent said yes, and 12 percent had no opinion.
- "If North Vietnam does try to take over South Vietnam again, do you think the United States should send troops to help South Vietnam, or not?" Seventy-nine percent were opposed to sending troops, while 13 percent favored such an action, and 8 percent had no opinion.

Kissinger later acknowledged that he had misjudged the willingness of the American people to defend the agreement. "But I admit this: we judged wrong. And what we judged wrong above all was our belief that if we could get peace with honor, that we would unite the American people who would then defend an agreement that had been achieved with so much pain. That was our fundamental miscalculation. It never occurred to me, and I'm sure it never occurred to President Nixon, that there could be any doubt about it, because an agreement that you don't enforce is a surrender; it's just writing down surrender terms."

Twenty-five Years Later

On the occasion of the twenty-fifth anniversary of the Paris agreement, the Nixon Center in Washington, D.C., convened a conference, "The Paris Agreement on Vietnam: 25 Years Later." Noticeable by their absence were those who in the intervening years had questioned "peace with honor." Kissinger attended and spoke about the many letters and private assurances given by Nixon to Thieu in which he promised to enforce the agreement: "I would simply ask some honest researcher sometime to compare the letters that President Nixon wrote to Thieu with the letters that still have not been published that President Kennedy or Johnson wrote to other leaders to see who made the bigger commitments. Or even other Presidents, in other circumstances. These were never treated as national commitments. These were expressions of the intentions of the President. Every senior member of the administration—including myself, the Secretary of Defense, the Secretary of State—is represented in compendiums of statements that said publicly every week that we intended to enforce the agreement. There was nothing new about that. . . . If I had any idea that all this was possible, I would not have participated in, and President Nixon would never have authorized, any sort of agreement. I believe it could otherwise have been maintained for a long enough period of time to give the South Vietnamese an opportunity, as the South Koreans were given, to develop their own future."

With respect to consultations with President Thieu, Kissinger's position remained unchanged: "There were all kinds of proposals that we made during that period—the last one made publicly in January 1972 by President Nixon when he disclosed the secret talks which had been going on, and which had been preceded by a secret proposal in May 1971 (all of which, incidentally, President Thieu, approved, probably thinking they would never be accepted). It was not as if we just slipped a proposal to the North Vietnamese that the South Vietnamese had never seen. In fact, I believe that Al Haig took every proposal to Saigon before we made it, and that was approved—although I will admit that the speed with which we moved at the end undoubtedly surprised the South Vietnamese."

The records that Kissinger and Nixon chose to omit from their respective memoirs offer a far more devious explanation. Hoang Duc Nha once employed a Vietnamese proverb to describe his dealings with Kissinger, translated as, "We are like frogs looking up from the darkness at the bottom of the well," meaning that the Vietnamese were in the dark about Kissinger's motives and intentions. Ever today, almost three decades since the Paris Accords were signed, Kissinger would prefer that we all remain, like the South Vietnamese, in the dark.

POSTSCRIPT

Did President Nixon Negotiate a "Peace with Honor" in Vietnam in 1973?

President Nixon presents his own version of the Vietnam fiasco. His contention is that despite policy failure by the prior president, the Nixon administration stemmed the tide. When the last United States troops were withdrawn and the Paris Peace Accords were signed in January 1973 between the two Vietnams, the South Vietnamese had achieved military victory. Although the victory was short-lived, Nixon argues that South Vietnam would have been saved except that the United States Congress, under the influence of the anti-war protestors and the liberal press, refused to send aid or support to any United States bombing missions.

Both Nixon and Kissinger have tried to control their tapes and papers in giving their own accounts of the Nixon presidency. In addition to *The Real War*, see the former president's *No More Vietnams* (Arbor House, 1985); and his autobiography *RN: The Memoirs of Richard Nixon* (Warner Books, 1978). Kissinger has condensed his two volumes of memoirs pertaining to Vietnam in *Ending the Vietnam War* (Simon and Schuster, 2003); condensed even further in his history of *Diplomacy* (Simon and Schuster, 1994). While both men argue that South Vietnam could have been saved, they give different accounts of the peace negotiations leading to the withdrawal of American troops in the winter of 1973. The rivalry between the two is fully explored in Robert Dallek, *Nixon and Kissinger: Partners in Power* (Harper Collins, 2007).

In the second reading, Larry Berman, professor of history at the University of California, Davis, has challenged the Nixon–Kissinger version of the ending of the Vietnam War. Through a careful use of declassified notes of key presidential advisers, that are located in the National Archives or Presidential libraries as well as translations of transcript-like narratives of documents from the Hanoi archives, Berman describes a story of "diplomatic deception and public betrayal" regarding the Paris Peace Accords supposedly ending the Vietnam War in January 1973.

Berman accepts the "decent interval" interpretation first advanced by CIA agent Frank Snepp in a book of the same title published in 1973. Both Kissinger and Nixon realized that once American troops were withdrawn, both sides would violate the cease-fire agreements and South Vietnam would lose the war within 2 years. Berman, however, adds a new twist to this view. Both Nixon and Kissinger knew that the South Vietnamese government was doomed to fail. But Nixon expected to resume bombing the North Vietnamese military to prevent the collapse of South Vietnam until after the president left office in 1977. But Congress refused to resume the bombing in the spring of 1973, and the president became embroiled in the Watergate scandal. Nixon resigned in August 1974, and the South Vietnamese government collapsed on April 30, 1975. The new president, Gerald Ford, had been unable to get Congress to send bombs, troops, or increased aid to South Vietnam.

The Vietnam War remains controversial both among historians and policy makers. President Nixon's interpretation gets support from Lewis Sorley, a third-generation graduate from West Point, a Ph.D. holder from Johns Hopkins, and a former CIA agent. *A Better War, the Unexamined Victories and Final Tragedy of America's Last Years in Vietnam* (Harcourt Brace & Co., 1999), argues that Nixon's policy makers and, in particular General Creighton Abrams, "dropped General Westmoreland's war of attrition and search-and-destroy missions in favor of a holistic approach aimed at 'pacifying' the population of South Vietnam." (Jeff T. Hay, *The Greenhaven Encyclopedia of the Vietnam War,* Greenhaven Press, 2004.) Militarily, the war was won, says Sorely, but Congress and a politically weakened Nixon negotiated a one-sided peace to ensure defeat for South Vietnam. Another military historian and former Vietnam War military commander, James H. Willbanks, supports some of Sorley's interpretation. *Abandoning Vietnam: How America Left and South Vietnam Lost Its War* (University Press of Kansas, 2004) argues that the South Vietnamese, with the aid of United States advisers and air power, held off the North Vietnamese military advances in 1972. But the Paris Peace Accords, negotiated by a politically weakened Nixon along with corrupt South Vietnamese political leaders and incompetent senior military leadership caused the demise of South Vietnam.

Professor Berman's interpretation is also challenged by Jeffrey Kimball who has written a comprehensive and detailed interpretation of *Nixon's Vietnam War* (University Press of Kansas, 1998). In his article for *The SHAFR Newsletter* (September 2001) "The Case of the 'Decent Interval': Do We Now Have a Smoking Gun?", Kimball feels that Berman misinterpreted some of his evidence. The "decent interval" was adopted in the fall of 1970 after his initial plan for a quick victory and withdrawal had failed and not in 1973 at the Paris Peace Talks as Berman claims.

Perhaps we will have a better assessment of Nixon's policies when all of his tapes along with Kissinger's correspondence are placed in the National Archives or the Nixon Presidential library.

The Vietnam War remains politically controversial. In the 2004 election, President George Bush had to prove he served in the Alabama National Guard during the war, while Senator John Kerry had to defend his patriotism as a former leader of the Vietnam Veterans against the War. In the summer of 2009, President Obama was weighing his options in Afghanistan. Should he send troops there? Republicans were reading Lewis Sorley's book for lessons on how to win while Democrats, including Obama, were reading Gordon M. Goldstein's *Lessons in Disaster: McGeorge Bundy and the Path to War in Vietnam* (Henry Holt and Co., 2008). Bundy was head of the National Security Council under both Presidents Kennedy and Johnson who, like former Secretary of Defense Robert F. McNamara, had second thoughts about escalating the war in 1965. See "A Battle of Two Books Rages," *The Wall Street Journal* (October 7, 2009).

There are thousands of books on the Vietnam War. The two best overviews are George C. Herring, *America's Longest War: The United States and Vietnam, 1950–1975,* 3rd ed. (McGraw Hill, 1996); and David L. Anderson, ed., *Shadows on the White House: Presidents and the Vietnam War, 1945–1975* (University Press of Kansas, 1993), which provide historical essays on the role of every President from Truman through Ford as regards to the Vietnam War.

Professor John Milton Cooper's monumental and massive *Woodrow Wilson: A Biography* (Knopf, 2009) is now the definitive biography of the current generation of historians. His earlier book *The Warrior and the Priest: Woodrow Wilson and Theodore Roosevelt* (Harvard University Press, 1984) presents Wilson as the realist and Theodore Roosevelt as the idealist. Cooper acknowledges his debt to the great diplomatic historian Thomas A. Bailey whose two books on *Woodrow Wilson and the Lost Peace* (The Macmillan Co., 1944) and *Woodrow Wilson and the Great Betrayal* (The Macmillan Co., 1945) were written as guidance for President Franklin Roosevelt to avoid the mistakes that Wilson made at home and abroad in his failure to gain ratification of the Treaty of Versailles. See also Bailey's summary of the second book from "Woodrow Wilson Wouldn't Yield," in *Essays Diplomatic and Undiplomatic of Thomas A. Bailey* (Appleton-Century-Crofts, 1969), which is also reprinted in volume 2 of the 13th edition of *Taking Sides . . . United States History.* Cooper's emphasis is different from Bailey. Where the latter wrote his books in the shadow of World War II, Cooper is responding to the emphasis placed on Wilson's psychological and physical well-being. In his last chapter of *Breaking the Heart of the World . . . ,* part of which is reprinted here, Cooper believes the League fight boils down to three interlocking propositions. "First, Wilson was ahead of his time. Second, Americans were not ready after World War I to make the full-scale commitment to collective security and international enforcement that Wilson demanded. Third, it took World War II to drive home the lessons that Wilson had tried to teach."

Cooper suggests some interesting alternatives to propositions two and three. In the 1920s, the country was divided between isolationism and internationalism with the majority holding no opinions. Could President Theodore Roosevelt have moved the country toward a stronger role in international affairs if he, instead of Harding, was elected president in 1920? As regards the lessons of World War II, did the Cold War mitigate the role of the United Nations in lessening tensions between the American and Soviet blocs?

In the end, Cooper lays most of the blame for the failure of the United States to satisfy the Treaty of Versailles and enter the League of Nations on Wilson. Lodge, says Cooper, was not responsible because playing politics like reading the entire treaty to an empty Senate and adding his 14 reservations were part of the Republican party's role as the loyal opposition.

Here Cooper departs from Bailey's critique of Lodge. In the final analysis, Cooper believes Wilson failed to compromise because of his stroke. If he was in better health, Wilson might have negotiated with Lodge as he had done on passing his New Freedom bills through Congress. Wilson was a high stakes gambler, but a more physically fit president would have called in Lodge's chips.

The most recent scholarship on Wilson can be found in two collections: John Milton Cooper, Jr., ed., *Reconsidering Woodrow Wilson: Progressivism,*

Internationalism, War and Peace (Woodrow Wilson Center Press, Johns Hopkins University Press, 2008) where the editor considers Wilson "to be one of the greatest legislators to sit in the White House." See also Cooper, Jr., "Whose League of Nations? Theodore Roosevelt, Woodrow Wilson, and World Order," in William N. Tilchin and Charles E. New, eds., *Artists of Power: Theodore Roosevelt, Woodrow Wilson, and Their Enduring Impact on U.S. Foreign Policy* (Praeger Security International, 2006). All the essays are worth reading.

The four best bibliographies of Wilson are as follows: the introduction to Lloyd E. Ambrosius's *Wilsonianism: Woodrow Wilson and His Legacy in American Foreign Relations* (Palgrave Macmillan, 2002), which is a collection of his articles from the leading realist Wilsonian scholar. John A. Thompson, a British scholar, has an up-to-date analysis of the Wilson scholarship in *Woodrow Wilson* (Pearson Education, 2002), a short, scholarly sympathetic study in the "Profiles in Power" series designed for student use. Advanced undergraduates should consult David Steigerwald, "The Reclamation of Woodrow Wilson," *Diplomatic History* (Winter 1999). Political science majors should consult Francis J. Gavin, "The Wilsonian Legacy in the Twentieth Century," *Orbis* (Fall 1997).

ISSUE 17

Has the Women's Movement of the 1970s Failed to Liberate American Women?

YES: F. Carolyn Graglia, from *Domestic Tranquility: A Brief Against Feminism* (Spence, 1998)

NO: Sara M. Evans, from "American Women in the Twentieth Century," in Harvard Sitkoff, ed., *Perspectives on Modern America: Making Sense of the Twentieth Century* (Oxford University Press, 2001)

ISSUE SUMMARY

YES: Writer and lecturer F. Carolyn Graglia argues that women should stay at home and practice the values of "true motherhood" because contemporary feminists have discredited marriage, devalued traditional homemaking, and encouraged sexual promiscuity.

NO: According to Professor Sara M. Evans, despite class, racial, religious, ethnic, and regional differences, women in America experienced major transformations in their private and public lives in the twentieth century.

In 1961, President John F. Kennedy established the Commission on the Status of Women to examine "the prejudice and outmoded customs that act as barriers to the full realization of women's basic rights." Two years later, Betty Friedan, a closet leftist from suburban Rockland County, New York, wrote about the growing malaise of the suburban housewife in her best-seller *The Feminist Mystique* (W.W. Norton, 1963).

The roots of Friedan's "feminine mystique" go back much earlier than the post–World War II "baby boom" generation of suburban America. Women historians have traced the origins of the modern family to the early nineteenth century. As the nation became more stable politically, the roles of men, women, and children became segmented in ways that still exist today. Dad went to work, the kids went to school, and Mom stayed home. Women's magazines, gift books, and the religious literature of the period ascribed to these women a role that Professor Barbara Welter has called the "Cult of True Womanhood." She describes the ideal woman as upholding four virtues—piety, purity, submissiveness, and domesticity.

In nineteenth-century America, most middle-class white women stayed home. Those who entered the workforce as teachers or became reformers were usually extending the values of the Cult of True Womanhood to the outside world. This was true of the women reformers in the Second Great Awakening and the peace, temperance, and abolitionist movements before the Civil War. The first real challenge to the traditional values system occurred when a handful of women showed up at Seneca Falls, New York, in 1848 to sign the Women's Declaration of Rights.

It soon became clear that if they were going to pass reform laws, women would have to obtain the right to vote. After an intense struggle, the Nineteenth Amendment was ratified on August 26, 1920. Once the women's movement obtained the vote, there was no agreement on future goals. The problems of the Great Depression and World War II overrode women's issues.

World War II brought about major changes for working women. Six million women entered the labor force for the first time, *many* of whom were married. "The proportion of women in the labor force," writes Lois Banner, "increased from 25 percent in 1940 to 36 percent in 1945. This increase was greater than that of the previous four decades combined." Many women moved into high-paying, traditionally men's jobs as policewomen, firefighters, and precision tool-makers. Steel and auto companies that converted over to wartime production made sure that lighter tools were made for women to use on the assembly lines. The federal government also erected federal childcare facilities.

When the war ended in 1945, many of these women lost their nontraditional jobs. The federal day-care program was eliminated, and the government told women to go home even though a 1944 study by the Women's Bureau concluded that 80 percent of working women wanted to continue in their jobs after the war.

Most history texts emphasize that women did return home, moved to the suburbs, and created a baby boom generation, which reversed the downward size of families in the years from 1946 to 1964. What is lost in this description is the fact that after 1947 the number of working women again began to rise, reaching 31 percent in 1951. Twenty-two years later, at the height of the women's liberation movement, it reached 42 percent.

When Friedan wrote *The Feminine Mystique* in 1963, both working-class and middle-class college-educated women experienced discrimination in the marketplace. When women worked, they were expected to become teachers, nurses, secretaries, and airline stewardesses—the lowest-paying jobs in the workforce. In the turbulent 1960s, this situation was no longer accepted.

In the following selection, F. Carolyn Graglia defends the traditional role of women in contemporary America. Women, she contends, should stay at home and practice the values of "true womanhood." Contemporary feminists, she argues, have devalued traditional homemaking, encouraged sexual promiscuity, and discredited marriage as a career for women. In the second selection, Sara M. Evans argues that in spite of class, racial, religious, ethnic, and regional differences, women in America experienced major transformations in their private and public lives in the twentieth century.

YES

F. Carolyn Graglia

Domestic Tranquility

Introduction

Since the late 1960s, feminists have very successfully waged war against the traditional family, in which husbands are the principal breadwinners and wives are primarily homemakers. This war's immediate purpose has been to undermine the homemaker's position within both her family and society in order to drive her into the work force. Its long-term goal is to create a society in which women behave as much like men as possible, devoting as much time and energy to the pursuit of a career as men do, so that women will eventually hold equal political and economic power with men. . . .

Feminists have used a variety of methods to achieve their goal. They have promoted a sexual revolution that encouraged women to mimic male sexual promiscuity. They have supported the enactment of no-fault divorce laws that have undermined housewives' social and economic security. And they obtained the application of affirmative action requirements to women as a class, gaining educational and job preferences for women and undermining the ability of men who are victimized by this discrimination to function as family breadwinners.

A crucial weapon in feminism's arsenal has been the status degradation of the housewife's role. From the journalistic attacks of Betty Friedan and Gloria Steinem to Jessie Bernard's sociological writings, all branches of feminism are united in the conviction that a woman can find identity and fulfillment only in a career. The housewife, feminists agree, was properly characterized by Simone de Beauvoir and Betty Friedan as a "parasite," a being something less than human, living her life without using her adult capabilities or intelligence, and lacking any real purpose in devoting herself to children, husband, and home.

Operating on the twin assumptions that equality means sameness (that is, men and women cannot be equals unless they do the same things) and that most differences between the sexes are culturally imposed, contemporary feminism has undertaken its own cultural impositions. Revealing their totalitarian belief that they know best how others should live and their totalitarian willingness to force others to conform to their dogma, feminists have sought to modify our social institutions in order to create an androgynous society in which male and female roles are as identical as possible. The results of the feminist juggernaut now engulf us. By almost all indicia of well-being, the institution of the American family has become significantly less healthy than it was thirty years ago.

Certainly, feminism is not alone responsible for our families' sufferings. As Charles Murray details in *Losing Ground,* President Lyndon Johnson's Great Society programs, for example, have often hurt families, particularly black families, and these programs were supported by a large constituency beyond the women's movement. What distinguishes the women's movement, however, is the fact that, despite the pro-family motives it sometimes ascribes to itself, it has actively sought the traditional family's destruction. In its avowed aims and the programs it promotes, the movement has adopted Kate Millett's goal, set forth in her *Sexual Politics,* in which she endorses Friedrich Engels's conclusion that "the family, as that term is presently understood, must go"; "a kind fate," she remarks, in "view of the institution's history." This goal has never changed: feminists view traditional nuclear families as inconsistent with feminism's commitment to women's independence and sexual freedom.

Emerging as a revitalized movement in the 1960s, feminism reflected women's social discontent, which had arisen in response to the decline of the male breadwinner ethic and to the perception—heralded in Philip Wylie's 1940s castigation of the evil "mom"—that Western society does not value highly the roles of wife and mother. Women's dissatisfactions, nevertheless, have often been aggravated rather than alleviated by the feminist reaction. To mitigate their discontent, feminists argued, women should pattern their lives after men's, engaging in casual sexual intercourse on the same terms as sexually predatory males and making the same career commitments as men. In pursuit of these objectives, feminists have fought unceasingly for the ready availability of legal abortion and consistently derogated both motherhood and the worth of full-time homemakers. Feminism's sexual teachings have been less consistent, ranging from its early and enthusiastic embrace of the sexual revolution to a significant backlash against female sexual promiscuity, which has led some feminists to urge women to abandon heterosexual sexual intercourse altogether.

Contemporary feminism has been remarkably successful in bringing about the institutionalization in our society of the two beliefs underlying its offensive: denial of the social worth of traditional homemakers and rejection of traditional sexual morality. The consequences have been pernicious and enduring. General societal assent to these beliefs has profoundly distorted men's perceptions of their relationships with and obligations to women, women's perceptions of their own needs, and the way in which women make decisions about their lives.

Traditional Homemaking Devalued

The first prong of contemporary feminism's offensive has been to convince society that a woman's full-time commitment to cultivating her marriage and rearing her children is an unworthy endeavor. Women, assert feminists, should treat marriage and children as relatively independent appendages to their life of full-time involvement in the workplace. To live what feminists assure her is the only life worthy of respect, a woman must devote the vast bulk of her time and energy to market production, at the expense of marriage and children. Children, she is told, are better cared for by surrogates, and marriage, as these feminists perceive it, neither deserves nor requires much attention; indeed, the very idea of a woman's "cultivating" her marriage seems ludicrous. Thus, spurred on by the women's movement, many women have sought to become male clones.

But some feminists have appeared to modify the feminist message; voices—supposedly of moderation—have argued that women really are different from men. In this they are surely right: there are fundamental differences between the average man and woman, and it is appropriate to take account of these differences when making decisions both in our individual lives and with respect to social issues. Yet the new feminist voices have not conceded that acknowledged differences between the sexes are grounds for reexamining women's flight from home into workplace. Instead, these new voices have argued only that these differences require modification of the terms under which women undertake to reconstruct their lives in accordance with the blueprint designed by so-called early radicals. The edifice erected by radical feminism is to remain intact, subject only to some redecorating. The foundation of this edifice is still the destruction of the traditional family. Feminism has acquiesced in women's desire to bear children (an activity some of the early radicals discouraged). But it continues steadfast in its assumption that, after some period of maternity leave, daily care of those children is properly the domain of institutions and paid employees. The yearnings manifested in women's palpable desire for children should largely be sated, the new voices tell us, by the act of serving as a birth canal and then spending so-called quality time with the child before and after a full day's work.

Any mother, in this view, may happily consign to surrogates most of the remaining aspects of her role, assured that doing so will impose no hardship or loss on either mother or child. To those women whose natures make them less suited to striving in the workplace than concentrating on husband, children, and home, this feminist diktat denies the happiness and contentment they could have found within the domestic arena. In the world formed by contemporary feminism, these women will have status and respect only if they force themselves to take up roles in the workplace they suspect are not most deserving of their attention. Relegated to the periphery of their lives are the home and personal relationships with husband and children that they sense merit their central concern.

Inherent in the feminist argument is an extraordinary contradiction. Feminists deny, on the one hand, that the dimension of female sexuality which engenders women's yearning for children can also make it appropriate and satisfying for a woman to devote herself to domestic endeavors and provide her children's full-time care. On the other hand, they plead the fact of sexual difference to justify campaigns to modify workplaces in order to correct the effects of male influence and alleged biases. Only after such modifications, claim feminists, can women's nurturing attributes and other female qualities be adequately expressed in and truly influence the workplace. Manifestations of these female qualities, feminists argue, should and can occur in the workplace once it has been modified to blunt the substantial impact of male aggression and competitiveness and take account of women's special requirements.

Having launched its movement claiming the right of women—a right allegedly denied them previously—to enter the workplace on an *equal* basis with men, feminism then escalated its demands by arguing that female differences require numerous changes in the workplace. Women, in this view, are insufficiently feminine to find satisfaction in rearing their own children, but too feminine to compete on an equal basis with men. Thus, having taken women out of their homes and settled them in the workplace, feminists have sought to reconstruct workplaces to create "feminist playpens" that are conducive to female qualities of sensitivity, caring, and empathy. Through this exercise in self-contradiction, contemporary feminism has endeavored to remove the woman from her home and role of providing daily care to her children—the quintessential place and activity for most effectively expressing her feminine, nurturing attributes.

The qualities that are the most likely to make women good mothers are thus redeployed away from their children and into workplaces that must be restructured to accommodate them. The irony is twofold. Children—the ones who could benefit most from the attentions of those mothers who do possess these womanly qualities—are deprived of those attentions and left only with the hope of finding adequate replacement for their loss. Moreover, the occupations in which these qualities are now to find expression either do not require them for optimal job performance (often they are not conducive to professional success) or were long ago recognized as women's occupations—as in the field of nursing, for example—in which nurturing abilities do enhance job performance.

Traditional Sexual Morality Traduced

The second prong of contemporary feminism's offensive has been to encourage women to ape male sexual patterns and engage in promiscuous sexual intercourse as freely as men. Initially, feminists were among the most dedicated supporters of the sexual revolution, viewing female participation in casual sexual activity as an unmistakable declaration of female equality with males. The women in our society who acted upon the teachings of feminist sexual revolutionaries have suffered greatly. They are victims of the highest abortion rate in the Western world. More than one in five Americans are now infected with a viral sexually transmitted disease which at best can be controlled but not cured and is often chronic. Sexually transmitted diseases, both viral and bacterial, disproportionately affect women because, showing fewer symptoms, they often go untreated for a longer time. These diseases also lead to pelvic infections that cause infertility in 100,000 to 150,000 women each year.

The sexual revolution feminists have promoted rests on an assumption that an act of sexual intercourse involves nothing but a pleasurable physical sensation, possessing no symbolic meaning and no moral dimension. This is an understanding of sexuality that bears more than a slight resemblance to sex as depicted in pornography: physical sexual acts without emotional involvement. In addition to the physical harm caused by increased sexual promiscuity, the denial that sexual intercourse has symbolic importance within a framework of moral accountability corrupts the nature of the sex act. Such denial necessarily makes sexual intercourse a trivial event, compromising the act's ability to fulfill its most important function after procreation. This function is to bridge the gap between males and females who often seem separated by so many differences, both biological and emotional, that they feel scarcely capable of understanding or communicating with each other.

Because of the urgency of sexual desire, especially in the male, it is through sexual contact that men and women can most easily come together. Defining the nature of sexual intercourse in terms informed by its procreative potentialities makes the act a spiritually meaningful event of overwhelming importance. A sexual encounter so defined is imbued with the significance conferred by its connection with a promise of immortality through procreation, whether that connection is a present possibility, a remembrance of children already borne, or simply an acknowledgment of the reality and truth of the promise. Such a sex act can serve as the physical meeting ground on which, by accepting and affirming each other through their bodies' physical unity, men and women can begin to construct an enduring emotional unity. The sexual encounter cannot perform its function when it is viewed as a trivial event of moral indifference with no purpose or meaning other than producing a physical sensation through the friction of bodily parts.

The feminist sexual perspective deprives the sex act of the spiritual meaningfulness that can make it the binding force upon which man and woman can construct a lasting marital relationship. The morally indifferent sexuality championed by the sexual revolution substitutes the sex without emotions that characterizes pornography for the sex of a committed, loving relationship that satisfies women's longing for romance and connection. But this is not the only damage to relationships between men and women that follows from feminism's determination to promote an androgynous society by convincing men and women that they are virtually fungible. Sexual equivalency, feminists believe, requires that women not only engage in casual sexual intercourse as freely as men, but also that women mimic male behavior by becoming equally assertive in initiating sexual encounters and in their activity throughout the encounter. With this sexual prescription, feminists mock the essence of conjugal sexuality that is at the foundation of traditional marriage.

Marriage as a Woman's Career Discredited

Even academic feminists who are considered "moderates" endorse doctrines most inimical to the homemaker. Thus, Professor Elizabeth Fox-Genovese, regarded as a moderate in Women's Studies, tells us that marriage can no longer be a viable career for women. But if marriage cannot be a woman's career, then despite feminist avowals of favoring choice in this matter, home-making cannot be a woman's goal, and surrogate child-rearing must be her child's destiny. Contrary to feminist claims, society's barriers are not strung tightly to inhibit women's career choices. Because of feminism's very success-ful efforts, society encourages women to pursue careers, while stigmatizing and preventing their devotion to child-rearing and domesticity.

It was precisely upon the conclusion that marriage cannot be a viable career for women that *Time* magazine rested its Fall 1990 special issue on "Women: The Road Ahead," a survey of contemporary women's lives. While noting that the "cozy, limited roles of the past are still clearly re-membered, sometimes fondly," during the past thirty years "all that was orthodox has become negotiable." One thing negotiated away has been the economic security of the homemaker, and *Time* advised young women that "the job of full-time homemaker may be the riskiest profession to choose" because "the advent of no-fault and equitable-distribution divorce laws" reflect, in the words of one judge, the fact that "[s]ociety no longer believes that a husband should support his wife."

No-fault divorce laws did not, however, result from an edict of the gods or some force of nature, but from sustained political efforts, particularly by the feminist movement. As a cornerstone of their drive to make women exchange home for workplace, and thereby secure their independence from men, the availability of no-fault divorce (like the availability of abortion) was sacrosanct to the movement. *Time* shed crocodile tears for displaced home-makers, for it made clear that women must canter down the road ahead with the spur of no-fault divorce urging them into the workplace. Of all *Time*'s recommendations for ameliorating women's lot, divorce reform—the most crying need in our country today—was not among them. Whatever hardships may be endured by women who would resist a divorce, *Time*'s allegiance, like that of most feminists, is clearly to the divorce-seekers who, it was pleased to note, will not be hindered in their pursuit of self-realization by the barriers to divorce that their own mothers had faced.

These barriers to divorce which had impeded their own parents, how-ever, had usually benefited these young women by helping to preserve their parents' marriage. A five-year study of children in divorcing families disclosed that "the overwhelming majority preferred the unhappy mar-riage to the divorce," and many of them, "despite the unhappiness of their parents, were in fact relatively happy and considered their situa-tion neither better nor worse than that of other families around them." A follow-up study after ten years demonstrated that children experienced the trauma of their parents' divorce as more serious and long-lasting than any researchers had anticipated. *Time* so readily acquiesced in the disadvantaging of homemakers and the disruption of children's lives be-cause the feminist ideological parameters within which it operates have excluded marriage as a *proper* career choice. Removing the obstacles to making it a *viable* choice would, therefore, be an undesirable subversion of feminist goals.

That *Time* would have women trot forward on life's journey con-strained by the blinders of feminist ideology is evident from its failure to question any feminist notion, no matter how silly, or to explore solutions incompatible with the ideology's script. One of the silliest notions *Time* left unexamined was that young women want "good careers, good marriages and two or three kids, and they don't want the children to be raised by strangers." The supposed realism of this expectation lay in the new wom-an's attitude that "I don't want to work 70 hours a week, but I want to be vice president, and *you* have to change." But even if thirty hours were cut from that seventy-hour workweek, the new woman would still be working the normal full-time week, her children would still be raised by surrogates, and the norm would continue to be the feminist version of child-rearing that *Time* itself described unflatteringly as "less a preoccupation than an improvisation."

The illusion that a woman can achieve career success without sac-rificing the daily personal care of her children—and except among the very wealthy, most of her leisure as well—went unquestioned by *Time*. It did note, however, the dissatisfaction expressed by Eastern European and Russian women who had experienced, as a matter of government policy, the same liberation from home and children that our feminists have un-dertaken to bestow upon Western women. In what *Time* described as "a curious reversal of Western feminism's emphasis on careers for women," the new female leaders of Eastern Europe would like "to reverse the com-munist diktat that all women have to work." Women have "dreamed," said the Polish Minister of Culture and Arts, "of reaching the point where we have the choice to stay home" that communism had taken away. But blinded by its feminist bias, *Time* could only find it "curious" that women would choose to stay at home; apparently beyond the pale of respectabil-ity was any argument that it would serve Western women's interest to retain the choice that contemporary feminism—filling in the West the role of communism in the East—has sought to deny them.

Nor was its feminist bias shaken by the attitudes of Japanese women, most of whom, *Time* noted, reject "equality" with men, choosing to cease work after the birth of a first child and later resuming a part-time career or pursuing hobbies or community work. The picture painted was that of the 1950s American suburban housewife reviled by Betty Friedan, except that the American has enjoyed a higher standard of living (particularly a much larger home) than has the Japanese. In Japan, *Time* observed, being "a housewife is nothing to be ashamed of." Dishonoring the housewife's role was a goal, it might have added, that Japanese feminists can, in time, accomplish if they emulate their American counterparts.

Japanese wives have broad responsibilities, commented *Time*, because most husbands leave their salaries and children entirely in wives' hands; freed from drudgery by modern appliances, housewives can "pursue their interests in a carefree manner, while men have to worry about support-ing their wives and children." Typically, a Japanese wife controls house-hold finances, giving her husband a cash allowance, the size of which, apparently, dissatisfies one-half of the men. Acknowledging that Japanese wives take the leadership in most homes, one husband observed that "[t]hings go best when the husband is swimming in the palm of his wife's hand." A home is well-managed, said one wife, "if you make your men feel that they're in control when they are in front of others, while in reality you're in control." It seems like a good arrangement to me.

Instead of inquiring whether a similar carefree existence might appeal to some American women, *Time* looked forward to the day when marriage would no longer be a career for Japanese women, as their men took over household and child-rearing chores, enabling wives to join husbands in the workplace. It was noted, however, that a major impediment to this goal, which would have to be corrected, was the fact that Japanese day-care centers usually run for only eight hours a day. Thus, *Time* made clear that its overriding concern was simply promoting the presence of women in the work force. This presence is seen as a good *per se*, without any *pro forma* talk about the economic necessity of a second income and without any question raised as to whether it is in children's interest to spend any amount of time—much less in excess of eight hours a day—in communal care. . . .

The Awakened Brünnhilde

. . . Those who would defend anti-feminist traditionalism today are like heretics fighting a regnant Inquisition. To become a homemaker, a woman may need the courage of a heretic. This is one reason that the defense of traditional women is often grounded in religious teachings, for the heretic's courage usually rests on faith. The source of courage I offer is the conviction, based on my own experience, that contemporary feminism's stereotypical caricature of the housewife did not reflect reality when Friedan popularized it, does not reflect reality today, and need not govern reality.

Feminists claimed a woman can find identity and fulfillment only in a career; they are wrong. They claimed a woman can, in that popular expression, "have it all"; they are wrong—she can have only some. The experience of being a mother at home is a different experience from being a full-time market producer who is also a mother. A woman can have one or the other experience, but not both at the same time. Combining a career with motherhood requires a woman to compromise by diminishing her commitment and exertions with respect to one role or the other, or usually, to both. Rarely, if ever, can a woman adequately perform in a full-time career if she diminishes her commitment to it sufficiently to replicate the experience of being a mother at home.

Women were *never* told they could *not* choose to make the compromises required to combine these roles; within the memory of all living today there were always some women who did so choose. But by successfully degrading the housewife's role, contemporary feminism undertook to force this choice upon all women. I declined to make the compromises necessary to combine a career with motherhood because I did not want to become like Andrea Dworkin's spiritual virgin. I did not want to keep my being intact, as Dworkin puts it, so that I could continue to pursue career success. Such pursuit would have required me to hold too much of myself aloof from husband and children: the invisible "wedge-shaped core of darkness" that Virginia Woolf described as being oneself would have to be too large, and not enough of me would have been left over for them.

I feared that if I cultivated that "wedge-shaped core of darkness" within myself enough to maintain a successful career, I would be consumed by that career, and that thus desiccated, too little of me would remain to flesh out my roles as wife and mother. Giving most of myself to the market seemed less appropriate and attractive than reserving myself for my family. Reinforcing this decision was my experience that when a woman lives too much in her mind, she finds it increasingly difficult to live through her body. Her nurturing ties to her children become attenuated; her physical relationship with her husband becomes hollow and perfunctory. Certainly in my case, Dr. James C. Neely spoke the truth in *Gender: The Myth of Equality:* "With too much emphasis on intellect, a woman becomes 'too into her head' to function in a sexual, motherly way, destroying by the process of thought the process of feeling her sexuality."

Virginia Woolf never compromised her market achievements with motherhood; nor did the Brontë sisters, Jane Austen, or George Eliot. Nor did Helen Frankenthaler who, at the time she was acknowledged to be the most prominent living female artist, said in an interview: "We all make different compromises. And, no, I don't regret not having children. Given my painting, children could have suffered. A mother must make her children come first: young children are helpless. Well, paintings are objects but they're also helpless." I agree with her; that is precisely how I felt about the briefs I wrote for clients. Those briefs were, to me, like helpless children; in writing them, I first learned the meaning of complete devotion. I stopped writing them because I believed they would have been masters too jealous of my husband and my children.

Society never rebuked these women for refusing to compromise their literary and artistic achievements. Neither should it rebuke other kinds of women for refusing to compromise their own artistry of motherhood and domesticity. Some women may agree that the reality I depict rings truer to them than the feminist depiction. This conviction may help them find the courage of a heretic. Some others, both men and women, may see enough truth in the reality I depict that they will come to regret society's acquiescence in the status degradation of the housewife. They may then accept the currently unfashionable notion that society should respect and support women who adopt the anti-feminist perspective.

It is in society's interest to begin to pull apart the double-bind web spun by feminism and so order itself as not to inhibit any woman who *could* be an awakened Brünnhilde. Delighted and contented women will certainly do less harm—and probably more good—to society than frenzied and despairing ones. This is not to suggest that society should interfere with a woman's decision to follow the feminist script and adopt any form of spiritual virginity that suits her. But neither should society continue to validate destruction of the women's pact by the contemporary feminists who sought to make us all follow their script. We should now begin to dismantle our regime that discourages and disadvantages the traditional woman who rejects feminist spiritual virginity and seeks instead the very different delight and contentment that she believes best suits her.

American Women in the Twentieth Century

In 1900, our foremothers predicted that the twentieth century would be the "century of the child." It might be more accurate, however, to call it the "century of women." Among the many dramatic changes in American society, it is hard to find an example more striking than the changes in women's lives on every level.

At the beginning of the twentieth century, women were challenging the confines of an ideology that relegated them to the private realm of domesticity. Despite the reality that thousands of women could be found in factories, offices, and fields—not to mention in a wide variety of political and reform activities—those ideas still held powerful sway both in law and in dominant notions of propriety. Over the course of the twentieth century, however, women in America emerged fully (though still not equally) into all aspects of public life—politics, labor force participation, professions, mass media, and popular culture. As they did so, they experienced a transformation in the fundamental parameters of their private lives as well—marriage, family, fertility, and sexuality. In complex ways, women transformed the landscapes of both public and private life so that at century's end we are left with a deeply puzzling conundrum about just what we mean by the terms *public* and *private*.

Women, of course, are part of every other social group. Deeply divided by race, class, religion, ethnicity, and region, they don't always identify with one another, and as a result women's collective identity—their sense of solidarity as women—has waxed and waned. Twice in this century, however, there has been a massive wave of activism focused on women's rights. We can trace the surges of change in women's status that accompanied each of these, one at the beginning and another near the end of the century.

Changes in women's lives were certainly driven by large structural forces such as the emergence of the postindustrial service economy, rising levels of education, and the exigencies of two world wars. Yet they have also been due to women's own self-organized activism in two great waves and in numerous ripples in between. In some instances, women fought for the right to participate in public life. In other instances, already present in public spaces, they struggled for equity. As a result of these struggles, American political and public life has undergone a series of fundamental transformations. Not only are women in different places at the end of the century then they were at the beginning, but also all Americans enter a new century shaped by the complexities of women's journey.

1900—Dawn of the Twentieth Century

At the beginning of the twentieth century, women's lives were defined primarily by their marital status, linked to race and class. If we take a snapshot (understanding that we are capturing a moment in a dynamic process of change), the normative adult woman—both statistically and in the images that pervaded popular culture—was married, middle class, and white. On average, women lived to 48.3 years; they married around age 22 and bore approximately four children. The vast majority of households consisted of male-headed married couples and their children.

In 1900 women's legal standing was fundamentally governed by their marital status. They had very few rights.

- A married woman had no separate legal identity from that of her husband.
- She had no right to control of her reproduction (even conveying information about contraception, for example, was illegal); and no right to sue or be sued, since she had no separate standing in court.
- She had no right to own property in her own name or to pursue a career of her choice.
- Women could not vote, serve on juries, or hold public office. According to the Supreme Court, Women were not "persons" under the Fourteenth Amendment to the Constitution that guarantees equal protection under the law.

These realities reflected an underlying ideology about women and men that allocated the public realms of work and politics to men and defined the proper place of women in society as fundamentally domestic. Confined to the realm of the home, women's duty to society lay in raising virtuous sons (future citizens) and dutiful daughters (future mothers). Over the course of the nineteenth century, however, women had pushed at the boundaries of their domestic assignment, both by choice and by necessity. They invented forms of politics outside the electoral arena by forming voluntary associations and building institutions in response to unmet social needs. In the 1830s, when women like Sarah and Angelina Grimké began to speak publicly against slavery, the mere appearance of a woman as a public speaker was considered scandalous. By 1900, however, women appeared in all manner of public settings, setting the stage for change in the twentieth century.

Signs of Change

A closer look at women's status in 1900 reveals trends that signal imminent change particularly in the areas of education, labor force participation, and sexuality. The coexistence of new possibilities alongside ongoing restrictions and discrimination laid the groundwork for challenges to the norms of female subordination.

Education   Women in 1900 had achieved a high degree of literacy. In fact, more girls than boys actually graduated from high school, probably because boys had access to many jobs that did not require significant education. When it came to higher education, however, women were seriously disadvantaged. They were overtly excluded from most professional education: only about 5 percent of medical students were women, and women's exclusion from legal education shows up in the fact that in 1920 only 1.4 percent of lawyers in the United States were female.

It is crucial to note, however, that in 1900 women constituted about 30 percent of students in colleges and universities, including schools for the growing female professions of nursing, teaching, librarianship, and social work. In the long run, this was a potent mix, as thousands of middle-class women embraced the opportunity to pursue higher education, which in turn generated new expectations. Education was a crucial force in creating the key leadership as well as a highly skilled constituency for the feminist mobilizations at either end of the century.

Labor Force Participation   In 1900, though wage labor was defined as a fundamentally male prerogative, women could be found in many parts of the labor force. Women's work outside the home, however, was framed by their marital status and overt discrimination based on race as well as sex.

- Approximately one in five women worked outside the home, a figure that was sharply distinguished by race: 41 percent nonwhite; 17 percent white.
- The average working woman was single and under age 25.
- Only 11 percent of married women worked outside the home (up to 15% by 1940), though the proportion among black women (26%) was considerably higher because discrimination against black men made it much harder for blacks to secure a livable income from a single wage.
- Available occupations were sharply limited. Most women who worked for wages served as domestics, farm laborers, unskilled factory operatives, or teachers. In fact, one in three women employed in nonagricultural pursuits worked in domestic service.
- Some new female-dominated professions, such as nursing, social work, and librarianship, were emerging. In addition, the feminization of clerical work, linked to the new technology of the typewriter and the record-keeping needs of growing corporate bureaucracies, signaled a dramatic trend that made the "working girl" increasingly respectable. By 1920 the proportion of women engaged in clerical work (25.6%) had surpassed the number in manufacturing (23.8), domestic service (18.2%), and agriculture (12.9%).

Sexuality and the Body   Late Victorians presumed (if they thought about it at all) that female sexuality should be confined entirely to marriage. Compared with today, there was very little premarital sex, and women were understood not to have much in the way of sexual desire. It was illegal to transmit information about contraception, though women clearly conveyed it anyway through networks of rumor and gossip. Within the dominant middle class even the simplest acknowledgments of female sexuality were suppressed into euphemism and other forms of denial. Body parts could not be named in polite company, so chicken "legs" and "breast," for example, became "dark meat" and "white meat." Female attire covered women's bodies with clothing that revealed some shape but very little skin.

Yet, as the twentieth century dawned with its emerging consumer culture, sexuality could no longer be so easily contained. Popular culture included vaudeville, dance halls, and a growing variety of public amusements (such as the brand-new movie theaters). In the past, women who frequented such places risked having a "bad reputation." Yet the growing popularity of public amusements within the "respectable middle class" was beginning to challenge such perceptions.

Women's bodies were also finding new visibility in athletics. In the wildly popular arenas of public competition such as baseball and boxing, athletics were virtually synonymous with masculinity. And yet women were beginning to play lawn tennis, field hockey, and gymnastics. Some even rode bicycles.

Race, Class, and Gender Ideals   Within the gender ideology of the urban middle class that emerged over the course of the nineteenth century, the "good woman" (and her antithesis) took on distinct characteristics associated with race and class. "Good" (white, Protestant, middle class) women embodied private virtues. They were chaste, domestic, pious, and submissive. "Bad" women were "low class"—immigrants, racial minorities—presumed to be promiscuous, bad mothers, and improper housewives largely on the basis of their presence in previously male-only public spaces (factories, saloons, dance halls). Such perceptions multiplied in the case of southern black women subjected to a regime of racial/sexual domination that included the constant threat of rape and the public humiliations of segregation. Yet, the denigration of lower-class and minority women on the basis of their presence in public was getting harder to sustain as growing numbers of supposedly "respectable" women showed up in the same, or similar, spaces.

The First Wave

This brief sketch of women's condition at the beginning of the century points to several forces for change that would bear fruit in the first few decades. The growth in women's education, their move into a wide variety of reform efforts as well as professions, laid the groundwork for a massive suffrage movement that demanded the most basic right of citizenship for women. The claim of citizenship was in many ways a deeply radical challenge to the ideology of separate spheres for men and women. It asserted the right of the individual woman to stand in direct relation to the state rather than to be represented through the participation of her husband or father. The growing power of the

women's suffrage movement rested both on women's collective consciousness, born in female associations, and on increased individualism among
women in an urbanizing industrializing economy.

While a small but crucial number of upper-middle-class women attended
college, where they developed a transformed awareness of their own potential
as women both individually and collectively, working-class immigrant and
African-American women experienced both individualism and collectivity in
very different ways. Forced to work outside the home in the least-skilled, lowest paying jobs, both they and their employers presumed that women's labor
force participation was temporary. Unions objected to their presence and
blocked them from apprenticeship and access to skilled jobs. Despite these
obstacles, when wage-earning women organized their own unions, often in
alliance with middle-class reformers, they exhibited awesome courage and
militancy. In the garment district of New York, for example, the "uprising of
the twenty thousand" in 1909 confounded the garment industry and led to
a new kind of industrial unionism.

By 1910, middle-class white reformers had formed increasingly effective
alliances with black and working-class women around the issue of women's
suffrage. The massive mobilization of American women in the decade before
the Nineteenth Amendment was ratified in 1920 included rallies of thousands of "working girls" and the organization of numerous African-American
women's suffrage clubs. Shared exclusion from the individual right of civic
participation symbolized their common womanhood. Following their victory, leaders of the National American Woman Suffrage Association joyfully
dismantled their organization and reassembled as the newly formed League
of Women Voters. Their new task, as they defined it, was to train women to
exercise their individual citizenship rights.

Such a reorientation seemed congruent with the popular culture of
the 1920s, which emphasized individual pleasures along with individual
rights. The development of a consumer economy, emphasizing pleasure
and using sexuality to sell, offered women other paths out of submissive
domesticity and into more assertive forms of individualism, paths that
did not require solidarity, indeed, undermined it. The female subculture
that relied on a singular definition of "woman" eroded. Female reform efforts remained a powerful force in American politics—laying much of the
groundwork for the emergence of a welfare state—but a broad-based movement for women's rights no longer existed after 1920. The pace of change
in areas like education and labor force participation also reached a plateau
and remained relatively unchanged for several decades after 1920. Modern
women were individuals. And "feminism" became an epithet.

The loss of female solidarity meant that women's organizations in
subsequent decades drew on narrow constituencies with very different
priorities. Professional women, lonely pioneers in many fields, felt the
continuing sting of discrimination and sought to eradicate the last ves-
tiges of legal discrimination with an Equal Rights Amendment (ERA). The
National Women's Party, one of the leading organizations in the struggle,
first proposed the ERA in 1923 for the vote. But they were opposed by

former allies, social reformers who feared that the protections for working women, which they had won during the Progressive era, would be lost. Though fiercely opposed to the ERA, reformers continued to advocate a stronger role for government in responding to social welfare. Many of them—with leaders like Eleanor Roosevelt—assumed key positions in the 1930s and shaped the political agenda known as the New Deal. In particular, their influence on the Social Security Act laid the foundations of the welfare state. Even among female reformers, however, alliances across racial lines remained rare and fraught with difficulty. As the progressive female reform tradition shaped an emergent welfare state, African-American voices remained muted, the needs of working women with children unaddressed.

The Second Wave

By mid-century the conditions for another surge of activism were under way. During the Second World War women joined the labor force in unprecedented numbers. Most significant, perhaps, married women and women over age 35 became normative among working women by 1950. Yet cold war culture, in the aftermath of World War II, reasserted traditional gender roles. The effort to contain women within the confines of the "feminine mystique" (as Betty Friedan later labeled this ideology), however, obscured but did not prevent rising activism among different constituencies of women. Under the cover of popular images of domesticity, women were rapidly changing their patterns of labor force and civic participation, initiating social movements for civil rights and world peace, and flooding into institutions of higher education.

The President's Commission on the Status of Women, established in 1961, put women's issues back on the national political agenda by recruiting a network of powerful women to develop a set of shared goals. They issued a report in 1963, the same year that Friedan published *The Feminine Mystique.* That report documented in meticulous detail the ongoing realities of discrimination in employment and in wages, numerous legal disabilities such as married women's lack of access to credit, and the growing problems of working mothers without adequate child care. In 1964, Title VII of the Civil Rights Act gave women their most powerful legal weapon against employment discrimination. An opponent of civil rights introduced Title VII, and many members of Congress treated it as a joke. But Title VII passed because the small number of women then in Congress fiercely and effectively defended the need to prohibit discrimination on the basis of "sex" as well as race, religion, and national origin.

The second wave emerged simultaneously among professional women and a younger cohort of social activists. Professionals, with the leadership of women in labor unions, government leaders, and intellectuals like Friedan, created the National Organization for Women (NOW) in 1966 to demand enforcement of laws like Title VII. A second branch of feminist activism emerged from younger women in the civil rights movement and the student new left. Civil rights offered a model of activism, an egalitarian and visionary language, an opportunity to develop political skills, and role models of courageous female leaders. Young women broke away in 1967 to form consciousness-raising groups and build on the legacy of the movements that had trained them.

The slogan, "the personal is political," became the ideological pivot of the second wave of American feminism. It drove a variety of challenges to gendered relations of power, whether embodied in public policy or in the most intimate personal relationships. The force of this direct assault on the public/private dichotomy has left deep marks on American politics, American society, and the feminist movement itself. Issues like domestic violence, child care, abortion, and sexual harassment have become central to the American political agenda, exposing deep divisions in American society that are not easily subject to the give-and-take compromises of political horse-trading.

From 1968 to 1975, the "Women's Liberation Movement," using the techniques of consciousness-raising in small groups, grew explosively. The synergy between different branches of feminist activism made the 1970s a very dynamic era. Feminist policymakers dubbed the years 1968 to 1975 "the golden years" because of their success in courtrooms and legislatures. These included the Equal Rights Amendment, which passed Congress in 1972 and went to the states; the 1973 Supreme Court decision legalizing abortion (*Roe v. Wade*); Title IX of the Higher Education Act, which opened intercollegiate athletics to women; the Women's Equity Education Act; and the Equal Credit Opportunity Act.

Women formed caucuses and organizations in most professional associations and in the labor movement. By the mid-1970s there were feminist organizations representing a broad range of racial groups as well—African-American women, Chicanas and Hispanic women, Asian-American women, Native American women. Women also built new organizations among clerical workers to challenge the devaluation and limited opportunities of traditional women's work.

With their new strength, women challenged barriers to the professions (law, medicine), to ordination within mainstream Protestant and Jewish denominations, and to the full range of traditionally male blue-collar occupations, from carpenters to firefighters and police. They filed thousands of complaints of discrimination, mounted hundreds of lawsuits, and also built thousands of new institutions—day-care centers, shelters for battered women, bookstores, coffeehouses, and many others. The new feminism drew on women's stories to rethink the most intimate personal aspects of womanhood including abortion rights, sexual autonomy, rape, domestic violence, and lesbian rights.

The second wave of feminism also changed the American language both through its own publications (of which there were hundreds, the largest of them being *Ms.*, first published in 1972) and through pressure on commercial publishing houses and mass media. New words entered the American lexicon—"Ms.," "firefighter," "sexism"—while uses of the generic masculine (mankind, brotherhood, policeman) suddenly seemed exclusive. In Women's Studies programs, which grew rapidly in the early 1970s, young scholars rethought the paradigms of their disciplines and initiated new branches of knowledge.

The second wave provoked a strong reaction, of course, revealing not only male hostility but also deep fissures among women themselves. Antifeminism became a strong political force by the late 1970s with the mobilization of Phyllis Schlafley's Stop-ERA and antiabortion forces. In the face of widespread cultural anxiety about equality for women and changing gender roles, the Equal Rights Amendment stalled after 1975 and went down to defeat in 1982 despite an extension of the deadline for ratification. Antifeminism drew on the insecurities of a declining economy in the wake of the Vietnam War and on the growing political power of the New Right which made cultural issues (abortion, the ERA, "family values," and homophobia) central. The 1980s, framed by the hostile political climate of the Reagan administration, nourished a growing backlash against feminism in the media, the popular culture, and public policy. As public spending shifted away from social programs and toward the military, female poverty increased sharply. The Reagan boom after 1983 did not touch the poorest, disproportionately female and racial minority, segments of the population.

At the same time, the 1980s witnessed the continued growth of women's presence in positions of public authority: Supreme Court justice, astronaut, arctic explorer, military officer, truck driver, carpenter, Olympic star, bishop, rabbi. Mainstream religious denominations began to rewrite liturgies and hymn books to make them more "inclusive." Despite regular announcements of the "death" of feminism, it would be more accurate to say that in the 1980s feminism entered the mainstream with new levels of community activism, sophisticated political fundraisers like EMILY's List, and broad political alliances on issues like comparable worth. Experimental "counterinstitutions" started in the 1970s (battered women's shelters, health clinics, bookstores, etc.) survived by adopting more institutionalized procedures, professionalized staff, and state funding. Women's Studies took on the trappings of an academic discipline.

Feminism was broad, diffuse, and of many minds in the 1980s. Legal and cultural issues grew more complex. Feminist theorists wrestled with the realities of differences such as race, class, age, and sexual preference, asking themselves whether the category "woman" could withstand such an analysis. The multifaceted activities that embraced the label "feminist"—policy activism, research think tanks, literary theory, music, art, spirituality—signaled the fact that the women's movement had lost some cohesiveness.

The testimony of Anita Hill during the 1991 hearings on the nomination of Clarence Thomas to the Supreme Court, however, catalyzed a new round of national conversation, complicated by the deep fissures of race and sex. The sight of a genteel black woman being grilled by a committee of white men who made light of this "sexual harassment crap" mobilized thousands of women to run for office and contribute to campaigns. In 1992 an unprecedented number of women were elected to public office.

2000—Dawn of a New Millennium

If we return to our original categories to describe women's situation at the end of the twentieth century, the contrast with 1900 could hardly be more dramatic. The average woman now can expect to live 79.7 years (65% longer than her great-grandmother in 1900), marry at age 24.5, and bear only about two children (if any at all). There are now decades in women's lives—both before and after the years of childbearing and child care—which earlier generations never experienced. As a result of the second wave of women's rights activism in the final decades of the twentieth century, in politics and law, labor force participation, education, and sexuality, women live in a truly different world. Yet, in each instance equity remains an elusive goal, suggesting the need for continued and revitalized activism in the twenty-first century.

Politics and Law

No longer defined by their marital status, women enjoy virtually the full range of formal legal rights. In addition to winning the right to vote in 1920, they achieved equal pay (for the same work) in 1963 and guarantees against discrimination in housing and employment in 1964 (Title VII of the Civil Rights Act). Since 1970 women have won the right to a separate legal identity; privacy rights regarding reproduction and bodily integrity; and rights to sue for discrimination in employment, to work when pregnant, to equal education, and to equal access to athletics. Whole new bodies of law have developed since the 1970s on issues like domestic violence and sexual harassment. Nonetheless, the failure of the Equal Rights Amendment (ERA) in 1982 means that women still have no constitutional guarantee of equality.

In the last twenty-five years we have also seen a dramatic growth in the numbers of female elected officials. In 1997 there were 60 women in Congress (11.2%)—14 of them women of color; 81 statewide executive officials (25%); 1,597 state legislators (21.5%); and 203 mayors of cities with population over 30,000 (20.6%). There are two women on the Supreme Court, 30 female circuit court judges (18.6%), and 107 female district court judges (17.2%).

Education

At the end of the twentieth century, 88 percent of young women ages 25 to 34 are high-school graduates. The transformations in primary and secondary education for girls cannot be captured in graduation numbers, however. They also reside in the admission of girls to shop and other vocational classes (and boys to cooking and sewing courses), in girls' participation in athletics, in curricula that—at least sometimes—emphasize women's achievements in the past, and in school counselors who no longer single-mindedly socialize girls for domesticity and/or nonskilled stereotypically female jobs.

In the arena of higher education women are closing in on equity. Today, 54 percent of all bachelor of arts degrees go to women; 25 percent of women aged 25 to 34 are college graduates. Most striking, the proportion of women in professional schools is now between 36 and 43 percent. The revolution of the late twenteeth century is evident in these figures, as most of the change occurred in the last three decades. Compare current numbers with those of 1960, when the proportion of women in law school was 2 percent (today 43%); medicine 6 percent (today 38%); MBA programs 4 percent (today 36%); Ph.D. programs 11 percent (today 39%), and dentistry 1 percent (today 38%).

Labor Force Participation

In stark contrast to a century ago, more than 61 percent of all women are in the labor force, including two-thirds of women with preschoolers and three-fourths of women with school-age children. Though African-American women continue to work at a higher rate than average (76% overall), the gap is clearly shrinking as the patterns that they pioneered are becoming the norm. With overt discrimination now outlawed, women practice virtually every occupation on the spectrum from blue collar to professional.

Yet alongside change, older patterns persist. Women remain concentrated in female-dominated, low-paid service occupations despite their presence in many professions and in traditionally male blue-collar occupations such as construction or truck driving. Although the exceptions are highly visible (tracked in the popular media frequently as interesting and unusual phenomena), 70 percent of women work either in the services industry (health and education) or in wholesale or retail trade. Women's median weekly earnings are still only 75 percent those of men—though there has been a dramatic gain since 1970 when they were 62.2 percent. (Note, however, that this change represents a combined gain for women of 17% and a 3% decline for men.)

Sexuality, Fertility, and Marriage

The late twentieth century has witnessed a sharp increase in single motherhood even as overall fertility has declined. One birth in three is to an unmarried woman; in 1970, that proportion was only one in ten. Sixty-nine percent of children live with two parents; 23.5 percent with mother only (for African Americans this is 52%).

Some of this single parenthood is due to divorce, something that was relatively rare in 1900 and today affects nearly one in every two marriages. The divorce rate seems to have peaked in 1980, however, and has declined somewhat since that time (in 1980 there were 5.2 divorces/1,000 population; today there are 4.4). Single motherhood is not the source of shame that it was in 1900, but it remains highly correlated with poverty.

If female sexuality was suppressed in 1900 (even though incompletely), at the end of the century sexual references and images saturate

American culture. It was not until the 1930s that birth control became legal in most states. In 1961 the birth control pill introduced the possibility of radically separating sexual experience from the likelihood of procreation. Then in 1973, the Supreme Court's *Roe v. Wade* decision legalized abortion. Today, premarital sex is common, even normative. According to the Alan Guttmacher Institute, in the early 1990s, 56 percent of women and 73 percent of men had sex by age 18.

As dramatic, homosexuality has become an open subject of public discourse, and lesbians—once completely hidden, even to one another—are creating new public spaces and organizations, fields of intellectual inquiry and theory, and families that rely on voluntary ties in the absence of any legal sanction. Lesbians have been a major constituency and source of leadership in the second feminist wave. Twenty years of visibility, however, is just a beginning. American society remains deeply, and emotionally, divided on the issue of homosexuality. Opposition to gay rights marks a key issue for the religious right, and open violence against lesbians and gay men continues.

Race and Class

The second wave grew directly from and modeled itself on the civil rights movement in the 1950s and 1960s. That movement, itself, relied heavily on the grass-roots (if relatively invisible) leadership of African-American women. In the last decades of the century, the voices of minority women have become increasingly distinct and powerful. Diversity among women, as in the society at large, has taken on new dimensions with a surge of immigration since the 1960s from Southeast Asia, East Africa, Central America, and other parts of the Third World. Predictions based on immigration and fertility suggest that by the middle of the next century whites will be only half the U.S. population. Women of color will become the new norm. Women remain deeply divided on racial grounds, but race is no longer defined as black and white.

Challenges to traditional conceptions of gender have also shaken the previous consensus on what constitutes a "good woman" (except perhaps to the right-wing traditionalists who still hold to a set of ideals quite similar to those that dominated American culture a century ago). Yet discomfort with women's move into public life is still widespread, and race and class stigmas remain. The massive growth of a welfare system whose clients are disproportionately women and children combines racial and gender stereotypes to create a new category of "bad women": single, minority, poor mothers. And wherever women appear in previously male-dominated environments, they remain suspect. In particular, the sharply polarized emotional response to Hillary Rodham Clinton during her time as first lady illustrates the undercurrent of anger at powerful, professional women. Radio talk shows have filled thousands of hours with hosts and callers venting their hostility toward this woman who, in their view, did not stay "in her place." But, of course, that is the open question at century's end: just what is "woman's place"?

Conclusion

This brief discussion of women in the twentieth century does not trace a smooth arc from the beginning of the century to the end. It is not simply about "progress" toward "equality." But it is, indeed, about a kind of sea change with unanticipated consequences and with dramatic acceleration in the last thirty years.

In the nineteenth century women created much of what today we call civil society. In the twentieth century they used that layer of society—which lies between formal governmental structures and private familial life—in an amazing variety of ways to reshape the landscape of American life. Virtually all of the public spaces previously presumed to belong properly to men—paid labor, higher education, electoral politics and public office, athletics—now incorporate a large and visible proportion of women. This theme of participation in public life, and the concomitant politicization of issues previously considered personal, runs through the entire century.

Such spectacular shifts have clearly been driven by large structural forces: the emergence of a postindustrial service economy, rising levels of education, two cataclysmic world wars, global power and national wealth on a level never imagined, changing patterns of marriage, fertility, and longevity. Yet the most dramatic changes can clearly be traced in equal measure to two large waves of women's activism.

The suffrage movement, by the 1910s, involved hundreds of thousands of women, branching out both tactically with the use of massive public parades and street corner speeches (females occupying public, political spaces) and in composition as it reached out to working women, immigrants, and minorities. That movement won for women the fundamental right of citizenship, the right to vote. And the Progressive movement on which it built laid the groundwork and provided many key players for the subsequent emergence of the welfare state. The impact of the second wave shows up in the astonishing acceleration of change in the last three decades of the century.

Each of these waves continued to surge forward in the decades after cresting. But each was also followed by a period in which the multiplicity of women's voices reasserted itself along with debates over the real meaning of equality. And each left much work undone for subsequent generations that face new issues and new dilemmas.

In the twenty-first century women will have choices that have never before been available, but they will not be easy. The twentieth century challenged our very definitions of male and female. Many of the signs of manhood and womanhood no longer function effectively. Work is no longer a manly prerogative and responsibility. Families are no longer constituted around a male breadwinner, a wife, and their children. More often they are two-income households (same or different sexes) or single-parent households. Large numbers of single men and women live alone. Yet "family values" have become a political code for attacks on welfare mothers, homosexuals, and nontraditional families (which, in fact, far outnumbered traditional ones). In the absence of significant societal or governmental support for women's traditional responsibilities, women assume a double burden. They participate in the labor force almost to the same degree as men, and yet work outside the home is still organized as though workers had wives to take care of household work, child care, and the myriad details of private life. Work outside the home makes few accommodations to the demands and priorities of family life.

The pioneering work of the twentieth century—as women made their way into hostile, male-dominated public spaces—remains unfinished. Most of the barriers have been broken at least once. But equity remains a distant goal. Achieving that goal is complicated by the fact that for the moment women are not a highly unified group. The contemporary struggles within feminism to deal with the differences among women are the essential precursor to any future social movement that claims to speak for women as a group. The very meanings of masculinity and femininity and their multiple cultural and symbolic references are now overtly contested throughout the popular culture.

Another legacy of the feminist movement that proclaimed that "the personal is political" is an unresolved ambiguity about just where the boundary between the personal and the political properly lies, and the dilemmas resulting from politicizing private life. At the end of the century, Americans faced a constitutional crisis rooted in the strange career of personal politics. For an entire year virtually everyone in the United States was riveted by the scandal concerning President Clinton, Monica Lewinsky, Kenneth Starr, and the American Congress. Behaviors that once would have been considered purely private (and gone unremarked by political reporters, for example) became the basis for impeachment. Who defended the distinction between public and private and who assaulted it? The tables seem to have turned with a vengeance as the right wing pried into intimate details about the president's sexual activities in a consensual relationship while the liberals (including feminist leaders) protested. The politicization of private life is indeed a double-edged sword. This should be no surprise, as conservative backlash since the 1970s has evidenced a clear willingness to use the power of the state to enforce its vision of proper private relationships on issues such as abortion, homosexuality, divorce, prayer in the schools, and the content of textbooks.

The recent history of feminism calls to our attention a number of dimensions in this crisis that should not go unnoticed. First, there have always been many members of society (racial and sexual minorities, welfare recipients, and women, to name only the most obvious) whose private behaviors have been scrutinized and regulated by those in power. By forcing these issues into public debate and evolving laws that might protect such groups (for example laws against sexual harassment) feminists have also removed the cover of silence that protected powerful men from public scrutiny for their private behaviors. That such laws were subsequently used in a campaign to unseat a president whose election was directly due to the votes of politically mobilized women resonates with irony.

Women's solidarity has waxed and waned across the twentieth century. It will certainly continue to do so in the twenty-first. The next wave of feminist activism will no doubt take a shape we cannot envision, just as no one at the dawn of the twentieth century could have imagined the battles that awaited them. That there will be another wave, however, is a safe prediction, given the unfinished agendas of the last century and the still unforeseen contradictions that future changes will create. The next wave will shape the new century.

Bibliography

William H. Chafe, *The American Woman: Her Changing Social, Economic, and Political Roles, 1920–1970* (New York: Oxford University Press, 1972), laid the groundwork for subsequent studies of twentieth-century women. Peter Filene examines the implications of changing definitions of womanliness and manliness on both sexes in *Him/Her Self: Sex Roles in Modern America*, 2nd ed. (Baltimore: Johns Hopkins University Press, 1986). Sara M. Evans, *Born for Liberty: A History of Women in America*, 2nd ed. (New York: Free Press, 1996) provides a general overview of women in American history.

The "first wave" of women's rights activism in the twentieth century is chronicled by Nancy F. Cott, *The Grounding of Modern Feminism* (New Haven, Conn.: Yale University Press, 1987); and Mari Jo Buhle and Paul Buhle, eds., *The Concise History of Woman Suffrage: Selections from the Classic Work of Stanton, Anthony, Gage, and Harper* (Urbana: University of Illinois Press, 1978). On women's role in the New Deal see Susan Ware, *Beyond Suffrage: Women in the New Deal* (Cambridge, Mass.: Harvard University Press, 1981). The critical eras of the 1940s and the cold war are examined in Susan Hartmann, *The Homefront and Beyond: American Women in the 1940s* (Boston: Twayne Publishers, 1982); and Elaine Tyler May, *Homeward Bound: American Families in the Cold War Era* (New York: Basic Books, 1988). There is a growing literature on the "second wave" of feminism. Some starting points would be Sara Evans, *Personal Politics: The Roots of Women's Liberation in the Civil Rights Movement and the New Left* (New York: Vintage, 1980); Alice Echols, *Daring to Be Bad: Radical Feminism in America, 1967–1975* (Minneapolis: University of Minnesota Press, 1989); and Donald Mathews and Jane De Hart, *Sex, Gender, and the Politics of ERA* (New York: Oxford University Press, 1990).

For more depth on the history of sexuality see John D'Emilio and Estelle B. Freedman, *Intimate Matters: A History of Sexuality in America* (New York: Harper & Row, 1988); on education see Barbara Solomon, *In the Company of Educated Women: A History of Women and Higher Education in America* (New Haven, Conn.: Yale University Press, 1985); on women in the labor force see Julia Blackwelder, *Now Hiring: The Feminization of Work in the United States, 1900–1995* (College Station: Texas A&M University Press, 1997). Some excellent starting points on racial minority and immigrant ethnic women include Vicki L. Ruíz, *From Out of the Shadows: Mexican Women in Twentieth-Century America* (New York: Oxford University

Press, 1999); on African-American women see Jacqueline Jones, *Labor of Love, Labor of Sorrow: Black Women, Work, and the Family from Slavery to the Present* (New York: Basic Books, 1985); and on Chinese women Judy Yung, *Unbound Feet: A Social History of Chinese Women in San Francisco* (Barkeley: University of California Press, 1995); Donna Gabaccia, *From the Other Side: Women, Gender, and Immigrant Life in the U.S., 1920–1990* (Bloomington: Indiana University Press, 1994).

For the most recent descriptions of women's status in all aspects of American life, see the series sponsored by the Women's Research and Education Institute in Washington, D.C., *The American Woman* (New York: W. W. Norton). This series has been updated biannually from its inception in 1987.

POSTSCRIPT

Has the Women's Movement of the 1970s Failed to Liberate American Women?

F. Carolyn Graglia's critique of contemporary feminism is a throwback to women of the late nineteenth and early twentieth century who opposed the women social workers and suffragettes who entered the man's world. Her book is a modern restatement of Barbara Welter's classic and widely reprinted article, "The Cult of True Womanhood," *American Quarterly* (Summer 1996).

Graglia argues that contemporary feminism ignores women's primary role in raising the children and preserving the moral character of the family. She blames contemporary feminism along with the Great Society's social programs for promoting a sexual revolution that has destroyed the American family by fostering sexually transmitted diseases and a high divorce rate.

Historian Sara M. Evans takes a long-range view of the women's liberation movement. By comparing the political, legal, and domestic situation of women in 1900 with today, Evans charts the successes and failures that were achieved by the two waves of feminist protest movements in the twentieth century.

At the beginning of the twentieth century, a number of middle-class women from elite colleges in the northeast were in the vanguard of a number of progressive reform movements—temperance, anti-prostitution, child labor, and settlement houses. Working in tandem with the daughters of first-generation immigrants employed in the garment industry, the early feminists realized that laws affecting women could be passed only if women had the right to vote. The suffragettes overcame the arguments of male and female antisuffragists who associated women voters with divorce, promiscuity, and neglect of children and husbands with the ratification of the Nineteenth Amendment in 1920.

The women's movement stalled between the two wars for a variety of reasons: Women pursued their own individual freedom in a consumer-oriented society in the 1920s, and the Great Depression of the 1930s placed the economic survival of the nation at the forefront. But the Second World War had long-range effects on women. Minorities—African Americans and Hispanics—worked for over 3 years in factory jobs traditionally reserved for white males at high wages; so did married white females, often in their thirties. Although the majority of these women returned to the home or took more traditional low-paying "women's" jobs after the war, the consciousness of the changing role of women during the Second World War would reappear during the 1960s.

Evans points out the two streams that formed the women's liberation movement from the mid-1960s. First were the professional women like Betty Freidan, who created the National Organization for Women (NOW) in 1966, who worked with women leaders in labor unions, government, and consciousness-raising groups to demand enforcement of Title VII of the 1965 Civil Rights Act, which banned discrimination in employment and wages. A second wing of feminist activists came from the civil rights and anti-war new left protest groups from the elite universities. Many of these women felt like second-class citizens in these movements and decided they had their own issues that they had to deal with.

Evans dubbed the years 1968 to 1975 "the golden years" because of the following successes: "Passage of the Equal Rights Amendment in Congress in 1972; the 1973 Supreme Court decision (*Roe v. Wade*) legalizing abortion; Title IX of the Higher Education Act which opened intercollegiate athletics to women; the Women's Equity Education Act; and the Equal Credit Opportunity Act."

Evans points out that the women's movement suffered a "backlash" in the 1980s as America became much more conservative. The new right blamed the increases in divorce, single parenthood, out-of-wedlock births, abortions, and open homosexuality on the cultural values of the 1960s. But by the beginning of the twenty-first century, middle-class women made substantial gains in the professions compared with 1960: Law school today 43 percent, 1960 2 percent; medicine today 38 percent, 1960 6 percent; MBA programs today 35 percent, 1960 4 percent; dentistry today 38 percent, 1960 1 percent; and Ph.D. programs today 39 percent, 1960 11 percent. Working-class women, however, have been much less successful in breaking into traditional blue collar jobs such as truck driving and construction.

Both the antifeminist Graglia and to a much less extent the pro-feminist Evans have been critiqued by moderate feminists like Elizabeth Fox-Genovese and Cathy Young, who contend that contemporary feminists have not spoken to the concerns of married women, especially women from poor to lower-middle-class families who must work in order to help support the family. Fox-Genovese's *Feminism Is Not the Story of My Life: How Today's Feminist Elite Have Lost Touch with the Real Concerns of Women* (Doubleday, 1996) is peppered with interviews of white, African American, and Hispanic Americans of different classes and gives a more complex picture of the problems women face today. Young, author of *Cease Fire! Why Women and Men Must Join Forces to Achieve True Equality* (Free Press, 1999), asserts that Graglia denies the real discrimination women faced in the job market in the 1950s. Furthermore, Graglia's critique of the sexual revolution is an attempt to restore a view of female sexuality as essentially submissive.

In 1998 Harvard University Press reprinted Betty Friedan's two later books—*The Second Stage* and *It Changed My Life*, both with new introductions with suggestions for the twenty-first century—which are critical of some of the directions that the women's movement took.

Important books and articles by activists with a historical perspective include Sara Evans, *Personal Politics: The Roots of Women's Liberation in the Civil Rights Movement and the New Left* (Vintage, 1979). This book is nicely summarized in "Sources of the Second Wave: The Rebirth of Feminism," in Alexander Bloom, ed., *Long Time Gone: Sixties America Then and Now* (Oxford, 2001). For a general overview of women's history, see Evans, *Born for Liberty: A History of Women in America*, 2nd ed. (Free Press, 1996); and Roger Adelson's *"Interview with Sara Margaret Evans," The Historian* (vol. 63, Fall 2000); Donna Gabaccia, *From the Other Side: Women, Gender and Immigrant Life in the U.S., 1920–1990* (Indiana University Press, 1994); and John D'Emilio and Estelle B. Freedman, *Intimate Matters: A History of Sexuality in America* (Harper & Row, 1988).

Review essays from various journals reflect the continuous battle over the importance of the women's movement. The neo-conservative magazine *Commentary* is constantly critical of feminism. See Elizabeth Kristol, "The Sexual Revolution" (April 1996); and Elizabeth Powers, "Back to Basics" (March 1999). Also critical is Daphne Patai, "Will the Real Feminists in Academe Stand Up," *The Chronicle of Higher Education* (October 6, 2000, pp. B6–9). Sympathetic to the movement is Christine Stansell, "Girlie Interrupted: The Generational Progress of Feminism," *The New Republic* (January 15, 2001); Andrew Hacker, "How Are Women Doing," *The New York Review of Books* (Fall 2000). See also Jo Freeman, "The Women's Liberation Movement: Its Origins, Structure, Activities, and Ideas," in Jo Freeman, ed., *Women: A Feminist Perspective*, 3rd ed. (Mayfield, 1984); Estelle B. Freedman, *No Turning Back: The History of Feminism and the Future of Women* (Balantine, 2001); and Susan Brownmiller, *In Our Time: Memoir of a Revolution* (Dial Press, 2000).

The best starting point is Ruth Rosen, *The World Split Open: How the Modern Woman's Movement Changed America* (Viking, 2000), written by a former Berkley activist for her students who were born in the 1980s.

Books that deal with the impact of the movement on specific groups include Johnnetta B. Cole and Beverly Gray-Sheftall, *Gender Talk: The Struggle for Women's Equality in African American Communities* (Balantine, 2003); Jacqueline Jones, *Labor of Love, Labor of Sorrow: Black Women, Work, and the Family from Slavery to the Present* (Basic Books, 1985); Vicki L. Ruiz, *From out of the Shadows: Mexican Women in Twentieth-Century Books* (April 11, 2002); and Kim France's review of Phyllis Chesler, *Letters to a Young Feminist* (Four Walls Eight Windows, 1998) in *The New York Times Book Review* (April 26, 1998, pp. 10–11).

ISSUE 18

Is the United States a Declining Power?

YES: Andrew J. Bacevich, from *The Limits of Power: The End of American Exceptionalism* (Metropolitan Books: Henry Holt and Company, 2008)

NO: Fareed Zakaria, from *The Post-American World* (W.W. Norton, 2009)

ISSUE SUMMARY

YES: Professor Andrew J. Bacevich, a West Point graduate and Vietnam veteran, believes that the United States has major problems because it has enlarged the power of the presidency and abuses its military power to create an informal empire in the energy-rich Persian Gulf in its pursuit of a consumer-dominated good life.

NO: Dr. Fareed Zakaria, a political commentator for CNN, believes the United States is still a great power in the post-industrial world because of its tremendous advantages in education, immigration, and scientific innovation.

A mericans generally don't like change. But it's the most constant factor in American history. The changes are measured against two ideal standards established by the founding fathers in 1787: (1) a representative and honest form of government run by men of character and virtue and (2) an economic system of laissez-faire capitalism where farmers and merchants compete fairly and honestly in an open market system with no interference from government. The reality is that each generation that has succeeded the founding fathers has never been able to live up to these ideals because they are impossible standards. Even the founding fathers floundered in the real world. During the earliest years of the Republic, the main issue was not decline but survival. Could a Republican form of government survive economically without the protection of the British mercantilist system? Could a federal system of government protect the liberty of its citizens and maintain order without disintegrating into anarchy? Did the North's victory in the Civil War end the constant threats of secession and prevent the decline of the American experiment with representative government? The answer to all these questions is yes.

This reader has focused on the issues affecting our history from the 1870s to the 1970s. In its broadest terms, the "Industrial Revolution" transformed the lives of all Americans who lived during these times. In 1910, a middle-class American baby would be born in a hospital, not at home. The delivery was made by a male medical doctor and not a female midwife. The family lived in a single-family house in a small city, not on a farm. The house contained two bedrooms, a parlor, one bathroom with a sink with pump water, and a toilet that may or may not flush. The ideal family (not always the reality) had clearly defined roles. Mom stayed home, the children attended grammar school, and the bright ones went to high school, while dad worked as a bookkeeper. Sunday was family day, a time for church picnics and an occasional trip to the closest city. This is a pretty idealistic portrait of middle-class America at the turn of the twentieth century, but it's not that far removed from reality. Urban life in 1910 was very different from farm life in 1850 and very different from a typical middle-class family in 2010.

Americans are constantly in search of the honest politician and the truly competitive economic system. When it is not found it's because of some conspiracy. Did John D. Rockefeller use force to eliminate his competitors in the oil distribution business? Did Jay Gould pay off the New York State legislature to gain access to land to build his railroad? Were urban Protestant laborers forced to work for minimal wages because business allowed Catholic and Jewish immigrants to compete for their jobs in the factories? Did the Jewish bankers from England control Wall Street and the gold standards? Did these banks control the cotton and grain exchanges and "screw" the farmers? Were old-line patrician families like the Adams and Roosevelts correct in their distrust of noveau riche tycoons like Diamond Jim Brady, Andrew Carnegie, and J. P. Morgan? Did nativist anti-Catholic and anti-Semitic complaints have any basis in reality or were they simplistic responses to a changed political and economic environment?

Since 1950, when the postindustrial society more or less originated, the American population has doubled from 150 to 300 plus million. Americans created the most affluent society that ever existed in history. While there have always been pockets of poverty, the upper and middle classes have never been better off. But is the good life about to end? Look at the negative side. Liberal critics point out that structural unemployment may remain at an all-time high at 8 percent; that the gap between rich and upper middle-class gets wider each decade; that the working class blue-collar workers have lost their factory jobs to automation and overseas competitors; that global warming is a real issue.

Conservatives also have their complaints. The deficit is out of control. Too many Americans want something for nothing. The work ethic is dead. Moral standards that permit abortion on demand and open prostitution are accepted as a matter of course. Terrorism is a real threat to Americans both in the Middle East and at home. Is it too late for Americans? Can we stop the government from taking away our second amendment rights to bear arms?

The final issue in the reader addresses the question of a declining America from two opposite views. Professor Andrew Bacevich thinks we've over-reached militarily in pursuit of a consumer-dominated good life. Political commentator Fareed Zakaria sees us still as a great power because of our advantages in education, immigration, and scientific innovation.

YES

Andrew J. Bacevich

The Limits of Power: The End of American Exceptionalism

Introduction: War Without Exits

For the United States, the passing of the Cold War yielded neither a "peace dividend" nor anything remotely resembling peace. Instead, what was hailed as a historic victory gave way almost immediately to renewed unrest and conflict. By the time the East-West standoff that some historians had termed the "Long Peace" ended in 1991, the United States had already embarked upon a decade of unprecedented interventionism. In the years that followed, Americans became inured to reports of U.S. forces going into action—fighting in Panama and the Persian Gulf, occupying Bosnia and Haiti, lambasting Kosovo, Afghanistan, and Sudan from the air. Yet all of these turned out to be mere preliminaries. In 2001 came the main event, an open-ended global war on terror, soon known in some quarters as the "Long War."

Viewed in retrospect, indications that the Long Peace began almost immediately to give way to conditions antithetical to peace seem blindingly obvious. Prior to 9/11, however, the implications of developments like the 1993 bombing of the World Trade Center or the failure of the U.S. military mission to Somalia that same year were difficult to discern. After all, these small events left unaltered what many took to be the defining reality of the contemporary era: the preeminence of the United States, which seemed beyond challenge.

During the 1990s, at the urging of politicians and pundits, Americans became accustomed to thinking of their country as "the indispensable nation." Indispensability carried with it both responsibilities and prerogatives.

The chief responsibility was to preside over a grand project of political-economic convergence and integration commonly referred to as globalization. In point of fact, however, globalization served as a euphemism for soft, or informal, empire. The collapse of the Soviet Union appeared to offer an opportunity to expand and perpetuate that empire, creating something akin to a global Pax Americana.

The indispensable nation's chief prerogative, self-assigned, was to establish and enforce the norms governing the post–Cold War international order. Even in the best of circumstances, imperial policing is a demanding task, requiring not only considerable acumen but also an abundance of determination. The

From *The Limits of Power: The End of American Exceptionalism* by Andrew J. Bacevich (Metropolitan Books, Henry Holt & Co., 2008), pp. 1–13, 177–182 (notes omitted). Copyright © Andrew J. Bacevich. Reprinted by arrangement with Henry Holt and Company, LLC.

preferred American approach was to rely, whenever possible, on suasion. Yet if pressed, Washington did not hesitate to use force, as its numerous military adventures during the 1990s demonstrated.

Whatever means were employed, the management of empire assumed the existence of bountiful reserves of power—economic, political, cultural, but above all military. In the immediate aftermath of the Cold War, few questioned that assumption. The status of the United States as "sole superpower" appeared unassailable. Its dominance was unquestioned and unambiguous. This was not hypernationalistic chest-thumping; it was the conventional wisdom.

Recalling how Washington saw the post–Cold War world and America's place in (or atop) it helps us understand why policy makers failed to anticipate, deter, or deflect the terrorist attacks of September 11, 2001. A political elite preoccupied with the governance of empire paid little attention to protecting the United States itself. In practical terms, prior to 9/11 the mission of homeland defense was unassigned.

The institution nominally referred to as the Department of Defense didn't actually do defense; it specialized in power projection. In 2001, the Pentagon was prepared for any number of contingencies in the Balkans or Northeast Asia or the Persian Gulf. It was just not prepared to address threats to the nation's eastern seaboard. Well-trained and equipped U.S. forces stood ready to defend Seoul or Riyadh; Manhattan was left to fend for itself.

Odd as they may seem, these priorities reflected a core principle of national security policy: When it came to defending vital American interests, asserting control over the imperial periphery took precedence over guarding the nation's own perimeter.

After 9/11, the Bush administration affirmed this core principle. Although it cobbled together a new agency to attend to "homeland security," the administration also redoubled its efforts to shore up the Pax Americana and charged the Department of Defense with focusing on this task. This meant using any means necessary—suasion where possible, force as required—to bring the Islamic world into conformity with prescribed American norms. Rather than soft and consensual, the approach to imperial governance became harder and more coercive.

So, for the United States after 9/11, was became a seemingly permanent condition. President George W. Bush and members of his administration outlined a campaign against terror that they suggested might last decades, if not longer. On the national political scene, few questioned that prospect. In the Pentagon, senior military officers spoke in terms of "generational war," lasting up to a century. Just two weeks after 9/11, Secretary of Defense Donald Rumsfield was already instructing Americans to "forget about 'exit strategies'; we're looking at a sustained engagement that carries no deadlines."

By and large, Americans were slow to grasp the implications of a global war with no exits and no deadlines. To earlier generations, place names like Iraq and Afghanistan had been synonymous with European rashness—the sort of obscure and unwelcoming jurisdictions to which overly ambitious kings and slightly mad adventures might repair to squabble. For the present generation, it has already become part of the natural order of things that GIs should be exerting themselves at great cost to pacify such far-off domains. For the average American tuning in to the nightly news, reports of U.S. casualties incurred in distant lands now seem hardly more out of the ordinary than reports of partisan shenanigans on Capitol Hill or brush fires raging out of control in Southern California.

How exactly did the end of the Long Peace so quickly yield the Long War? Seeing themselves as a peaceful people, Americans remain wedded to the conviction that the conflicts in which they find themselves embroiled are not of their own making. The global war on terror is no exception. Certain of our own benign intentions, we reflexively assign responsibility for war to others, typically malignant Hitler-like figures inexplicably bent on denying us the peace that is our fondest wish.

This book challenges that supposition. It argues that the actions of Saddam Hussein and Osama bin Laden, however malevolent, cannot explain why the United States today finds itself enmeshed in seemingly never-ending conflict. Although critics of U.S. foreign policy, and especially of the Iraq War, have already advanced a variety of alternative explanations—variously fingering President Bush, members of his inner circle, jingoistic neoconservatives, greedy oil executives, or even the Israel lobby—it also finds those explanations inadequate. Certainly, the president and his advisers, along with neocons always looking for opportunities to flex American military muscle, bear considerable culpability for our current predicament. Yet to charge them with primary responsibility is to credit them with undeserved historical significance. It's the equivalent of blaming Herbert Hoover for the Great Depression or of attributing McCarthyism entirely to the antics of Senator Joseph McCarthy.

The impulses that have landed us in a war of no exits and no deadlines come from within. Foreign policy has, for decades, provided an outward manifestation of American domestic ambitions, urges, and fears. In our own time, it has increasingly become an expression of domestic dysfunction—an attempt to manage or defer coming to terms with contradictions besetting the American way of life. Those contradictions have found their ultimate expression in the perpetual state of war afflicting the United States today.

Gauging their implications requires that we acknowledge their source: They reflect the accumulated detritus of freedom, the by-products of our frantic pursuit of life, liberty, and happiness.

Freedom is the altar at which Americans worship, whatever their nominal religious persuasion. "No one signs odes to liberty as the final end of life with greater fervor than Americans," the theologian Reinhold Niebuhr once observed. Yet even as they celebrate freedom, Americans exempt the object of their veneration from critical examination. In our public discourse, freedom is not so much a word or even a value as an incantation, its very mention is enough to stifle doubt and terminate all debate.

The Limits of Power will suggest that this heedless worship of freedom has been a mixed blessing. In our pursuit of freedom, we have accrued obligations and piled up debts that we are increasingly hard-pressed to meet. Especially since the 1960s, freedom itself has undercut the nation's ability to fulfill its commitments. We teeter on the edge of insolvency, desperately trying to balance accounts by relying on our presumably invincible armed forces. Yet there, too, having exaggerated our military might, we court bankruptcy.

The United States today finds itself threatened by three interlocking crises. The first of these crises is economic and cultural, the second political, and the third military. All three share this characteristic: They are of our own making. In assessing the predicament that results from these crises, *The Limits of Power* employs what might be called a Niebuhrean perspective. Writing decades ago, Reinhold Niebuhr anticipated that predicament with uncanny accuracy and astonishing prescience. As such, perhaps more than any other figure in our recent history, he may help us discern a way out.

As pastor, teacher, activist, theologian, and prolific author, Niebuhr was a towering presence in American intellectual life from the 1930s through the 1960s. Even today, he deserves recognition as the most clear-eyed of American prophets. Niebuhr speaks to us from the past, offering truths of enormous relevance to the present. As prophet, he warned that what he called "our dreams of managing history"—born of a peculiar combination of arrogance and narcissism—posed a potentially mortal threat to the United States. Today, we ignore that warning at our peril.

Niebuhr entertained few illusions about the nature of man, the possibilities of politics, or the pliability of history. Global economic crisis, total war, genocide, totalitarianism, and nuclear arsenals capable of destroying civilization itself—he viewed all of these with an unblinking eye that allowed no room for hypocrisy, hokum, or self-deception. Realism and humility formed the core of his worldview, each infused with a deeply felt Christian sensibility.

Realism in this sense implies an obligation to see the world as it actually is, not as we might like it to be. The enemy of realism is hubris, which in Niebuhr's day, and in our own, finds expression in an outsized confidence in the efficacy of American power as an instrument to reshape the global order.

Humility imposes an obligation of a different sort. It summons Americans to see themselves without binders. The enemy of humility is sanctimony, which gives rise to the conviction that American values and beliefs are universal and that the nation itself serves providentially assigned purposes. This conviction finds expression in a determination to remake the world in what we imagine to be America's image.

In our own day, realism and humility have proven in short supply. What Niebuhr wrote after World War II proved truer still in the immediate aftermath of the Cold War: Good fortune and a position of apparent preeminence placed the United States "under the most grievous temptations to self-adulation." Americans have given themselves over to those temptations. Hubris and sanctimony have become the paramount expressions of American statecraft. After 9/11, they combined to produce the Bush administration's war of no exits and no deadlines.

President Bush has likened today's war against what he calls "Islamofascism" to America's war with Nazi Germany—a great struggle waged on behalf of liberty. That President Bush is waging his global war on terror to preserve American freedom is no doubt the case. Yet that commitment, however well intentioned, begs several larger questions: As actually expressed and experienced, what is freedom today? What is its content? What costs does the exercise of freedom impose? Who pays?

These are fundamental questions, which cannot be dismissed with a rhetorical wave of the hand. Great wartime presidents of the past—one thinks especially of Abraham Lincoln speaking at Gettysburg—have not hesitated to confront such questions directly. That President Bush seems oblivious to their very existence offers one measure of his shortcomings as a statesman.

Freedom is not static, nor is it necessarily benign. In practice, freedom constantly evolves and in doing so generates new requirements and abolishes old constraints. The common understanding of freedom that prevailed in December 1941 when the United States entered the war against Imperial Japan and Nazi Germany has long since become obsolete. In some respects, this must be cause for celebration. In others, it might be cause for regret.

The changes have been both qualitative and quantitative. In many respects, Americans are freer today than ever before, with more citizens than ever before enjoying unencumbered access to the promise of American life. Yet, especially since the 1960s, the reinterpretation of freedom has had a transformative impact on our society and culture. That transformation has produced a paradoxical legacy. As individuals, our appetites and expectations have grown exponentially. Niebuhr once wrote disapprovingly of Americans, their "culture soft and vulgar, equating joy with happiness and happiness with comfort." Were he alive today, Niebuhr might amend that judgment, with Americans increasingly equating comfort with self-indulgence.

The collective capacity of our domestic political economy to satisfy those appetites has not kept pace with demand. As a result, sustaining our pursuit of life, liberty, and happiness at home requires increasingly that Americans look beyond our borders. Whether the issue at hand is oil, credit, or the availability of cheap consumer goods, we expect the world to accommodate the American way of life.

The resulting sense of entitlement has great implications for foreign policy. Simply put, as the American appetite for freedom has grown, so too has our penchant for empire. The connection between these two tendencies is a causal one. In an earlier age, Americans saw empire as the antithesis of freedom. Today, as illustrated above all by the Bush administration's efforts to dominate the energy-rich Persian Gulf, empire has seemingly become a prerequisite of freedom.

There is a further paradox: The actual exercise of American freedom is no longer conducive to generating the power required to established and maintain an imperial order. If anything, the reverse is true: Centered on consumption and individual autonomy, the exercise of freedom is contributing to the gradual erosion of our national power. At precisely the moment when the ability to wield power—especially military power—has become the sine qua non for preserving American freedom, our reserves of power are being depleted.

One sees this, for example, in the way that heightened claims of individual autonomy have eviscerated the concept of citizenship. Yesterday's civic obligations have become today's civic options. What once rated as duties—rallying to the country's defense at times of great emergency, for example—are now matters of choice. As individuals, Americans never cease to expect more. As members of a community, especially as members of a national community, they choose to contribute less.

Meanwhile, American political leaders—especially at the national level—have proven unable (or unwilling) to address the disparity between how much we want and what we can afford to pay. Successive administrations, abetted by Congress, have deepened a looming crisis of debt and dependency through unbridled spending. As Vice President Dick Cheney, a self-described conservative, announced when told that cutting taxes might be at odds with invading Iraq, "Deficits don't matter." Politicians of both parties certainly act as if they don't.

Expectations that the world beyond our borders should accommodate the American way of life are hardly new. Since 9/11, however, our demands have become more insistent. In that regard, the neoconservative writer Robert Kagan is surely correct in observing that "America did not change on September 11. It only became more itself." In the aftermath of the attacks on the World Trade Center and the Pentagon, Washington's resolve that nothing interfere with the individual American's pursuit of life, liberty, and happiness only hardened. That resolve found expression in the Bush administration's with-us-or-against-us rhetoric, in its disdain for the United Nations and traditional American allies, in its contempt for international law, and above all in its embrace of preventive war.

When President Bush declared in his second inaugural that the "survival of liberty in our land increasingly depends on the success of liberty in other lands," he was in effect claiming for the United States as freedom's chief agent the prerogative of waging war when and where it sees fit, those wars by definition being fought on freedom's behalf. In this sense, the Long War genuinely qualifies as a war to preserve the American way of life (centered on a specific conception of liberty) and simultaneously as a war to extend the American imperium (centered on dreams of a world remade in America's image), the former widely assumed to require the latter.

Yet, as events have made plain, the United States is ill-prepared to wage a global war of no exits and no deadlines. The sole superpower lacks the resources—economic, political, and military—to support a large-scale, protracted conflict without, at the very least, inflicting severe economic and political damage on itself. American power has limits and is inadequate to the ambitions to which hubris and sanctimony have given rise.

Here is the central paradox of our time: While the defense of American freedom seems to demand that U.S. troops fight in places like Iraq and Afghanistan, the exercise of that freedom at home undermines the nation's capacity to fight. A grand bazaar provides an inadequate basis upon which to erect a vast empire.

Meanwhile, a stubborn insistence on staying the course militarily ends up jeopardizing freedom at home. With Americans, even in wartime, refusing to curb their appetites, the Long War aggravates the economic contradictions that continue to produce debt and dependency. Moreover, a state of perpetual national security emergency aggravates the disorders afflicting our political system, allowing the executive branch to accrue ever more authority at the expense of the Congress and disfiguring the Constitution. In this sense, the Long War is both self-defeating and irrational.

Niebuhr once wrote, "One of the most pathetic aspects of human history is that every civilization expresses itself most pretentiously, compounds its partial and universal values most convincingly, and claims immortality for its finite existence at the very moment when the decay which leads to death has already begun." Future generations of historians may well cite Niebuhr's dictum as a concise explanation of the folly that propelled the United States into its Long War.

In an immediate sense, it is the soldier who bears the burden of such folly. U.S. troops in battle dress and body armor, whom Americans profess to admire and support, pay the price for the nation's collective refusal to confront our domestic dysfunction. In many ways, the condition of the military today offers the most urgent expression of that dysfunction. Seven years into its confrontation with radical Islam, the United States finds itself with too much war for too few warriors—and with no prospect of producing the additional soldiers needed to close the gap. In effect, Americans now confront a looming military crisis to go along with the economic and political crises that they have labored so earnestly to ignore.

The Iraq War deserves our attention as the clearest manifestation of these three crises, demonstrating the extent to which they are inextricably linked and mutually reinforcing. That war was always unnecessary. Except in the eyes of the deluded and the disingenuous, it has long since become a fool's errand. Of perhaps even greater significance, it is both counterproductive and unsustainable.

Yet ironically Iraq may yet prove to be the source of our salvation. For the United States, the ongoing war makes plain the imperative of putting America's house in order. Iraq has revealed the futility of counting on military power to sustain our habits of profligacy. The day of reckoning approaches. Expending the lives of more American soldiers in hopes of deferring that day is profoundly wrong. History will not judge kindly a people who find nothing amiss in the prospect of endless armed conflict so long as they themselves are spared the effects. Nor will it view with favor an electorate that delivers political power into the hands of leaders unable to envision any alternative to perpetual war.

Rather than insisting that the world accommodate the United States, Americans need to reassert control over their own destiny, ending their condition of dependency and abandoning their imperial delusions. Of perhaps even greater difficulty, the combination of economic, political, and military crisis summons Americans to reexamine exactly what freedom entails. Soldiers cannot accomplish these tasks, nor should we expect politicians to do so. The onus of responsibility falls squarely on citizens. . . .

Containment during the Cold War did not preclude selective engagement. Nor should it today. A strategy of containment should permit and even underwrite educational, cultural, and intellectual exchanges. It should provide opportunities for selected students from the Islamic world to study in the West. And it ought to include a public diplomacy component. Yet however worthy, such initiatives will have a marginal effect at best. Our ability to influence perceptions and attitudes across the Islamic world will remain limited.

By extension, Americans ought to give up the presumptuous notion that they are called upon to tutor Muslims in matters related to freedom and the proper relationship between politics and religion. The principle informing policy should be this: Let Islam be Islam. In the end, Muslims will have to discover for themselves the shortcomings of political Islam, much as Russians discovered the defects of Marxism-Leninism and Chinese came to appreciate the flaws of Maoism—perhaps even as we ourselves will one day begin to recognize the snares embedded in American exceptionalism.

President Bush's freedom agenda has attracted negligible international support. As a result, when it comes to liberating the Greater Middle East, the United States finds itself stuck doing most of the heavy lifting. A strategy that aims to contain violent extremists would likely be far more agreeable to American allies and could be persuaded to shoulder a greater portion of the load.

The president's insistence that war provides the best antidote to terror has made it difficult to locate a point of concurrence between ourselves and others who share the view that Islamic extremism poses a problem, while defining the solution to that problem differently. The president's reluctance even to acknowledge the existence of other equally important problems where "the parochial and the general interest" just might intersect has further complicated the effort to forge a basis for collaboration. Repairing the legacy of the Bush years will surely require renewed attention to such problems, two of which loom especially large: nuclear weapons and climate change.

For the United States, abolishing nuclear weapons ought to be an urgent national security priority. So, too, should preserving our planet. These are the meta-challenges of our time. Addressing them promises to be the work of decades. Yet ridding the world of nuclear weapons is likely to prove far more plausible and achievable than ridding the world of evil. Transforming humankind's relationship to the environment, which will affect the way people live their daily lives, can hardly prove more difficult than transforming the Greater Middle East, which requires changing the way a billion or more Muslims think.

In lieu of President Bush's misguided global war on terror, these two issues offer points of concurrence that can provide the basis for sound strategy. In each case, realism rather than idealism—not "do-goodism" but self-interest—provides the impetus for action. The idea is not to save the world but to provide for the well-being of the American people. That others might credit the United States with promoting the common good, thereby refurbishing U.S. claims to global leadership, ranks at best as a secondary, although by no means trivial, potential benefit.

Nuclear weapons are unusable. Their employment in any conceivable scenario would be a political and moral catastrophe. For the United States, they are becoming unnecessary, even as a deterrent. Certainly, they are unlikely to dissuade the adversaries most likely to employ such weapons against us—Islamic extremists intent on acquiring their own nuclear capability.

If anything, the opposite is true. By retaining a strategic arsenal in readiness (and by insisting without qualification that the dropping of atomic bombs on two Japanese cities in 1945 was justified), the United States continues tacitly to sustain the view that nuclear weapons play a legitimate role in international politics—this at a time when our own interests are best served by doing everything possible to reinforce the existing taboo against their further use.

Furthermore, the day is approaching when the United States will be able to deter other nuclear-armed states, like Russia and China, without itself relying on nuclear weapons. Modern conventional weapons possess the potential to provide a more effective foundation for deterrence. They offer highly lethal, accurate, responsive second-strike (or even first-strike) capabilities. Precision conventional weapons also carry fewer of the moral complications that make nuclear weapons so inherently problematic. Hence, they have the added advantage of being usable, which enhances credibility.

By the end of the Cold War, the United States had accumulated a stockpile of some 23,000 nuclear weapons. By 2007, that number stood at an estimated 5,736 warheads of various types. Although the reduction appears impressive, this represents less an achievement than a gesture—like the chronic cigarette smoker who goes from three packs a day to two and fancies that he has his habit under control. Even if one assumes that nuclear weapons possess any real utility, what conceivable target set would require more than 100 warheads to destroy? Far more severe cuts in the U.S. arsenal, shrinking the total to a couple hundred at most, are in order.

When it comes to nuclear weapons, the point of concurrence between the parochial and the general interest seems clear: Such weapons should be entirely eliminated. Presidents from Harry Truman's day to the present have bemoaned their very existence and have repeatedly promised to work for their abolition. Now might actually be the moment to act on that promise.

Climate change likewise poses a looming threat to America's well-being—and the world's. Here, the point of concurrence between the national and international common good seems self-evident: It lies in moving aggressively to reduce the level of emissions that contribute to global warming.

The United States ranks among the world's worst polluters—here we confront one unfortunate by-product of American freedom as currently practiced. Acting alone, Americans cannot curb climate change. Yet unless the United States acts, the chances of effectively addressing this global threat are nil.

Preserving the environment means reducing the global consumption of fossil fuels while developing alternative energy sources. In addition to saving the planet, leadership in this arena will enhance national security. Among other things, reducing oil imports could reduce the flow of dollars to the Islamists who wish us ill, something that ought to be the very cornerstone of a strategy of containment. Perfect security is an illusion. Yet, when it comes to keeping security problems within tolerable limits, self-sufficiency has a value greater than even the largest army.

No doubt undertaking a serious, long-term, national effort to begin the transition to a post–fossil fuel economy promises to be a costly proposition. Yet, whereas spending trillions to forcibly democratize the Islamic world will achieve little, investing trillions in energy research might actually produce something useful. From the Manhattan Project to the space race to the development of the Internet, large-scale technological innovation has tended to be an American strong suit. By comparison, when it comes to large-scale efforts to engineer political, social, and cultural change abroad, the American track record has never been better than mixed. Since September 2001, it has been downright abysmal.

A concerted effort to abolish nuclear weapons will entail some risk. A concerted effort to reduce the effects of climate change implies considerable inconvenience and even sacrifice, at least in the near term. Yet, a people for whom freedom has become synonymous with consumption and self-actualization evince little appetite for either risk or sacrifice—even if inaction today increases the prospect of greater risks and more painful sacrifices tomorrow.

As long as Americans remain in denial—insisting that the power of the United States is without limits—they will remain unlikely to do any of these things. Instead, abetted by their political leaders, they will continue to fancy that some version of global war offers an antidote to Islamic radicalism. The United States will modernize and enhance its nuclear strike capabilities while professing outrage that others should seek similar capabilities. Americans will treat climate change as a problem to be nickel-and-dimed. They will guzzle imported oil, binge on imported goods, and indulge in imperial dreams. All the while, Washington will issue high-minded proclamations testifying to the approaching triumph of democracy everywhere and forever.

Meanwhile, the American people will ignore the imperative of settling accounts—balancing budgets, curbing consumption, and paying down debt. They will remain passive as politicians fritter away U.S. military might on unnecessary wars. They will permit officials responsible for failed policies to dodge accountability. They will tolerate stupefying incompetence and dysfunction in the nation's capital, counting on the next president to fix everything that the last one screwed up. In Niebuhr's words, they will cling to "a culture which makes 'living standards' the final norm of the good life and which regards the perfection of techniques as the guarantor of every cultural as well as every social-moral value." Above all, they will venerate freedom while carefully refraining from assessing its content or measuring its costs.

"The trustful acceptance of false solutions for our perplexing problems," Niebuhr wrote a half century ago, "adds a touch of pathos to the tragedy of our age." That judgment remains valid today. Adamantly insisting that it is unique among history's great powers, the United States seems likely to follow the well-worn path taken by others, blind to the perils that it courts through its own feckless behavior.

For all nations, Niebuhr once observed, "The desire to gain an immediate selfish advantage always imperils their ultimate interests. If they recognize this fact, they usually recognize it too late." Both parts of this dictum apply to the United States today—and in spades. To extend however slightly the here and now, Americans are increasingly inclined to write off the future. So they carry on, heedless of the consequences even for themselves, no less for their children or grandchildren.

Thus does the tragedy of our age move inexorably toward its conclusion. "To the end of history," our prophet once wrote, "social orders will probably destroy themselves in the effort to prove that they are indestructible." Clinging doggedly to the conviction that the rules to which other nations must submit don't apply, Americans appear determined to affirm Niebuhr's axiom of willful self-destruction.

Fareed Zakaria

The Post-American World

The Rise of the Rest

This is a book not about the decline of America but rather about the rise of everyone else. It is about the great transformation taking place around the world, a transformation that, though often discussed, remains poorly understood. This is natural. Changes, even sea changes, take place gradually. Though we talk about a new era, the world seems to be one with which we are familiar. But in fact, it is very different.

There have been three tectonic power shifts over the last five hundred years, fundamental changes in the distribution of power that have reshaped international life—its politics, economics, and culture. The first was the rise of the Western world, a process that began in the fifteenth century and accelerated dramatically in the late eighteenth century. It produced modernity as we know it: science and technology, commerce and capitalism, the agricultural and industrial revolutions. It also produced the prolonged political dominance of the nations of the West.

The second shift, which took place in the closing years of the nineteenth century, was the rise of the United States. Soon after it industrialized, the United States became the most powerful nation since imperial Rome, and the only one that was stronger than any likely combination of other nations. For most of the last century, the United States has dominated global economics, politics, science, and culture. For the last twenty years, that dominance has been unrivaled, a phenomenon unprecedented in modern history.

We are now living through the third great power shift of the modern era. It could be called "the rise of the rest." Over the past few decades, countries all over the world have been experiencing rates of economic growth that were once unthinkable. While they have had booms and busts, the overall trend has been unambiguously upward. This growth has been most visible in Asia but is no longer confined to it. That is why to call this shift "the rise of Asia" does not describe it accurately. In 2006 and 2007, 124 countries grew at a rate of 4 percent or more. That includes more than 30 countries in Africa, two-thirds of the continent. Antoine van Agtmael, the fund manager who coined the term "emerging markets," has identified the 25 companies most likely to be the world's next great multinationals. His list includes four companies each from Brazil, Mexico, South Korea, and Taiwan; three from India; two from China; and one each from Argentina, Chile, Malaysia, and South Africa.

Look around. The tallest building in the world is now in Taipei, and it will soon be overtaken by one being built in Dubai. The world's richest man is Mexican, and its largest publicly traded corporation is Chinese. The worlds biggest plane is built in Russia and Ukraine, its leading refinery is under construction in India, and its largest factories are all in China. By many measures, London is becoming the leading financial center, and the United Arab Emirates is home to the most richly endowed investment fund. Once quintessentially American icons have been appropriated by foreigners. The world's largest Ferris wheel is in Singapore. Its number one casino is not in Las Vegas but in Macao, which has also overtaken Vegas in annual gambling revenues. The biggest movie industry, in terms of both movies made and tickets sold, is Bollywood, not Hollywood. Even shopping, America's greatest sporting activity, has gone global. Of the top ten malls in the world, only one is in the United States; the world's biggest is in Beijing. Such lists are arbitrary, but it is striking that only ten years ago, America was at the top in many, if not most, of these categories.

It might seem strange to focus on growing prosperity when there are still hundreds of millions of people living in desperate poverty. But in fact, the share of people living on a dollar a day or less plummeted from 40 percent in 1981 to 18 percent in 2004, and is estimated to fall to 12 percent by 2015. China's growth alone has lifted more than 400 million people out of poverty. Poverty is falling in countries housing 80 percent of the world's population. The 50 countries where the earth's poorest people live are basket cases that need urgent attention. In the other 142—which include China, India, Brazil, Russia, Indonesia, Turkey, Kenya, and South Africa—the poor are slowly being absorbed into productive and growing economies. For the first time ever, we are witnessing genuinely global growth. This is creating an international system in which countries in all parts of the world are no longer objects or observers, but players in their own right. It is the birth of a truly global order.

A related aspect of this new era is the diffusion of power from states to other actors. The "rest" that is rising includes many nonstate actors. Groups and individuals have been empowered, and hierarchy, centralization, and control are being undermined. Functions that were once controlled by governments are now shared with international bodies like the World Trade Organization and the European Union. Nongovernmental groups are mushrooming every day on every issue in every country. Corporations and capital are moving from place to place, finding the best location in which to do business, rewarding some governments while punishing others. Terrorists like Al Qaeda, drug cartels, insurgents, and militias of all kinds are finding space to operate within the nooks and crannies of the international system. Power is shifting away from nation-states, up, down, and sideways. In such an atmosphere, the traditional applications of national power, both economic and military, have become less effective.

The emerging international system is likely to be quite different from those that have preceded it. One hundred years ago, there was a multipolar order run by a collection of European governments, with constantly shifting alliances, rivalries, miscalculations, and wars. Then came the bipolar duopoly of the Cold War, more stable in many ways, but with the superpowers reacting and overreacting to each other's every move. Since 1991, we have lived under an American imperium, a unique, unipolar world in which the open global economy has expanded and accelerated dramatically. This expansion is now driving the next change in the nature of the international order.

At the politico-military level, we remain in a single-superpower world. But in every other dimension—industrial, financial, educational, social, cultural—the distribution of power is shifting, moving away from American dominance. That does not mean we are entering an anti-American world. But we are moving into a *post-American world*, one defined and directed from many places and by many people.

What kinds of opportunities and challenges do these changes present? What do they portend for the United States and its dominant position? What will this new era look like in terms of war and peace, economics and business, ideas and culture?

In short, what will it mean to live in a post-American world? . . .

America's Long Run

First, however, it is essential to note that the central feature of Britain's decline—irreversible economic deterioration—does not really apply to the United States today. Britain's unrivaled economic status lasted for a few decades; America's has lasted more than 130 years. The U.S. economy has been the world's largest since the middle of the 1880s, and it remains so today. In fact, America has held a surprisingly constant share of global GDP ever since. With the brief exception of the late 1940s and 1950s—when the rest of the industrialized world had been destroyed and America's share rose to 50 percent!—the United States has accounted for roughly a quarter of world output for over a century (32 percent in 1913, 26 percent in 1960, 22 percent in 1980, 27 percent in 2000, and 26 percent in 2007).[1] It is likely to slip, but not significantly, in the next two decades. In 2025, most estimates suggest that the U.S. economy will still be twice the size of China's in terms of nominal GDP (though in terms of purchasing power, the gap will be smaller).

This difference between America and Britain can be seen in the burden of their military budgets. Britannia ruled the seas but never the land. The British army was sufficiently small that the German chancellor Otto von Bismarck once quipped that, were the British ever to invade Germany, he would simply have the local police force arrest them. Meanwhile, London's advantage over the seas—it had more tonnage than the next two navies put together—came at ruinous cost to its treasury. The American military, in contrast, dominates at every level—land, sea, air, space—and spends more than the next fourteen countries put together, accounting for almost 50 percent of global defense spending. Some argue that even this understates America's military lead against the rest of the world because it does not take into account the U.S. scientific and technological edge. The United States spends more on defense research and development than the rest of the world put together. And, crucially, it does all this without breaking the bank. Defense expenditure as a percent of GDP is now 4.1 percent, lower than it was for most of the Cold War. (Under Eisenhower, it rose to 10 percent of GDP.) The secret here is the denominator. As U.S. GDP grows larger and larger, expenditures that would have been backbreaking become affordable. The Iraq War may be a tragedy or a noble endeavor, depending on your point of view. Either way, however, it will not bankrupt the United States. The war has been expensive, but the price tag for Iraq and Afghanistan together—$125 billion a year—represents less than 1 percent of GDP. Vietnam, by comparison, cost 1.6 percent of American GDP in 1970 and tens of thousands more soldiers' lives.

American military power is not the cause of its strength but the consequence. The fuel is America's economic and technological base, which remains extremely strong. The United States does face larger, deeper, and broader challenges than it has ever faced in its history, and the rise of the rest does mean that it will lose some share of global GDP. But the process will look nothing like Britain's slide in the twentieth century, when the country lost the lead in innovation, energy, and entrepreneurship. America will remain a vital, vibrant economy, at the forefront of the next revolutions in science, technology, and industry—as long as it can embrace and adjust to the challenges confronting it.

The Future Is Here

When trying to explain how America will fare in the new world, I sometimes say, "Look around." The future is already here. Over the last twenty years, globalization has been gaining breadth and depth. More countries are making goods, communications technology has been leveling the playing field, capital has been free to move across the world. And America has benefited massively from these trends. Its economy has received hundreds of billions of dollars in investment—a rarity for a country with much capital of its own. Its companies have entered new countries and industries with great success and used new technologies and processes, all to keep boosting their bottom lines. Despite two decades of a very expensive dollar, American exports have held ground.

GDP growth, the bottom line, has averaged just over 3 percent for twenty-five years, significantly higher than in Europe. (Japan's averaged 2.3 percent over the same period.) Productivity growth, the elixir of modern economics, has been over 2.5 percent for a decade now, again a full percentage point higher than the European average. The United States is currently ranked as the most competitive economy in the world by the World Economic Forum. These rankings have been produced every year since 1979, and the U.S. position has been fairly constant, slipping sometimes in recent years to small northern European countries like Sweden, Denmark, and Finland (whose collective population is twenty million, less than that of the state of Texas). America's superior growth trajectory might be petering out, and perhaps its growth will be more "normal" for an advanced industrial country for the next few years. But the general point—that America is a highly dynamic economy at the cutting edge, despite its enormous size—still holds.

Look at the industries of the future. Nanotechnology—applied science dealing with the control of matter at the atomic or molecular scale—is considered likely to lead to fundamental breakthroughs over the next fifty years. At some point in the future, or so I'm told, households will construct products out of raw materials, and businesses will simply create the formulas that turn atoms into goods. Whether this is hype or prescience, what is worth noticing is that by every conceivable measure, the United States dominates the field. It has more dedicated nanocenters than the next three nations (Germany, the United Kingdom, and China) combined, and many of its new centers focus on narrow subjects with a high potential for practical, marketable applications—such as the Emory-Georgia Tech Nanotechnology Center for Personalized and Predictive Oncology. At market exchange rates, government nanotech funding in the United States is almost double that of its closest competitor, Japan. And while China, Japan, and Germany contribute a fair share of journal articles on nanoscale science and engineering topics, the United States has issued more patents for nanotechnology than the rest of the world combined, highlighting America's unusual strength in turning abstract theory into practical products.

The firm Lux, led by Dr. Michael Holman, constructed a matrix to assess countries' overall nanotech competitiveness. Their analysis looked not just at nanotechnology activity but also at the ability to "generate growth from scientific innovation." It found that certain countries that spend much on research can't turn their science into business. These "Ivory Tower" nations have impressive research funding, journal articles, and even patents, but somehow don't manage to translate this into commercial goods and ideas. China, France, and even Britain fall into this category. A full 85 percent of venture capital investments in nanotechnology went to U.S. companies.

Biotechnology—a broad category that describes the use of biological systems to create medical, agricultural, and industrial products—is already a multibillion-dollar industry. It, too, is dominated by the United States. More than $3.3 billion in venture financing went to U.S. biotech companies in 2005, while European companies received just half that amount. Follow-on equity offerings (that is, post-IPO) in the United States were more than seven times those in Europe. And while European IPOs attracted more cash in 2005, IPO activity is highly volatile—in 2004, U.S. IPO values were more than four times Europe's. As with nanotechnology, American companies excel at turning ideas into marketable and lucrative products. U.S. biotech revenues approached $50 billion in 2005, five times greater than those in Europe and representing 76 percent of global revenues.[2]

Manufacturing has, of course, been leaving the United States, shifting to the developing world and turning America into a service economy. This scares many Americans and Europeans, who wonder what their countries will make if everything is "made in China." But Asian manufacturing must be viewed in the context of a global economy in which countries like China have become an important part of the supply chain—but still just a part.

The *Atlantic Monthly* writer James Fallows spent a year in China watching that manufacturing juggernaut up close, and he provides a persuasive explanation— one well understood by Chinese businessmen—of how outsourcing has strengthened American competitiveness. Most Americans, even management experts, have not heard of the "smiley curve." But Chinese manufacturers know it well. Named for the U-shaped smile on the simple 1970s cartoon of a happy face, ☺, the curve illustrates the development of a product, from conception to sale. At the top left of the curve one starts with the idea and high-level industrial design—how the product will look and work. Lower down on the curve comes the detailed engineering plan. At the bottom of the U is the actual manufacturing, assembly, and shipping. Then rising up on the right of the curve are distribution, marketing, retail sales, service contracts, and sales of parts and accessories. Fallows observes that, in almost all manufacturing, China takes care of the bottom of the curve and America the top—the two ends of the U—which is where the money is: "The simple way to put this—that the real money is in the brand name, plus retail—may sound obvious," he writes, "but its implications are illuminating." A vivid example of this is the iPod: it is manufactured mostly outside the United States, but the majority of value added is captured by Apple, Inc. in California. The company made $80 in gross profit on a 30-gigabyte video iPod that retailed (in late 2007) for $299. Its profit was 36 percent of the estimated wholesale price of $224. (Add to that the retail profit if it was sold in an Apple store.) The total cost of parts was $144. Chinese manufacturers, by contrast, have margins of a few percent on their products.

America's Best Industry

"Ah yes," say those who are more worried, "but you're looking at a snapshot of today. America's advantages are rapidly eroding as the country loses its scientific and technological base." For some, the decline of science is symptomatic of a larger cultural decay. A country that once adhered to a Puritan ethic of delayed gratification has become one that revels in instant pleasures. We're losing interest in the basics—math, manufacturing, hard work, savings—and becoming a postindustrial society that specializes in consumption and leisure. "More people will graduate in the United States in 2006 with sports-exercise degrees than electrical-engineering degrees," says General Electric's CEO, Jeffrey Immelt. "So, if we want to be the massage capital of the world, we're well on our way."

No statistic seems to capture this anxiety better than those showing the decline of engineering. In 2005, the National Academy of Sciences released a report warning that the United States could soon lose its privileged position as the world's science leader. In 2004, the report said, China graduated 600,000 engineers, India 350,000, and the United States 70,000. These numbers were repeated in hundreds of articles, books, and blogs, including a *Fortune* cover story, the *Congressional Record*, and speeches by technology titans like Bill Gates. And indeed, the figure does seem like cause for despair. What hope does the United States have if for every qualified American engineer there are 11 Chinese and Indian ones? For the cost of one chemist or engineer in the United States, the report pointed out, a company could hire 5 well-trained and eager chemists in China or 11 engineers in India.

The only problem is that the numbers are wildly off the mark. A journalist, Carl Bialik of the *Wall Street Journal*, and several academics investigated the matter. They quickly realized that the Asian totals included graduates of two- and three-year programs—people getting diplomas in simple technical tasks. A group of professors at the Pratt School of Engineering at Duke University traveled to China and India to collect data from governmental and nongovernmental sources and interview businessmen and academics. They concluded that eliminating graduates of two- or three-year programs halves the Chinese figure, to around 350,000 graduates, and even this number is probably significantly inflated by differing definitions of "engineer" that often include auto mechanics and industrial repairmen. Bialik notes that the National Science Foundation, which tracks these statistics in the United States and other nations, puts the Chinese number at about 200,000 degrees per year. Ron Hira, a professor of public policy at the Rochester Institute of Technology, puts the number of Indian graduates at 120,000–130,000 a year. That means the United States actually trains more engineers per capita than either India or China does.

And the numbers don't address the issue of quality. As someone who grew up in India, I have a healthy appreciation for the virtues of its famous engineering academies, the Indian Institutes of Technology (IIT). Their greatest strength is that they administer one of the world's most ruthlessly competitive entrance exams. Three hundred thousand people take it, five thousand are admitted—an acceptance rate of 1.7 percent (compared with 9 to 10 percent for Harvard, Yale, and Princeton). The people who make the mark are the best and brightest out of one billion. Place them in any educational system, and they will do well. In fact, many of the IITs are decidedly second-rate, with mediocre equipment, indifferent teachers, and unimaginative classwork. Rajiv Sahney, who attended IIT and then went to Caltech, says, "The IITs' core advantage is the entrance exam, which is superbly designed to select extremely intelligent students. In terms of teaching and facilities, they really don't compare with any decent American technical institute." And once you get beyond the IITs and other such elite academies—which graduate under ten thousand students a year—the quality of higher education in China and India remains extremely poor, which is why so many students leave those countries to get trained abroad.

The data affirm these anecdotal impressions. In 2005, the McKinsey Global Institute did a study of "the emerging global labor market" and found that a sample of twenty-eight low-wage countries had approximately 33 million young professionals[3] at their disposal, compared with just 15 million in a sample of eight higher-wage nations (the United States, United Kingdom, Germany, Japan, Australia, Canada, Ireland, and South Korea). But how many of these young professionals in low-wage countries had the skills necessary to compete in a global marketplace? "Only a fraction of potential job candidates could successfully work at a foreign company," the study reported, pointing to several explanations, chiefly poor educational quality. In both India and China, it noted, beyond the small number of top-tier academies, the quality and quantity of education is low. Only 10 percent of Indians get any kind of postsecondary education. Thus, despite enormous demand for engineers, there are relatively few well-trained ones. Wages of trained engineers in both countries are rising by 15 percent a year, a sure sign that demand is outstripping supply. (If you were an employer and had access to tens of thousands of well-trained engineers coming out of colleges every year, you would not have to give your employees 15 percent raises year after year.)

Higher education is America's best industry. There are two rankings of universities worldwide. In one of them, a purely quantitative study done by Chinese researchers, eight of the top ten universities in the world are in the United States. In the other, more qualitative one by London's *Times Higher Educational Supplement*, it's seven. The numbers flatten out somewhat after that. Of the top twenty, seventeen or eleven are in America; of the top fifty, thirty-eight or twenty-one. Still, the basic story does not change. With 5 percent of the world's population, the United States absolutely dominates higher education, having either 42 or 68 percent of the world's top fifty universities (depending which study you look at). In no other field is America's advantage so overwhelming.[4]

A 2006 report from the London-based Centre for European Reform, "The Future of European Universities," points out that the United States invests 2.6 percent of its GDP in higher education, compared with 1.2 percent in Europe and 1.1 percent in Japan. The situation in the sciences is particularly striking. A list of where the world's 1,000 best computer scientists were educated shows that the top ten schools are all American. U.S. spending on R&D remains higher than Europe's, and its collaborations between business and educational institutions are unmatched anywhere in the world. America remains by far the most attractive destination for students, taking 30 percent of the total number of foreign students globally. All these advantages will not be erased easily, because the structure of European and Japanese universities—mostly state-run bureaucracies—is unlikely to change. And while China and India are opening new institutions, it is not that easy to create a world-class university out of whole cloth in a few decades. Here's a statistic about engineers that you might not have heard. In India, universities graduate between 35 and 50 Ph.D.'s in computer science each year; in America, the figure is 1,000.

Learning to Think

If American universities are first-rank, few believe that the same can be said about its schools. Everyone knows that the American school system is in crisis and that its students do particularly badly in science and math, year after year, in international rankings. But the statistics here, while not wrong, reveal something slightly different. America's real problem is one not of excellence but of access. Since its inception in 1995, the Trends in International Mathematics and Science Study (TIMSS) has become the standard for comparing educational programs across nations. The most recent results, from 2003, put the United States squarely in the middle of the pack. The United States beat the average score of the twenty-four countries included in the study, but many of the countries ranked below it were developing nations like Morocco,

Tunisia, and Armenia. Eighth-graders did better than fourth-graders (the two grades measured) but still lagged behind their counterparts in countries like Holland, Japan, and Singapore. The media reported the news with a predictable penchant for direness: "Economic time bomb: U.S. teens are among worst at math," declared the *Wall Street Journal*.

But even if the U.S. scores in math and science fall well below leaders like Singapore and Hong Kong, the aggregate scores hide deep regional, racial, and socioeconomic variation. Poor and minority students score well below the American average, while, as one study noted, "students in affluent suburban U.S. school districts score nearly as well as students in Singapore, the runaway leader on TIMSS math scores." These are the students who then go on to compete for and fill the scarce slots in America's top universities. The difference between average science scores in poor and wealthy school districts *within* the United States, for instance, is *four to five times greater* than the difference between the U.S. and Singaporean national averages. In other words, America is a large and diverse country with a real inequality problem. This will, over time, translate into a competitiveness problem, because if we cannot educate and train a third of the working population to compete in a knowledge economy, it will drag down the country. But we do know what works. The large cohort of students in the top fifth of American schools rank along with the world's best. They work hard and have a highly scheduled academic and extracurricular life, as anyone who has recently been to an Ivy League campus can attest.

I went to elementary middle, and high school in Mumbai, at an excellent institution, the Cathedral and John Connon School. Its approach (thirty years ago) reflected the teaching methods often described as "Asian," in which the premium is placed on memorization and constant testing. This is actually the old British, and European, pedagogical method, one that now gets described as Asian. I recall memorizing vast quantities of material, regurgitating it for exams, and then promptly forgetting it. When I went to college in the United States, I encountered a different world. While the American system is too lax on rigor and memorization—whether in math or poetry—it is much better at developing the critical faculties of the mind, which is what you need to succeed in life. Other educational systems teach you to take tests; the American system teaches you to think.

It is surely this quality that goes some way in explaining why America produces so many entrepreneurs, inventors, and risk takers. In America, people are allowed to be bold, challenge authority, fail, and pick themselves up. It's America, not Japan, that produces dozens of Nobel Prize winners. Tharman Shanmugaratnam, until recently Singapore's minister of education, explains the difference between his country's system and America's. "We both have meritocracies," Shanmugaratnam says. "Yours is a talent meritocracy, ours is an exam meritocracy. We know how to train people to take exams. You know how to use people's talents to the fullest. Both are important, but there are some parts of the intellect that we are not able to test well—like creativity, curiosity, a sense of adventure, ambition. Most of all, America has a culture of learning that challenges conventional wisdom, even if it means challenging authority. These are the areas where Singapore must learn from America."

This is one reason that Singaporean officials recently visited U.S. schools to learn how to create a system that nurtures and rewards ingenuity, quick thinking, and problem solving. As the *Washington Post* reported in March 2007, researchers from Singapore's best schools came to the Academy of Science, a public magnet school in Virginia, to examine U.S. teaching methods. As the students "studied tiny, genetically altered plants one recent afternoon, drawing leaves and jotting data in logbooks," the Singaporean visitors "recorded how long the teacher waited for students to answer questions, how often the teenagers spoke up, and how strongly they held to their views." Har Hui Peng, a visitor from Singapore's Hwa Chong Institution, was impressed, as the *Post* noted. "Just by watching, you can see students are more engaged, instead of being spoon-fed all day," said Har. The *Post* article continued, "[In Singapore], she said, the laboratories are fully stocked but stark, and the students are bright but reluctant to volunteer answers. To encourage spontaneity, Hwa Chong now bases 10 percent of each student's grade on oral participation."

While America marvels at Asia's test-taking skills, Asian countries come to America to figure out how to get their kids to think. Top high schools in Beijing and Shanghai are emphasizing independent research, science competitions, and entrepreneur clubs. "I like the way your children are able to communicate," said Rosalind Chia, another Singaporean teacher on tour in the States. "Maybe we need to cultivate that more—a conversation between students and teachers." Such change does not come easily. Indeed, Japan recently attempted to improve the flexibility of its national education system by eliminating mandatory Saturday classes and increasing the time dedicated to general studies, where students and teachers can pursue their own interests. "But the Japanese shift to *yutori kyoiku*, or relaxed education," the *Post* says, "has fueled a back-to-basics backlash from parents who worry that their children are not learning enough and that test scores are slipping." In other words, simply changing curricula—a top-down effort—may lead only to resistance. American culture celebrates and reinforces problem solving, questioning authority, and thinking heretically. It allows people to fail and then gives them a second and third chance. It rewards self-starters and oddballs. These are all bottom-up forces that cannot be produced by government fiat. . . .

The native-born, white American population has the same low fertility rates as Europe's. Without immigration, U.S. GDP growth over the last quarter century would have been the same as Europe's. America's edge in innovation is overwhelmingly a product of immigration. Foreign students and immigrants account for 50 percent of the science researchers in the country and, in 2006, received 40 percent of the doctorates in science and engineering and 65 percent of the doctorates in computer science. By 2010, foreign students will get more than 50 percent of all Ph.D.'s awarded in every subject in the United States. In the sciences, that figure will be closer to 75 percent. Half of all Silicon Valley start-ups have one founder who is an immigrant or first-generation American. America's potential new burst of productivity, its edge in nanotechnology, biotechnology, its ability to invent the future—all rest on its immigration policies. If America can keep the people it educates in the country, the innovation will happen here. If they go back home, the innovation will travel with them.

Immigration also gives America a quality rare for a rich country—hunger and energy. As countries become wealthy, the drive to move up and succeed weakens. But America has found a way to keep itself constantly revitalized by streams of people who are looking to make a new life in a new world. These are the people who work long hours picking fruit in searing heat, washing dishes, building houses, working night shifts, and cleaning waste dumps. They come to the United States under terrible conditions, leave family and community, only because they want to work and get ahead in life. Americans have almost always worried about such immigrants—whether from Ireland or Italy, China or Mexico. But these immigrants have gone on to become the backbone of the American working class, and their children or grandchildren have entered the American mainstream. America has been able to tap this energy, manage diversity, assimilate newcomers, and move ahead economically. Ultimately, this is what sets the country apart from the experience of Britain and all other historical examples of great economic powers that grow fat and lazy and slip behind as they face the rise of leaner, hungrier nations.

The Macro Picture

Many experts, scholars, and even a few politicians worry about a set of statistics that bode ill for the United States. The savings rate is zero, the current-account deficit, trade deficit, and budget deficit are high, median income is flat, and commitments for entitlements are unsustainable. These are all valid concerns and will have to be addressed by Washington. If America's economic system is its core strength, its political system is its core weakness. But the numbers might not tell us everything we need to know. The economic statistics that we rely on give us only an approximate, antiquated measure of an economy. Many of them were developed in the late nineteenth century to describe an industrial economy with limited cross-border activity. We now live in an interconnected global market, with revolutions in financial instruments, technology, and trade. It is possible that we're not measuring things correctly.

It used to be a law of macroeconomics, for example, that in an advanced industrial economy there is such a thing as NAIRU—the nonaccelerating inflation rate of unemployment. Basically, this meant that unemployment could not fall below a certain level, usually pinned at 6 percent, without driving inflation up. But for the last two decades, many Western countries, especially the United States, have had unemployment rates well below levels economists thought possible. Or consider that America's current-account deficit—which in 2007 reached $800 billion, or 7 percent of GDP—was supposed to be unsustainable at 4 percent of GDP. The current-account deficit is at dangerous levels, but we should also keep in mind that its magnitude can be explained in part by the fact that there is a worldwide surplus of savings and that the United States remains an unusually stable and attractive place in which to invest.

Harvard University's Richard Cooper even argues that the American savings rate is miscalculated, painting an inaccurate picture of massive credit card debt and unaffordable mortgages. While many households do live beyond their means, the picture looks healthier at the aggregate level, Cooper argues. Private

U.S. savings, which includes both household saving (the "often-cited" low figure of about 2 percent of personal income) and corporate saving, reached 15 percent in 2005. The decrease in personal saving, in other words, has been largely offset by an increase in corporate saving. More important, the whole concept of "national saving" might be outdated, not reflecting the reality of new modes of production. In the new economy, growth comes from "teams of people creating new goods and services, not from the accumulation of capital," which was more important in the first half of the twentieth century. Yet we still focus on measuring capital. The national accounts, which include GDP and traditional measures of national saving, were, Cooper writes, "formulated in Britain and the United States in the 1930s, at the height of the industrial age."

Economists define saving as the income that, instead of going toward consumption, is invested to make possible consumption in the future. Current measures of investment focus on physical capital and housing. Cooper argues that this measure is misleading. Education expenditures are considered "consumption," but in a knowledge-based economy, education functions more like savings—it is spending forgone today in order to increase human capital and raise future income and spending power. Private R&D, meanwhile, isn't included in national accounts at all, but rather considered an intermediate business expense—even though most studies suggest that R&D on average has a high payoff, much higher than investing in bricks and mortar, which counts under the current measures as savings. So Cooper would also count as savings expenditure on consumer durables, education, and R&D—which would give the United States a significantly higher savings rate. The new metric worldwide would raise the figure for other nations as well, but the contribution of education, R&D, and consumer durables to total savings "is higher in the United States than in most other countries, except perhaps for a few Nordic countries."[5]

With all these caveats, the United States still has serious problems. Many trends relating to the macroeconomic picture are worrisome. Whatever the savings rate, it has fallen fast over the past two decades. By all calculations, Medicare threatens to blow up the federal budget. The swing from surpluses to deficits between 2000 and 2008 has serious implications. For most families, moreover, incomes are flat or rising very slowly. Growing inequality is the signature feature of the new era fueled by a triple force—the knowledge economy, information technology, and globalization. Perhaps most worryingly, Americans are borrowing 80 percent of the world's surplus savings and using it for consumption. In other words, we are selling off our assets to foreigners to buy a couple more lattes a day. These problems have accumulated at a bad time because, for all its strengths, the American economy now faces its strongest challenge in history. . . .

Notes

1. These numbers are based on market exchange rates, not adjusted for living standards. The numbers in PPP dollars would be 19 percent in 1913, 27 ercent in 1950, 22 percent in 1973, 22 percent in 1998, and 19 percent in 2007. The PPP numbers also show the same pattern, of American power being relatively stable at around 20 percent of global GDP.

2. Of course, information from public companies represents only part of the picture, because more than three-quarters of the world's 4,203 biotech companies are held privately. Europe has a larger share of the world's private biotech companies, representing 42 percent of the total (compared with 31 percent in America). The United States, by contrast, is home to a greater share of public biotech companies (50 percent versus Europe's 18 percent), perhaps indicating the greater maturity of the U.S. market.

3. MGI's figure includes graduates trained in engineering, finance and accounting, life science research, and "professional generalists," such as call center operatives. Young professionals are defined as graduates with up to seven years of experience.

4. The right-wing attack on American universities as being out-of-touch ivory towers has always puzzled me. In a highly competitive global environment, these institutions dominate the field.

5. Consumer durables, education, and R&D amount to 8.6 percent, 7.3 percent, and 2.8 percent of GDP, respectively. Adding this to the 15 percent saved by more traditional means yields just over 33 percent of GDP in national savings.

POSTSCRIPT

Is the United States a Declining Power?

Fareed Zakaria is one of our more perceptive political television and magazine commentators. Born in India and educated in elite Indian schools, he immigrated to the United States and attended Yale and Harvard before editing and writing for *Newsweek Internationale*.

Zakaria believes we are now in the third great tectonic shift since 1500. The Renaissance, Reformation, and scientific revolutions were the first, the industrial revolution dominated by the United States from the 1880s through the 1980s was the second, while the third revolution since the 1990s is "the rise of the rest—China, India, Brazil, Russia—sharing wealth and power with the United States."

Zakaria does not believe that the United States is a declining power. He rejects comparisons with the decline of England in the twentieth century because the United States has a much stronger economic and population base to remain a major power in the postindustrial world. Three areas where the United States dominates the rest of the world include education, science, and a diverse population.

No social scientist can dispute that the United States contains the world's best undergraduate and research universities because so many immigrants, including Zakaria, clamor for student visas to attend our colleges. While our grammar and high schools have been disparaged for poor teaching and lower standards, the author points out that our suburban schools as opposed to our inner city high schools are among the best in the world. As the Singaporean minister of education points out, "We have a meritocracy of test takers, you have a meritocracy of thinkers and doers."

Both the universities and the government along with many businesses support our talented entrepreneurs with research and development (R&D) in "nanotechnology-applied science dealing with the control of matter at the atomic or molecular scale" as well as biotechnology which is a multibillion-dollar industry that creates medical, agricultural, and industrial products.

Immigration, according to Zakaria, has provided America's edge in innovation. Foreign students have taken advantage of our superior higher education system. By 2010, foreign students will earn more than 50 percent of all Ph.D.s, including 75 percent in the sciences. Many of these students remain in the United States, start up new companies in nanotechnology and biotechnology, become citizens and create a "brain drain" from the country of origins.

Critics of Zakaria might complain that he is too optimistic and plays down some of America's current problems. While he is good on the long-term prognosis, there are a number of immediate issues that need to be dealt with.

Like most economists and political observers, Zakaria was caught off guard by the collapse of Wall Street and the large investment banking houses in the fall of 2008 as revealed in his new preface to the paperback edition of *The Post-American World*. The debt issue is not dealt with adequately even if we need new economic indicators to measure capital in today's economy. We don't know whether high unemployment is temporary or a structural casualty in the new economy. If structural, how many workers will be available to pay the retirement and health benefits of an aging population? Finally, Zakaria doesn't seem to be much concerned with a bloated military budget which he deems a minor concern.

Both Zakaria and Bacevich are concerned with a broken political system. Zakaria's chief worry is that the two political parties have become so ideologically polarized into liberal and conservative factions, compromise, which is the heart of our political system, has become broken. Bacevich, on the other hand, believes that Democracy is broken because the large power of the executive branch has created an imperial presidency that presides over an informal global empire run by the American military.

Unlike Zakaria, Professor Bacevich believes that the "exceptional American political and economic" system which we created in the late eighteenth and nineteenth centuries has come to an end. America's present-day obsession with consumer goods has allowed our government to use the military to create an informal empire in the Middle East in search of oil and other energy-related resources. Consequently, Americans refuse to deal with two major problems that could destroy our world—the proliferation of nuclear weapons and the issue of global warming. Bacevich is not very optimistic about America's future. He quotes the famous Protestant theologian Reinhold Niebuhr: "One of the most pathetic aspects of human history is that every civilization expresses itself most pretentiously, computes its partial and universal values most convincingly, and claims immortality for its finite existence at the very moment when the decay which leads to death has already begun." (*Beyond Tragedy* [New York, 1937]).

In addition to Niebuhr's *Irony of History* (New York, 1952), which informed many post-World War II scholars, Bacevich has incorporated the concept of an informal American empire from the diplomatic historian William Appleman Williams' *The Tragedy of American Diplomacy*, 2nd ed. (Dell Publishing, 1972), whose seminars and books created "the Wisconsin school of diplomacy"—a generation of new left scholars still dominant in the field. Bacevich wrote a new introduction to the 50th anniversary of *The Tragedy of American Diplomacy*.

Ironically, Bacevich is a Catholic Conservative, a West Point graduate, a Vietnam veteran, and a parent who lost his son in combat in 2007 in the Iraq War. A professor of history and international relations at Boston University, he writes for a number of magazines, including Pat Buchanan's *The American Conservative* which supports a conservative domestic policy but also a neo-isolationist foreign policy. His critique of the neoconservative foreign policy of the Bush administration can be found in *The New American Militarism: How Americans Are Seduced by War* (Oxford, 2005). In a footnote on p. 235, the author cites Bruce Berkowitz on *The New Face of War* (New York, 2003) which cites CIA data calculating annual worldwide military spending at approximately $750 billion with the then-current Pentagon budget at $380 billion or more than 50 percent of the world's military outlays.

The bibliography of the postindustrial economy is enormous and constantly changing. Somewhat optimistic are the books by *New York Times'* columnist Thomas Friedman. Two of significance are: *The World is Flat* (Farrar, Straus, and Giraux, 2005) and *Hot, Flat, and Crowded: Why We Need a Green Revolution and How It Can Renew America* (Farrar, Straus, and Giraux, 2008). A student guide to Friedman is the portrait of him, "The Bright Side: The Relentless Optimism of Thomas Friedman," in *The New Yorker* (November 10, 2008) by Ian Parker. On a daily basis, a reader can gain a liberal optimistic view from the editorial pages of *The New York Times* and a more pessimistic conservative outlook from the editorial pages of *The Wall Street Journal*. Finally, reporter James Fallows supports Zakaria in "How America Can Rise Again," *The Atlantic Monthly* (January/February, 2010).

Contributors to This Volume

EDITORS

LARRY MADARAS is a professor of history emeritus at Howard Community College in Columbia, Maryland. He received a B.A. from the College of Holy Cross in 1959 and an M.A. and a Ph.D. from New York University in 1961 and 1964, respectively. He has also taught at Spring Hill College, the University of South Alabama, and the University of Maryland at College Park. He has been a Fulbright Fellow and has held two fellowships from the National Endowment for the Humanities. He is the author of dozens of journal articles and book reviews.

JAMES M. SoRELLE is a professor of history and former chair of the Department of History at Baylor University in Waco, Texas. He received a B.A. and M.A. from the University of Houston in 1972 and 1974, respectively, and a Ph.D. from Kent State University in 1980. In addition to introductory courses in United States and world history, he teaches advanced undergraduate classes in African American history, the American civil rights movement, and the 1960s, as well as a graduate seminar on the civil rights movement. His scholarly articles have appeared in the *Houston Review, Southwestern Historical Quarterly,* and *Black Dixie: Essays in Afro-Texan History and Culture in Houston* (Texas A&M University Press, 1992), edited by Howard Beeth and Cary D. Wintz. He also has contributed entries to *The New Handbook of Texas, The Oxford Companion to Politics of the World, Encyclopedia of African American Culture and History, The Encyclopedia of the Confederacy,* and *The Encyclopedia of African American History.*

AUTHORS

RICHARD M. ABRAMS is a professor of history at the University of California, Berkeley, where he has been teaching since 1961. He has been a Fulbright professor in both London and Moscow and has taught and lectured in many countries throughout the world, including China, Austria, Norway, Italy, Japan, Germany, and Australia. He has published numerous articles in history, business, and law journals, and he is the editor of *The Shaping of Twentieth Century America: Interpretive Essays,* 2nd ed. (Little, Brown, 1971) and the author of *The Burdens of Progress* (Scott, Foresman, 1978). His most recent book is *America Transformed: Sixty Years of Revolutionary Change, 1941–2001* (Cambridge University Press, 2006).

ANDREW J. BACEVICH, a professor of history and international relations at Boston University, retired from the U.S. Army with the rank of colonel. He is the author of *The New American Militarism,* among other books. His writing has appeared in *Foreign Affairs, The Atlantic Monthly, The Nation, The New York Times, The Washington Post,* and *The Wall Street Journal.*

LARRY BERMAN, professor and director of the University of California Washington Center, has written two previous books on Vietnam, *Planning a Tragedy and Lyndon Johnson's War,* and has appeared in several major television documentaries on the war. He lives in Davis, California, and Washington, D.C.

ROGER BILES is a professor in and chair of the history department at East Carolina University in Greenville, North Carolina. He is the author of *The South and the New Deal* (University Press of Kentucky, 1994) and *Richard J. Daly: Politics, Race, and the Governing of Chicago* (Northern Illinois Press, 1994).

CARL M. BRAUER received his Ph.D. in history from Harvard University in 1973 and has taught at the University of Missouri, Brown University, and the University of Virginia. He also served as a research fellow in the Institute of Politics at the John F. Kennedy School of Government. Since 1991, he has been a freelance historian and biographer. He is the author of *Presidential Transitions: Eisenhower Through Reagan* (Oxford, 1986) and has written a number of commissioned histories for both private and public institutions.

NICK BRYANT earned his Ph.D. from Oxford University where he developed a fascination for politics in the United States. He has served as a correspondent for the British Broadcasting Corporation in Washington, D.C., New Delhi, and most recently, in Sydney, Australia.

JOHN C. BURNHAM teaches the history of American science at the Ohio State University and is the author of *Lester Frank Ward in American Thought* and *Psychoanalysis and American Medicine.*

WILLIAM G. CARLETON (1903–1982) was professor emeritus at the University of Florida and author of the widely used textbook on *The Revolution in American Foreign Policy.*

JOHN MILTON COOPER, JR., Professor of History at the University of consin is the author of numerous books on World War I and Vers including the definitive biography of *Woodrow Wilson: A Biography* (A A. Knopf, 2009).

DAVID T. COURTRIGHT has written numerous articles on United Stat Western history and is a professor of history at the University of Nor Florida. He is the author of *Single Men and Social Disorder from the Fronti to the Inner City* (Harvard University Press, 1996).

CARL N. DEGLER is the Margaret Byrne Professor Emeritus of American History at Stanford University in Stanford, California. He is a member of the editorial board for the Plantation Society, and he is a member and former president of the American History Society and the Organization of American Historians. His book *Neither Black nor White: Slavery and Race Relations in Brazil and the United States* (University of Wisconsin Press, 1972) won the 1972 Pulitzer Prize for history.

ROBERT R. DYKSTRA is professor of history and public policy at the State University of New York, Albany. A specialist in nineteenth-century American social and political history, he is the author of two books on the trans-Mississippi West, most recently *Bright Radical Star: Black Freedom and White Supremacy on the Hawkeye Frontier* (Cambridge: Harvard University Press, 1993). He is currently engaged in a long-term project on black-family demography in post-Civil War Virginia.

SARA M. EVANS is Distinguished McKnight University Professor of History at the University of Minnesota, where she has taught women's history since 1976. She is the author of several books including *Personal Politics: The Roots of Women's Liberation in the Civil Rights Movement and the New Left* (1979) and *Born for Liberty: A History of Women in America*, 2nd ed., (1997). Born in a Methodist parsonage in South Carolina, she was a student activist in the civil rights and antiwar movements in North Carolina and has been an active feminist since 1967.

LEON FINK is a professor of history at the University of North Carolina at Chapel Hill and the author of numerous books and articles on labor history.

BURTON W. FOLSOM is a professor of history at Hillsdale College in Michigan and senior historian at the Foundation for Economic Education in Irvington, New York. He is a regular columnist for *The Freeman* and has written articles for *The Wall Street Journal* and *American Spectator*, among other publications. He lives in Michigan.

GEORGE M. FREDRICKSON was the Edgar E. Robinson Professor of U.S. History Emeritus at Stanford University and the preeminent American scholar on the history of race. He was the author of *The Inner Civil War: Northern Intellectuals and the Crisis of the Union* (Harper and Row, 1965), *White Supremacy: A Comparative Study of American and South African History* (Oxford University Press, 1981), and *Black Liberation: A Comparative History* s *in the United States and South Africa* (Oxford University

.DDIS is the Robert A. Lovett Professor of History at Yale University, ew Haven, Connecticut. He has also been Distinguished Professor, ory at Ohio University, where he founded the Contemporary nstitute, and he has held visiting appointments at the United Naval War College, the University of Helsinki, Princeton University, xford University. He is the author of many books, including *We Now v: Rethinking Cold War History* (Oxford University Press, 1997).

S. GORDON is a specialist in business and financial history whose articles have appeared in numerous prominent magazines and newspapers for the past 20 years. He is a contributing editor to American Heritage and since 1989 has written the "Business of America" column. His other books include *Hamilton's Blessing: The Extraordinary Life and Times of Our National Debt* (Walker, 1997), *The Great Game: The Emergence of Wall Street as a World Power, 1653–2000* (Scribner, 1999), and *A Thread Across the Ocean: The Heroic Story of the Transatlantic Cable* (Walker, 2002).

F. CAROLYN GRAGLIA is a trained lawyer, writer, and lecturer whose articles and books challenge the viewpoint of the modern women's movement.

OSCAR HANDLIN was the Carl M. Loeb Professor of History at Harvard University in Cambridge, Massachusetts, where he has been teaching since 1941. A Pulitzer Prize–winning historian, he has written or edited more than 100 books, including *Liberty in Expansion* (Harper & Row, 1989), which he coauthored with Lilian Handlin, and *The Distortion of America*, 2nd ed. (Transaction Publishers, 1996).

RICHARD HOFSTADTER (1916–1970) was a professor of history at Columbia University and is considered to be among the best American historians of the post–World War II generation. His books *The American Political Tradition and the Men Who Made It* (Alfred A. Knopf, 1948) and *The Age of Reform: From Bryan to F.D.R.* (Alfred A. Knopf, 1955) are considered classics.

DAVID E. KYVIG is a professor of history at Northern Illinois University. He was awarded the Bancroft Prize for his work *Explicit and Authentic Acts: Amending the U.S. Constitution, 1776–1995*.

ARTHUR S. LINK was a professor at Princeton University. He is the editor-in-chief of the Woodrow Wilson papers and the author of the definitive multi-volume biography of President Wilson.

RICHARD L. McCORMICK is president of Rutgers University in New Brunswick, New Jersey. He received his Ph.D. in history from Yale University in 1976, and he is the author of *The Party Period and Public Policy: American Politics from the Age of Jackson to the Progressive Era* (Oxford University Press, 1986).

RICHARD NIXON was our 37th president who was twice elected and ended America's participation in the Vietnam War. In August 1974, he was forced to resign after he was impeached by the House of Representatives. He wrote almost a dozen books in retirement.

ROBERT J. NORRELL holds the Bernadotte Schmitt Chair of Excellence in the history department at the University of Tennessee, Knoxville. He is the author of *Reaping the Whirlwind: The Civil Rights Movement in Tuskegee* (1985) and *The House I Live In: Race in the American Century* (Oxford University Press, 2005).

J. RONALD OAKLEY was a professor of history at Davidson County Community College in Greensboro, North Carolina.

ARNOLD A. OFFNER is Cornelia F. Hugel Professor of History and head of the history department at Lafayette College. He is the author of *American Appeasement: United States Foreign Policy and Germany, 1933–1938* (1969) and *Origins of the Second World War: American Foreign Policy and World Politics, 1917–1941* (1975); and with Theodore A. Wilson coedited *Victory in Europe, 1945: The Allied Triumph over Germany and the Origins of the Cold War* (1999). He has recently completed a book-length study of President Harry S. Truman and the origins of the Cold War.

JODY PENNINGTON is an associate professor in Media and Cultural Studies at the University of Aarhus in Denmark. He is the author of *Sex in American Film* (Praeger, 2007). In 2008, he was President of the Denmark Association of American Studies.

CHARLES POSTEL is an assistant professor of history at San Francisco University where he specializes in politics, reform movements, populism, and the Gilded Age and Progressive Era. His first book was *Power and Progress: Populist Thought in America* (University of California Press, 2002). His most recent book on *The Populist Vision,* excerpted in this reader, won the Bancroft Prize and Frederick Jackson Turner Award in 2008.

HEATHER COX RICHARDSON is professor of history at the University of Massachusetts, Amherst. Her other books include *The Greatest Nation of the Earth: Republican Economic Policies during the Civil War* (Harvard University Press, 1997) and *West from Appomattox: The Reconstruction of America after the Civil War* (Yale University Press, 2007).

DONALD SPIVEY is professor of history and Cooper Fellow in the history department at the University of Miami. He received his Ph.D. from the University of California, Davis (1976). He is the editor of *Sport in America: New Historical Perspectives* (Greenwood Press, 1985) and the author of *The Politics of Miseducation: The Booker Washington Institute of Liberia, 1929–1984* (University Press of Kentucky, 1996). He is currently working on a biography of Leroy "Satchel" Paige.

ROBERT A. THEOBALD was a retired rear admiral before his death. He was the commanding officer of Flotilla One, Destroyers, Pacific Fleet, and was present at the Pearl Harbor attack. He testified on behalf of Admiral Husband E. Kimmel before the Roberts Commission, which had accused Kimmel of "dereliction of duty."

ROBERTA WOHLSTETTER is a historian and a member of the Steering Committee of the Balkan Institute, which was formed to educate the public on the nature of the crisis in the Balkans and its humanitarian, political, and military consequences. She has earned the Presidential Medal of Freedom, and she is coauthor of *Nuclear Policies: Fuel Without the Bomb* (Harper Business, 1978).

MARK WYMAN is professor of history at Illinois State University and the author of *Round-Trip to America: The Immigrant Returns to Europe, 1880–1930* (Cornell University Press, 1993).

FAREED ZAKARIA is the host of CNN's Fareed Zakaria GPS and editor of *Newsweek Internationale*. His previous book was *The New York Times* bestseller *The Future of Freedom*.

HOWARD ZINN was a civil rights protester and peace activist with a Ph.D. from Columbia University. He taught for many years at Spelman College and Boston University and was immensely popular with the students. He has written hundreds of articles, but *A People's History of the United States* (HarperCollins, 1980, 1999) has sold enough copies to make a millionaire out of a Socialist.